John Charles Frémont Botanical Explorer

FRONTISPIECE. Drawing of *Arctomecon californicum* Torr. & Frém. in Frém., by Nick Pooley. The illustration is mounted on a sheet, NY, labeled, "Fremont's Expedition to California, 1843–4. No. 429. May 3, 1844. Arctomecon Californicum. Torr. Specimen lost by Nick Pooley—or the Lithographer. It was the only one collected by Fremont! Found at a place called Las Vegas, near the Rio Virgen, in southern Utah—Lat. 36°10'."

John Charles Frémont

John Charles Frémont Botanical Explorer

Stanley L. Welsh

Missouri Botanical Garden Press

MONOGRAPHS IN SYSTEMATIC BOTANY

FROM THE MISSOURI BOTANICAL GARDEN

Volume 66

ISBN 0-915279-49-5
ISSN 0161-1542

AUTHOR'S ADDRESS

Life Science Museum and Department of Botany
Rm. 290 MLBM
Brigham Young University
Provo, Utah 84602, U.S.A.

TABLE OF CONTENTS

Abstract[1]

The five expeditions of John Charles Frémont are reviewed, the plant names cited in the Frémont reports are emphasized, the botany of the expeditions is discussed, and a checklist of plant species taken during the expeditions is presented. Numerous plant specimens were collected by Frémont on the first, second, and third expeditions. Many new genera and species were described from those collections. Plant specimens were taken on all five expeditions. An itinerary of dated and datable specimens is presented for the first three expeditions. Plants known to have been taken on the fourth and fifth expeditions are listed in their entirety. The checklist consists of a comprehensive listing of plants from all of the expeditions based on both literature and herbarium specimens. The herbaria at The New York Botanical Garden and at the Gray Herbarium of Harvard University are the primary sources of specimen citations. Contemporary literature is the source of most of the bibliographic information, including data on type specimens and other specimens. Frémont collections include some 163 plants later named as species or varieties. He also collected the specimens on which some 19 genera were ultimately based in whole or in part.

Se repasan las cinco expediciones de John Charles Frémont, se enfatizan los nombres de las plantas citados en los informes de Frémont, se describe la botánica de las expediciones, y se presenta una lista comprobatoria de las especies de plantas coleccionadas en las expediciones. Varias especies de plantas fueron coleccionadas por Frémont en la primera, la segunda, y la tercera expediciones. Muchos géneros y especies nuevos se describieron según esas colecciones. Especies de plantas se coleccionaron en todas las cinco expediciones. Un itinerario de especímenes fechados y fechables se presenta para las primeras tres expediciones. Se hace una lista comprensiva de las plantas que se sabe que fueron coleccionadas en las expediciones cuatro y cinco. La lista comprobatoria consiste en una citación comprensiva de las plantas de todas las expediciones basada tanto en la literatura como en las especimenes del herbario. Los herbarios en el "New York Botanical Garden" y el "Gray Herbarium" de la universidad de Harvard son las fuentes principales de las citaciones de las especímenes. La literatura del siglo XIX es la fuente de la mayoría de la información bibliográfica, incluso la información sobre los especímenes de tipo y otros especímenes. Las colecciones de Frémont incluyen unas 163 plantas nombradas luego como especies o variedades. Él también coleccionó los especímenes según los cuales 19 géneros se han basado en parte o en su totalidad.

[1]Abstracts are presented in the most common languages used on the Frémont expeditions.

Les cinq expéditions de John Charles Frémont sont revisés, les noms des plantes citées dans les comptes rendus de Frémont sont accentués, la Botanique des expéditions est discuté, et une liste de contrôle des espèces des plantes acquises pendant les expéditions est presentée. Nombreux spécimens de plantes turent collectionés par Frémont sur la première, la deuxième et la troisième expéditions. Beaucoup de genres et des espèces étaient décrits dans ces collections. Spécimens de plantes étaient pris sur tous les cinq expéditions. Un itinéraire daté et datable de spécimens est presenté pour les trois premières expéditions. Les plantes surement prises sur la quatrième et cinquième expéditions sont enumérées en entier. La liste de contrôle est composée d'une énumération compréhensive des plantes de tous les expéditions basée sur la littérature aussi bien que les spécimens d'herbier. Les herbiers à New York Botanical Garden et à Gray Herbarium de l' Université d' Harvard sont les sources principales des citations de spécimens. La littérature contemporaine est la source de la plupart de l'information bibliographique, y compris les données des spécimens types et d'autres spécimens. Les collections de Frémont incluent 163 plantes qui étaient nommées plus tard comme espèce ou variété. En fin de compte, il a collectionné aussi les spécimens sur lesquels 19 genres étaient basées en tout ou en partie.

CHAPTER I

INTRODUCTION

> "I speak often of the grass and flowers, but I have learned to value the one and the other lends a beauty to the scenery which I do not like to omit, and the reader can always imagine for himself the brightness they give when once he has had described the glorious flowers of this country, where the most lovely hues are spread in fields over both hill and plain" (Frémont, 1887: 479).

Overview

During the U.S. Civil War there were at least three Union General officers who had made contributions to the understanding of the botany of the American West: George H. Thomas, Rock of Chicamauga (commemorated by *Eriogonum thomasii* Torr.); William H. Emory, antagonist of Frémont at his court-martial (commemorated by *Hyptis emoryi* Torr.); and John C. Frémont. Plant specimens taken by each of them in the American West are in the herbarium of The New York Botanical Garden, sometimes mounted together on the same sheets. Two of the officers, Thomas and Emory, served more or less ably during the war. Only Frémont left a record of more failures than successes. Thomas had opportunity thrust upon him at Chicamauga and at Nashville where he defeated John Bell Hood despite the perception by Lincoln and Grant that he had "The Slows," i.e., that he would not move until ready; Emory served for the most part splendidly, but some criticized his actions at the battle of Cedar Creek and his role in Louisiana; Frémont failed largely in his assignment as General of the Army of the West at St. Louis, played a mediocre role in charge of the Mountain Division in West Virginia and Virginia against General Stonewall (Thomas J.) Jackson, and resigned in a huff when General John Pope was advanced ahead of him. Practically all books dealing with the Civil War contain references to Frémont, especially those concerned with the early years of that tearing, valiant but morbid conflict.

Frémont's tenure as appointed governor of the territory of Arizona, 1879–82, was clouded by his attention to personal mining, land development, and railroad promotion schemes, whereby he tried to regain his lost fortunes. He spent more time away from the governor's job than on the job, but nevertheless failed in his personal investment schemes. His life beyond the governorship was spent in relative poverty in California, where he lived on his wife's earnings from writing.

Prior to the war, in 1856, Frémont was defeated in his bid for the presidency of the United States, as first candidate of the Republican party. He was also the presidential candidate of the Radicals during the 1864 election, when Abraham Lincoln's future was unsure due to failures in conduct of the Civil War. John Charles withdrew his candidacy only when Lincoln's chances improved following successful battles, primarily the taking of Atlanta, prior to the election of 1864.

In financial, political, and military affairs, Frémont may be judged lacking. He was bright, ambitious, vain, arrogant, and lacked judgment at certain times when prudent action was critical for success, both his and that of the country. This man was often courageous when courage was not called for and cautious to the point of reticence when courageous action was required. Further, his wife, Jessie, and his influential father-in-law, Thomas Hart Benton, powerful Senator from Missouri, were both assets and liabilities. They supported the career of Frémont but provided targets for detractors. And Frémont would ultimately fall out of Senator Benton's favor.

Frémont, as General of the Army of the West, issued a document in August 1861, which, among other things, contained an emancipation proclamation, freeing the slaves of Missouri secessionists. This action came at a time when President Lincoln was doing a balancing act with the Border States, trying to retain them within the Union. Asked by Lincoln to retract the proclamation, Frémont refused. Jessie carried the refusal to Lincoln personally, and in her heated defense of John Charles guaranteed his dismissal by being arrogant also. Lincoln did not act soon to relieve him, but first gave him every chance to be successful.

All of the events outlined have overshadowded the important topographic and botanical contributions of Frémont, derived from his exploration of the American West. The first three expeditions, prior to his court-martial and resignation from the Army at the end of the third journey, were especially important.

Frémont had been trained in the art and science of topographical work by Joseph Nicolas Nicollet, who made pioneer surveys of that part of the United States between the Mississippi and Missouri Rivers, including all or parts of North and South Dakota, Minnesota, Wisconsin, Illinois, Iowa, and Missouri (map by Nicollet & Frémont, 1843). Nicollet understood the broad aspects of such surveys, and insisted on having a botanist, Karl Geyer, attached to the expeditions. When funds were not available from the government to pay for the botanical services, Nicollet paid Geyer personally. The example was not lost on bright and impressionable John Charles. Indeed, when Nicollet was unable to complete the survey of that portion of Iowa along the Des Moines River in the summer of 1841, Frémont was sent to accomplish it, and Geyer accompanied him. On each of the Nicollet expeditions Frémont had an opportunity to observe Geyer at work, and those observations would serve western American botany well during future trips.

The work with Nicollet had prepared Frémont for the important task of providing maps for the settlement of much of the American West. Americans were moving west in increasing numbers, some to the Oregon Territory, where the United States had a legitimate claim, and others to California, where the claim was clouded or lacking. Maps of the route to Oregon were either lacking or of very poor quality. Those provided with the reports of the first and second expeditions closed the gap between the edge of the American frontier along the Missouri River and the west coast of the continent. That of the second expedition also showed the outline of the Great Basin, and clearly demonstrated the extent of Alta California in its broadest sense. The third expedition map was marked with routes across Colorado, Utah, Nevada, and through northern California into southern Oregon. The gap between the second and third expeditions was closed.

The first expedition in 1842, lasting six months from the time Frémont left Washington City, began near the mouth of the Kansas River, present Kansas City, Kansas, and proceeded west along that river and across the divide to the Platte River, near Grand Island, Nebraska. The route (Figures 1 and 3) was then west to the junction of the North and South Platte Rivers, up the south Fork to St. Vrain's Fort, in Colorado, then north to Fort Laramie, Wyoming. West from that fort the route followed up the North Platte to the Sweetwater River and west to South Pass, and northwest to the Wind River Mountains, Sublette County, Wyoming. The return route was back to Fort Laramie and down the Platte to the Missouri.

The second expedition (Figure 2), 1843–44 (14 months in duration), began like the first at the mouth of the Kansas, followed up the Kansas, up the Republican Fork, and over the divide to the South Platte and St. Vrain's Fort. Southward to Pueblo, back to St. Vrain's Fort, the party moved then northwestward into Wyoming, west to Idaho, south to the Great Salt Lake, back to Fort Hall, and west along the Snake River, ultimately to The Dalles. South from that place they moved to south-central Oregon, then almost due east to the Great Basin, and south along the west side of the Basin to the vicinity of present Carson City. From there the men, cold and suffering, and their equally suffering mules and horses, crossed the Sierra Nevada in January and February of 1844. At Sutter's Fort they recuperated and refitted prior to going south up the San Joaquin Valley, across a pass near Tehachapi Pass, into the Mohave Desert. They crossed the desert on the Spanish Trail through eastern California, southern Nevada, and Utah (Figure 4), then all still parts of Alta California, Mexico. From Utah Lake they proceeded across northeastern Utah and northwestern Colorado, and into southern Wyoming. At the Platte they turned southward into the great parks of Colorado, finally arriving at the Arkansas River, which was followed downward to Bent's Fort. From there the route was across the prairie lands of eastern Colorado and Kansas back to Westport.

The expedition was amazing for its length, estimated at more than 5500 miles, and for the difficulty of the country traversed. The agony of hours, days, weeks, and months in the saddle cannot be estimated.

The third expedition (Figure 5), 1845–47 (some 22 months in duration), began again at the mouth of the Kansas River, with a huge entourage, including the contingent of Lieutenants James W. Abert and William G. Peck, who had different goals than those of Frémont. They would separate at Bent's Fort, Otero County, Colorado, in August 1845. Frémont went west up the Arkansas past Pueblo and into the mountains, crossed the divide to the Grand (Colorado) River and thence to the head of the White River in western Colorado. The White River was followed downstream into Utah to its confluence with the Green. The route was then up the Duchesne River to near its head and over the divide to the Provo River, down which the group followed to Utah Lake and beyond to Great Salt Lake. The party then turned west across the salt flats of the Great Salt Lake desert and into Nevada. Across Nevada they traveled to Walker Lake and over the Sierra Nevada in November. Frémont was again at Sutter's Fort with a portion of his party of

62 armed men; the remainder under Joseph Walker proceeded to the south and crossed by another pass into California. The two groups met again near Monterey early in 1846 and were invited out of the country by the Californians. After some show of force, Frémont's party moved slowly up the Sacramento River to Lassen's, Tehama County. And, as spring came on the men and animals moved northward to Modoc County, and finally into Klamath County, Oregon.

There Frémont was overtaken by messengers telling him to return at once to California. The war with Mexico, which would add California to the United States, was imminent, and Frémont would be involved in it. The political, not very likeable, Frémont would emerge. He acted decisively (e.g., killing Indians) when decisive action was unnecessary and indecisively (e.g., not actually joining the Bear Flag rebellion) when decisive action was necessary. He is both lauded and despised for his action and lack thereof. His arrogance, vanity, and quest for wealth were sources of his ultimate downfall. Frémont had collaborated with Commodore Stockton of the U.S. Navy in initial stages of the California war, portions of which succeeded well. Out of Frémont's vision, a nemesis was to appear in the form of General Stephen Watts Kearny (Figure 6, route of Army of the West). Frémont chose to side with Stockton instead of admitting subservience to General Kearny. The fault is not entirely his, but he could have come away in grand style by application of finesse and a willingness to collaborate. Instead, he left California under house arrest, a condition that was made formal upon his arrival at Fort Leavenworth, Kansas, late in 1847. At his court-martial in Washington City, Frémont was found guilty of mutiny and could have been dismissed from the Army. President Polk approved the sentence but canceled the punishment. Frémont resigned in a huff. He had demanded and expected exoneration.

The resignation would change the course of topographic and botanical exploration for much of the following decade. The topographic expeditions would be led by others less qualified than Frémont.

The fourth expedition (Figure 7), 1848–49 (privately financed), was a disaster and is related here only because of its meager botanical importance. It was undertaken by Frémont, partly at least, to demonstrate his continued viability as a topographer, and partly with the hope of continued governmental support. The story of the fourth expedition is both simple and tragic. The party moved from the Missouri River on 21 October 1848 to Bent's Fort, Otero County, Colorado, on 21 November. The start was too late in the year, and tragedy could have been avoided only by competent planning, care, and preparation, all of which were missing. The competent men of the second and third expeditions were mainly not present, and the ill-prepared and poorly led party moved up the Arkansas, crossed the Sangre de Cristo range, and proceeded into the San Luis Valley. At the head of the Rio Grande are the San Juan Mountains. The winter was unusually severe. The party was turned back by a wall of snow and ice, high winds and high elevations, and in retreat left behind 10 men and 120 mules.

The retreat was to Taos, New Mexico. As soon as he could reorganize and refit, Frémont and those of the party who would still follow him moved south along the Gila track into Arizona, Sonora, back into Arizona, and into southern California.

The fifth expedition (Figure 8), 1853–54 (again privately financed), was the result of hopeful expectations by Thomas Hart Benton that Frémont might lead one of the railroad surveys. Frémont was in Europe when a letter from Benton told him to come home, in expectation of such an assignment. The Secretary of War, Jefferson Davis, would hardly appoint anti-slavery Frémont on the recommendation of his anti-slavery father-in-law. The assignment went to Captain John W. Gunnison. Frémont, not to be discouraged by such an event, decided to go anyway.

Captain Gunnison and his party were already well into the field before Frémont arrived. Frémont would demonstrate once and for all that he could cross the Colorado Rockies in mid-winter. Frémont had been ill and joined the party late on 30 October 1853 on the Saline Fork of the Kansas, and on 1 November the party of men and animals were finally under way toward Bent's Fort. The entourage entered the Rockies on 3 December. Frémont never published an account of the expedition. The most complete record was published by Carvalho, his dageurreotypist. On 14 December they crossed Cochetopa Pass, following the route of Captain Gunnison, who had preceded them through this very region some months earlier. The route was then along the Gunnison River to the vicinity of Delta, Colorado, then north to Grand Junction, where the men plunged with their horses into the ice-margined Grand (Colorado) River. Ahead of them lay more than a hundred miles of the most desolate land in North America. The route was across the gray, sparsely vegetated tracts of Mancos Shale to the Green River, a route with few water holes and little vegetation for their stock. Beyond the Green River the route did not improve. They traversed dry desertic country with few water holes, crossed mountain ranges, and passed through valleys until they finally came to the pioneer village of Parowan, Utah.

When finally able to travel again, the survey party moved across southern Nevada into California. Frémont's contributions were essentially completed. He was 41 years of age.

What were his contributions? His able topographers, Charles Preuss of the first, second, and fourth expeditions, and Edward M. Kern of the third, had contributed maps useful in colonization of the West. The maps of the first and second expeditions were especially useful in the settlement of Oregon and in the Mormon migration. More to the point of this presentation are his botanical contributions. The first expedition yielded 22 new taxa, the second 79, the third 52, the fourth 10, the fifth 1 taxon, and there are 3 whose expedition is unknown. A total of 19 new genera were based on the Frémont gatherings. The collections extant at The New York Botanical Garden, Gray, Missouri Botanical Garden, and U.S. National herbaria have yielded specimens from 108 families of vascular plants, 448 genera, and 1064 species and/or infraspecific taxa, from among 2129 known specimens or literature citations.

By late 20th century standards it is difficult to evaluate the contributions of Frémont. The principal purpose of the Frémont expeditions was topographic, i.e., the production of maps of previously unmapped or poorly mapped regions of the American West. Measurements of latitude and longitude were essential to accurate construction of maps. Such measurements are more easily described than done. Frémont stood for hours in the snow to take measurements of the satellites of Jupiter and other astronomical bodies.

Weather conditions often precluded observations of the sun or of the stars, and the chronometer was not without its flaws. To such observations were added measurements of air temperature and barometric pressure, and water samples were taken for analysis of mineral content. Mineral and fossil samples were collected and taken along with the baggage of the expedition. Collection of plants was a chore added to all of the others of the expedition, not the least of which involved caring for cattle, horses, mules, and men. Feeding large numbers of people was often simplified. The five expeditions were supported by roughly 25, 42, 62, 33, and 25 persons respectively, and in some cases the food for the day was solved by killing another mule. On portions of the second and fifth expeditions a horse or a mule was eaten by the entourage each day and a half. On both of those expeditions there were too many days and too few horses or mules. Unfortunately, on the fourth expedition the carcasses of frozen horses were left behind in the mountains and could not be eaten. The options for the men were two: stay and freeze to death, or walk towards the settlements and survive long enough to be saved.

The chief advantage of the personnel of the expeditions was that they could and did eat anything. A skunk made a part of a meal for one of the messes of the second expedition as it was approaching Utah. The dog Clammet was eaten on the crossing of the Sierra Nevada in February 1844, not the first dog to be eaten. Preuss, the dour, pessimistic realist, would not eat horse, mule, or dog at first, but did finally when there was no other choice. In fact he reached the point when he considered a mule's head boiled all night a delicacy, as long as salt was available. Too often, when the men were forced from want of wild game to eat their pack and riding animals, those same animals had been subjected to weeks or months of privation, and starving men were fed starving animals, barely able to move along themselves.

Mosquitoes and other biting flies and vermin plagued the Frémont expeditions as they still do modern ones. In more modern times there are numerous repellents to at least mitigate the attacks of insects. In Frémont's time the men spent much time at each of the warm season camps standing in the smoke of their fires, trying to escape clouds of biting flies and mosquitoes.

Horses and mules had to be cared for first. They were the part of the expedition responsible for carrying it along. In spite of the care of wranglers reared with animals and knowing of their needs since early youth, there were cases of lost animals, times when several of them returned to a favored campsite, even though guarded. Some were taken by Indians, who viewed them not so much as beasts of burden but as walking larders.

The parties consisted, in large part, of Creole and French Canadian voyageurs, who were paid from 62½ cents to $1.00 per day. These mostly very young men had already spent few to many years on the western frontier. The men spoke French, to Frémont's pleasure, knew how to survive in primitive conditions, could eat anything, were competent horsemen and riflemen, and could survive the rigors of weather, insects, and all other troubles of the frontier. Without them the Frémont expeditions would have failed at the start.

Accompanying the voyageur core of his parties were such men as Kit Carson, whom Frémont met by chance on his way up the Missouri at the beginning of the first expedition. Carson was on the second and third expeditions also. Alex Godey was on the second, third, and fourth expeditions. Thomas (Brokenhand) Fitzpatrick was largely answerable for the success of the second expedition; he was responsible for the baggage and animals. Without his loyal dedication the party would have failed. Joseph Walker joined the second expedition after it had arrived in southern Utah in the spring of 1844 and was also on the third expedition. Walker knew much of the West, and had preceded Frémont to California, across the Sierra Nevada, by several years. Richard Owens, Kit Carson's partner, who joined the third expedition, was a very able person. Charles Preuss complained constantly but did the work, made the observations to keep the log of each day's journey, and finally summarized the information to form maps. Hunters, mainly Delaware Indians, accompanied the second, third, and fifth expeditions. These men were hardy, resourceful, and courageous. Without them the Frémont expeditions would have been much more difficult—perhaps impossible. They came home, months later from the almost disastrous fifth expedition, not having any lasting ill effects from the journey, finding it not as hard as wintering with their own tribe.

Not all of the men came back. Only the first expedition was free of human casualties. Jean Baptiste Tabeau and François Badeau died on the second expedition, the half-breed Denny, Delaware Indian Crane, and Basil Lajeunesse were killed by Klamath Indians on the third expedition, and ten men, including the faithful Rafael Proue, who had been on all four expeditions, died on the fourth journey. Oliver Fuller died of exposure and starvation on the fifth expedition.

Horses and mules suffer from all of the failings attributed to the men they serve. They have minds of their own, and people who work with them look to a benevolent deity for special consideration after having worked with them. Animals require food, water, and rest. These along with cattle and dogs suffered with the men, served as food, and died of fatigue and starvation along the way. The Frémont routes were strewn with the carcasses of his animals.

Each day the animals, whether pack, riding, or draught, would be rounded up, caught, and fitted with bridles, hackamores, saddles, or harnesses. Baggage would be arranged and packed, and finally tied on the animals or placed in carts. Food was prepared for breakfast, with an arrangement for a lunch near midday. The evening meal was probably prepared with greatest care and required more time than other meals. Wood was gathered and fires started as the animals were unpacked and camp set up. Often most of the men slept in a single large lodge of buffalo hides, with a separate small one for Frémont.

Amidst all of the unpacking and preparations, the plants were collected and pressed. Dry plants were removed from the presses at intervals and packed separately in material that was at least somewhat waterproof. The fact that plants were taken at all is a tribute to John Charles, devoted collector. Once dried and packed away there was no certainty that they would reach the east and the caring eyes of eager botanists. A pack mule carrying some of the plants fell into a chasm in the Sierra Nevada on the second expedition. Neither animal nor pack was recovered. A flood on the Smoky Hill Fork of the Kansas inundated the camp, including packets of dried plants taken from Sutter's in California eastward to Colorado. Many were destroyed.

The plants of the first expedition were taken by a naïve John Charles; he did not make prior arrangements for their disposition at the end of the trip. An acquaintance, Benedict Jaeger, suggested that the plants be sent to Dr. John Torrey, professor of chemistry at Princeton and Columbia. Somewhat presumptuously the plants were sent prior to receiving an affirmative reply from Torrey. Torrey and colleague Asa Gray of Harvard University were grasping at straws, as it were. Specimens from the American West, were rare as hen's teeth, being represented mainly by collections of Meriwether Lewis and William Clark, David Douglas, Thomas Drummond, John Richardson, and Thomas Nuttall. Both Torrey and Gray were closely bound to their institutions, and were known, fairly or unfairly, as herbarium or closet botanists. Each was eagerly and intently awaiting the arrival of other materials, which were then compared to the meager assemblage of specimens already at hand. All botanical works available were searched in detail for clues to the identity of western American plants, and many of them were regarded as conspecific with Old World ones.

Frémont apologized for the quality of the first expedition plants, and Gray suggested to Torrey that a botanist be sent with Frémont on subsequent expeditions. Not until the fourth expedition did a botanist, Frederick Creutzfeldt, accompany Frémont, and then not to Frémont's satisfaction. Creutzfeldt apparently did not keep track of where the specimens were collected and allowed them to be wet repeatedly. No matter who collected the plants they are credited to Frémont. In spite of the conditions under which the first expedition plants were collected and despite the lack of a botanist, the collections are not especially poor. Locality data were evidently kept by Frémont in his daily journal, and many of the first expedition plants, published in large part in 1843 by Dr. Torrey, were assigned localities.

The larger second and third expeditions each had increased tasks. Frémont either was unable to devote as much attention to locality data, or at least the locality data accompanying the specimens did not reach Dr. Torrey. Nevertheless, Frémont continued to take plants throughout the second expedition, even during the precarious and life-threatening crossing of the Sierra Nevada, when he collected the type of *Libocedrus decurrens* Torrey. Following the disastrous flood on the Smoky Hill Fork of the Kansas, he was determined to replace the soaked, moldy, damaged specimens from the second expedition. The third expedition would, he hoped, make up for the destroyed ones from the earlier expedition.

No complete itinerary of the third expedition was ever published, due to the unhappy events following the California war. Camp was established at Westport, Kansas, on 23 June 1845, and the day following the expedition was under way. Dates from specimens indicate that plants were taken routinely across Kansas and eastern Colorado. The party arrived at Bent's Fort, Otero County, Colorado, on 2 August. Following refitting and parting with the Abert and Peck contingent, Frémont moved west on 16 August. By 25 September the party was in Utah, having taken plants across the mountains and valleys of Colorado. The next known record of plants was on 2 or 3 October, along the Provo River, Utah, and the next following were taken one day west of Donner Pass, probably in Placer County, California. Gathering of plants continued more or less through the winter of 1845–46, but increased when the group was forced into days of idleness along the valley of the Sacramento River, especially at Lassen's ranch near present Vina, Tehama County, California. The men were at the ranch on at least three occasions during the height of the spring flowering season, and the plants reflect the spring flora of the region, rich in beautiful flowers. Lupines, gilias, redbud, mints, clovers, oaks, louseworts, and various liliaceous plants were gathered. Enough of them bear dates or specific places to which dates can be assigned to give indications of the large numbers of plants collected.

Collecting essentially ended with the beginning of Frémont's involvement with the California war. The plants taken were not forgotten, however. Frémont had been disappointed with the events of the second expedition when part of the plants were destroyed, almost at the point of salvation. He had apologized to Torrey for the bedraggled appearance of the first expedition specimens. Now he would see that the specimens would arrive safely in Torrey's hands. The specimens were bound in packets and placed in tin boxes. The ends were then soldered shut, and placed within wooden boxes, each bound up in a green cow hide. Boxes were sent by ship to Panama, carried across the isthmus, and shipped from there to New York. The specimens arrived in excellent condition, to be shared by Dr. Torrey with Dr. Gray for determination and publication of novelties.

Plants of the first expedition were published in their entirety in an appendix to the first report in 1843 (Torrey, 1843). Only new genera, species, and infraspecific taxa taken on the second expedition were published. There were just too many of them and too little time to do them justice in the appendix of the second expedition report in 1845 (Frémont, 1845). Now the third expedition's specimens had arrived, the plants were in very good condition, but they could not be published, even in part, as had those from earlier expeditions. The only publication authorized by the Senate following the third expedition was the *Geographical Memoir*, which did not contain the usual botanical appendix. It is evident that Torrey again provided the determinations to fill in the botanical names left blank in Frémont's notes and ultimately in the Memoir. The materials forming the bases of new taxa taken by Frémont on the third expedition would appear in various journals over a period covering more than half a century.

The third expedition collections yielded only somewhat fewer new taxa than did those of the second expedition. Following collection and examination, much time is necessary to establish a taxonomic concept. This depends on the expertise of the particular botanist, the status of knowledge of a particular genus, the presence of literature to allow valid comparisons, and the presence of sufficient herbarium material for comparison. The taxa described as new by Torrey, Gray, George Bentham, Sereno Watson, Per Axel Rydberg, Edward Tuckerman, and Willis Jepson were only a part of the new taxa within the Frémont collections at the time of their collection. Many taxa were described later on the basis of materials taken by other workers, which, unknown to the later workers, were first taken by Frémont and his contemporaries.

In a letter to Torrey prior to the fourth expedition, Frémont wrote: "I have good reasons for believing that I shall receive aid from the government in carrying on the work, and am now making my arrangements in that expectation. Perhaps you will be able to give me the approximate amount which we shall require for our botany, as I should like to include it in the general estimate" (NY!; copy BRY!). He hoped to raise sufficient money to complete investigations for a botanical publication, essentially a flora of California.

How Frémont expected to complete such a flora is not known. Certainly the belated start and tragic events in the San Juan Mountains of Colorado did not offer opportunity to complete floristic studies. The botanical contributions from that expedition, few as the specimens are, were made possible by the tragedy; the party was forced south into springtime, when plants were blooming and collections were possible. Creutzfeldt's botany (though attributed to Frémont), provided science with materials on which 10 new taxa were based in whole or in part. Governmental support was not forthcoming, and the hoped-for flora was a vanishing dream. Nevertheless, the Frémont specimens would add to the body of knowledge on which the Flora of California (Brewer, et al., 1876) would be based.

The fifth expedition, begun late in 1853, would add the final few specimens to be taken by Frémont. By the time he arrived in the field on 31 October 1853, the man who laid the tracks he would follow through much of the winter, John W. Gunnison, was already dead. Gunnison, leading the expedition Frémont had sought, arrived at the Rocky Mountains months earlier, and blazed a trail westward, surveying for a route for a railroad to the Pacific. On 26 October, while camped along the Sevier River in Utah, his small party was ambushed by Indians. Killed were Gunnison, Creutzfeldt, and Richard Kern. Both Creutzfeldt and Kern had been with Frémont on the disastrous fourth expedition. The Gunnison expedition then fell to E. G. Beckwith, whose group had been separated from the main Gunnison contingent at the time of the disaster.

The ill-advised but not ill-prepared fifth expedition traversed the mountainous country in midwinter, when collecting of plants is poor at best. The few plants taken on the expedition were collected late, either in western Nevada or southeastern California. One new genus, *Syntrichopappus*, with its new species, *S. fremontii*, was named by Asa Gray from plants taken on this final trip.

Following the first expedition Frémont had written to Torrey asking if it were not possible for one who was not a botanist to stand in the shadow of one who was and publish with them? In this manner he invited his inclusion as coauthor of the 18 new species published in the appendix of the second report. Thus the association in botanical authorship of Torrey and Frémont came into being. In spite of his affiliation with Torrey in this manner, Frémont should not be considered a botanical professional. He was, however, an ardent and dedicated plant collector. His collections became part of an ever-expanding database that allowed interpretation of the botany of the West. His place in the botany of this region is certainly assured.

Frémont's achievement was in leading small groups of men beyond the frontier in the American West. His flaws of character—arrogance, conceit, vanity, lack of judgment—cannot diminish the importance of his contributions to botany, among which are more than 40 plants bearing his name, and botanists today continue to regard him highly for his work, performed under the most arduous of conditions.

Biography

More than a century has passed since the death of John Charles Frémont, and it has been a century and a half since his first topographical expedition. The American West has changed much since that time, the land has filled with people, civilization has progressed, and the understanding of the region has increased dramatically. Much of the American West was poorly explored and maps were poor and often misleading. Frémont, in five expeditions, left a legacy of information that aided in the settlement of this vast region. He left the comforts of home and family and endured untold hardships to follow the endless rocky and sagebrush-choked expanses of the western wilderness. Maps, climatic information, camp localities, and distances were based on the endeavors of Frémont and his men, and the data provided were used by pioneers who surged into the American West during the great migrations of the middle nineteenth century. The fatigue and excitement in organizing of the surveys, the time spent in the saddle, the distances covered, and the separation from home and family cannot now, in this age of swift travel and computers, be easily understood. The distances were vast; the party on horseback would plod from morning to dusk and still be in the same valley, not so much from want of speed but from sheer extent of the land. Neither food nor lodging was available; everything necessary to the expedition had to be carried or obtained by whatever means possible. Specimens collected on the way, with some notable exceptions, had to be carried along to the conclusion of the trip, since there were few places from which they could be sent home. The fact that any of the frail, dry, pressed plant specimens survived the expeditions is a tribute to the men who collected, dried, protected, and carried them along.

This review is an attempt to look at one aspect of Frémont's life and works aside from topographical and political facets of his life. That aspect, his botanical contributions, cannot be separated from his expeditions, however. The plants collected by Frémont were carried by pack animals, typically mules, through the sparsely populated lands of the West and delivered to botanists in the eastern United States. There the fragile specimens were fitted into the array of plants that arrived from partially explored land, and their descriptions and names became part of American botany. This account of the plants taken, and of their disposition and place within the framework of botany, would be incomplete without an overview of the life and times of Frémont, and, especially, without a detailed review of his expeditions of exploration and discovery. The locations where plants were taken is of great scientific interest. If plants are described as new, their place of discovery, i.e., the type locality, is of importance in allowing them to be relocated with some accuracy. This work attempts to place as many as possible of the Frémont plants at their points of discovery. The existence of the specimens in herbaria at the present time raises enquiries about their collector and his life and times. No attempt will be made to account for the plant fossils taken by Frémont.

John Charles Frémont was many things—topographer, mathematician, pathfinder and explorer, scientist and skilled observer, political candidate, governor, senator, military officer, administrator, entrepreneur, and husband and father, among others. Hidden within his list of roles are those of botanical pioneer, collector, and coauthor. While much has been written about his complex personality and amazing life, his role in botany is somewhat obscured within the large bibliography (Upham, 1856; Bigelow, 1856; Dellenbaugh, 1914; Egan, 1977; Nevins, 1956; Herr, 1987; Rolle, 1991) of his life and works. McKelvey (1955), in her monumental work, summarized some of it, and Jackson and Spence (1970) devoted much energy in their brilliant and exhaustive work to noting his botanical contributions. In the index of Jackson and Spence (1970) references are given to all scientific plant names included in Frémont's accounts, and where possible their modern equivalents have been determined, often in conjunction with botanical historian Joseph Ewan. The most detailed, professional, and complete works on Frémont, on which the narrative of this treatment is based in large part, are the series of books by Jackson and Spence (1970), Jackson (1973), Spence and Jackson (1973a, 1973b), and Spence (1984).

The popular or semipopular and serious historical biographies of John Charles and Jessie range from the "guilded" accounts by Upham and Bigelow to the fine works of Dellenbaugh, Egan, Nevins, and Herr (a brilliant biography of Jessie), and finally to the less than factual treatment by Rolle. None of these works give due credit to the role of John Charles as a botanical collector, a role, it must be admitted, secondary to the topographic surveys, the main objectives of the expeditions. Frémont's botanical exploration, his collections, together with his written materials and those publications by others reflecting on his role in botany form the basis of this work. An attempt is made herein to place his botanical contributions in perspective.

A person's beginnings should not of necessity be complex. Frémont's origins were, however. He was born on 21 January 1813 in Savannah, Georgia, the illegitimate son of Jean Charles Fremon and Anne Beverley Whiting Pryor. Anne's husband, Major John Pryor, was still living. When Pryor and Anne were married, he was 62, and she was 17. Divorce appeal to the Virginia legislature by Pryor was denied on 13 December 1811, and Pryor died in 1823, some five years after Fremon's death (Jackson & Spence, 1970: xxiv). In 1815 and 1817, respectively, a daughter and a second son were born to the Fremons. By 1818 Charles Fremon was dead, and Anne and her children, then residing in Norfolk, Virginia, later moved to Charleston, South Carolina.

John Charles, called Charley by his friends, would add a terminal "t" to his surname when he was about 25; and later still the acute accent was added to the "e." He went to school in Charleston, where he received a classical education. He was "a boy of fine features topped by a beautiful mass of curly, dark hair; and his light blue eyes and olive-colored skin made him stand out" (Egan, 1977: 7). He was drawn to people of influence and came under the guidance of Joel Roberts Poinsett (1779–1851), who had served as United States minister to Mexico. It was Poinsett who helped John Charles secure a position as teacher of mathematics on a naval vessel, the U.S. sloop of war *Natchez*, on a cruise down the coast of South America. The assignment lasted for two years, until June 1835.

Poinsett again influenced Frémont's future by aiding him with an assignment as assistant engineer for a survey of a route for a railroad from Charleston to Cincinnati. In 1836 Frémont was engaged in still another survey; this time he ventured into the Cherokee lands in North Carolina, Tennessee, and Georgia. While these surveys were in progress, Joel Poinsett was appointed Secretary of War by President Martin Van Buren. Poinsett was contacted by John Charles and was again aided by this influential ally with an appointment to the Nicollet survey. The 25-year-old Frémont had applied for a commission, and at the request of Poinsett he was later appointed Second Lieutenant in the United States Topographical Corps. His work with the Nicollet survey, initially as a civilian, began in April 1838, when he received notice from Lieutenant Colonel John James Abert, Bureau of Topographical Engineers, to report to St. Louis (Jackson & Spence, 1970: 3). Abert would be honored by John Charles on the second expedition; a lake in Oregon was named for him. Joseph Nicolas Nicollet (1786–1843) was an amazingly competent topographer, who became a close friend and ally of John Charles. Nicollet is remembered in botany by the genus *Nicolletia* (see Appendix I).

Nicollet was to make a survey of the territory lying between the Mississippi and Missouri Rivers. Frémont would be his student in the guise of an assistant (at $4.00 per day). Nicollet introduced John Charles to Pierre Chouteau, Jr. (1789–1865), of the American Fur Company (also called P. Chouteau, Jr., and Company), among others. That introduction would serve Frémont well in later expeditions, when St. Louis would be the starting and ending point. Accompanying this expedition was Karl Andreas Geyer (1809–53), 29, a botanist from Dresden, Germany, who came to North America in 1834. Geyer was employed privately by Nicollet. The party arrived at Fort Snelling (in present Minneapolis-St. Paul), Minnesota, on 25 May 1838. The fort was then an outpost at the edge of civilization. At the hamlet of Mendota baggage was transferred to two-wheeled carts drawn by draught animals, and the men were mounted on horses or mules for their survey of the plains country. They determined positions of the various features, mapped them, took notes, and kept records of the country as the party moved from place to place, ending the season upon their return to St. Louis in December of 1838. In St. Louis Nicollet made preparations for the next season of mapping and surveying. Frémont went to Washington City to report to Poinsett.

In March of 1839 Colonel Abert instructed Lieutenant Frémont to go to St. Louis as soon as possible (Jackson & Spence, 1970: 45). The Nicollet expedition that second year was to explore the area west of the Mississippi and north of the Missouri, with headquarters at present-day Pierre, South Dakota. Geyer was hired at government expense, for $2.00 per day. Accompanying this expedition was Etienne Provost (ca. 1782–1850), a mountain man with experience in the Rocky Mountains and the Great Basin, where he is credited with discovery of the Great Salt Lake (Jackson & Spence, 1970: 68). Discussions between Provost and Frémont are unrecorded, but the two of them must have spoken of the Great Salt Lake and the surrounding region, places that would attract Frémont during later expeditions.

The mapping expedition worked in what is now North Dakota during the summer and surveyed the region around Devil's Lake. From there the survey party moved to the southeast to Lac que Parle in Minnesota. They reached the steamboat landing near Fort Snelling on the first of November, but Frémont missed the last steamboat of the season and was obliged to make an overland march to St. Louis, in winter, a prologue to events on subsequent expeditions when winter travel was a necessity. The two expeditions with Nicollet had prepared him to make astronomical observations, sketch topography, learn the names of plants and see how specimens were collected and cared for in the field, observe soils and minerals, and make maps (Nicollet & Frémont map, 1843). He was thus prepared as a topographer.

Frémont returned to Washington toward the end of 1839. There, with Nicollet, he attended a meeting with Secretary of War Poinsett and President Martin Van Buren. Nicollet had already given a glowing account of Frémont's performance on the two journeys of exploration to the upper Midwest. President Van Buren was the first of several presidents to be known personally by Frémont. He then accompanied Nicollet to Baltimore for a rest and change of pace. While there John Charles learned of the death of his brother Frank, from complications following an accidental gunshot wound. His sister Elizabeth had died eight years earlier. He traveled to Charleston to be by his mother's side during this time of sorrow.

Now, John Charles was the lone survivor of the issue of his parents. He returned to Washington, leaving his mother in Charleston. In Washington he moved with Nicollet into the residence of Ferdinand Rudolph Hassler (1770–1843), superintendent of the United States Coast Survey. Hassler, then 70 years of age, was to become a good friend and ally. He provided offices for his guests in the Coast Survey building, which was near his residence.

A visitor to the Hassler home was the senior senator from Missouri, Thomas Hart Benton (1782–1858), a man convinced of the necessity for western expansion of the United States. Benton's dream of a United States extending from the Atlantic to the Pacific came within the vision of Lieutenant Frémont. The still youthful topographer now dreamed of providing the maps and information that would be essential for emigrants moving west. And, perhaps equally important to this handsome, single young man, Frémont was invited to dinners with the Benton family, where he heard Senator Benton and his friends discuss the grand ideas of empire and western expansion.

John Charles became well acquainted with the Senator and his wife, Elizabeth, and with some of their children. The older girls were attending a boarding school in Georgetown, however. Frémont went with Eliza, one of the Benton daughters, to listen to music at the school. There he first saw Jessie Benton (1824–1902), only 15 years of age. The first sight overwhelmed Frémont, then 26. He waxed poetic in prose that has persisted in his writings. "She made the effect that a rose of rare color or beautiful picture would have done" he said (Frémont, 1887: 66; Herr, 1987: 58). His life was forever changed by that encounter. The couple met again some months later, and, later still, the Bentons noted that a bond existed between this couple so separated by age. Mrs. Benton objected to the relationship, and Senator Benton was not very pleased by the attentions of Frémont to this bright and attractive young girl.

Objections to the match between Jessie and John Charles involved the age difference, Jessie's youth, and the prospects of John Charles, who had no money and whose career in the Army would offer slow promotion and a migratory life-style. Senator Benton, as father not friend, told John Charles that, in any event, marriage would have to wait for a year at least. There was no alternative for Frémont, but to agree.

At this point, on 4 June 1841, John Charles received orders from Colonel Abert to go immediately to St. Louis to arrange for a survey of the lower Des Moines River area in Iowa, country not previously mapped. Frémont was sent in place of Nicollet, who was ill. He returned to St. Louis, and with the help of Chouteau's American Fur Company prepared for the expedition. Once again he hired Karl Geyer as botanist of the expedition (Frémont, 1887: 68).

Frémont, Geyer, and party surveyed the course of the Des Moines River, noting its rich growth of native herbs, grasses, and trees and shrubs. Geyer made plant collections and notes on the vegetation of the country. Summer passed quickly and by mid-August Frémont was back in Washington City, where he again visited the Benton home, ostensibly to tell Senator Benton of his successful adventure in Iowa, but in reality to see Jessie. At this time completion of the Nicollet surveys fell to John Charles, because of Nicollet's continued declining health.

Due to the work responsibility and the reluctance of the parents, John Charles and Jessie should have had little chance to continue their romance. The two must have met more than by chance, however, because the entire manuscript document of Frémont's report on the Des Moines was submitted in Jessie's hand (Jackson & Spence, 1970: 96). Were it not for the intervention of Mrs. John J. (Maria) Crittenden, wife of the senator from Kentucky, they would have had little if any possibility of meeting privately. The couple were allowed to meet secretly at her home. And it was Maria Crittenden who arranged for the wedding services for the impulsive couple, who had decided not to wait out the year dictated by Senator Benton (Frémont, 1887: 69; Herr, 1987: 62). The ceremony was conducted by a Catholic priest, Father Joseph Van Horseigh, after two protestant ministers, frightened by the potential consequences, refused to perform the ceremony (Jackson & Spence, 1970: 103). At the Crittenden home on 19 October 1841, 17-year-old Jessie was married to John Charles, then 28. After some time of living as if unmarried, Jessie at the family home and Frémont in his own quarters, John Charles and Jessie visited with Nicollet, who was confined to his room, still ill. Nicollet told them not to continue the sham, but to let the Bentons know as soon as possible that they were married. This the husband and wife did, confronting Benton in his home the next morning. After an initial heated objection, Benton welcomed them into his house, and he informed the distraught Mrs. Benton of the marriage and future living arrangements of the couple. A somewhat different account of the breaking of the news and the living arrangements is given elsewhere (Herr, 1987: 64–65). John Charles now had the family he had so long lacked, a family tied to the course of destiny of the United States. His beloved Jessie was a remarkable young woman, who would become an extension of the hopes and dreams of John Charles and of her father—"a lady who sometimes took matters into her own hands and not always, I believe, to her husband's eventual benefit"

(McKelvey, 1955: 753). For now she would be the devoted young bride left behind when her energetic husband left on his faraway, romantic trips of exploration.

By the end of 1841, Frémont's previous experiences as a teacher of mathematics on the sailing ship off South America, surveyor, and explorer-topographer had prepared him to begin his life's work. His ties to the powerful Senator Benton, Poinsett, Nicollet, Hassler, and other influential people also placed him in a position of prominence; he was at center stage, where he could shine like a star or fail ignominiously. In the future John Charles would do both, without understanding how circumstance and the very people who had promoted his career had both helped and hindered him. He was, however, competent in his own right and worked diligently to achieve the immediate goals. A portion of his earlier work included an introduction to pioneer botanical methodology. He would in the future collaborate with the principal plant taxonomists of the period and participate in publication of portions of his botanical gatherings.

Joel Roberts Poinsett is acknowledged in Frémont's memoirs (1887: 22) as "one of the distinguished men of the day, of broad and liberal mind, refined by study and much travel. While Minister to Mexico his cultivated taste led him to interest himself in the luxuriant flora of that country. Known in a graver way through his public works and service, it has chanced that his name has been kept familiarly present and most popularly known by the scarlet Poinsettia which he contributed to botany." Poinsett was Frémont's influential older friend who promoted his career at critical times, and who was greatly admired and trusted by John Charles. The botanical interest of Poinsett could hardly have been lost on bright and impressionable John Charles. Certainly the example set by Nicollet in the hiring of Karl Geyer as botanist on the first and subsequent topographical expeditions between the Mississippi and Missouri Rivers was not lost on him either.

Indeed, Frémont was responsible for hiring the members of the second Nicollet expedition and also the shorter third expedition to Iowa. Nicollet had paid privately for Geyer's remuneration on the first (Frémont, 1887: 34). The second was at government expense ($2.00 per day), as was part of the Iowa trip ($1.50 per day by the government and an additional $100 paid privately by Nicollet). Nicollet was determined to have a botanist along on the expedition; he considered such a person an absolute necessity to the understanding of a geographical survey. Frémont obviously was impressed with the need to include botanical observations as a part of the investigations conducted. Collecting and collections would become an obsession.

Frémont (1887: 20) notes: "I remember, once along the banks of the Des Moines, a botanist with me stooped down and grasped the clustered head of a low flowering plant. Under the broad leaves lay coiled a rattlesnake, close to his hand. Geyer escaped, but it gave him a spasm that made him dig his heels into the ground and jerk his arms nervously about as he threw off the shock. Always afterward he looked for snakes among his flowers." The training received informally from Geyer would allow him to identify many of the plants of the prairies, plains, and mountains in the following years. Always sensitive to the plants of the areas traversed, he must have questioned and observed Geyer intensively during their three expeditions. Certainly the collections of the first Frémont expedition reflect a competence both in collecting and recording of botanical information.

Unfortunately that level of competence did not carry over completely to the larger second and third expeditions, wherein a great many more plants were taken but the collection data are comparatively fewer.

It is not my intention here to whitewash the record of Frémont, who was imperfect in many ways. It is my intention to attempt to understand his attributes and imperfections as they relate to his botanical contributions. Geyer did not consider Frémont to be a botanist, writing in a letter to William Jackson Hooker of Kew Gardens in 1845 that "neither he [Frémont] nor any of his party understood any thing about botany" (McKelvey, 1955: 755), but McKelvey admits that Geyer was "somewhat prone to belittle," and that Frémont would not take him along on the 1842 expedition, possibly because of Geyer's poor personality and his inability to get along with people generally. Could Geyer's evaluation not have been a case of sour grapes? And, what is it that defined a botanist in that era, or in any other, in fact? Certainly there was, and is, no one possible definition. In contemporary terms a botanist is whoever considers himself thusly, and usually excludes all whose training is different. Frémont alluded several times to his botanical interest. Those who would criticize him for not knowing many of the plants, even the common ones, and for his reliance on pioneer taxonomic botanists John Torrey (1796–1863), Asa Gray (1810–88), and others, betray an ignorance of process and practice of collecting and identifying plants. Frémont walked from one botanical region to another, in each of which it would require a lifetime to know most of the taxa. Indeed, in the century and a half since Frémont's expeditions, taxonomic problems along the routes he walked still persist, despite the devotion of generations of botanists since his time.

Living among Indians, some of whom had little if any previous contact with whites, had engendered both liking and understanding. Indians were to be respected, but not always trusted. Frémont would both welcome them and fight (and perhaps kill) them. And, regardless of the circumstances, he would observe how the Indians lived and record their livelihood, manners, customs, food, dress, and other aspects of their culture or heritage.

The previous ventures made from the base at St. Louis and his contacts with the Chouteau family were valuable assets. The Chouteaus, a long-established family in St. Louis with ties to the fur trade, were able to supply information, supplies, and men for Frémont's expeditions. Frémont enjoyed the mixed group of voyageurs who lived capably in the rough-and-tumble existence of the frontier and beyond. The men worked hard, spoke several languages, ate almost anything, and were, generally speaking, illiterate. He was now ready for the first grand adventure led by himself.

Materials dealing with the expeditions are taken from several primary sources, among them Frémont's personal published records of the 1842, 1843–44, and 1845–47 expeditions, published diaries and biographies by others on those and later expeditions, and published accounts by other authors who have drawn from those publications and from other sources. All sources are in the accompanying list of literature cited. Frémont tells his own story better than anyone else; therefore, to the extent possible the following treatment is quoted or paraphrased from the published Frémont journals. The results of the first, second, and third expeditions were published during Frémont's lifetime. Materials from the fourth and fifth expeditions are from Frémont where such documentation exists, and from other sources where Frémont is silent.

The quotations in the following account are reproduced faithfully as they appeared in the original publications cited in the list of references. Whether the inconsistencies are the result of hurried preparation of the Frémont manuscripts or errors by the typographer is not of consequence, but there are numerous incongruities. There is no consistent use of italics for scientific names, generic names mainly are in lowercase throughout, sometimes the author's names are italicized when the Latin names are not, punctuation is frequently placed within the parentheses instead of following, and spelling is often antiquated or merely wrong. Whatever the case, the quotes attempt to retain the peculiarities. Editorial comments and corrections are included in brackets. The traditional "sic" is not employed.

Chapter II

First Expedition—1842

Frémont was aware that the influential westerners, including Senator Thomas Hart Benton, had agreed that the time had come to put into action their views concerning Oregon. Senator Benton had decided that an expedition ought to be sent to open the way for the emigration then commencing. Whoever would fill the country with immigrants would control the destiny of the region. He intended that Joseph Nicollet should be at its head and that Frémont should be his assistant. While one objective of the expedition (Figure 1) would be to survey and describe a route of migration, a major objective, at least in the mind of Senator Benton, involved guaranteeing United States rights to territory bordering the Pacific, especially Oregon.

Nicollet would not be able to head such an expedition. He had become not only Frémont's superior and teacher, but his friend. He acknowledged the work of Frémont in the map of the hydrography of the upper Mississippi basin, prepared following years of extensive and intensive field and laboratory work (see Nicollet & Frémont, 1843, map citation), but his health had continued to decline, and the mantle of leadership fell logically on John Charles, who would need help of other professionally trained people in the future. Such a person, who would accompany him on his first, second, and fourth expeditions, was introduced to him by his friend Ferdinand Hassler. The man, "a strange figure—a shock of light curly hair standing up thick about his head, and a face so red that we attributed it to a wrong cause instead of to the cold and nervousness and anxiety which turned his speech into stammering," was Charles Preuss (1803–1854), a German and a skilled topographer (Frémont, 1887: 70). Preuss was as much in need of a paying position as Frémont was in need of help in working up the final results of the Nicollet surveys in the Dakotas, Minnesota, and Iowa. Preuss could not do the complicated mathematical computations, but Frémont hired him anyway and did the calculations himself.

Charles Preuss was an accomplished topographer who would more than match Frémont's generosity by his selfless, if complaining, service during three expeditions in the future. Additionally, Preuss kept a diary that has been translated and published (Gudde & Gudde, 1958). From his writings Preuss could never quite accept the conditions of life as they were—if conditions were bad now, they would be worse later. Yet, if times were really dire, Preuss could find in the situation something grand to live by. There were times when his descriptions of the botany of a region surpassed those of Frémont. He would prove to be Frémont's alter ego. Frémont did not report events that went wrong; Preuss would add those events, providing a more balanced picture of places and happenings. His topographical skills are indicated in the maps of the first and second expeditions.

The death of President William Henry Harrison made difficult the task of obtaining funds for the expedition to explore the country between the Missouri River and the Rocky Mountains, "in aid of and auxiliary to the Oregon emigration" (Frémont, 1887: 71). President John Tyler, though evidently not opposed to emigration to Oregon, kept much to himself, and the funding was obtained through delicate political maneuvering. During March 1842 Frémont went to New York to obtain necessary instruments and other materials, including an India-rubber boat with inflatable compartments.

On 2 May 1842 Frémont departed Washington City, leaving Jessie, then 18, with her parents. Following his arrival in St. Louis on 22 May, he began the task of outfitting for the expedition. Horses were acquired and equipment procured for the day-to-day tasks of the journey. Valuable and experienced men were selected, among them Clement Lambert, J. B. L'Esperance, J. B. Lefevre, Benjamin Potra, Louis Gouin, J. B. Dumes, Basil Lajeunesse, François Tessier, Benjamin Cadotte, Joseph Clement, Daniel Simonds, Leonard Benoit, Michel Morly, Baptiste Bernier, Honoré Ayot, François Badeau, Louis Menard, Joseph Ruelle, Moise Chardonaisse, Auguste Janisse, and Rafael Proue.

Wages paid ran from \$.62½ to \$1.85¾ per day, but most were for \$1.00 per day or less. In addition to these Creole and Canadian voyageurs, Charles Preuss, Lucien Bonaparte Maxwell (1818–1875), Henry Brandt, and Randolph Benton (12-year-old son of Senator Benton) joined Frémont on their trip by steamboat up the Missouri River to the mouth of the Kansas River. On the boat Frémont had the good fortune to meet Kit (Christopher) Carson (1809–1868). So pleased was John Charles with the meeting that, following some inquiry, he hired Carson as guide. "I presume the reports he [Frémont] received were favorable, for he told me he would engage me, paying me one hundred dollars per month" (Quaife, 1935: 66). The future of Carson and his role from this time forward were due to his association with Frémont on the expeditions. Jackson and Spence (1970: 170) note that there were others in the original party or who were added later but not indicated in the above roster, i.e., Registe Larente (who went only part way), Osea Hasrmiyo (hired near the mouth of the Laramie), and François Latulippe, who was encountered en route on 29 June (along the Platte River, present Dawson County, Nebraska) and hired immediately. Others would be added to the expedition from time to time. Some would leave it prior to completion of this and subsequent expeditions. Guides, usually Indians from various tribes, would be hired and carried along for a time.

Kit Carson had gone east from Bent's Fort (present Otero County, Colorado) to the Missouri with wagons belonging to Messrs. Bent and St. Vrain. He visited with friends and acquaintances and took a trip to St. Louis. From there he "took a steamer for the Upper Missouri, and—as luck would have it—Colonel Frémont, then a Lieutenant, was aboard the same boat" (Carter, 1968: 81). After some discussion Frémont offered him employment at \$100 per month, good wages for the time. "During the expedition, I [Carson] performed the duties of guide and hunter" (Quaife, 1935: 68; Carter, 1968: 84). His role was to be much greater than that of mere guide and hunter. Frémont trusted Carson, four years his senior, explicitly and was accompanied by him on all special occasions.

Scientific equipment consisted of barometers to determine elevation, thermometers to measure air and water temperature, chronometers to determine longitude, and astronomical instruments to determine latitude. Photographic equipment, including cameras and wet plates, was also a part of the materials to be transported. Frémont would try his hand at photography in the Wind River mountains, without success. Preuss noted (Gudde & Gudde, 1958) that he arrived at Chouteau's Landing, now a part of Kansas City, Missouri, on 4 June 1842. He pitched his tent and made the first barometric observations. "Weather good. Food bad. Beverages are coffee, tea, and water." Equipment and extra baggage were carried in carts. The armed and mounted party set out on the morning of Friday, 10 June 1842, from the trading house of Mr. Cyprian Chouteau, 12 miles above the mouth of the Kansas River, on a route west along the south side of the river. The route would continue through Kansas until 21 June (McKelvey, 1955: 757).

The men and animals forded the Kansas River roughly 100 miles above its mouth and followed up the Big Blue River, and its tributary the Little Blue River, for some distance. The route then crossed to the Platte River, which the party followed west to the junction of the South Platte. The South Platte was followed west to St. Vrain's Fort. Throughout the trek astronomical observations were made at critical points, and barometrical and temperature measurements were recorded. Preuss worked hard each day to record the topographical features and correlate them with calculations of latitude and longitude.

Frémont (1845: 13) took occasion on 18 June 1842 to record the plants observed in the rolling, virgin prairie. He was then near the mouth of the Vermillion, which enters the Kansas River from the north in Pottawatomie County (McKelvey, 1955: 757). The group left their encampment on the river bottom early on the 19th, proceeding on to the rolling country, and he recorded many beautiful plants in flower, among which "*amorpha canescens* was characteristic," and "enlivened the green of the prairie." At the heads of the ravines were seen occasional thickets of "*salix longifolia*, the common willow of the country." They made 19 miles and camped along a small creek. Location of the camp was determined as 39°30′40″ north, 96°14′49″ west.

Early on the morning of 20 June the men and animals were again under way along the Big Vermillion to the Big Blue River, in or near Marshall County, Kansas. Frémont (1845: 13) noted: "Whenever the soil was good and protected from the winds, in the creek bottoms and ravines, and on the slopes they [plants] flourished abundantly; among them the amorpha, still retaining its characteristic place." They crossed the Big Vermillion at 10 a.m. The drainage had a rich bottom of about a mile in breadth, one-third of which was occupied by timber. Antelope and deer were seen during the day, and Preuss wrote: "A prairie chicken was shot. If the cook cannot prepare it any better than the turtle [cooked earlier], let him gulp it down himself" (Gudde & Gudde, 1958: 9).

They continued west on 21 June. Along the route "*amorpha* has been a very abundant but variable bloom—in some places bending beneath the weight of purple clusters; in others without a flower. It seems to love best the sunny slopes with a dark soil and southern exposure. Every where the rose is met with, and reminds us of cultivated gardens and civilization. It is scattered over the prairies in small bouquets, and, when glittering in the dews and waving in the pleasant breeze of the early morning, is the most beautiful of the prairie flowers. The *artemisia*, absinthe, or prairie sage, as it is variously called, is increasing in size, and glitters like silver as the southern breeze turns up its leaves to the sun. All these plants have their insect inhabitants, variously colored; taking generally the hue of the flower on which they live. The artemisia has a small fly accompanying it through every change of elevation and latitude; and wherever I have seen the *asclepias tuberosa*, I have always remarked, too, on the flower a large butterfly, so nearly resembling it in color as to be distinguishable at a little distance only by the motion of its wings" (Frémont, 1845: 14).

Plant names in Frémont's daily journals, at least many of them, were left blank to be filled in ultimately, only after Dr. Torrey had made the necessary determinations, although at that time no authority on plants had been approached for such determinations. This practice should not, however, be construed as a lack of botanical knowledge, although most of the plant species were indeed new to John Charles; it is a routine practice for plant collectors to leave identifications vacant while in the field. Practically no one knows all plants observed, even with modern keys readily available. Frémont had only his previous few seasons of experience with plants similar to those encountered in easternmost portions of his explorations. West of the 105th meridian of longitude the botanical world changes; east of that line the climate is moist, to the west it is arid. The 105th meridian is a fixed imaginary line, but the change of climate across the invisible boundary (which, in actuality, shifts back and forth) is reflected by the vegetation.

From 22 June to 8 July the route was in Nebraska (McKelvey, 1955: 757). On 22 June the entourage moved forward 24 miles and camped on the Little Blue, near Powell, Jefferson County, Nebraska. On this day Preuss (Gudde & Gudde, 1958: 12) recorded, "Like every day—monotonous prairie ahead of us and behind us." On the 23rd they reached a very beautiful wooded stream, about 35 feet wide, called Sandy Creek, tributary to the Little Blue, in or near Adams County, Nebraska. "The country has become very sandy, and the plants less varied and abundant, with the exception of thc *amorpha*, which rivals the grass in quantity, though not so forward as it has been found to the eastward" (Frémont, 1845: 14). Later in the day he added, "The bed of a little creek was perfectly dry, and, on the adjacent sandy bottom, *cacti*, for the first time, made their appearance" (Frémont, 1845: 14). They traveled 28 miles and camped again on the Little Blue.

The next day, 24 June, elk were seen frequently and deer bounded from the groves. Elk were a common part of the fauna of the prairies and plains far to the east of their 20th-century montane distribution. The road in the afternoon was over the upper prairies, several miles from the river, and camp was set up at sunset on one of its small tributaries, "where an abundance of prele (*equisetum*) afforded fine forage to our tired animals" (Frémont, 1845: 15). The men and animals had traveled 31 miles, a long and tiring experience, later to become almost routine. Preuss (Gudde & Gudde, 1958: 13) remarked: "I should prefer to ride on alone and think, when the work permits, of old times than to have this rabble around me. If I only had a few congenial fellows, Germans of course, with me, we could make this monotonous prairie life agreeable enough. But so completely alone among these twenty-five people!" At least some Germans accompanied later expeditions, but Preuss then complained of other matters.

On 25 June the route was again to the westward along the Little Blue River, and Frémont noted, "the road of the day had kept the valley, which is sometimes rich and well timbered, though the country is generally sandy. Mingled with the usual plants, a thistle (*carduus leucographus*) had for the last day or two made its appearance; and along the river bottom, *tradescantia* (*virginica*) and milk plant (*asclepias syriaca*) in considerable quantities" (Frémont, 1845: 16). He continued, "our march to-day had been twenty-one miles and the astronomical observations gave a chronometric longitude of 98°22′12″, and latitude 40°26′50″." They were moving forward at seven in the morning of 26 June, and in about five miles reached a fork of the Blue, where the road leaves the river and crosses over to the Platte.

"No water was to be found on the dividing ridge and casks were filled and the animals were allowed a short repose. The road led across a high and level prairie ridge, where were but few plants and those principally thistle (carduus leucographus,) and a kind of dwarf artemisia" (Frémont, 1845: 16). The Platte River was reached on 26 June, evidently near the present location of Fort Kearney, Kearney County, Nebraska (McKelvey, 1955: 758). The fort, initially called Fort Childs, was built in 1848. It was later named in honor of Frémont's nemesis of the third expedition, although the spelling, an alternative one, is not as Kearny spelled it. "Change of soil and country appeared here to have produced some change in the vegetation," he noted. "*Cacti* were numerous, and all the plants of the region appeared to flourish among the warm hills. Among them the *amorpha*, in full bloom, was remarkable for its large and luxuriant purple clusters" (Frémont, 1845: 16). Their campsite on the Platte was about 21 miles below the head of Grand Island. Its location was determined as 40°41′06″ north, 98°45′49″ west. Preuss (Gudde & Gudde, 1958: 14) grumbled; "Low, wet prairie. Legions of mosquitos."

After proceeding 18 miles along the bottoms of the Platte River on 27 June, camp was made near the head of Grand Island. "The soil here is light and rich, though in some places rather sandy; and, with the exception of a scattered fringe along the bank, the timber, consisting principally of poplar, (*populus monilifera*,) elm, and hackberry, (*celtis crassifolia*,) is confined almost entirely to the islands" (Frémont, 1845: 17). Preuss was unhappy with their progress (Gudde & Gudde, 1958: 14): "Now it is already four weeks since we left St. Louis, and what a short distance we have covered!"

Torrey (1843, preface; see appendices) notes: "Crossing over from the waters of the Kansas, Lieutenant Frémont arrived at the Great Platte [26 June 1842], two hundred and ten miles from its junction with the Missouri. The valley of this river, from its mouth to the great forks, is about four miles broad, and three hundred and fifteen miles long. It is rich, well timbered, and covered with luxuriant grasses. The purple *liatris scariosa*, and several *asters*, were here conspicuous features of the vegetation. I was pleased to recognize, among the specimens collected near the forks, the fine large-flowered asclepias, that I described many years ago in my account of Jame's Rocky Mountain Plants, under the name of *A. speciosa*, and which Mr. Geyer also found in Nicollet's expedition. On the Lower Platte, and all the way to the Sweet Water, the showy *cleome integrifolia* occurred in abundance."

The party continued westward along the Platte, recording the events of travel and the sights of the country. On 2 July the morning was "cool and smoky." Crossed that day were a number of hollows, "timbered principally with box elder, (*acer negundo*,) poplar, and elm" (Frémont, 1845: 21). And, further: "In the vicinity of these places there was a bluish grass, which the cattle refused to eat, called by the voyageurs '*herbe salee*,' (salt grass.)" "Camped among millions of mosquitos," complained Preuss (Gudde & Gudde, 1958: 18). They were at the Forks of the Platte, Lincoln County, Nebraska, in the evening of 2 July 1842.

The party had seen many buffalo and wolves and were subsisting on buffalo meat. Prior to arrival at St. Vrain's Fort, west of the juncture of the South Platte on 4 July, Frémont chose to divide his party. The cavalcade of men, horses, and wheeled carts were at a point only a few miles from where the road crossed to the North Fork of the Platte, and most of the party and baggage were sent that way toward Fort Laramie. Frémont and six others, Preuss included (to his dismay), moved up the South Platte. "Antelope were tolerably frequent, with a large gray hare" (Frémont, 1887: 94). The group crossed into Colorado on that day (McKelvey, 1955: 759). On the next day, 6 July, Preuss was allowed to return to the main party along the north branch of the Platte. He could not take the pace set by Frémont, who had traveled 40 miles on the first day away from the main party. Preuss was 39 years of age, and considered himself old, a not unlikely supposition when compared with the young people in the party.

On 9 July the men with Frémont had their first faint glimpse of the Rocky Mountains. Frémont and the small advanced party were at St. Vrain's Fort, in present Weld County, Colorado, by late evening on the 10th. Leaving the fort, bound for Fort Laramie 125 miles away, they moved along the valley of the South Platte, before cutting northward across drainages issuing from the high plains (see Chapter VII for intervening dates and localities). The date of 13 July was noted by Frémont (1843: 32–33) for its lack of wood, and the use of "*bois de vache*" as fuel on which the meal of the previous evening was cooked. That evening there still was no wood and more buffalo chips were used to cook the evening meal, and "I amused myself with hunting for plants among the grass." John Charles collected plants on both 12 and 14 July 1842 (see itinerary Chapter VII), but none are recorded from the 13th. Possibly he found none to his liking.

On 15 July the small party arrived at the Platte River some 13 miles below Fort Laramie. Following the road they arrived late that evening at Fort Laramie. The fort was located near the juncture of the Laramie and Platte Rivers, in western Goshen County, Wyoming. It is a pretty place where short-grass prairie rolls against gentle slopes of surrounding hills. The rivers are lined with cottonwood, and the fort was perched on the terrace between the North Platte and the Laramie River. There Frémont found the larger part of his party camped, awaiting him and others of the advance party. The baggage party, which had arrived on the 13th, had met Jim Bridger (1804–1881) during their journey and had been entertained by him with tales of the country the expedition was to penetrate later. Sioux Indians to the west were reputedly openly hostile, and the route would be dangerous. The men would be in Wyoming continuously from 14 July to 5 September.

Near the juncture of the Laramie River with the Platte, "the singular leguminous plant, the *kentrophyta montana* of Nuttall was first seen, and then occurred at intervals to the Sweet Water river" (Torrey, 1843, preface).

Negotiations were undertaken at Fort Laramie, where the party stayed for five days, waiting for a guide to accompany them for some distance to the west, and Brant and Randolph Benton were left at the fort along with a portion of baggage, field notes and observations, and several instruments. The threat of hostile Indians was not enough to prevent the western thrust of the party. Preuss was sure that he was marching into the mouth of death or even something worse: "I see no honor in being murdered by this rabble. But all that is too late now" (Gudde & Gudde, 1958: 29).

Frémont and his men left Fort Laramie on 21 July and proceeded west to a point where (Frémont, 1887: 121) they could view a canyon, "where the Platte issues from the Black Hills [Laramie Mountains]." The next morning Frémont and Basil Lajeunesse, his favorite among the voyageurs, entered the canyon. The scenery was unlike any Frémont had seen, a place of great beauty, with pines, cherry, and grains de boeuf (*Shepherdia argentea*). Their Indian guide led them off the main road for a day or two, during which time Frémont made several important plant collections (Frémont, 1845: 47). Torrey (1843, preface) states: "The route along the North fork of the Platte afforded some of the best plants in the collection. The *senecio rapifolia*, Nutt., occurred in many places, quite to the Sweet Water; *lippia* (*zapania*) *cuneifolia* (Torr. in James's plants, only known before from Dr. James's collection;) *cercocarpus parvifolius*, Nutt.; *eriogonum parvifolium*, and *caespitosum*, Nutt.; *shepherdia argentea*, Nutt., and *geranium Frémontii*, a new species, (near the Red Buttes,) were found in this part of the journey." Red Buttes are near present Casper, Wyoming.

West of the Laramie River "the place of grass is usurped by the artemisia and other odoriferous plants, to whose growth the sandy soil and dry air of this elevated region seems highly favorable." The party had passed into the shrub steppe lands of Wyoming and the "extraordinary abundance of the artemisias" (Frémont, 1887: 123) was a conspicuous fact of the landscape. Westward still the Frémont party finally encountered a small band of Sioux Indians, who were intimidated by the size and the preparations of the explorer's party. Gaining what information was possible from two of the Sioux, the party again advanced westward. The account for the next few days is replete with descriptions of the country, including the names of plant species: *Psoralea esculenta*, asters, and *Shepherdia argentea*. The group was near present Glendo, Platte County, Wyoming, on 22 July, at Deer Creek near Glen Rock, on 26 July, and at Red Buttes adjacent to Casper, Natrona County, on 29 July.

Frémont decided to reduce the baggage and make a rapid move west to South Pass (in present Frémont County, Wyoming) and the Wind River Mountains, whose southwest side is in Sublette County, Wyoming. The carts were dismantled and much of the unnecessary equipment cached at Goat Island, not far from Alcova, Natrona County, Wyoming, and on the morning of 30 July the party left the course of the Platte to cross over to the Sweetwater, bypassing the gorge that held the narrowly entrenched, swift, and boulder-strewn portion of the Platte below its junction with the Sweetwater, a portion of which is now beneath Pathfinder Reservoir, so named after one of Frémont's sobriquets. "Along the Sweet Water, many interesting plants were collected, as may be seen by an examination of the catalogue; I would, however, mention the curious *oenothera Nuttallii*, Torr. and Gr.; *eurotia lanata* Mocq.; (Diotis lanata, *Pursh*,) which seems to be distinct from *E. ceratoides*; *thermopsis montana*, Nutt; *gilia pulchella*, Dougl.; *senecio spartioides*, Torr. and Gr.; a new species, and four of five species of wild currants, (*ribes irriguum*, Dougl., &c.) Near the mouth of the Sweet Water was found the plantago eriophora, Torr., a species first described in my Dr. James's Rocky Mountain Plants. On the upper part, and near the dividing ridge, were collected several species of *castilleja*; *penstemon micrantha*, Nutt.; several *gentians*; the pretty little *androsace occidentalis*, Nutt; *solidago incana*, Torr. and Gr.; and two species of *eriogonum*, one of which was new" (Torrey, 1843, preface).

Camp for the night of 31 July was about a mile below "Rock Independence" (Frémont 1887: 134). Five miles beyond that famous landmark (Natrona County, Wyoming) the party came to a place called Devil's Gate, where the Sweetwater cuts through the point of a granite ridge. By 3 August they had their first view of the Wind River Mountains. On 4 August the "first magpie" was seen, and numerous bright-colored flowers had made the river bottom look as gay as a garden (Frémont, 1887: 135).

On 5 August (Friday) Preuss complained again: "Frémont is roaming through the mountains collecting rocks and is keeping us waiting for lunch. I am hungry as a wolf. That fellow knows nothing about mineralogy or botany. Yet he collects every trifle in order to have it interpreted in Washington and to brag about it in his report. Let him collect as much as he wants—if he would only not make us wait for our meal."

South Pass was attained on the 8th, and Frémont noted that they "were obliged to watch very closely to find the place at which we had reached the culminating point" so broad and flat was the pass itself. The entourage traveled beyond the pass to the Little Sandy (Sublette County, Wyoming), prior to camping. The Little Sandy is a tributary of the Green River, which flows south to join the Colorado. The party was at the Big Sandy the following day. "Along Little Sandy, a tributary of the Colorado of the West, were collected a new species of *phaca* (*P. digitata*), and *parnassia fimbriata*" (Torrey, 1843, preface).

Warmth of midsummer had given way to indications of autumn on the high plains, and water had frozen during the night of 9 August. The season for exploration was passing quickly, and there was reason for haste. The Wind River Mountains, standing nearby, provided the motivation for a final rush to complete the expedition before winter should close the survey summarily. The party was now skirting the southwest flank of the Wind Rivers, crossing the drainages of the numerous small streams that lead to the Green River. The expedition finally reached one of the lakes near present Pinedale, Wyoming, "set like a gem in the mountains." At the foot of the lake, Frémont was transfixed by the scene: "With nothing between us and their feet to lessen the effect of the whole height, a grand bed of snow-capped mountains rose before us, pile upon pile, glowing in the bright light of an August day. 'Never before,' said Preuss, 'in this country or in Europe, have I seen such magnificent, grand rocks'" (Frémont, 1887: 140).

The statement is, perhaps, more eloquent than the reality of the situation. From the foot of Frémont Lake, at least, the snowcapped peaks of the Wind River Mountains are largely obscured by an intervening, pine-covered front range. More distant views show the magnificence of the range to better advantage, a line of snowcapped peaks trending northwest-southeast, contrasting with tones of earth, vegetation, and blue sky typical of Wyoming. The range is truly beautiful, and that beauty was conveyed adequately by Frémont, in spite of what Preuss was thought to have said, or what he recorded in his diary.

The entry for Thursday, 4 August 1842, by Preuss (Gudde & Gudde, 1958: 33) contradicts: "Whoever has seen Switzerland and expects something similar here is bound for a great disappointment." Practically everything disappointed Preuss; but his discernment of beauty (Gudde & Gudde, 1958: 37) was not always jaded by his generally sour disposition: "Noon. We camp here at a lovely little lake at the foot of the mountains. The shores are covered with aspen and fir. The finest trout swim in the crystal clear water; I wish we had them in the frying pan. In the foreground are cliffs about seven hundred feet high, with the more distant snow peaks towering beyond." His description more closely matches the scenery as seen by me in 1991. Continuing, Preuss pleaded plaintively, "Oh, I wish I were home again!"

Torrey (1843, preface) notes: "On the morning of the 11th of August, they entered the defiles of the Wind river mountains, a spur of the Rocky mountains, or northern Andes, and among which they spent about eight days. On the borders of a lake, embosomed in one of the defiles, were collected *sedum rhodiola*, DC., (which had been found before, south of Kotzebue's sound, only by Dr. James;) *senecio hydrophilus*, Nutt.; *Vaccinium uliginosum*; *betula glandulosa*, and *B. occidentalis*, Hook.; *eleagnus argentea*, and *shepherdia Canadensis*."

On 12 August, 15 people, including John Charles, moved to explore the mountain range, leaving 10 members of the party at base camp. It seemed to Frémont as though "nature had collected all her beauties together in one chosen place. We were overlooking a deep valley, which was entirely occupied by three lakes, and from the brink the surrounding ridges rose precipitously five hundred and a thousand feet, covered with the dark green of the balsam pine [mainly lodgepole pine, *Pinus contorta* Loud.], relieved on the border of the lake with the light foliage of the aspen" (Frémont, 1845: 64–65). The men moved from obstacle to obstacle as they mounted ever upward. Preuss (Gudde & Gudde, 1958: 39) recorded: "Before our eyes there unfolded a lovely landscape, with three mountain lakes surrounded by cliffs.—Oh, these mosquitoes!—The mountains were partly covered by spruce and fir; in the valley only aspen can be seen." Frémont (1845: 65) noted: "The depths of this unexplored forest were a place to delight the heart of a botanist. There was a rich undergrowth of plants, and numerous gay-colored flowers in brilliant blossom." He noted later, while supper was being prepared, "I set out on an excursion in the neighborhood, accompanied by one of my men. We wandered about among the crags and ravines until dark, richly repaid for our walk by a fine collection of plants, many of them in full bloom" (Frémont, 1845: 65). During the exploration of the peak Frémont mentions plants again and again but seldom uses their scientific names. He was beyond his experience with these alpine materials, not present in any of his previous travels. Seldom, however, does he mention a collection of plants. The impossible-to-please Preuss wrote (Gudde & Gudde, 1958: 39): "As interesting as these mountains are, they cannot at all be compared to the Alps of Switzerland. No glaciers, ice lakes, avalanches, or waterfalls are to be seen. A little snow on the peak—that is all."

Nothing would do but to reach the summit of this spectacular range, and Frémont and party proceeded to do just that. Food was low, and one summit turned out to be the precursor of another still higher one beyond. Suffering from lack of food and nearly depleted of reserve energy the young men nevertheless endured. "The flora of the region we had traversed since leaving our mules was extremely rich, and, among the characteristic plants, the scarlet flowers of the *Dodecatheon dentatum* [a name applied by Frémont to several species of this genus] everywhere meet the eye in great abundance. A small green ravine, on the edge of which we were encamped, was filled with a profusion of alpine plants in brilliant bloom" (Frémont, 1887: 146). The summit was attained on 15 August. Barometrical observations gave the elevation of the summit as 13,570 feet above sea level. Frémont Peak is cited on modern maps as 13,730 feet in elevation. From his vantage point he could view the Tetons, far to the west. Both the peak and the beautiful lake below it were named in honor of Frémont.

Evidently Gannett Peak is the highest in the range (Gudde & Gudde, 1958: 40), and Jackson and Spence (1970: 270) assert that Frémont was not on what is now called Frémont Peak, but more likely he was on one farther north called Woodrow Wilson Peak, just south of Gannett Peak. It was presumptuous, perhaps, that the peak was called Frémont's Peak on the maps of the expedition; after all, who would name such a feature after himself? Whether the name was supplied by Frémont or his cartographer is not clear, but the choice of epithet was a source of derision of Frémont by Bancroft (1889) and Rolle (1991), who thought that others might be more deserving than this latecomer on the scene. Be that as it may, Frémont was there, and those who would criticize him were not. Gudde and Gudde (1958: 45) maintain: "Frémont apparently did not name the mountain for himself. It was either bestowed by his friends in Washington, or Preuss placed the name on the map on his own responsibility."

Torrey (1843, preface) writes: "The vegetation of the mountains is truly alpine, embracing a considerable number of species common to both hemispheres, as well as some that are peculiar to North America. Of the former, Lieutenant Frémont collected *pleum* [*Phleum*] *alpinum*; *oxyria reniformis*; *Veronica alpina*; several species of *salix*; *carex atrata*; *C. panicea*; and immediately below the line of perpetual congelation, *silene acaulis*, and *polemonium caeruleum*, *β* Hook. Among the alpine plants peculiar to the western hemisphere, there were found *oreophila myrtifolia*, Nutt.; *aquilegia caerulea*, Torr.; *pedicularis ciliata* James; *silene Drummondii*, Hook.; *menziesia empetriformis*, *potentilla gracilis*, Dougl.; several species of *pinus*; *frasera speciosa*, Hook.; *dodecatheon dentatum*, Hook.; *phlox muscoides*, Nutt.; *senecio Frémontii*, n. sp., Torr. and Gr.; four or five *asters*, and *vaccinium myrtilloides* Mx.; the last seven or eight very near the snow line. Lower down the mountain were found *arnica angustifolia*, Vahl.; *senecio triangularis*, Hook.; *S. subnudus*, DC.; *macrorhynchus troximoides*, Torr. and Gr.;

helianthella uniflora, Torr. and Gr.; and *linosyris viscidiflorus*, Hook." A more complete listing of collections from the Wind River Mountains is given in the discussion of botanical results of the first expedition (Chapter VII). The five days spent in the Wind River Mountains would yield a collection of plant specimens representing more than 60 taxa. It was the most productive period for collection of plants in all of Frémont's expeditions.

Now began the return eastward toward home, family, and report and map preparation. By 23 August the party reached its previous encampment at Independence Rock, on which Frémont engraved an impression of the Christian cross. Of this, McKelvey (1955: 765) noted that "Someone, I know not who, once made the comment that only by the introduction of ships had humanity added to the beauty of nature." The natural exfoliation of the granite rock would remove the cross within a short time, but the rock would be marked by many others, a kind of newspaper rock, and it still bears plaques dedicated to many of those who passed it by. The plaques themselves are considered by some as a form of defacement.

Here began Frémont's famous and foolhardy attempt to survey the Platte from the river itself. The India-rubber boat was inflated, placed in the water, and loaded with gear. The attempt was a failure, due to low water. Back at the Platte proper, the boat was launched again to float through the narrows formed by entrenchment of the river into the hills. The rubber boat bearing Frémont, Preuss, and five of his ablest men (Clement, de Couteau, Basil, Ayot, and Benoit, according to Preuss) moved with great speed into the canyon. After an initial near disaster, the men embarked yet again; Frémont was determined to run the river, mainly perhaps because he could not turn back. After several narrow escapes the boat finally capsized, dumping men and equipment into the river. The most valuable journals and other materials were recovered, and no one died. But arms and ammunition had been lost, and it was now imperative that the soaked survivors reach Goat Island at the foot of the canyon, where they were to meet those sent overland with the animals and other baggage.

Fortunately, the overland party had waited for them at Goat Island, and they were fed and reclothed before nightfall. How many times the men of the expedition had used the inflatable boat prior to this attempt is not recorded, but the men must have been both optimistic and naïve concerning its safety. Otherwise, Frémont would not have included as part of the cargo valuable items such as journals and notes on the expedition. Certainly the journals and other items so precious to the expedition should have been carried on the pack animals around the narrows.

After gathering up as many of their belongings as they could recover from along the river, following their disastrous boat ride, the men and animals reached Cache Camp, not far from Alcova, Natrona County, Wyoming, on 26 August and found their cached carts and other equipment undisturbed. The carts were retrieved from their burial sites, assembled, and loaded in quick order. Beyond Cache Camp the group moved on to the ford of the Platte, where camp was made for the night. Late rains gave a verdure to the country to the east, which had been parched for lack of rain a month earlier. Now the expedition ran eastward as rapidly as possible, the cold nights indicating that winter was not far behind them. On the last day of August the party reached Fort Laramie, where they were greeted by their friends, especially by Brandt and Benton, who had waited rather anxiously during their absence of some 42 days. Carson left the party at Fort Laramie (Quaife, 1935: 68) and returned several hundred miles to his residence in Taos, New Mexico. The group remaining with John Charles left Fort Laramie on 3 September, proceeding down the Platte, "which was glorious with the autumnal splendor of innumerable flowers in full and brilliant bloom" (Frémont, 1887: 160).

Following another failed attempt at navigating the Platte, then at a low period in its annual fluctuating flow, the party arrived at Grand Island on 18 September. Continuing on down the Platte the Loupe Fork of the Platte was reached on the 24th. This stream joins the Platte at Columbus, Nebraska (Gudde & Gudde, 1958: 73). The Missouri River was reached on the 30th, some 520 miles from Fort Laramie. Frémont supervised the completion of a boat at Bellevue, Iowa, across from the mouth of the Platte. Surplus equipment and supplies of the expedition were sold at Bellevue, and the men embarked down the Missouri on the boat, equipped with 10 oars. St. Louis, their goal of several months, was reached on 18 October. By the 29th Frémont was reunited with his family at Washington City.

During the remainder of 1842 and the early months of 1843 Frémont was engaged in the preparation of a report and maps of the routes of the expedition. Admitting trouble with the writing, he turned again to Jessie as scribe for his dictated thoughts. The ideas in the reports are those of John Charles, but the words belong to Jessie. She was then only a few months past her 18th birthday. Despite her youth Jessie had an excellent mastery of the English language, and her words flow in the narrative of the expedition. Jessie made Frémont's dictation of the narrative come alive for her and for her readers; she wrote words that breathed of the green prairie, its blue sky, billowing clouds, and flowing waters.

Preuss was busy preparing the maps of the expedition (Figure 3), on which would be marked the campsites where grass, water, and wood were to be found, all for the benefit of future emigrants moving west. Plant specimens taken on the expedition were sent by Frémont to John Torrey at the suggestion of Benedict Jaeger, lecturer on natural history at Princeton (Jackson & Spence, 1970: 130).

The report of the first expedition, containing the botanical treatment by Torrey, was submitted to Colonel J. J. Abert on 1 March 1843.

CHAPTER III

SECOND EXPEDITION—1843–44

Missouri River to Fort Hall

The second and most productive expedition of exploration by John Charles Frémont was designed to "connect the reconnaissance of 1842, with the surveys of Commander Charles Wilkes on the coast of the Pacific ocean, so as to give a connected survey of the interior of our continent." It was imperative that the route between South Pass in Wyoming and The Dalles in Oregon be surveyed. Families were already moving over the land on their way to Oregon Territory. Others would follow in quick succession, and all needed maps of the route.

Little time elapsed between the completion of the report of the first expedition, submitted for publication on 1 March 1843, and Frémont's arrival on 17 May "at the little town of Kansas, on the Missouri frontier, near the junction of the Kansas river with the Missouri river" (Frémont, 1845: 105). Frémont, then 30 years of age, and Jessie, still 18, had had little time together as husband and wife. Now Frémont was away on another expedition. He remained at Kansas for two weeks completing preparations for the second expedition. His party this time consisted of Thomas (Broken Hand) Fitzpatrick (referred to by Frémont as Mr. Fitzpatrick; 1799–1854), guide (Favour, 1962; Hafen, 1973); Charles Preuss, topographer; Theodore Talbot and Frederick Dwight, tourists; and the following men: Alexis Ayot, François Badeau (d. 1844), Oliver Bernier, John A. Campbell, John G. Campbell, Manuel Chapman, Ransom Clark, Philibert Corteau, Michel Crelis, William Creuss, Clinton Deforest, Baptiste Derosier, Basil Lajeunesse (d. 1846), François Lajeunesse, Henry Lee, Louis Menard, Louis Montreuil, Samuel Neal, Alexis Pera, James Power, faithful Rafael Proue (d. 1849), Oscar Sarpy, Baptiste Tabeau (d. 1844), Charles Taplin, Baptiste Tesson, Auguste Vasquez, Joseph Verrot, Patrick White, Tiery Wright, Louis Zindel (a German in charge of the howitzer), and Jacob Dodson. Jacob Dodson was "a free young colored man." Jackson and Spence (1970: 428) cite Dodson as being 18 years of age, devoted to the Benton family, and the personal servant of Frémont on both the second and third expeditions.

Badeau, Bernier, Basil Lajeunesse, Menard, and Proue had accompanied Frémont on the 1842 expedition also. Theodore Talbot would become a First Lieutenant in the Army (Hendrickson, 1990: 42), and would be stationed at Fort Moultrie in Charleston Harbor, just prior to the Fort Sumter incident that opened the Civil War. Jessie Frémont would correspond with his mother throughout the second expedition (Herr, 1987).

A brief biographical sketch of Fitzpatrick (1799–1854), called Broken Hand or White Hair by the Indians, is given in Jackson and Spence (1970: 222). He was, according to them, an Irish immigrant who became one of the greatest of the mountain men. The Rocky Mountain Fur Company was organized by Fitzpatrick, Bridger, and others in 1830.

When the beaver were depleted, he quit trapping and served as guide for some early emigrant trains and expeditions. He was to prove invaluable to Frémont on this expedition. Thomas Fitzpatrick's role as guide was to be assumed by Kit Carson (Quaife, 1935; Estergreen, 1962), and Fitzpatrick became leader of the larger part of the expedition, with the task of bringing the baggage party along, a not inconsiderable and independent assignment that required skill, hard work, and devotion. Frémont trusted this older man implicitly, and he never failed in his responsibility during the entire expedition. In a very real sense, Thomas Broken Hand Fitzpatrick is the unsung hero of the second expedition.

This mounted and well-armed party (with Halls' carbines), equipped with the famous or infamous 12-lb. brass howitzer furnished by the orders of Colonel Stephen Watts Kearny, not following official procedure (Herr, 1987: 87–90), from the arsenal at St. Louis, began the long journey west from Kansas, now within Kansas City, Kansas, on 29 May 1843. The howitzer would haunt the men who had to carry it along during the expedition, and its acquisition would provide a cloud that would cast a shadow over Frémont in times to come. McKelvey (1955: 844) notes, "This howitzer served no purpose, was never used, and finally was abandoned many, many miles from St. Louis; actually it did more harm to Frémont than to anyone else!" The howitzer in fact was used on a number of occasions to be noted later in the narrative; however, McKelvey's other contentions were, unfortunately, true.

The course chosen (Figure 2) differed from that of the earlier year so that "the problem of a new road to Oregon and California . . . might be solved" (Frémont, 1845: 106). The route would follow up the valley of the Kansas River and then to the head of the Arkansas, which they would follow to some pass in the mountains.

By 4 June the party of mounted men, teams pulling 12 carts, extra riding horses and mules, and at least some cattle for use as food, crossed Otter Creek, a tributary of the Kansas that enters from the south. Here they observed "five or six Kansas women, engaged in digging prairie potatoes, (*psoralea esculenta*)" (Frémont, 1845: 107). Smoky Hill Fork, the principal southern fork of the Kansas in present Geary County, Kansas, was reached on 8 June, and the group remained there until the 11th. Their course was now along the Republican Fork of the Kansas. By 14 June the expedition was 265 miles from the mouth of the Kansas and had attained an elevation of 1520 feet. In spite of the progress, the pace had been too slow to allow them to continue with the expedition schedule as Frémont perceived it.

Frémont again divided the party on 16 June 1843, similar to the division of the previous season. With Frémont, accompanied by Charles Preuss and 15 men, all heavily armed, went the howitzer. The remainder of the party, consisting of 25 men in the charge of Fitzpatrick, brought up the rear with the baggage, carts, animals, and most of the supplies. It is curious that Frémont's assumption seems to have been that the baggage party, with most of the horses, mules, and supplies, required less protection than did he and his men.

On the first evening after the division Frémont and his small group encamped at a little stream (a tributary of Solomons Fork of the Smoky Hill Fork), where a single dry cottonwood provided wood for the evening fire. He noted, "bunch grass, (festuca,) and Buffalo grass, (*sesleria dactyloides.*) Amorpha canescens (*lead plant*) continued the characteristic plant of the country, and a narrow-leaved *lathyrus* occurred during the morning in beautiful patches. *Sida coccinea* occurred frequently, with a *psoralia* [*Psoralea*] near *psoralia floribunda*, and a number of plants not hitherto met, just verging into bloom" (Frémont, 1845: 108). He recorded the presence of the wild sensitive plant "(*shrankia angustata*)," which occurred frequently in the prairie, and later that day "*Amorpha*, with the *psoralea*, and a dwarf species of *lupinus*," became the characteristic plants.

On 21 June, the men killed their first buffalo, "a large old bull" (Frémont, 1845: 109). Antelope were seen during the day, and the party encamped on one of the tributaries of the Republican. In the morning the plants were few, "and with the short sward of the buffalo grass, which now prevailed every where, giving to the prairies a smooth and mossy appearance, were mingled frequent patches of a beautiful red grass, (*aristida pallens*,) which had made its appearance only within the last few days." At evening the party camped within a few miles of the main fork of the Republican, "on a little creek, where the air was fragrant with the perfume of *artemisia filifolia*," which they had seen for the first time (Frémont, 1845: 109).

On 22 June Frémont, his men, animals, and equipage proceeded along a fork of the Republican where camp was made on the banks, "well wooded with ash-leaved maple, (*negundo fraxinifolium*,) elm, cottonwood, and a few white oaks" (Frémont, 1845: 109). The journal entry for the next day states: "At noon, on the 23d, we descended into the valley of a principal fork of the Republican, a beautiful stream with a dense border of wood, consisting principally of varieties of ash, forty feet wide and four feet deep. It was musical with the notes of many birds, which, from the vast expanse of silent prairie around, seemed all to have collected here. We continued during the afternoon our route along the river, which was populous with prairie dogs, (the bottoms being entirely occupied by their villages,) and late in the evening encamped on its banks. The prevailing timber is a blue-foliaged ash, (*fraxinus*, near *F. Americana*,) and ash-leaved maple. We gave to this stream the name of Prairie Dog river [in or near Harlan County, Nebraska]" (Frémont, 1845: 109). That evening they camped "where the air was fragrant with the perfume of *artemisia filifolia*."

By 30 June Frémont and his small party arrived at a bluff overlooking the South Fork of the Platte, and "the nature of the country had entirely changed. Bare sand hills every where surrounded us" and "the plants peculiar to a sandy soil made their appearance." On 1 July they had their first clear view of Long's Peak, sentinel-like in the west. Camp that night was at the mouth of Bijou Creek, Morgan County, Colorado. St. Vrain's Fort (near present-day Milliken, Weld County, Colorado) was reached on 4 July. There Lucien Maxwell was sent on a long ride to Taos in New Mexico to purchase horses and supplies, there being none of the former and few of the latter at the fort. Maxwell was supposed to meet them at a rendezvous on the Arkansas later in the summer, and presumeably he did. Oscar Sarpy left the party at the fort to return to the states.

Traveling up the South Fork of the Platte, they reached a place where three forks come together (Denver County, Colorado) on 8 July, and continued on up the easternmost fork. Pines and aspen were encountered, mixed with cottonwood, "and there was excellent grass and rushes for the animals" (Frémont, 1845: 112). Many flowers were in blossom, among them blue flax and a tall, handsome species of *gilia* [*G. aggregata*], with slender red-scarlet flowers, which appeared the previous day for the first time and was very frequent that day. Due to paucity of game and low reserves of meat the party turned east along the high ground between the Platte and the Arkansas, where a buffalo was killed. Snow fell heavily in the mountains during the night. The exploring party continued east during 10 July, crossing the "Kioway" River. They turned southward on the 11th, and saw a few small bushes of sagebrush, but the characteristic plant was "*esparcette*, (*onobrychis sativa*) [likely *Hedysarum boreale* Nutt. or possibly *Oxytropis lambertii* Pursh and *O. sericea* Nutt. in Torr. & A. Gray]." Some of the men encountered a foraging grizzly bear, which charged when they approached it. Fortunately, no one was injured.

Southward they crossed the divide into the Arkansas drainage, at an elevation of about 7500 feet, and about 40 miles from Pike's Peak. The course was southwest on 12 July. The wagon road to the settlements on the Arkansas River was encountered, and the party encamped in the afternoon on the "*Fontaine-qui-bouit* [or Boiling Spring, now Fountain Creek] river." And "during the morning a tall species of *gilia*, with a slender white flower [probably *Gilia longiflora* (Torr.) G. Don], was characteristic; and in the later part of the day, another variety of *esparcette* (wild clover,) having the flower white [*Oxytropis sericea* ?], was equally so" (Frémont, 1845: 115).

At noon on 13 July Frémont noted that "our animals [were] luxuriating on rushes (*equisetum hyemale*)" (Frémont, 1845: 115). The rushes involved were more likely species of *Juncus*, *Carex*, and other plants of moist habitats; members of the genus *Equisetum* are known to be poisonous, especially to horses. "A variety of cactus made its appearance, and a plant resembling *mirabilis jalapa*, with a handsome *convolvulus* I had not hitherto seen, (*calystegia*.)" (Frémont, 1845: 115).

"Continuing down the River [Fontaine-qui-bouit] we encamped at noon on the 14th at its mouth, on the Arkansas River [Pueblo County, Colorado], a short distance above our encampment, on the left bank of the Arkansas, is a pueblo [present Pueblo] (as the Mexicans call their civilized Indian villages)" (Frémont, 1845: 116). Here Frémont learned from his messenger Maxwell that Indian troubles at Taos and vicinity had disrupted any possibility of obtaining remounts and supplies. Not by chance, Kit Carson was at Pueblo, and Frémont was happy to take him into service again as guide (Quaife, 1935: 73–74). Carson was dispatched to Bent's Fort (Otero County, Colorado, see Hyde, 1968), east along the Arkansas, for supplies. From that fort Carson was to rendezvous with Frémont at St. Vrain's Fort by the shortest possible route, a difficult but routine task for Carson.

Kit Carson had gone to Bent's Fort in January 1843, and then departed for Taos. In February he married Señorita Josepha Jaramilla, a daughter [then 15 or possibly only 13] of Don Francisco Jaramilla. He remained in Taos till April, then started for Missouri with Bent and St. Vrain. Frémont had passed Bent's Fort prior to Carson's return. Carson rode after him, to "have a talk. But when Frémont saw me again and requested me to join him,

I could not refuse, and again entered his employ as guide and hunter. I was sent back to the fort to purchase mules, I bought ten head" (Carter, 1968: 84–88).

Leaving Pueblo the party traveled to the northwest to the Front Range, then northward to St. Vrain's Fort, which was reached on 23 July. There Frémont and the exploring party were reunited with Mr. Fitzpatrick and the supporting party, who had followed behind the more rapidly moving advance party. Kit Carson, having moved very quickly with 10 good mules equipped with pack saddles, was there also. Carson was not one to hold up the expedition. The party was again split, with Fitzpatrick continuing in charge of the baggage train, scheduled to meet again at Fort Hall, in present-day Idaho. Frémont and his smaller group would move to the west along the drainage of the Cache la Poudre River.

Prior to arriving at St. Vrain's Fort, between 16 and 23 July 1843, Frémont recorded plant species several times in his report. "*Ipomoea leptophylla*, in bloom, was a characteristic plant along the river, generally in large bunches, with two to five flowers on each. Beautiful clusters of the plant resembling *Mirabilis jalapa* [*M. multiflora* (Torr.) A. Gray in Torr.] were numerous, and *Glycyrrhiza lepidota* was characteristic of the bottoms" along Fontaine-qui-bouit River on 16 July. "Currants, nearly ripe, were abundant, and among the shrubs which covered the bottom was a very luxuriant growth of chenopodiaceous shrubs four to six feet high" (Frémont, 1887: 183). They were at Fontaine-qui-bouit springs on the 18th. Trees noted in the vicinity are reported on 19 July: "The trees in the neighborhood were birch, willow, pine, and an oak resembling *quercus alba*. In the shrubbery along the river are currant bushes (*ribes*,) of which the fruit has a piney flavor; and on the mountain side, in a red gravelly soil, is a remarkable coniferous tree, (perhaps an *abies*,) having the leaves singularly long, broad, scattered, with bushes of *spireae ariaefolia*." During the morning of 19 July the party "traveled up the eastern fork of the Fontaine-qui-bouit river, our road being roughened by frequent deep gullies timbered with pine, and halted at noon on a small branch of the stream, timbered principally with the narrow-leaved cottonwood, (*populus angustifolia*,) called by the Canadians [Frémont's voyageur companions] Liard amere [bitter cottonwood]" (Frémont, 1887: 183).

Summer's unparalleled beauty was apparent on 20 July: "We continued our march up the stream, along a green sloping bottom, between pine hills on the one hand, and the main Black hills on the other, toward the ridge which separates the waters of the Platte from those of the Arkansas. As we approached the dividing ridge, the whole valley was radiant with flowers; blue, yellow, pink, white, scarlet, and purple vied with each other in splendor. *Esparcette* was one of the highly characteristic plants, and a bright-looking flower (*gaillardia aristata*) was very frequent; but the most abundant plant along the road today was geranium maculatum, which is the characteristic plant on this portion of the dividing ground. Crossing to the waters of the Platte, fields of blue flax added to the magnificence of this mountain garden" (Frémont, 1845: 119). In the drainage of the Platte, followed later in the day, Frémont observed "*Achillea millefolium* (milfoil). This was one of the most common plants during the whole of our journey, occurring in almost every variety of situation. I had noticed it on the lowlands of the rivers, near the coast of the Pacific, and near to the Snow among the mountains of the *Sierra Nevada*" (Frémont, 1845: 119).

Two Delaware Indians had accompanied the Frémont party as far as St. Vrain's Fort. Now the Indians decided to return home, leaving the party short of competent hunters. Almost providentially, Alexander (or Alexis) Godey, who would prove to be fearless, trustworthy, and able, was at St. Vrain's and was hired to replace them. Godey was a Creole Frenchman of St. Louis, a very able man, probably Kit Carson's equal. Certainly Godey and Carson formed an almost matched pair throughout the 1843–44 saga. Frémont's advance party at that time consisted of Charles Preuss, Kit Carson, Basil Lajeunesse, François Badeau, J. B. Bernier, Louis Menard, Rafael Proue, Jacob Dodson, Louis Zindel, Henry Lee, Baptiste Derosier, François Lajeunesse, and Auguste Vasquez. Evidently Alex Godey would have to prove his worth with the baggage contingent. The small Frémont party was here joined by a Snake Indian woman (Sally) with two children, whose husband (Baptiste Exervia or Xervier) had been killed a few days earlier (fide Dr. Stephen L. Clark, a descendent of Sally).

The baggage contingent was scheduled to rejoin Frémont later at Fort Hall, or some other place. They were under the able direction of Thomas Fitzpatrick, "an old mountaineer," who worked easily with the 40 men. The two parties "separated at [St. Vrain's] Fort. Fitzpatrick took charge of the main camp, carts, etc. and went to [Fort] Laramie" (Quaife, 1935: 75) prior to turning west on the route toward Fort Hall.

Frémont, Carson, and the remainder of the advance party left St. Vrain's Fort on 26 July, were along the Cache la Poudre River on the 28th, and by the evening of the 29th had camped in sight of "the great Laramie plains" (Frémont, 1845: 122). On 31 July the group emerged on a small tributary of the Laramie River, where the flora became perfectly magnificent, and camped that night on the Laramie. At noon on 2 August halt was made on the most western fork of the Laramie River. There Frémont first encountered the yampah (*Perideridia*), which he found "the Snake woman [Sally] engaged in digging in a low timbered bottom of the creek" (Frémont, 1845: 124). Indians to the west considered it "the best among the roots used for food." Frémont (or rather Torrey?) mistook the plant for parsley, referring to it by the scientific name, "anethum graveolens." He notes that a tributary of the Colorado, resorted to for collection of the roots of this plant, is referred to as the "Yampah." That river, now called the Yampa, flows into the Green River in Uintah County, Utah. By afternoon, travel had become difficult, as the road was dotted with sagebrush, the rough, stiff, tough bushes hindering the passage of men and animals.

They camped the evening of 2 August on a principal fork of the Medicine Bow River, near Medicine Butte. The group traveled toward the North Fork of the Platte on 4 August, through sagebrush and some thin grasses. The efficacy of the howitzer as a pacifier was apparent on 5 August when the camp was charged by about 70 mounted Arapaho and Cheyenne Indians. When the Indians saw the armed men and the howitzer, they quickly made signs of peace (Frémont, 1845: 126). The route on 6 August continued through "artemisia bushes," in rugged, barren, and uninteresting country. The passage the following day "was through a continued and dense field of *artemisia*, which now entirely covered the country" (Frémont, 1845: 127). "Within fifty miles of the Sweet Water, the country changed into a vast saline plain, in many places extremely level, occasionally resembling the flat sandy beds of shallow lakes. Here the vegetation consisted of a shrubby growth, among which were several varieties of chenopodiaceous plants; but the characteristic shrub was Fremontia vermicularis, with smaller saline shrubs, growing with singular luxuriance and in many places holding exclusive possession of the ground" (Frémont, 1845: 128).

By the evening of 9 August the small group of men, with the howitzer, were encamped on the Sweet Water, about 20 miles west of Devil's Gate in southwest Natrona County, Wyoming. At this point they were 315 miles from St. Vrain's Fort. The route was then along the course of the Sweetwater to where the road to Oregon diverged toward the Green River. During the night of 12 August water froze in their lodge. On 16 August the party crossed the Green River (northwest Sweetwater County, Wyoming) and followed southward along the west bank, "of which the islands and shores are handsomely timbered with cottonwood" (Frémont, 1845: 129). Frémont notes that the Green River was known as the "Seeds-ke-dee-agie, or Prairie Hen river; a name which it received from the Crows, to whom its upper waters belong, and on which this bird is still very abundant." Late on 16 August Black's Fork of the Green River was reached. On the 17th the party was at Ham's Fork, which was "wooded with thickets of red willow, and in the bottom is a tolerably strong growth of grass." Frémont comments: "Since crossing the great dividing ridge of the Rocky mountains, plants have been very few in variety, the country being covered principally with artemisia." On 18 August the Snake woman Sally took leave of the party, expecting to find some of her relatives at nearby Bridger's Fort (Fort Bridger, Uinta County, Wyoming). Now Frémont and his men would have to erect the lodges each night, a task previously done by Sally. The crossing of the Green River is in the Seedskedee National Wildlife Refuge, a few miles south of Fontanelle Dam. The bottoms and uplands are still, during the last decades of the twentieth century, abundant habitat for large numbers of prairie chickens.

The small group of men traveled 32 miles on 18 August before encamping on a salt creek. "One of our mules died here, and in this portion of our journey we lost six or seven of our animals. The grass which the country had lately afforded was very poor and insufficient; and animals which have been accustomed to grain became soon weak and unable to labor, when reduced to no other nourishment than grass" (Frémont, 1845: 131). Possibly at least a portion of the problem with animals in this region was due to their consumption of poisonous plants, which are common in the vicinity. After leaving camp on the 19th, they passed over a low range of hills, "near a grove of low cedar," and descended upon one of the heads of Ham's fork, called the Muddy (Uinta County, Wyoming), where they halted for midday. Fossils and coal marked a portion of the route in the afternoon. The men and animals, and the team with the wheeled howitzer, traveled 28 miles on a dusty road through smoky, oppressively hot weather and noted again that "Artemisia was characteristic among the few plants." Smoke is not just a product of modern industrialized nations; historically it occurred each year from uncontrolled fires, both those caused naturally and those by people. Frémont notes smoky conditions several times.

At noon on the 20th, the group halted at the last main fork of Muddy Creek, at an elevation of 7200 feet, and in the afternoon the route continued on the same excellent road, up the left or northern fork of the stream toward its head, to a pass that the barometer placed at 8230 feet above the sea. The party descended on the west side and camped near water, where the emigrant stock had eaten the grass "as completely as if we were again in the midst of the buffalo" (Frémont, 1845: 132). The Bear River Valley (Lincoln County, Wyoming), reached on the morning of the 21st, offered a greater variety of vegetation and a change from the interminable artemisia. "The stream is here 200 feet wide, fringed with willows and occasional groups of hawthorns" (Frémont, 1845: 132). The party continued along the Bear River throughout the day and set up camp after traveling some 26 miles. "Antelope and elk were seen during the day on the opposite prairie; and there were ducks and geese in the river."

The next morning, about three miles from their encampment, they "reached Smith's fork [Cokeville, Lincoln County, Wyoming]), a stream of clear water, about 50 feet in breadth. It is timbered with cottonwood, willow, and aspen, and makes a beautiful debouchement through a pass about 600 yards wide, between remarkable mountain hills, rising abruptly on either side, and forming gigantic columns to the gate by which it enters Bear river valley" (Frémont, 1845: 133). They halted at noon in a fertile bottom, "where the common blue flax was growing abundantly, a few miles below the mouth of Thomas's fork, one of the larger tributaries of the river." In the afternoon the group came to a scene recorded by Frémont (1845: 133) as follows: "The edge of the wood, for several miles along the river, was dotted with the white covers of emigrant wagons, collected in groups at different camps, where the smokes were rising lazily from the fires, around which the women were occupied in preparing the evening meal, and the children playing in the grass; and herds of cattle, grazing about in the bottom, had an air of quiet security, and civilized comfort, that made a rare sight for the traveller in such a remote wilderness."

The men and animals arrived at an Indian encampment on the 23rd, where, after an initial charge by excited warriors, camp was made and the men traded for horses. "We obtained from them also a considerable quantity of berries of different kinds, among which service berries were the most abundant; and several kinds of roots and seeds, which we could eat with pleasure, as any kind of vegetable food was gratifying to us. I ate here, for the first time, the *kooyah*, or *tobacco root*, (*valeriana edulis*) the principal edible root among the Indians who inhabit the upper waters of the streams on the western side of the mountains. It has a very strong and remarkably peculiar taste and odor, which I can compare to no other vegetable that I am acquainted with, and which to some persons is extremely offensive" (Frémont, 1845: 135). Preuss was offended by kooyah, which he characterized as the "most horrid food he had ever put in his mouth" (Frémont, 1845: 135). The observation is supported by modern encounters with this plant, which smells not unlike a wet bed or excessively bad body odor, even following years of storage as dry specimens in a herbarium cabinet. The party continued along the valley of the Bear River on the 24th, noting that blue flax "is the most characteristic plant of the Bear river valley" (Frémont, 1845: 135).

Volcanic rock was encountered on the morning of 25 August, the first they had seen. After a journey of six miles the expedition arrived at Beer (Soda) Springs (Caribou County, Idaho). Here the Bear River reaches its northernmost point before turning south toward the Great Salt Lake. Frémont investigated the area around Beer Springs, took a sample of the water, and wandered about "among the cedars, which occupy the greater part of the bottom towards the mountains" (Frémont, 1845: 135). Beer or Soda Springs is now drowned in the waters of the reservoir at Soda Springs, Idaho. On the morning of the 26th the party moved on down the immigrant road toward Fort Hall for a short distance prior to halting where the road left the Bear River Valley. Frémont had noted on 21 August his intention to travel to the Great Salt Lake, about which little accurate information was available. He had indicated while still in St. Louis that the Great Salt Lake was one of his main goals of the expedition. Reasons for the visit to the lake could well have been based on discussions with Provost during the Nicollet expedition. Ever the explorer, Frémont states (1845: 139): "An examination of the great lake which is the outlet of this river, and the principal feature of geographical interest in the basin, was one of the main objects contemplated in the general plan of our survey, and I accordingly determined at this place to leave the road, and, after having completed a reconnaissance of the lake, regain it subsequently at Fort Hall."

The small advance party turned away from the Oregon trail toward the Great Salt Lake, following the Bear River, and on the evening of 26 August they encamped on the Bear River near some Indian lodges. Frémont was there introduced to the camas root (bulb) for the first time. They halted at noon on the 27th "in the ravine of a pretty little stream, timbered with cottonwood of a large size, ash-leaved maple, with cherry and other shrubby trees. Among the plants occurring along the line of the road during the day, *epinettes des prairies* (grindelia squarrosa) was in considerable abundance, and is among the very few plants remaining in bloom—the whole country having now an autumnal appearance, in the crisped and yellowish plants and dried-up grass" (Frémont, 1845: 140). On 28 August travel was along the valley, which was about five or six miles wide, where a skunk was killed, that "made a supper for one of the messes." Frémont noted that the river there was bordered occasionally with fields of cane, probably *Phragmites australis* (Cav.) Trin. ex Steudel. During the day's march of 27 miles, they had viewed Cache Valley in present-day Franklin County, Idaho, and Cache County, Utah, and had seen the mountain range (Wellsville Mountains) where the Bear River exited. On 29 August the party discovered a trail trending west toward three marked gaps in the bordering range.

Frémont and his small entourage overtook a party of Shoshone Indians, who indicated that the road through the chain of mountains was "a very excellent one, leading into a broad valley which ran to the southward" (Frémont, 1845: 141). The party was now at the northern boundary of what was to become Utah. They halted at noon along a stream issuing from a most beautiful valley "of trees and shrubs—aspen, maple [*Acer grandidentatum* Nutt.], willow, cherry [*Prunus virginiana* L.], and elder [*Sambucus caerulea* Raf.]; a fine verdure of smooth short grass spread over the remaining space to the bare sides of the rocky walls" (Frémont, 1845: 141). According to Jackson and Spence (1970: 483), Frémont had turned away from the Bear River at Standing Rock Pass, had gone up Weston Creek, and then down Deep Creek to the valley of the Malad, roughly paralleling the Idaho-Utah border.

The morning of 30 August dawned clear and cold, the temperature at sunrise being 39 degrees. Constant thunderstorms during the night had intensified the cold, as had the elevation, which by barometer reading was 5580 feet. The party moved west in the morning and came upon a Shoshone village. A meridian observation of the sun indicated the latitude of the village as 42°14′22″, just north of the present Utah-Idaho boundary. They halted on the river (possibly Deep Creek, a tributary of the Malad River), "which was lightly wooded with cherry, willow, maple, service berry [*Amelanchier alnifolia* Nutt.], and aspen [*Populus tremuloides* Michx.]" (Frémont, 1845: 143). The men had stopped near the Indian village, because they wished to "purchase from them some roots and berries." The Indians were short of just about everything, were very lean themselves, and could not supply all of the items needed by Frémont and his men, who were also running low on food supplies. "Among the roots we obtained here, I could distinguish only five or six different kinds; and the supply of the Indians whom we met consisted principally of yampah, (anethum, graveolens,) tobacco root, (valeriana,) and a large species of thistle, (cirsium Virginianum,) which now is occasionally abundant and is a very agreeably flavored vegetable" (Frémont, 1845: 146).

Yampah (*Perideridia*) was evidently a staple food of the Indians in this region. It was used along with the malodorous *Valeriana edulis* Nutt. ex. Torr. & A. Gray, and the thistle was probably *Cirsium scariosum* Nutt., the meadow thistle common through much of the West.

The party proceeded five miles beyond the village and camped on the same river (east of Malad, Oneida County, Idaho). "The Indians informed us that we should reach the big salt water, after having slept twice and travelling in a south direction" (Frémont, 1845: 146). Evidently the Indians traveled more quickly than did Frémont and his men. They would be closer to the lake after having slept twice, of course, but it was still some days before the lake would be seen. The stream had here entered a nearly level plain or valley (Malad Valley) of good soil, eight or ten miles broad, to which no termination was to be seen, and lying between ranges of mountains, which, on the right, were grassy and smooth, unbroken by rock, and lower than on the left, where they were rocky and bald, increasing in height to the southward.

The weather on 31 August was clear and cool. The party moved down the creek they had been following for about five miles to where it joined with the Roseaux (French for reed) or Reed (Malad) River. The men and animals then turned southward and followed the foot slope of the mountains in a route paralleling the river. Halt at noon was "at a swampy spring, where there were good grass and abundant rushes. Here the river was forty feet wide, with a considerable current; and the valley a mile and a half in breadth; the soil being generally good, of a dark color, and apparently well adapted to cultivation. The day had become bright and pleasant with the thermometer at 71°. By observation, our latitude was 41°59′31″, and the elevation above the sea 4670 feet" (Frémont, 1845: 146).

The party was now in Box Elder County, Utah, possibly at Oregon Springs, but the elevation noted is about 300 feet too high. "Towards evening, our way was somewhat obstructed by fields of *artemisia*, which began to make their appearance here, and we encamped on the Roseaux, the water of which had acquired a decidedly salt taste, nearly opposite a canon gap in the mountains, through which the Bear River enters the valley" (Frémont, 1845: 147). It rained in the evening and the artemisia, the only wood available, was too wet to burn.

The morning of 1 September was stormy and cold. Traveling between Roseaux and Bear rivers, the party continued to descend the valley, which expanded gradually in width. They traveled along the slopes that afforded them no view of their goal, the Great Salt Lake. "On this upper plain the grass was everywhere dead; and among the shrubs with which it was almost exclusively occupied, (artemisia being the most abundant,) frequently occurred handsome clusters of several species of *dietaria* [*Machaeranthera*] in bloom. *Purshia tridentata* was among the frequent shrubs. Descending to the bottoms of Bear river, we found good grass for the animals, and encamped about 300 yards above the mouth of Roseaux, which here makes its junction, without communicating any of its salty taste to the main stream, of which the water remains perfectly pure. On the river are only willow thickets, (*salix longifolia*,) [*Salix exigua* Nutt.] and in the bottoms plants are canes, solidago, and helianthi, and along the banks of Roseaux are fields of *malva rotundifolia* [possibly a species of *Sidalcea*]" (Frémont, 1845: 147). His camp that night was about midway between modern Bear River City and Corinne, in Box Elder County, Utah.

On 2 September the party ferried people, equipment, and the carriage and 12-lb. howitzer across the Roseaux River in their inflatable rubber boat, a contraption some 18 feet long that must have required great effort to inflate. While the others of the party continued southward, Frémont and Basil Lajeunesse paddled down the Bear River, thinking that perhaps in the course of the day they might reach the outlet at the lake. For five or six hours John Charles and Basil paddled slowly the winding course of the sluggish river as it meandered over the nearly level approach to Great Salt Lake. The pair came upon several families of Indians busy with weirs or nets made of canes and rushes for the purpose of catching fish. The progress was so laboriously slow that Frémont chose to abandon the attempt. They cached the boat some distance below the Indian encampment and proceeded on foot for some miles (the estimate of 15 is too great, but it probably seemed that far) to overtake the others. "A plentiful supper of aquatic birds, and the interest of the scene, soon dissipated fatigue" (Frémont, 1845: 148). Observations of the satellites of Jupiter gave his position along the Bear River as west of present-day Brigham City, Utah (see charts of observations for 3 September in the appendix of the 1843 Frémont report).

Basil was sent back for the boat, accompanied by several other men and horses. "On the dry salt marsh here, is scarce any other plant than *salicornia herbacea*" (Frémont, 1845: 149). The men returned with the boat in the afternoon, bringing also a small quantity of roots and some meat, which had been obtained from the Indians encountered the day earlier. The men continued along the Bear River for about three miles in the afternoon but found an obstacle to any further travel in that direction. The stream branched into several channels, and the low grounds were covered with water. Rushes and canes in the marshes prevented them from seeing the lake. The Bear River was bordered by a "fringe of willows and canes, among which were interspersed a few plants; and scattered about on the marsh was a species of *uniola*, closely allied to *U. spicata* [saltgrass, *Distichlis spicata* (L.) Greene] of our sea coast. The whole morass was animated with multitudes of water fowl, which appeared to be very wild—rising for the space of a mile round about at the sound of a gun, with a noise like distant thunder. Several of the people waded out into the marshes, and we had to-night a delicious supper of ducks, geese, and plover" (Frémont, 1845: 149). Elevation of their camp was at 4200 feet; they were approximately at the level of the surface of the lake, but the men still could not see it.

On 4 September, as the party was preparing to proceed, Kit Carson rode into camp with flour and a few other articles of food, enough for two or three days—"a scanty but very acceptable supply." Kit had ridden to Fort Hall from Beer Springs to obtain supplies, which were very scarce, and had ridden at great speed to catch up with Frémont, who had turned south to explore the Great Salt Lake and was almost out of food. Mr. Fitzpatrick, with the slower baggage contingent, had not arrived at Fort Hall by the time Carson left to find John Charles on the Bear River. The still poorly supplied party then returned up the Bear River for five or six miles before finding a crossing to the east side of the channel. The people and baggage were crossed to the east bank in the boat. Camp that night was on the east bank of the Bear River, where they had crossed.

Before them was the salt marsh that bordered the east side of the Great Salt Lake—level, bare, and whitened in places by saline efflorescences, with here and there a pool of water. The riverbank supported a narrow strip of vegetation, consisting of "willows, helianthi, roses, flowering vines, and grass; bordered on the verge of the great marsh by a fringe of singular plants, which appear to be a shrubby salicornia [*Allenrolfea*, see Appendix I], or a genus allied to it" (Frémont, 1845: 150). After attempting to traverse directly toward what appeared to be a peninsula at the lake's edge, the men and animals, still with the howitzer on its wheeled carraige, turned toward the higher ground at the foot of the mountains to the east. There the group halted at noon "on a beautiful little stream of pure and remarkably clear water, with a bed of rock *in situ*, on which was an abundant water plant with a white blossom. There was good grass in the bottoms; and amidst a rather luxuriant growth, its banks were bordered with a large showy plant (*eupatorium purpureum*,) which I here saw for the first time. We named the stream Clear Creek [possibly Willard Creek]." They continued on a plainly traveled trail southward along the foot of the mountain, encountering a leguminous plant "(*glycyrrhiza lepidota*)." "Near a rocky point of the mountain [Pole Patch], at a large spring of pure water, were several hackberry trees, (*celtis*,) probably a new species, the berries still green; and a short distance farther, thickets of sumach (*rhus*)" (Frémont, 1845: 150). Netleaf hackberry (*Celtis reticulata* Torr.) and sumac (*Rhus glabra* L.) still grow there today. "In about seven miles from Clear creek, the trail brought us to a place at the foot of the mountains where there issued with considerable force ten or twelve hot springs [Utah Hot Springs, north of present Ogden, Utah], highly impregnated with salt." Leaving the hot springs, the party veered to the southwest to the Weber River where the camp was set up. "This river, . . . was 100 to 150 feet wide, with high banks, and very clear pure water, without the slightest indication of salt" (Frémont, 1845: 151). The description of the lower Weber by Frémont is a far different one than the murky stream, depleted by numerous diversions and enriched by nutrients, of the late twentieth century.

On the morning of 6 September the group proceeded westward toward Little Mountain, the peninsular butte referred to days earlier, "across a low shrubby plain, crossing in the way a slough-like creek with miry banks, and wooded with thickets of thorn (*crataegus*) which were loaded with berries [*Crataegus douglasii* Lindl.]." In time they reached Little Mountain and ascended to its summit. The lake was immediately adjacent to the mountain, "the waters of the Inland Sea, stretching in still and solitary grandeur far beyond the limit of our vision. It was one of the great points of the exploration" (Frémont, 1845: 151). Frémont then compared this view with that of Balboa when he and his followers first beheld the great "Western ocean." "It was certainly a magnificent object, and a noble terminus to this part of our expedition; and to travellers so long shut up among mountain ranges, a sudden view over the expanse of silent waters had in it something sublime. Several large islands raised their high rocky heads out of the waves; but whether timbered, was still left to our imagination, as the distance was too great to determine if the dark hues upon them were woodland or naked rock."

The view from the burned-over summit of Little Mountain today is less than spectacular. Salt-evaporation ponds and mineral extraction plants preclude a close approach to the lake. Cheatgrass is the principal plant occupying Little Mountain, but occasional clumps of pricklypear cactus indicate that native vegetation once grew there. The islands in the lake appear to be merely bare rock to this observer. But in fairness to Frémont, his view and expectations of the island, romanticized by space and time between actual observation and final prose of his report, appear to have been fanciful at best and unnecessarily optimistic at worst. The romantic mind of Jessie, scribe of the report, should not be ruled out. The entry by Preuss (Gudde & Gudde, 1958: 88–89) for 8 September is unequivocal: "We ferried with our miserable rubber boat to the next island, which Frémont christened Disappointment Island because he expected game there but did not find it. None of the rest of us were so crazy as to expect that on a bare rock without trees or water. One could clearly see that both were lacking." Bancroft (1889) criticized Frémont's exploration of the Great Salt Lake and his claim to being the first to boat upon its surface, a sentiment evidently supported by McKelvey (1955), who quoted him. According to Jackson and Spence (1970: 502), "William H. Ashley's men had sailed around the lake in skin canoes in 1826." One must consider, however, that Frémont was not a historian; instead he was an explorer who understood that in point of space and time he was removed from the contemporary civilization—his party at the lake was far from the civilized world; they were alone. The lack of a historical background does not itself constitute a crime. Of being an impulsive, egocentric romanticist his contemporaries and those since might judge him guilty. Nevertheless he was there; his critics were not!

In spite of what he thought he saw from the summit of Little Mountain, Frémont and party prepared to set up camp and explore Great Salt Lake (Miller, 1948; Neff, 1928).

"During the day the clouds had been gathering black over the mountains to the westward, and, while we were looking, a storm burst down with sudden fury upon the lake, and entirely hid the islands from our view. So far as we could see, along the shores there was not a solitary tree, and but little appearance of grass; and on Weber's fork, a few miles below our last encampment, the timber was gathered into groves, and then disappeared entirely. As this appeared to be the nearest point to the lake where a suitable camp could be found, we directed our course to one of the groves, where we found a handsome encampment, with good grass and an abundance of rushes, (*equisetum hyemale*) [probably *Juncus*, *Carex*, and grasses]" (Frémont, 1845: 151).

The day of 7 September 1843 was spent in preparation for the intended exploratory voyage of Great Salt Lake. The party constructed a corral for the animals from timbers felled along the Weber River and a little fort for the people who were to remain. Then the men worked at repairing the India-rubber boat and filling it with air. At this point seven of the party were sent to Fort Hall because supplies of food were insufficient for the entire party to remain. The returning men were guided by François Lajeunesse, a seasoned mountain man, who led them astray. The four-day journey turned into a week-long trek. The boating expedition would consist of Charles Preuss, Kit Carson, J. B. Bernier, Basil Lajeunesse, and, of course, John Charles. François Badeau, Baptiste Derosier, and Jacob Dodson were left in charge of the camp. Preuss (Gudde & Gudde, 1958: 88) indicated that four men stayed to guard the camp; the fourth is not identified. "The bottoms along the river were timbered with several kinds of willow, hawthorn, and fine cottonwood trees (*populus canadensis*) with remarkably large leaves, and sixty feet in height by measurement" (Frémont, 1845: 152). This is the species of cottonwood that would be collected by him at Lassen's in present Tehama County, California, in 1846 and named in honor of Frémont decades later by Sereno Watson (1875).

Supper on the evening of the seventh consisted of "*yampah*, the most agreeably flavored of the roots, seasoned by a small fat duck, which had come in the way of Jacob's rifle." The small group of men remaining discussed the possibilities of the adventure about to begin. Fancied growth on the large islands was "a tangled wilderness of trees and shrubbery, teeming with game of every description that the neighboring region afforded, and which the foot of a white man or Indian had never violated." But, for the present, the India-rubber boat was a troubling reality. The seams were only pasted together, not sewed like those on the boat of the first expedition. This one was coming apart and had to be reinflated on a continuing basis.

September 8 dawned clear and calm. Instruments, water, and gear were placed into the boat, and the party was away down the course of the Weber River at sunrise. Late in the day they were near the outlet to the lake, in very shallow water, and were forced to wade and pull the boat. Camp that evening was on a low point among rushes and young willows, near the mouth of the Weber River. "The stillness of the night was enlivened by millions of water fowl" (Frémont, 1845: 153).

The morning of 9 September was also clear and calm. The men dragged the boat over a mud flat about a mile wide, sinking to their knees in the evil-smelling slime at every step. They came finally to a small black ridge on the bottom "beyond which the water became suddenly salt, beginning gradually to deepen, and the bottom was sandy and firm. It was a remarkable division, separating the fresh water of the rivers from the briny water of the lake, which was entirely saturated with common salt" (Frémont, 1845: 153). The men boarded the boat, with its leaky rubber cylinders, and began their journey upon the Inland Sea. Their immediate goal was the near island, which was reached in a few hours of rowing. At the island they were fascinated by the accumulation of the skins of worms, about the size of a grain of oats (possibly castings of the brine fly), which had been washed up by the waters of the lake. The barometer and other instruments were taken to the summit of the island, "a bare rocky peak [Castle Rock], 800 feet above the lake." From there the various topographic features of both the lake and the mountains to the east were surveyed. These corresponding features had been surveyed from Little Mountain also. Preuss was able to construct a reasonably accurate map of the basin of the Great Salt Lake from those measurements. The island turned out to be merely a rocky hill, "on which there is neither water nor trees of any kind; although the *Fremontia vermicularis* [*Sarcobatus vermiculatus* (Hook.) Torr.], which was in great abundance, might easily be mistaken for timber at a distance [this is a fanciful justification]. The plant seemed to delight in a congenial air, growing in extraordinary luxuriance seven or eight feet high, and was very abundant on the upper parts of the island, where it was almost the only plant. This is eminently a saline shrub; its leaves have a very salt taste; and it luxuriates in saline soils, where it is usually a characteristic. It is widely diffused over all this country. A chenopodiaceous shrub, which is a new species of **Obione**, (O. rigida, *Torr. & Frém.*,) was equally characteristic of the lower parts of the island. These two are the striking plants on the island, and belong to a class of plants which form a prominent feature in the vegetation of this country. On the lower parts of the island, also, a prickly pear of very large size was frequent. On the shore near the water, was a woolly species of *phaca*; and a new species of umbelliferous plant (*leptotaenia*) was scattered about in very considerable abundance. These constituted all the vegetation that now appeared upon the island" (Frémont, 1845: 156).

Obione rigida is an earlier manuscript name for *Atriplex confertifolia* (see Appendix I). The woolly *Phaca* is probably the same as that collected by members of the Stansbury (1852; Madsen, 1981) expedition to the lake in 1849 and later named *Phaca mollissima* var. *utahensis* Torr. [*Astragalus utahensis* (Torr.) Torr. & A. Gray]. The *Leptotaenia* has been identified; it is *Lomatium dissectum* (Nutt.) Math. & Const. Latitude and longitude determinations were made by Frémont, indicating the location of their camp was along the northeast shore of this commalike island, which was named "Disappointment." The epithet supported Frémont's feeling about the place that differed so vastly from his dreams. It is today named Fremont Island, so designated by Howard Stansbury, has an area of about five square miles, and has been grazed in winter by sheep. The principal vegetation today is *Bromus tectorum* L., the introduced Old World cheatgrass first collected in Utah in 1894 by Marcus E. Jones (Welsh et al., 1987).

The party stayed the night of 9 September on the island, free from threat of attack by Indians or any other creature that might stir in the night. By morning of 10 September the surf was breaking heavily on the shore. Following a hurried breakfast, the boat was quickly launched and reloaded. The men crowded into the boat with its leaky cylinders and paddled out onto the wave-tossed surface. Luckily, but not without some consternation (Quaife, 1935: 77), they regained the eastern shore of the lake on the mud flat adjacent to Little Mountain. Even now boaters on Great Salt Lake, far better equipped than Frémont and his men, are endangered by the windswept waters; search parties and rescues and recovery of drowning victims are commonplace. Preuss and Lajeunesse proceeded on foot to the camp some miles distant (the nine miles estimated by Frémont seems excessive), and Basil returned with horses for the boat and baggage.

"*Linosiris graveolens* [*Chrysothamnus nauseosus* (Pallas) Britt.], and another new species of **Obione**, (O. confertifolia—*Torr. & Frém.*,) [*Atriplex confertifolia* (Torr. & Frém.) Wats.] were growing on the low grounds, with interspersed spots of unwholesome salt grass, on a saline clay soil, with a few other plants" (Frémont, 1845: 157). This and *Pterochiton occidentale* are the earliest plant types collected within Utah. The return to camp was through the lowlands bordering the lake and the lower reaches of the Weber River. "The low plain through which we rode to camp was covered with a compact growth of shrubs of extraordinary size and luxuriance. The soil was sandy and saline; flat places, resembling the beds of ponds, that were bare of vegetation, and covered with a powdery white salts, being interspersed among the shrubs. Artemisia tridentata was very abundant, but the plants were principally saline; a large and vigorous chenopodiaceous shrub [*Atriplex canescens* (Pursh) Nutt. var. *occidentale* (Torr. & Frém.) Welsh & Stutz, based on *Pterochiton occidentale*], five to eight feet high, being characteristic, with Fremontia vermicularis, and a shrubby plant which seems to be a new *salicornia* [*Allenrolfea occidentalis* S. Wats.]" (Frémont, 1845: 157).

At the camp the returning men were greeted by a shot fired from the howitzer by the men left there. During the exploratory party's absence, the camp tenders had become uneasy about Frémont's fate on the lake, and celebrated the group's return by firing the howitzer.

Five gallons of water brought from the lake was boiled down at the camp on the lower Weber River on 11 September. The five gallons yielded fourteen pints of a very fine-grained and very white salt, consisting almost entirely of sodium chloride. Preuss (Gudde & Gudde, 1958: 89) further explains: "We found plenty of salt and have boiled down some of it. I believe that three, or certainly four, pounds of water make one pound of salt. I have never seen anything like it. We found the salt fifteen feet deep near the island." Observations at the camp placed it along the river approximately two miles west of the community of West Weber, at 41°15′50″, 112°06′43″. They had breakfasted on yampah, and had only "kamas" for supper; "but a cup of good coffee still distinguished us from our *Digger* acquaintances" (Frémont, 1845: 158). The collections of Frémont were, in part, corroborated by Stansbury (1852) and Durand (1869).

The morning of 12 September was clear and calm, and the party resumed its journey back along the path they had followed in reaching the Weber campsite. The small party struck the foothills a little south of the hot springs and camped that evening on Clear (Willard?) Creek. "This creek is here unusually well timbered with a variety of trees. Among them were birch (*betula*,) the narrow-leaved poplar (*populus angustifolia*,) several kinds of willow (*salix*,) hawthorn (*crataegus*,) [*C. douglasii* Lindl.] alder (*alnus viridis*) [*Alnus incana* Willd.] and *cerasus* [probably *Prunus virginiana*], with an oak allied to *quercus alba* [*Q. gambelii* Nutt., almost at its northernmost limits, then still undescribed], but very distinct from that or any other species in the United States. We had tonight a supper of sea gulls [probably *Larus californicus*, the species later designated as the Utah state bird], which Carson killed near the lake" (Frémont, 1845: 158).

The party of hungry travelers continued up the valley of the Bear River on 13 September, crossing various small streams. One of the streams broke into several channels in the lowlands, "and the irrigated bottom of fertile soil was covered with innumerable flowers, among which were purple fields of *eupatorium purpureum*, with helianthi, a handsome solidago (*S. canadensis*,) and a variety of other plants in bloom." Camp that evening was in the vicinity of present Deweyville on the Bear River at 41°42′43″, 112°05′12″. Frémont noted that the men were in low spirits due to hunger, their food supply having dwindled to practically nothing. After about four miles of travel on the 14th, they crossed the Bear River where it enters the valley near the present community of Fielding and proceeded to a campsite that had served as a lunch stop on the way south. "The people this evening looked so forlorn, that I gave them permission to kill a fat young horse which I had purchased with goods from the Snake Indians, and they were very soon restored to gaiety and good humor. Mr. Preuss and myself could not yet overcome some remains of civilized prejudices, and preferred to starve a little longer; feeling as much saddened as if a crime had been committed" (Frémont, 1845: 159). Preuss's (Gudde & Gudde, 1958: 89) record of the event was more laconic: "Frémont tried a little of the horse meat yesterday."

On 15 September the party again moved northward along Malad Valley, retracing their southward route of a few days earlier. An Indian encampment of two families of Snake Indians was encountered, from whom some kooyah was purchased. The families had been gathering seeds and roots of thistle. Later, they met an Indian with the carcass of an antelope, which was also purchased. Following arrival in camp, where preparations were being made to eat the antelope, Baptiste Tabeau rode into camp with news that Mr. Fitzpatrick had arrived from Fort Hall and was camped nearby. He had brought flour, rice, and dried meat, "and even a little butter." The combined party ate heartily and slept well that night. Neither Frémont nor Preuss record the joy of the reunion with Fitzpatrick and his supply of food. The men with Frémont must have also been comforted by the increased security guaranteed by the larger combined force, and it must have been a time of recounting stories of the adventures of the parties during their separation, each having had unique experiences of interest to the other. Frémont's silence is a matter-of-fact response to his trust in Fitzpatrick; he had been expected to do his job well.

With no time to lose, the combined party was up before sunrise on 16 September and continued north again. The noon stop was made near some Indian lodges, where purchase was made of about a bushel of service berries. Frémont enticed an Indian boy to show him the kooyah plant, which proved to be "*valeriana edulis*." The route north was, according to Jackson and Spence (1970: 483), up the Malad and Little Malad Rivers, over a divide to the Bannock and down that stream to the Snake River. John Charles did not hesitate in the choice of route. Fitzpatrick merely retraced his steps to Fort Hall. In the afternoon of the 16th the divide separating the Great Basin drainage from that of the Snake River was crossed; the Frémont and Fitzpatrick party was in Power County, Idaho.

Frémont (1845: 160) summarized his views of the basin encompassing the Great Salt Lake: "I can say of it, in general terms, that the bottoms of this river, (Bear,) and of some of the creeks which I saw, form a natural resting and recruiting station for travellers, now, and in all times to come. The bottoms are extensive; water excellent; timber sufficient; the soil good, and well adapted to the grains and grasses suited to such an elevated region. A military post, and a civilized settlement, would be of great value here; and cattle and horses would do well where grass and salt so much abound. The lake will furnish exhaustless supplies of salt. All the mountain sides here are covered with a valuable nutritious grass, called bunch grass, from the form in which it grows, which has a second growth in the fall. The beasts of the Indians were fat upon it; our own found it a good subsistence; and its quantity will sustain any amount of cattle, and make this truly a bucolic region." That optimistic description must have sounded very good to people in the United States looking for an opportunity to come west. The bunch grasses would be grazed heavily in the first decades following settlement, and they would be replaced by sagebrush, which was already plentiful nearby.

An Indian family on horseback was encountered, returning from an outing to gather service berries. Plants of service berry were scattered about on the hills, "and the upper parts of the pass was timbered with aspen; (*populus trem.*,) the common blue flowering flax occurring among the plants" (Frémont, 1845: 160). The group with Frémont passed over a divide and descended "by a very steep slope, into a broad open valley—good soil; from four to five miles wide; coming down immediately upon one of the headwaters of the Pannack [Bannock] river, which here loses itself in a swampy ground" (Frémont, 1845: 160).

In the afternoon of 17 September the party entered the valley of the Pannack River, which was there a mile and a half wide, fertile, and bordered by smooth hills. Camp was made that night on the river, its position determined as 42°44′40″, 112°29′52″. The next day, 18 September, the expedition emerged on the plains of the "Columbia [actually the Snake River plains]" and came in site of the famous "Three Buttes," which were some 45 miles distant. "Covered as far as could be seen with artemisia, the dark and ugly appearance of this plain obtained for it the name of *Sage Desert*; and we were agreeably surprised, on reaching the Portneuf river, to see a beautiful green valley with scattered timber spread out beneath us, on which, about four miles distant, were glistening the white walls of the fort" (Frémont, 1845: 161). At Fort Hall the combined Frémont and Fitzpatrick party rejoined those portions of their company that had come behind them with most of the baggage and those sent earlier from Great Salt Lake. The distance between the Missouri River and Fort Hall, via Fort Laramie, was computed by Frémont as 1323 miles.

The reunited party stayed in the vicinity of the fort on 19 September, where Frémont traded for several horses and five oxen. One of the latter was butchered and served to restore the "good humor" of the men following a dark and gloomy day of disagreeable weather. Snow and rain fell in the night, and on the morning of the 20th it was again raining and there was snow on the ground. The morning of the 21st the weather cleared, but rainfall again on the morning of the 22nd was an unmistakable warning to Frémont an early winter was imminent. Several members of the party were prevailed upon to return voluntarily, as John Charles wrote it, to the east. At least some portion of the men leaving here were evidently glad to depart, not wishing to spend another hour working with the expedition. They had other responsibilities at St. Louis and were anxious to leave the party. Those returning were C. Deforest, Henry Lee, J. Campbell, Wm. Creuss, A. Vasquez, A. Pera, Patrick White, B. Tesson, M. Crelis, François Lajeunesse, and Basil Lajeunesse. Basil was one of his best and most reliable voyageurs and a favorite, and Frémont regretted very much his return. It is possible that at least some portion of the plant specimens were sent eastward with the returning men. Henry Lee had been entrusted with letters, which he was supposed to deliver to Jessie, but which he lost in swimming a river en route home (Herr, 1987: 94). So many of the early collections are missing that one wonders if plant specimens met the same fate. How these men prevailed in reaching St. Louis, a considerable undertaking by itself, is not recorded.

Of Fort Hall Frémont writes: "It is in a low, rich bottom of a valley, apparently 20 miles long, formed by the confluence of Portneuf river with Lewis's fork [Snake River] of the Columbia, which it enters about nine miles below the fort, and narrowing gradually to the mouth of the Pannack river, where it has a breadth of only two or three miles." The party was at a major turning point of the expedition.

Fort Hall to The Dalles

The two parties, east- and westbound, separated on the morning of 22 September. That evening the westbound group camped on the bank of the Lewis Fork of the Columbia at the mouth of the Pannack. The air on the 23rd was laden with snow that turned to rain, which melted the snow along the valley but not in the adjacent hills. The party remained in camp, where Frémont took hourly barometrical observations from sunrise to midnight. This was "an inauspicious commencement of the autumn, of which this was the first day." On this date Preuss (Gudde & Gudde, 1958: 90), who had gone hungry with the others of the Salt Lake group, noted, "We have plenty to eat again—five oxen, sugar, coffee, flour for a short time, and butter." They moved west on 24 September through lands occupied by artemisia, that plague of the Snake River country, and at noon camped among willows at the upper end of some islands near American Falls (Power County, Idaho) of the Snake River. "Among the willows here, were some bushes of Lewis and Clark's currant, (*ribes aureum.*)" (Frémont, 1845: 164). On 25 September the entourage traveled 14 miles through country where grass was scanty, rocks and sagebrush were abundant, and the rugged banks supported scattered "cedars." Another oxen was butchered for food. The barometer indicated an elevation of 4400 feet. Even this smaller party consumed an immense quantity of meat and other food.

Rain fell during the night, making the morning of the 26th cool. Frémont's party traveled some four miles to a "picturesque stream," which he named Fall Creek. After a detour on a wrong route, they returned to the river and continued west to a stream called

Raft River, which drains from a range of that same name mostly in northwestern Utah. Raft River enters the Snake in Cassia County, Idaho. On the morning of 27 September the party again was divided, with Frémont running ahead and Brokenhand Fitzpatrick bringing the heavy baggage and carts. John Charles's explanation for the division of the group is hardly understandable: "Since leaving the American falls, the road had frequently been very bad; the many short, steep ascents, exhausting the strength of our worn-out animals, requiring always at such places the assistance of the men to get up each cart, one by one; and our progress with twelve or fourteen wheeled carriages, though light and made for the purpose, in such a rocky country, was extremely slow; and I again determined to gain time by a division of the camp. Accordingly, to-day the parties again separated, constituted very much as before—Mr. Fitzpatrick remaining in charge of the heavier baggage" (Frémont, 1845: 166). Splitting the party would allow him to travel more quickly, but it would certainly place a hardship on those left behind with the heavy loads. If the carts could be gotten up only with difficulty, how would Fitzpatrick with a smaller contingent succeed? But Frémont would not be concerned with how the baggage party got along. Now he and the smaller group were free of the burdensome carts; they traveled 20 miles following the abandonment of the baggage party before stopping for the evening meal that was cooked over a sagebrush fire. "Mingled with the artemisia was a shrubby and thorny chenopodiaceous plant [probably shadscale, *Atriplex confertifolia*]" (Frémont, 1845: 166).

After an uncomfortable day's ride of 25 miles, the westbound group with Frémont camped on the evening of the 28th in a sheltered place with an abundance of firewood. The road had been good and the journey uneventful, with the exception of some difficulty at Goose Creek. The country was densely covered with artemisia. The road traveled on the 29th was extremely rocky and bad. Later the road entered sandy country and travel improved. Sagebrush "covered the river plain so far as the eye could reach, and, with their uniform tint of dark gray, gave to the country a gloomy and sombre appearance" (Frémont, 1845: 167). Preuss (Gudde & Gudde, 1958: 91) agreed: "Nothing to be seen anywhere on the plain or the mountains except artemisia." They camped at Rock Creek after having traveled 24 miles.

On 30 September camp was made on the escarpment above the entrenched Snake River, at 42°38′44″, 114°25′04″ (Twin Falls County, Idaho), and the animals, except for one of the oxen that was killed for food, were driven down a steep ravine to the river bottom where there was "tolerably good grass bordering the water." Across from camp there was a subterranean river that burst forth from the face of the escarpment. The morning of 1 October was spent in launching the inflatable boat on the Snake River. The men rowed to the north shore and examined the subterranean river. In the afternoon the journey was resumed, and the party proceeded west for 17 miles. Camp was made about one mile below "*Fishing Falls*" near the lodges of Snake Indians. Frémont's men were able to exchange goods for dried salmon. Salmon were still in the river, and the party watched as the Indians paddled about in boats made of rushes. Downstream on 2 October a series of falls and rapids was encountered. "In about seven miles we reached the most beautiful and picturesque fall (Shoshone or Twin falls?) I had seen on the river"

(Frémont, 1845: 169). Even Preuss (Gudde & Gudde, 1958: 92) was impressed: "This Snake River is interesting, I must confess, no matter how awful the country around it may be. The most beautiful little waterfalls, twenty to forty feet high. Then steep, volcanic, rocky shores along which one can travel for days without being able to find a place to get to the stream." The road on 3 October was broken by ravines. In the afternoon they arrived at the ford (Three Island Crossing, near present Glenns Ferry, Elmore County, Idaho) where the road crosses to the right (north) bank of the Snake River. The ford proved to be impassable, and the inflatable boat was again put to use. The animals were forced into the water and swam to the north bank. All other baggage, howitzer included, and the men were carried in the inflatable boat. Their location at camp on the north bank was determined to be 42°55′58″ north, 115°04′46″ west. The advance group of men were 208 miles west of Fort Hall by road. How Fitzpatrick and the heavy baggage crossed the river is not recorded.

On 4 October the road turned north of the Snake River onto a plain covered by artemisia, "but *Purshia tridentata* makes its appearance here on the hill sides and on bottoms of the creeks—quite a tree in size, and larger than the artemisia" (Frémont, 1845: 170). They camped that night three miles up the bed of a creek where there was wood and grass. Travel was slow on 5 October because of the rocky road. After traveling about nine miles, several smoking hot springs (present Hot Springs, east of Mountain Home, Elmore County, Idaho) were encountered, with a temperature measured at 164°. Despite the lateness of the season, there were a few helianthi in bloom. The ground around the springs was warm and the place was green with vegetation. Camp that night was on a stream, "which was probably Lake river [Bennett Creek]" (Frémont, 1845: 171). The stream was lined with willows and a few cottonwoods, and "along the banks were canes, rose bushes, and clematis, with Purshia tridentata and artemisias on the upper bottom. The sombre appearance of the country is somewhat relieved in coming unexpectedly from the dark rocks upon these green and wooded watercourses, sunk in chasms; and, in the spring, the contrasted effect must make them beautiful" (Frémont, 1845: 171). The next morning, 6 October, the region of volcanic rocks through which the group had traveled for the past two days was left behind, and the party progressed into a land where granitic rocks dominated the landscape. "Here, the character of the vegetation was very much changed; the artemisia disappeared almost entirely, showing only at intervals towards the close of each day, and was replaced by Purshia tridentata, with flowering shrubs, and small fields of *dietaria divaricata*, which gave bloom and gaiety to the hills. These were every where covered with a fresh and green short grass, like that of early spring. This is the fall or second growth, the dried grass having been burnt off by the Indians; and wherever the fire has passed, the bright-green color is universal" (Frémont, 1845: 171). They camped on a small stream after a journey of 22 miles.

Travel on 7 October was pleasing to Frémont because the trail was on high ground above the gray sagebrush plain, which he was happy to be away from, "even for a day." In the course of the day the men suddenly came in sight of "the broad green line of the valley of the *Riviere Boisee*, (wooded river,) black near the gorge where it debouches into the plains, with high precipices of basalt, between walls of which it passes, on emerging from the mountains. Descending the hills, after traveling a few miles along the high plain, the road brought us down upon the bottoms of the river, which is a beautiful rapid stream, with clear mountain water, and, as the name indicates, well wooded with some varieties of timber—among which are handsome cottonwoods" (Frémont, 1845: 172). Indians from nearby camps came to trade dried and fresh fish during the evening. On 8 October the party traveled about 26 miles, and the next day 24 miles. Fort Boise was reached on 10 October. There the road crossed the Boise River, and the route was again through interminable artemisia. Frémont and his men traveled on a very good road during the 11th and reached about sunset the "*Riviere aux Malheurs*, (the unfortunate or unlucky river,)" having crossed the Snake River again (Frémont, 1845: 174). The Malheur River is in Malheur County, Oregon. The 12th dawned clear and calm, but the temperature was 23°. During the day the group crossed Birch River and descended to the Snake River. Their camp was at 44°17′36″, 116°56′45″ at an elevation determined as 1880 feet. They were in Oregon, west of present-day Payette, Idaho.

On 13 October the Snake River was departed as the men and animals, and the howitzer, moved westward in Oregon. The country was mountainous, with steep ascents and descents common. "The mountains were covered with good bunch grass, (*festuca*;) the water of the streams was cold and pure; their bottoms were handsomely wooded with various kinds of trees; and huge and lofty and picturesque precipices were displayed where the river cut through the mountains." Camp for the night was "among large timber, principally birch, which had been recently burnt and blackened, and almost destroyed by fire" (Frémont, 1845: 176). The road continued badly on the 14th, and Frémont marveled that the wagons in the emigrant trains ahead of them had gotten through at all, being without help. There is no hint, however, of any concern for Mr. Fitzpatrick and the men bringing along his own baggage carts and animals. The party had been following the general course of the Burnt River and on 15 October crossed the dividing ridge between that river and the Powder River. "From the summit here, the whole horizon shows high mountains; no high plain or level is to be seen; and on the left, from south around by the west to north, the mountains are black with pines; while, through the remaining space to the eastward, they are bald with the exception of some scattered pines" (Frémont, 1845: 177). Frémont was watching for a landmark, a tree (*l'arbre seul*, the lone tree), which he had been told should be in this vicinity and "on arriving at the river [Powder], we found a fine tall pine stretched on the ground, which had been felled by some inconsiderate emigrant axe" (Frémont, 1845: 172).

Ice a quarter of an inch thick formed inside the sleeping lodge during the night, and in the morning of the 16th the thermometer stood at 16°F. Preuss (Gudde & Gudde, 1958: 93) had been thinking of going home, which now seemed to be a remote possibility: "Since it is now certain that we shall not get home this winter, I am making plans in my spare time of how to spend all the money I shall have earned by next spring," while Frémont laments that the annual vegetation is now nearly gone, "almost all the plants being out of bloom." The men could see the Blue Mountains on the left during the 16th, and they were even closer on the 17th. The company crossed affluents of the Powder River in the morning along a good road, passing through very deep, black soil, and climbed the divide separating the Powder River from Grand Ronde (Great Circle) drainage (Union County, Oregon). "On either side, the mountains here are densely covered with tall and handsome trees; and, mingled with the green of a variety of pines, is the yellow of the European larch (*pinus larix,*) [*Larix occidentalis* Nutt.] which loses its leaves in the fall. From its present color, we were enabled to see that it forms a large proportion of the forests on the mountains, and is here a magnificent tree, attaining sometimes the height of 200 feet, which I believe is elsewhere unknown" (Frémont, 1845: 178). In the afternoon a divide was reached "from which we obtained a good view of the *Grand Rond* [Ronde]—a beautiful level basin, or mountain valley, covered with good grass, on a rich soil, abundantly watered, and surrounded by high and well-timbered mountains; and its name descriptive of its form—the great circle" (Frémont 1845: 178). The valley is in Union County, Oregon. That evening camp was on the banks of one of the tributaries of the Grand Ronde River. The elevation of the camp was determined to be 2940 feet.

The route left the emigrant trail on the 18th, and camp that evening was near the north end of the Grand Ronde valley. An Indian trail led through the region, and Frémont wished to determine if it would not be a better road than that followed by the emigrants. The camp was at 45°26′47″ north, 117°28′26″ west (several miles northeast of present La Grande, Oregon). The party halted at noon on 19 October on a branch of the Grand Ronde River at the foot of the Blue Mountains. After noon travel was resumed, and the route began to ascend the slopes of the Blues. The camp that night was without water, and pretty but not comfortable. The morning of 20 October was frosty, and the animals had not eaten during the night, having been tied to trees. An early start was made, and the men and animals traveled "among pines, which were more dense than yesterday, and still retained their magnificent size. The larches cluster together in masses on the sides of the mountains, and their yellow foliage contrasts handsomely with the green of the balsam and other pines. After a few miles we ceased to see any pines, and the timber consisted of several varieties of spruce, larch, and balsam pine [fir], which have a regular conical figure. These trees appear from 60 to nearly 200 feet in height; the usual circumference being 10 to 12 feet, and in the pines sometimes 21 feet. In open places near the summit, these trees became less high and more branching, the conical form having a greater base" (Frémont, 1845: 180). Camp that evening was near some springs on the mountainside, beyond the summit. The party made only six miles on 21 October, due to the necessity of cutting a road through thick timber. "During the days' journey, the barometer was broken; and the elevations above the sea, hereafter given, depend upon the temperature of boiling water. Some of the white spruces which I measured to-day were twelve feet in circumference, and one of the larches 10; but eight feet was the average circumference of those measured along the road" (Frémont, 1845: 181).

On 22 October the party was on the western margin of the Blue Mountains along affluents of the Umatilla River. Preuss (Gudde & Gudde, 1958: 94) describes the situation: "For four days we have been wandering in the Blue Mountains because we took the wrong route and had to hew our path through the firs. Although I had to walk, these have been the most agreeable days for me. The weather is fine (terribly cold during the night, to be sure) and the mountains are beautiful. Balsam firs and larches are the predominant trees, up to two hundred feet tall." Frémont could detect the course of the "Walahwalah river" across the plain toward the Columbia River. They camped in a meadow where water, he noted, was to be had "only by descending a bad ravine, into which we drove our animals, and had much trouble with them, in a very close growth of small pines. Mr. Preuss had walked ahead, and did not get into camp this evening" (Frémont, 1845: 182). That evening Preuss (Gudde & Gudde, 1958: 94) wrote in his diary: "I am sitting alone here at Walla Walla Creek and have to go to bed hungry. I have started two fires, and am lying between them on a bed of leaves. It will surely get cold. This morning it was 19° Fahrenheit, and since I have nothing to cover myself, I had to build two fires." On 23 October, Frémont (1845: 182) notes: "After cutting through two thick bodies of timber, in which I noticed some small trees of *hemlock* spruce [likely *Tsuga heterophylla* (Raf.) Sarg.], (*perusse*,) the forest became more open, and we had no longer any trouble to clear a way. The pines here were 11 or 12 feet in circumference, and about 110 feet high, and appeared to love the open grounds."

Charles Preuss was found well but tired and hungry at about 4 o'clock in the afternoon at a bottom along the Walla Walla River. Their camp was just south of the Oregon-Washington boundary east of the community of Milton-Freewater (Umatilla County, Oregon). On the 24th they crossed the Walla Walla and proceeded through hilly country with good bunch grass. "In six miles we crossed a principal fork, below which the scattered water of the river was gathered into one channel; and passing on the way several unfinished houses, and some cleared patches, where corn and potatoes were cultivated, we reached, in about eight miles farther, the missionary establishment of Dr. [Marcus] Whitman, which consisted, at this time, of one *adobe* house—i.e. built of unburnt bricks, as in Mexico" (Frémont, 1845: 182). The group passed quickly beyond the mission and camped on the river about four miles below. [According to Jackson and Spence (1970: 552), the mission site is seven miles west of Walla Walla, Washington, near U.S. highway 12, and is currently a National Historic Site administered by the National Park Service.]

The account for 25 October is brief: "The weather was pleasant, but the road to-day had in it nothing of interest; and the country offered to the eye only a sandy, undulating plain, through which a scantily timbered river takes its course." On the same date Preuss's diary (Gudde & Gudde, 1958: 95) records: "I was so disappointed after all that to-do about the Walla Walla settlement. I actually believed we would find a sort of paradise. But it is not much better than all the miserable country we have crossed. . . . Only one thing I can praise: good potatoes in abundance. Last night we ate them twice. Kit put another potful on the fire before we went to sleep." On 26 October Nez Perce Fort was reached, a trading establishment of the Hudson Bay Company situated a few hundred yards above the junction of the Walla Walla River with the Columbia. From the South Pass to the Fort was about 1000 miles, and 2000 miles from the mouth of the Kansas. The men had certainly ridden much farther than that. The party remained there for some "few days," after which: "Having reinforced our animals with eight fresh horses, hired from the post, and increased our stock of provisions with dried salmon, potatoes, and a little beef, we resumed our journey down the left bank of the Columbia, being guided on our road by an intelligent Indian boy, whom I had engaged to accompany us as far as the Dalles" (Frémont, 1845: 184). Evidently the men and animals departed for The Dalles on 28 October, following a poor road through deep sands. Camp that evening was on the riverbank with little grass and less timber. Mt. St. Helens was first viewed on 29 October, and on that date the party crossed the Umatilla River. The camp for the evening again had little grass, and wood was purchased from Indians, there being none available otherwise. The last day of October dawned cold and clear, but clouds formed as the sun rose. Mount Hood was in view all day to the southwest as they traveled again on bad roads.

That night camp was again on the river, and *Purshia tridentata* was used for firewood. "Among the rocks which formed the bank, was very good green grass" (Frémont, 1845: 185). November 1 brought a clear view of Mount Hood, glowing in the sunlight. The route continued on down the river. At noon on 2 November the John Day River was crossed, a clear and beautiful stream, with a swift current and a bed of rolled stones (Frémont, 1845: 185). Camp that night was in a grassy hollow, without water despite the proximity of the great Columbia. Following a two hour's ride on 3 November through fertile, hilly country, the party descended again to the river bottom, along which they resumed travel, and in about four miles reached the ford of the Fall River "(*Riviere aux Chutes*,) [Deschutes River, boundary between present Sherman and Wasco counties, Oregon], a considerable tributary of the Columbia" (Frémont, 1845: 185–86). Their journey this day was 17 miles. The route turned inland from the river, as it ran within a gorge, and arrived finally at the "*Dalles of the Columbia.*" This was the termination of the land party's journey along the Columbia. Frémont wrote to Mr. Fitzpatrick, who followed some days rearward, to abandon the carts at the Walla Walla missionary station and to proceed as soon as possible to The Dalles with pack saddles and animals, a not inconsiderable assignment with which Brokenhand and his hardy companions would comply.

Frémont, accompanied by Preuss, Bernier, and Jacob Dodson, proceeded downriver in a canoe manned by three Indians from the family who owned the canoe, leaving the others of the advance party under Carson's direction (Quaife, 1935: 77) to await the arrival of Fitzpatrick and the baggage party. The purpose of the trip was to obtain supplies and information from Fort Vancouver. Frémont (1845: 174) noted: "Being now upon the ground explored by the South Sea expedition under Captain [Charles] Wilkes, and having accomplished the object of uniting my survey with his, and thus presenting a connected exploration from the Mississippi to the Pacific, and the winter being at hand, I deemed it necessary to economize time by voyaging in the night, as is customary here, to avoid the high winds, which rise with the morning, and decline with the day." Preuss (Gudde & Gudde, 1958: 97) noted: "Last night [7 November] we arrived here at Fort Vancouver. I hope it will be our westernmost destination, from which we shall turn back. . . . They say that one can get everything here that one's heart desires. God knows we need quite a few things."

The return journey by canoe continued on 11, 12, 13 November. On 14 November the entry contains the following: "A gentleman named Luders, a botanist from the city of Hamburg, arrived at the bay I have called by his name while we were occupied in bringing up the boats. I was delighted to meet at such a place a man of kindred pursuits; but we had only the pleasure of a brief conversation, as his canoe, under the guidance of two Indians, was about to run the rapids; and I could not enjoy the satisfaction of regaling him with a breakfast, which, after his recent journey, would have been an extraordinary luxury. All of his few instruments and baggage were in the canoe, and he hurried around by land to meet it at the Grave-yard bay; but he was scarcely out of sight, when, by the carelessness of the Indians, the boat was drawn into the midst of the rapids, and glancing down the river, bottom up, with the loss of every thing it contained. In the natural concern I felt for his misfortune, I gave the little cove the name of Luders bay." Alluded to here is the fact that, in spite of the assertions of others, Frémont considered himself to be something of a botanist. The name Luders Bay is no longer in use for this feature, which "would have been a short distance below Stevenson, Wash." (Jackson & Spence, 1970: 570).

On 18 November Frémont was back at The Dalles, engaged with the party in making preparations for their return home. Little did they realize the course of the trail before them or where it led. Frémont and his men, with their large cavalcade of animals, were about to embark on an improbable and next-to-impossible journey, south to south-central Oregon, then east into the Great Basin. Following along the west side of the Great Basin to the vicinity of present Carson City, Nevada, the party would turn west across the Sierra Nevada into the Great Valley of California, thence southward up the valley of the San Joaquin where they would recross the Sierra Nevada into the Mohave Desert. Beyond that parched barrier the route would cut diagonally across Utah and into Colorado where the men and animals would proceed through the parks of the Rocky Mountains. Finally their route would be onto the plains and to the Missouri River. Final destination would be St. Louis, where the party would disband.

"Three principal objects were indicated, by report or by maps, as being on this route; the character or existence of which I wished to ascertain, and which I assumed as landmarks, or leading points, on the projected line of return" (Frémont, 1845: 196). These were the Klamath Lake, a lake called Mary's, and the reputed "*Buenaventura* river." They would be investigated along the line of return then contemplated, "a great part of it absolutely new to geographical, botanical, and geological science—and the subjects of reports in relation to lakes, rivers, deserts, and savages hardly above the condition of mere wild animals, which inflamed desire to know what this *terra incognita* really contained" (Frémont, 1845: 196). The party now consisted of 25 persons "—American, French, German, Canadian, Indian [including a young Chinook, William, from The Dalles], and colored—and most of them young, several being under twenty-one years of age." Preuss was then 40 years of age and considered himself to be old and decrepit.

Mr. Fitzpatrick, with Theodore Talbot, Alex Godey, and the larger baggage contingent of men and animals, arrived on 21 November. The wheeled carts had been abandoned upriver (much to the dismay of Preuss, who now had to ride a horse or mule), pack animals and saddles had been procured, and the men and animals had arrived at The Dalles in good order. The trials and difficulties of Mr. Fitzpatrick and the baggage party are nowhere recorded, but the problems must have been monumental. Now, with the switch from loading carts to loading pack animals a new dimension had been added to the daily work load.

The change from hauling baggage in carts to the use of pack animals was no small change. Large numbers of horses and mules would serve to carry the baggage, all of which must be packed with great care and secured to pack saddles—a work of great labor, requiring both skill and enduring patience. Animals were loaded with packs each morning and unloaded every night. The horses and mules were then hobbled and turned to graze. Each morning the animals were rounded up, caught, saddled, and prepared for loading. The routine of packing and loading took much of the time early each morning and had to be accomplished prior to movement of the party. The work became routine, and neither Frémont nor Fitzpatrick, nor even Preuss, mention the daily chores of camp.

Jackson and Spence (1970: 574) discuss the possibility that the "Buenaventura" river was a feature added as the manuscript was in preparation at the conclusion of the trip and allude to the possibility of Jessie Benton Frémont's flair for the dramatic being somehow involved. Be that as it may, the search for the fabled river was a recurring theme in the published account of Frémont's journal.

The Dalles to Sutter's Fort

The party arose early on 25 November following completion of preparations for their long and roundabout trip homeward. Their baggage was stowed on horses or mules, which gave them greater mobility than they had experienced previously. The only wheeled vehicle was the howitzer, which was to prove ultimately too great an inconvenience; it would be abandoned in the Sierra Nevada. At noon the mounted party, its cavalcade including some "California cattle" and 104 mules and horses, was under way amidst cold and snow flurries. Evening came early in the shortened days of late autumn, and the party camped at "*Tinanens* creek," where pasture of new short grass was available for their livestock and timber plentiful for fire. Water froze in their tents that night, and in the morning it was 20°F. Next morning they proceeded up a tributary of the Tinanens to the divide with the "Fall river" (Deschutes). "The creeks we had passed were timbered principally with oak and other deciduous trees" (Frémont, 1845: 198). The expedition, with its large contingent of horses, mules, and cattle, camped that night on a branch of the Deschutes River. To spare the horses for anticipated future hardships, the men walked for much of the day; "and Mr. Fitzpatrick and myself [Frémont] made the days' journey on foot."

Frémont (1845: 198) recorded on 27 November: "A fine view of Mount Hood this morning; a rose-colored mass of snow, bearing S.85° W. by compass. The sky is clear, and the air cold; the thermometer 2°.5 below zero; the trees and bushes glittering white, and the rapid stream filled with floating ice." The mounted entourage, pack animals, and howitzer ascended from the river valley to an elevated upland called the "Taih [Tigh] prairie," which was sprinkled with some scattered pines (Frémont, 1845: 199). "To our right we had always the mountains [Cascade Range], from the midst of whose dark pine forests the isolated snowy peaks were looking out like giants. They served us for grand beacons to show the rate at which we advanced on our journey." Camp was made back on the Deschutes River, where an "ox" was killed and butchered for food. The position of the camp was determined to be 45°06′45″, 121°02′43″, in Wasco County, near present Warm Springs. The following morning, 29 November, the party came to a "considerable branch [Warm Springs River] of Fall river," which was descended to some hot springs. The men and animals, with baggage and the howitzer, forded the tributary and proceeded south along the Deschutes to a camp on a small effluent. On 30 November men and animals had journeyed only a short distance when their path was blocked by a deeply entrenched tributary of the Deschutes, likely the Metolius River (now a portion of a reservoir created by a dam). They descended to the river with much difficulty, having to lower the heavy and cumbersome howitzer by hand, and camped early in an open bottom among the pines, a short distance below a lodge of Indians (Frémont, 1845: 200). The air must have resounded with expletives in many languages as the men struggled with the howitzer.

The party forded the river a short way above their camp on 1 December and again camped early at a marshy site where grass was available for their stock. The Indian guide had indicated that grass was in short supply beyond, and an attempt was being made to conserve what energy remained in their animals. Preuss (Gudde & Gudde, 1958: 99) wrote on this date: "Here I am in the mountains, sitting on an old fir trunk, with thin snow around me and a mule beside me, waiting for the caravan. I had to give up my place in the wagon. Frémont said that progress was too slow on the bad roads and gave the wagon away. Yet the cannon causes just as much delay, and unless he presents it to someone as he did the wagon, we shall move ahead slowly." On 2 December, "We traveled to-day over a very stony, elevated plain, about which were scattered cedar and pine, and encamped on another large branch of the Fall river" (Frémont, 1845: 201). Frémont went ahead with the howitzer on 3 December, again leaving Mr. Fitzpatrick with the remainder of the party. Dissatisfaction with the progress of the previous few days evidently was the reason. Animals have minds of their own, and this was the case on 4 December, when the men awoke to find that the animals had turned back, "although a number were hobbled." Recovering them took most of the morning, delaying the start southward until noon. The party was then in the vicinity of present Bend, Oregon. "After passing for several miles over an artemisia plain, the trail entered a beautiful pine forest through which we traveled for several hours; and at about 4 o'clock descended into the valley of another large branch, on the bottom of which were spaces of open pines, with occasional meadows of good grass, in one of which we encamped" (Frémont, 1845: 202). Among the timber at the campsite Frémont reported "larches [*Larix occidentalis* Nutt.] 140 feet high, and over 3 feet in diameter." For 5 December he recorded: "To-day the country was all pine forest, and beautiful weather made our journey delightful. . . . The timber was uniformly large; some of the pines measuring 22 feet in circumference at the ground, and 12 to 13 feet at 6 feet above" (Frémont, 1845: 202). Camp was set up early, and in the evening Mr. Fitzpatrick and the baggage party rejoined them. Possibly Frémont wanted them to catch up and help with the howitzer?

During 6 December a village of Nez Perce Indians was encountered. Camp was established on a southern smaller branch of the river in early evening. Travel on 7

December was through pine forest and meadowland along the stream. Frémont described rich soil, excellent water, meadows, and noble forests. The position of their camp that evening was 43°30′36″, 121°30′50″, in the vicinity of present Deschutes and Klamath counties boundary, not far from The Timbers. On 8 December the expedition crossed the last branch of the Fall River, issuing, like all the others they had crossed, in a southwesterly direction from the mountains. Their direction was a little east of south, the trail leading constantly through pine forests (Frémont, 1845: 203). The campsite lacked grass, and the horses had to use snow for water. "These pines [*Pinus lambertiana* Dougl., sugar pine] are remarkable for the red color of the bolls; and among them occurs a species, of which the Indians had informed me when leaving the Dalles. The unusual size of the cone (16 or 18 inches long) had attracted their attention; and they pointed it out to me among the curiosities of the country. They are more remarkable for their large diameter than their height, which usually averages only about 120 feet. The leaflets [needles] are short—only two or three inches long, and five in a sheath; the bark of a red color" (Frémont, 1845: 203). Travel on 9 December was much the same as on the 8th—again there was little grass and the animals fared badly.

On 10 December "the country began to improve; and about 11 o'clock we reached a spring of cold water on the edge of a savannah, or grassy meadow, which our guides informed us was an arm of the Tlamath [Klamath] lake [actually Klamath Marsh, 25 or 30 miles north of the lake; fide Gudde & Gudde, 1958: 99]; and a few miles further we entered upon an extensive meadow, or lake of grass, surrounded by timbered mountains. . . . It was a picturesque and beautiful spot, and rendered more attractive to us by the abundant and excellent grass, which our animals, after traveling through pine forests, so much needed; but the broad sheet of water which constitutes a lake was not to be seen" (Frémont, 1845: 203).

Camp was on a low point covered with pines. Being concerned by reports of the hostility and courage of the Indians in this area, and noting smoke arising from various points in the vicinity, Frémont had the howitzer fired twice, after which the smokes immediately disappeared. The latitude of the camp was determined to be 46°56′51″, and so they were not at Klamath Lake proper, but considerably north of that lake, about on a line due east of Crater Lake, Klamath County, Oregon. Frémont and some of the men visited an Indian village in the large meadow near their camp. The men marveled at the ability of the Indians to use grass to make mats, shoes, and hats. Preuss (Gudde & Gudde, 1958: 101) stated hopefully: "From here we turn east and start our direct journey home." Their horses were in sufficiently poor condition that Frémont decided to stay in camp for the remainder of 11 December. The next day they proceeded across the grassy "lake" basin and camped in a sheltered cove along its east side, where grass was available for the animals. Among the pines here were some five or six feet in diameter (Frémont, 1845: 206).

Their goal now was to turn east to the shores of reputed Mary's Lake or the river Buenaventura, where it was hoped the party could recruit their horses and find release from the cold of winter; and possibly, as Preuss had stated, proceed directly across the Great Basin toward home. Their route for the next few days would, indeed, be almost directly eastward. The way on 13 December was obstructed by fallen trees and snow up to a foot deep made difficult going for the mules pulling the howitzer. Camp was made along a stream that night where there was good grass. Observations indicated their position as 42°51′26″, 121°20′42″, still well to the northeast of Klamath Lake, east of present Kirk (probably in Lake County), Oregon. The party rode for seven hours on the 14th through a thick snowstorm, through pine forests, to where they came upon the headwaters of another stream, on which there was grass. The snow lay deep on the ground, and only the high swamp grass appeared above. The Indians accompanying them were thinly clad and had suffered from the cold during the day. That evening they told Frémont that the snow was getting too deep on the mountain, and they could not be induced to go further (Frémont, 1845: 206). The Indian guides departed on 15 December, and the expedition proceeded eastward in a pine forest in deep snow, which made travel slow and laborious. At this encampment they killed a cow, which had been getting poorer each day, "but the meat was rather tough."

Travel on the 16th was through snow "about three feet deep, which, being crusted, very much cut the feet of our animals" (Frémont, 1845: 207); the route was through a pine forest, partially obscured by falling snow. The party was traveling in what is today the Frémont National Forest. Toward noon the men rode out of the forest at the edge of a high vertical and rocky wall, where they could see green prairie country, "in which a beautiful lake, some twenty miles in length, was spread along the foot of the mountain" (Frémont, 1845: 207). The shores of the lake were bordered with green grass. "Shivering on snow three feet deep, and stiffening in a cold north wind, we exclaimed at once that the names of Summer Lake and Winter Ridge should be applied to these two proximate places of such sudden and violent contrast" (Frémont, 1845: 207). The features, both of which are in Lake County, Oregon, bear those names today.

"Viewed from our elevation, the face of the country exhibited only rocks and grass, and presented a region in which the artemisia became the principal wood, furnishing to its scattered inhabitants fuel for their fires, building material for their huts, and shelter for the small game which ministers to their hunger and nakedness" (Frémont, 1845: 207). The expedition was on the northwest border of the Great Basin, their camp at 42°57′22″ was almost due east of their locality on 13 December. The days were now very short, and night had fallen before the men and animals made their descent to the valley floor. The way was steep and presented numerous obstacles for a wheeled cart. Consequently, the howitzer was left halfway up the mountain, to be recovered the next morning.

Preuss (Gudde & Gudde, 1958: 102) reports from the Summer Lake camp: "Yesterday I ate, without knowing it, the meat of an unborn calf. However, it was very tender." The calf was undoubtedly from the cow with "meat rather tough."

By noon on 17 December the men had reassembled all of their baggage and traveled a short distance along the west shore of Summer Lake, following an Indian trail. They continued on that trail on 18 December, crossing small streams that entered from Winter Ridge, and camped "near the eastern point of the lake, where there appeared between the hills a broad and low connecting hollow with the country beyond" (Frémont, 1845: 208). For the next few weeks the party would be continuously in the Great Basin.

On 19 December the party proceeded in an easterly direction and came upon a rapid stream (possibly the Chewaucan River) of pure water, "roaring along between banks overhung with aspens and willows" (Frémont, 1845: 208). They followed down the stream to a marsh, or dry lake, encountering high reeds and rushes, where "large patches of ground had been turned up by the squaws in digging for roots, as if a farmer had been preparing the land for grain" (Frémont, 1845: 208). The expedition moved across the marshy land onto a bordering plain covered with artemisia, prior to camping before sundown on a creek where there was tolerably good grass.

The next morning, 20 December, after traveling for a few hours down the stream on which they had camped the previous night, and rounding a point of a hill came in view of another large lake (Abert Lake), which is bordered on its east side by a precipitous ridge (Abert Rim). "Spread out over a length of 20 miles, the lake, when we first came in view, presented a handsome sheet of water; and I gave it the name of Lake Abert, in honor of the chief of the corps to which I belonged. The white efflorescences which lined the shore like a bank of snow, and the disagreeable ordor [odor] that filled the air as soon as we came near, informed us too plainly that the water belonged to one of those fetid salt lakes which are common in the region" (Frémont, 1845: 209). The water was not drinkable, but nevertheless Preuss recorded (Gudde & Gudde, 1958: 103), "Drank stinking salt water at Abert Lake." Camp was made on the shore, but there was little grass for the stock. Firewood consisted of chenopodiaceous shrubs, "which burned with a quick bright flame." On 21 December the long column of mounted men, pack animals, and the howitzer proceeded along the lake to a low place where there was a shore, holes with pure water, and grass for the animals. Camp was established, and the party stayed there through the remainder of the day, during which time they ascertained that the lake had no outlet. Lake Abert is southeast of Summer Lake, and it appears probable that Frémont was attempting a direct move homeward across the northern Great Basin. Lake Abert was left behind on 22 December.

This was the time of the winter solstice, and the days were at their shortest. From this point on the days would get longer, but for the next few critical weeks the change in length of daylight would be neglegible; the days would be too short and the nights too long. The men and animals traveled southward to avoid rocky ridges to the east and halted that night on the sagebrush plain without either grass or water. Fortunately, rain fell during the night, allowing the animals to have some water. The camp was at a site where Indians had made enclosures of sagebrush. On 23 December the country had "a very forbidding appearance, presenting to the eye nothing but sage and barren ridges" (Frémont, 1845: 210). That description applies to much of the Great Basin, a sea of sagebrush marked with north-south trending island ranges. Continuing on, they found a lake surrounded by mud, which made approach impossible. Near the southern end of the lake were some hollows where bushes and small trees were discovered, in such situations, a sure sign of water. They found there several springs, "and the hill side was well sprinkled with a species of *festuca*—a better grass than we had found for many days" (Frémont, 1845: 210). The "*festuca*" of Frémont, here and probably elsewhere in his accounts, was more likely a species of *Elymus*, a wheatgrass that grows in bunches.

Probably the expedition was in the Warner Lakes vicinity, still in Lake County, Oregon. On 24 December they arrived at a small lake observed from a high point during the previous day. The water was tolerably pure, and camp was made where abundant grass was available for their livestock. The route was still as much easterly as southerly.

Christmas was celebrated by the firing of rifles and the howitzer (its fourth and last recorded use). The name Christmas was bestowed on the lake, one of those in the Warner Lakes (Lake County, Oregon) group (either Hart or Crump Lake), according to Jackson and Spence (1970: 596). The route continued southward in the course of the day, along a well used Indian trail, after an abortive attempt to travel in a more easterly direction was blocked by country so rough as to appear impassable.

Dozens of north-south trending ranges in the Great Basin play a role in the ease of travel in that northern extension of the Basin and Range Province. It is easier to travel in the valleys parallel to the ranges than to cross them from valley to valley. At this point in the expedition the men and animals were led naturally southward. Perhaps they hoped that winter would be less difficult to the south. For whatever reason, the expedition continued southward on 26 December, through country made up of small basins holding lakes of water entering from the mountains, and camped that night on a stream of fresh water adjacent to a ridge. "It was bordered with grassy bottoms and clumps of willows, the water partially frozen." Their camp was on the 42nd parallel, which is the boundary between Oregon and Nevada (and California, too). "To-night a horse belonging to Carson, one of the best we had in the camp, was stolen by the Indians" (Frémont, 1845: 211). They crossed over a divide on 27 December and descended into another basin, on the playa of which no water was found, and encamped among the sage on the bordering plain, where the snow was still about one foot deep. In the snow the grass was remarkably green, and that night the animals fared tolerably well (Frémont, 1845: 211). The party had passed into Nevada, in present Washoe County, but then part of Alta California, Mexico. Whether or not a decision had already been made to abandon the attempt at a direct way homeward, the route from this place forward would be to the south, along valleys bordered by the north-south trending ranges of the western Great Basin.

Their road on 28 December was down a level valley between steep ridges. "Artemisia was the principal plant, mingled with Frémontia and other chenopodiaceous shrubs. The artemisia was here extremely large, being sometimes a foot in diameter and eight feet high" (Frémont, 1845: 212). In fact, the plants were so large that Frémont's men frightened some Indians whose sagebrush lodges were encountered suddenly and unexpectedly in the tall shrubbery. After a journey of 24 miles camp was set up on a sheltered hillside, where there was bunch grass. Southeasterly travel on 29 December was hampered by a heavy snowstorm. Entering a drainage channel, the men and animals followed it to a willow grove in a meadow where there was water and forage for their animals. The snow was deep and the night was very cold. The party followed the little stream present at the campsite for several hours on the morning of 30 December in a southeasterly direction. The expedition was then forced to detour away from the stream by a narrow canyon through which it flowed, but came upon it again below the canyon. "The water had now more the appearance of a flowing creek; several times we passed groves of willows, and we began to feel ourselves out of all difficulty. From our position, it was reasonable to conclude that this stream would find its outlet in Mary's lake, and conduct us into a better country" (Frémont, 1845: 213). That night camp was established along the stream, where there was abundant grass, but the men were disappointed on 31 December when, after a few hours' ride, the valley opened out and the stream drained into yet another dry bottom. The party traveled beyond the dry valley, through a pass, into still another broad valley where they were able to obtain water by cutting ice. Grass for the animals was unpalatable, however. "Here we concluded the year 1843, and our new year's eve was rather a gloomy one. The result of our journey began to be very uncertain; the country was singularly unfavorable to travel; the grasses being frequently of a very unwholesome character, and the hoofs of our animals were so worn and cut by the rocks, that many of them were lame, and could scarcely be got along" (Frémont, 1845: 213).

In spite of the new year, with its promise of better things to come, the route on New Year's day 1844 continued southward, and offered little change from the previous day. The trail was still bad, broken by gullies and impeded by sagebrush. Grass was essentially nonexistent. The men and animals proceeded toward a "black cape, at the foot of which a column of smoke indicated hot springs." On 2 January the party was on the road early, through country hidden by falling snow. Again travel was made difficult by the poor condition of the trail. The weather cleared a little by noon, and the men and animals arrived at the hot springs discovered the day previously. "There was a large field of the usual salt grass here, peculiar to such places. The country otherwise is a perfect barren, without a blade of grass" (Frémont, 1845: 214). Camp that night was dry and without grass, among snow-covered sagebrush. Weakened by lack of food, constant use, and the difficult road, several mules gave out and a horse was left on the trail.

A dense fog barred their vision on 3 January making it difficult for the men to find their horses, and they were detained in camp until late in the day. "Our position had now become a serious one. We had reached and run over the position where, according to the best maps in my possession, we should have found Mary's lake, or river. We were evidently on the verge of the desert which had been reported to us; and the appearance of the country was so forbidding, that I was afraid to enter it, and determined to bear away to the southward, keeping close along the mountains, in the full expectation of reaching the Buenaventura river. This morning I put every man in camp on foot—myself, of course, among the rest—and in this manner lightened by distribution the loads of the animals" (Frémont, 1845: 214).

The group was in the vicinity of the Black Rock and Smoke Creek deserts, not far from present Gerlach, Washoe County, Nevada. Now there was no choice but to continue their southward journey. Dense fog persisted on 4 January, and the party traveled only a few miles before camping where there was some grass but no water. They faced more of the same on 5 January and were now in very poor condition. Fog continued unabated on 6 January. Nevertheless, Frémont, with Preuss and Carson, climbed the mountain adjacent to camp to a point above the fog. There the men could see a column of steam arising about 16 miles away, and decided to proceed in that direction. They arrived at the spring after a laborious journey and found abundant grass and hot springs. "In the immediate neighborhood, the valley bottom is covered almost exclusively with chenopodiaceous shrubs, of greater luxuriance, and larger growth, than we have seen them in any preceding part of the journey" (Frémont, 1845: 215).

The entry in the Preuss journal (Gudde & Gudde, 1958: 103) for 5 January 1844 discloses the thoughts of a man in despair: "We've been sitting here for three days, wrapped in fog, on a miserable plateau surrounded by bare hills. The animals are dying, one after the other. Very little grass, snow instead of water. We have turned more to the southwest. We shall probably cross over to California. It appears to be impossible to move with such animals through the plains in winter, almost without grass and water. What a Christmas and New Year we have had this year!" The Preuss statement indicates that the decision had been made, at least tentatively, for the expedition to attempt to reach the valley of California (they were already in Alta California).

Their circumstances had become progressively more serious. Of the 15 animals lost since leaving The Dalles, nine had died or been abandoned within the previous few days. It was obvious that something different must be done, and so a plan was devised to scout ahead for the next campsite prior to moving from the one then occupied. "Taking with me Godey and Carson, I made to-day a thorough exploration of the neighboring valleys, and found a ravine in the bordering mountains a good camping place, where was water in springs, and a sufficient quantity of grass for a night. Overshading the springs were some trees of the sweet cottonwood, which, after a long interval of absence, we saw again with pleasure, regarding them as harbingers of a better country. To us, they were eloquent of green prairies and buffalo" (Frémont, 1845: 215). The men were back at the camp at sunset, after a ride of about 40 miles. The group remained at this place through 8 January, because Mr. Fitzpatrick had found, "a few miles distant a hollow of excellent grass and pure water, to which the animals were driven, as I remained another day to give them an opportunity to recruit their strength" (Frémont, 1845: 216). Latitude of the boiling springs camp was determined as 40°39′46″.

On 9 January they moved to the cottonwood camp discovered two days earlier. "Among the shrubs on the hills were a few bushes of *ephedra occidentalis*, which afterwards occurred frequently along our road, and, as usual, the lowlands were occupied with artemisia" (Frémont, 1845: 216). Reconnaissance ahead was continued on 10 January, with the camp following behind. The scouts found and marked a campsite for the main party, and Frémont rode southward to see what the next basin might contain. There he discovered a "sheet of green water, some twenty miles broad. It broke upon our eyes like the ocean. The neighboring peaks rose high above us, and we ascended one of them to obtain a better view. The waves were curling in the breeze, and their dark-green color showed it to be a body of deep water" (Frémont, 1845: 216). On their journey to the lake on 11 January the men saw herds of mountain sheep, and "encamped on a little stream at the mouth of the defile, about a mile from the margin of the water, to which we hurried down immediately. The water is so slightly salt, that, at first we thought it fresh, and would be pleasant to drink when no other could be had" (Frémont, 1845: 216). Frémont initially thought this might be the long sought Mary's Lake, but decided that it fit neither the position nor the descriptions of setting for that. [According to Gudde &

Gudde (1958: 104), Mary's Lake was Humboldt Sink, about 50 miles east; Humboldt River was called Mary's River by trappers.] That night they halted at what appeared to be a favorite camping place for Indians.

By 13 January the route was along the lakeshore, and the howitzer was proving more difficult to transport, as their path ascended to a narrow track along the cliffs above the lake. Camp was made where there was abundant fresh green grass, and the howitzer, left behind again, was brought into camp on the morning of the 14th. It was becoming ever harder for the men and animals to bring this useless burden with them. "There were chenopodiaceous and other shrubs along the beach; and, at the foot of the rocks, an abundance of *ephedra occidentalis*, whose dark-green color makes them evergreens among the shrubby growth of the lake. Towards evening the snow began to fall heavily, and the country had a wintery appearance" (Frémont, 1845: 217). The party moved only nine miles on 14 January, a day of warm sun and rapidly melting snow, and camped opposite a remarkable rock in the lake. "It rose, according to our estimate, 600 feet above the water; and, from the point we viewed it, presented a pretty exact outline of the great pyramid of Cheops . . . and I called it Pyramid lake" (Frémont, 1845: 217). The elevation of the lake was determined as 4890 feet. The last of the cattle driven from The Dalles was killed for food. From this point on the expedition, for weeks to come, the supply of meat, unless game or fish could be found, would consist of flesh of dogs, horses, and mules.

Pyramid Lake is in Washoe County, Nevada, now within the Pyramid Lake Indian Reservation (Jackson & Spence, 1970: 605). The lake is about 25 miles long and from 4 to 11 miles wide. It is fed by the Truckee River and has no outlet.

On 15 January, accompanied by an Indian who had come to their camp, the party moved toward groves of cottonwood at the mouth of a river indicated by their guide. There they came to an Indian village and traded for large fish, which were referred to as a "salmon trout [*Salmo clarki*, the Lahontan cutthroat trout]. . . . Their flavor was excellent—superior, in fact, to that of any fish I have ever known. They were of extraordinary size—about as large as the Columbia river salmon—generally from two to four feet in length" (Frémont, 1845: 218). Frémont and his men camped near the Indian village and ate fish. Of Pyramid Lake, Preuss (Gudde & Gudde, 1958: 104) notes: "It teems with the most magnificent salmon trout. For a few farthings we bought a whole load of them from the Indians. I gorged myself until I almost choked." Preuss had all he could eat for once, of food to his liking, a memorable event to be savored and remembered during hard times in the future. The latitude of their camp was 39°51′13″, near present Nixon, Nevada. Pyramid Lake native trout still inhabit the lake, and the fish are as good eating, though apparently not as large or abundant, now as they were in Frémont's time.

"This morning [16 January] we continued our journey along this beautiful stream, which we naturally called the Salmon Trout river [Truckee]. . . . the stream was handsomely timbered with large cottonwoods; and the waters were very clear and pure" (Frémont, 1845: 219). The men camped after 18 miles under large cottonwoods in the river bottom, "where there was tolerably good grass." On 17 January they left the river, "which here issues from the mountains on the west. With every stream I now expected to see the great Buenaventura; and Carson hurried eagerly to search, on every one we reached, for beaver cuttings, which he always maintained we should find only on waters that ran to the Pacific" (Frémont, 1845: 219). In 20 miles the party came to another large stream (Carson River, probably in Lyon County, Nevada), timbered with cottonwood, and flowing also out of the mountains, but running more directly eastward.

On 18 January the mounted men, pack animals, and those caring for the howitzer, followed the Carson River downstream, hoping it would prove a branch of the Buenaventura. Frémont rode out with Fitzpatrick and Carson to reconnoitre the country. Upon their return, Frémont examined the animals and found their hooves to be in poor condition. The men had converted all extra iron into nails to secure the animals' shoes. Now there was no more iron, and spare shoes could not be used. Because of the apparent problems of attempting to traverse the Great Basin toward home, Frémont decided to proceed west into the great valley of California, where there was the possibility for refitting. Horses without shoes are a liability to themselves and to men dependent on them for riding or pulling. Carson (Quaife, 1935: 79) noted that, "We were nearly out of provisions but we had to cross the mountains, let the consequences be what they may." Latitude of the camp was 39°19′21″ north.

On 20 January the party moved upstream and camped in Carson Valley along Carson River near the mountains. A route up the river was investigated, but because of weather conditions Frémont decided against forcing a passage through at this point, which would have led them along the route followed by Walker in 1833 and 1843, saving the party the long and wearing detour to the south (Jackson & Spence, 1970: 612). The group again turned to the south on 21 January, where, after 24 miles, they camped on another large stream, Walker River, near present Yerington, Nevada. "It ran through broad bottoms, having a fine meadow-land appearance." The next week of travel was difficult and trying, leading to one unsatisfactory westward route after another. At the end of that arduous week the party would be back almost to their beginning point of 22 January. Exact location of the route is subject to speculation and interpretation, but it is unimportant with regard to botanical considerations, with the possible exception of the collection locality for the type material of *Pinus monophylla*. The report for the days of meandering is summarized below.

The party traveled, on 22 January, up Walker River for about 14 miles. There the stream forked, with one branch from the southwest and the other from the south-southeast. The men again surveyed a possible route west from the camp but again decided to move southward because of snow in the mountains. The camp was at 5020 feet and latitude 38°49′54″. The route on the next day, 23 January, was along the course of the branch other than the one surveyed, the East Walker River, where the party laboriously crossed a low divide and ultimately descended into the valley of still another stream. Camp was established after a journey of 24 miles. There followed several attempts to force a crossing of the Sierra Nevada. The men and animals would proceed up one drainage, cross a divide, move along another drainage, cross another divide, until they finally found one where the crossing was possible, but by far the hardest.

An Indian of advanced age, "a sort of forlorn hope," came into camp on the morning of 24 January. "He brought with him in a little skin bag a few pounds of the seeds of a pine tree, which to-day we saw for the first time, and which Dr. Torrey has described as a new species, under the name of *pinus monophyllus*; in popular language, it might be called the *nut pine*. We purchased them all from him. The nut is oily, of very agreeable flavor, and must be very nutritious, as it constitutes the principal subsistence of the tribes among which we were now traveling" (Frémont, 1845: 221). The expedition passed up the valley of the creek on which they had camped, through hills clothed with nut pine. The route of the stream finally became impasssable, and the party was forced to climb upwards to a pass from which they descended into a broad valley where camp was set up. The creek was frozen, and holes were cut to allow the animals to drink. "The banks are lightly wooded with willow, and on the upper bottoms are sage and Fremontia with *ephedra occidentalis*, which begins to occur more frequently" (Frémont, 1845: 222).

A month had passed since the winter solstice and the days were now perceptably longer. Still in the depths of winter, the expedition was in great peril. The morning of 25 January was cold and bright, and the party moved up the valley into snow six inches deep. "The timber consists principally of nut pines (*pinus monophyllus*,) which here are of a larger size—12 to 15 inches in diameter; heaps of cones lying on the ground, where the Indians have gathered the seeds" (Frémont, 1845: 222). The men and animals struggled upward to a pass where the snow depth reached three to four feet. The route ahead could be discerned, however. "After a hard days' march of 27 miles, we reached the river some time after dark, and found the snow about a foot deep on the bottom—the river being entirely frozen over. We found a comfortable camp, where there were dry willows abundant, and we soon had blazing fires. A little brandy, which I husbanded with great care, remained, and I do not know any medicine more salutary, or any drink (except coffee) more agreeable, than this in a cold night after a hard days' march. Mr. Preuss questioned whether the famed nectar even possessed so exquisite a flavor. All felt it to be a reviving cordial" (Frémont, 1845: 223).

Temperature on 26 January was -2°F, "but the sky was bright and pure, and the weather changed rapidly into a pleasant day of summer. I remained encamped, in order to examine the country, and allow the animals a day of rest, the grass being good and abundant under the snow" (Frémont, 1845: 223). According to Gudde and Gudde (1958: 104) their camp was near Bridgeport in Mono County, California. Frémont and Carson set out to explore a possible route across the Sierra Nevada. They saw a promising route and returned to camp. The campsite was determined to be at 38°18′01″. "Leaving the camp to follow slowly [on 27 January], with directions to Carson to encamp at the place agreed on, Mr. Fitzpatrick and myself continued the reconnaissance" (Frémont, 1845: 224). Hot springs were discovered during the course of the day, and the expedition came to yet another pass. On 28 January the party climbed through the pass and "after a hard days' journey of 12 miles, encamped on a high point where the snow had been blown off, and the exposed grass afforded a scanty pasture for the animals. . . . Tonight we did not succeed in getting the howitzer into camp. This was the most laborious day we had yet passed through; the steep ascents and deep snow exhausting both men and animals" (Frémont, 1845: 224).

The howitzer had been an object of travail over much of the country since leaving The Dalles. Now, Frémont came to a hill where it became too difficult to bring the gun along any further; its time had run out somewhere along the headwaters of the Walker River in Mono County, California (Reveal & Reveal, 1985). The remainder of the party camped before arriving at where Frémont was camped in the company of Indians, who told him that he was still in the Great Basin and that yet another great divide separated him from the Pacific drainages. When the rear group caught up with Frémont, they came without the howitzer. It must have been a relief to have this millstone removed. No one records the joy of those charged with bringing it along, even though John Charles must have been disappointed. That he did not attempt to have it recovered is an indication that the situation of the party was serious indeed. The men must have been ecstatic, although their worn and precarious position likely dampened any thoughts of celebration. The story of the howitzer, including its ultimate disposition and present whereabouts, has been the subject of numerous enquiries and publications. None seem pertinent to plant taxonomic considerations. However, one must consider what might have happened had they been able to arrive at Sutter's Fort with the field piece. The Californians evidently felt some concern with the arrival of the party of armed men even without a cannon.

On 30 January, accompanied by an Indian guide, the men and animals descended the river to a broad valley. Frémont and party were shown the point where some whites had been encamped prior to embarking through the Sierra Nevada some years earlier. "With our late start we made but ten miles, and encamped on the low river bottom, where there was no snow, but a great deal of ice; and we cut piles of long grass to lay under our blankets, and fires were made of large dry willows, groves of which wooded the stream" (Frémont, 1845: 227). From their camp the men could see the gap through which they were to pass the next day.

After traveling 12 to 14 miles on the 31st, the struggling men had reached the upper part of the pass when it began to snow heavily. And, after a difficult march in the extreme cold, during which their Indian guides departed for less difficult regions, the party again camped on a river where there was grass for their animals. Before them was the central ridge of the Sierra Nevada. "We had made a forced march of 26 miles, and three mules had given out on the road. Up to this point, with the exception of two stolen by Indians, we had lost none of the horses which had been brought from the Columbia river, and a number of these were still strong and in tolerably good order. We had now 67 animals in the band" (Frémont, 1845: 227). Attrition had reduced the herd size by 37 animals, somewhat more than a third of those that had left The Dalles. Discussions with Indians who came into camp indicated that the route across the Sierra Nevada was impossible due to deep snow. Undaunted, Frémont nevertheless obtained a guide; they would try for a crossing, no matter how difficult. A dog that had been their *compagnon de voyage* from the valley of the Bear River was killed for food, "and it made a strengthening meal for the greater part of the camp." Preuss did not comment on that development, but he would later, when another dog was killed for food.

On 2 February the party crossed the stream and began their ascent of the high backbone of the Sierra Nevada. "The people were unusually silent; for every man knew that our enterprise was hazardous, and the issue doubtful" (Frémont, 1845: 229). The snow deepened rapidly, and it soon became necessary to break a road. For this service, a party of ten was formed, mounted on the strongest horses; each man in succession opening the road on foot, or on horseback, until he and his horse became fatigued, then he stepped aside; and as the others passed ahead, he took his station in the rear. The men camped that night on the banks of a little stream in about four feet of snow. Kit Carson found an open hillside with sufficient grass for the animals. Trees of the single-leaf pinyon were here giving way to heavy timber, "and there were some immense pines on the bottom, around the roots of which the sun had melted away the snow; and here we made our camps and built huge fires." They had traveled 16 miles and were at an elevation of 6760 feet.

The route of 3 February was along another drainage, but the snow was so deep in the bottom that the men and animals were forced to travel on the steep hillside. They proceeded in the same manner as on the day before, but made only seven miles. The camp was made near some springs at the foot of a high, steep incline. "The springs were shaded by the boughs of a lofty cedar, which here made its first appearance; the usual height was 120 to 130 feet, and one that was measured near by was 6 feet in diameter" (Frémont, 1845: 230).

Horses were taken by Baptiste Tabeau to grass several miles back along the trail, there being none at the camp. The men spent the remainder of the day beating down a road to the foot of the hill, a mile or two distant. This camp was evidently along the East Carson River (Alpine County, California), near where it is joined by Markleeville Creek (Jackson & Spence, 1970: 627). Frémont went ahead with three men on 4 February, each with a horse to break a trail in the deep snow. After much difficulty on a steep hillside, encrusted with snow, they reached a bench in the hollow. From there the men could see into a basin, "some ten miles across, whose bottom presented a field of snow. At the further or western side rose the middle crest of the mountain, a dark-looking ridge of volcanic rock."

The men attempted in the afternoon to force a road in the direction of a pass that their Indian guide indicated was on the route. After a few hundred yards the men and horses gave out, and it seemed that the deep snows would prevent the crossing. Frémont returned a short distance and met the faithful and steadfast Mr. Fitzpatrick. The camp had been attempting to catch up with Frémont during the day, but only the strongest of the horses had made it up the steeply sloping mountainside. Hearing of the disposition and troubles of the remainder of the camp: "I therefore immediately encamped on the ground with my own mess, which was in advance, and directed Mr. Fitzpatrick to encamp at the springs, and send all the animals, in charge of Tabeau, with a strong guard, back to the place where they had been pastured the night before" (Frémont, 1845: 231).

The party was in dire circumstances, but Frémont was an optimist; he had been in tight places before. The men were, after all, mainly young and in the vigor of their lives. The condition of the animals was not yet critical, and there was hope that they would be able to proceed again later. Tomorrow would be another day—a better day.

On 5 February the main party was occupied in bringing up the baggage and animals. Indians had, for some days, run circles around the floundering Frémont party on snowshoes made of willows and bark. Now Frémont had sledges and snowshoes made (Quaife, 1935: 79); he was determined to explore the mountain ahead, and the sledges were to be used in transporting baggage. Men would haul the baggage; the horses would, if luck held, bring themselves. Their latitude was 38°42′26″, not far from present Markleeville, Alpine County, California. Elevation, determined by boiling water, was 7400 feet.

The next day, 6 February, Frémont, Carson, and Mr. Fitzpatrick started out with a reconnoitering party on snowshoes. The men trampled a trail to be used later, should their survey demonstrate the feasibility of traveling across the divide. Finally, the trio and others traversed the broad, snowy valley and climbed a peak at the side of the pass they suspected as being on their route. "Far below us, dimmed by the distance, was a large snowless valley, bounded on the western side, at the distance of about a hundred miles, a low range of mountains, which Carson recognised with delight as the mountains bordering the coast" (Frémont, 1845: 232). To say that the members of the exploring party were ecstatic at the prospects is probably an understatement. The men were still a long way from achieving the valley, but at least Frémont and his companions could see where they wanted to go. Valleys were visible where there was no snow, that plague of the immediate region and an almost insurmountable obstacle to travel in these mountains in winter. To reach the divide with the entire party, including baggage and animals, would require another two weeks of incredible labor and hardship, but they had viewed the promised land. It was late in the day when the small party turned toward their camp.

The air in the failing light of the setting sun quickly became cold, and one of the men began to suffer from frozen feet. A fire was started in the trunk of a dry old cedar, and Mr. Fitzpatrick remained with the ailing man until his clothes were dry, and then straggled into camp at nightfall.

Carson (Quaife, 1935: 79) stated: "Upon reaching the end of the snow, we could see the green valley of the Sacramento, and in the distance the Coast Range. I had been there seventeen years before, and knew the place well. Our feelings can best be imagined when we obtained a view of such a beautiful country. We returned to the place from which we had sent back our animals, and with nothing to eat but mule meat commenced the work of making the road. In fifteen days our task was accomplished, and we sent back for the animals. Driven by hunger, they had eaten one another's tails and the leather of the pack saddles, in fact everything they could lay hold of. They were in a deplorable condition and we would frequently kill one to keep it from dying, then use the meat for food."

The men now worked as a body getting the animals and baggage to the pass. The animals were the main problem, since the horses and mules could not negotiate the deep snow; "and it was supposed that, after all the baggage had been drawn with the sleighs over the trail we had made, it would be sufficiently hard to bear our animals. At several places, between this point and the ridge, we had discovered some grassy spots, where the wind and sun had dispersed the snow from the sides of the hills, and these were to form resting places to support the animals for a night in their passage across" (Frémont, 1845: 232). The depth of the snow was about 5 feet, but in places it had accumulated to depths as great as 20 feet. Thus the relay of baggage, men, and animals was commenced. Frémont moved forward first with one of the sleighs to the first grassy spot about four miles distant. The indomitable Fitzpatrick remained at the previous advance camp to form an intermediate station between Frémont's location and that of the animals.

On 8 February the weather was clear and extremely cold; "3° below zero; 1° higher, when his [the sun's] rays struck the lofty peaks; and 0° when they reached our camp." The baggage sleighs, pulled by men rather than their pack animals, arrived at the grassy site at about midmorning. Part of the load was stored at the grassy site, and Frémont moved another mile and a half to the foot of the slope beyond the far side of the open bottom. Bernier and Godey had been sent the day previous to climb a still higher peak. They returned this day "hungry and fatigued." There is no account of how the pair had survived a night in the open under the prevailing conditions, but most certainly they endured incredible suffering. Tea and sugar from Frémont's dwindling stock were given to the men who arrived with two other sleighs in the afternoon. Clouds that had gathered in the afternoon were of sufficient concern to Frémont to cause him to send part of the men back to Fitzpatrick with instructions to bring the animals up the following morning. Those remaining with Frémont were Preuss, Talbot, Carson, and Jacob. Bernier and Godey had evidently recovered sufficiently to return with the other men. Elevation of Frémont's camp was determined as 7920 feet.

Snow began to fall before morning on 9 February. The trail was soon covered, and Frémont remained in camp all day. The weather improved in the afternoon, and by evening men with four sleighs arrived with bedding for the men. Frémont notes the suffering from want of salt, and the weakness of the men from insufficient food.

Taplin was sent back to Mr. Fitzpatrick with a few other men on 10 February, while Frémont proceeded forward with three sleighs loaded with baggage. They made camp at the foot of the last mountain ridge. According to Jackson and Spence (1970: 633): "The party was at the foot of Elephant's Back, on the western side of Faith Valley, probably near Forestdale Creek." Frémont notes that "the forest here has a noble appearance; the tall cedar [*Calocedrus decurrens* (Torr.) Florin, the incense cedar] is abundant; its greatest height being 130 feet, in circumference 20, three or four feet above the ground; and here I see for the first time the white pine [*Pinus lambertiana* Dougl., sugar pine], of which there are some magnificent trees. Hemlock spruce [*Tsuga mertensiana* (Bong.) Carr., mountain hemlock] is among the timber, occasionally as large as 8 feet in diameter four feet above the ground; but, in ascending, it tapers rapidly to less than one foot at a height of 80 feet. I have not seen any higher than 130 feet, and the slight upper part is frequently broken off by the wind. The white spruce [*Abies concolor* (Gord. & Glend.) Lindl., white fir] is frequent; and the red pine (*pinus colorado* of the Mexicans,) [possibly *Pinus ponderosa* Dougl., ponderosa pine] which constitutes the beautiful forest along the flanks of the Sierra Nevada to the northward, is here the principal tree, not attaining a greater height than 140 feet, though with sometimes a diameter of 10. Most of these trees appeared to differ slightly from those of the same kind on the other side of the continent" (Frémont, 1845: 233). In spite of their precarious position Frémont continued to observe and record the botany of the region. The camp elevation, determined by the boiling point of water, was 8050 feet.

"Putting on our snow shoes, we spent the afternoon in exploring a road ahead. The glare of the snow, combined with great fatigue, had rendered many of the people nearly blind; but we were fortunate in having some black silk handkerchiefs, which, worn as veils, very much relieved the eye" (Frémont, 1845: 233).

On 11 February, Fitzpatrick tried to bring the horses along the almost obliterated trail. He failed, however, when the animals broke through and floundered in the deep snow. Now the men would carve shovels from tree trunks and pack the trail prior to another attempt. Preuss (Gudde & Gudde, 1958: 107) notes of this day: "We are now completely snowed in. The snowstorm is on top of us. The wind obliterates all tracks, which, with incredible effort we make for our horses. The horses are about twenty miles behind and are expected to arrive tonight—or rather they are now no longer expected."

On 12 February, Frémont reported: "We made mauls, and worked hard at our end of the road all day" (Frémont, 1845: 234). Preuss (Gudde & Gudde, 1958: 107) elaborated: "We started immediately to stamp down the snow as hard as we could with our feet and with clubs. We then threw dense branches over the track. In the meantime, five men were ordered back with the horses to a place where there was good grass and water, that is, twelve miles east of Fitzpatrick's camp. Several horses were slaughtered immediately so that the men might preserve their strength and so that the small amount of flour and peas could be used sparingly. The flour was no longer to be used to make bread, but was to be cooked with horse soup. Fitzpatrick had already killed a lean animal and had sent us part of it, together with the bad news. I ate some of it yesterday for the first time. I really cannot say whether it tasted good or bad. It was without fat, which, however, is said to have only a disagreeable taste. Without salt, nothing has any flavor to me, so to speak."

The labor continued on 13 February, when Frémont held a conference with Fitzpatrick and suffered at the thoughts of some Indians who passed on snowshoes during the day on their way west after fish. The dog "Tlamath" was killed and cooked along with some horse meat and peas for dinner. Evidently Frémont had put aside his aversion to eating horse. Of the death of the dog, Preuss (Gudde & Gudde, 1958: 107) dutifully reports: "The meat failed to appear for such a long time that Alex [Godey] was afraid that he would have to go to work without a meat breakfast. So he took hold of the little dog Clammet and slaughtered him." Preuss noted that he was weak and tired easily, attributing this to the lack of salt in his diet. Apart from that lack, and the cold and snow, the men were working at a high elevation where oxygen is in shorter supply and where any exertion is wearing.

"With Mr. Preuss, I ascended to-day [14 February] the highest peak to the right; from which we had a beautiful view of a mountain lake [Lake Tahoe] at our feet, about 15 miles in length, and so entirely surrounded by mountains that we could not discover an outlet" (Frémont, 1845: 234). Locality of the camp was determined as 38°41′57″, 120°25′57″ (El Dorado County, California). On 15 February, Preuss (Gudde & Gudde,

1958: 110) indicated that 51 of the remaining 63 animals were brought across the four miles of stamped path, and "the little dog tasted all right, but the great good news is that the men have bartered rock salt from the Indians." Preuss was in fine spirits—there was salt and even dog meat wasn't too bad; how times had changed!

By 16 February the party had succeeded in getting the horses to the first grassy hill, and Frémont crossed the dividing ridge with Jacob to ascertain a route for the expedition on the California side of the Sierra Nevada. They camped that night on the west side, but most of the party was still in the Great Basin drainage side of the divide. Frémont and Jacob continued to reconnoiter down the west side of the Sierra Nevada on 17 February, while the men and animals were slowly moved up to the pass. When Frémont and Jacob arrived back at camp that night all of the animals (57 in number, by attrition) were at a grassy spot nearby.

While Frémont and Jacob were west of the divide, Preuss (Gudde & Gudde, 1958: 110) was still in camp; he wrote that his mule Jack, who had been killed for food sometime earlier, had been consumed, but that he had not eaten any of it. He further stated, "Today a horse will be killed, and since we have salt now, I shall eat with relish." Times were indeed difficult, but Preuss was now thriving amidst untold hardships.

According to Preuss, the party remained in camp, resting and preparing for the final assault, during 18 February; "The horses are now near by on a snow-free hill, where grass is said to be rather plentiful." His appetite had returned and "the horse meat is all right as long as the salt holds out." On the 19th the party worked to complete the road and bring up the baggage; "and, on the afternoon of the next day, *February* 20, 1844, we encamped with the animals and all the *materiel* of the camp, on the summit of the Pass in the dividing ridge, 1,000 miles by our traveled road from the Dalles of the Columbia." Temperature of boiling water indicated an elevation of 9338 feet at the pass. "Latitude 38°44′; longitude 120° 28′." The expedition was in present El Dorado County, California.

The weakened men and starving animals traveled only six miles on 21 February, but they were then beyond the crest of the range. At this point there were 53 surviving animals serving as transport and as a walking, albeit thin and skeletal, larder. In spite of the state of the animals and men John Charles turned his attention to plants. "The grass was better than we had yet seen, and we were encamped in a clump of trees twenty or thirty feet high, resembling white pine" (Frémont, 1845: 236). Near the camp for the night Frémont observed, "among the few plants that appeared here, was the common blue flax. To-night, a mule was killed for food" (Frémont, 1845: 237). Travel on 22 February was over crusted snow in part, but much time was spent in improving a road for men and animals. That night they killed another mule—"now our only resource from starvation." Preuss records on this date that a horse was eaten "every day and a half."

Difficult as travel had been that day, the next day was even worse. Frémont was hardly a complainer, but of 23 February he said: "This was our most difficult day: we were forced off the ridges by the quantity of snow among the timber, and obliged to take the mountain sides, where, occasionally, rocks and a southern exposure afforded us a chance to scramble along" (Frémont, 1845: 237). Axes and mauls again were used to make a road through the snow. Frémont and Carson both had an icy bath when Frémont slipped and fell into a river, and Carson went in after him.

On 24 February Frémont arose at 3:00 a.m. for an astronomical observation. The determined locality of their camp was 38°46′58″, 120°34′20″, still in El Dorado County, California, not far from present Placerville. Temperature under clear skies was 2° below the freezing point. The way down improved as the day progressed; snow gave way to bare gound, patches at first and finally overall. A path was found, which they were able to follow, and there was green grass, a good prospect. "The character of the forest continued the same; and, among the trees, the pine with sharp leaves and very large cones was abundant, some them being noble trees. We measured one that had 10 feet diameter, though the height was not more than 130 feet. All along, the river was a roaring torrent, its fall very great; and, descending with a rapidity to which we had long been strangers, to our great pleasure oak trees appeared on the ridge, and soon became very frequent; on these I remarked unusually great quantities of mistletoe. Rushes began to make their appearance; and at a small creek where they were abundant, one of the messes was left with the weakest horses, while we continued on" (Frémont, 1845: 238). It is probable that on 24 February 1844 Frémont collected the specimen later cited as the type of *Libocedrus decurrens* (see Chapter VII and Appendix I).

Frémont now demonstrated increased interest in the change of vegetation. "Continuing on, we halted a moment at one of these rivulets, to admire some beautiful evergreen trees [*Quercus wislizenii* A. DC., interior live oak], resembling live oak, which shaded the little stream. They were forty to fifty feet high, and two in diameter, with a uniform tufted top; and the summer green of their beautiful foliage, with the singing birds, and the sweet summer wind which was whirling about the dry oak leaves nearly intoxicated us with delight; and we hurried on, filled with excitement, to escape from the horrid region of inhospitable snow, to the perpetual spring of the Sacramento" (Frémont, 1845: 238). Their camp was determined to be at 3864 feet elevation. In just four days the party had descended more than a mile in elevation. "Another horse was killed to-night, for food." This event made Preuss hope "that the eating of horse meat would soon be over."

Leaving the loyal and dependable Mr. Fitzpatrick to bring along the baggage, animals, and most of the men, John Charles again chose to move on ahead. With him went Preuss, Talbot, Carson, Derosier, Towns, Proue, and Jacob. "We took with us some of the best animals, and my intention was to proceed as rapidly as possible to the house of Mr. Sutter, and return to meet the party with a supply of provisions and fresh animals" (Frémont, 1845: 239). Thus, Fitzpatrick was left with a very difficult job, one he was to accomplish with the least able of the animals, most of the baggage, and many more starving men.

Frémont and party made 12 miles before camping near some Indian huts along the American River in the early afternoon of 25 February. "The bottom was covered with trees of deciduous foliage, and overgrown with vines and rushes. On the bench of the hill near by, was a field of fresh green grass, six inches long in some of the tufts which I had the curiosity to measure. The animals were driven here; and I spent part of the afternoon sitting on a large rock among them, enjoying the pauseless rapidity with which they luxuriated in the unaccustomed food. The forest was imposing to-day in the magnificence of the trees: some of the pines, bearing large cones, were 10 feet in diameter; cedars also abounded, and we measured one 28½ feet in circumference four feet from the ground. This noble tree seemed here to be in its proper soil and climate. We found it on both sides of the Sierra, but most abundant on the west" (Frémont, 1845: 239). One wonders how Fitzpatrick and his party of weakened men and animals spent that afternoon. Plodding west most likely!

Frémont and his small contingent continued to descend the stream on 26 February. Camp was made near nightfall along the banks of a tributary to the main drainage, and "here we saw, on the lower hills, the first flowers in bloom, which occurred suddenly, and in considerable quantity; one of them a species of *gilia*" (Frémont, 1845: 239). Preuss (Gudde & Gudde, 1958: 114) notes cheerfully on 28 February, "Day before yesterday I found the first flowers." The men camped that evening in rain, "and, the horses, standing about in the rain, looked very miserable." Fording the stream the next morning, the worn and starving men and animals proceeded to a grassy slope where they stopped only about a mile from the camp. There a mule was killed and butchered for food. Its head was placed in a container of boiling water and after some hours "made a passable soup for famished people."

The 28 February diary entry of Preuss (Gudde & Gudde, 1958: 114) states: "When cooked all night, a mule head is a delicacy." Preuss had come a long way from his compunction about eating horse, mule, and dog. Now even boiled mule's head was "a delicacy." Frémont's favorite horse, Proveau, could not keep up due to weakness. The horse was left with Jacob to bring on, and Frémont moved ahead, having divided his party yet again. Evidently even the best horses, those taken by Frémont, were not in very good condition. It was imperative that he reach Sutter's and return with supplies and fresh animals.

In spite of the poor condition of the party and their animals, Frémont continued to observe plants and to comment on them. "A new and singular shrub, which had made its appearance since crossing the mountain, was very frequent to-day. It branched out near the ground, forming a clump eight to ten feet high, with pale-green leaves of an oval form, and the body and branches had a naked appearance, as if stripped of the bark, which is very smooth and thin, of a chocolate color, contrasting well with the pale green of the leaves [probably a species of *Arctostaphylos*]" (Frémont, 1845: 240). Frémont's narrative continued: "The day was nearly gone; we had made a hard days' march, and found no grass. Towns became light-headed, wandering of into the woods without knowing where he was going, and Jacob [having caught up] brought him back. Near night-fall we descended into the steep ravine of a handsome creek thirty feet wide, and I was engaged in getting the horses up the opposite hill, when I heard a shout from Carson, who had gone ahead a few hundred yards—'Life yet,' said he, as he came up, 'life yet; I have found a hill side sprinkled with grass enough for the night.' We drove along our horses, and encamped at the place about dark, and there was just room enough to make a place for shelter on the edge of the stream. Three horses were lost to-day—Proveau; a fine young horse from the Columbia, belonging to Charles Towns; and another Indian horse which carried our cooking utensils; the two former gave out, and the latter strayed off into the woods as we reached camp" (Frémont, 1845: 240).

The condition of men and animals dictated that they remain in camp on 29 February. Derosier volunteered to retrieve Proveau. He found the pack horse was near the camp also. As night fell, Derosier had not returned, but he returned during the night. Leaving Derosier to follow, presumably bringing along the ailing Proveau, Frémont and the others moved six miles onward and camped again. The men and their thin mounts were descending the foot slopes of the Sierra Nevada, into springtime. On 1 March, insects were active and flowers were coming into bloom. "Among those which appeared most numerously to-day was *dodecatheon dentatum* [a name applied to several species of shooting-star by Frémont, see Appendix I]" (Frémont, 1845: 240). Charles Towns was still delirious and went to swim in the river "as if it were summer, and the stream placid, when it was a cold mountain torrent foaming among the rocks." Derosier came into camp in the evening, also delirious. "The times were severe when stout men lost their minds from extremity of suffering—when horses died—and when mules and horses, ready to die of starvation, were killed for food. Yet there was no murmuring or hesitation" (Frémont, 1845: 240). Conditions were serious indeed. There is no report of the suffering of Fitzpatrick and the baggage party, whose condition was worse than that of Frémont and the advance party.

Preuss (Gudde & Gudde, 1958: 115) wrote on 29 February: "The weather is beautiful now, but I did not like the great circle around the moon last night. Otherwise, I am in the best of spirits. The mule-meat bullion gives some strength after all. Until now, we fools have been pouring it away and have eaten only the dry, woody meat. As long as salt and coffee last, this life can be called wonderful." Preuss is remarkable; in these dire circumstances he ponders the wonderful nature of his existence. In the afternoon Preuss had time to contemplate his situation: "What influence weather can have on a man! Under the circumstances, I feel quite satisfied in this magnificent spring weather and mountain air. The water gurgles at my feet; green trees, live oaks, and many kinds of conifers are all around." In the worst of times Preuss had become an optimist.

Preuss had gone ahead during the day of 2 March and was unaware of the early camp by Frémont and men; he was lost yet again. He noted (Gudde & Gudde, 1958: 117) on 3 March: "This is beginning to get serious. I couldn't find the others again, and I am alone here, about twelve miles down the river. They must have taken another route, and I have to look out for myself now." And later, "Since yesterday I have not eaten a thing except a few sweet onions which I just scratched out of the ground. At the same time, I found an ants' nest, a portion of which I bit off and swallowed. Nor do I have any tobacco. How will this end?"

On 3 March the party followed the trail of Preuss for some distance to where he had camped the previous night. He had continued downstream. "At every step the country improved in beauty; the pines were rapidly disappearing, and oaks became the principal trees of the forest. Among these, the prevailing tree was the evergreen oak, (which, by way of distinction, we shall call the *live oak*;) and with these, occurred frequently a new species of oak bearing a long slender acorn, from an inch to an inch and a half in length, which we now began to see formed the principal vegetable food of the inhabitants of this region" (Frémont, 1845: 240). Frémont noted the encouraging signs of greater abundance of food—heaps of acorn hulls near some Indian huts and plentiful grass. They stopped to let the animals feed and rest, and that afternoon another horse was butchered for food. "He was a good animal, and had made the journey round from Fort Hall." The next sentence shows Frémont's dedication to botanical observations: "*Dodecatheon dentatum* continued the characteristic plant in flower; and the naked looking shrub, already mentioned continued characteristic, beginning to put forth a small white blossom" (Frémont, 1845: 242). The men who had been searching for Preuss returned empty-handed.

On 4 March Frémont and his small party moved rapidly downriver with the intention of getting ahead of Preuss. The men with Frémont had still discovered no sign of him when they halted at noon in the shade of evergreen oaks. By evening, when camped was established, Preuss was still missing. Frémont was greatly concerned for him; "and, for a large reward, Derosier [who had recovered his senses] volunteered to go back on the trail." He was to proceed back for a day and a half, in which time he might meet Mr. Fitzpatrick with the baggage animals. Fitzpatrick, far in the rear, was directed by Frémont to aid in the search for Preuss, should Derosier contact him. On that day the lonesome Preuss walked about "seven or eight miles," and dug a few roots and onions with his pocket knife. He also ate the legs of some frogs captured in shallow puddles he had crossed in the day's walk.

Frémont and his remaining men, in the meantime, continued downriver on 5 March. They surprised and surrounded three Indian women who were engaged in filling baskets with a small, leafy plant "(*erodium cicutarium*)," which was then beginning to bloom. The erodium covered the ground "like a sward of grass." The evening camp was at a place of great beauty, and Frémont fittingly named it "Beautiful Camp." Toward evening Preuss came in, having traveled 25 miles that day, but not having seen Derosier. Indians had provided him with some acorns, and he finally came upon the tracks of Frémont's horses, which he followed to the present camp. Of his arrival in camp, Carson (Quaife, 1935: 81) notes, "Four days later the old man [Preuss was 41] found us. His pockets were full of acorns, and he had had no other food since he left us. We were all rejoiced at his return, for he was much respected by the party."

Erodium cicutarium (L.) L'Her., also called storksbill or filaree, was likely introduced during the 18th century or earlier by Spaniards, who brought it from the Mediterranean. It was certainly abundant in the Alta California of Frémont, who mentions it repeatedly beyond this initial sighting (Jackson & Spence, 1970: 649).

On 6 March the pasturage had improved sufficiently that the horses had regained some of their strength. The party now traveled rapidly, over four miles per hour, "four of us riding every alternate hour." Soon they came upon the tracks of cattle, much to their delight, because they knew settlements could not be far away. "From the upland we descended into broad groves on the river, consisting of the evergreen, and a new species of white oak with a large tufted top, and three to six feet in diameter" (Frémont, 1845: 244). "We made an acorn meal at noon, and hurried on; the valley being gay with flowers, and some of the banks being absolutely golden with the Californian poppy, (*eschscholtzia crocea*)" (Frémont, 1845: 244). On a bluff above the river they came upon an adobe house with glass windows. Only Indians were at the house, and Frémont was disappointed.

Civilization was indeed nearby. Hurrying on, they met an Indian who spoke Spanish and who guided them to Sutter's Fort. John Augustus Sutter, owner of the fort and considerable property, welcomed them and made them comfortable. "He gave us a most frank and cordial reception—conducted us immediately to his residence—and under his hospitable roof we had a night of rest, enjoyment, and refreshment, which none but ourselves could appreciate." Preuss was pleased to be alive and to have food again. He summarized (Gudde & Gudde, 1958: 119) his stay at Sutter's Fort as follows: "Drinks, fish, bread, butter, milk, beef, pork, potatoes, wonderful salmon." Carson indicated (Quaife, 1935: 81) that when they arrived at Sutter's they were "nearly naked, and in as poor a condition as men possibly could be."

Frémont was delighted to be at Sutter's, "But the party left in the mountains with Mr. Fitzpatrick were to be attended to; and the next morning [7 March], supplied with fresh horses and provisions, I hurried off to meet them. On the second day [Frémont's days are off here] we met, a few miles below the forks of the Rio de los Americanos; and a more forlorn and pitiable sight than they presented cannot well be imagined. They were all on foot—each man, weak and emaciated, leading a horse or mule as weak and emaciated as themselves. They had experienced great difficulty in descending the mountains, made slippery by rains and melting snows, and many horses fell over precipices, and were killed; and with some were lost the *packs* they carried. Among these, was a mule with the plants which we had collected since leaving Fort Hall, along a line of 2,000 miles traveled. Out of 67 horses and mules with which we commenced crossing the Sierra, only 33 reached the valley of the Sacramento, and they only in a condition to be led along" (Frémont, 1845: 245). That any animals made it through to Sutter's is remarkable. All would have perished, had it not been for the care given them by Fitzpatrick and his men.

Although Frémont (1845: 4) notes that "we lost fourteen horses and mules," it is not certain that that many of the pack animals fell over precipices and were killed; most were killed and eaten by the starving men. Some 57 animals were alive as of 17 February and 33 arrived at Sutter's. The loss of 14 over precipices would have allowed only 10 animals to be eaten by the men between then and their arrival at Sutter's. Somehow, the number 14 lost by accident does not appear factual; some plants taken between Fort Hall and Sutter's did survive (see Appendix IV), possibly still in a plant press not on the ill-fated mule. The number of plant specimens lost is open to conjecture, but the number could have been great, if, as seems probable, the pack contained specimens taken prior to arrival at Fort Hall. A camp was made as soon as the parties met, and Fitzpatrick and the men accompanying him ate their first good meal in weeks, "beef, excellent bread, and delicious salmon." The combined party camped on the "8th" at the junctions of the two rivers, the Sacramento and Americanos, Sacramento County, California. There they would begin preparations for the trip home a second time. Now the beginning point for the return trip was further away than when they began the first attempt at The Dalles some months earlier. The men were in want of everything. Mules, horses, and cattle had to be collected, and the mill was at work day and night, to make sufficient flour. The blacksmith shop was also busy making horse shoes and bridle bits; and pack saddles, ropes, and bridles, and all other little equipments of the camp, were again to be provided. The delay was one of repose and enjoyment for the tired half-starved men (Frémont, 1845: 247). No matter how much repose the men might have gained by wintering in the Great Basin, they could not have obtained the materials necessary for continuing the trip homeward. The travail in reaching California made possible the successful completion of the journey.

Sutter's Fort to Utah Lake

Their first move following refitting was made on 22 March, when they moved near the settlement of John Sinclair (d. 1849), "on the left bank of the Rio de los Americanos." Five men left his party here. Derosier, one of his best men who had earlier suffered mentally and physically, wandered off from the camp and did not return. There is nothing really mysterious or surprising about his disappearance, even though Carson (Quaife, 1935: 81–82) indicates that one of the men, probably Derosier, being deranged "jumped up, perfectly wild, and inquired for his mule. Although it was tied close by him, he started to the mountains to look for it. Some time later, when his absence became known, men were sent in search of him. We looked through all the neighborhood, and made inquiries of the Indians, but could hear nothing of him." It seems probable that Derosier simply did not let John Charles know that he would not continue with the expedition, and chose to avoid being found. After the harrowing experience of the past few weeks it is surprising that more of the party did not abandon the expedition at this place of opportunity and plenty. Others took their leave at this time with the knowledge of John Charles. Jackson and Spence (1970: 657) note that Derosier finally turned up at Sutter's, and that he reached Jefferson, Missouri, on 21 November 1845. His wife, Therese, had been paid $45 by Frémont, and the remainder was paid to him upon his return.

The party was finally under way in earnest on 24 March, only 16 days following arrival at Sutter's, with 130 horses and mules, and 30 cattle, "five of which were milch cows." A "*vaquero*, an Indian boy, was furnished by Mr. Sutter to aid in handling the cavalcade, . . . great part of which were nearly as wild as buffalo; and who was, besides, very anxious to go along with us" (Frémont, 1845: 248). The direct route was to the east, but the Sierra Nevada was too great a barrier for them to attempt another crossing, clothed as it still was in winter snows. The expedition would move to the south several hundred miles, to a pass at the head of the San Joaquin river. Frémont outlined his expected route homeward: "This pass, reported to be good, was discovered by Mr. Joseph Walker. To reach it our course lay along the valley of the San Joaquin—the river on our right, and the lofty wall of the impassable Sierra on the left. From that pass we were to move southeastwardly, having the Sierra then on the right, and reach the '*Spanish trail*,' deviously traced from one watering place to another, which constituted the route of the caravans from *Puebla de los Angeles*, near the coast of the Pacific, to *Santa Fe* of New Mexico. From the pass to this trail was 150 miles. Following that trail through a desert, relieved by some fertile plains indicated by the recurrence of the term vegas, until it turned to the right to cross the Colorado, our course would be northeast until we regained the latitude we had lost in arriving at the Eutah [Utah] lake, and thence to the Rocky mountains at the head of the Arkansas. This course of traveling, forced upon us by the structure of the country, would occupy a computed distance of two thousand miles before we reached the head of the Arkansas; not a settlement to be seen upon it; and the names of places along it, all being Spanish or Indian, indicated that it had been but little trod by *American* feet. Though long, and not free from hardships, this route presented some points of attraction, in tracing the Sierra Nevada—turning the Great Basin, perhaps crossing its rim on the south—completely solving the problem of any river, except the Colorado, from the Rocky mountains on that part of our continent—and seeing the southern extremity of the Great Salt lake [reference to Utah Lake, a mistake discussed later], of which the northern part had been examined the year before" (Frémont, 1845: 248). Frémont would deviate from the route as described above; he would not cross Walker Pass.

The dates for the first several days after leaving Sutter's Fort are not readily applicable to the places reported in Frémont's journal. Dates on herbarium labels indicate arrival at the various river crossings and camps along the rivers at different dates than are reported in the following summary. It seems probable that the dates on the specimens (see Chapter VII) are correct and that Frémont attempted to recapitulate the daily events at some later date than their actual happenings.

The journal descriptions for both the 1843–44 and 1845–47 expeditions demonstrate that Frémont either never clearly understood the names of the streams south of the American Fork in California or that the entries were composed at later dates, when the information was no longer clear in his mind. In any event, the dates and places are jumbled.

Camp on the first night was along the "*Rio de los Cosumnes*." The route was through evergreen and deciduous oaks in groves. Preuss (Gudde & Gudde, 1958: 120) indicates that he rode 45 miles without stopping on 27 March, adding that it was a valley paradise: "Grass, flowers, trees, beautiful clear rivers, thousands of deer, elk, wild horses, wonderful salmon." The year previous, such a ride nearly killed Preuss. Now it was merely another day to be enjoyed. On 28 March they traveled 28 miles and halted in a bottom adjacent to a ford of the "*Rio de los Mukelemnes*" [San Joaquin County, California]. Label data on plants at this river are dated 25–26 March, so one or the other of the dates is in error. Frémont described the bottoms as "broad, rich, and extremely fertile; and the uplands are shaded with oak groves. A showy *lupinus* [*Lupinus albifrons* Benth.] of extraordinary beauty, growing four to five feet in height, and covered with spikes in bloom, adorned the banks of the river, and filled the air with a light and grateful perfume" (Frémont, 1845: 248–49).

The huge entourage was at "*Arroyo de las Calaveras*, (Skull creek,) a tributary of the San Joaquin and Sacramento rivers," on 26 March, still in San Joaquin County. The place was made beautiful by groves of oak and the grassy sward beneath. *Ammole* (soap plant) [*Chlorogalum pomeridianum* (DC.) Kunth, collected, according to label data, at the Mokelumne River] replaced grass near the river. Of this species Munz (1970) states: "The bulbs were roasted and eaten by the Indians; uncooked they have lather-producing properties in water. Crushed material of the plant was used in streams to stupify fish." A vine with small white flowers "(*melothria*?) [*Marah fabaceus* (Naud.) Greene]" called *la yerba buena,* "gives name to an island and town in the bay, was to-day very frequent on our road—sometimes running on the ground or climbing on trees" (Frémont 1845: 249). Jackson and Spence (1970: 659) note that the "yerba buena" that gave San Francisco its name is *Satureja douglasii* (Benth.) Briq., not the tentative *Melothria* of Frémont. He did, however, collect specimens of the *Satureja* also (see Appendix I).

The party continued south through the beauty of springtime in the San Joaquin Valley. "About 1 o'clock [on 27 March] we came again among innumerable flowers; and a few miles further, fields of the beautiful blue-flowering *lupine*, which seems to love the neighborhood of water, indicated that we were approaching a stream. We here found this beautiful shrub in thickets, some of them being 12 feet in height. Occasionally three feet in circumference, and 10 feet high; the whole covered with spikes of flowers, the perfume of which is very sweet. A lover of natural beauty can imagine with what pleasure we rode among these flowering groves, which filled the air with a light and delicate fragrance" (Frémont, 1845: 249). Live oaks, with branches reclining on the ground, California poppy ("of a rich orange color"), elk, and bands of antelope rounded out the day. They arrived (28 or 29 March) at the Stanislaus River, which was in flood, and traveled about five miles up that stream prior to camping, without having found a ford. At the camp *Erodium cicutarium*, some eight or ten inches high, was in bloom.

On 30 March the party returned back down the Stanislaus (the present boundary between San Joaquin and Stanislaus Counties, California) for 17 miles, "and again encamped without having found a fording place." The group followed downstream another eight miles on 31 March, camped, killed several cattle, and used their skins to make boats to ferry their baggage across the river. The Indian vaquero deserted them there. The dates for the preceding few days are unclear, as the dates are run together in Frémont's journal. Apparently Frémont was still not back on track when they moved 10 miles on 1 April to the "*Rio de la Merced*, (river of our Lady of Mercy)" (according to Jackson & Spence, 1970: 661, actually the Tuolumne, still in Stanislaus County). The place showed evidence of elk, wild horses, and grizzly bear. The men saw during that day one band of elk with about 200 head. On 2 April they built a boat to ferry their baggage across the river, and the next day traveled near the San Joaquin River. Multitudes of wild fowl, mainly geese, were disturbed and the party encountered large bands of elk, antelope, and wild horses. The men camped near the river that night, and on 4 April, after an early rain storm, "continued up the San Joaquin." As they moved upriver, Frémont noted that the oak trees had disappeared and were replaced by large willows. The encampment that night was near a clump of trees on the river where there was good grass. "The prairies along the left bank are alive with immense droves of wild horses." Position of this camp was determined as 37°08′00″, 120°45′22″, not far from present Merced, in the county of the same name.

Travel was resumed on 5 April. "During the earlier part of the days' ride, the country presented a lacustrine appearance; the river was deep, and nearly on a level with the surrounding country; its banks raised like a levee, and fringed with willows. Over the bordering plain were interspersed spots of prairie among fields of *tule* (bulrushes,) which in this country are called *tulares*, and little ponds" (Frémont, 1845: 251). They traveled 37 miles and camped again on the river. This campsite was determined to be at 36°49′12″, 120°28′34″, in Fresno County. Halt was called after 15 miles of travel on 6 April under shade of sycamore trees along the river. The source of the San Joaquin River arises to the southeast of this place, and Frémont forded the river and camped on its south bank, "where droves of wild horses were raising clouds of dust on the prairie."

"We made, on the 7th, a hard march in a cold chilly rain from morning until night—the weather so thick that we traveled by compass." Preuss (Gudde & Gudde, 1958: 122) says of this date: "This was the hardest day of the entire journey. We made fifty miles, from one river to another. Continual cold rain from morn till night." "This was a *traverse* from the San Joaquin to the waters of the Tule lakes, and our road was over a very level prairie country" (Frémont, 1845: 252). The journey continued in the company of wolves prowling about after young antelope, which had not yet strength to run fast. Late in the afternoon timber was discovered, groves of oak trees on a dry *arroyo*. "Riding on through the timber, about dark we found abundant water in small ponds, 20 to 30 yards in diameter, with clear deep water and sandy beds, bordered with bog rushes (*juncus effusus*,) and a tall rush (*scirpus lacustris*) 12 feet high, and surrounded near the margin with willow trees in bloom; among them one which resembled *salix myricoides*. The oak of the groves was the same already mentioned, with small leaves, in form like those of the white oak, and forming, with the evergreen oak, the characteristic trees of the valley" (Frémont, 1845: 252).

On 8 April the expedition reached the principal tributary of the "Tule lakes," and detoured upstream several miles to a ford. They camped among oak groves on the river, at 36°24′50″, 119°41′40″, near present Hanford, Kings County, California. The party continued south on 9 April through rotten ground initially and through timbered arroyos and oak groves to their encampment among a collection of streams. These ran through rushes and willows, thick with blackbirds. The day of 10 April was good traveling and the party made 40 miles, although the country was uninteresting. "In the evening the face of the country became hilly; and, turning a few miles up towards the mountains, we found a good encampment on a pretty stream hidden among the hills, and handsomely timbered, principally with large cottonwoods, (*populus*, differing from any in Muchaux's Sylva.) [This comment undoubtedly came from Torrey, and the observation was correct.] The seed vessels of this tree were now just about bursting." An Indian pointed out a trail for the journey of 11 April, which proved to be good and carefully chosen, as the country was otherwise rough and could have been crossed only with difficulty. "Instead of grass, the whole face of the country is closely covered with *erodium cicutarium*, here only two or three inches high. Its height and beauty varied in a remarkable manner with the locality, being, in low places which we passed during the day, around streams and springs, two and three feet in height" (Frémont, 1845: 253). Camp was made that night on a large creek, where Frémont noticed "in bloom, for the first time since leaving the Arkansas waters, the *mirabilis Jalapa* [likely *Mirabilis multiflora* or a near ally]."

The road on 12 April was through sandy country with meager vegetation. "*Ephedra occidentalis*, which we had first seen in the neighborhood of the Pyramid lake, made its appearance here, and in the course of the day became very abundant, and in large bushes" (Frémont, 1845: 253). The group encountered a swift stream (later named Kern River by Frémont, after Edward M. Kern of the third expedition) and followed it upwards for several miles to where they camped at a site with scanty grass. "In greater part, the vegetation along our road consisted now of rare and unusual plants, among which many were entirely new [whether new to science or to Frémont is unclear]. Along the bottoms were thickets consisting of several varieties of shrubs, which made here their first appearance; among these was *Garrya elliptica* (Lindley,) [likely *G. fremontii* Torr., though mainly a plant of dry slopes] a small tree belonging to a very peculiar natural order, and, in its general appearance, (growing in thickets,) resembling willow. It now became common along the streams, frequently supplying the place of *salix longifolia*" (Frémont, 1845: 253). On 13 April (in Kern County, California) they continued upstream for a few miles and crossed to the south side. From there the men and animals proceeded southeasterly over broken country to a stream, which they designated "Pass creek," and ascended toward a pass high above. "The stream enlarged rapidly, and the timber became abundant as we ascended. A new species of pine made its appearance, with several kinds of oaks, and a variety of trees; and the country changing its appearance suddenly and entirely, we found ourselves again traveling among the old orchard-like places. Here we selected a delightful encampment in a handsome green oak hollow, where, among the open bolls of the trees, was an abundant sward of grass and pea vines" (Frémont, 1845: 254).

Into this camp rode an Indian, "well dressed, with long spurs, and a *sombrero*, and speaking Spanish fluently." The Indian was able to give Frémont information he so sorely needed about the route beyond the Sierra Nevada. He agreed to travel with the party for two days prior to his departure from their route to proceed to "*San Fernando*." Their position was determined as 35°17′12″, 118°35′03″; this is east of present Bakersfield, Kern County, California, not far from Tehachapi Pass. On 14 April the guide joined them en route, and the the huge party continued their ascent along a stream, "which was enriched by a profusion of flowers, and handsomely wooded with sycamore, oaks, cottonwood, and willow, with other trees, and some shrubby plants. In its long strings of balls, this sycamore differs from that of the United States, and is the *platanus occidentalis* of Hooker—a new species, recently described among the plants collected in the voyage of the Sulphur [actually *Platanus racemosa* Nutt.]. The cottonwood varied its foliage with white tufts, and the feathery seeds were flying plentifully through the air. Gooseberries, nearly ripe, were very abundant on the mountain; and as we passed the dividing grounds, which were not very easy to ascertain, the air was filled with perfume, as if we were entering a highly cultivated garden; and, instead of green, our pathway and the mountain sides were covered with fields of yellow flowers, which here was the prevailing color. Our journey to-day was in the midst of an advancing spring, whose green and floral beauty offered a delightful contrast to the sandy valley we had just left" (Frémont, 1845: 255). The ride through such beautiful country delighted Frémont, who contrasted the exquisite flowering land through which they traveled, not only with the sandy valley but with the snowy mountains of the Sierra Nevada immediately above them to the east and those that only a short time previously had provided a travail of snowy, wet, cold hardship and had become imprinted clearly in his memory.

During the 14th the summit of the pass, still in Kern County, California, was reached. It was a place where the bleak view to the east contrasted with the floriferous greenery of the land just passed. According to Gudde and Gudde (1958: 123) and Jackson and Spence (1970: 668) this was Oak Creek Pass, not Tehachapi Pass (and certainly not Walker Pass, a pass much farther to the north, as intimated earlier by Frémont), which is nearby to the north about five or six miles. The land to the east presented a dreary sight, a scene of bald rocks and any color but green. At this point, John Charles and his men had followed the Sierra Nevada and Cascade ranges from the Columbia River to this pass, traveled on both sides of the north-south axis of the Sierra Nevada, and, unbelievably, crossed the Sierra Nevada in midwinter. Disproved was the existence of the fabled river Buenaventura, which was supposed to drain from the west base of the Rocky Mountains westward into San Francisco Bay. Now Frémont was to leave the Sierra and plunge into one of the truly dry regions of the continent, with his tried and true men and his still half-wild cavalcade of horses and cattle. Botanically they had entered a whole new regime—beyond the experience of Frémont and to a large extent unexplored as to its plant species. The discoveries would be unique, just how unique Frémont could not have guessed. Now was the time when fanciful dreams of the future might have been justified.

The beginning of the homeward route for Preuss was in sight at the summit of the pass. He wrote: "The same mountain range which a short time ago caused us such misery we crossed in one day today, through a most beautiful pass covered with trees and flowers. To the right and left the snow-capped mountains stared us in the face but could not frighten us. Hummingbirds and warm spring air made us laugh at the snow. Now, to be sure, all this glory is gone. We are camping on the east side of the mountains, have a desert ahead of us, and must prepare for a miserable journey for the next months" (Gudde & Gudde, 1958: 122). In returning to forlorn territory, Preuss had regained at least part of his former disgruntled nature.

Descending from the pass, they reached a country of fine grass, where "*erodium cicutarium* finally disappeared, giving place to an excellent quality of bunch grass. Passing by some springs where there was a rich sward of grass among groves of large black oak" (Frémont, 1845: 256). Later in the day, after crossing a low mountain range and descending a hollow where a spring gushed out, they were "struck by the sudden appearance of *yucca* trees [*Yucca brevifolia* Engelm.], which gave a strange and southern character to the country, and suited well with the dry and desert region we were approaching. Associated with the idea of barren sands, their stiff and ungraceful form makes them to the traveller the most repulsive tree in the vegetable kingdom. Following the hollow, we shortly came upon a creek timbered with large black oak, which yet had not put forth leaf. There was a small rivulet of running water with good grass" (Frémont,

1845: 256). Preuss merely notes for this yucca: "The *Pisang*, a tree I knew before only from paintings, cuts a sorry figure" (Gudde & Gudde, 1958: 123).

The arborescent yucca, called Joshua tree less than a quarter century later by the Mormons, did not affect Frémont or Preuss with its subtle charm and anthropoid forms. Individual plants are architecturally beautiful, and even old senescent trees, with drooping branches, are not lacking altogether in aesthetic value. The trees stand like people with arms outstretched and, when viewed on ridges in the distance, deceive travelers into imagining that they are accompanied by other humans. The species would await a scientific name for another 27 years, when it was finally named and described by George Engelmann (Watson, 1871). Evidently Frémont did collect samples of this remarkable plant, but the specimens consist of leaves only.

The Indians who had accompanied their guide left them on 15 April, and the party continued down the creek, crossed a spur ridge, and descended onto a plain. Their guide stretched his hand toward the desert and said: "'There are the great *llanos*, (plains;) *no hay agua*; *no hay zacate—nada*; there is neither water nor grass—nothing; every animal that goes out upon them, dies'" (Frémont, 1845: 256). As if in contemplation of their chances of crossing such a formidable obstacle Frémont described the entourage. "Our cavalcade made a strange and grotesque appearance; and it was impossible to avoid reflecting upon our position and composition in this remote solitude. Within two degrees of the Pacific Ocean; already far south of the latitude of Monterey; and still forced on south by a desert on one hand, and a mountain range on the other; guided by a civilized Indian, attended by two wild ones from the Sierra; a chinook from the Columbia; and our own mixture of American, French, German—all armed; four or five languages heard at once; above a hundred horses and mules, half wild; American, Spanish, and Indian dresses and equipments intermingled—such was our composition. Our march was sort of a procession. Scouts ahead, and on the flanks; a front and rear division; the pack animals, baggage, and horned cattle, in the center; and the whole stretching a quarter of a mile along our dreary path. In this form we journeyed; looking more like we belonged to Asia than to the United States of America" (Frémont, 1845: 257). Frémont was intrigued by the similarity of the American West with Asia, and made reference to it on various occasions, even though he had not been to Asia. The hand of Jessie, with her flair for the dramatic, is suspected.

Their route took them south across the plain, on which grew yucca trees as far as the eye could see. "Several new plants appeared, among which was a zygophyllaceous shrub (*zygophyllum Californicum*, Torr. & Frém.) [the creosote bush, *Larrea tridentata* (DC.) Cov.] sometimes 10 feet in height; in form, and in the pliancy of its branches, it is rather a graceful plant. Its leaves are small, covered with a resinous substance; and, particularly when bruised and crushed, exhale a singular but very agreeable and refreshing odor. This shrub and the *yucca*, with many varieties of cactus, make the characteristic features in the vegetation for a long distance to the eastward. Along the foot of the mountain, 20 miles to the southward, red stripes of flowers were visible during the morning, which we supposed to be variegated sandstones. We rode rapidly during the day, and in the afternoon emerged from the *yucca* forest at the foot of an *outlier* of the Sierra before us, and came among the fields of flowers we had seen in the morning, which consisted principally of the rich orange-colored Californian poppy, mingled with other flowers of brighter tints" (Frémont, 1845: 257). Camp for the night was set up near a spring among granite boulders, among which grew "borders of buckwheat [*Eriogonum fasciculatum* Benth.], with their white blossoms." The camp was situated at 34°41′42″, 118°20′00″, in the vicinity of present Lancaster, Los Angeles County, California.

The Indian guide left them on the morning of 17 April, after pointing out a distant butte at the foot of which water could be found. They continued eastward "through a succession of valleys, and came into a most beautiful spot of flower fields: instead of green, the hills were purple and orange, with unbroken beds, into which each color was separately gathered. A pale straw color, with a bright yellow, the rich red orange of the poppy mingled with fields of purple, covered the spot with a floral beauty; and, on the border of the sandy deserts, seemed to invite the traveller to go no further. Riding along through the perfumed air, we soon after entered a defile overgrown with the ominous *artemisia tridentata*, which conducted us into a sandy plain covered more or less densely with forests of *yucca*" (Frémont, 1845: 258). Camp was on the banks of a swiftly running stream, but there was no grass for the animals. It is evident that previous experience with the sagebrush ("*artemisia tridentata*"), of days of monotonous riding through vast expances, had caused Frémont to use the term ominous.

On 18 April 1844 "some parties were engaged in hunting up the scattered horses, and others in searching for grass above; both were successful, and late in the day we encamped among some spring heads of the river, in a hollow which was covered with only tolerably good grasses, the lower ground being entirely overgrown with large bunches of the coarse stiff grass, (*carex sitchensis*)" (Frémont, 1845: 258). *Carex* is, of course, a sedge—a grasslike plant—not a grass. The identity of the coarse stiff grass is unknown; possibly it was *Sporobolus airoides* (Torr.) Torr. The locality of the camp was determined as 34°27′03″, 117°13′00″, near present Victorville, San Bernardino County, California.

Preuss had a difficult time on 17 April: "My Polly ran against a cactus, jumped high in the air, and threw me off. My hips were blue this morning. I lost this diary and other things; luckily, I recovered everything this morning. Bad, bad region! Sand and Yucca trees and cactus." Preuss had returned to his normal condition, the situation was bad as expected. The party continued: "Traveling close along the mountain, we followed up, in the afternoon of the 19th, another stream, in hopes to find a grass patch like that of the previous day, but were deceived; except some scattered bunch grass, there was nothing but rock and sand; and even the fertility of the mountains seemed withered by the air of the desert. Among the few trees was the nut pine, (*pinus monophyllus*)" (Frémont, 1845: 258). McKelvey (1955: 872) suggests that it might have been here that the type material of the single-leaf pinyon was taken. Other data, including the collection number of the type specimen, indicate that the supposition is correct (see Appendix I).

The route on the 20th continued to the east and, after a difficult march of 18 miles, led them to the Spanish Trail. The rate of travel increased because of the nature of the trail, and the men and animals hurried on to a large stream some 15 miles beyond their juncture. Because the river was timbered with cottonwoods and had tolerable grass, the party remained in camp on 21 April to give the animals a chance to eat and rest from the difficult trip of the previous month. The past, in this case, was indeed prologue; the country ahead was dry except for occasional springs, and grass would be in short supply throughout the desert country. In spite of the limited and contradictory information obtained in California concerning the Spanish Trail, Frémont found the road beyond this camp to be the "roughest and rockiest road we had ever seen in the country, and which nearly destroyed our band of fine mules and horses." Position of this camp of two nights was determined as 34°34′11″, 117°13′00″, somewhere between present Victorville and Barstow.

The morning of the 22nd was clear and bright, and a snowy peak in the Sierra Nevada to the southward shone out high and sharply defined. The route was along the banks of a stream (the Mohave River) vegetated with cottonwoods and willows until the stream gradually dwindled away, absorbed by the sand. Camp was made after traveling 20 miles, at an old encampment along the Spanish Trail, about 16 miles southwest of Barstow, California. Their route on 23 April continued along the Mohave River, which, in the course of the day, dried entirely. The route was then along the dry river bed for some 16 miles where the water reappeared in low places in the channel, which were timbered with cottonwood and willow. There they came to still another customary campsite along the Spanish Trail.

At this point in the narrative of his journey, Frémont (1845: 260) presents an apology of sorts for the remainder of the report: "Our journey homeward was fruitful in incident; and the country through which we traveled, although a desert, afforded much to excite the curiosity of the botanist; but limited time, and the rapidly advancing season for active operations, oblige me to omit all extended descriptions, and hurry briefly to the conclusion of this report." Description of vegetation, flowers, and other incidentals beyond this point in the published narrative are reduced to a minimum. The glowing descriptions of the earlier portions seldom extend to the report beyond this entry. One is forced to wonder whether the observations were recorded and merely left out because of constraints of time or other exigencies, or whether they were not made. The rate of collection, if the dated and datable specimens taken by Frémont are indicative, did not change much following this date. He continued to collect on a rather regular schedule.

The camp was moved some eight miles on 24 April to another site still on the course of the Mohave River. "The caravans sometimes continue below, to the end of the river, from which there is a very long *journada* of perhaps sixty miles, without water. Here a singular and new species of acacia [*Prosopis odorata* (Torr. in Frém.) Torr. & Frém. in Frém. emend. Welsh], with spiral pods or seed vessels, made its first appearance; becoming henceforward, for a considerable distance a characteristic tree. It was here comparatively large, being about 20 feet in height, with a full and spreading top, the lower branches declining towards the ground. It afterwards occurred of smaller size, frequently in groves, and is very fragrant. It has been called by Dr. Torrey *spirolobium odoratum*. The zygophyllaceous shrub [creosote bush, *Larrea tridentata* (DC.) Cov.] had been constantly characteristic of the plains along the river; and here, among many new plants, a new and very remarkable species of eriogonum (*eriogonum inflatum*, Torr. & Frém.) made its first appearance" (Frémont, 1845: 260). Three cattle were killed and the meat was dried in preparation for the crossing of the desert. Indians who had joined them earlier engaged in a great feast, utilizing every part of the animals except the bones.

Frémont and his group of men were joined at this camp by two Mexicans, "*Andreas Fuentes*," an adult, and "*Pablo Hernandez*," a boy of 11. The two were the survivors of a party of six, including Fuentes's wife and Pablo's father and mother, who had been killed by Indians at a camp some 60 miles distant. The Mexicans possessed about 30 horses, of which some were taken by the Indian assailants and the remainder had been herded by Fuentes and the boy to a point not far from the Frémont camp. Frémont welcomed the man and the boy into camp, into his own mess, and offered whatever aid he could give. At some later time he hired Fuentes as a voyageur. Both accompanied the party to St. Louis. The two must have looked upon Frémont and his party as their saviors, who chanced to be nearby when help was so desperately needed.

After regaining the Spanish Trail on 25 April the Frémont party with the two new members proceeded along it in a northeasterly direction. The route was rough and the party toiled along "oppressed with thirst and a burning sun. But, throughout this nakedness of sand and gravel, were many beautiful plants and flowering shrubs, which occurred in many new species, and with greater variety than we had been accustomed to see in the most luxuriant prairie countries; this was a peculiarity of this desert. Even where no grass would take root, the naked sand would bloom with some rich and rare flower, which found its appropriate home in the arid and barren spot. Scattered over the plain, and tolerably abundant, was a handsome leguminous shrub, three or four feet high, with fine bright-purple flowers [the indigobush, *Psorothamnus fremontii* (Torr.) Barneby]. It is a new *psoralea*, and occurred frequently henceforth along our road" (Frémont, 1845: 262). Frémont's observation of the great species diversity of these desert areas compared with those of the most luxuriant prairies is correct and botanically astute. His description of the Mohave desert is likewise more than adequate.

Springtime temperatures in the Mohave desert fluctuate greatly both daily and from day to day. Frontal systems sweep from west to east across the region, giving sequences of days with temperature approaching or even surpassing 100° Fahrenheit, alternating with others in the 50°s. One is uncomfortably warm, taking off clothing one day and reaching for a coat the next. Violent winds accompany some of the frontal systems, picking up gigantic roostertail plumes of dust from the valley floors. Clear cloudless skies are normal. Summers in the Mohave are hot and dry. It is fortunate that John Charles crossed it before the searing heat of that season.

Upon their arrival, after about 25 miles, at the spring "*Agua de Tomaso*," (Bitter Spring) where the horses had been left by Fuentes and Pablo, it was found that the horses were gone. Carson, Godey, and Fuentes went after the horses, following the tracks of the animals and of the Indians who had taken them. Carson (Quaife, 1935: 83) had expected to be joined by others of Frémont's men, but when none volunteered the trio set out. Frémont and party camped at the spring, which had been dug out to increase its flow and make it usable by previous travelers or by Indians. Fuentes returned in the evening, his horse having failed 20 miles from camp. Carson and Godey, unperturbed by the loss of Fuentes, continued in pursuit. The position of the camp where Frémont and his men waited was determined as 35°13′08″, 116°23′28″, in the vicinity of present Baker, California. While in this camp, Frémont evidently pressed a specimen of *Eriogonum maculosum* A. Heller (#235).

Carson and Godey returned to camp on 26 April, driving a band of horses "recognised by Fuentes to be part of those they had lost. Two bloody scalps, dangling from the end of Godey's gun, announced that they had overtaken the Indians as well as the horses" (Frémont, 1845: 262). The Indians had been ambushed and the horses recovered. Carson and Godey had ridden about 100 miles in their adventure, all in about 30 hours. Possibly their action did indeed right a wrong that had been committed by the Indians, but it seems probable that their action was to plague the party until it left the Mohave Desert in the corner of present Utah.

Preuss (Gudde & Gudde, 1958: 127) was disgusted: "Two scalps from the hands of Alex Godey. Are these whites not much worse than the Indians? . . . To me such butchery is disgusting, but Frémont is in high spirits." It appears to this writer that the ambush of the Spanish people, the killing of the men, and the abduction of the women, followed by the retribution of Carson and Godey, had changed Frémont's attitude regarding at least certain Indians. In the future some would receive his wrath. At the present, near the end of the 20th century, it is easy to be judgmental, but perhaps not so easy to be just. The Indians, Mexicans, and members of Frémont's party were all survivors in a world we can glimpse only through the pages of history: each of them made do with what was available. It seems that every animal, and human for that matter, was fair game.

The party moved again in the late afternoon of 27(?) April, with the intention of traveling all night to avoid the heat, which was oppressive to both men and animals. The men rode on in the warmth of a moonlit night, "directly towards the north star, we journeyed now across an open plain between mountain ridges. . . . The plain appeared covered principally with *zygophyllum Californicum* already mentioned; and the line of our road was marked by the skeletons of horses, which were strewed to a considerable breadth over the plain." They camped at the entrance of a canyon, in what appeared to be a good location because of the presence of water. Morning demonstrated that the campsite was poor; it was a saline area with some long unwholesome grass, the water too salty to drink. Another spring nearby provided water of drinkable quality, but too little grass to sustain the herd. There were thickets of "*spirolobium odoratum* (acacia) in bloom, and very fragrant" (Frémont, 1845: 264). The reference to acacia is, of course, to *Prosopis*. There is, however, the possibility that he encountered the catclaw, *Acacia greggii* A. Gray, in portions of the Mohave. Usually it blooms late, following that of the mesquites; and, no specimens of it collected by Frémont are in the Torrey collection at New York.

They traveled for about 8 miles on 28(?) April to the bed of a large creek "of salt and bitter water, running in a westerly direction, to receive the stream bed we had left. It is called by the Spaniards *Amargosa*—the bitter water of the desert. Where we struck it, the stream bends; and we continued in a northerly course up the ravine of its valley, passing on the way a fork from the right, near which occurred a bed of plants, consisting of a remarkable new genus of *cruciferae* [*Oxystylis lutea* Torr. & Frém. in Frém., (Capparaceae), which looks like a mustard superficially], was taken at this place [south of Shoshone, San Bernardino County, California]. Gradually ascending, the ravine opened into a green valley, where, at the foot of the mountain, were springs of excellent water. We encamped among groves of the new *acacia*, where there was an abundance of grass for the animals. This was the best camping ground we had seen since we struck the Spanish trail" (Frémont, 1845: 262). They had traveled 12 miles. Throughout the day the party had been following the present route of highway 127, proceeding north from Baker toward Shoshone and Death Valley (Jackson & Spence, 1970: 683).

On 29 April the party reached the camp in which the Indians had ambushed the Mexicans, designated as "*Archilette*." The party traveled some 7 miles from the previous camp to this site. There the bodies of the men were discovered, but not of the women, whom they assumed had been taken captive by the Indians. However, Carson (Quaife, 1935: 85; Carter, 1968: 93) reported that "a party [possibly the Walker group] traveling in our rear found their bodies very much mutilated and staked to the ground." Frémont renamed the site "*Agua de Hernandez*" in honor of Hernandez, who was killed in the fight. This place, about 92 miles west of Las Vegas, Nevada, in Inyo County, California, was later called "Resting Springs." Latitude was reported as 35°51′22″.

The group traveled 24 miles on 30 April, across the Nopah Range through Emigrant Pass and partway across Pahrump Valley, to a little stream that came out of the mountains on the left, "very slightly wooded with cottonwood, willow, and acacia, and a few dwarf oaks; and grass was nearly as scarce as water. A plant with showy yellow flowers (*Stanleya integrifolia*) [*S. pinnata* Pursh] occurred abundantly at intervals for the last two days, and *eriogonum inflatum* was among the characteristic plants." They camped that night at Stump Spring, Clark County, Nevada (Jackson & Spence, 1970: 684).

"May 1.— The air is rough, and overcoats pleasant. The sky is blue, and the day bright. Our road was over a plain, towards the foot of the mountain; zygophyllum californicum, now in bloom with a small yellow flower, is characteristic of the country; and *cacti* were very abundant, and in rich fresh bloom, which ornaments this poor country" (Frémont, 1845: 265). Camp was made at a spring, Mountain Spring, in a pass in the Charleston or Spring Mountains where there was grass but little water. Noted here were "nut pine, cedars, and a dwarf species of oak [? *Quercus turbinella* Greene]; and among the shrubs were *Purshia tridentata*, *artemisia*, and *ephedra occidentalis*." Shrubs were in bloom, "with flowers of white, yellow, red, and purple." The animals suffered from the rocky trails and from lack of water and grass. The expedition traveled 12 rough miles on 2 May, crossed a mountain, and descended to a creek bottom with much-welcomed water and grass. This locality, Cottonwood Spring, is near the site of present Blue Diamond, Nevada (Jackson & Spence, 1970: 685). Indian tracks were noted, but no Indians were seen.

On 3 May the men and animals reached the springs at "*las Vegas* [The Meadows]—a term which the Spaniards use to signify fertile or marshy plains, in contradistinction to *llanos*, which they apply to dry and sterile plains. Two narrow streams of clear water, four or five feet deep gush suddenly, with a quick current, from two singularly large springs; these and other waters of the basin, pass out in a gap to the eastward. The taste of the water is good, but rather too warm to be agreeable; the temperature being 71° in the one, and 73° in the other. They, however, afforded a delightful bathing place" (Frémont, 1845: 266). This is at the present Las Vegas, Clark County, Nevada, and it was here that Frémont collected several new species, among them the beautiful *Arctomecon californicum* (frontispiece) and the unusual selenophyte *Astragalus preussii*. Ahead of them lay one of the most desolate stretches of their journey, across parched land in a creosote bush vegetation type—a vast waterless, bleak land, where mountains display raw geological strata not softened by vegetation. These ranges, which change hue with the time of day, are starkly beautiful; probably less so when one has insufficient water.

The journey began again on the morning of 4 May, "earlier than usual, traveling in a northeasterly direction across the plain from Las Vegas. The new acacia (*spirolobium odoratum*) has now become the characteristic tree of the country; it is in bloom, and its blossoms are very fragrant. The day was still, and the heat, which soon became very oppressive, appeared to bring out strongly the refreshing scent of the zygophyllaceous shrubs and the sweet perfume of the acacia. The snowy ridge we had just crossed [Charleston or Spring Mountains] looked out conspicuously in the northwest. In about five hours ride, we crossed a gap in the surrounding ridge, and the appearance of skeletons of horses very soon warned us that we were engaged in another dry *jornada*, which proved the longest we made in all our journey—between fifty and sixty miles without a drop of water. Travellers through countries affording water and timber can have no conception of our intolerable thirst while journeying over the hot yellow sands of this elevated country, where the heated air seems to be entirely deprived of moisture. We ate occasionally the *bisnada* [a plant shown them earlier by Fuentes, who was still with them and was in Frémont's employ], and moistened our mouths with the acid of the sour dock, (*rumex venosus*) [*Rumex hymenosepalus* Torr., canaigre]. Hourly expecting to find water, we continued to press on until towards midnight, when, after a hard and uninterrupted march of 16 hours, our wild mules began running ahead; and in a mile or two we came on a bold running stream—so keen is the sense of that animal, in these desert regions, in scenting at a distance this necessity of life [water is odorless, but the vegetation associated with it is not!]. According to the information we had received, Sevier river was a tributary of the Colorado; and this, accordingly, should have been one of its affluents. It proved to be the *Rio de los angeles* (river of the Angels) [Muddy River]—a branch of the Rio Virgen (river of the Virgin)" (Frémont, 1845: 266).

The distance they had traveled is 49 miles by modern highway map. By their trail it would certainly have been longer; their speed averaged somewhat more than three miles per hour, a remarkable rate. In the late 20th century one can cover the same distance in air-conditioned comfort in somewhat less than one hour. The river, of course, is in no way connected to the Sevier, a Great Basin stream heading far to the east of their position, still in the Basin and Range Province.

John Charles and his men stayed at the Muddy River camp through 5 May to allow the animals rest and sustenance. Indians crowded around, probably with knowledge of the events far to the southwest, and Frémont's men went armed all day to keep them out of the camp and away from the horses, which they seemed intent on stealing. The Indians made threatening gestures and were evidently hostile. "They were barefooted, and nearly naked; their hair gathered up into a knot behind; and with his bow, each man carried a quiver with thirty or forty arrows partially drawn out. Besides these, each held in his hand two or three arrows for instant service. Their arrows are barbed with a very clear translucent stone, a species of opal, nearly as hard as the diamond; and, shot from their long bow, are almost as effective as a gunshot" (Frémont, 1845: 267). The Indians spoke a dialect "of the *Utah*." One can only surmise Frémont's feelings about the abandoned howitzer at this time when it might have served as an excellent pacifier. Additionally, these local inhabitants did not share the earlier compunction of Frémont and Preuss against eating horses and mules; instead, horses and mules were simply viewed as walking food. Frémont took time out from concerns with the Indians to collect the specimens on which would be based the name *Dalea fremontii* Torr. in A. Gray, the Frémont indigo-bush (now *Psorothamnus fremontii* (Torr.) Barneby).

Frémont and party left the encampment at the Muddy River on 6 May, "through the same desolate and revolting country, where lizards were the only animal, and the tracks of the lizard eaters [the Indians] the principal sign of human beings." After traveling for 20 miles, "we reached the most dreary river [Virgin River] I have ever seen—a deep and rapid stream, almost a torrent, passing swiftly by, and roaring against obstructions. The banks were wooded with willow, acacia, and a frequent plant of the country already mentioned, (*Garrya elliptica*,) growing in thickets, resembling willow, and bearing a small pink flower. Crossing it we encamped on the left [south] bank, where we found a very little grass" (Frémont, 1845: 268).

They killed their three remaining, tired, hungry, and thin steers for food; the milk cows had long since been consumed, and the party was now out of traditionally eaten livestock. Possibly Frémont was husbanding the large horse herd in anticipation of the 1845 expedition. The horses and mules were too valuable to be eaten, unless circumstances became dire.

Elevation of the camp, near present Mesquite, Clark County, Nevada, by boiling point of water was determined to be 4060 feet (much too high; it is less than 3000 feet). Latitude was determined as 36°41′33″. Certainly the plant noted was not *Garrya ellipitica*, and probably not even a *Garrya*. Members of that genus grow mainly on dryish to dry sites in mountains along the route of Frémont's march, and the pink color noted for the flowers is likewise questionable, more so because *Garrya* traditionally blooms much earlier in the season and has greenish flowers. The identity of the pink-flowered plant remains a mystery. Frémont's assessment of the dreary river is, unfortunately, correct. The river runs through a broad valley filled with almost level alluvial deposits that form low mesas and buttes. Eastward are the stark and rugged mountains of the Beaver Dam and Virgin ranges. At the time of Frémont's visit the river was in flood, and presented a difficult barrier to cross. Why they crossed to the south bank is not known, but evidently the Spanish Trail north of the river was not well marked.

Frémont (1845: 268) states that "for several days we continued our journey up the river." This observation is in error, because by 8 May, two days after they first reached the Virgin, they were in a camp not far from present Littlefield, Mohave County, Arizona. The time interval might have seemed to be very long, however, because the Indians, to whom Frémont refers as "*Diggers*," were constantly in evidence. Animals left behind were summarily driven off and slaughtered for food by the Indians.

The entourage had traveled 28 miles upriver from their first camp to that of 8 May. There "we encamped at a little grass plat [on the south side of the river], where a spring of cool water issued from the bluff [the spring is still there]. On the opposite or north side was a grove of cottonwoods at the mouth of a fork [Beaver Dam Wash, at Littlefield, Mohave County, Arizona], which here enters the river. On either side the valley is bounded by ranges of mountains, every where high, rocky, and broken. The caravan road was lost and scattered on the sandy country, and we had been following an Indian trail up the river. The hunters the next day [9 May] were sent out to reconnoitre, and in the mean time we moved a mile farther up, where we found a good little patch of grass. There being only sufficient grass for the night, the horses were sent with a strong guard in charge of [Jean Baptiste] Tabeau to a neighboring hollow, where they might pasture during the day; and, to be ready in case the Indians should make any attempt on the animals, several of the best horses were picketed at the camp. In a few hours the hunters returned, having found a convenient ford in the river, and discovered the Spanish trail on the other side" (Frémont, 1845: 268).

Except for loss by attrition, with the possible exception of Baptiste Derosier, whose circumstances and condition were at that time unknown, Frémont had been fortunate in preservation of the lives of those who struggled with him on this and earlier expeditions. Now, that record of success in spite of hardship was to change. "I had been engaged in arranging plants [the only account of actually being involved in pressing plants in his journal]; and, fatigued with the heat of the day, I fell asleep in the afternoon, and did not awake until sundown. Presently Carson came to me, and reported that Tabeau, who early in the day had left his post, and, without my knowledge, rode back to the camp we had left [across from the mouth of Beaver Dam Creek], in search of a lame mule, had not returned. While we were speaking, a smoke rose suddenly from the cottonwood grove below, which plainly told us what had befallen him; it was raised to inform the surrounding Indians that a blow had been struck, and to tell them to be on their guard" (Frémont, 1845: 268–69).

Carson and some men went to find Tabeau and the mule he had been pursuing. The mule was found mortally wounded, with an arrow in its side. A small puddle of blood indicated that Tabeau might also have been killed. The search continued on 10 May, when Frémont, Mr. Fitzpatrick, Carson, and several other men returned along the track. The search party not only found where Tabeau had been wounded and had struggled, but also identified where his body had been dragged to the banks of the Virgin and thrown into it. All of his belongings had been taken by the Indians. They had struck a blow, possibly in retribution for the attack by Carson and Godey some days earlier.

Of the death of Tabeau, Preuss (Gudde & Gudde, 1958: 130) reports: "Yesterday afternoon [9 May] we lost one of our best men in a miserable manner. One can say that he lost his young life because of the horseshoes of a mule. In order to save these, he rode back where he thought he could find the animal. Only a mile from camp he was killed with arrows by hidden Indians and thrown into a rapid river."

Frémont mourned the loss of Tabeau, who "had been one of our best men, and his unhappy death spread a gloom over our party." Indeed, one can only wonder that many, if not all, of the party could not have been included in the "best men" category. These men were survivors, after all, of an impossible and incredibly dangerous journey through a strange land. Carson (Quaife, 1935: 86; Carter, 1968: 95) said of Tabeau, "He was a brave, noble-souled fellow, and I was saddened by his death." A notched peak visible from the site of the massacre, at my suggestion, now bears the name "Tabeau Peak," published in the Decision List for 1992 by the United States Board on Geographic Names.

Now Frémont would live up to his admonition regarding mention of vegetation; from this point forward only the most cursory of descriptions would be made. His observations would lack the completeness of those heretofore. The party would hurry on; suddenly, there seemed to be an urgency to their movement. "We wished to avenge his death; but the condition of our horses, languishing for grass and repose, forbade an expedition into unknown mountains." The Indians, having taken their toll, had now made off. Could it be that the death of Tabeau reminded Frémont of the precariousness of his position? Might that not explain his sudden push homeward? Or is it possible that they were merely short of meat and hurried on before the food supply ran out again? Thoughts of Jessie and home could not have escaped him and might have hastened his drive toward St. Louis. He was about to leave the late springtime of the Mohave, and, following an interval, move into the fresh springtime at higher elevations northward in Utah. There he would take many plants; thus, his rush homeward did not preclude wholly his quest for botanical specimens.

"Our camp [of 9–10 May] was in a basin below a deep canon—a gap of two thousand feet deep in the mountain—through which the *Rio Virgen* passes [Virgin River Narrows], and where no man or beast could follow it [present Interstate 15 traverses it]. The Spanish trail, which we had lost in the sands of the basin, was on the opposite [north] side of the river. We crossed over to it, and followed it northwardly toward a gap which was visible in the mountain [Beaver Dam Mountains in present Washington County, Utah]. We approached it by a defile, rendered difficult for our barefooted animals by the rocks strewed along it; and here the country changed its character. From the time we entered the desert, the mountains had been bald and rocky; here they began to be wooded with cedar and pine [i.e., Utah juniper and single-leaf pinyon or nut pine—the same *Pinus monophylla* of his western Nevada experience], and clusters of trees gave shelter to birds—a new and welcome sight—which could not have lived in the desert we had passed" (Frémont, 1845: 269). The party had passed up the Beaver Dam Slope and entered a drainage leading to a divide (possibly up Bull Dog Knolls or more likely Castle Cliffs drainages), and as elevation up Beaver Dam Slope increased, the expedition left behind the creosote bush and Joshua tree community. This amazing plant community of Joshua, creosote bush, and numerous other shrubs and cacti had become commonplace to Frémont during the almost four weeks since his party had entered it, and he hardly could have been as impressed with leaving it as with encountering pines and junipers as he moved up hill to the pass through the Beaver Dam Mountains. The Mohave plants symbolized the hardships endured while crossing through grassless stretches of drought, heat, and hostile Indians. The party had, in passing the divide over the Beaver Dam Mountains, left the deserts of the Basin and Range Province behind them, if only momentarily.

The pass at the head of Castle Cliff Wash is clothed by a mixed community of chaparral intermingling with pinyon and juniper. In the chaparral is Frémont mahonia (or barberry), cliff rose, manzanita, and Garrya. Some or all of these must have been in full flower when the expedition went through the pass. It seems likely that some of them were collected there, especially the cliff rose.

Beyond the Beaver Dam Mountains the group descended toward the narrow valley of the Santa Clara River, and "we saw before us a snowy mountain [Pine Valley Mountains], far beyond which appeared another more lofty still [Markagunt Plateau]" (Frémont, 1845: 269). They were for the time being in the Colorado Plateau Province, which Frémont would visit again under other circumstances during both his third and fifth expeditions in 1845 and 1854 respectively. The grateful party halted for the night where there was good grass and abundant clear water on the Santa Clara. The next day, 11 May, dawned cloudy and cool, and was followed with a rain shower, their first in 27 days since entering the desert. Travel was over a rough trail on 11 May along the Santa Clara, but was made more pleasant by the very country through which they marched. "The stream is prettily wooded with sweet [Frémont] cottonwood trees—some of them of large size; and on the hills, where the nut pine is often seen, a good and wholesome grass occurs frequently. This [sweetly scented, resinous] cottonwood [*Populus fremontii* Wats.], which is now in fruit, is of a different species from any in Michaux's Sylva. Heavy dark clouds covered the sky in the evening, and a cold wind sprang up, making fires and overcoats comfortable" (Frémont, 1845: 269). The reference to Michaux's Sylva is certainly from John Torrey. The species would later be named in Frémont's honor by Sereno Watson (1875). The cottonwood still forms a riparian forest along Santa Clara River, where its rounded, contiguous canopies shade the ground in umbrella fashion.

The route followed the Santa Clara on 12 May to where the stream forked, and then up the right-hand fork, which is the main channel of the Santa Clara River. Camp was on the summit of the ridge dividing the drainage of the Santa Clara from the Great Basin, the hydrologically closed northern extension of the Basin and Range Province. The Bull Valley Mountains lie to the west and the Pine Valley Mountains to the east. "We considered ourselves as crossing the rim of the basin; and, entering it at this point, we found here an extensive mountain meadow [site of the infamous Mountain Meadows massacre in 1857], rich in bunch grass, and fresh with numerous springs of clear water, all refreshing and delightful to look upon. It was, in fact, that *las Vegas de Santa Clara*, which had been so long presented to us as the terminating point of the desert, and where the annual caravan from California to New Mexico halted and recruited for some weeks" (Frémont, 1845: 270). John Charles noted that the meadow was about a mile wide and some ten miles long [possibly a little too large, from modern perspective]. It must have seemed something of a paradise after the experiences of the past month in the desert. The expedition had traveled 550 miles in just 28 days, averaging slightly less than 20 miles per day. "Having reached the resting place of the *Vegas de Santa Clara*, we had complete relief from the heat and privations of the desert, and some relaxation from the severity of camp duty. Some relaxation, and relaxation only—for camp guards, horse guards, and scouts are indispensable from the time of leaving the frontiers of Missouri until we return to them" (Frémont, 1845: 270). Preuss (Gudde & Gudde, 1958: 131) wrote: "The animals live well now, and we fare badly. Flour soup and bread. Wish I were in the land of the buffalo!" Preuss had recovered completely.

The journal account of the days do not here add up. The notation for 13 May (Frémont, 1845: 271) indicates that they remained at the Mountain Meadows for one day to rest and refresh themselves prior to moving in a northwesterly direction into the margin of the Escalante Desert. Evidently the route crossed the Antelope Range east of present Newcastle and skirted west of the Three Peaks Hills and north to the gap in the Red Hills west of Parowan. The expedition turned east through this gap and camped on the night of 16 May at the north edge of dry Little Salt Lake. Spence (1976: 291) contends that the route was somewhat different: "Passing north of the Antelope Range and east to Iron Springs, he reached present Enoch at the divide between Cedar and Parowan valleys near the southern end of Little Salt Lake." The map by Preuss supports the first described route, not that in Spence.

Preuss (Gudde & Gudde, 1958: 132), still obsessed with food, noted: "When a bookbinder is so down and out that he has to eat his own paste, he is still better off than we are now—he has made his paste of better flour."

On the morning of 17 May the Frémont party left the Spanish Trail, which proceeded eastward across the Markagunt Plateau and on to the east. Frémont and party turned north away from that trail. Unknown to them at the time was the fact that the head of Parowan Valley, in which they had camped, received its water from a drainage later to be named Frémont Wash. That wash would be followed westward by Frémont in his winter expedition of 1854.

The party had been joined some days earlier, after leaving Mountain Meadows, by Joseph Reddeford Walker (1798–1876), guide to Captain Benjamin Louis Eulalie de Bonneville's (1797–1878) 1832 expedition (Irving, 1986), and a company of eight men, who now continued north with Frémont. The Frémont-Walker party moved north along the foot of the Markagunt Plateau (called Wah-satch range or chain by Frémont) to the east, which is replaced northward by the Tushar Mountains along the hingeline of Utah, a geological feature that effectively separates eastern from western Utah. Northward the Wasatch Mountains are the principal feature along the hingeline. "The mountain presented itself to us under the form of several ridges, rising one above the other, rocky, and wooded with pine and cedar; the last ridge covered with snow. Sevier river, flowing northwardly to the lake of the same name, collects its principal waters from this section of the Wah-satch chain. We had now entered a region of great pastoral promise, abounding with fine streams, the rich bunch grass, soil that could produce wheat, and indigenous flax growing as if it had been sown. Consistent with the general character of its bordering mountains, this fertility of soil and vegetation does not extend far into the

Great Basin" (Frémont, 1845: 271). Along this trail, which essentially follows the route of present Interstate 15, they met the Ute Indian chief Walker, whose name source, Mr. Joseph Walker, was present to make the introduction. Frémont and Chief Walker exchanged presents of blankets. The party had also met other Indians, who sold them some beaver tails to eat, much to the satisfaction of Preuss.

Frémont was not, at this time, within the drainage of the Sevier River, which was over the mountain range to the east. His party paralleled its route, however. He was moving along the east margin of the Great Basin. On 23 May the expedition reached the Sevier River, a deep and meandering stream whose banks lacked timber, only driftwood being available along the shore and that apparently in short supply. Immediately north of where it was intersected by the Frémont party the river turns to the west then southwest to Sevier Lake, now a dry saline pan, rarely with a few inches of water that soon evaporates. "After searching in vain for a fordable place, we made little boats (or, rather, rafts) out of bull rushes, and ferried across. These rafts are readily made, and give a good conveyance across a river. The rushes are bound in bundles, and tied hard; the bundles are tied down upon poles, as closely as they can be pressed, and fashioned like a boat, in being broader in the middle and pointed at the ends. The rushes, in being tubular and jointed, are light and strong" (Frémont, 1845: 272). The rafts were fashioned, it seems likely, after those that Frémont had seen in use by Indians on the Snake River the previous autumn. The rafts were rowed back and forth, carrying the effects from the southeast bank to the northeast one.

The river crossing was near the site of present Yuba Dam, where it turns west toward Sevier Lake, at 39°22′19″. "We had here the misfortune to lose one of our people, François Badeau, who had been with me in both expeditions; during which he had always been one of my most faithful and efficient men. He was killed in drawing towards him a gun by the muzzle; the hammer being caught, discharged the gun, driving the ball through his head. We burried him on the banks of the river" (Frémont, 1845: 272). Utah became the permanent resting place of this remarkable man of the Frémont party. It was Badeau, along with Derosier and Dodson, who kept camp on the Weber River while Frémont explored the Great Salt Lake. Following his death and the disappearance of Derosier, only Dodson of the trio remained with the party. The entry for this day by Preuss (Gudde & Gudde, 1958: 132) is short and unsympathetic: "Ferrying across Sevier River in a tuleboat. Badeau shot and killed himself through carelessness."

Badeau's grave was noticed for some years following his death by others passing through the region. It was on the riverbank at the foot of a low ridge near present Yuba Dam. The ridge at the base of which Badeau was buried, at my suggestion, now bears the official designation "Badeau Ridge," published in the 1992 Decision List of The United States Board on Geographic Names.

"Crossing the next day (24 May) a slight ridge along the river, we entered a handsome mountain valley covered with fine grass, and directed our course towards a high snowy peak [Mount Nebo, southernmost peak in the Wasatch Range], at the foot of which lay the Utah lake. . . . At noon we fell in with a party of Utah Indians coming out of the mountain, and in the afternoon encamped on a tributary of the [Utah] lake, which is separated from the waters of the Sevier by very slight dividing grounds. . . . Early the next day we came in sight of the lake; and, as we descended to the broad bottoms of the Spanish fork, three horsemen were seen galloping towards us, who proved to be Utah Indians—scouts from a village, which was encamped near the mouth of the river. . . . We encamped near them, on the Spanish fork, which is one of the principal tributaries to the [Utah] lake" (Frémont, 1845: 273). Later camp was moved because the Indians became troublesome. "Here the principal plants in bloom were two, which were remarkable as affording to the Snake Indians—the one an abundant supply of food, and the other the most useful among the applications which they use for wounds. These were the kooyah plant, growing in fields of extraordinary luxuriance, and *convallaria stellata* [*Smilacina stellata* (L.) Desf.], which, from the experience of Mr. Walker, is the best remedial plant known among those Indians. A few miles below us was another village of Indians, from which we obtained some fish—among them a few salmon trout [the lake phase of *Salmo clarki utah*, now extinct in the lake], which were very much inferior in size to those along the Californian mountains. The season for taking them had not yet arrived; but the Indians were daily expecting them to come up out of the lake" (Frémont, 1845: 273).

This native Utah Lake trout was harvested in huge quantities by Mormon settlers. Aside from heavy utilization by settlers, its demise is attributed to diversion of the spawning streams for irrigation and to pollution of the lake. By the 1930s it was extinct.

Frémont here made an error, probably because of time constraints or other problems connected with his hurried trip homeward, in assuming that Utah Lake was an arm of Great Salt Lake (Figure 4). He could not accommodate in his mind that Utah Lake was fresh and Great Salt Lake saturated with salt. Determination of the boiling point of water might have indicated that the difference in elevation was some 288 feet. Perhaps his thermometer was misplaced (it is in evidence again on 29 May), and the previous calculation of elevation by that method on the Virgin River was in error by a greater margin than the difference noted here. Whatever the reason, no measurement of elevation was taken. Frémont would learn in October 1845, on his third expedition, that Utah Lake is joined to Great Salt Lake by the Jordan River [Frémont's designation was Hughes Creek]. Publication of the error in the 1845 report preserved it for posterity. Other observations were succinct and accurate.

Frémont (1845: 276) noted: "In the eastern part of the Basin, containing Sevier, Utah, and the Great Salt lakes, and the rivers and creeks falling into them, we know there is good soil and good grass, adapted to civilized settlements. In the western part, on Salmon Trout River, and some other streams, the same remark may be made." Most of the Great Basin, if not all of it, was considered to be a portion of Alta (Northern) California, a completely separate issue from that of Oregon country, to which a valid territorial claim by the United States existed, even though it was mainly occupied by the British. And, Frémont had tied the survey of the route to Oregon to that of the Wilkes Expedition, who had surveyed up the Columbia to near The Dalles. The way was open from the border states at the Missouri to the Pacific, and emigrants by the thousands followed the mapped route. Frémont's published reports and maps from the first and second expeditions became a deciding factor for Brigham Young and others of the Mormon hierarchy, who chose to settle in the Great Basin (Frémont, 1887: 415; Egan, 1977: 155).

Utah Lake to St. Louis

Except for closing the gap between Utah Lake and Great Salt Lake, Frémont had passed entirely around the Great Basin, which has no surface connection to the sea. This was a remarkable feat, to which the accomplishment of crossing the Basin would be added the year following. Now he would proceed in the direction of St. Louis and his beloved Jessie. On 27 May the party rode eastward, ascending Spanish Fork Canyon, following a good trail. They camped that evening along one of the tributaries of the Spanish Fork, adjacent to "strata of bituminous limestone [Green River Formation oil shales]" (Frémont, 1845: 277). "In a few miles from this encampment we reached the head of the stream; and crossing, by an open and easy pass [Soldier Summit], the dividing ridge which separates the waters of the Great Basin from those of the Colorado, we reached the head branches of one of its larger tributaries, which, from the decided color of its waters, has received the name of White river" (Frémont, 1845: 278). Back in the Colorado Plateau Province, they followed up the White River and crossed the Avintaquin Ridge, which forms the divide between the Uinta Basin and Price River drainages. The men could see the Uinta Mountains (called by Frémont the Bear River range) from the divide summit. The party descended quickly into the spring-flowering season of the Uinta Basin, along a tributary of the Strawberry River (branch of the Uintah according to Frémont).

On 30 May the route was down the affluent [possibly Avintaquin or Timber canyons] on which the group had camped. Arriving at a place where three streams came together, the men and animals forded the main stream, the Strawberry River, and ascended Red Creek. From that drainage they crossed the intervening highland to the east and camped on the Duchesne River, Duchesne County, Utah. "The water was very clear, the stream not being yet swollen by the melting snows; and we forded it without any difficulty" (Frémont, 1845: 278). Proceeding down the river next day, the camp for the evening was on the left (north or east) bank of the Duchesne. The site of this camp of 31 May was determined as 40°18′53″, 112°18′30″, in the vicinity of modern Duchesne. The longitude reading is in error by approximately two degrees; the site is nearer 110°, not 112°. On 1 June the men and animals left Duchesne fork, and, "after traversing a broken country for about sixteen miles, arrived at noon at another considerable branch, a river of great velocity, to which the trappers have improperly given the name of Lake Fork" (Frémont, 1845: 278). The stream drains from a series of alpine lakes, some miles to the north. "After infinite difficulty, and the delay of a day, we succeeded in getting the stream bridged, and got over with the loss of one of our animals" (Frémont, 1845: 278).

The route was then along the south-facing foot slope of the Uinta Mountains, at right angles to the entrenched streams draining from that range. Snowmelt had raised the steams to dangerous flood level. The tired, hungry, and worn group moved eastward across a broken country, of which the higher parts were rocky and timbered with Utah juniper and two-needle pinyon pine, *Pinus edulis* Engelm., and the lower parts covered with good grass. On 3 June, in the afternoon, the party reached Fort Uinta, a trading post belonging to Mr. Antoine Roubideau [or Robidoux, 1794–1860], on the Uinta River. The stream was nearly as rapid and difficult as the Lake fork, divided into several channels, which were too broad to be bridged. With the aid of guides from the fort, they succeeded, with very great difficulty, in fording the rapid stream, and encamped near the fort, which was situated a short distance above the junction of two branches of the river. Their position was determined as 40°27′44″, 109°56′42″, which agrees with the approximate location of present Whiterocks, Uintah County, Utah.

Frémont made several important plant collections during the journey across the Uinta Basin, despite the difficulties of travel and fording of streams during the preceding days. The plants were, in fact, the first ever for the Uinta Basin. *Gilia stenothrysa* Torr. was taken between the Duchesne River and Lake Fork, and *Senecio multilobatus* Torr. & A. Gray was collected on one of the islands in the Uinta River adjacent to Fort Uinta.

Frémont (1845: 279) described the trading post as "a motley garrison of Canadian and Spanish *engages* and hunters, with the usual number of Indian women." He was able to obtain a small supply of sugar, coffee, dried meat, and a cow, which was a very acceptable change from the *pinoli* on which they had subsisted for some weeks past. He strengthened his party by the addition of Auguste Archambeau [1817–1882], "an excellent voyageur and hunter, belonging to the class of Carson and Godey."

Preuss was pleasantly surprised by the provisions obtainable at the fort: "We had been told that Uintah Fort is always poorly stocked with supplies. Yet day before yesterday we succeeded in purchasing there several pounds of coffee and sugar, a sack of dried meat, toro, some tallow, and best of all, a fat cow. The latter was slaughtered last night, and we had a magnificent breakfast this morning" (Gudde & Gudde, 1958: 135).

On the morning of the 5th Frémont and his men left Fort Uinta, and continued east over a broken country, which provided a rich addition to the botanical collection; specimens of *Eriogonum ovalifolium* Nutt. and *Penstemon fremontii* Torr. & A. Gray were collected during the day. Following a ride of 25 miles, they were again checked by another stream, Ashley Creek, where they were detained by high water until noon of the next day (Frémont, 1845: 279). The camp was in the vicinity of present Vernal, Uintah County, Utah, at 40°28′07″, 109°27′07″. The men and animals forded Ashley Creek on the afternoon of 6 June and traveled 15 miles to a site on the side of Diamond Mountain, where they camped for the last time in Utah. At that site was found excellent and abundant grass of a type that had not previously been encountered. It was a "species of *elymus*, which had a purgative and weakening effect upon the animals" (Frémont, 1845: 279).

The next day, 7 June, the party crossed through small valleys on the broad, parklike summit of Diamond Mountain to a steep, rocky ravine through which they descended to Brown's Hole. The Hole or Park is a broad valley along the Green River through which passes the present Colorado-Utah boundary. Despite the swiftness, breadth, and depth of the Green River (called Colorado by Frémont), the party crossed it without serious difficulty. The men repaired a skin boat purchased a few days earlier at Fort Uinta and, after a delay of a day, reached the opposite banks with much less delay than had been encountered on the streams in the Uinta Basin. Their camp on the east bank was at

40°46′27″, a latitude possible only if they were already in Moffatt County, Colorado. The elevation determination of 5150 feet is possibly at least 200 feet too low. The men surprised some mountain sheep during the day, and the hunters killed several. Greasewood (*Sarcobatus vermiculatis—Frémontia vermicularis* of Frémont's report) and other chenopodiaceous shrubs were noted by John Charles along Vermillion Creek, a tributary of the Green River adjacent to their camp on the east bank. They followed up the drainage of Vermillion Creek on 9 June and camped for the night. The water was brackish and the grass "indifferent." "A few scattered cedar [juniper] trees were the only improvement of the country on the following day [10 June]; and at a little spring of bad water, where we halted to noon, we had not even the shelter of these from the hot rays of the sun," Frémont wrote. "At night we encamped in a fine grove of cottonwood trees on the banks of the Elk Head [actually the Little Snake] river, the principal fork of the Yampah river, commonly called by the trappers the Bear river" (Frémont, 1845: 280).

On the 11th the party continued up the Elk Head River, a considerable stream, 50 to 100 yards wide, handsomely and "continuously wooded with groves of the narrow-leaved cottonwood, (*populus angustifolia*;) with these were thickets of willow and grain du boeuf. The characteristic plant along the river is *F. vermicularis*, which generally covers the bottoms; mingled with this, are saline shrubs and artemisia" (Frémont, 1845: 280). The description could apply to vast stretches of stream bottoms in the montane West. Three antelope were killed in the afternoon, and camp was set up a little below a branch of the river called St. Vrain's fork. The group left the river on 12 June and turned east across open country. Ahead of them could be seen the high mountains of the Continental Divide, and the face of the country began to improve. The river bottoms and the hills were covered with grass, and among the usual varied flora of the mountain region, the blue flowers of a *Lupinus* sometimes stained the hillsides. In the course of the morning buffalo were seen for the first time that year, and the men "welcomed the appearance of two old bulls with as much joy as if they had been messengers from home; and when we descended to noon on St. Vrain's fork [Battle Creek], an affluent of Green river, the hunters brought in mountain sheep and the meat of two fat bulls" (Frémont, 1845: 281). Camp for the night was almost luxurious, situated among aspen adjacent to a spring of cold water. The hunters killed two buffalo cows near the camp, elk and antelope were seen, and herds of buffalo kicked up dust nearby. It was a land of plenty, but potentially dangerous due to its use by Indians as both hunting and war grounds. Preuss could now live in comfort again; there was plenty of food, including "marrow-bones, tongue, etc."

On 13 June the group proceeded to the east and crossed a dividing ridge, from the summit of which they could see a drainage extending eastward—Pullam's fork, a tributary of the Platte River. "Issuing from the pines in the afternoon," Frémont wrote, "we saw spread out before us the valley of the Platte, with the pass of the Medicine Butte beyond, and some of the Sweet Water mountains; but a smoky haziness in the air entirely obscured the Wind River chain" (Frémont, 1845: 281). Their position was then about two degrees (circa 138 miles) from South Pass, and the party could have easily proceeded on a direct route toward home. Southward were the parks of the Colorado Rockies, however, and they beckoned Frémont; he might not have this opportunity again. They would move to the south into the parks and peaks of the Colorado Rockies. For now the route continued in an easterly direction, and camp was again in a grove of trees. "The country had now become very beautiful—rich in water, grass, and game; and to these were added the charm of scenery and pleasant weather" (Frémont, 1845: 282). Their route on the 14th was along the foot of a range of mountains, where they crossed numerous streams. "These were variously wooded with groves of aspen and cottonwood, with willow, cherry, and other shrubby trees. Buffalo, antelope, and elk, were frequent during the day; and in their abundance, the latter sometimes reminded us slightly of the Sacramento valley" (Frémont, 1845: 282). The men and animals forded a creek called Potter's fork and camped on another, which Frémont for obvious reasons called Beaver Dam. Their route crossed the Continental Divide in the Sierra Madre range, and the party descended to the valley of the North Platte in Carbon County, Wyoming (Jackson & Spence, 1970: 711).

On the morning of 14 June the men gave chase to a grizzly bear. One of the men, Fuentes, attempted to lasso the animal, but the loop slipped off, and the bear escaped into the dense thickets of the creek (Frémont, 1845: 282). It is probably fortunate, even providential, that the lasso fell free. The minds of men, sometimes, seem to escape from the reality of how to let go of such an animal once caught. The choices are few—kill the bear or give it the lasso! The Platte River was encountered during the afternoon (Jackson County, Colorado). "It was apparently deep, with a moderate current, and wooded with groves of large willow" (Frémont, 1845: 282). The entourage ascended the valley of the Platte, which narrowed as they proceeded. Upon passing through a narrows the party entered "New Park [North Park]—a beautiful circular valley of thirty miles diameter, walled in all round with snowy mountains, rich with water and with grass, fringed with pine on the mountain sides below the snow line, and a paradise to all grazing animals" (Frémont, 1845: 282). Walden, Colorado, occupies the center of this valley.

On the morning of 16 June the group traveled south along the main branch of the Platte, crossing numerous smaller affluents. By evening the men and animals were in the south end of the park, where the position of the camp was determined as 40°33′22″. On the 17th a path was discovered leading to a pass back over the Continental Divide to the south. "The trail led among the aspens, through open grounds, richly covered with grass, and carried us over an elevation of about 9,000 feet above the level of the sea" (Frémont, 1845: 283). The trail descended from the pass into the drainage of the Grand (now Colorado) River. Frémont had a large herd of horses, and they must have been tempting to the Indians. Following a long day's journey and being apprehensive of Indian attack, camp was on a small creek (Muddy Creek). Frémont referred to this area as "Old [Middle] Park" and noted that "it is more or less broken into hills, and surrounded by the high mountains, timbered on the lower parts with quaking asp and pines" (Frémont, 1845: 283). On the morning of 18 June they met a party of Arapahos in search of game and roots. The Indians were not especially friendly, and Frémont quickly moved his camp into a defensive position along the bottoms of the Grand River. The camp was immediately confronted by about 200 Indians, "mounted, painted, and armed for war. We planted the American flag between us; and a short parley ended in a truce, with something more than the usual amount of presents" (Frémont, 1845: 283). A compromise was worked out, and next morning Frémont and his group descended the river for about eight miles, near where the Grand River issues from the Park, near Gore Canyon, in the vicinity of Kremmling, Grand County, Colorado (Jackson & Spence, 1970: 714). The baggage was ferried to the south side, with men and animals crossing by swimming, and the party followed up a tributary stream about eight miles and camped. The route continued up the stream (Blue) during 20 June, through many foaming tributaries, and camp was set in an aspen grove. On the 21st the men had a delightful ride on a good trail through fragrant pines, among which they saw numerous buffalo. The hunters brought the meat of seven buffalo cows into camp. Continuing upward in the afternoon, the men followed the trail into an open place among pines, where they camped and soon fortified. "The mountains exhibit their usual varied growth of flowers, and at this place I noticed, among others, *thermopsis montana*, whose bright yellow color makes it a showy plant. This has been a characteristic in many parts of the country since reaching the Uintah waters. With fields of iris were *aquilegia caerulea*, violets, esparcette [likely *Oxytropis*], and strawberries" (Frémont, 1845: 285).

The expedition encountered a party of trappers, who wished to join the larger Frémont group for safety. Indians arrived soon afterward to encourage Frémont and the trappers to join them in an attack on the Ute Indians, who were camped in South Park, south of mountains over which Frémont was to travel. The Indians were to attack by another pass than the one the party was entering, and Carson told them that the party with Frémont was too far along the trail to turn back and ally with them. The Indians returned, apparently satisfied with the explanation. The camp was above 10,000 feet elevation, "and still the pine forest continued, and grass was good." John Charles and his group crossed the divide after a short ride on the morning of 22 June. Camp was established beyond the pass at 39°20′24″, near present Hoosier Pass, Summit County, Colorado. Their descent into South Park the next day, 23 June, was along a small drainage. The region was beautiful and parklike, with level meadows, pines, and aspens. The peacefulness was not long-lasting, though, for the Frémont party met still another party of Indians, who proved to be Ute women moving away from their village, which was under attack by the Arapahos on the other side of the ridge. The better part of valor is to know when to get out of a place, and they bypassed the area where fighting was under way, marched for 15 miles, and camped in a site that was soon fortified. The men could see Pikes Peak plainly in the afternoon. On 24 June they moved southeasterly for 10 miles and crossed a ridge, leaving South Park behind. The new terrain proved to be difficult, and during the day their trek, over ridges and through drainages, was hard and wearing. "Aspens and pines were the prevailing timber; on the creeks, oak was frequent; but the narrow-leaved cottonwood, (*populus angustifolia*,) of unusually large size, and seven or eight feet in diameter, was the principal tree" (Frémont, 1845: 287).

The route was through rough but botanically interesting country until the evening of 27 June, when the mountains were finally left behind. On the morning of 28 June camp was made at the foot of the mountains on a tributary of the Arkansas River in the vicinity of present Canon City, Colorado. In the afternoon the men and animals descended the stream, along the bottoms, "which were densely wooded with oak, and in the evening encamped near the main river." They continued on 29 June, and after meeting a party of Arapahos, arrived before sunset at Pueblo, 13 months to the day following their departure from Kansas.

The men and animals moved rapidly down the valley of the Arkansas River on 30 June, and on 1 July they arrived at Bent's Fort, east of present La Junta, Otero County, Colorado. Carson, Walker, and two others of the party left Frémont at Bent's Fort; the men all lived nearby. Kit Carson left on 4 July for Taos (Quaife, 1935: 87). Frémont and the reduced party proceeded some 20 miles on 5 July, meeting on the way a large number of Sioux and Cheyenne Indians returning from a battle with the Delaware Indians. John Charles and men left the Arkansas on 6 July and moved northeasterly toward the Kansas. On the evening of the eighth the diminished party of men were camped on the Smoky Hill Fork of the Kansas River, probably in Cheyenne County, Colorado, and on the day following moved down the Smoky Hill Fork, which became wooded with occasional groves of cottonwood. On 10 July they were again among buffalo and stopped to provision themselves with meat.

"A few days afterwards, we encamped [13 July 1844, Logan County, Kansas], in a pleasant evening, on a high river prairie, the stream being less than a hundred yards broad. During the night we had a succession of thunder storms, with heavy and continuous rain, and towards morning the water suddenly burst over the banks, flooding the bottoms, and becoming a large river, five or six hundred yards in breadth. The darkness of the night and incessant rain had concealed from the guard the rise of the water; and the river broke into the camp so suddenly, that the baggage was instantly covered, and all our perishable collections almost entirely ruined, and the hard labor of many months destroyed in a moment" (Frémont, 1845: 289).

Preuss (Gudde & Gudde, 1958: 139) recorded: "The herbarium, to be sure, is in a deplorable condition. The plants are beginning to sprout again. To dry the herbarium and everything else we are having a day of rest today, a Sunday." Almost within touch of civilization and home, this disaster amounted to a tragedy of the worst kind. Botanists since have mourned the damage done to the specimens taken at such cost and destroyed or damaged so quickly.

The expedition moved again eastward on 17 July, encountering a village of Pawnee Indians on the way. Frémont anticipated that the Indians would be friendly, but they proved to be rude and insolent. After some difficulty Frémont's party extricated themselves from the Indians and moved some 15 miles beyond, where they stopped and camped. "The country through which we had been traveling since leaving the Arkansas river, for a distance of 260 miles, presented to the eye only a succession of far-stretching green prairies, covered with the unbroken verdure of the buffalo grass, and sparingly wooded along the streams with straggling trees and occasional groves of cottonwood; but here the country began perceptibly to change its character, becoming a more fertile, wooded, and beautiful region, covered with a profusion of grasses, and watered with innumerable little streams, which were wooded with oak, large elms, and the usual varieties of timber common to the lower course of the Kansas river" (Frémont, 1845: 289). As they continued farther eastward, the country changed again. "The beautiful sward of the buffalo grass, which is regarded as the best and most nutritious found on the prairies, appeared now only in patches, being replaced by a longer and coarser grass, which covered the face of the country luxuriantly. The difference in the character of the grasses became suddenly evident as the weakened condition of our animals, which began sensibly to fail as soon as we quitted the buffalo grass" (Frémont, 1845: 289). At this point, almost at the close of an incredibly dangerous and difficult journey, Alexis Ayot was shot through the leg accidentally and crippled for life.

The party abandoned the course of the Kansas River and moved east to the wagon road from Santa Fe to Independence. On the last day of July the men camped again in the little town of Kansas on the banks of the Missouri. There ended the expedition. No one had been ill during all of the 14 months of the journey, but one had been seriously injured and two of the party had been killed.

On 1 August Frémont and party were aboard a steamboat gliding down the Missouri. The animals had been placed on pasture in anticipation of the expedition of 1845. Frémont reached St. Louis on 6 August 1844, and the 21-year-old Jessie was awaiting him, following an absence that must have seemed like an eternity. There the party finally disbanded, most of them living in the area. Andreas Fuentes remained in St. Louis, and Pablo Hernandez was placed with the Benton family. The Chinook Indian from the Dalles accompanied Frémont to Washington, prior to attending school to learn to read and write; arrangements were finally made to return him to the Columbia.

The report was submitted to Colonel J. J. Abert, chief of the Corps of Topographical Engineers, on 31 March 1845.

CHAPTER IV

THIRD EXPEDITION—1845–47

The results of the first and second expeditions became available almost immediately in Senate publications. However, because of the circumstances dealing with the return of Frémont to face a court-martial and his subsequent resignation from the Army, the summary account of the third expedition was published initially as a *Geographical Memoir* (Frémont, 1848). That publication was in support of a map of Oregon and California, and unlike the reports of the two earlier expeditions, is in a geographical, not chronological, format. A chronology of sorts is included within the discussions of the geographical subdivisions, but it is disconnected and lacks the crispness of the earlier reports. In his *Memoirs* Frémont (1887) relied on the *Geographical Memoir* written almost three decades earlier, on unpublished notes, on what he considered as other relevant material, and on his memory. He was, in part, justifying his not always justifiable role in history. The events were placed back into chronological sequence in the *Memoirs*. The itinerary as recorded in the *Memoirs* is followed herein, but the memoirs of both 1848 and 1887 form the basis of the account.

John Charles had been away for more than 14 months on the second expedition, and Jessie worried about his safe return. She had been expecting him since February of 1844 and had placed a lighted candle in the window each night. By August she was deeply concerned. During his absence his mentor, Joseph Nicolas Nicollet, had died (September 1843), as had his good friend Ferdinand Hassler (November 1843).

Frémont did not tarry long in St. Louis. Upon his arrival in Washington, he had reported to General Winfield Scott and called upon the Secretary of War, Mr. Wilkins. Charles Preuss, now the owner of a comfortable home purchased, it is suspected, with the money earned on the long journey of 1843–44, "had been assigned the congenial labor of making up the maps" (Frémont, 1887: 413). Astronomical observations taken on the expedition were computed with the aid of Joseph C. Hubbard, who assisted John Charles also in additional trials of the sextant. Frémont, again aided by Jessie, worked on the report of the expedition in a small wooden house, not far removed from their living quarters in Washington City. "There was but brief time in which to do this writing. In the evenings the note-books were consulted, and the work thought out and prepared for the morning. Jacob kept up the camp habit and very early brought me coffee; and punctually at nine o'clock Mrs. Frémont joined me at the workshop" (Frémont, 1887: 414). Following completion of the report of the second expedition Frémont was fully occupied with preparations for the third.

With the able support and help of the influential father-in-law, Thomas Hart Benton, and wife, Jessie, and with his successful completion of two laborious expeditions, Frémont had become famous. As an established professional he was free to plan, with the cooperation of the Corps of Topographical Engineers, his own expeditions (Eisenhower, 1989: 210). His prestige and good luck had allowed him to attract very able men to the expeditions, men who practically guaranteed his success.

Much of the area contemplated for inclusion in the survey was in Mexican territory. Spence and Jackson (1973a: xxii) note that the written orders of Frémont do not mention that he was to enter California, i.e., Mexican territory. He was directed to: "'strike the Arkansas as soon as practicable, survey the Red River without our boundary line, noting particularly the navigable properties of each,' and 'determine as near as practicable the points at which the boundary line of the U.S. and the 100th degree of longitude west of Greenwich strikes the Arkansas, and the Red River.'" Essentially, he was to direct the efforts of the expedition in 1845 to the region around Bent's Fort. That he conceived a grander expedition is evinced by his "Notice to the Reader," which had prefaced the one-volume edition of his first and second reports: "The third expedition, now commencing, will be directed to that section of the Rocky mountains which gives rise to the Arkansas, the Rio Grande del Norte, and the Rio Colorado of California; and will extend west and southwest of that section, so as to examine the country towards the Pacific Ocean, ascertain the lines of communication between the mountains and the ocean in that latitude, and complete the examination of the Great Salt Lake and of the interesting region which embosoms it" (Frémont, 1845: 3). "And in arranging this expedition, the eventualities of war were taken into consideration" (Frémont, 1887: 422). Spence and Jackson (1973a: xxii) point out that there were many hints that he had broader and confidential orders to proceed beyond the headwaters of the Arkansas.

Frémont (1887: 422) indicates long after the fact the concern of the United States over possession of California should war with Mexico take place. Great Britain was apparently still in contention with the United States over Oregon and might place a claim on portions of California in any conflict between the States and Mexico. John Charles stated, also after the fact, that a plan was worked out whereby a Marine lieutenant would be sent to find him and his party should war be forthcoming. He would then move to tie California to the United States.

Although Frémont's *Memoirs* give no complete roster of those who joined him on this expedition, Spence and Jackson give a list (1973a: 487–88). I will not repeat the list of participants, but include biographical information for those who were named in the *Memoirs*. These men were thrust into events that gave many prominent roles in history.

Accompanied by Jacob and William Chinook (the Indian from The Dalles), John Charles left Jessie in Washington City with her mother, who was ill, and proceeded westward to initiate the third expedition. Many men from previous journeys again joined him. In the party were Alex Godey, twelve Delaware Indian hunters (two, James Swanok or Swanuck and James Sagundai, were chiefs), Edward M. Kern (1823–1863, topographer replacing Charles Preuss), two army Lieutenants (James William Abert, 1820–1897, and William Guy Peck), James McDowell (nephew of Mrs. Benton), and Theodore Talbot. Joseph Walker again joined the party, later, along the upper White River in western Colorado. Names of some of the other Delaware Indians include: James Connor, Delaware Charley, Wetowaka, Crane, Solomon Everett, Bob Skirkett, Richard Brown, and Jim

Simmonds (Carter, 1968: 104). Old Bill Williams accompanied the party as far as the Great Salt Lake desert (Carter, 1968: 100).

The huge entourage of men, riding and draught animals, and cattle reached Bent's Fort, their "real point of departure," on the Arkansas River in Colorado, on 2 August 1845. A messenger was sent to Kit Carson, who was working at establishing a stock farm on the Cimarron River, tributary of the Arkansas. Carson and his partner Richard L. Owens (or Owings, 1812–1902) must not have been too enthralled with their enterprise since, upon hearing that John Charles was again in the vicinity, they sold their holdings at once and joined him. Of Godey, Carson, and Owens, Frémont noted: "The three, under Napoleon, might have become Marshals, chosen as he chose men" (Frémont, 1887: 427). Frémont and his party left Bent's Fort on 16 August 1845, a "party of sixty; mostly experienced and self-reliant men, equal to any emergency likely to occur and willing to meet it" (see Figure 5 for their westward route). The group did not include the Lieutenants Abert and Peck, who, along with Thomas Fitzpatrick had parted to explore and map along the Arkansas River prior to returning east. Perhaps they fulfilled the stipulations of Frémont's orders to explore and map that region. In keeping with the example set by Frémont prior to arrival at Bent's Fort, Abert collected plants also. Specimens taken by Abert following his departure from Frémont are also in the herbarium at The New York Botanical Garden.

By 20 August the men with Frémont were at the mouth of Fountain Creek near Pueblo, Pueblo County, Colorado. There John Charles set up a "portable transit," with which he determined their position as 38°15′18″, 104°42′41″. On 26 August, camp was made at the mouth of "Great Canyon" (Royal Gorge, near Canon City, Frémont County, Colorado). Their camp of 2 September was near the head of the Arkansas (near the continental divide), in Mexican territory. Position of the camp was determined as 39°20′38″, 106°27′15″, in or near Lake County, Colorado. The weather was delightful and the country beautiful. Frémont described the "fresh and green, aspen groves and pine woods" the "clear rushing water," and "cool streams sparkling over rocky beds" (Frémont, 1887: 428). Passing the night of the 4th of September on Piney River, Eagle County, Colorado, an affluent of Grand River, of the Colorado of the Gulf of California, they encamped the next day on the same river at "Williams Fishery," at latitude 39°39′12″, longitude 106°44′21″. They caught there "a singular fish, which was called buffalo-fish from a hump on the back, rising straight up immediately behind the head" [probably the razor-back sucker, *Xyrauchen texanus* (Abbott), according to Dennis Shiozawa, personal communication] (Frémont, 1887: 428).

Frémont does not describe the next portion of his journey, but Carson did: "Then to head of White River [12 September, Rio Blanco County, Colorado], down it to near where it empties into Green River [near present Ouray, Uintah County, Utah, on 25 September]. Crossed Green River and went on to the Winty [Uinta River, actually the Duchesne], up it to near where it comes out of the mountain [Lake Fork on 27 September and Duchesne Fork on 29 September, both in Duchesne County, Utah], left it, crossed the mountain [by a pass near the head of Wolf Creek, Wasatch County, Utah], and on to Provost Fork [Provo River, Wasatch County, Utah]. . . . We took down Provost to the

Little Utah Lake [Utah Lake, Utah County, Utah], which empties into the Great Salt Lake, followed its outlet to near the Great Salt Lake" (Carter, 1968: 96).

The camp on 2 October was on a "fork of the Provost," probably Center Creek, east of present Heber, Wasatch County, Utah. Latitude and longitude determinations were made at various positions on the Provo River on both 4 and 6 October. By 10 October the men and animals were at Utah Lake, probably at the mouth of American Fork Creek (called Pinquam Creek by Frémont), Utah County, Utah. On 12 October the party was at the outlet of Utah Lake, at the beginning of Hughes Creek, now the Jordan River. On 13 October the men, animals, and baggage arrived at the south margin of the Great Salt Lake, near the mouth of the Jordan River, Salt Lake County, Utah. There Frémont made his camp, "some distance south of our former encampment [of September 1843, which had been along the lower Weber River, west of present Ogden, Weber County, Utah]." The site of the encampment near the shore of the Great Salt Lake was made the second principal station for longitude. Measurements taken at the station indicated a longitude of 112°06′08″ (slightly west of the Salt Lake City center, which would be established in less than two years by Brigham Young and his band of Mormon pioneers, who used the report and map of the second expedition as a prime basis for settling in Utah), and a latitude of 40°45′53″. The men stayed in the area for two weeks, exploring the valley and Great Salt Lake, including a trip to Antelope Island. "We could find in it [the lake] no fish, or animal life of any kind, the larvae which were accumulated in beds on the shore being found to belong to winged insects [probably the brine fly]. On the contrary, the upper lake—the Timpanogos [Utah]—which discharges into this by a stream [Jordan River] about thirty-five miles long, is fresh water, and affords large trout and other fish in great numbers" (Frémont, 1887: 430). Frémont had here corrected his error of the previous year, when he had concluded that Utah Lake was an arm of the Great Salt Lake, resulting in later contention between Frémont and Brigham Young (Frémont, 1887: 415).

Frémont described the nature of the land around the lake and noted that the weather was mild during the first part of October. "On the 15th it began to rain in occasional showers which whitened with snow the tops of the mountains on the southeast side of the lake valley. Flowers were in bloom during all the month. About the 18th, when we visited the large island [Antelope] in the south of the lake, *helianthus*, several species of *aster*, *erodium cicutarium*, and several other plants were in fresh and full bloom; the grass of the second growth was coming up finely, and vegetation generally betokened the lengthened summer of the climate" (Frémont, 1887: 431). Rain continued throughout 16–18 October, after which the weather settled into a fine Indian summer, terminated by more rain at the month's end. On 23 October the camp moved to a spring in one of the valleys opening southward from the lake, and on 25 October the camp was moved to another valley near the southwestern shore of Great Salt Lake, about fifty miles from the longitude station creek. The locality of this third camp was determined as 40°38′17″, 113°05′09″, which is south of Clive, on the west side of the Cedar Mountains, Tooele County, Utah. The route westward was across the grain of the Great Basin, with its north-south trending mountain ranges separated by broad valleys. Each range presents high peaks and low passes. Upon attaining the summit in a forest of juniper and pinyon the route descends monotonously into another broad valley clothed with sagebrush and other shrubs. Crossing Nevada, even today, one is struck with the succession of rugged mountains and broad valleys, all subtly and charmingly beautiful. On horseback the trip must have seemed both monotonous and endless. Neither Joseph Walker nor Kit Carson knew anything of the route immediately ahead of them.

"Nearly upon the line of our intended travel, and at the further edge of the desert, apparently fifty to sixty miles away, was a peak-shaped mountain [Pilot Peak]. This looked to me to be fertile, and it seemed safe to make an attempt to reach it" (Frémont, 1887: 432). Separating them from Pilot Peak was the Great Salt Lake desert, a stretch of dry, saline pans marked here and there with shallow pools of salt water and areas of mud, which would try the minds and souls of this and later groups who would pass through it. "I arranged that Carson, [Auguste] Archambeau, and [Lucien] Maxwell [and Basil Lajuenesse, fide Quaife, 1935: 89] should set out at night, taking with them a man having charge of a pack-mule with water and provisions, and make for the mountain. I to follow with the party the next day and make one camp out into the desert. They to make a signal by smoke in case water should be found. The next afternoon, when the sun was yet two hours high, with the animals rested and well watered, I started out on the plain. As we advanced this was found destitute of any vegetation except sage-bushes [likely *Allenrolfea*, *Atriplex*, and other chenopodiaceous species], and absolutely bare and smooth as if water had been standing upon it." Then he added, "Sometime before morning I made camp in the sage-brush, lighting fires to signal Carson's Party. Before daybreak Archambeau rode in; the jingling of his spurs a welcome sound indicating as it did that he brought good tidings. They had found at the peak pure water and grass, and wood abundant. The gearing up was quickly done and in the afternoon we reached the foot of the mountain, where a cheerful little stream broke out and lost itself in the valley. The animals were quickly turned loose, there being no risk of their straying from the grass and water. To the friendly mountain I gave the name of Pilot Peak" (Frémont, 1887: 433). Position of the peak was determined as 41°00′28″, 114°11′09″, in present Elko County, Nevada.

Frémont notes that the route later became known as the Hastings Cutoff, named for Lansford Warren Hastings, who encouraged emigrant parties to follow Frémont's trail. Among them was the ill-fated Donner Party, only a year behind Frémont. The salt flats of the Great Salt Lake desert would be a dismaying, discouraging, and practically impossible barrier to the pioneer parties that would follow him. It would become a trail of tears, sorrow, hardship, and woe, littered with discarded supplies and equipment and carcasses of dead livestock. The crossing was little more than routine for the Frémont party, consisting as it did mainly of young men mounted on horses or mules, with their baggage packed on animals, not carried in heavy wheeled wagons or carts.

While John Charles and his men were struggling to cross the salt flats of western Utah events were transpiring in far away Washington City that would change the course of the expedition and the history of the nation. In late October 1845 President Polk had conferred with Senator Benton regarding the extension of United States law to Oregon and the possibility of California coming into the Union. As President Polk understood the situation, Britain was threatening the United States's position along the Pacific Coast, and he confided that he had sent instructions to Consul Larkin and others in California. On the very day that Frémont and his men rested at Pilot Peak, President Polk had summoned First Lieutenant Archibald H. Gillespie, U.S. Marine Corps, to visit him at the White House. Some days earlier Gillespie had been designated to carry dispatches to Consul Larkin, but now he was appointed "special agent" and would carry a package from Senator Benton to John Charles. Eisenhower (1989: 43) notes that "Gillespie left the White House convinced that his real mission was to help Frémont encourage the Californios to rise up against the Mexican government." The die was cast; the conspiracy that would involve John Charles and his men would serve to entrap them in a situation too grand for them to understand.

The group rested at Pilot Peak for a day and on 1 November they resumed their journey. That night the camp was at a spring whose position was determined as 40°43′49″, 114°26′22″, also in Elko County, Nevada. On 2 November they arrived at yet another spring, now Mound Spring, which Frémont named Whitton, honoring "one of my men who discovered it" (Frémont, 1887: 433). Camping places determined the course of their route. Men would be sent out in the morning searching for a place that offered water and sufficient grass along the line of march. On 8 November camp was made on a stream at 40°17′16″, 115°46′00″, which Frémont named Crane's Branch (possibly Huntington Creek, Elko County, Nevada) after one of his Delaware hunters, and later determined to be affluent to the Humboldt River, also named by John Charles, after Baron Alexander von Humboldt (1769–1859). Winter was imminent, and wishing to get the most out of the short time available to them, Frémont again divided the party. One party, under Edward Kern (Carson says Theodore Talbot was in charge) and guided by Joseph Walker, was to survey the Humboldt River prior to proceeding to Walker Lake where the two parties were to be reunited. The party with Kern and Talbot had the greatest number of animals with it, there being water and grass along the Humboldt. The valley of the Humboldt also provided a low- elevation route westward toward Walker Lake.

A subsidiary reason for division of the parties is apparent in the size of the horse and mule herd, both those being ridden and those in reserve. Any cattle still being driven along to be used as food would add to the assemblage. Food for them would always be a consideration. By dividing the party the need for such a large amount of fodder at each camp site would be reduced.

Frémont and 10 men, including Carson and some of the Delawares, moved directly southwestward across the Basin. According to Spence and Jackson (1973a: 45): "After dividing his party, he led his own detachment south and west. Passing south of Franklin Lake, he went into Ruby Valley and across the Humboldt [Ruby] Mountains, probably by Harrison Pass. Proceeding south over tortuous ground, he went through Ruby Pass into Diamond Valley and camped on 11 Nov. at Connor Spring, named after one of his Delawares, James Connor. Continuing a southwest course, south of present Eureka, Nevada, he skirted the Monitor Range and crossed the Toquima Range into Big Smoky Valley. Following along the east side of the Toyabe Mountains, he rounded them at the southern end and proceeded to the east shore of Walker Lake [Mineral County, Nevada]."

On 16 November 1845, while the two arms of the expedition traveled their separate ways across the ranges and valleys of Nevada, messenger Gillespie began his journey from New York to California. Eisenhower (1989:44) writes: "Gillespie was an ambitious man. Just how ambitious would be revealed at the end of his journey." Frémont and his men would move forward to a destiny not of their planning.

Somewhere west of Crane's Branch, camp was set up at a spring, which Frémont named for the Delaware Chief Sagundai. There they encountered an ancient Indian woman, apparently alone and starving, to whom meat and other supplies was given. Other Indians would not be treated so kindly. "On the 24th we encamped at our rendezvous on the [Walker] lake where beds of rushes made good pasturage for our animals. Three days afterward the main party arrived. The men and animals of both parties were all in good health, and neither had met with serious accident. But the scarcity of game had made itself felt, and we were now all nearly out of provisions. It was now almost midwinter [still autumn by calendar], and the open weather could not be expected to last" (Frémont, 1887: 439). And, "I was in the neighborhood of the passage which I had forced across it [the Sierra Nevada] a year before, and I had it on my mind. Heavy snows might be daily expected to block up the passes, and I considered that in this event it would be hopeless to attempt a crossing with the material of the whole party. I therefore decided again to divide it, sending the main body under Kern and Talbot to continue southward along the lake line and pass around the Point of the California Mountain into the head of the San Joaquin valley." Walker, who was now on familiar ground, was to serve again as guide, with the meeting place in the valley of Lake Fork, a tributary of Tulare Lake, agreed upon. Frémont must have considered that his arrival at Sutter's with a small contingent of men would not create any serious objection from the Mexicans. The ultimate arrival of the other approximately 45 heavily armed members of the expedition would cause them to ask questions. John Charles must have taken that into account in the division of the party.

The parties at Walker Lake were near the west side of the Great Basin, having traversed its grain and perceived its general nature and structure. Frémont described the Great Basin in the 1848 *Memoir*: "East of the Sierra Nevada, and between it and the Rocky Mountains, is that anomalous feature of our continent, the Great Basin, the existence of which was advanced as a theory after the second expedition, and is now established as a geographical fact. It is a singular feature: a basin of some five hundred miles diameter every way, between four and five thousand feet above the level of the sea, shut in all around by mountains, with its own system of lakes and rivers, and having no connexion whatever with the sea. Partly arid and sparsely inhabited, the general character of the Great Basin is that of desert, but with great exceptions, there being many parts of it very fit for the residence of a civilized people; and of these parts, the Mormons have lately established themselves in one of the largest and best." And, "The interior mountains conform to the law which governs the course of the Rocky mountains, and of the Sierra Nevada, ranging nearly north and south, and present a very uniform character of abruptness, rising suddenly from a narrow base of ten to twenty miles, and attaining an elevation of two to five thousand feet above the level of the country. They are grassy and wooded, showing snow on their summit peaks during the greater part of the year, and affording small streams of water from five to fifty feet wide, which lose themselves, some in lakes, some in the dry plains, and some in the belt of alluvial soil at the base; for these mountains have very uniformly this belt of alluvion, the wash and abrasion of their sides, rich in excellent grass, fertile, and light and loose enough to absorb small streams" (Frémont, 1848: 7, 8). A better summary description of the Great Basin portion of the Basin and Range Province is difficult to find almost a century and a half after it was written.

With a group of 15, including once again several Delawares, Frémont would leave the Great Basin and cross the Sierra Nevada to Sutter's Fort to refit and, with abundant supplies, relieve the larger portion of his outfit southward. Frémont headed for the Truckee River, which he had called Salmon-Trout river the previous year. He was at the river by 1 December and at its head on 4 December. "Our effort had been to reach the pass before a heavy fall of snow, and we had succeeded. All night we watched the sky, ready to attempt the passage with the first indication of falling snow; but the sky continued clear. On our way up, the fine weather which we had left at the foot of the mountains continued to favor us, and when we reached the pass the only snow showing was on the peaks of the mountains" (Frémont, 1887: 439). Frémont now crossed in a few days the range of mountains that had taken them weeks to pass through a year earlier. Such are the vagaries of climate that the Donner Party did not have such luck, were snowed in, and resorted to cannibalism in the winter of 1846–47. The locality of the pass (Truckee, later Donner, Pass) was determined as 39°17′12″, 120°15′20″.

At the pass, the small party with John Charles moved away from the trail leading into Bear River, the preferred route of later settlers. The route the next day, 6 December, was over good terrain. Gaining a broad leading ridge they traveled through the silence of a pine forest where many of the trees were of great height and uncommon size. "The tall red columns standing closely on the clear ground, filtered, flickering sunshine from their summits far overhead, gave the dim religious light of cathedral aisles, opening out on every side, one after the other, as we advanced." Later, in early spring, these same grounds are covered with a "blue carpet of forget-me-nots. The pines of the European forests would hide their diminished heads amidst these great columns of the Sierra. A species of cedar (*Thuya gigantea*) [*Calocedrus decurrens*, the incense cedar] occurred often of extraordinary bulk and height. *Pinus Lambertiani* was one of the most frequent trees, distinguished among cone-bearing tribes by the length of its cones, which are sometimes sixteen or eighteen inches long. The Indians eat the inner part of the burr," and Frémont noticed large heaps of them where they had been collected (Frémont, 1887: 440). The beauty of the scene was likely enhanced by poetic Jessie.

Frémont continued: "Leaving the higher ridges we gained the smoother spurs and descended about 4000 feet, the face of the country rapidly changing as we went down. The country became low and rolling; pines began to disappear, and varieties of oak, principally an evergreen resembling live oak, became the predominating forest growth. The oaks bear great quantities of acorns, which are the principal food of all the wild Indians; it is their bread-fruit tree." And, "The sweetest and best acorns, somewhat resembling Italian chestnuts in taste, are obtained from a large tree belonging to the division of white oaks, distinguished by the length of its acorn, which is commonly an inch and a half and sometimes two inches. This long acorn characterizes the tree, which is a new species and is accordingly specified by Dr. Torrey as *Quercus longiglanda* (Torr. and Frém.)—long-acorn oak [*Q. lobata* Nee, the valley oak]. This tree is very abundant and generally forms the groves on the bottom-lands of the streams; standing apart with a green undergrowth of grass which gives the appearance of cultivated parks. It is a noble forest tree, sixty to eighty feet high with a summit of wide-spreading branches, and frequently attains a diameter of six feet; the largest that we measured reached eleven feet. The evergreen oaks generally have a low growth with long branches and spreading tops." The citation of *Quercus longiglanda* noted above is quoted from the 1887 *Memoirs*, where it was taken out of context from the 1848 *Memoir*. The 1848 citation, included below, is important from a nomenclatural point of view; it is the place of official publication for the name *Quercus longiglanda*.

On 8 December they camped on a stream called Hamilton's Creek (named for Aaron Hamilton, one of the voyageurs of the expedition) at an elevation of 500 feet above the sea. The men and animals had entered a springlike region teeming with fresh grass and flowers. They camped early and took their time, spending about four days to reach the valley. On the ninth the group reached Grimes Rancho on the "*Rio de los Americanos*," near Sutter's Fort, a place last seen by them little more than a year and a half earlier. "Captain Sutter received me with the same friendly hospitality which had been so delightful to us the year before. I found that our previous visit had created some excitement among the Mexican authorities. But to their inquiries he had explained that I had been engaged in a geographical survey of the interior and had been driven to force my way through the snow of the mountains simply to obtain a refuge and food where I knew it could be had at his place, which was by common report known to me" (Frémont, 1887: 441).

Frémont stayed in the vicinity of Sutter's only a few days to obtain horses, cattle, and various other supplies prior to departing southward on 14 December. The party, now consisting of 16—one Pablo, possibly a vaquero, had been added at Sutter's—moved southeasterly toward the Cosumne River and camped that night about eight miles above the "junction of the Cosumne with the Mokelumne River, which a few miles below enters a deep slough in the tide-water of the San Joaquin delta" (Frémont, 1887: 442; 1848: 16). The route continued along ground familiar from the previous year, but this time the streams were low, and fording was easy. Leaving the Mokelumne River on 16 December, the Frémont party traveled about 20 miles through "open woods of white oak, crossing in the way several stream-beds, among them the Calaveras Creek [near present Stockton, California]" (Frémont, 1887: 442). Camp for the night was in a grove of large white oaks, "previously mentioned as *quercus longiglanda* (*Torr. and Frém.*). This oak is a new species, belonging to the division of white oaks, distinguished by the length of the acorn, which is commonly an inch and a half and sometimes two inches. This long acorn characterizes the tree, which has accordingly been specified by Dr. Torrey as *quercus longiglanda*—(long-acorn oak.) The tree attains frequently a diameter of six feet, and a height of eighty feet, with a wide spreading head." A footnote supporting the above quote (Frémont, 1848: 17) records: "The names of plants in this memoir rest on the authority of Dr. Torrey, by whom they have been examined."

The description and citation of place, name, and authority is sufficient to serve as both effective and valid publication of a new species, *Quercus longiglanda* Torr. & Frém., the only species published in the 1848 *Memoir*. Additionally, there are specimens to serve as types for the name (see Appendix I). [Latin as the language of description under the *International Code of Botanical Nomenclature* did not become necessary until 1935.]

On 17 December the group rode about 16 miles over open prairie partly covered with bunch-grass, "the timber reappearing on the rolling hills of the river Stanislaus in the usual belt of evergreen oaks." That night camp was in a grove of large white oaks. The next day (18 December) the party moved south again through evergreen and other oaks intermingled with some shrubbery. Among the undergrowth was a lupine of extraordinary size, not yet in bloom. Later the men approached the Tuolumne River (To-wal-um-ne of Frémont). The hills were covered with "a species of geranium (*erodium cicutarium*), in the language of the country *alfalferia*, a valuable plant for stock and considered very nutritious. With this was interspersed good and green bunch-grass, and a plant commonly called *bur-clover* [possibly a species of *Medicago*]. This plant, which in some places is very abundant, bears a spirally twisted pod, filled with seeds that remain on the ground during the dry season, well preserved" (Frémont, 1887: 442; 1848: 17). Camp was made on the Tuolumne among white oaks "of the new species [*Q. lobata*, called by Torrey *Q. longiglanda*, see above]." Indians from the vicinity soon became reconciled to the presence of Frémont and his men. Near the Indian huts were "*acorn cribs*, each containing some twenty or thirty bushels." Excellent grass was found at the campsite, which was on broad bottoms of alluvial land, among open-wooded, large white oaks of the new species (Frémont, 1887: 442; 1848: 17). On 18 December, after traveling 17 miles, the party reached the Aux-um-ne, another large affluent to the San Joaquin. They then continued about 6 miles up the stream, with their goal the head of the Lake Fork of the Tulare, where they expected to meet the Kern-Talbot contingent (Frémont, 1848: 18). Next day, 19 December, the party continued southeasterly: "In a few hours we reached a beautiful country of undulating upland, openly wooded with oaks, principally evergreen, and watered with small streams which together make the **Mariposas River**" (Frémont, 1887: 442). The bold rendering of "Mariposas River" seems to indicate Frémont's own later interest in this region, which he purchased prior to leaving for the east in 1847, and on which gold would be discovered. The name Mariposas is not in the 1848 account (see Frémont, 1848: 18).

Continuing along, they came upon tracks of Indians with horses. Richard Owens, Lucien Maxwell, and two Delawares were sent to investigate. They were evidently attacked by Indians and under siege when Frémont and others (the party totaled 16 men) went to their rescue. Frémont and his men were driving a small herd of cattle ahead of them for the relief of the Walker-Talbot-Kern party, should they be encountered as was expected. The cattle and horses of the expedition must have been tempting to the Indians.

In the morning (20 December), following a night of tension and guard duty, the men turned down one of the streams away from the Indian villages. A running fight took place between a solitary Indian, probably a messenger, and Maxwell, who killed him. Once away from the oak belt, where the villages were situated, Frémont and his small party turned again to the south. Camp was set up that evening at an elevation of 1000 feet, at 37°07′47″. The men had seen elk during the day, "making at one time a broken band several miles in length." Their route on 21 December continued in a southeasterly direction, toward the upper Joaquin. "On the trees along these streams as well as on the hills I noticed *mosses*" (Frémont, 1887: 448; 1848: 18). In the afternoon the men and animals succeeded in fording the San Joaquin River. Rain fell in the evening, marking the beginning of spring. The "*Tulare Lake*" River was reached on 22 December. "This is the Lake Fork [King's River]; one of the largest and handsomest streams in the valley, being about one hundred yards broad and having perhaps a larger body of fertile lands than any one of the others. It is called by the Mexicans the *Rio de los Reyes*. The broad alluvial bottoms were well wooded with several species of oaks" (Frémont, 1887: 448).

Somewhere on Lake Fork Frémont expected to find Kern (or Talbot, as Carson asserts) and Walker with the bulk of the expedition. He and his men camped on the river for a day and on 24 December entered the mountains. "We forced our way up among the head springs of the river [King's, Fresno County, California] and finally stood upon the flat ridge of naked granite which made the division of the waters and was 11000 feet above the sea. . . . Here and there a pine or two, stunted and twisted, and worried out of shape by the winds, and clamping itself to the rock. But immediately below we encamped in the sheltering pine woods which now were needed, for towards evening the weather threatened change" (Frémont, 1887: 450). The day following, 31 December 1845, the men and animals traveled only a short distance before camping, because the cattle had sore feet and were in poor condition to travel. Indians had killed one of their mules during the night (Frémont noted that Pablo's mule had been killed by Indians on this date on the collection label of *Platanus racemosa*, see Appendix I; possibly Pablo was a vaquero hired to herd the cattle). New Year's Eve was marked by a snowfall. Abandoning their cattle in the snow on the mountain, Frémont and his men made their way to lower ground. By 3 January 1846 the small contingent with Frémont was camped at an elevation of 4500 feet, and by 7 January they were back on the lower reaches of Lake Fork, in the vicinity of Tulare Lake, without having found the Walker-Kern-Talbot contingent.

Rain in the valley had changed the face of the land. Now there were flowers: "Several humble plants, among them the golden-flowered violet (*viola chrysantha*) and *erodium cicutarium*, the first valley flowers of the spring, and which courted a sunny exposure and warm sandy soil, were already in bloom on the southwestern hill slopes. In the foot-hills of the mountains the bloom of the flowers was earlier" (Frémont, 1887: 451; 1848: 19). Herds of elk, antelope, and wild horses were encountered. Several of the latter were killed for food and were very fat. The fare of the previous winter had convinced Frémont of the value and edibility of horse flesh. Now wild horses were killed for food, when other animals were available.

"During a journey through the valley, between the head of the Tulare lakes and the mouth of the San Joaquin, from the 19th January to the 12th February, the mean temperature was 38° at sunrise and 53° at sunset, with frequent rains. At the end of January, the river bottoms, in many places, were thickly covered with luxuriant grass, more than half a foot high. The California poppy, (*Eschscholtzia Californica,*) the characteristic plant of the California spring; *nemophila insignis* [*N. menziesii* Hook. & Arn.], one of the earliest flowers, growing in beautiful fields of a delicate blue, and *erodium cicutarium*, were beginning to show a scattered bloom. Wild horses were fat, and a grisly bear, killed on 2d February, had four inches thickness of fat on his back and belly, and was estimated to weigh a thousand pounds" (Frémont, 1848: 19).

The Frémont party now searched up the San Joaquin Valley but still failed to find Kern, Walker, Talbot, and the remainder of their entourage. There was little to be gained in searching further, and Frémont returned down the San Joaquin to Sutter's Fort, where they arrived on 15 January without many of their mounts. Of their return Carson (Quaife, 1935: 92) indicates, "All of us were afoot, having lived principally on the meat of wild horses that we killed on the march." At this point, on 19 January 1846, Frémont took eight of his men on a visit to Yerba Buena (San Francisco), traveling under authority of a passport issued by Captain Sutter, and he became acquainted with Americans in the consular service. There he was able to write a letter to Jessie, in which he summarized their progress to date. He went with Vice-Consul William Alexander Leidesdorff (1810–1848) to Monterey, arriving on 27 January, where he met with Consul Thomas Oliver Larkin (1802–1858), who, unknown to Frémont, was, or soon would be, under instructions to "'exert the greatest vigilance in discovering and defeating any attempts which may be made by Foreign Governments to acquire a control'" over California (Spence & Jackson, 1973a: xxii). There he found that Governor Pio Pico (1801–1894) was absent at Los Angeles, and with Mr. Larkin called upon the "commanding general, Don Jose Castro (ca. 1810–60), the prefect, alcalde, and ex-Governor Juan Bautista Alvarado [1809–1882]" (Frémont, 1887: 454). He informed them that he was surveying a route from the United States to the Pacific Ocean, that the object was geographical, made in the interests of science and commerce, and that the party was composed of civilians, not soldiers. He asked permission to refit his expedition, and the request was readily granted.

In the *Geographical Memoir* Frémont (1848: 35) states: "In the latter part of *January*, 1846, a few shrubs and flowers were already in bloom on the sandy shore of Monterey bay (lat. 36° 40′). Among these were the California poppy, and *nemophila insignis*. On the 5th of February I found many shrubs and plants in bloom, in the coast mountains bordering St. Joseph's valley, between Monterey and the bay of San Francisco; and vegetation appeared much more green and spring-like, and further advanced, than in the plains. About the middle of February I noticed the *geranium* [probably *Erodium*] in flower in the valley; and from that time vegetation began generally to bloom."

While the small party was at San Jose, Carson indicated, "we heard that they [Talbot, Kern, and Walker party] were on the San Joaquin, and Frémont sent me with two men to meet them. We found them and guided them to San Jose" (Quaife, 1935: 93). By 15

February the Walker-Kern-Talbot contingent was reunited with Frémont's party "in the valley of San Jose, about thirteen miles south of the village of that name on the main road leading to Monterey, which was about sixty miles distant" (Frémont, 1887: 454). The principals of the two parties each had a different Lake Fork in mind, and the Kern-Talbot-Walker combine had placed the rendezvous at some lakes about 80 or 90 miles southeast of the Tulare Lakes. They had evidently come by way of Walker Pass and had been in camp in the valley of Kern River, another affluent of the Tulare Lake, near the summit of the Sierra Nevada from 27 December to 17 January. The camp was along a river to which Frémont gave the name Kern, in honor of Edward. On 19 January, the Kern-Walker-Talbot party descended to the Cosumne River where they camped, awaiting the arrival of Frémont. Walker continued down the valley where he met Kit Carson and Richard Owens, who were looking for him. The route for the separate party had not been especially difficult. Frémont gave the name of Owens to a lake along the east side of the Sierra Nevada, which he had then not seen.

The combined party moved onto a vacant rancho belonging to former sea captain William Fisher (d. 1850), where they remained for some time, purchasing horses, obtaining supplies, and refitting. The camp site was determined as 37°13′32″, 121°39′08″, Santa Clara County, California.

"The fertile valley of San Jose is a narrow plain of rich soil lying between equally fertile ranges from two thousand to three thousand feet high, covered on one side with wild oats, and wooded on the range toward the sea. The valley is openly wooded with groves of oak free from underbrush, and after the spring rains covered with grass. On the west it is protected from the chilling influence of the northwest winds by the *Cuesta de los Gatos*—Wild-Cat Ridge—which separates it from the coast" (Frémont, 1887: 456). Camp was moved on 22 February (Frémont erroneously recorded March) to Wild-Cat Ridge on the road to Santa Cruz, "and again on the 23d near the summit."

The botanical wonders of California astounded Frémont as the following description taken from the *Geographical Memoir* (1848: 36) indicates: "The mountains were wooded with many varieties of trees, and in some parts with heavy forests. These forests are characterized by a cypress (*taxodium*) of extraordinary dimensions, which I have already mentioned among the trees in the Sierra Nevada as distinguished among the forest trees of America by its superior size and height. Among many we measured in this part of the mountain a diameter of nine or ten feet was frequent, sometimes eleven; but going beyond eleven only in a single tree, which reached fourteen feet in diameter. Above two hundred feet was a frequent height. In this locality the bark was very deeply furrowed and unusually thick, being fully sixteen inches on some of the trees. It was now in bloom, flowering near the summit, and the flowers consequently difficult to procure. This is the staple timber-tree of the country, being cut into both boards and shingles, and is the principal timber sawed at the mills. It is soft and easily worked, wearing away too quickly to be used for floors; but it seems to have all the durability which anciently gave the cypress so much celebrity. Posts which had been exposed to the weather three-quarters of a century since the foundation of the Missions, showed no marks of decay in the wood and are now converted into beams and posts for private dwellings. In California this tree is called the *Palo Colorado*, Redwood [*Sequoia sempervirens* (D. Don) Endl.]. It is the king of trees."

Nowhere else in North America was there such an assemblage of plants, and Frémont was much impressed by them, as were all others who saw these grand trees in their almost pristine state.

Frémont continues with a description of the lofty evergreen oaks, with smooth white bark and close-grained hardwood. He notes its preference for north slopes, where it reached 4 feet in diameter and 100 feet in height. "Another remarkable tree in these woods is called in the language of the country *Madroña* [*Arbutus menziesii* Pursh]. It is a beautiful evergreen with large, thick, and glossy digitated leaves; the trunk and branches reddish colored and having a smooth and singularly naked appearance, as if the bark had been stripped off. In its green state the wood is brittle, very heavy, hard, and close-grained; it is said to assume a red color when dry, sometimes variegated, and susceptible of a high polish. This tree was found by us only in the mountains. Some measured nearly four feet in diameter and were about sixty feet high" (Frémont, 1887: 458; 1848: 37).

Camp was moved on 25 February to the western point of Monterey Bay, where the weather turned rainy, persisting to the end of the month. On 1 March the journey along the coast was resumed and the men found a forest of *palo colorado* at the foot of the mountain, which became noted for the great size and height of the trees. "I measured one," Frémont wrote, "which was 275 feet in height and fifteen feet in diameter, three feet above the base. Though this was distinguished by the greatest girth, other surrounding trees were but little inferior in size and still taller. Their colossal height and massive bulk give an air of grandeur to the forest. These trees grow tallest in the bottom lands, and prefer moist soils and north hillsides. In situations where they are protected from the prevailing northwest winds, they shoot up to a great height; but wherever their heads are exposed, these winds appear to chill them and stop their growth. They then assume a spreading shape, with larger branches, and an apparent broken summit" (Frémont, 1848: 37). The description of the ecological setting of the forest shows Frémont to be an astute observer.

The land between Santa Cruz and Monterey, and the plains of St. John, a grand grassland, which had been eaten down by the large herds of cattle, was now green with its regrowth. Flowers had begun to blossom, and in the valleys of the mountains bordering the Salinas plains, a plain some 50 miles in length along the Salinas river, wild oats were three feet high and well headed, by the 6th of March (Frémont, 1848: 37). The huge entourage with its numerous livestock had to keep moving. There was insufficient forage in any given place for such a large group of animals.

By 3 March the men and animals, a large, impressive, and potentially dangerous expedition—from the standpoint of the Californians—had moved to the (William E. P.) Hartnell rancho, which was on a small creek bed well out on the plain. They were now passing Monterey, which was about 25 miles distant. Frémont was moving toward a pass between the San Joaquin Valley and the western branch of the Salinas River—and, as it turned out, toward trouble. He had with him only a small number of men when he met with officials and asked for permission to refit; now he was leading a large contingent of men, all of them armed.

Political issues were about to become a feature of Frémont's third expedition. Those issues are an aside from the account of botanical, personal, and geographical interests presented herein, which indicate much of the hardship of botanical exploration. His reasons for bringing the exploring party to the central valley of California are not clear. It seems certain that there were implied instructions to be on hand should war break out between Mexico and the United States, and it is certain that John Charles was intent on returning to California during this expedition; he had arrived there by the most direct route. The reasons for his being there, including his topographical pursuits, are open to conjecture.

Explorer Frémont, it is certain, had developed interests in California other than exploration. That Frémont was interested in the natural history is evident in the botanical descriptions noted above, and his ability as a topographer and student of botany was evident from previous works. He was personally interested in settling in California, where he had discussed selecting a place for himself and for his mother. Other personal ambitions are not as obvious, but a place in the sun was certainly not beyond his consideration.

One must believe that Frémont, with more than 60 (40 according to Carson) armed men—outfitting and taking their time in a foreign country, near its capital city of Monterey—might arouse suspicions and give the appearance of a hostile force. Such an interpretation might cause the local Mexican officials much anxiety. How much concern was developed is not the issue here. The Californians did act, with some justification, since General Castro was by that time aware of both the large Frémont contingent and of the impending war between his country and the United States. Frémont gave the appearance of settling in for a long stay, a position not understandable to the Californians, who had granted him permission for a temporary stay to refit.

On 3 March 1846, while Frémont was camped at the Hartnell rancho, a Lieutenant Chavez, accompanied by two men, arrived in camp with a message from General Castro, "ordering me [Frémont and party] forthwith out of the department, and threatening force in the event that I should not instantly comply with the order" (Frémont, 1887: 459). Copies of two letters ejecting him from the districts are reproduced in Spence and Jackson (1973a: 74, 75), and neither, read in context of the 20th century, seems especially objectionable—Frémont is in trespass and he was to leave at once, under threat of force. To this order, Frémont responded by refusing to comply and sent the message back to the General with his messenger. Perhaps Frémont reasoned that resistance would mark the beginning of the end of Mexican rule in California, and perhaps it did. Whatever the reasoning, and that might involve nothing more than the stiffening of the back of this young topographic officer supported by a strong paramilitary force, Frémont went into a fortified encampment atop a peak (Frémont or Gabilan Peak) in the Gabilan Range and raised the American flag. A party of armed Mexicans rode near the fortified camp but retreated before coming within range of the armed Americans.

After three days the Americans decided to move. Frémont explains: "Thinking I had remained as long as the occasion required, I took advantage of the accident [the flag pole fell] to say to the men that this was an indication for us to move camp, and accordingly I gave the order to prepare to move. The protecting favor which the usage of all civilized governments and peoples accords to scientific expeditions imposed on me, even here, a corresponding obligation; and I now felt myself bound to go on my way, having given General Castro sufficient time to execute his threat. Besides I kept always in mind the object of the Government to obtain possession of California and would not let a proceeding which was mostly personal put obstacles in the way" (Frémont, 1887: 460).

Consul Larkin had also reinforced his decision to move on, by pointing out that Frémont knew his government instructions and believed he would follow them. Several messages passed between Larkin and John Charles in which Frémont's options were discussed. Generally, Larkin thought he should move. In the end cooler heads prevailed, but Captain Frémont was now up to his elbows in the politics of California. He had taken an arrogant stand, surrounded as he was with some of the most able people in the world—his frontiersmen. Evidently Frémont's back stiffened because he was so sure of his men and their abilities, and he was unused to being ordered about by anyone. Certainly Frémont's men were a match, or more than a match, for what the Californians could raise on short notice to force them from the territory. From the Californians point of view it was undoubtedly perceived that any armed encounter might lead to the acquisition of the region by the United States. It is almost certain that the Californians were glad not to have a confrontation, and they did not press Frémont's retreating party.

The party left the fortified encampment on 10 March 1846 and proceeded leisurely toward the valley of the San Joaquin, which was reached on 11 March (Frémont, 1887: 470; 1848: 38). They "found almost a summer temperature and the country clothed in the floral beauty of spring." Traveling by short stages they reached the Tuolumne River, whose position was determined as 37°25′53″ north and 120°35′55″ west, on the evening of the 14th. The latitude and longitude are those of the Merced River, not the Tuolumne.

"By the middle of March, the whole valley of the San Joaquin was in the full glory of spring; the evergreen oaks were in flower, *geranium cicutarium* was generally in bloom, occupying the place of grass, and making the uplands a close *sward*. The higher prairies between the rivers presented unbroken fields of yellow and orange colored flowers, varieties of *Layia* and *Eschscholtzia Californica*, and large bouquets of the blue flowering *nemophila* nearer the streams. These made the prevailing bloom, and the sunny hill slopes to the river bottoms showed a varied growth of luxuriant flowers. The white oaks were not yet in bloom" (Frémont, 1848: 20). The Stanislaus River was reached on 21 March 1846. From there it was not far to Sutter's, where the party "remained several days on the Rio de los Americanos, to recruit our animals on the abundant range between the Sacramento and the hills" (Frémont, 1848: 21).

On 24 March the expedition left the American River 10 miles upstream from its mouth and traveled "a little east of north" in the direction of the Bear River settlements. "The road led among oak timber, over ground slightly undulating, covered with grass intermingled with flowers" (Frémont, 1848: 20). They traveled about 30 miles on 25

March to "[Sebastian] Keyser rancho, on the Bear River; an affluent of the *Feather* River, the largest tributary of the Sacramento. The route lay over an undulating country—more so as our course brought us nearer the mountains—wooded with oaks and shrubbery in blossom, with small prairies intervening. Many plants were in flower and among them the California poppy was unusually magnificent. It is the characteristic bloom of *California* at this season, and the Bear River bottoms, near the hills, were covered with it" (Frémont, 1848: 22). Almost 40 years later, he added, "the blue fields of nemophyla [*Nemophila*] and this golden poppy represent fairly the skies and gold of California" (Frémont, 1887: 471).

On 26 March the group reached the Feather River (Yuba County, California), after a journey of 16 miles, at a point about 20 miles above its junction with the Sacramento. They were near the mouth of the Yuba (present Marysvale), and Indians helped them across the deep river. "Extending along the bank in front of the [Indian] village, was a range of wicker cribs, about twelve feet high, partly filled with what is there the Indians' staff of life—acorns. A collection of huts, shaped like bee hives, with naked Indians sunning themselves on the tops, and these acorn cribs, are the prominent objects in an Indian village" (Frémont, 1848: 22). The Indians of the great valley of California had developed an entire way of life based on acorns and wild game, including salmon, which came up the rivers in great numbers each year.

Travel resumed on 27 March "up the right bank of the river, which was wooded with large white and evergreen oaks, interspersed with thickets of shrubbery in full bloom" (Frémont, 1848: 22). Camp on 28 March was made on Butte Creek, following a march of about 15 miles. "It has large, fertile bottoms, wooded with open groves, and having a luxuriant growth of pea vine among the grass. The oaks here were getting into general bloom" (Frémont, 1887: 472). The party traveled 20 miles on 29 March and camped on Pine Creek, "another fine stream, with bottoms of fertile land, wooded with groves of large and handsome oaks, some attaining to six feet in diameter, and forty to seventy feet in height" (Frémont, 1848: 23). March 30 found the party continuing its move up the Sacramento Valley, the road through an upland prairie of the Sacramento, this with a yellowish, gravelly soil, generally two or three miles from the river, and twelve or fifteen miles from the foot of the eastern mountains (Frémont, 1848: 23). That afternoon camp was pitched on Deer Creek, another of the affluents of the Sacramento (near Vina, Tehama County, California). "It has the usual broad and fertile bottom-lands common to these streams, wooded with groves of oak and a large sycamore (*platanus occidentalis*) [*Platanus racemosa* Nutt., including *P. californica* Benth.], distinguished by bearing its balls in strings of three to five, and peculiar to California" (Frémont, 1887: 473, 1848: 23). The position of their camp, adjacent to a farm of a Peter Lassen (1800–1859; for whom a peak and county were later named), was determined as 39°57′00″, 121°56′44″; elevation was 560 feet.

The group remained in the camp at Deer Creek for six days, until 5 April. "Salmon was now abundant in the Sacramento. Those which we obtained were generally between three and four feet in length, and appeared to be of two distinct kinds. It is said that as many as four different kinds ascend the river at different periods. The great abundance in which this fish is found gives it an important place among the resources of the country. The salmon crowd in immense numbers up the Umpqua, Tlamath, and Trinity Rivers, and into every little river and creek on the coast north of the Bay of San Francisco [Frémont, 1848: 24]; and up the San Joaquin River, into the Stanislaus, beyond which the Indians say they do not go" (Frémont, 1887: 474).

The trip north was resumed on 5 April, and the group camped again on a stream. "It is a handsome place, wooded with groves of oak, and along the creek are sycamore, ash, cottonwood, and willow" (Frémont, 1887: 474). The journey on 6 April continued along the Sacramento, which they crossed in canoes, prior to camping on a creek wooded mainly with large oaks. "The snowy peak of Shastl [Mount Shasta] bore directly north, showing out high above the other mountains" (Frémont, 1887: 474).

Travel was toward Mount Shasta on 7 April, between mountain ranges whose peaks were snow covered. The range to the east bore the peaks called "*the Sisters*," and that to the west had a prominent peak, which Frémont named "**Mount Linn**" (Castle Crags) in remembrance of his friend from Missouri, the late Senator Lewis Fields Linn, who advocated inclusion of Oregon within the United States. "Leaving the Sacramento at a stream called Red Bank Creek, we entered on a high and somewhat broken upland, timbered with at least four varieties of oaks, with *manzanita* [*madroña*?] (*arbutus Menziesii*) and other shrubbery interspersed" (Frémont, 1887: 475). And, "A remarkable species of pine [possibly the digger pine, *Pinus sabiniana* Dougl.], having leaves in threes (sometimes six to nine inches long), with bluish foliage, and a spreading, oak-shaped top, was scattered through the timber. I have remarked that this tree grows lower down the mountains than the other pines, being found familiarly associated with oaks, the first met after leaving the open valleys, and seeming to like a warm climate. It seems that even among inanimate things association levels differences. This tree, growing among oaks, forgets its narrow piny form and color, and takes the spreading shape of the oaks, their broad summits and lesser heights. Flowers were as usual abundant. The splendid California poppy characterized all the route along the valley. A species of clover was in bloom, and the berries of the *mansanita* were beginning to redden on some trees, while others were still in bloom" (Frémont, 1887: 475; 1848: 25). The expedition camped that night at an elevation of 1000 feet on Cottonwood Creek, whose bottoms were wooded with oaks and cottonwoods.

On 8 April the cavalcade continued for 16 miles up the valley. It rained during the day, and snow was apparent on the mountains, but by midmorning of 9 April the rain had stopped. The men crossed the river in boats, the animals evidently forced to swim, and proceeded eastward "toward the foot of the Sierra. The Sacramento bottoms here are broad and prettily wooded, with soil of a sandy character. Our way led through a very handsome, open woods, principally of oaks, mingled with a considerable quantity of the oak-shaped pine. Interspersed among these were bosquets or thickets of *mansanita*, and an abundant white flowering shrub [*Ceanothus*?], now entirely covered with small blossoms. The head of the valley here (lower valley) is watered by many small streams, having fertile bottom-lands, with a good range of grass and acorns. In about six miles we crossed a creek twenty or twenty-five feet wide, and several miles farther descended into the broad bottoms of a swift stream about twenty yards wide, called Cow Creek [Shasta County, California], so named as being the range of a small band of cattle, which ran off here from a party on their way to Oregon" (Frémont, 1887: 476–77; 1848: 26).

Frémont discusses the division of the Sacramento Valley into two parts, upper and lower. "The division is strongly and geographically marked. The Shastl peak stands at the head of the lower valley, in the forks of the river, rising from a base of about 1,000 feet, out of a forest of heavy timber. It ascends like an immense column upwards of 14,000 feet" (Frémont, 1848: 25). This is instructive regarding the designation "Upper Sacramento" on plant specimen labels, although it is apparent that materials from the vicinity of Lassen's were sometimes marked as "upper Sacramento" also.

On 10 April 1846 a hailstorm burst upon them, whitening the face of the country and bringing with it an unseasonable cold. The party now retraced its steps back to Lassen's, on Deer Creek (or River), which was reached on the evening of 11 April. "The Sacramento bottoms between Antelope and Deer river were covered with oats, which had attained their full height, growing as if sown fields. The country here exhibited the maturity of spring. The California poppy was everywhere forming seed-pods, and many plants were in flower and seed together. Some varieties of clover were just beginning to bloom. By the middle of the month the seed-vessels of the California poppy which, from its characteristic abundance, is a prominent feature in the vegetation, had attained their full size; but the seeds of this and many other plants, although fully formed, were still green-colored, and not entirely ripe. At this time I obtained from the San Joaquin valley seeds of the poppy, and other plants, black and fully ripe, while they still remained green in this part of the Sacramento—the effect of a warmer climate in the valley of the San Joaquin" (Frémont, 1887: 477, 1848: 26). Frémont does not explain how he received the seeds from the San Joaquin; possibly they were sent to him by someone knowing of his interest in plants.

At Lassen's, where the party remained from 11 to 24 April, Frémont set up the transit and determined the location as 39°47′04″, and 120°56′44″. Many of the plants taken on the expedition were from this vicinity. Spring had arrived, and the flowers were blooming in great variety. Frémont, a fancier of beautiful things, especially flowering plants, must have been enthralled by the beauty. Numerous specimens bear the notation "Upper Sacramento." Whether they were from the upper Sacramento as defined by Frémont or from the upper part of the lower Sacramento, as is likely, is difficult to determine, except for those having dates.

Carson (Quaife, 1935: 95; Carter, 1968: 101) indicates that the men were not just resting or collecting plants during this long encampment, however. Settlers, having received a threat from Indians in the vicinity, real or merely perceived, solicited Frémont's aid. He obliged them by attacking the Indians, resulting in "a perfect butchery," according to Carson. It is difficult to believe from this vantage point in time that the "butchery" was justifiable or necessary.

From Lassen's, the expedition moved north toward Oregon, where Frémont hoped to join the present survey with that of two years earlier and perhaps to continue toward home. The large group of men and animals left the Sacramento along one of the many affluents of that river, south of present Redding, through regions of abundant grass and acorns, and encamped among oak groves in the evening. Bears were in evidence near the camp, and four were killed by the hunters. Latitude of the camp was 40°38′58″, and elevation 1080 feet. On 27 April they "found a good way along a flat ridge; there was a pretty stream in a mountain valley on the right, and the face of the country was already beginning to assume a mountainous character, wooded with mingled oak and long-leaved pine, and having a surface of scattered rocks, with grass or flowers, among them the three-leaved poppy, its parti-colored blossoms waving on the long stem above the grass, and gaining for itself the name of *mariposas* [*Calochortus*?], already mentioned of its resembling living butterflies. I speak often of the grass and flowers, but I have learned to value the one and the other lends a beauty to the scenery which I do not like to omit, and the reader can always imagine for himself the brightness they give when once he has had described the glorious flowers of this country, where the most lovely hues are spread in fields over both hill and plain" (Frémont, 1887: 479).

The next day, 28 April, the group crossed one of the high ridges, where "snow and the great pine *Lambertiani* appeared together, and an hour before noon we reached a pass in the main ridge of the Sierra Nevada, in an open pine forest at an elevation of only four thousand six hundred feet, where the snow was in patches and the deciduous oaks were mingled with the pines" (Frémont, 1887: 479). Frémont noted that they were then at the upper limit of the oak region, in a pass at about the 40th parallel. From the pass the party descended into a valley between ridges of the Sierra Nevada, one with a fundamentally different climate from that encountered in the valley of the Sacramento. Camp on 29 April was at 40°58′43″, 121°07′59″ (Lassen County, California); that of 30 April, in "*Round Valley*," was at 41°17′17″, 121°01′23″ (near present Lookout, Modoc County, California). The camp of 1 May was at the edge of a lake that Frémont named "Lake Rhett" (present Clear Lake), the position of which was determined as 41°48′49″, 121°15′24″ (Modoc County, California). The hunter Archambeau left the party in search of game on the morning of 2 May and did not return until the evening of 4 (?) May, worn and hungry, but otherwise faring satisfactorily, having been "led off and entangled among the hills." Camp was moved on 5 May to a stream (Lost River) flowing into Lake Rhett, which Frémont named McCrady (after one of his boyhood friends in Charleston, South Carolina).

"In the forenoon of the sixth we reached the Tlamath [Klamath] Lake [Klamath County, Oregon] at its outlet, which is by a fine, broad stream, not fordable" (Frémont, 1887: 483). There they discovered Indians who had houses (permanent huts, fide Frémont). Arrival of the expedition took the Indians by surprise, and although they appeared friendly, Frémont did not trust them. The scenery was intriguing and the lake beautiful, and John Charles was captivated by the scene: "It was all wild and unexplored, and the uninvaded silence roused curiosity and invited research. Indigenous, the Indians like the rocks and trees seemed part of the soil, growing in a state of rude nature like the vegetation, and like it nourished and fed by nature. And so it had been back to a time of which nothing was known. All here was in the true aboriginal condition, but I had not time now for idling days, and I had to lose the pleasure to which the view before me invited" (Frémont, 1887: 483). The men of the party were ferried across the outlet by Indians in canoes. Camp that night was on a stream that Frémont afterward named Denny's Branch.

On 7 May the group proceeded between the lake and the foot of the mountains. The route along the lake was continued again on 8 May. At this point in the journal, Frémont implores the reader to fairness and indicates his intended activity in this region. He is now only 20 miles from his December 1843 camp at the Klamath Marsh, and in closing that distance his survey would have come full circle. And, he had expected to continue his survey in the Cascade Mountains as spring progressed. All of that changed when into the light of his fire rode two horsemen. They were Californians Samuel Neal and Levi Sigler, both known to John Charles. The two were messengers from a United States officer and confidential government agent, Lieutenant Archibald H. Gillespie (1813–1873), U.S. Marine Corps, who had been pursuing Frémont with dispatches. Neal told Frémont that Gillespie was in danger of being attacked and killed by Indians, who had demonstrated their intent by attempting to cut off Neal and Sigler.

A relief party, consisting of 10 men—Carson, Lucien Maxwell, Owens, Godey, Basil Lajeunesse, Frémont, and four of the Delawares—was formed to start the next morning in search of Gillespie (Egan, 1977: 328). At dawn the small group started on the trail back along the lake margin, traveled for 45 miles, and encamped in a meadow surrounded by trees along a small stream. Grass was good and there Frémont intended to wait. At about sundown four men, one of them Gillespie, came into camp. He brought the first news from home that Frémont had received in some 11 months. Lieutenant Gillespie, under orders from the President and the Secretary of the Navy, had traveled some 600 miles in search of Frémont. "He was directed to find me wherever I might be" (Frémont, 1887: 488).

The War Bill indicating a state of war with Mexico would not be signed into law by President Polk until 13 May 1846, a fact that would not become known to Frémont for some months. Indeed, it was not until 17 August 1846 that a ship arrived at Los Angeles bearing dispatches that war between the United States and Mexico had finally been declared (Eisenhower, 1989: 218). Frémont would become a part of a struggle dictated by political considerations far removed from him in remote California.

The medusa-headed and octopus-armed corpus of American politics had closed upon this man of destiny. He would not be the same again—change he would, and change he did. The political consideration would become overwhelming and he would never again be the botanically and geographically oriented explorer, even though he was only partway along the track of his third expedition and two more would follow. He would demonstrate once and for all that people with a scientific bent are at their best when unfettered by politics. Frémont had married into a family where politics was a way of life, but John Charles was not expert at political processes; he was out of his league in that arena. Despite the promptings of his wife, Senator Benton, and many others or perhaps because of them, John Charles would fail from the start as a politician. He was at least equally matched in arrogance by his wife, and surpassed in both arrogance and need for self-aggrandizement by his father-in-law, Senator Benton (Eisenhower, 1989: 162). Their needs and desires, including a considerable baggage of enemies, would serve to hinder as much as help him.

From this point, rational descriptions of geographical and botanical features are replaced by somewhat irrational justifications and partial truths or downright lies concerning his partisan and, perhaps, politically sanctioned activities. "The mission on which I had been originally sent to the West was a peaceful one, and Mr. [George] Bancroft [Secretary of the Navy] had sent Mr. Gillespie to give me warning of the new state of affairs and the designs of the President [James Polk]. Mr. Gillespie had been given charge of dispatches from the Secretary of the Navy to Commodore [John] Sloat, and had been purposely made acquainted with their import. Known to Mr. Bancroft as an able and thoroughly trustworthy officer, he had been well instructed in the designs of the Department and with the purposes of the Administration, so far as they related to California" (Frémont, 1887: 488).

Frémont's duties as explorer were set aside, and he was given the knowledge that the "Government intended to take California." He continued: "The time has come. England must not get a foothold. We must be first. Act; discreetly, but positively. . . . Now it was officially made known to me that my country was at war [with Mexico, a date impossible for Gillespie or Frémont to know at their meeting], and it was so made known expressly to guide my conduct." The quotes presented here were made long after the fact, when Frémont most certainly knew that war had not yet been declared by the time of arrival of Lieutenant Gillespie.

He decided to return at once to California, "in order to bring to bear all the influences I could command" (Frémont, 1887: 488). And, at this point the geographical expedition effectively ended, in spite of an official termination noted by Frémont as the "Buttes." The men of the party were about to become Indian fighters and ruffians, killing and looking for fights, one of which was about to be thrust upon them. The question remains as to the nature of the instructions or lack thereof. When questioned later by Commodore Sloat as to his orders, Frémont could not produce written orders supporting his position. Spence and Jackson (1973a: xxviii–xxix) state: "It is entirely possible that Polk verbally and confidentially instructed Gillespie to order Frémont and his armed *voyageurs* to be on hand in California to help seize it when news of American hostilities arrived." Gillespie had not chased after the Frémont party for several hundred miles merely to chat. He had been sent by the President specifically to find John Charles and his men, and he had already delivered the wishes of the President to both Commodore Sloat and Consul Larkin. Indications are that Sloat had orders to raise the American flag in California, if circumstances warranted that action, and evidently those orders involved suspicions that the British were in a position to intercede in California.

According to Carson (Quaife, 1935: 96) Frémont "set up till twelve or one o'clock reading the letters which he had received from the states," undoubtedly considering the consequences of the messages and messengers. He was asleep when Carson awakened the camp with the cry, "Indians!" The marauders had killed both Basil Lajeunesse and the half-breed Denny. In the fight that ensued the Delaware Indian Crane was killed also, struck by "four arrows in the chest" according to Carson (Quaife, 1935: 97). A Klamath chief was killed as the fight progressed, and another of the Delaware Indians was wounded. Basil Lajeunesse was a favorite of John Charles, who often accompanied him in small parties. He would be sorely missed. Grief-stricken, and undoubtedly shocked by the vicious attack, the sorrowful survivors buried their dead companions and rejoined the main body of their party. The following day camp was moved three miles and the site was fortified. Locality of the camp was determined as 42°36′45″, 121°58′45″ (near mouth of Williamson River, Klamath County, Oregon). On the next day the group followed around the lake shore to the extreme northwestern bay and again fortified their camp.

On the day following, Carson and Owens, with 10 men, were sent ahead to reconnoitre the position of an Indian encampment at the inlet of the lake, probably not peopled with those whose ambush resulted in the deaths of Crane, Basil, and Denny. Nevertheless, a battle was begun, and Frémont and the remaining men joined the struggle. Fourteen of the Indians were killed and the village and its supplies destroyed. The next day a lone Indian was killed by the Delaware, (James) Sagundai, whose action along with that of Frémont possibly saved Carson, whose gun misfired. Locality of their camp, on a river that Frémont named after John Torrey (now Williamson River), was determined as 42°41′30″, 121°52′08″. "To this river I gave the name of my friend, Professor Torrey, who, with all the enthusiasm that goes with a true love of science, had aided me in determining the botany of the country" (Frémont, 1887: 495). Two days later the party camped on another stream near the south end of the lake; the stream was named by Frémont "We-to-wah," after another of the Delaware. The mouth of the creek was at 42°21′43″, 121°41′23″.

Some days later (ca. 20 May?) the party crossed a pass into the head of the lower Sacramento Valley "and, descending, entered into a truly magnificent forest. It was composed mainly of a cypress [*Sequoia*] and a lofty white cedar (*Thuya gigantea*) one hundred and twenty to one hundred and forty feet high, common in the mountains of California. All were massive trees, but the cypress was distinguished by its great bulk. None were seen so large as are to be found in the coast mountains near Santa Cruz, but there was a greater number of large trees—seven feet being a common diameter—carrying the bulk eighty or a hundred feet without a limb" (Frémont, 1887: 498, 1848: 31). Frémont continues: "At the elevation of about three thousand feet the timber had become more open, the hills rolling, and many streams made pretty bottoms of rich grass; the black oaks in full and beautiful leaf were thickly studded among the open pines, which had become much smaller and fewer in variety, and when we halted near midday, at an elevation of two thousand two hundred feet, we were in one of the most pleasant days of early spring, cool and sunny, with a pleasant breeze, amidst a profusion of flowers; many trees in dark summer foliage, and some still in bloom. Among these the white spikes of the horse-chestnut [*Aesculus californica* (Spach) Nutt.], common through all the oak regions, were conspicuous" (Frémont, 1887: 498, 1848: 32).

After a long period during which dates were not recorded, for whatever reason, the journal mentions that on 25 May the party again was at Lassen's, where they remained for two days prior to moving to the rancho of Neal. There the political dragon again confronted Frémont, and he transformed into the engaged, but hardly efficient or convincing politician; now he would become involved in the intrigues that would lead to the addition of Alta California to the United States. Frémont notes the end of the geographic survey at the "Buttes," using the justification of the last of the latitude and longitude determinations. On 30 May camp was established near the "Buttes of the Sacramento [Sutter County, California]." Locality was determined as 39°12′03″, 121°38′04″. "The hunters always left the camp before daylight, and were in by nine o'clock, after which the sun grew hot. Game was very fat and abundant; upward of eighty deer, elk, and bear were killed in one morning" (Frémont, 1848: 27). It is little wonder that much of the wild game in the great valley of California was extirpated. Designating the hunters as overzealous might indeed understate the case.

Beyond the above entry the *Memoir* of 1848 includes summaries of the various geographic regions, with accounts of climate, fertility, and resources. The areas covered include San Francisco Bay, including the Golden Gate, which Frémont named, the western slope of the Sierra Nevada, and the coastal country north of San Francisco Bay. The Great Basin, its rivers and fertile areas are described and contrasted with the great valley of California. It is an interesting and worthy document, with numerous insights that are modern, even at the end of the 20th century. The topographic information was combined with that of the two previous expeditions and with information from other surveys. The results were presented in a map of the American West, a map that would be useful to thousands of people moving west. In spite of the quality of the report and map, it is unfortunate that the report was not in the format of the two previous ones. That no botanical report accompanied the 1848 *Memoir* is a shame.

The narrative presented herein now shifts from covering botanical and related interests to the political ones also, with the justification that events beyond this point in the life of Frémont were to have a vast effect on the botanical exploration of the West, as will be demonstrated later in this account. And, with rare exceptions, Frémont did not record botanical features or collect additional plant specimens.

The Mexican government seemed to play into the hands of the American settlers, for whom Frémont became a rallying point. American settlers were effectively stripped of property and privilege in a "Banda" forwarded "by Don Manuel Castro, Prefect of Monterey, to his Sub-Prefect in San Francisco, and transmitted by the latter to the U. S. Vice-Consul at that port, Leidesdorff, to be by him made known to the American settlers" (Frémont, 1887: 503). The banda solidified the ranks of the Americans, causing them to take a stand in their own defense. Frémont (1887: 516) notes: "My camp at the Buttes [near present Marysvale, California] became a rendezvous for the settlers, and a centre of information for me and of confidence for them." General José Castro (1810–1860) had made an attempt to organize the Indians against the settlers and against the Frémont party. Now Frémont would try to anticipate the Indians and demonstrate to them "that Castro was far and I was near." In retrospect, it seems that his stand bordered on the fanatical, and what was to happen can hardly be explained in terms of rational 20th-century thought—Frémont set out to kill Indians! The men of his party attacked the first of the Maidu villages encountered along the west bank of the Sacramento, killing several of the reputed hostiles. "With scarcely a halt we rode on towards the other *rancherias* [Indian ranchos], but the news of our attack apparently reached these as soon as ourselves, for the Indians were escaping from their villages as we rode in among them. Before the close of the day nearly all the *rancherias* had been visited and the Indians dispersed" (Frémont, 1887: 517). And, "We had surprised them assembled in the height of their war ceremonies. . . . This was a rude but necessary measure to prevent injury to the whites. And it had the effect I intended" (Frémont, 1887: 520). One doubts that he had made many friends among the Indians.

While still encamped at the Buttes, events were transpiring at great distance that would inflict a great blow to the plans of John Charles. On 2 June 1846 Colonel Stephen Watts Kearney received orders to lead a force from Fort Leavenworth to Santa Fe. This order was in keeping with the progress of the war with Mexico, in which considerable progress had been made, and the move was to take control of New Mexico and add it to the United States. Kearney was to then move on to California. President Polk expected that Commodore John D. Sloat's naval forces would seize the ports of Upper California (Eisenhower, 1989: 105).

Camp was moved on 8 June from the Buttes to an earlier encampment on the American River, which was reached on 12 June. A trip was made to "Sutter's Landing," on 13 June, where supplies requisitioned earlier from U.S. Navy ship *Portsmouth* in San Francisco Bay were to be delivered. Lieutenant Gillespie had been there some hours earlier with the stores, and with communication from Commander John Berrien Montgomery [1794–1873], but finding Frémont not in evidence, he had detoured up the American River. Outlined in the correspondence was the possibility of the Frémont party's traveling south to Santa Barbara prior to returning to the States and of having a U.S. war ship standing by at that place in case of need. Frémont would wait for the return of Gillespie for some days before reading that communication. In the meantime he would stay at the Landing. It was in this period, 14–15 June 1846, that he collected the material later designated as *Philadelphus fremontii* Rydb.

The role of Frémont and his men in the California war is treated in some detail by other works on his life cited earlier in this account. Eisenhower (1989: 211) notes that "Frémont, to whom the men were fanatically loyal, was at best a loose cannon on the deck." Perhaps that judgement is somewhat wide of the mark, but close enough to summarize his role in the taking of California. Certainly his association with the California war was a bittersweet experience, one that he would have to defend constantly in the remainder of his life. The other players on the scene, Gillespie, Sloat, Stockton, and Kearney, if not loose cannons were close enough, by contemporary standards, to be painted with the same brush. Perhaps it is a failing of the human condition, not mere conceit, arrogance, stubbornness, jealousy, or greed, that led the players to act as they did. They were removed from each other and from orders from Washington by days, weeks, or even months. And, in other wars of the century, even where better communications were available, the Civil War for example, the engagements were often a comedy of errors, the winning side determined as much by chance as by careful planning. Arrogance and jealousy of commanding officers played important roles in all conflicts of the time.

Botanical specimens taken following mid-June 1846 are few indeed, and to recount the happenings of the war seems unnecessary. The outcome of that war, however, most certainly affected botanical exploration of the American West during the following decade. Frémont had formed an association with Commodore Robert F. Stockton (1795–1866) of the U.S. Navy, and had cooperated with him in the taking of California. Late in the proceedings, after California was more or less in the American control, a nemesis, Brigadier General Stephen Watts Kearny (1794–1848) of the United States Army, who had been moving relentlessly toward California for some months, would appear on the scene. Shortly following the arrival of Kearny, a disagreement developed as to who had precedence over Frémont and his men, General Kearny or Commodore Stockton. Frémont, stubborn to the point of being ridiculous, chose to align himself with Stockton. Because of that and other factors, including failure to turn over official papers to Kearny, he was charged with mutiny, tried by court-martial, and found guilty. In a rage, he resigned his commission, even though President Polk remitted his sentence of dismissal. His resignation from the Army most certainly placed other men in prominent roles in the exploration of the American West, exploration that included taking of plants to add to the growing number of specimens on which interpretation of botany would be based. Exploration of the Great Salt Lake would fall to Captain Howard Stansbury (1852) and that of the Pacific Railroad Survey to Captain John W. Gunnison; Frémont could have had both under different circumstances. He was the best prepared explorer for these two expeditions, and could have done admirable work.

The third expedition thus became one of both glory and disaster. It was his best of times but not quite his worst of times; the fourth expedition would fulfill the latter designation.

CHAPTER V

FOURTH EXPEDITION—1848–49

Upon his resignation from the Army following the court-martial, Frémont hoped that the government would continue to support his geographical explorations as a civilian. An attempt was made to secure government funding to allow him to continue. A bill to that effect was passed by the Senate but defeated in the House of Representatives. In a letter to John Torrey dated 24 February 1848 (Spence & Jackson, 1973a: 479) Frémont wrote: "When I resigned my commission of Lt. Col. of Cavalry, I gave up also my commission in the Topl. Engineers, which had in fact been vacated by my acceptance of the former. I have therefore entirely withdrawn from the public service, but I am deeply gratified with being able to say to you that our work will still go on, and that I even hope to be able to give it a greater extent and beauty than we had before anticipated. This, although only a hope at present, will, I have great reason to believe be verified, and in the mean time I am permitted to assure you that there will be no interruption in working up the materials that we have already collected." On 2 March 1848 Frémont again wrote to Torrey (Spence & Jackson, 1973a: 481): "I shall leave this city in the course of next month for the Missouri frontier, thence to California with an exploring party, taking a direct route to the bay of San Francisco. I have not thought of abandoning our intended work, and will immediately endeavor to obtain necessary means."

There would be a considerable interruption in "working up the materials we have already collected." The work would not be completed in the lifetime of either Torrey or Frémont. John Charles did not leave for the frontier in the course of the next month. Five months would pass, as he would be involved completely in other work, prior to his leaving for the frontier. Those five months of delay would prove disastrous for the expedition.

While working to complete the *Geographical Memoir*, containing the results of the 1845–47 expedition, Frémont was obviously planning yet another trip. Rationale for the fourth expedition seems to have involved, at least in some part, a need to demonstrate his continued viability and value following the court-martial. It is evident that the previous expeditions were both satisfying and beneficial to Frémont personally; he could be his own boss away from the annoyances and intrigues of life in the civilized world. Unfortunately, too much of the preparation or lack thereof was tried in too little time, and the ill-prepared, ultimately disastrous expedition moved to its beginning—too late.

John Charles, in another letter to Torrey, wrote that he hoped to make additional plant collections, and had arranged for Richard H. Kern "of Philadelphia, a brother of the artist [Edward M. Kern] who accompanied the last expedition, [to] go with me on this, and from what I have seen of his work you may anticipate beautiful drawings" (Spence & Jackson, 1973a: 484).

The fourth expedition would be privately financed, and some participants, at least, would provide their own equipment and probably furnish their services free (Spence, 1984: xxii). Included in this category were Henry King (d. 1849), Andrew Cathcart, Thomas E. Breckenridge, Micajah McGehee (1824–1880), and the brothers Kern (Richard Hovendon, Edward Meyer, and Benjamin Jordan). A summary of the surnames of those involved with the 1848 expedition is included in Spence (1984: 52) and Favour (1962: 176–78). Of special note are Charles Preuss, of the first and second expeditions; Alex Godey, who was so important in the second and third expeditions; Edward Meyer Kern, artist-topographer of the third expedition; Charles Van Linneus Taplin (1819–1855) of the second and third expeditions; and Rafael Proue, who had been with Frémont on all of his expeditions and would accompany him on this, Proue's final one (Hafen & Hafen, 1960). And, after the urgings of Torrey and Gray to take a botanist, one would finally be hired—Frederick Creutzfeldt (Welsh, 1982b). Private financing was forthcoming, with some difficulty, and John Charles was involved with matters unresolved following the third expedition, namely trying to convince Congress to make payment on accounts dating from his service as governor of California. These matters delayed him in Washington until late summer. By early September Frémont, accompanied by Jessie, their daughter Lily and baby son Benton, was on his way to St. Louis. Leaving their daughter in St. Louis, the family embarked by steamboat for Kansas Landing, where they arrived on 8 October. The infant, Benton, had died during the interval. Still mourning the death of Benton, Jessie left at the breakup of the camp on 20 October, to return to St. Louis prior to returning east, where she embarked by ship via Panama to California to rendezvous with John Charles.

"The story of the fourth expedition is simple and tragic" (Spence, 1984: xxiv). From Choteau's Landing (Westport) on 21 October 1848, the party moved on to Bent's Fort on 21 November, and at Pueblo, some days later, employed Old Bill (William Sherley) Williams (1787–1849), then 66 years of age, as guide, and proceeded on to the Colorado Rockies and into an unusually harsh winter. Lacking was the leadership and fortitude that had been with Frémont during the difficult crossing of the Sierra Nevada in the winter of 1844. Fitzpatrick, Carson, Tabeau, and others who had served so valiantly then were absent now. Old Bill Williams did not (or could not) serve the party well, and was blamed by Frémont for the failure; but the expedition was poorly planned, poorly prepared, and poorly executed. There are indications that Old Bill had wanted to go by a pass that might have been possible, but that John Charles had insisted on a more direct route westward south of the 38th parallel. Whatever the case, Frémont, and not Old Bill Williams, must bear the major responsibility for its failure. It seems that the expedition collapsed a little at a time, imperceptibly at first, then crashed at the end, like a starving horse that still appears viable until it collapses in death. The expedition went into the mountains, met more than its match, and came straggling out—leaving behind 10 dead men and 120 dead mules. This story of hardship, privation, and disaster would be recorded in some detail by Frémont; it would haunt him always.

The men and animals crossed the Sangre de Cristo Mountains, evidently through Robideau Pass, then went up the San Luis Valley, headwaters of the Rio Grande, and came up against the final obstacle, the San Juan Mountains (Figure 7). These are formidable mountains, passable in other seasons and possibly even during some winters, but not during the winter of this unconscionable attempt. Winter had arrived early with deep snow and low temperatures accompanied by high winds in the upper elevations. No one could have anticipated that the winter would be so severe. The problem was not, however, the severity of the winter—it was, rather, the lateness of the start. Had the party arrived at the mountain passes in September or even in October the story could have ended in another Frémont triumph.

Perhaps the best, but still sketchy and one-sided account of this disaster by Frémont, is that recorded in letters he wrote to Jessie (J. B. Frémont, 1878: 69–81), which presumably she received while still in Panama, en route to California. The published account is evidently one of several versions sent by Frémont to Senator Benton and others (Upham, 1856: 279–296, essentially identical to that of J. B. Frémont); it differs in some slight respects from the version recorded in Spence (1984: 75–86). Possibly the hand of the romantic Jessie in her published version accounts for much of the difference, which is mostly irrevelant.

Frémont and his men, with 120 mules (many carrying corn to feed them in times of scarcity) left Pueblo, Colorado, about the 25th of November, expecting to reach the snowless, low-elevation Grand River tributaries in the course of a few weeks. Bill Williams, who had intended to spend the winter at Pueblo was engaged as guide. An early winter closed in on the party as it moved west from Pueblo. Deep snow and freezing winds took their toll on both men and animals. By about the 11th of December the men and their animals were in the mountains attempting to cross a high mountain pass. Even the river bottoms, which were followed as the lowest elevation routes through the country, had deep snow reaching to the bellies of the horses and mules. Snow fell continuously, and the cold was extreme.

The attempt was made to cross the high passes of the Colorado Rockies, and the mules and men began to fail. Bill Williams nearly froze to death, according to Frémont, and dead mules were evident at the camp sites and along the trails tramped into the snow. Upward the party straggled, finally camping at above 12,000 feet elevation. Snow continued to fall, and cold temperatures did not moderate. Food for the animals had long since been exhausted, and sparse grass could be found only on the highest ridges where snow was blown free by high winds. Down slope the snow was so deep that the animals merely floundered and finally fell dead from lack of food and extreme cold.

Retreat was the only viable alternative for the men, but not for the animals. All of them died prior to the return of the men, carrying the baggage, down to the Del Norte. A plan for the salvation of the men of the expedition involved sending a relief party to the Spanish settlements in New Mexico. A relief party consisting of King, Brackenridge, Creutzfeldt, and Bill Williams was sent toward the settlements on 26 December 1848. In just one month the expedition had to admit defeat. Why they waited so long has been a matter of conjecture.

While awaiting the return of the relief party, the men carried more of their baggage to the Del Norte. The situation was desperate. Rafael Proue laid down in the trail and froze to death. After sixteen days had elapsed from King's departure and no sign that they were about to return with help, Frémont with Godey (and his nephew), Charles Preuss, and Saunders (Frémont's black servant) set out for the Spanish settlements also.

Frémont had the good luck to encounter some Ute Indians, one of whom served as guide and provided four weak horses to carry their meager baggage and food supply. On the sixth day after leaving camp, at about sunset, Frémont discovered a little smoke in a grove of timber off the river, and thinking perhaps it might be the relief party on its return, they went to see who was at the fire. At the fire were Creutzfeldt, Brackenridge, and Williams, in miserable condition. They had been starving, and King had starved to death a few days before. His remains were some six or eight miles above, near the river. The surviving men joined with Frémont and his small party, which made its way to the settlement on the Red River, which was reached on 29 January, the tenth day after leaving their camp in the mountains. They had traveled about 100 miles.

The morning after reaching the Red River town, Godey and Frémont rode on to the Rio Hondo and Taos in search of animals and supplies. Godey collected animals and supplies, and with the help of four Mexicans, set out to save the men back along the trail. Meeting the first of the survivors along the trail, Godey provided them with food and other supplies and then pressed on until all of those still alive were accounted for. Ten men, including Rafael Proue, had died of starvation and exposure.

Frémont would not or could not return back along the trail to aid in the recovery of his men. There are indications (Herr, 1989) that one of his legs was frostbitten, to the extent that he would suffer from the injury for years to come.

The hero of this sorry event is clearly Alex Godey. Having endured the rigors of the expedition himself, and knowing full well the harrowing circumstances awaiting him, he nevertheless returned to the sorrowful scenes of desolation as rescuer. He carried food and other supplies to keep the men alive and brought extra horses to carry them to safety.

Several members of the expedition kept diaries for at least portions of the trip, and most are published. All of those are reviewed in the work of Spence (1984). The Charles Preuss diary was published by Gudde and Gudde (1958), but it is somewhat disappointing following his accounts of the first two expeditions, where his personality is so apparent. This one gives the feeling that it was composed afterward, with dates filled in from memory; it is not the vintage Preuss.

It was not until 9 February 1849 that the last of the survivors arrived at Taos. The tragedy was not at an end, but for the time being the stragglers back along the track had been saved. Benjamin Kern and Bill Williams, with a party of Mexicans, returned back into the mountains in a few days to recover their belongings, and both were killed, reputedly by Ute Indians. Richard would suffer a similar fate along with botanist Frederick Creutzfeldt before the passing of half a decade on still another expedition noted later in this work. Frémont moved rapidly to gain new supplies and livestock before leaving by the southern route along the Del Norte to the Gila in southern Arizona and to Sonora, Mexico, prior to turning north to Tucson, Arizona, and west to southern

California. Not all of the party chose to continue to go with him; some harbored ill feelings toward Frémont, he had let them down in a critical situation and some would never forgive him. More will be said of the fourth expedition in the section on botany, not so much because of the contributions of Frémont but with the movement of men, including botanist Frederick Creutzfeldt and artist Richard Kern, to the Gunnison expedition.

Frémont would return to Washington as the short-term anti-slavery senator from California early in 1850. With gold mined from The Mariposas and the senatorial position, his future seemed assured. He would not, however, be re-elected to that office, and money, which at times he possessed in great abundance, was a fleeting entity in Frémont's hands.

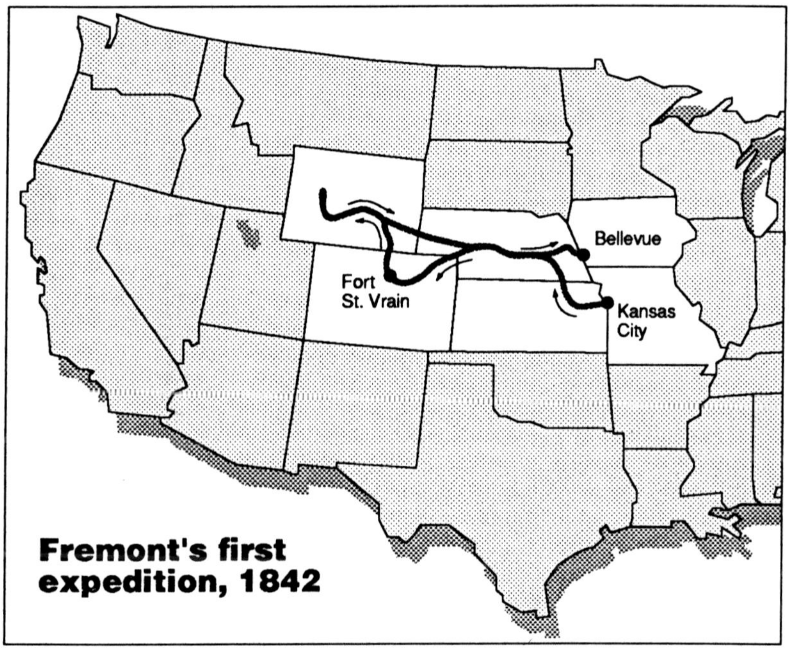

FIGURE 1. Route of the first expedition, 1842.

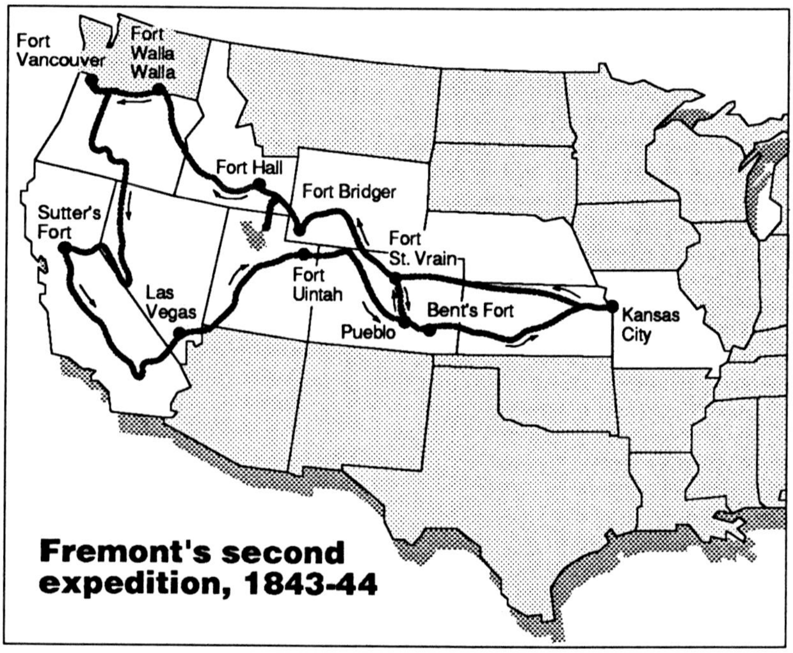

FIGURE 2. Route of the second expedition, 1843–44.

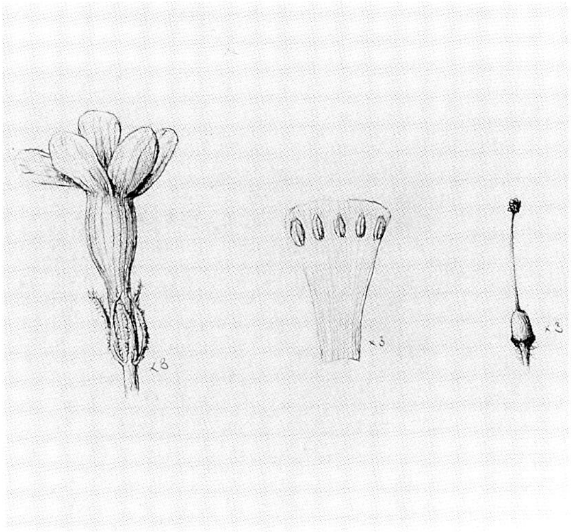

FIGURE 18. Drawing at NY taken from lectotype of *Amsonia tomentosa* Torr. & Frém. in Frém. (artist unknown).

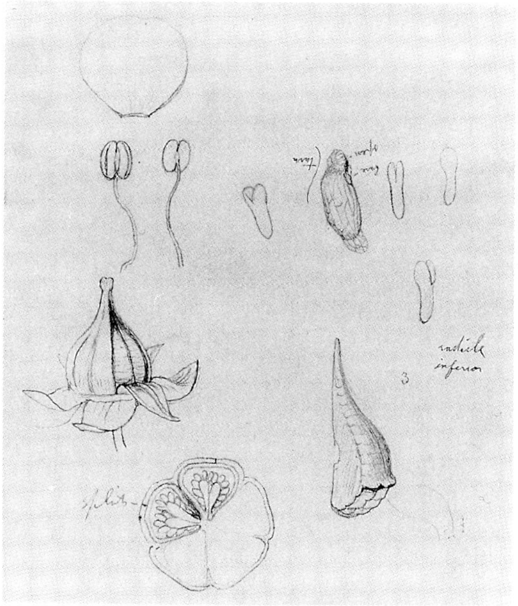

FIGURE 19. Pencil sketch showing detail reconstructed by John Torrey from the specimens of *Carpenteria californica* Torr. taken late in the season by Frémont, NY.

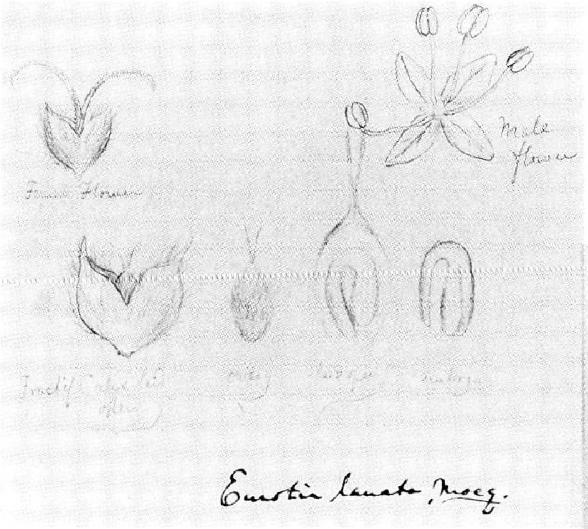

FIGURE 20. Pencil sketch of details of flowers, fruit, seed, and embryo of *Ceratoides lanata* (Pursh) J. T. Howell. The sketch is attached to a sheet bearing four mounted specimens, one by Dr. James of Long's 1st Expedition, one by Abert in 1846 and two by John Charles Frémont, one on the first and one on the third expedition, NY.

FIGURE 21. Specimens (syntypes) of *Chorizanthe brevicornu* Torr. taken by Frémont "Probably from the Gila," NY.

FIGURE 22. Sheet of *Eriogonum annuum* Nutt. with two collections by Frémont, both from the third expedition, NY. On 29 July 1845, Frémont was three days' ride east of Bent's Fort (Otero Co., Colorado), and he reached Piney Creek of the Grand River on 4 September 1845.

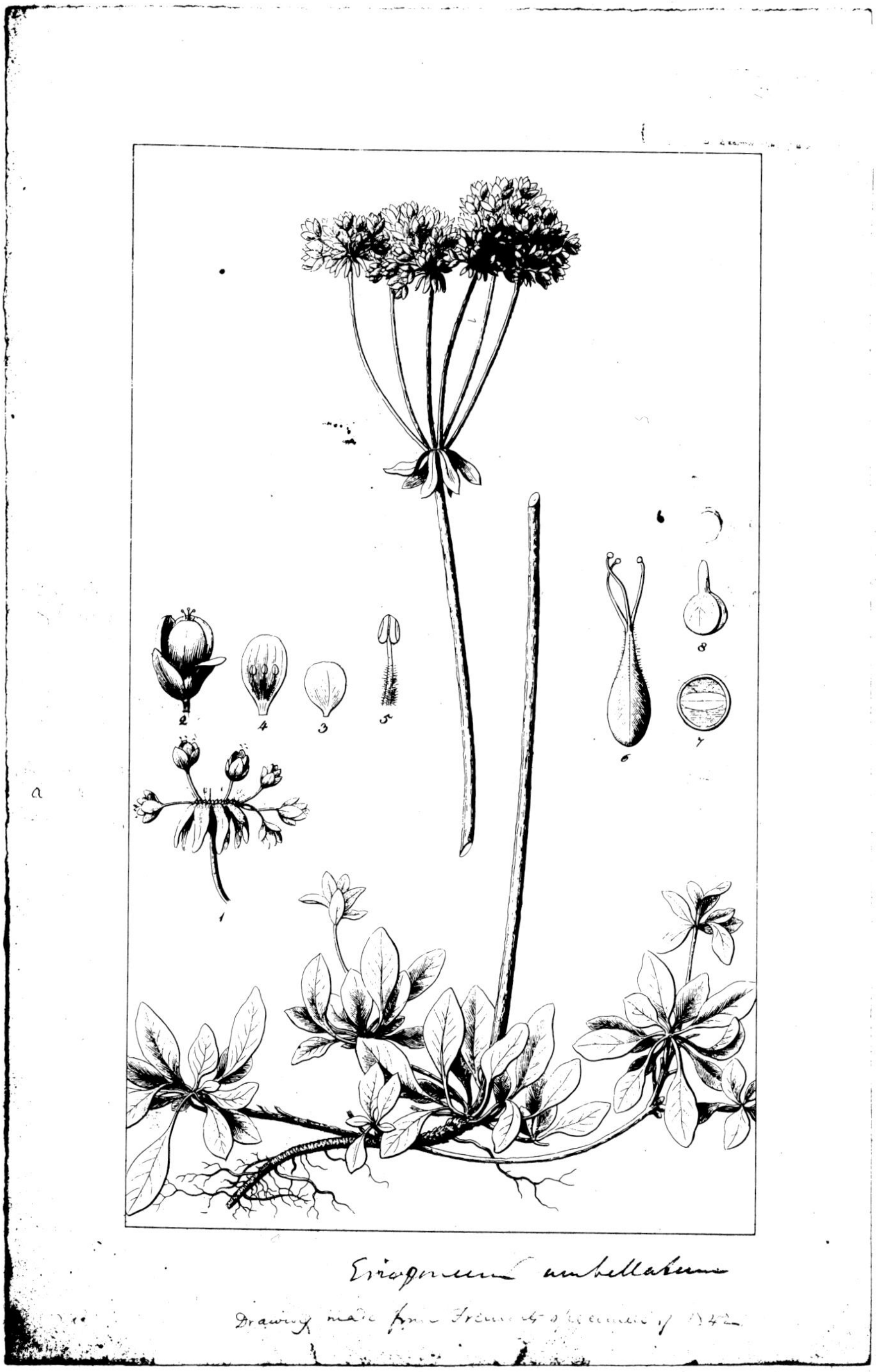

FIGURE 23. Print of *Eriogonum umbellatum* Torr. "Drawing made from Frémont's specimen of 1842," NY. With notations by John Torrey. The Frémont collection was taken on 7 August 1842, one day's journey east of South Pass, Frémont Co., Wyoming.

FIGURE 24. Syntype of *Franseria deltoidea* Torr., with Torrey's sketches of floral parts, NY.

FIGURE 25. Type of *Ipomoea leptophylla* Torr. in Frém., NY. On 24 July 1842, Frémont moved west from the La Bonte River junction with the North Fork of the Platte, near present Douglas, Converse Co., Wyoming.

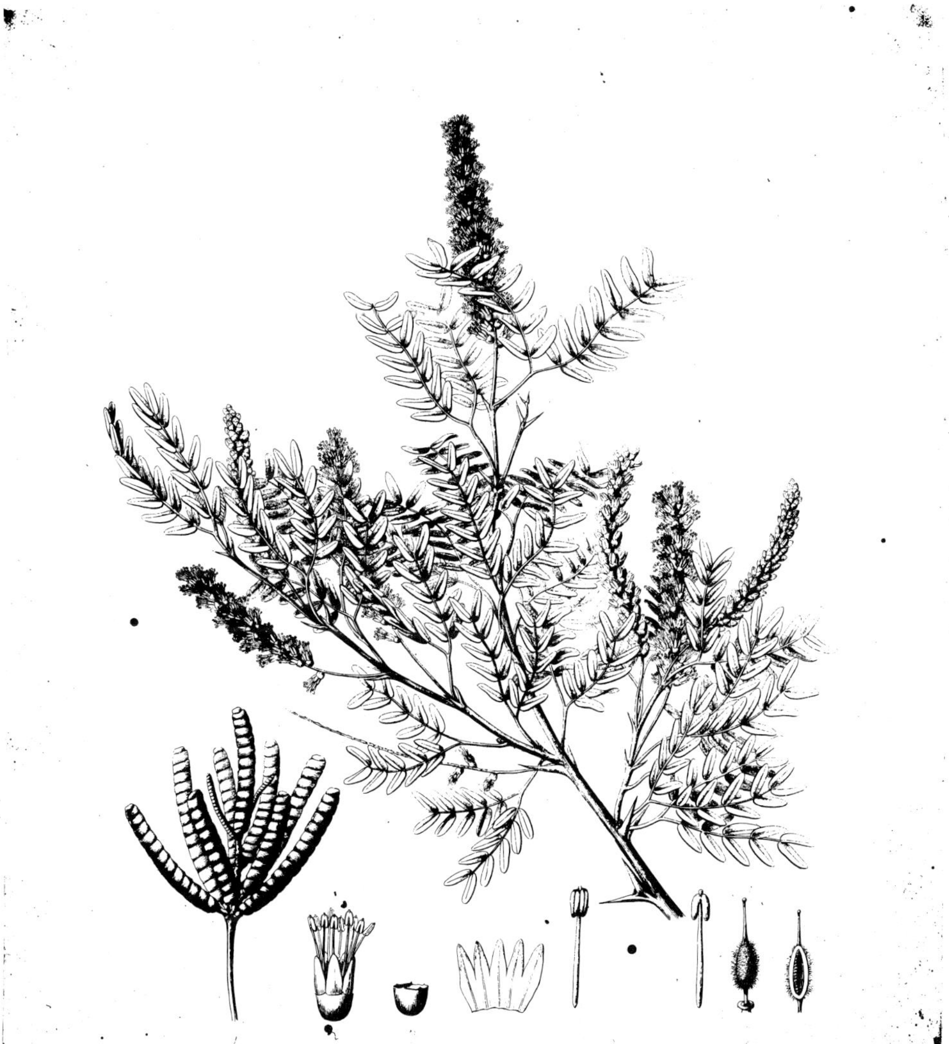

FIGURE 26. Print of *Prosopis odorata* (Torr. in Frém.) Torr. & Frém. in Frém. emend. Welsh, NY. This shows the mixed collection of fruit of screwbean, type of the species, and flowering branch of the honey mesquite.

FIGURE 27. Sheet of *Quercus gambelii* Nutt., NY. The specimen was taken in Spanish Fork Canyon, Utah Co., Utah on 21 May 1844. It is one of the first known plant specimens to be collected in Utah County.

FIGURE 28. Diagnostic sketches of fertile portions of *Fremontia* Torr. (i.e., *Sarcobatus*), NY. The material on which the genus is based was taken by Frémont on 30 July 1842, near Alcova, Natrona Co., Wyoming.

FIGURE 29. John Charles Frémont, modified from an engraving by J.Rogers Sc. 381 B. W. N. York, used as frontispiece in C. W. Upham's 1856 "Life, Explorations, and Public Service of John Charles Frémont." Boston: Tichnor and Fields.

CHAPTER VI

FIFTH EXPEDITION—1853–54

John Charles, Jessie, and family were in Paris, France, when they received a letter from Thomas Hart Benton indicating that Congress had finally approved surveys of the main routes for construction of a railroad to the Pacific. The routes had to be both practical and economical. Benton advised Frémont to return from Europe and to apply for a place on the survey of that region between the 38th and 39th parallels. Frémont was admirably prepared for such an assignment, since he had already surveyed both ends of the area of concern. Benton even contacted Secretary of War Jefferson Davis to suggest that Frémont should be included. Davis did not respond favorably to Benton's suggestions and instead appointed Captain John W. Gunnison leader of the survey. Certainly the abolitionist views of Senator Benton and of John Charles did not help the case with Jefferson Davis, who in a few short years would be president of the Confederacy.

Time had not waited for Frémont, who had become increasingly tied to events arising from the purchase of the property known as The Mariposas in California in 1847. Prior to leaving Sutter's Fort under house arrest for the long ride to Fort Leavenworth, Kansas, Frémont had arranged for the purchase of the property. Gold was discovered on The Mariposas, following the initial discovery at Sutter's. Frémont became, overnight as it were, a wealthy person. He engaged in numerous ventures, many with side issues resulting in litigation, and there was the constant fight to prove up on the land grant claims of The Mariposas, which consisted of some 70 square miles of land at the head of the Mariposa River, Mariposa County, California.

While Frémont was involved with his private life, other expeditions were in progress. Probably as a consequence of Frémont's retirement from the military and certainly as a result of his summary explorations of the Great Salt Lake, an expedition was mounted to explore that region. The expedition could well have been assigned to Frémont, who knew the region better than anyone in the Topographical Corps of the Army. Instead the expedition was placed under the direction of Captain Howard Stansbury (1806–1863), Corps Topographical Engineers, U. S. Army (Stansbury, 1852). The Stansbury expedition left Fort Leavenworth on 31 May 1849 and arrived in Utah in late August or early September. Assisting Stansbury was Lieutenant John W. Gunnison, who would be named in 1853 to command the very expedition that Frémont had hoped for. The botanical results of the Stansbury expedition have been reviewed by Welsh (1987) and Tiehm (1987).

Now, despite the loss of the appointment to lead the exploration of the central route for a practical and economical railroad, Frémont would return and prepare for a survey anyway, financed in part personally and in part by other private individuals. Perhaps he still had thoughts of recovering his stature as famous explorer gained from the first two highly successful expeditions especially. He must have expected some positive economic gain from the venture, or possibly the allure of camp life was sufficiently attractive to cause him to attempt another such venture, although he claimed this was not the case. At 40 years of age he was certain of the rigors of the wilderness, a fact that his injury from the fourth expedition constantly reminded him of. Another winter beyond the frontier must have seemed a little too much. His reasons were not made clear, but the venture was undertaken in spite of the failure of the fourth expedition and his disgraceful treatment following the third expedition.

While Frémont was in New York, he engaged the services of artist and dageurreotypist Solomon Nunes Carvalho (on 23 August 1853) for the coming expedition. Evidently Frémont had been embarrassed by the numerous journals recording his grisly trip of 1848–49, or, possibly, he wanted to garner all possible commercial advantage to himself. In any event, he forbade Carvalho (1815–1897) and others from keeping journals during the expedition of 1853–54. In spite of that prohibition, Carvalho (1857) was later able to publish an account of the journey, whether from letters, as is indicated in the preface of his work, or from a secretly kept journal is speculative. And, it is from his account of the expedition that most of the information has been derived. Unfortunately, Frémont published only fragments of the record of the fifth expedition, and his reasons for not publishing a complete account have remained obscure.

The itinerary is generally described, but there is a consistent lack of dates. Consequently, much familiarity with the country through which the 1853–54 expedition traveled is necessary to determine even approximate times of events and places. No map showing camp sites was produced at the close of the expedition either, so dates are impossible to infer from map localities. The account presented below is taken from the version printed in 1954 by The Jewish Publication Society of America, Philadelphia.

Carvalho left New York on 5 September 1853, "having in charge the daguerreotype apparatus, painting materials" (Carvalho, 1857), and went to St. Louis, to Colonel Brant's house. Later, on the day of his arrival, he boarded a steamer for Kansas. He did not arrive at Kansas until 14 September. From there his baggage was moved to Westport, a few miles away. Ten Delaware Indians were chosen to go with the party, among whom was "a chief named Solomon, who had been with him [Frémont] before, and for whom Col. Frémont felt a great friendship" (Carvalho, 1857: 85). The Indians were to join the party near the Kansas River, "about one hundred miles westward, on 27 Sept. Evidently twelve Delaware were in the party, at one time or another" (Spence, 1984: 403). Spence notes that Solomon had been with Frémont on the third expedition.

The party evidently left Westport on 23 September, proceeded westward past the Shawnee Mission a few miles and camped for the night. A Max Strobel joined the party there as assistant topographer. Frémont, being ill, returned to Westport, and finally to St. Louis, while the party continued west to the point chosen to meet the Delaware hunters. Frémont would try to rejoin them there. Sometime in October 1853 Jessie received a telegram indicating that John Charles was ill, too sick to continue, and had returned to St.

Louis. Jessie hurried to his side and found him to be suffering from "inflamatory rheumatism in his frostbitten leg" (Herr, 1989: 232).

Travel of the expedition sans Frémont on 24 September was through open prairie. On the morning of 25 September, Carvalho (1857: 90) rode out onto the prairie to watch the sunrise, and he wrote eloquently: "Gradually the eastern horizon assumed a warmer hue, while some floating clouds along its edge, developed their form against the luminous heavens. The dark grey morning tints were superseded by hues of the most brilliant and gorgeous colors, which almost as imperceptibly softened, as the glorious orb of day commenced his diurnal course, and illumined the vault above; a slight rustling of the long grass, caused by a deliciously pleasant zephyr, which made it move in gentle undulation, was all that disturbed the mysterious silence that prevailed."

When the contingent came to the place they were to meet the Delaware Indians, on 27 September, Carvalho (1857: 91) recorded: "To-day we met our Delawares, who were awaiting our arrival. A more noble set of Indians I never saw, the most of them six feet high, all mounted and armed *cap-a-pie*, under command of Captain Wolff, a 'Big Indian,' as he called himself." And, "They became very much attached to Col. Frémont, and every one of them would have ventured his life for him." The combined party stayed at the encampment until the end of September, awaiting John Charles's arrival. After two days Strobel arrived with a letter from Frémont, who had been forced, in consequence of his continuing illness, to return to St. Louis. The party was instructed by Frémont to move camp to the "Saline fork of the Kansas River, where there were plenty of buffalo, and remain there until he joined us, which he hoped would be in a fortnight."

The impatient group of men were still in their camp on the Saline Fork on 20 October, when it was necessary to send to Fort Riley for supplies. By 30 October the men were still in camp, both more anxious and more impatient, while prairie fires raged about them, filling the air with smoke. Through the smoke and fire on 31 October came Frémont, Solomon, and Doctor Ober (Ebers), "Col. Frémont's 'cook'" (Carvalho, 1857: 119). Dr. Ebers was a physician who accompanied the party to treat the ailing Frémont.

In the *Memoirs* Frémont (1887: 27–28) wrote a few meager entries concerning with the 1853–54 expedition. Under the date of 25 October 1853 he records: "Went to Union town and nooned. This is a street of log-cabins. Uniontown is called a hundred miles from Kansas." On 26 October, he continued: "High wind and sleet. Clouds scudding across the sky. About two o'clock we reached the pretty little Catholic Mission of St. Mary's. . . . A clear sky promises a bright day for to-marrow. Learned here some of the plants, which are medicinal among the Indians. Among them *Asarum Canadensis* [*A. canadense* L.]—jewelweed [probably *Impatiens capensis* Meerb.]—a narcotic; and *Oryngium Aquaticum* [possibly *Orontium aquaticum* L., but not of the Great Plains], the great remedy of the Pottawatamies for snake-bites." On 27 October he noted: "White frost covers the ground this morning. Sky clear and air still." Three days later John Charles arrived through the smoke into camp where the party anxiously awaited him. One wonders if the above citations by Frémont of the 1853–54 expedition were not the only ones he recorded personally, or, if not, why they were the only ones he chose to include in his memoirs. The fourth and fifth expedition journals were to be included in volume two of his memoirs, a volume never published. One can only wonder at what they might have contained or what they would have been based upon. The inclusion of plant names in the fragmentary record indicates that botany would again have been a theme.

On 1 November 1853 Frémont and company moved toward Bent's new fort (later Fort Lyon, following purchase by the government) near Big Timbers (downriver from Las Animas, Bent County), Colorado. William Bent, owner of the fort, was well known to John Charles, and from him were obtained the provisions to carry the party through the mountains. Carvalho (1857: 132) reports: "Col. Frémont procured from him fresh animals for all the men, leaving behind us those which were thought unable to go through. At this time Mr. Bent had but a small quantity of sugar and coffee; he supplied us, however, with all he could spare, and a considerable quantity of dried buffalo meat, moccasins and overshoes for all the men; a large buffalo-skin lodge, capable of covering twenty-five men, and one small one for Col. Frémont; buffalo robes for each man besides stockings, gloves, tobacco, etc." The party would be much better prepared than was the 1848 expedition, but still they could not carry sufficient supplies for so protracted an exploration. The party of 25 men, working hard, would require huge quantities of food, rich in fat and protien, but the men were hopefully expectant of living off the land. The Delaware Indians, hunters of renown, were among the insurance policies of this expedition. They would provide meat from wild animals if any were to be had. The country through which they were to pass was to prove a poor one with regard to edible wild game, or any other animals, in that season. One suspects that there were later doubts about leaving any animals behind at Bent's Fort; all could have been eaten.

Evidently Frémont's leg was so much better that he decided not to take Doctor Ebers with him. The exploring party traveled up the Arkansas River, passed the ruins of Bent's original fort, and struck the mouth of the Huerfano River (Pueblo County), which they followed into the Huerfano Valley, "which is by far the most romantic and beautiful country I ever beheld" (Carvalho, 1857: 136). The party entered the mountains on 3 December. They then crossed a pass beyond which lay the San Louis Valley (Alamosa County, Colorado), and into this they descended. The route was then along the valley toward its head, where the entourage crossed Saguache Creek and entered Saguache Valley (Saguache County, Colorado) (Spence, 1984: 428). The route continued westward to the Continental Divide at Cochetopa Pass on 14 December (Upham, 1856: 330). The men and animals had been following the route of Captain Gunnison, who had preceded them through this very region some months earlier. Now they followed down along the course of the river that would bear Gunnison's name. This was in the Colorado River drainage, which had eluded Frémont on his 1848 journey.

Supplies had already begun to run low, and without sufficient wild game along the route the men were killing horses to eat. The trail was south of the Gunnison River, approximately along the route of present U.S. Highway 50. One of their camps was near a Ute Indian village, probably in the Uncompahgre Valley, where Frémont bartered with the Indians for food and other items. Later the Indians claimed that a supposedly wild horse killed by the party some 20 miles distant in reality belonged to one of them. Frémont offered to pay for it, but not with gunpowder that might be used against them.

Next morning Carvalho traded for a young healthy horse, giving a pair of blankets, an exhausted pony, and other items in exchange. His own horse Pungo had been slaughtered for food three days earlier, and Carvalho was riding one of the baggage animals. He probably had second thoughts about giving up the worn-out horse later, when there were not enough animals to carry the men. Game was scarce, and the little that could be procured could not appease the appetites of the group. The men ate one horse or mule each day and a half, and in the end there were too many days and too few horses and mules.

After leaving the Indian encampment, the expedition traveled for 30 miles and again camped. The camp was soon surrounded by another group of armed Indians, demanding payment for the butchered horse a second time, stating that the horse did not belong to the person at the other encampment but to one of them. Frémont would not listen to or be threatened by them, reasoning that the Indians must be out of powder or otherwise they would have attacked the camp and taken the supplies. From these Indians they obtained several strong horses to add to their dwindling supply. The horses were all later eaten by the men. Following along the Uncompahgre River, the party reached the Gunnison River (near present Delta). The expedition then followed the course of the Gunnison to the Grand (present Colorado) River near where Grand Junction (Mesa County), Colorado, now stands. Ice stood out from the banks of the river, narrowing the flowing stream to about two hundred yards in width. To allow the animals to keep their footing, the men carried sand out onto the smooth ice. Two of the Delaware Indians swam through the icy waters to the north bank and built a fire on that side, so that the others might be warmed quickly. The men on the south bank rode their horses onto the ice and forced them to plunge into the frigid water, clinging desperately to their animals as they swam to the far side of the river. Immediately after emerging from the water, the men headed for the roaring fire, where they stood shivering until their clothes dried on them.

The men now faced perilous conditions. Their supply of horses diminished with each passing day, and they were still almost 300 miles away from pioneer Mormon settlements. To make matters even worse, the route west from the vicinity of Grand Junction traverses one of the most bleak and desolate landscapes in western America, almost devoid of wildlife. Cretaceous sandstones, interspersed with clays and beds of coal, form prowlike and castellated abutments in a long, sweeping line of the Tavaputs Plateau on the north. The broad valley is in Mancos Shale, clothed thinly with salt desert shrubs. The beautiful, snow-capped La Sal Mountains lie almost menacingly to the south. The Colorado River becomes entrenched in a deep gorge not far west of Grand Junction, and its route turns to the southwest into the great Canyonlands of the Colorado Plateau. The saline clay plain has few waterholes and practically no running streams. Food for the thin and starving horses and mules was limited to the sparse covering of salt desert shrubs, mainly salt bushes (species of *Atriplex*). Fortunately there were few barriers, except for readily bypassed, deeply entrenched dry drainages, for the men and their animals to cross. This was the land the expedition would have to cross immediately on their way to the Green River.

The Frémont party was again (or still) on the tracks of the Gunnison expedition, which they followed westward. Somewhere west of present Crescent Junction, Grand County, Utah, the route diverged from the Gunnison track and turned to the southwest to the Green River, across from its juncture with the San Rafael River. After crossing the Green River (into Emery County, Utah) the progressively weaker party immediately went to an Indian camp on the west side. "We found that they lived on nothing else but grass-seed [likely that of *Stipa hymenoides* Trin., the Indian ricegrass], which they collected in the fall. Their women parch it, and grind it between stones. In this manner it is very palatable, and tastes very much like roasted peanuts. This, their only article of food, was very scarce, and we could procure only a small supply" (Carvalho, 1857: 168). The men bartered what they could and obtained some of the meal and a lame horse, the latter being immediately butchered for food.

Upon leaving the Green River the route was along the San Rafael River toward huge sandstone hogbacks forming the "tooth-in-jaw" eastern margin of the San Rafael Swell, a huge anticline, through which is entrenched the river. Unless one was willing to pass northward around this geological barrier, the route west was effectively blocked by the hogback ridges of the San Rafael Swell. Later surveyors for railroad routes would avoid the swell after one abortive attempt across its northern end, the evidence of which can still be seen in cut-and-fill slopes and structures. The northern route would be north of the 39th parallel, which Frémont somehow discerned as the northern limits of his survey.

With the way westward blocked and with that to the northwest untenable, the party turned to the southwest along the gently inclined east foot of the San Rafael Swell, with the San Rafael Reef of saw-toothed hogbacks to the west. They crossed the Muddy River northwest of present Hanksville, near its juncture with Salt Creek, and it seems probable that they turned west along Salt Creek and up the foot slope of Thousand Lake Mountain, which they crossed before the route descended into Rabbit Valley northeast of present Frémont, Wayne County, Utah. Crossing the Awapa Plateau, the party descended into Grass Valley, near present Koosharem, and turned south down the drainage. To the west was a huge snow-covered mountain (Monroe Mountain), which blocked their way. Southward Otter Creek, the stream in Grass Valley, Piute County, Utah, joins the East Fork of the Sevier River north of present Antimony. Following along the East Fork of the Sevier, the party moved west to its juncture with the main branch of the Sevier at present Kingston, Piute County, Utah. The massive, snowclad peaks of the Tushar Mountains stood sentinel-like to the west, again blocking the direct path westward, and again the party turned to the south, up the main course of the Sevier River. The struggling party, some of them again walking—the horses or mules they had been riding having been killed for food—passed present Circleville and entered the cliff-margined narrows through which present highway 89 runs, crowded by the river. Evidently at the mouth of Chokecherry Creek, within the narrows of Circleville Canyon, through which the Sevier River passes, the group—worn, hungry, freezing, and desolate—turned west and wearily climbed the southeast flank of the Tushar Mountains toward a low pass.

Carvalho (1857: 186) notes that after they left the Green River, "the whole party was on foot." Lack of food made them weaker each day. They were suffering from the cold, especially from frozen feet. The men and animals of the expedition were in such poor condition, that they determined to cache part of the baggage (including Caravalho's daguerrotypes) to lighten the load, which according to Spence (1984: 467), they did in Grass Valley, along Otter Creek (near present Koosharem, Utah). The men could all ride again, but thereafter whenever a horse or mule gave out or was killed for food, the man who had been riding it had to walk. To preserve the strength of the horses and mules as much as possible, the men chose to walk and lead them. When an animal was killed, it was divided into 20 parts, 10 for the Indians and 10 for the balance of the party. The ration had to last for six meals, i.e., two days. Often it was consumed in one day, and those who did not choose to ration themselves were forced to go without food until the next horse or mule was killed. As the days passed, more of the party were again on foot. And each day the surviving men and animals became more gaunt and nearer starvation.

Probably while camped at the mouth of Chokecherry Creek, Carvalho assisted Frémont in making an astronomical observation to determine their position. Frémont remained for hours making the observations, using the light from a candle provided by Carvalho. "The next morning, Col. Frémont told me that Parowan, a small settlement of Mormons, forty rods square, in the Little Salt Lake Valley, was distant so many miles in a certain direction, immediately over this great mountain of snow; that in three days he hoped to be in the settlement, and that he intended to go over the mountain, at all hazards" (Carvalho, 1857: 193). The route westward was up the steep drainage of Chokecherry Creek, through the broad meadow-clad Dog Valley to the divide of Frémont Pass, and then down Frémont Wash to Parowan or Little Salt Lake Valley, Iron County, Utah. Deer tracks were seen in the snow, and the Delawares, with newly found energy and enthusiasm, were soon out hunting. After some hours one of them, Weluchas, came in with a deer across his saddle. The deer are traditionally poor at that time of year; it was then the first week of February. But no matter how poor the animal, it was better than the flesh of starving horses and mules.

The route for the previous hundred miles was through what is in modern times some of the best big game lands of Utah, but no previous mention of deer or antelope was included by Carvalho. Indications are that game was indeed very scarce during this period.

In spite of the nearness of the party to the pioneer village of Parowan and the encouragement derived from the deer, the travail was not at an end. Oliver Fuller died in the saddle on 7 (or 6) February, filling the camp with despair. His body was rolled in some blankets and cached in the snow, to be buried a few days later by a party of Mormons from Parowan (at a point about 1.5 miles east along Frémont Wash from Muley Point, the prominence on the east side of Parowan Valley near its north end). Soon thereafter they came upon ruts in the snow made by wagon wheels; civilization could not be far away. Late at night on 8 (or 7, see Upham, 1856: 330) February 1854 the starving party, suffering from cold and exhaustion, straggled into Parowan, Iron County, Utah, and salvation. The Mormons welcomed John Charles. The young men of the village turned out en masse and went immediately back along the trail to bring in the stragglers, took them individually into their homes, helped to clean them up, fed them, and provided warm places to sleep—the first inside a dwelling in many months of living in the wilderness. No one, not even Frémont, was able to leave immediately to continue the journey, although apparently the Delawares all arrived in relatively good condition. Carvalho was taken in by an English shoemaker, Mr. William Heap, a polygamist with two wives, with whom he stayed for two weeks, at a cost of $1.50 per day, paid by Colonel Frémont, who was hosted by Mormon Stake President John Calvin Lazelle Smith and his family (Spence, 1984: 468).

John Charles wrote a letter (Upham, 1856: 329–333) to Senator Benton, dated 9 February 1854, in which the condition of the men was noted: "The Delawares all came in sound, but the whites of my party were all exhausted and broken up, and more or less frost-bitten. I lost one, Mr. Fuller of St. Louis, Missouri, who died on entering this valley. He died like a man, on horseback, in his saddle, and will be buried like a soldier, on the spot where he fell."

By 21 February, Frémont and the bulk of the party were sufficiently recovered and resupplied to continue toward California. Carvalho and some others could not continue because they were weak and afflicted with diarrhea. On the same day that Frémont left Parowan, Carvalho did too, but toward Salt Lake City, with a party of Mormons on their way north to attend the annual April conference of the Mormon Church. Carvalho was able to purchase sugar, tea, and coffee from Henry Lunt, prominent church official in the region. He arrived at Salt Lake City on 1 March 1854. There Carvalho met Lieutenant E. G. Beckwith, then in charge of the Gunnison Expedition.

On 25 October 1853 the Gunnison party was camped along the Sevier River, west of present Deseret, Millard County, Utah, when they were attacked by Indians. Killed in the attack were Captain Gunnison, artist Richard Kern, and botanist Frederick Creutzfeldt. Both Kern and Creutzfeldt had been with Frémont on the fourth expedition of 1848. The death of Kern, at the hands of a disgruntled band of Ute Indians, is coincidental, his brother Benjamin having been killed by other Indians five years earlier. Only Edward (Hine, 1962) of the Kern trio survived the expeditions of western exploration. Beckwith invited Carvalho to "mess at their table, at E. T. Benson's, one of the Mormon apostles" (Beckwith, 1855: 206).

Frémont had been able to obtain horses and mules through an arrangement whereby the animals and supplies were paid out of tithing money then in hand, by Mormon Bishop Tarleton Lewis, who took in exchange from the expedition leader a draft on a California bank, ultimately to be deposited to the account of Governor Brigham Young. "On his return to Washington, JCF called on the Utah territorial delegate, John Bernheisel, and thanked him for the kindness he had received from the Mormon people" (Spence, 1984: 469).

The route from Parowan to California is outlined by Spence (1984: 475). The party traveled past Cedar City, entered the Antelope Range via Leach Canyon, traversed the range, passed present New Castle, and entered the Escalante Desert. The trail passed up Shoal Creek to its source, almost on the present boundary between Utah and Nevada, where Frémont and his men left the Great Basin and passed back into the Basin and Range Province within the Colorado drainage. Westward they descended into Clover

Valley via Clover Creek. The route was upstream along Clover Creek and over a divide into Meadow Valley Wash. Continuing westward they crossed Stampede Gap and Dry Lake Valley and entered the drainage of the White River, tributary of the Colorado drainage system in the Basin and Range Province. Up the White River Valley to approximately the 38th parallel, the route struck westward across Timber Pass back into the Great Basin in the Seaman Range, entered Coal Valley, and trended southwest across the Golden Gate Range to Garden Valley. It then traversed Sand Spring Valley, through the gap at the north end of the Worthington Mountains. "Turning west after clearing the southernmost projections of the Quinn Canyon and Reveille ranges, the expedition crossed the Kawich Mountains via Cedar Pass and descended to the floor of Cactus Flat" (Spence, 1984: 476).

From Cactus Flat the Frémont party went west over the Palmetto Mountains via Lida Pass, crossed Fish Lake Valley, ascended the White Mountains, and crossed into Owens Valley, near present Big Pine, California. It was then early spring, on or about 21 March, and snow blocked the passes westward. Turning southward, the party followed the trail of the Talbot-Kern portion of Frémont's 1845 expedition until opposite Owens Peak, then turned west and crossed the Sierra Nevada on 1 April over Bird Spring Pass, 10 miles south of his goal of Walker Pass.

Frémont was in San Francisco by 16 April 1854. "The season did not permit of extensive zoological, botanical or geological researches" (Spence, 1984: 474). Frémont had passed his 41st birthday somewhere between Cochetopa Pass and Parowan, possibly near the Green River crossing. The close of the fifth expedition marked the end of an era in his life. He would progress to other things, but a single word might be used to summarize his years beyond the expeditions—failure. The results of the fifth expedition are difficult to judge. Certainly John Charles had demonstrated that it was feasible to cross the Rocky Mountains in mid-winter, by ordinary means, vindicating, at least in part, the failure of the fourth expedition. And, he was able to add a few specimens to the large herbarium of his previous expeditions. Perhaps the fifth journey was a success after all; it is too bad that John Charles chose not to publish a complete account.

In two years, 1856, he would be the presidential candidate for the Republican Party; he would run for the office of president and lose, but in so doing he would set the stage for the election of Abraham Lincoln in 1860. James Buchanan, winner of the 1856 election, a man frozen by indecision, would prove incapable for the job, but then too, perhaps, John Charles would not have done better. The events of history over the previous decades had polarized the nation into two camps; probably the Civil War was inevitable. Abolitionist Frémont was in trouble with a huge segment of the nation during his campaign for the presidency, one reason for his defeat. The people of the South would not have looked kindly upon his election, possibly resulting in a Civil War some four years earlier than the date following the election of Lincoln.

Appointed by Lincoln as general in the Civil War (Bradford, 1984; Foote, 1986; Freeman, 1970; Hart, 1958; Herr, 1987; Long, 1971; McPherson, 1988; Rolle, 1991), Frémont would fail in his role as commander of the Army of the West, fall from favor because of inaction, graft, insensivity to the general good of the nation, and other failures, and be replaced by an impatient and considerate President Abraham Lincoln, who gave Frémont every benefit of the doubt prior to dismissing him. Later, with hope that Frémont would serve well somewhere, and under considerable political pressure, Lincoln would reappoint John Charles commander of the Mountain Division in West Virginia and Virginia; here Frémont would act indecisively in campaigns against Confederate General Stonewall Jackson, who out-generaled him. On 17 June 1862, the disappointed Frémont, with feelings hurt, arrogantly resigned his command when General John Pope was advanced ahead of him (Long, 1971). Ten days later President Lincoln accepted the resignation. Few were unhappy to see him leave command, even though he was to be retained in the Army for more than a year beyond his resignation; perhaps he could serve elsewhere, but his rank was senior to practically all others in the Army, an untenable condition, and his role as a Civil War soldier was at an end, long before that devastating and bloody struggle came to its grinding halt. Responsible for the appointment of U.S. Grant to a position in the Army of the West, Grant was somewhat resentful of Frémont's removal (Long, 1952: 360). The view of history indicates that John Charles did not serve well under either of his Civil War appointments. Perhaps too much had been expected.

In 1864, the disgruntled and vindictive Frémont accepted the nomination by Republican party radicals, and by others unhappy with Lincoln's handling of the war, as candidate for the presidency, at a meeting held some days prior to the regular Republican political convention. In his acceptance speech John Charles denounced Lincoln, who was fighting to preserve the Union with a diverse group of generals, many of whom were, for a variety of reasons, as incompetent and as impossible to deal with as Frémont had been. One by one Lincoln replaced most of them as he had John Charles. Only when the fortunes of war turned clearly to the Union (General William T. Sherman's capture of Atlanta) did Frémont withdraw, throwing support to the Republican party, but still bitterly denouncing Lincoln (McPherson, 1988). He would not, at least, serve as spoiler of Lincoln's bid for a second term. Still later, during 1879–82, Frémont would serve ineffectively as appointed governor to the Territory of Arizona; his role there was primarily a private one, trying through various mining and investment schemes in that Territory to recoup the lost fortunes from his failed California ventures. The results of those attempts guaranteed his failure as governor of the territory, and did not result in the recouping of his fortunes.

In spite of Frémont's misfortunes, this man of intelligence, obvious charm, and numerous faults (Herr, 1987: 92) would never be better than when leading his small parties of exploration. There he could and did make the decisions without interference from others. When involved with the workaday world of politics or finance, Frémont was largely ineffectual. Spence (1976: 288) noted: "Too often one lets Frémont's later failures cloud his earlier achievements. In admitting that his character was flawed by vanity and by hunger for recognition and financial gain, one tends to forget the dedication and discipline of his work of the 1840s. The wonder is that he was able to accomplish as much as he did. An exploring expedition required organization: as leader, Frémont provided this—and he handled the logistics, oversaw the mapping, conducted the geodetic surveying, arranged the defense, and maintained the records. Late at night he shot readings on the stars, sometimes standing waist-deep in snow, work he regarded as routine." To this long list of tasks, which would have been impossible for most expedition leaders, must be added the collection of plants, a task often too great in contemporary terms for expeditions with multiple tasks.

The time spent on expeditions was taken from John Charles's marriage to Jessie Benton. "Frémont was absent five of their first six and a half years of wedded life. Not until 1860 could Jessie write: 'I feel now as if we were a complete & Compact family & really Mr. Frémont used to be only a guest—dearly loved & honored but not counted on for worse as well as better'" (Spence, 1976). His years following the Civil War and those in New York and California with Jessie, though often troubled (there are accounts of his infidelity), must have been filled with much contentment and certainly with many regrets (Herr, 1987). John Charles Frémont, aged 77, died of peritonitis in New York City on 13 July 1890 and is buried in Rockland County, New York. Jessie did not have the means to have him returned to California for burial and could not afford to travel to New York for his funeral. She would survive him by a dozen years and be his staunch defender to the end. Jessie and most of Frémont's family are appropriately interred adjacent to the remains of John Charles, in a lovely spot overlooking the Hudson River.

CHAPTER VII

BOTANY OF THE EXPEDITIONS

The contributions to understanding of western American topography undoubtedly constitute the most important works of John Charles Frémont. It is also apparent, however, that among his most lasting and most important works are those in the field of botany, a field largely ignored by his biographers. Plants were taken on all five expeditions, and those formed a portion of the data base on which western American botany was interpreted. The late Susan Delano McKelvey (1955: 754) noted that, "many of his activities along lines other than topographical are even now subjects for controversy," and that, "our interest in Frémont's travels arises from the fact that on his first three journeys he collected plants which were described by John Torrey. There is reason to suppose that he made some collections on his fourth expedition as well but, as far as I know, no report was published upon them."

Frémont was indeed controversial—he almost invited controversy living in the spotlight with a family at least as controversial as he was—and much of the rhetoric used by his accusers was justified. Even if controversial, he was seldom dull. Nevertheless, McKelvey, a capable botanist in her own right, merely summarized Frémont's botanical contributions, doing little more than listing the botanical names included in the accounts of the first three expeditions. There is no indication that she made an effort to search out exactly what his contributions were in fact, a problem made understandable and excusable by the size and complexity of her magnificent undertaking. However, Frémont made collections on all five expeditions, and those collections are reported herein.

The published accounts by Frémont demonstrate conclusively that he was dedicated to the collection of plants, continuing to take them even during the most difficult periods of the expeditions, such as the crossing of the Sierra Nevada in the winter of 1844, while some of his men were engaged in killing Indians at Lassen's in the spring of 1846, and at the beginning of the rebellion in California later in 1846. An examination of the many specimens that survived the perils of travel and wear and tear of the expedition demonstrates even more conclusively the dedication of John Charles. Such devotion to a task is difficult, if not impossible, to instill in some persons unless there is some stimulus to initiate the action. It seems that some people have an innate potential for collection; John Charles Frémont (Figures 9, 29) was such a person. Obviously bright and quick to understand the potential for increasing knowledge and adding to his own prestige, Frémont could not have avoided recognition of the examples set by his benefactor, Joel Roberts Poinsett, and by his leader, teacher, and trusted friend, Joseph Nicolas Nicollet. It was Poinsett for whom the *Poinsettia* was named, and it was Nicollet who hired Karl Geyer to collect and prepare lists of plants of the regions surveyed in the north-central part of the United States. Why John Charles did not choose to annex a botanist to his early expeditions is open to speculation. Karl Geyer was evidently available but was not a very agreeable companion, a fact that must have influenced Frémont against taking him.

It was to John Torrey (1796–1873; Figure 11), and through him to Asa Gray (1810–1888; Figure 12), that Frémont turned for initial identifications for the botanical appendices of his reports. Later, George Bentham (1800–1884; Figure 13), Frederick Michael Liebman (1813–1856), Edward Tuckerman (1817–1886), Joseph Decaisne (1807–1882), and Sereno Watson (1826–1892; Figure 14) would work on specimens taken by John Charles. Still later, following the turn of the century, Per Axel Rydberg (1860–1931; Figure 15) and Willis L. Jepson (1867–1946) would name a few novelties based on the Frémont specimens (see Appendix I for species and bibliographic citations). Torrey alone would name 43 specific or infraspecific taxa and 7 genera based on Frémont's collections; Torrey and Gray 21 and 6 genera; Gray alone 37 and 2 genera; Torrey and Frémont 19 and 4 genera; Bentham 16; Watson 15; Rydberg 6; and Decaisne, Liebman, Tuckerman, and Jepson 1 each. All except Rydberg have taxa based on Frémont material still recognized at some taxonomic standing.

Even pending receipt of the Frémont materials of the 1842 collection from Kansas west to the Wind River Mountains, Torrey (Jackson & Spence, 1970: 130), in a letter to Gray dated 18 November 1842, suggested sending a collector with him on a presumed second expedition to the West. Torrey (Jackson & Spence, 1970: 130) notes: "How would it do to send a collector with him. [Melines C.] Leavenworth [1796–1862] wishes to go somewhere—& this place might suit *him*—but not *us* in all respects." Gray (Jackson & Spence, 1970: 133) responded on 5 December 1842 by saying, "I wish we had a collector to go with Frémont. It is a great chance. If none are to be had, Lieut. F. must be *indoctrinated*, & taught to collect both dried spec. & seeds. Tell him he shall be immortalized by having the 999th Senecio called S. Frémontii; that's *poz.*, for he has at least two new ones." The fact that Frémont was indoctrinated to collect seeds is evident in the number of plants grown at the botanical garden at Cambridge, which bear the notation "e sem. Frémont." The honor of having species named after him must have been especially gratifying.

John Charles's letter (Figure 10) to Torrey dated 16 November 1842 appears presumptuous at first examination. He opens the letter, "I transmit to you by to-day's Cars a Collection of Plants which I have made during the present year in the course of a Geographical Exploration to the Rocky Mountains." He indicates later in that correspondence that the plants were being sent by Professor Benedict Jaeger (1789–1869), who would have by this time contacted Dr. Torrey. He presumes, on the hearsay of Professor Jaeger, that Torrey will be willing and able to provide "a Catalogue in a few weeks." Frémont does apologize for the liberty he had taken. More will be said of this later. Indeed, Professor Jaeger had contacted Dr. Torrey a few days previous to the arrival of Frémont's letter. In a letter to Asa Gray, quoted by McKelvey (1955: 767), Torrey notes that he had received Jaeger's communication and that Jaeger had advised that the Frémont collections would be sent to him. Torrey is quoted as indicating that Frémont "writes something like a foreigner." In anticipation of the arrival of the box of specimens, Torrey had already made a division—the Compositae and such duplicates of the others, if there be any, would be sent to Gray for his collection.

Without waiting for a reply, Frémont (Figure 10) in the letter to Torrey noted above stated: "Should these plants possess any interest for you, I trust that they will be an apology for the liberty I have taken. It is probable that next year I shall be sent to continue these Explorations to the Pacific, & I shall be very much gratified if you will take some interest in my researches & enable me to give to any thing I may find interesting in your science, the authority of your name." Thus the correspondence opened; it would continue for several years.

Frémont was presumptuous in his approach to Torrey, as others have been to taxonomic botanists since that time. Identifications are always required in surveys and explorations, and the determinations are required immediately, even though the material is frequently poor and sometimes impossible to identify.

There would not be a botanist on the first three expeditions, and that of the fourth, Frederick Creutzfeldt, proved unsatisfactory to Frémont. Frémont would do the collecting, as Preuss noted in his diary, often to the disgust of those left waiting supper and other tasks as well. It is difficult to believe that John Charles was not aided by other members of the party, as is often the case when someone begins collecting as a part of a larger group. And, when that person is the leader of the expedition, it would be presumptuous, indeed, to assume that he alone collected everything. In fact, some of the notes attached to the specimens of the first expedition, at least, seem not to be in Frémont's handwriting, and one at least contains misspellings not consistent with the careful and correct spelling of Frémont.

George Engelmann (1809–1884) wrote from St. Louis to Asa Gray on 4 June 1843: "Frémont was here beginning of May for nearly 2 weeks and I assisted him in his preparations and gave him instructions for geological & botanical researches and collections. He will if possible ascend the Arkansas to its sources, pass over to Lake Bonneville and then to the Columbia. He said he was not authorized to take any botanist with him" (Jackson & Spence, 1970: 346). From this quotation it is apparent that Frémont had intended to visit the Great Salt Lake prior to departing on the second expedition.

Plants were evidently collected in plant presses, carried on pack animals or in carts from camp to camp, dried without artificial heat, and taken from the presses when dry. The dried specimens were then packed in bundles and protected as much as possible from the ravages of the expeditions. Those of the first expedition were not numbered; those of the second and third expeditions were numbered, but the numbers were apparently placed on them some time following pressing—seldom do the dates correspond to the numerical sequence. It seems that the plants were somewhat jumbled from their collection sequence then numbered. Fourth and fifth expedition specimens were not numbered. Dates appear on relatively few of the specimens. This shortfall in information often leaves one guessing as to collection locality. Some specimens are dated but not numbered, allowing one to find the location in the accounts of the explorations.

Botanical names were left blank in the journals of the expeditions and were added subsequently into the Frémont reports (Jackson & Spence, 1970: 346): "The labels which are affixed to the plants [in shipment to Torrey] will enable us to assign them their exact localities on a Topographical Map of the country which I am now engaged in constructing." Several of the extant specimens do bear the original tiny tags, often with a number, but sometimes with locality data only, written in either ink or pencil. Some of the tags, ordinary writing paper cut into strips, were slit and slipped over the end of the specimen or they were tied with an overhand knot to the stems. Torrey could then identify the plant and return the name corresponding to the number in Frémont's notes back to John Charles. However, many of the specimens lack numbers and others evidently arrived at Dr. Torrey's residence without label information; this, in some part at least, accounts for the application of obvious wrong determinations at various places in the manuscript. Rushes became *Equisetum*, and often *E. hyemale*, when, in reality, the plants referred to more likely belonged to species of *Juncus*, *Scirpus*, and various grasses. *Garrya elliptica* was reported from places where it is not now known and where there is no reason to believe that it existed during the expeditions—along the Virgin River, for example.

Another letter to Torrey (NY!; BRY!) dated 22 March 1848 states: "After taking the trouble to gather plants I do not think we ought to lose them, even the scattered fragments which I find here & there in my note books." The scraps were to be sent to Torrey, and "I shall therefore send you such as I find; and will beg you to return them to me with a name if you have leisure. It may happen that I can make the knowledge useful." In this manner the majority of the scientific names of plants came into the published accounts of the explorations. His need for botanical determinations was again emphasized in a letter from Jessie (Spence, 1984: 74–75) to Torrey dated 29 May 1848: "Mr. Frémont is so pressed to finish his little memoir for the Senate, that he has asked me to send you the enclosed remnants of plants. They are the earliest flowering plants of the Joaquin valley (Cal.) and he would be much obliged if you could send him very soon, their names."

John Charles was always pressed by deadlines for publication of the reports of the expeditions, and his letters to John Torrey contain plaintive pleadings for names of plant genera and species. He sometimes questioned Dr. Torrey about details in the manuscript prior to their publication. In one of his letters to Torrey (Jackson & Spence, 1970: 165) he inquires: "In *Equisetum arvense* of the Catalogue, is '*arvense*' right? Among the plants collected on the Sandy river, (branch of the Green River) on our return [from the first expedition], was a portion of an *artemisia* (?) can you tell me if this *is* an artemisia, & if so, what one?"

Genera of conifers were not well defined in the botanical world of Frémont's time. Pines, firs, and spruces were all "pines," and "cedars" included junipers and other genera of the Cupressaceae. Cypress was called variously *Thuya* (*Thuja*; including *T. gigantea*) or *Taxodium* (later known as *Sequoia sempervirens* (Lamb.) Endl.). It also seems clear that Frémont did not see the big tree, *Sequoiadendron giganteum* (Lindley) Buchholz, during his early expeditions, or, if so, he did not record those huge and fantastic plants. He would see them later, but the tree subsequently known as the "Frémont Tree" (Rolle, 1991: 264) is a coast redwood. Neither did he record seeing the Monterey Cypress, even though he was in Monterey on several occasions. That lack of report might be excused because of his other interests during those visits.

No contemporary 19th-century American botanist knew the western flora well, and most knew it hardly at all. And, no 20th-century botanist is familiar with all of that flora, despite the collections of hundreds of thousands of specimens by thousands of students of botany in the time since Frémont and his caravans moved across the vast reaches of the American West. By the 1840s only a relatively small number of plants had made their way to the eastern herbaria, and consequently all botanists of this period were pioneering from a very small data base. Because Torrey and his premier student, Asa Gray, recognized the need for great numbers of collections from the West, they grasped at every opportunity to view the scraps of plants brought back by various explorers. And scraps the specimens often were, because of the exigencies of collecting in the wilderness, in part, and because of the training, or lack thereof, of the explorers, few of whom were botanists by training or otherwise. Annotations on the Frémont specimens reflect the evolution of botanical thought in western North America over the century and a half since the plants were collected. That evolution continues at the present and will in the future. It is the nature of taxonomic botany that all treatments are preliminary.

For whatever reason, Frémont was the nearest thing to botanist on the first, second, and third expeditions, even though both Torrey and Gray encouraged him to take a botanist on later journeys. The colorful Charles Preuss wondered at Frémont for his diligence in collecting plants and other natural history artifacts. The Preuss reference is an indication of Frémont's devotion to collecting, even though Preuss stated his opinion that Frémont was "not a botanist." Nevertheless, Frémont collected flowering plants with showy flowers as well as those with very tiny and inconspicuous ones. Oaks were a favorite, possibly because the samples could be collected from horseback; they are represented in the collection in numbers disproportionate to the number of species present. Or, possibly Frémont had received instructions from Torrey to gather as many oaks as possible. It is certain that they became a special interest for Frémont. Additionally he collected conifers, some ferns, and even a couple of lichens. The lichens, both at NY, are *Alectoria fremontii* Tuckerman and *Letharia columbiana* (Nutt.) Thoms.

First Expedition—1842

"The collection of plants submitted to me [Torrey] for examination, though made under unfavorable circumstances, is a very interesting contribution to North American Botany" (Torrey, 1843: 79). The preface to the publication of 1843 *Catalogue of Plants* begins with the above sentence, which is supported by the letter dated 5 December 1842 from Asa Gray to Dr. Torrey: "The parcel of Compositae &c. of the Far West [collected by Frémont in 1842] just came in, I have looked over the Compos. with some excitement. Some few new, and the old help out Nuttall's scraps &c. very well. Tetradymia's this side of the Rocky Mts.!! Some new Senecio's, especially from the Mountain near the snow line. How I would like to botanize up there! I will give you an account of these Compos. soon, and send back the spec. as you desire, selecting one for myself where it will bear it. Pray remember me in this matter as regards the other families of this collection" (Jackson & Spence, 1970: 133).

"Nuttall's scraps" referred to are the plant collections taken by Thomas Nuttall (1786–1859), who had accompanied the Wyeth expedition of 1834–35 along much of the route followed by the Frémont expedition of 1842. Nuttall was an amazing botanical explorer, whose meager collections represented the botany of the intermontane West for generations. His numerous new entities were mainly published in the *Flora of North America* by Torrey and Gray (1838). His collections, like those of Frémont, were taken under circumstances where space and weight of baggage were at a premium. The inability to move swiftly caused Frémont to abandon carts and revert to pack animals for their rush west from below Goat Island, near present Alcova, Natrona County, Wyoming, on the upper Platte in the summer of 1842.

Pressing equipment is always scarce in such situations, and the specimens are often mere fragments or small representatives of the species. This writer has tried to collect while using a horse for conveyance and has experienced the great difficulty involved with dismounting to collect and remounting afterwards. The collector's companions either keep moving, obliging him to play catchup, or they are all delayed. The presses are always packed on another animal, and they are not readily accessible for use until camp is reached for the night. Frémont was evidently able to press some plants collected during noon haltings, however. Possibly many of the plants taken earlier in the day were pressed during the evening stop.

The collecting season advanced as Frémont moved westward. A drought had settled over the lands adjacent to the upper Platte, and flowers of mid-summer were few indeed. Only immediately adjacent to seeps, springs, and along banks of rivers and tributaries was there much in the way of collectable plants. Even the high-altitude flora of the Wind River mountains was passing its prime by the time Frémont began collecting there on 12 August 1842. The rather long list of specimens taken there (see itinerary below) shows Frémont's attempt to take a representative sample of the flora. The late summer and early autumn flora was in full array along the Platte, with its depauperate deciduous summer woodland flora, and on the adjacent prairies. Frémont would continue to collect plants far into the season, almost to the end of the expedition. He was ever aware of the vegetation, both for its utilitarian and aesthetic values.

The foray into the Wind River Mountains was one of hardship, and the men were inadequately supplied with provisions, especially with food. Even the rush homeward, pushed onward by frosty nights of late summer, did not deter him from taking specimens. That any plants were taken at all is an indication of the enthusiasm of Frémont, the collector. He noted in a letter to Torrey (11 March 1843, NY; BRY!): "I claim no other credit than what may be due to having collected them [the specimens] under circumstances of considerable hardship and privation." And further, "When you join to these things the various duties which were constantly claiming my attention, you will readily make an allowance for the bad condition of the collection I sent to you." The determinations were completed in time for publication as an appendix to the 1843 report. The list is the only one published in its entirety for the five expeditions of Frémont. It consists of

371 taxa (460 specimens), among 57 families of dicots, 10 of monocots, 2 of conifers (Pinaceae and Cupressaceae, both included under Coniferae), and 2 families of vascular cryptogams (Equisetaceae and Filices). The number of taxa recognized in this work, 371, is not identical in composition to the Torrey list in the 1843 report appendix and family summary, due mainly to reduction of some names to synonymy and to recognition of others not treated by Torrey.

For many of the taxa included in the 1843 list Torrey was able to provide a collection date or collection period. The dates of specimens from this and later expeditions can be correlated with the travel of the respective expeditions as outlined both in Frémont's published accounts and on the maps (Frémont, 1843; Frémont & Preuss, 1845; Preuss, 1846; Preuss, 1848) of Frémont, and Frémont and Preuss, which were probably all drawn by Preuss; hence, the emphasis of locality data in the narrative of this report. It is apparent that the procedure worked out by Frémont and Torrey was neither simple nor always workable. As pointed out previously, the plants with tags, some with meager locality data, were sent to Torrey, who would provide determinations to Frémont, and evidently he would then send locality information or additional locality information to Torrey. The most manifest difficulty with the procedure involved the loss or jumbling of tags accompanying the plants, or their lack in the beginning.

It is easy to underestimate the need for data when making plant collections. One cannot, of course, anticipate all future requirements, but there should be a basic minimum of information accompanying each specimen. The core information provided by Frémont, essentially none, was usual for the period. Assignment of approximate locality was not difficult, however, e.g., "Wind River mountains," or "Upper Platte." However, the narrative and map of the first expedition allow one to estimate more closely the regions of collection. Historians still argue about actual routes and peaks climbed by Frémont, members of his parties, and those of other explorers. Botanical researchers should not expect to be different from historians. However, the bulk of the specimens collected on the first expedition were provided with dates of collection in the published account by Dr. Torrey. From that information it is possible to determine at least state and county where many of the plants were taken.

The dried specimens were divided between Torrey and Gray. The latter worked on members of the sunflower family and on other members of the gamopetalae, especially. Torrey worked with most other groups. And, because of different demands upon their time and differences in completion dates, the results could not consistently be included within the appendix of the report of the expedition. Nevertheless, Torrey published more than half of the novelties in the botanical appendix to the Frémont report of the first expedition. Others appeared in volume two of the *Flora of North America* (Torrey & Gray, 1843). Places of publication of the remainder of the 1842 novelties include de Candolle's *Prodromus* Volume 10 (Bentham, 1846), the botanical appendix to the *Report on Geological Exploration of the Fortieth Parallel* (Watson, 1871), and *Proceedings of the American Academy*, volume 10 (Watson, 1875). Some 22 new taxa were proposed, exclusive of the abortive attempt at commemoration of John Charles with the genus *Fremontia* Torr., which was almost immediately recognized as a synonym of *Sarcobatus*.

Possibly the most startling find among the 1842 materials is the beautiful *Actinella grandiflora* Torr. & A. Gray in A. Gray [*Hymenoxys grandiflora* (Torr. & A. Gray) Parker]. This low, shaggy, white tomentose perennial with huge floral heads, matching in size those of a common sunflower, is among the most showy of the high-elevation plants in the American West. About half of the taxa named from the first expedition are still recognized at some taxonomic rank.

New taxa described from the 1842 expedition to the Wind River Mountains are as follows:

Abronia micrantha Torr. in Frém.
Actinella grandiflora Torr. & A. Gray in A. Gray
Amarella ventorum Rydb.
Aster adscendens var. *fremontii* S. Wats.
Castilleja lineariifolia Benth. in DC.
Chenopodium fremontii S. Wats.
Clematis fremontii S. Wats.
Eritrichium crassisepalum Torr. & A. Gray
Fremontia Torr. in Frém.
Gentiana fremontii Torr. in Frém.
Gnaphalium strictum Torr. in Frém.
Hendecandra multiflora Torr. in Frém.
Ipomoea leptophylla Torr. in Frém.
Mimulus jamesii β fremontii Benth. in DC.
Penstemon strictus Benth. in DC.
Phacelia leucophylla Torr. in Frém.
Senecio filifolius β fremontii Torr. & A. Gray
Senecio fremontii Torr. & A. Gray
Senecio lanceolatus Torr. & A. Gray
Senecio spartioides Torr. &. A. Gray
Sium incisum Torr. in Frém.
Thalictrum megacarpum Torr. ex Rydb.
Townsendia fremontii A. Gray

Torrey must have had more complete information on dates and places of collection than are recorded on the specimen labels or on sheets that lack a standard label. Dates of collection reported by Torrey (1843) and recorded on the extant herbarium specimens provide an almost day-by-day itinerary of the 1842 expedition. The first expedition was the best of Frémont's journeys with regard to locality information. Localities can be inferred from the dates and vice versa. While many of the Frémont collections can, therefore, be ascribed to sites within modern counties, sometimes the inclusive dates are too broad for pinpoint accuracy. Plotting of localities is aided by correlation of dates with the Frémont and Preuss maps (see map citations).

The exigencies of collecting during such a horse-bound expedition dictate that most specimens be taken, as noted previously, at the evening campsite or, less commonly, during the noon halt; some few specimens bear the notation "noon halt." Because Frémont traveled no more than 40 miles per day the site of collection on a given day cannot be far from the evening campsite.

Following is an itinerary of the 1842 expedition and plants taken by date. The names, with some exceptions, are those reported in the Torrey (1843) botanical appendix. Modern equivalents are given in the botanical appendix to this work. During the six-month expedition (four months actually in the field) specimens are known to have been taken on at least 56 dates (almost 50 percent of the days of the expedition). A total of 285 collections, more than half of those known, can be assigned to a date, and hence to a modern locality.

10 June departed Westport (present Kansas City), Kansas.

19 June—Big Vermillion of the Kansas River, near Pottawatomi County, Kansas.
Asclepias tuberosa
Ceanothus mollissimus

20 June—Big Blue River of the Kansas, probably Marshall County, Kansas.
Acerates angustifolia
Acerates longifolia
Anatherix viridis
Batschia gmelinii
Elymus virginicus
Geum virginianum
Oenothera missouriensis
Oenothera speciosa
Oxybaphus nyctaginea
Phlox pilosa
Polytaenia nuttallii

21 June—Big Blue River of the Kansas, Marshall County, Kansas.
Malva pedata
Petalostemon violaceum

22 June—Little Blue River of the Kansas, near Powell, Jefferson County, Nebraska.
Acerates longifolia
Agrostis michauxiana
Cacalia tuberosa
Carex aurea
Elymus canadensis
Euphorbia obtusata
Plantago gnaphaloides
Psoralea argophylla
Spartina cynosuroides
Specularia amplexicaulis
Thalictrum dasycarpum

23 June—Little Blue River of the Kansas, near Adams County, Nebraska.
Hymenopappus scabiosaeus
Malva involucrata
Psoralea argophylla

24 June—Little Blue River of the Kansas, near Adams County, Nebraska.
Rosa arkansana

26 June—Platte River, near present Fort Kearney, Kearney County, Nebraska.
Lepachys columnaris
Onosmodium molle
Talinum parviflorum (Platte Ridge)

27 June—Platte River, near head of Grand Island, Kearney County, Nebraska.
Oxytropis lambertii

28 June—Platte River, south of present Lexington, Dawson County, Nebraska.
Lobelia spicata

29 June—Platte River, south of present Cozad, Dawson County, Nebraska.
Acerates angustifolius
Amplectrum hyemale
Aristida pallens
Astragalus mollissimus
Chenopodium pratericola
Cleome integrifolia
Helianthus petiolaris
Lepidium ruderale
Onosmodium molle
Sagittaria sagitifolia
Sida coccinea

2 July—Forks of the Platte, Lincoln County, Nebraska.
Asclepias speciosa
Asclepias verticillata
Astragalus gracilis
Calystegia sepium
Cleome integrifolia
Eretrichium crassisepalum
Hendecandra multiflora
Hordeum jubatum
Lysimachia ciliata
Monarda pectinata
Myosotis glomeratus
Opuntia missouriensis
Penstemon albidum
Polygala alba
Psoralea campestris
Psoralea floribunda
Salvia azurea
Sisyrinchium anceps
Stachys aspera

4 July—South Platte, ca. 40 miles west of Platte forks, present Keith County, Nebraska.
Erysimum asperum
Euphorbia polygonifolia
Gaura coccinea
Nycterium luteum
Orobanche fasciculata
Penstemon caeruleum

8 July—Sand Hills, South Platte, near Brush, Morgan County, Colorado.
Gilia longiflora
Linum rigidum
Phlox hoodii (*P. andicola*)

10 July—St. Vrain's Fort, near Milliken, Weld County, Colorado.
Aplopappus spinulosus
Chenopodium album
Mentha canadensis
Scutellaria galericulata

12 July—Near present Greeley, Weld County, Colorado.
Abronia mellifera
Chenopodium album
Lippia cuneifolia
Sisyrinchium anceps
Sium incisum
Verbena bracteata
Verbena hastata
Verbena stricta

14 July—Horse Creek, north of Cheyenne, Laramie County, Wyoming.

Chenopodium subglabrum
Heterotheca villosa
Mentha canadensis
Mentzelia nuda
Mimulus alsinoides
Oenothera albicaulis
Salix amygdaloides
Yucca angustifolia

20 July—Fort Laramie, Goshen County, Wyoming.

Penstemon cobaea

22 July—Horseshoe Creek, near present Glendo, Platte County, Wyoming.

Beckmannia eruciformis
Cercocarpus parviflorus
Eriogonum caespitosum
Eriogonum ovalifolium
Gerardia tenuifolia
Heterotheca villosa
Ipomoea leptophylla
Thelesperma megapotamicum

23 July—Upper North Fork of the Platte, Black Hills, mouth of La Bonte Creek, near present Orin, Converse County, Wyoming.

Erysimum chieranthoides
Physalis pubescens
Physalis pumila
Polanisia trachysperma

24 July—North Fork of the Platte, between La Bonte Creek and La Prele Creek, Converse County, Wyoming.

Eriogonum effusum
Ipomoea leptophylla
Psoralea lanceolata

25 July—North Fork of the Platte, west of La Prele Creek, Converse County, Wyoming.

Mulgedium pulchellum

26 July—Deer Creek, Black Hills, Upper North Fork of the Platte, near Glen Rock, Converse County, Wyoming.

Artemisia ludoviciana
Helianthus maxmiliani
Helianthus petiolaris
Nasturtium palustre
Oenothera drummondii
Olione [*Obione*] *canescens*
Polygonum viviparum
Rorippa islandica
Rumex salicifolius

27 July—Upper North Fork of the Platte, east of Evansville, probably in Natrona County, Wyoming.

Platanthera leucophaea

28 July—Platte Bottom, near Evansville, Natrona County, Wyoming.

Asclepias speciosa
Atriplex argentea

29 July—Red Buttes, adjacent to Casper, Natrona County, Wyoming.

Rhus trilobata
Petalostemon candidum
Polemonium caeruleum
Sphaeralcea coccinea

30 July—Upper North Fork of the Platte (Cache Camp), near Alcova, Natrona County, Wyoming.

Cerasus virginiana
Fremontia vermicularis ("Excursion to the Pass, near mouth of the Sweetwater")
Gilia inconspicuua
Oenothera trichocalyx
Phacelia leucophylla

31 July—Camp was along the Sweetwater, ca. one day's journey east of Independence Rock, Natrona County, Wyoming.

Agoseris glauca
Crepis runcinata
Glaux maritima
Oxytropis plattensis (Goat Island)
Phaca elegans (Goat Island)
Plantago eriopoda (mouth of Sweetwater)
Ranunculus cymbalaria
Wyethia scabra

1 August—Near mouth of the Sweetwater, at Independence Rock, Natrona County, Wyoming.

Abronia micranthum
Lupinus caudatus

2 August—Sweetwater River, west of Devil's Gate, Natrona County, Wyoming.

Ribes cereum
Ribes irriguum

3 August—Sweetwater River, west of Jeffery City, Frémont County, Wyoming.

Iris missouriensis
Iva axillaris
Ribes lacustre
Stachys aspera

4 August—Sweetwater River, southwest of Carmody Lake, Frémont County, Wyoming.

Amarella ventorum
Gentiana arctophila β densiflora
Heterotheca villosa
Polygonum amphibium
Polygonum aviculare
Potentilla pensylvanica
Senecio rapifolius

5 August—Sweetwater River, southeast of Atlantic City, Frémont County, Wyoming.

Amelanchier diversifolia var. *alnifolia*
Androsace filiformis
Androsace occidentalis
Astragalus hypoglottis
Castilleja flava
Orthocarpus luteus
Ribes aureum
Thermopsis montana

7 August—Sweetwater River, adjacent to South Pass, Frémont County, Wyoming.

Edosmia gairdneri
Erigeron glabellus
Eriogonum fremontii
Eriogonum umbellatum
Penstemon micranthum
Penstemon strictus
Potentilla gracilis
Spiranthes cernua

8 August—Sweetwater River, Frémont County to Little Sandy Creek, Sublette County, Wyoming across South Pass.

Castilleja pallida
Gentiana affinis
Linum rigidum
Parnassia fimbriata (Little Sandy Creek)
Phaca digitata

12 August—Frémont Lake, Wind River Mountains, Pinedale, Sublette County, Wyoming.

Phaca longifolia
Psoralea tenuiflora

12–17 August—Wind River Mountains, from base camp at Frémont Lake, Pinedale, Sublette County, Wyoming (several specimens bear specific dates during this period and are here combined for simplification; most were collected during 13–15 August 1842).

Abies lasiocarpa
Actinella grandiflora
Allium reticulatum
Aquilegia caerulea
Arctostaphylos uva-ursi
Arenaria congesta
Arnica angustifolia
Betula glandulosa
Betula occidentalis
Castilleja miniata
Ceanothus velutinus
Cornus stolonifera
Deschampsia caespitosa
Dodecatheon dentatum
Elaeagnus argentea
Equisetum arvense
Eriogonum brevicaule
Eutoca sericea
Festuca ovina
Frasera speciosa
Gentiana fremontii
Heracleum lanatum
Linosyris viscidiflorus
Lupinus argenteus
Mimulus alsinoides
Mimulus lewisii
Musineum tenuifolium
Oreophila myrtifolia
Oxyria reniformis
Pedicularis surrecta
Phaca longifolia
Phleum alpinum
Phlox muscoides
Phyllodoce empetriformis
Pinus alba
Pinus near *balsaminea*
Pinus flexilis
Polemonium caeruleum β humile
Populus tremuloides
Potentilla gracilis
Pulmonaria ciliata
Rubus strigosus
Salix glauca
Sedum rhodiola
Senecio hydrophilus
Senecio subnudus
Senecio triangularis
Shepherdia canadensis
Sibbaldia procumbens
Silene drummondii

Solidago virga-aurea var. *multiradiata*
Symphoricarpos vulgaris
Veronica alpina β

15 August—Wind River Mountains, the day the summit was reached, Sublette County, Wyoming.

Carex atrata
Carex panicea
Phaca astragalina
Phlox muscoides
Senecio fremontii
Silene acaulis
Vaccinium myrtilloides
Vaccinium uliginosum

16 August—Frémont Lake, Sublette County, Wyoming, departure date.

Aster adscendens var. *fremontii*
Aster andinus
Aster glacialis
Aster salsuginosus

20 August—East of South Pass, southwest of Carmody Lake, Frémont County, Wyoming.

Gilia aggregata
Linosyris graveolens

21 August—Sweetwater River, vicinity of Jeffery City, Frémont County, Wyoming.

Cleome integrifolia
Populus angustifolia
Senecio spartioides

22 August—Sweetwater River, west of Devil's Gate, Frémont County, Wyoming.

Aster novae-belgiae

25–31 August—North Fork of the Platte, from near Alcova, Natrona County, through Converse and Platte counties, into Goshen County, Wyoming.

Castillejaleariifolia
Eriogonum brevicaule ("*E. fremontii*")
Galium boreale

27 August—Deer Creek, near Glenrock, Converse County, Wyoming.

Tetradymia canescens

28 August—La Prele Creek (Black Hills, Platte Valley), west of Douglas, Converse County, Wyoming.

Negundo aceroides

29 August—Black Hills of the Platte, one day's journey west of La Bonte River, Converse County, Wyoming.

Lepidium ruderale
Liatris punctata

3 September—Laramie River at Fort Laramie, Goshen County, Wyoming.

Andropogon nutans
Aplopappus spinulosus
Gutierrezia euthamiae
Machaeranthera tanacetifolia
Solidago missouriensis

4 September—North Fork of the Platte, west of Scotts Bluff, Scotts Bluff County, Nebraska.

Amphicarpaea monoica
Brickellia grandiflora
Cycloloma platyphyllum
Eriogonum annuum
Juncus echinatus
Liatris spicata
Lobelia siphilitica
Pachypodium integrifolium
Polygonum aviculare
Polygonum persicaria
Suaeda maritima

5 September—Near Chimney Rock, Scotts Bluff County, Nebraska.

Senecio filifolius β fremontii Torr. & A. Gray

9 Septemer—North Fork of the Platte, near present Keystone, Keith County, Nebraska.

Gentiana affinis

11–13 September—Forks of the Platte, near present North Platte, Lincoln County, Nebraska.

Apios tuberosa
Euphorbia marginata
Psoralea tenuiflora

16 September—Sand hills of the Platte, 20 miles below the Forks, Lincoln County, Nebraska.

Gilia longiflora

17 September—Platte River, one day's journey west of Grand Island, Nebraska.

Darlingtonia brachycarpa

18 September—Platte River, at Grand Island, in or near Kearney County, Nebraska.

Oenothera rhombipetala

19 September—Grand Island, Platte River, probably in Hall County, Nebraska.

Populus monilifera
Salix lutea
Vitis riparia

27 September—Lower Platte, three day's journey west of Platte mouth, Nebraska.

Liatris squarrosa

30 September—Mouth of the Platte, Sarpy or Cass County, Nebraska.
Cassia chamaechrista *Lespedeza capitata*

The devotion and competence of Frémont as a collector under very difficult circumstances, where plant pressing material and dried specimens were carried from Cache Camp to the Wind River Mountains and returned on pack animals, are much in evidence. This first expedition, with Frémont acting as botanist, was to produce the most satisfying collection to later workers. Frémont would not achieve either the accuracy or completeness of reporting on subsequent trips.

Second Expedition—1843–44

Seasons of collection on Frémont's second expedition were late spring, summer, and autumn of 1843, winter of 1843–44, and spring and summer of 1844. The spring and summer season of 1843 were passed on the prairies and plains of central Kansas and Colorado, and in the Rocky Mountains of Colorado, Wyoming, Utah, and Idaho. The expedition spent most of the autumn and winter between Fort Hall, Idaho, and Sutter's Fort, California. The trip down the San Joaquin Valley in California was into an advancing spring of 1844, which continued across the Mohave Desert to the corner of Utah. The northward part of the route across Utah and the advance of the party into the high-elevation forests and alpine tundra of the Rocky Mountains of Colorado kept the party enclosed in almost perpetual springtime, until they descended into summer along the Arkansas drainage and proceeded onto the Great Plains. The expedition was, thus, exceptionally suited to the collection of plants at those times when they are most identifiable, when they are in full flower. Only that portion from Fort Hall to Sutter's was undertaken at a time when most plants are beyond flowering and fruiting stages.

The second expedition was more ambitious than the first, covered more country, and encountered greater hardships. Fate, not necessarily kind or fair, both smiled and frowned upon this expedition. Most of the men, except for Jean Baptiste Tabeau and Francois Badeau, made it through well, by the hardest exertion, but the plant specimens did not fare so well. At least part of the specimens taken between Fort Hall and Sutter's was reputedly lost when a pack mule plunged from a ridge into a torrent and was killed; the pack containing the specimens was not recovered (Torrey, 1853: 3). Some plant specimens exist from the portion of the route from Fort Hall to Sutter's; one wonders how many plants were taken between Fort Hall and Sutter's and how many of them, if any, were lost in actuality. The specimens surviving the trip from Fort Hall to Sutter's were obtained along the Snake River in Idaho or in the Sierra Nevada, and were possibly still in a plant press or in a pack not carried by the animal that was killed. Even if the account is factual, there might not have been too many plants taken between Fort Hall and Sutter's in the pack of the lost animal, the route to that point having been made during autumn and winter when collection of large amounts of material would have been difficult indeed.

The estimate of total collections for 1843 is relatively large, possibly as many as 789. Only about a quarter of them are extant in herbaria. It is probable that a great many of the early collections were lost, possibly when the mule fell into the canyon, but they could have been destroyed prior to that time or later during the flood of the Kansas. Nearing home, on the Smoky Hill Fork of the Kansas River, most of the collection was soaked during a sudden flood. Only a portion of the plants were salvaged from the packets of mold delivered to Dr. Torrey, whose disappointment is apparent in the preface (cited above) to the publication of new genera and species from the expedition. "In the departments of geological and botanical science," Frémont wrote, "I have not ventured to advance any opinions on my own imperfect knowledge of those branches, but have submitted all my specimens to the enlightned judgment of Dr. Torrey, of New Jersey, and Dr. Hall, of New York, who have kindly classified and arranged all that I was able to submit to them. The botanical observations of Dr. Torrey will be furnished in full hereafter, there not being time to complete them now" (Frémont, 1845: 4). John Charles continued with a more complete description of the accidents of the second expedition, "Unhappily, much of what we had collected was lost by accidents of serious import to ourselves, as well as to our animals and collections. In the gorges and ridges of the Sierra Nevada, of the Alta California, we lost fourteen horses and mules, falling from rocks or precipices into chasms or rivers, bottomless to us and to them, and one of them loaded with bales of plants collected on a line of two thousand miles of travel; and when almost home, our camp on the banks of the Kansas was deluged by the great flood which, lower down, spread terror and desolation on the borders of the Missouri and Mississippi rivers, and by which great damage was done to our remaining perishable specimens, all wet and saturated with water, and which we had no time to dry." That many specimens were lost is evident from the plants now present in herbaria versus the total possible from the collection numbers recorded on specimens. The proportion of specimens from early in the expedition gives indication of a rather gradual attrition of the collection as it was carried from place to place. A disproportionately greater number of specimens are extant from the latter part of the expedition.

Frémont was very disappointed that the botanical specimens of the expedition had met with such disasters, a continual theme in his letters to Torrey and others. On 15 September 1844 he wrote to Dr. Torrey (NY!, BRY!): "From California to the forks of the Kansas river, I had made a collection which could have been full of interest to you. I have never seen anything comparable to the profusion and variety of plants in the country thro' which I passed. I am satisfied that *very* many of the plants & shrubs, as well as several trees were entirely new, & I had with great labor ascertained from the Indians the medicinal qualities of many, and had obtained all those which they used in any way for food. Both these latter I was also acquainted from having used them myself, and the use of the former had witnessed in several important cases. I had carefully studied the vegetation through every mile of the regions travelled and made full notes." The notes had survived, but many of the plants were ruined.

In the letter to Torrey (NY!; BRY!), Frémont continued: "Though in the course of our journey the Bales of plants had been twice wet, yet they were in very beautiful order when we encamped on the upper waters of the Kansas on 13th of July [Logan County, Kansas], in the course of which night it began to rain violently & towards morning the river which was 100 yards wide suddenly broke over its banks, becoming in less than 5 minutes more than half a mile in breadth. Everything we had was thoroughly soaked. We were obliged to move camp to the Bluffs in a heavy rain which continued for several days and our fine collection was entirely ruined. I have never had a severer trial of my fortitude. I brought them along and such as they are I send them to you. They are broken up & mouldy and decayed, and to day I tried to change some of them, but found it better to let them alone. Perhaps your familiarity with plants may enable you to make something out of them. You will find them labelled with numbers which correspond to the numbers of notes in my books, which I will copy & send to you in case you can do anything with them." Both disappointment and sorrow are evident. In a letter (MO; BRY!) to George Engelmann in St. Louis, Missouri, dated 22 October 1844, Frémont wrote: "I found the plants in such a miserable condition when I arrived that I could not even change them but sent them direct to Dr. Torrey. The greater part were entirely ruined; he [Torrey] says he thinks he will be able to identify a number of them, & judging from the collection he says we have sustained a great loss as the botanical riches of the country are very great. Among the collection are several specimens of new trees—Dr. Torrey & Dr. Gray are jointly engaged in endeavoring to make what they can out of them. But my misfortune on this occasion will be a safeguard to me on the next trip." John Charles was an unrealistic optimist; one can never quite match a collection from a previous year with that of a later one. Seasons change, times of encounter of the species are different, and opportunity is never the same again. One can truly be at a place only once!

"When Captain Frémont set out on his second expedition," Torrey observed, "he was well provided with paper and other means for making extensive botanical collections; and it was well understood that, on his return we should conjointly, prepare a full account of his plants, to be appended to his report. About 1,400 species [collections, more likely] were collected, many of them in regions not before explored by any botanist. In consequence, however, of the great length of the journey, and the numerous accidents to which the party were exposed, but especially owing to the dreadful flood of the Kansas, which deluged the borders of the Missouri and Mississippi rivers, more than half of his specimens were ruined before he reached the borders of civilization. Even the portion saved was greatly damaged; so that, in many instances, it has been extremely difficult to determine the plants. As there was not sufficient time before publication of Captain Frémont's report for the proper study of the remains of his collection, it has been deemed advisable to reserve the greater part of them to incorporate with the plants which we expect he will bring with him on returning from his third expedition, upon which he has just set out" (Torrey in Frémont, 1845: 311).

Many of the specimens taken by John Charles during the second expedition were numbered. Evidently at least two number series are represented, one for the year 1843, totaling 789 numbers, and one for 1844, totaling 626, with each series beginning with the number one. Only 250 collections are known currently to bear numbers, many others do not. The number series for the year 1843 is very incomplete, that of 1844 is more so. However, complete or not, there is a jumbling of numbers and dates (see Appendix IV). For example, *Balsamorhiza bolanderi*, no. 7, is indicated as being taken on 12 March 1844, while *Libocedrus decurrens*, no. 33, is dated 25 February 1844. There are places where the numbers evidently coincide with dates for short sequences, but in others they are unintelligibly jumbled.

Total collections for the 1843–44 expedition number 1415. Perhaps that is the source of the number 1400 derived by Dr. Torrey. Of the 1400 species reported, Torrey states that more than half were destroyed. In research leading to this treatment the present author has been able to account for not more than 379 taxa (552 specimens, including duplicates) from the second expedition, and almost a fifth of the taxa are represented by type specimens. It is likely that about two-thirds of the collection was destroyed.

Brewer (1880: 556) summarized the contributions of Frémont to the understanding of the flora of California as follows: "Capt. John C. Frémont traversed the continent in 1843 by way of Great Salt Lake and Humboldt River, crossed the Sierra Nevada in midwinter, just south of Lake Tahoe, and entered California in February, 1844, descending the South Fork of the American River. Late in March he set out on his return, passed southward along the eastern edge of the great valley, recrossed the Sierra Nevada at Tehachapi Valley and Frémont's Pass, thence to the Mohave and Virgin Rivers, and eastward, taking with him the earliest collection that had been made in any portion of the Sierra Nevada Range. In the report of this expedition (usually known as his second expedition), Dr. Torrey described about thirty species and four new genera. On the next (or third) expedition of 1845 to 1847 he made much more extensive collections, but unfortunately many of the specimens were lost by an accident in the mountains. The specimens saved amounted to about six hundred numbers, and contained many new species, some of which were described by Dr. Torrey in 'Plantae Fremontianae' in the 'Smithsonian Contributions' for 1850."

Brewer seems to have mistakenly attributed the reported accidents of the second expedition collections to those of the third expedition materials. Thus, probably the 600 numbers applied to the second expedition, not the third, a likely assumption when somewhat more than half that number are known to exist currently. Frémont makes no mention of particular troubles with the collections on the third expedition, even though indications are that a great many of the specimens from that expedition were destroyed also. Bigelow (1856: 324, 469) quotes from a report to the Senate of the United States by Senator Breese that "More than one thousand specimens in botany, a great number in geology and mineralogy, with engravings of birds and animals, and remarkable scenery, and a large collection of the skins of birds with the plumage preserved, have been as the committee are informed, brought home [from the third expedition] to enrich the stores and add to the sum of human knowledge. The botanical specimens examined by Dr. Torrey are deemed by him of great value and worth of the expense of European engraving, if not done by our own government." The number "more than a thousand" is approached by the actual number of specimens currently known to exist in the herbaria of the United States from the third expedition (see Appendix III).

Despite hopes that the loss of the second expedition specimens would be made up on the third expedition, no complete list of plants for the second expedition was ever published, nor for the third.

Torrey had asked Frémont to provide a preface to the botanical appendix of the first expedition, and Frémont had declined, although he did provide a brief description of the route and of some of the problems involved. Later, following receipt of the completed preface, John Charles proposed that Torrey and he might collaborate in the future: "I have purposely delayed replying to an occasional enquiry in some of your letters as to whether or not I should be able to take with me a botanist, in order that I might be in possession of information, which would enable me to give you a definite answer. I find for various strong reasons, that I shall not be able to do so, but still I contemplate doing something for your favorite science. Can we not do something together? Is it not customary sometimes for collectors, unskilled as myself to publish their plants in partnership with, & under the shadow of, the standard names in science. I do not know if I am asking too much, but if I am not, I should be glad if you would write to me on the subject, and I think something good may be done" (letter of 21 March 1843, Jackson & Spence, 1970: 165–66). Possibly Frémont wanted the glory both of discovery and publication. He sometimes wore his vanity like a badge of honor.

That the second expedition was incredible is to understate the case. Veering from the route of most pioneer plant collectors, John Charles took the first plants from the region around the Great Salt Lake, including the type material of the shadscale, *Atriplex confertifolia* (Torr. & Frém.) S. Wats. The route of the party essentially bisected Oregon on a route that passed from north to south to near the southern margin of the state, passed eastward into the Great Basin, and followed its western margin south to near present Carson City, Nevada. There the expedition turned west, and in the final assault of three weeks of almost super-human endeavor they crossed the Sierra Nevada in February of 1844. Retrospect indicates that men as well as animals should have perished; all men, but by no means all animals, made it through to Sutter's, albeit in weakened and starving condition.

Those who would criticize, as some historians have, the decision by John Charles to cross the snowy ridges of the Sierra Nevada, thereby endangering his men, instead of turning eastward across the Great Basin or wintering at Pyramid Lake, have failed to understand either men or horses and mules. Whether they stayed or turned eastward, both men and animals required refitting—the men with food, clothing, and equipment, and the animals with shoes, tackle, and pack apparatus. Months of waiting for the snows of the Sierra Nevada to melt could have done little to improve the status of the expedition. They had to get to some place as quickly as possible for refitting; Frémont had little choice. To stay at Pyramid Lake or elsewhere in the basin, to wait out the winter, could have spelled disaster for the expedition, which had accomplished so much to that point. The party was already at risk prior to the attempt at crossing.

The ride south from Sutter's to the vicinity of Tehachapi Pass in southern California was through the California springtime, during March and April. The flowers dazzled the eye, and the descriptions in the narrative constantly turn to the botanical theme. The great oaks and the huge lupines were referred to again and again. Filaree, practically omnipresent, was described in its various growth forms. The general lushness of vegetation was to be contrasted with the Mohave Desert east of the pass, where Frémont and Preuss both commented on the unlovely Joshua tree, and Preuss was disgusted by the cactus that caused his Polly to unseat him hard upon the ground. Even there John Charles was delighted with the diversity of vegetation as well as the great bands of color from the blossoms of plant species. His party had entered a different world botanically, a region from which few if any plant specimens had been taken previously, and from which came the most interesting plants described in his collections. It was only by luck that Frémont was able to collect so many species of plants within the Mohave Desert. Rains occur irregularly and the plants are keyed to respond to the amount and timing of the precipitation. The year 1844, despite lack of precipitation during the expedition's crossing of the Mohave desert, was one of at least moderate rainfall, and the desert had responded with a varied flowering vegetation, even though grasses for forage were in short supply. A year earlier or later might have found the vast tracts of the Mohave barren, such are the vagaries of the climate and vegetative response in desert lands.

The Mohave Desert, which the Indian guide described eloquently in Spanish as "*no hay agua*; *no hay zacate—nada*," yielded type specimens of at least 27 new taxa, including:

Amphipappus fremontii Torr. & A. Gray in A. Gray
Amsonia tomentosa Torr. & Frém.
Aplopappus tortifolius Torr. & A. Gray
Arctomecon californicum Torr. & Frém. in Frém.
Astragalus arthu-schottii A. Gray
Astragalus fremontii A. Gray ex Torr.
Astragalus preussii A. Gray
Baileya multiradiata var. *nudicaulis* A. Gray
Berberis fremontii Torr.
Coleogyne ramosissima Torr.
Dalea arborescens Torr. ex A. Gray
Dalea fremontii S. Wats.
Emplectocladus fasciculatus Torr.
Eriogonum inflatum Torr. & Frém.
Franseria dumosa A. Gray in Frém.
Geraea canescens Torr. & A. Gray in A. Gray
Hymenoclea salsola Torr. & A. Gray in A. Gray
Lepidium flavum Torr.
Lepidium fremontii S. Wats.
Meconella californica Torr. & Frém.
Monoptilon bellidiformis Torr. & A. Gray in A. Gray
Nama demissum A. Gray
Nicolletia occidentalis A. Gray in Frém.
Oenothera deltoides Torr. & Frém. in Frém.
Oenothera claviformis Torr. & Frém.
Oxystylis lutea Torr. & Frém.
Oxytheca perfoliata Torr. & A. Gray
Spirolobium odoratum Torr.
Thamnosma montana Torr. & Frém.

More information is presented in the botanical appendix (Appendix I) on these and other species taken by John Charles during the second expedition.

Plant specimens were taken from along the route through Utah in May and June of 1844. The track led northward from Washington County in the southwestern corner of the state, through Iron, Millard, and Utah counties. Plants were collected in all of those counties, the first for each of them. A collection of *Lycium pallidum* Miers was made at the night camp of 10 May 1844 along the Santa Clara River. *Eriogonum caespitosum*

Nutt. was taken near Mountain Meadows, and *Cryptantha humilis* (Greene) Payson was collected near present Fillmore. At or near Utah Lake several species were collected (see itinerary below).

The first plants from the Uinta Basin of northeastern Utah were collected during June 1844, and the place would remain essentially unbotanized until the second decade of the 20th century (Spence, 1976; Welsh, 1982a). Collected there were the types of *Actinella depressa* Torr. & A. Gray in A. Gray, *Gilia stenothyrsa* A. Gray, *Penstemon fremontii* A. Gray, and *Senecio multilobatus* Torr. & A. Gray. Frémont also collected several other taxa during his trip across the Uinta Basin, including *Leptodactylon pungens* (Torr.) Nutt. on the Duchesne River and *Iris missouriensis* Nutt. along Ashley Creek on 6 May.

New genera named on the basis of the 1843–44 collections include *Anisocoma* Torr. & A. Gray in A. Gray, *Amphipappus* Torr. & A. Gray in A. Gray, *Arctomecon* Torr. & Frém. in Frém., *Calliachyris* Torr. & A. Gray in A. Gray, *Emplectocladus* Torr., *Coleogyne* Torr., *Geraea* Torr. & A. Gray in A. Gray, *Hymenoclea* Torr. & A. Gray in A. Gray, *Monoptilon* Torr. & A. Gray in A. Gray, *Nicolletia* A. Gray in Frém., *Oxystylis* Torr. & Frém. in Frém., *Pterochiton* Torr. & Frém. in Frém., and *Thamnosma* Torr. & Frém. in Frém.

Altogether the collections yielded type material for 79 plant taxa. Places of publication other than the botanical appendix to the 1845 report by Torrey and Frémont include: Proceedings of the American Academy volume 1, 1848, by Torrey and Gray in A. Gray; Memoirs of the American Academy II, volume 4, 1849, by Torrey and Gray in A. Gray; volume 5, 1855, by S. Watson. Boston Journal of Natural History, volume 5, by Torrey and Gray in A. Gray 1845, volume 4, 1849. Oversigt over det Kongelige danske videnskabernes Selskabs Forhandlinger og dets medlemmer arbeider, 1854, by Frederick Michael Liebman. Proceedings of the American Academy [Daedalus], volume 6, 1862–64, by A. Gray; volume 8, 1870–73, by A. Gray. Pacific Railroad Report, volume 4, 1857, by A. Gray ex Torrey. Botany of the U. S. and Mexican Boundary, 1859, by Torrey or by A. Gray in Torrey. Smithsonian Contributions to Knowledge, volume 6, 1853, by Torrey. De Candolle's Prodromus, volumes 10 and 14, 1846 and 1856, by G. Bentham. Proceedings of the Academy of Natural Sciences of Philadelphia, volume 1863, 1864, by A. Gray. Report of U.S. Geological Exploration of the Fortieth Parallel, Botany, 1871, by S. Watson.

The taxa were published by six authors over a period of 26 years in 10 different periodicals, but in 14 different volumes. Reasons for the length of time involved in recognition and publication of the taxa from the second expedition involve the condition of the collection, the time necessary for publication, Frémont's rush to prepare for other expeditions, and the progress of botanical revisions and monographs in which new taxa were published. John Charles had pleaded with Torrey to complete the botanical determinations through the winter of 1844–45. Despite the pressure applied in the letters, Torrey could not complete the determinations, and neither could Gray. Certainly Frémont had no conception of the tasks and time involved with such a project. He had been spoiled by Torrey's swift response following the first expedition. Now, circumstances and the size of the project had changed. There was no possibility of the botanists finishing their work in time for it to be published in its entirety.

In spite of the specimens lost with the death of the mule in the Sierra Nevada and the flood on the Kansas River the second expedition yielded Frémont's greatest contribution to botany. New taxa collected on the second expedition include:

Acerates latifolia Torr. & Frém. in Frém.
Actinella depressa Torr. & A. Gray in A. Gray
Amphipappus fremontii Torr. & A. Gray in A. Gray
Amsonia tomentosa Torr. & Frém. in Frém.
Anisocoma acaulis Torr. & A. Gray in A. Gray
Aplopappus tortifolius Torr. & A. Gray in A. Gray
Arctomecon californicum Torr. & Frém. in Frém.
Astragalus arthu-schottii A. Gray
Astragalus fremontii A. Gray ex Torr.
Astragalus preussii A. Gray
Atriplex breweri S. Wats.
Baileya multiradiata var. *nudicaulis* A. Gray
Balsamorhiza bolanderi A. Gray
Berberis fremontii Torr.
Blitum californicum S. Wats.
Brodiaea multiflora Benth.
Calliachyris fremontii Torr. & A. Gray in A. Gray
Chaenactis fremontii A. Gray
Clematis fremontii S. Wats.
Cleomella obtusifolia Torr. & Frém. in Frém.
Coleogyne ramosissima Torr.
Collinsia bartsiifolia Benth. in DC.
Cordylanthus laxiflorus A. Gray
Cowania stansburyana Torr.
Dalea arborescens Torr. ex A. Gray
Dalea fremontii Torr. ex A. Gray
Echinospermum (*Lappula*) *fremontii* Torr. in A. Gray
Emplectocladus fasciculatus Torr.
Eriogonum cordalum Torr. & Frém. in Frém.
Eriogonum inflatum Torr. & Frém. in Frém.
Eriogonum polifolium Benth. in DC.
Eriogonum reniforme Torr. & Frém. in Frém.
Eriogonum strictum var. *lachnogynum* Benth. in DC.
Eritrichium glomeratum var. (?) *fulvocanescens* A. Gray ex S. Wats.
Eunanus fremontii Benth. in DC.
Frankenia jamesii Torr. ex A. Gray
Franseria dumosa A. Gray in Frém.
Geraea canescens Torr. & A. Gray in A. Gray
Gilia aurea var. *decora* A. Gray
Gilia stenothyrsa A. Gray
Gilia tenuiflora Benth. var. *latiflora* A. Gray
Hosackia argophylla var. *fremontii* A. Gray
Hymenoclea salsola Torr. & A. Gray in A. Gray
Lepidium flavum Torr.
Lepidium fremontii S. Wats.
Libocedrus decurrens Torr.
Lithospermum multiflorum Torr. ex A. Gray
Lupinus ornatus var. *glabratus* S. Wats.
Lycium torreyi A. Gray
Machaeranthera fremontii Rydb.

Malvastrum fremontii Torr. ex A. Gray
Meconella californica Torr. & Frém. in Frém.
Monoptilon bellidiformis Torr. & A. Gray in A. Gray
Nama demissa A. Gray
Navarretia setosissima Torr. & A. Gray ex Torr.
Nicolletia occidentalis A. Gray in Frém.
Obione confertiflora Torr. & Frém. in Frém.
Oenothera canescens Torr. & Frém. in Frém.
Oenothera claviformis Torr. & Frém. in Frém.
Oenothera deltoides Torr. & Frém. in Frém.
Oenothera fremontii S. Wats.
Oxystylis lutea Torr. & Frém. in Frém.
Oxytheca perfoliata Torr. & A. Gray
Penstemon ambiguus β foliosus Benth. in DC.
Penstemon fremontii Torr. & A. Gray
Penstemon nitidus β major Benth. in DC.
Penstemon secundiflorus Benth. in DC.
Phacelia fremontii Torr. in Ives
Pinus monophylla Torr. & Frém. in Frém.
Potentilla pectinisecta Rydb.
Prosopis odorata Torr. & Frém. in Frém.
Pterochiton occidentale Torr. & Frém. in Frém.
Pyrrocoma foliosa A. Gray
Salazaria mexicana Torr.
Sanicula tuberosa Torr.
Senecio multilobatus Torr. & A. Gray in A. Gray
Strombocarpa odorata Torr. in Frém.
Thamnosoma montana Torr. & Frém. in Frém.

Departure of the second expedition from Westport, Kansas, was on 29 May 1843. The party moved up the valley of the Kansas to Smoky Hill Fork, across the divide northwestward to the Republican Fork, and on to the valley of the South Platte, where they arrived at St. Vrain's Fort, Weld County, Colorado, on 4 July 1843. From that fort the party moved south in Colorado to the Fountain Creek tributary of the Arkansas River. They arrived at its mouth at present Pueblo on 15 July, then returned up Fountain Creek to the Arkansas-South Platte Divide, and were back at St. Vrain's Fort on 23 July. From St. Vrain's Fort the party moved to the Cache la Poudre River (tributary of the South Platte), which was followed to the divide with the Laramie River. Camp was on a tributary of the Laramie River, Albany County, Wyoming, on 30 July. By 12 August the expedition had reached the Sweetwater River (tributary of the North Platte), west of Devil's Gate, Natrona County, Wyoming. The expedition crossed the Green River near the mouth of Sandy Creek, Sweetwater County, Wyoming, on 16 August, at Blacks Fork on 17 August, Bear River, Lincoln County, Wyoming, on 22 August, Beer (Soda) Springs, Caribou County, Idaho, on 25 August, and entered Utah on 1 September.

The details of the itinerary repeated at this point are necessary to understand the rather complicated moves of the expedition not accounted for in the itinerary presented below from dated or datable collections. Fortunately one of the maps by Preuss (see map citations) has the course plotted for the expedition.

The second expedition was larger than the first, increasing the problems of transport and provision that accompany a larger group. Too, the expedition was burdened by the 12-pound brass howitzer and its accoutrements. Possibly because of the greater obstacles of moving more men, baggage, and animals over a greater distance, less attention was paid to collection of plants; more of them arrived without locality data, although most of them were numbered, at least initially. This is especially true in the early part of the expedition. The expedition was to last for 14 months, and Frémont was evidently more fascinated with the flora of the Rocky Mountains and Alta California than with those of the prairies and plains. Specimens are known to have been taken on only 75 of the more than 400 days of the expedition, with 141 datable or probably (those marked by circa) datable collections.

Below is the itinerary of the 1843–44 expedition and plants taken by date.

29 May 1843—Party leaves Westport, near the mouth of the Kansas River, Kansas.

2 June—Small tributary of the Kansas, ca. 4 days W of Westport, Kansas.
Machaeranthera canescens no. 10

25 June—Rawlins County, Kansas.
Sophora nuttalliana no. 206

27 June—Republican Fork of the Kansas, Kansas.
Oenothera latifolia no number

10 July—St. Vrain's Fort, Weld County, Colorado.
Antennaria microphylla

12–18 July—Fountain Creek, Pueblo County, Colorado.
Aster occidentalis no. 449
Quercus gambelii no. 464
Tripterocalyx micrantha no number

20 July—Near head of Fountain Creek (north of present Colorado Springs) El Paso County, Colorado.
Abies concolor no. 426
Lithospermum multiflorum no. 442
Machaeranthera fremontii no. 421

23 July—St. Vrain's Fort, Weld County, Colorado.
Eriogonum umbellatum var. *majus* no. 400

28 July—Northern Larimer County, Colorado.
Paronychia jamesii no. 493

30 July—Near head of Laramie River, vicinity of Glendevey, Larimer County, Colorado.
Juniperus scopulorum no. 526

31 July—Upper Laramie River, Albany (?) County, Wyoming.
Penstemon laricifolius no. 553 (circa)

8 August—Carbon County, Wyoming.
Suaeda torreyana no. 622

12 August—Sweetwater, probably Frémont County, Wyoming.
Atriplex powellii no. 621

19 August—Muddy River, tributary to Ham's Fork, Uinta County, Wyoming.
Artemisia longiloba no. 660 *Artemisia tridentata* no. 659

22 August—Mouth of Smith's Fork, Lincoln County, Wyoming.
Aster occidentalis no. 666

3 September—Box Elder (?) County, Utah.
Distichlis spicata no. 672

4 September—Near Brigham City, Box Elder County, Utah.
Salicornia herbacea no. 677

5 September—Near Brigham City, Box Elder County, Utah.
Allenrolfea occidentalis no. 760

9 September—Frémont Island, Great Salt Lake, Weber County, Utah.
Leptotaenia multifida no. 764 *Pterochiton occidentale* no number
Obione rigida no. 767

10 September—Little Mountain to Weber River, Weber County, Utah.
Obione confertifolia no. 761

11 September—Shore of Great Salt Lake, Weber County, Utah.
Cordylanthus laxiflorus no. 759

17 September—Bannock River, Power County, Idaho.
Lupinus leucophyllus no. 734

24 September—American Falls, Snake River, Power County, Idaho.
Asclepias speciosa no. 724

6 October—Snake River, probably Elmore County, Idaho.
Chaenactis douglasii no. 789
Eriogonum strictum var. *lachnostegium* no. 786

7 October—North of Mountain Home, Elmore County, Idaho.
Gayophytum diffusum no. 782

8 October—Plains of Boisse River (a branch of the Snake), Elmore (?) County, Idaho.
Phlox aculeata no. 784

1844
24–25 February—Sierra Nevada, probably Eldorado County, California.
Chamaebatia foliolosa no. 37, 52
Libocedrus decurrens no. 33
Quercus chrysolepis no. 22

29 February—Sierra Nevada, probably Eldorado County, California.
Pellaea mucronata no. 60 (circa)

4 March—American Fork of the Sacramento River, Eldorado (?) County, California.
Meconella californica nos. 39, 44 (circa)
Nemophila heterosepala no. 42

5 March—American Fork of the Sacramento River, Sacramento (?) County, California.
Thysanocarpus curvipes no. 43

8 March—American Fork of the Sacramento River, Sacramento County, California.
Gilia tricolor no. 26

12 March—Mouth of American Fork, Sacramento River, Sacramento County, California.
Balsamorhiza bolanderi no. 7
Chlorogalum pomeridianum no. 14 (circa)
Montia perfoliata no. 10

14 March(?)—Valley of the San Joaquin, Sacramento County, California.
Dichelostemma pulchellum no. 173 (probably 24 March or later)

15 March—Mouth of American Fork, Sacramento River, Sacramento County, California.
Marah fabaceus no. 114

24 March—Cosumne River (Calaveras Creek, on specimen label), Sacramento County, California.
Dichelostemma pulchellum no. 131

24–25 March—Cosumne River, probably in Sacramento County, California.
Triteleia laxa no. 98

25–26 March—Mokelumne River and (?) Calavaras Creek, probably San Joaquin County, California.
Agoseris heterophylla no. 87
Chamaebatia foliolosa no number
Chlorogalum pomeridianum no. 81
Erodium macrophyllum no. 85
Lupinus albifrons no. 129
Lupinus bicolor no. 78
Marah fabaceus no. 80
Triteleia grandiflora no. 41, 79

28 March—Stanislaus River, Stanislaus County, California.
Marah fabaceus no. 152
Phacelia douglasii no. 155 (circa)
Polygala alba no. 153 (circa)

29 March—Stanislaus River, Stanislaus County, California.
Lupinus densiflorus no. 147
Quercus lobata no. 149

10 April—Northeast of Bakersfield, Kern County, California.
Nicolletia occidentalis no. 220 (circa)
Orthocarpus purpurascens no. 232
Trifolium depauperatum no. 235 (circa)

13 April—Kern River to the pass, Kern County, California.
Echinospermum (*Lappula*) *fremontii* no number
Eriogonum polifolium no. 297
Geraea canescens no. 293
Hymenoclea salsola no. 298 (circa)

14 April—Oak Creek or Tehachapi Pass, Kern County, California.
Quercus douglasii no. 314

15 April—East side Oak Creek Pass, south of Tehachapi Pass, Kern County, California.
Dalea arborescens no number
Yucca brevifolia no. 271

17–18 April—Mohave Desert, near Victorville, San Bernardino County, California.
Lepidium fremontii no. 316
Purshia tridentata no number
Salvia dorrii no. 349

19 April—Mohave Desert, near Victorville, San Bernardino County, California.
Pinus monophylla no. 367

23 April—Mohave River, near Barstow, San Bernardino County, California.
Franseria dumosa no. 334
Rafinesquia californica nos. 332, 335

23–24 April—Mohave Desert, Mohave River, San Bernardino County, California.
Abronia turbinata no. 339
Astragalus arthu-schottii no. 338
Franseria dumosa no. 374
Lepidium flavum no number
Lupinus argenteus no. 333

24–25 April—Mohave River, San Bernardino County, California.
Camissonia boothii subsp. *desertorum* no. 337
Hemerocallis undulata no. 363

25 April—Bitter Spring, north of Barstow, San Bernardino County, California.
Eriogonum inflatum no. 392

25–27 April—North of Barstow, San Barnardino County, California.
Eriodictyon angustifolium no. 334
Eriogonum maculatum no. 235 (near Agua de Tomaso)
Lepidium fremontii no. 390

28 April—Amargosa River, south of Shoshone, in San Bernardino County, California.
Oxystylis lutea no. 386

29 April—Resting (Hernandez) Spring, Inyo County, California.
Baileya multiradiata no number

30 April–1 May—Stump Spring, Pahrump Valley, Clark County, Nevada.
Coleogyne ramosissima no. 409
Navarretia setosissima no. 414

1 May—Mountain Spring, Spring (Charleston) Mountains, Clark County, Nevada.
Calochortus kennedyi no. 402
Hymenoclea salsola no. 400, 401 (circa)
Phlox longifolia no. 431
Salvia dorrii no. 407

2 May—Spring at Blue Diamond, Clark County, Nevada.
Thamnosma montana no. 405

3 May—Springs at Las Vegas, Clark County, Nevada.
Arctomecon californicum no. 429
Astragalus fremontii no. 424
Astragalus preussii no number
Eriogonum fasciculatum var. *polifolium* no. 427
Prosopis odorata no. 419 (circa)

4 May—Near Las Vegas, Clark County, Nevada.
Salazaria neomexicana no. 433

5 May—Muddy River, near Moapa, Clark County, Nevada.
Berberis fremontii no. 432 (at or near this locality)
Dalea fremontii no. 417

10 May—Washington County, Utah.
Amelanchier utahensis no. 442 (circa)
Coleogyne ramosissima no. 443 (circa)
Phlox austromontana no. 447
Purshia mexicana no. 444 (circa)

11 May—Santa Clara, Washington County, Utah.
Lycium pallidum no. 474

12 May—Vegas de Santa Clara, Mountain Meadows, Washington County, Utah.
Physaria acutifolia nos. 419, 420

15 May—Iron Co., Utah
Phlox austromontana no. 468

16 May—"Wasatch Mountains," near Little Salt Lake, Iron County, Utah.
Eriogonum caespitosum no. 470

21 May—"Western side of Wahsatch Mts." near present Fillmore, Millard County, Utah.
Cryptantha humilis no. 522

24–26 May—Utah Lake, Utah County, Utah
Crataegus douglasii var. *rivularis* no. 511
Mahonia repens no. 530
Plectritis macrocera no number
Valeriana edulis no number

27–31 May—Utah County, Utah.
Thermopsis montana no. 504

27 May—Spanish Fork Canyon, Utah County, Utah.
Phacelia linearis no. 505
Ribes aureum no. 502

28 May—Spanish Fork Canyon, Utah County, Utah.
Quercus gambelii no. 506

31 May—Duchesne River, Duchesne County, Utah.
Leptodactylon pungens no. 484
Penstemon nitidus β major (*P. pachyphyllus*) no. 485

1 June—Between Duchesne River and Lake Fork, Duchesne County, Utah.
Cryptantha flava no. 557 (possibly 3 June)
Gilia stenothyrsa no. 556

3 June—Island in Uinta River, Fort Uintah (Whiterocks), Uintah County, Utah.
Zigadenus sp. (*Anticlea*) no number
Senecio multilobatus no. 549
Townsendia fremontii no. 548 (circa)

5 June—East of Fort Uintah (Whiterocks), Uintah County, Utah.
Eriogonum ovalifolium no. 536
Penstemon fremontii no. 540

6 June—Ashley Creek, Uintah County, Utah
Iris missouriensis no. 488

7 June—Diamond Mountain, Uintah County, Utah.
Actinella depressa no number

10 June—Little Snake River, Moffatt County, Colorado.
Acerates latifolia no. 584

12 June—Carbon County, Wyoming.
Lupinus plattensis no. 578
Swertia perennis no. 583

16–17 June—North Park, Jackson County, Colorado.
Potentilla plattensis no. 564
Thlaspi montana no. 561
Thalictrum occidentale no. 571 (circa)

7 July—Cheyenne County, Colorado (?).
Penstemon ambiguus β foliolosa no. 623

The expedition returned to the Missouri River on 31 July 1844, ending a highly successful trip so far as new taxa are concerned. The paucity of dated or datable specimens known from the rather sizeable collection of the expedition indicates that Frémont was more involved with other matters than with collection of plants. Despite the loss of specimens due to accident and flood, the plants from the second expedition yielded more new genera, species, and varieties, than any other of the expeditions.

Third Expedition—1845–47

As early as 15 September 1844, Frémont (letter NY!, BRY!) indicated to Torrey that another expedition was in the planning stages. "From the moment the plants were lost [in the flood along the Kansas], I had formed a determination which has been strengthened by your letter—to return immediately to the interesting regions I have described to you, with the main and leading object of making anew such a collection as will enable us to give a perfect description of the vegetable character of the whole region. Its interest will of course be increased by large additions in geography & geology as we shall run an entirely new line in going out. I beg that you will keep this plan in view in your examination of the plants I now send you, as we may possibly be able to connect them with those I shall gather next year. Silence is one of the elements of success, and therefore I know that you will excuse me for telling you that I mention this plan only to yourself & shall speak of it to no one else."

The need for secrecy is difficult to understand. Frémont described the scope of the third expedition in the "Notice to the Reader" preface to the combined report of the first and second expeditions (Frémont, 1845: 3), which appeared shortly after his departure for the third expedition. Return to California was described as being a part of the plan for the third expedition. The aura of the impending war with Mexico or mere political expediency might account for the initial secrecy. Clearly Frémont had in mind going back to where his damaged or destroyed plant specimens had been taken, i.e., to Alta California, Mexico. Indeed, there are indications that Frémont hoped to return to California again soon. Some 60 or 70 mules and horses had been left in pastures on the frontier in Kansas, mules and horses that could reasonably have been added to the meager larder for the hungry men of the second expedition following the killing of the last cattle along the Mohave River. The next real supply of meat was the cow purchased at Robideau's Fort in the Uinta Basin of northeastern Utah. The animals were being saved for a future expedition, and soon prior to his return to civilization Frémont was making arrangements to move west again in 1845. He would be better prepared to do botanical collecting on this trip than on either of the two previous expeditions, and the "fatality" that had attended the plants on the second trip would apparently not be as serious during this expedition. Torrey (1853: 4) does indicate, however, that "very large collections were also made in his [Frémont's] Third Expedition in 1845 and the two following years, but again, notwithstanding every precaution, some valuable packages were destroyed by the numerous and unavoidable mishaps of such a hazardous journey." This together with the Brewer note record the loss of some portion of the third expedition specimens, but neither states clearly which specimens were destroyed, those sent from Bent's Fort or those taken later in California. While the itinerary reconstructed from the dated and datable specimens, and from the numbered specimens, does not show any significantly large gaps that would be accounted for by the destruction of specimens, neither does that for the second expedition.

It seems evident that Frémont began a numbered sequence of plant specimens collected soon after his departure from Westport. The numerical sequence was continuous until his arrival at Pueblo, Colorado, which became a major geographic site of the expedition, and, despite Frémont's designation of Bent's Fort as the actual beginning point of the journey, it was at Pueblo that the number sequence apparently began again. The new number series begun at Pueblo was continued to the Sierra Nevada, where still a third number sequence was initiated. Each number sequence commenced with the number one. The numbers were, as previously, written on tags attached to the plants sometime later, and the numbers were recorded in Frémont's diary. There is a mix-up of dates versus numbers, but one can often place specimens in approximate collection localities using even the jumbled sequence of numbers versus dates.

If the assumption is made that some 537 specimens were collected between Westport and Pueblo, almost four-fifths of them are presently unaccounted for. These were the specimens supposedly sent east from Bent's Fort; the loss of some specimens and the presence of others are difficult to explain—all should have been lost or a greater number would be found in herbaria. From Pueblo to the Sierra Nevada an additional potential of 464 specimens were numbered. Existing specimens number slightly more than a quarter of that number. Some 379 numbered and unnumbered specimens exist from the 1845–46 California collection; almost three-quarters of the potential collection of 511. Thus, one must accept at face value Dr. Torrey's evaluation of the destruction that accompanied even this most careful of the expeditions.

Despite the larger number of specimens and their care, the third expedition would not equal the second one in novelties ultimately based on Frémont's collections. According to Jackson and Spence (1970: xlvi), Frémont had "sent back hundreds of species of plants from both Bent's Fort & San Francisco," but only a few were ever treated in print. The proportion of the third expedition collection sent from Bent's Fort is not known. Perhaps all specimens that were dry were returned. It is difficult to reconcile the great number of missing numbers with the information that specimens were sent back from the fort. Those sent from there are disappointing in several ways—paucity of surviving material and lack of precise collection data, although their collection began while the party was still at Westport, Kansas, on 20 June. Their interpretation is made more difficult by the fact that no map of the Kansas-eastern Colorado portion of the trip was ever published.

Jackson and Spence (1970: xlvi) note that "Torrey wrote a fellow scientist, Jacob Whitman Bailey, a description of how the Frémont third expedition specimens sent from California were packed. 'There were two huge cases—filled with tin cases.' They were soldered up after being filled with plants—then guarded by a strong frame of wood, & finally sowed up in a green cowhide." In a letter to Torrey (1 November 1847, NY!, BRY!) Frémont says: "I was obliged to leave them [the specimens] behind in California, but expect them by the first vessel which shall arrive. As soon as I receive them I will put them at your disposition." Exactly how many specimens and represented taxa the cases contained remains unknown. Hundreds of species, as indicated by Jackson and Spence, might have indeed been the case, but it is difficult to ascertain now that the numbers were very large. Brewer (1880: 556) states inconclusively that there were about 600 numbers. The Bigelow (1856: 324, 469) quote cited earlier indicates that "more than a thousand" plant specimens resulted from the third expedition. Materials from the third expedition in the botanical appendix, include some 454 taxa from among the 980 known specimens. It is doubtful that there are a great many more specimens extant in the herbaria of this or other countries.

Frémont, it seems, made sure that the California plants that had survived the ravages of the expedition would not again arrive in damaged and moldy condition. But, the way to publication was strewn with new obstacles. The results of his potentially greatest journey of exploration and botanical contributions, richer even than those of the second expedition, remained unpublished due to his involvement in political intrigue directed toward acquisition of Alta California by the United States. Many of the taxa in his 1845–46 collections would later be based on collections by still others. Frémont's disastrous role in the acquisition of California interrupted botanical exploration, and no complete account of his collections has been published until now. Those that were published are scattered in lists of specimen citations in numerous revisions and monographs.

The plant specimens went initially to John Torrey, who had hopes that funding would be forthcoming to allow publication of a summary report of the botany of the second and third expeditions. The court-martial had already been completed prior to arrival of the plant specimens from the third expedition. In his letter to Torrey (24 February 1848, NY!, BRY!) Frémont noted: "I have therefore entirely withdrawn from the public service, but I am deeply gratified with being able to say to you that our work will still go on, and that I even hope to be able to give to it a greater extent and beauty than we had before anticipated. This, although only a hope at present, will, I have great reason to believe, be verified, and in the mean time I am permitted to assure you, that there will be no interruptions in working up the materials that we have already collected." The hoped-for identifications and publication were not to be realized.

The only publication authorized by the Senate following the third expedition was the *Geographical Memoir* (Frémont, 1848), which did not contain the usual botanical appendix. It is evident that Torrey again provided the determinations to fill in the botanical blanks in Frémont's notes and ultimately in the *Geographical Memoir*. The materials forming the bases of new taxa taken by Frémont on the third expedition would appear in various journals over a period covering more than half a century.

The novelties included four new genera: *Carpenteria* Torr., *Fremontia* Torr., *Sarcodes* Torr., and *Spraguea* Torr. Torrey tried again to honor Frémont with a genus, having been thwarted by the obstacle of an earlier generic name for the common but unlovely *Fremontia vermicularis* of the first expedition. Now he created a later homonym, a name that could not then stand by reason and could not now by stipulations of the International Code of Botanical Nomenclature. The name was replaced later by *Fremontodendron* Cov., a logical and acceptable substitute. The species *Fremontodendron californicum* (Torr.) Cov. of the Sterculiaceae is a plant of great beauty, unlike *Sarcobatus vermiculatus* with its inconspicuous flowers, and it stands as a much more fitting tribute to Frémont—devoted collector.

Other specimens, from 1845–46 especially and 1847 perhaps, were deposited in various places, in the Torrey herbarium, the Gray herbarium, the Engelmann herbarium, the U.S. National Herbarium, and some elsewhere (see herbarium designations in Appendix I & III). Many of them were cited later in various publications by Torrey, Gray, and Watson. Later workers have tended to ignore them, except for the types. Contemporary 20th-century workers prefer to cite specimens by state and county, at least. This is often impossible to do with the Frémont collections, and thus they have frequently been ignored or placed at the ends of lists of exsiccatae.

Notwithstanding the problems associated with them, these specimens proved vitally important to Torrey, Gray, Bentham, Watson, Tuckerman, Decaisne, Rydberg, and Jepson and are often cited in their summary revisions and papers dealing with new taxa in the American West. At least some of the 1845–47 specimens appear in the list of plant species appended to this work. It has not been possible, on the basis of literature, to assign all cited material to a particular expedition or year. Identifications of the specimens have been verified by using standard modern floras for Kansas, Colorado, Wyoming, Utah, and California.

New taxa named from specimens taken during the third expedition to California from 1845–47 include:

Alectoria fremontii Tuckerman
Allium serratum S. Wats.
Amauria dissecta A. Gray
Anogra cinerea Rydb.
Anticlea fremontii Torr.
Antirrhinum vagans A. Gray
Asclepias fremontii Torr. ex A. Gray
Bahia lanata var. *grandiflora* A. Gray
Calycadenia fremontii A. Gray in Torr.
Calycadenia pauciflora A. Gray in Torr.
Carpenteria californica Torr.
Carum kelloggii A. Gray
Ceanothus decumbens S. Wats.
Chaenactis heterocarpa Torr. & A. Gray in A. Gray
Chenopodium olidum S. Wats.
Dichaeta fremontii Torr. ex A. Gray
Eriogonum corymbosum Benth. in DC.
Eriogonum effusum var. *rosmarinoides* Benth. in DC.
Eriogonum nudum var. *pubiflorum* Benth. in DC.
Eriogonum obtusum Benth. in DC.
Eriogonum polyanthum Benth. in DC.
Eriogonum umbellatum var. *majus* Benth. in DC.
Eriogonum virgatum Benth. in DC.
Fremontia californica Torr.
Fritillaria pluriflora Torr. in Benth.
Garrya fremontii Torr.
Godetia amoena var. *albicaulis* Jepson
Hemizonia virgata A. Gray
Heteromeles fremontiana Decaisne
Hosackia argophylla var. *fremontii* A. Gray
Lepidium alyssoides A. Gray
Lilium canadense var. *puberulum* Torr.
Oenothera hispidula S. Wats.
Pedicularis procera A. Gray
Penstemon watsonii A. Gray
Philadelphus fremontii Rydb.
Populus fremontii S. Wats.
Potentilla etomentosa Rydb.
Prunus fremontii S. Wats.
Pycnanthemum californicum Torr. in Durand
Quercus chrysolepis Liebm.
Quercus longiglanda Torr. & Frém. in Frém.
Sarcodes sanguinea Torr.
Scutellaria antirrhinoides var. *californica* A. Gray
Senecio eurycephalus Torr. & A.Gray
Sidalcea candida A. Gray
Sidalcea diplocypha var. *β minor* A. Gray
Smelowskia fremontii S. Wats.

Sphaeralcea pedata Torr. in A. Gray
Spraguea umbellata Torr.
Stropholirion californicum Torr.
Styrax californica Torr.

The third expedition moved through the Great Plains in the summer of 1845 when the prairies and plains flora was at the height of flowering. Westward the expedition moved upward into the mountains in August and September as autumn was moving downward. The men and animals then traversed the peculiar exposed geological strata of the Colorado Plateau, where species of *Eriogonum* line the formations. Plants were sampled at intervals as the season progressed. By the time the party chose to move swiftly west from the Great Salt Lake autumn was advancing, and they raced to cross the Sierra Nevada before snows of winter closed the passes. Once west of the divide, on the California side of the range, Frémont began collecting again and collected throughout the winter season. When spring came early, as it does in the Great Valley of California, collecting intensified. Arrival at Lassen's in Tehama County along the upper Sacramento was during that part of springtime when the flowers were blooming in all their glory. Despite all of the distractions of the expedition Frémont concentrated on taking as many plants as possible. A glimpse of that flora appears among his collections.

According to Egan (1977: 288), who cites Isaac Cooper, the third expedition began on 23 June 1845, when the huge entourage, comprising Lieutenants Abert and Peck and their men and the Frémont party, moved to a camp near Westport, where they stayed until 26 June. The combined party likely retraced the homeward track of the previous year's expedition, moving along the Santa Fe Trail to a point near present Lindsburg, McPherson County, Kansas. There they could follow the track along the Smoky Hill Fork of the Kansas into present Cheyenne County, Colorado. From there the men and animals turned southwesterly and crossed to the Arkansas River east of Bent's Fort, present Otero County, Colorado, where they arrived on 2 August 1845.

At Bent's Fort the group with Lieutenants Abert and Peck, consisting of 34 men guided by Thomas Brokenhand Fitzpatrick, left Frémont and proceeded with a survey of the Purgatory, Red, and Canadian Fork of the Arkansas rivers, before returning to St. Louis (Egan, 1977: 292–93).

Following the departure of Lieutenant Abert and his men, Frémont left Bent's Fort on 16 August 1845 with an entourage of 200 pack animals in the train, 150 loose horses (remounts for those being ridden), and 250 head of cattle (Egan, 1977: 295). This large number of animals was in addition to those being ridden by the more than 60 men in the group. It is some wonder that Frémont was able to devote any time to the collection of plants. He does not mention that he did so, but there are dated specimens that indicate collections of botanical specimens before and after his arrival at Bent's Fort.

The following itinerary of the 1845–47 expedition indicates plants taken by date.

23 June 1845—Camp moved to near Westport, Kansas.

20 June—Westport, Kansas.
Galium circaezans no number

30 June—Prairies, four days west of Westport, along the Santa Fe Trail, Kansas.
Phlox pilosa no. 15
Psoralea argophylla no. 15

3 July—Near Santa Fe Road, Kansas.
Carya tomentosa no. 24

4 July—Near Santa Fe Road, Kansas.
Amaranthus arenicola no. 138

5 July—Near Santa Fe Road, Kansas.
Hypericum sphaerocarpum no. 49, 51
Liatris punctata no. 48
Quercus macrocarpa nos. 39, 41

6 July—Near Santa Fe Road, Kansas.
Hypericum sphaerocarpum no. 34

8 July—Near Santa Fe Road, Kansas.
Callirhoe alceoides no. 54

11 July—Turkey Creek, Kansas.
Calystegia sepium no. 108
Cirsium undulatum no. 86
Ruellia humilis no number

12 July—West of Turkey Creek, Kansas.
Penstemon buckleyi no. 118

15 July—Branch of Smoky Hill Fork, Kansas.
Mentzelia oligosperma no. 123

18 July—Branch of Smoky Hill Fork, Kansas.
Senecio riddellii no. 170
Vitis riparia no. 168

19 July—Smoky Hill Fork (?), Kansas.
Haplopappus spinulosus no number
Mentzelia nuda no. 149
Verbena bipinnatifida no. 147

20 July—Smoky Hill Fork (?), Kansas.
Oenothera latifolia no number

23 July—Smoky Hill Fork (?), Kansas.
Asclepias speciosa nos. 93, 94

24 July—Smoky Hill Fork (?), Kansas.
Eriogonum effusum var. *rosmarinoides* no. 181

25 July—Smoky Hill Fork (?), Kansas.
Cucurbita foetidissima nos. 198, 202
Oenothera canescens no. 192
Oenothera serrulata no. 201
Salvia reflexa nos. 201, 202
Solidago mollis nos. 189, 190

27 July—Five day's journey east of Bent's Fort, probably in eastern Colorado (a Sunday).
Atriplex canescens no. 209
Linum rigidum var. *berlandieri* no. 207

29 July—Four day's journey east of Bent's Fort, Colorado.
Chenopodium album no. 239
Eriogonum annuum no. 239

30 July—Three day's journey east of Bent's Fort, Colorado.
Abronia fragrans no. 227
Dalea nana nos. 130, 221
Euphorbia marginata nos. 112, 241
Euphorbia missurica nos. 102, 234

31 July—Upper Arkansas, east of Bent's Fort, Colorado.
Mentzelia nuda no. 243

14 August—Bent's Fort, Otero County, Colorado.
Citrullus lanatus no. 37 (from second number series, possibly taken in Pueblo County on 18–20 August)

15 August—Bent's Fort, Otero County, Colorado.
Alternanthera lanuginosa no. 455

2–16 August—Bent's Fort, Otero County, Colorado.
Aster oblongifolius no. 498
Eriogonum effusum no. 486 (circa)
Lepidium alyssoides no. 480 (circa)
Machaeranthera canescens no. 481 (circa)
Monolepis nuttalliana no. 477
Pedicularis procera no. 478 (circa)
Ribes aureum no. 490
Stanleya integrifolia no. 423

16–20 August—Between Bent's Fort and Upper Pueblo, Otero to Pueblo counties, Colorado.
Alternanthera lanuginosa no. 455
Anogra cinerea nos. 202, 234
Atriplex canescens no. 433
Eriogonum annuum no. 454
Helianthus petiolaris no. 34

18–20 August—Arkansas bottoms, Fountain Creek, Pueblo County, Colorado.
Cardamine cordifolia no. 429
Helianthus petiolaris no. 34
Mirabilis multiflora no. 1
Rumex maritimus var. *fuegineus* no. 426 (circa)

21 August—Mouth of canyon above Pueblo (near Canon City), Pueblo County, Colorado.
Potentilla pseudosericea no. 218 (circa)

22 August—Upper Arkansas, two day's journey west of Pueblo [Fontaine-qui-bouit], Pueblo County, Colorado.
Artemisia filifolia nos. 62, 63
Mentzelia nuda no number
Rhus aromatica no number

28 August—West of Canon, Frémont County, Colorado.
Aster laevis no. 394
Salix amygdaloides no. 402a
Salix exigua no. 402b
Salix monticola no. 402
Sarcobatus vermiculatus no. 401

2 September—Headwaters of the Arkansas, in South Park (Bahia Salada) Chaffee or Lake counties, Colorado.
Amauria dissecta no number
Eriogonum alatum no. 288
Eriogonum cernuum no. 289
Eriogonum umbellatum var. *majus* no. 237
Gentiana affinis no. 128 (circa)
Senecio eremophilus no. 380

4–11 September—Piney Creek, Eagle County, Colorado (Grand River and tributaries).
Eriogonum corymbosum no. 248
Vicia americana no. 257

12–25 September—White River, Rio Blanco County, Colorado and Uintah County, Utah.
Alnus incana no. 422
Chenopodium olidum no. 382
Lupinus caudatus no. 406
Rumex occidentalis no. 384 (circa)
Sidalcea candida nos. 407, 410 (both circa)

2 or 3 October—Provo River, Wasatch County, Utah.
Acer grandidentatum no. 305

4 December—Donner Pass, probably Placer County, California.
Sedum obtusum no number

5 December—One day west of Donner Pass, probably Placer County, California.
Alectoria fremontii no. 491
Quercus chrysolepis no number

6 December—Two days west of Donner Pass, probably Placer County, California.
Chamaebatia foliolosa no number

9 December—Grimes Rancho, near Sutters, Sacramento County, California.
Senecio douglasii no. 9

14 (?) December—Cosumne River, Sacramento County, California.
Quercus lobata no. 14

15 December—Mokelumne River, San Joaquin County, California.
Quercus wislizenii no number (2 specimens; a third sheet cites date as 18 Dec.)

17 December—Stanislaus River, Stanislaus County and Merced River, Merced County, California.
Quercus lobata nos. 4, 7
Quercus wislizenii no. 15

22–23 December—King's River (Lake Fork), Fresno County, California.
Arctostaphylos tomentosa no. 20
Quercus lobata no. 8

24–25 December—King's River (Lake Fork), Fresno County, California.
Quercus chrysolepis nos. 22(?), 29
Quercus wislizenii no. 16

25 December—King's River (Lake Fork), Fresno County, California.
Quercus wislizenii no number (2 specimens)

26 December—King's River (Lake Fork), Fresno County, California.
Quercus chrysolepis nos. 29, 35

29 December—King's River (Lake Fork), Fresno County, California.
Phyllodoce breweri no. 40

31 December—King's River (Lake Fork), Fresno County, California.
Platanus racemosa no. 110 (circa)

21 January 1846—Near Monterey, Monterey County, California.
Lupinus chamissonis no number

31 January—Near Monterey, Monterey County, California.
Keckiella breviflora no number
Salvia mellifera no number

22 February—Wild Cat Ridge, Santa Cruz County, California.
Picea engelmannii nos. 117, 235 (possibly elsewhere)

23 February—Wild Cat Ridge, Santa Cruz County, California.
Cardamine angulata nos. 151, 154
Thermopsis macrophylla no. 153 (circa)
Dodecatheon conjugens no. 105

25 February—Santa Cruz, Santa Cruz County, California.
Oenothera ovata no. 125

26 February—Santa Cruz, Santa Cruz County, California.
Arctostaphylos tomentosa no. 145
Solanum umbelliferum no. 120

28 February—Santa Cruz, Santa Cruz County, California.
Anticlea fremontii no. 157
Ribes sanguineum no. 159 (circa)
Marah fabaceus no number

2 March—Santa Cruz, Santa Cruz County, California.
Calandrina ciliata no. 160

11 March—San Joaquin Valley, San Benito County, California.
Ceanothus cuneatus no number

14 March—Cosumne River, Sacramento County, California.
Dichelostemma pulchellum no. 173

16–17 March—Between Stanislaus and Mokelumne rivers, San Joaquin County, California.
Phacelia cicutaria no. 186 (circa)
Triteleia laxa nos. 184, 260

18 March—Mokelumne River, San Joaquin County, California.
Quercus wislizenii no number

19 March—Mokelumne River, San Joaquin County, California.
Lomatium utriculatum no. 197

20 March—Cosumne River, Sacramento County, California.
Acer negundo var. *californica* no number

27 March—Feather River, Yuba County, California.
Calochortus luteus nos. 209, 213
Fritillaria pluriflora no. 213 (circa)

2 April—Deer Creek, at Lassen's, near Vina, Tehama County, California.
Salix lasiolepis no number

5 April—Sacramento River, at Lassen's, near Vina, Tehama County, California.
Gilia achilleifolia no. 241
Lupinus bicolor no. 242 (circa)
Populus fremontii nos. 243, 244 (circa)
Rubus ursinus no. 239

7 April—Cottonwood Creek, vicinity of Redding, Shasta County, California.
Quercus agrifolia no. 247

8 April—Cow Creek, vicinity of Redding, Shasta County, California.
Cercis occidentalis no. 181
Lupinus albifrons no number
Quercus agrifolia no. 300
Quercus tinctoria var. *californica* no number
Toxicodendron diversilobum no. 298

9 April—Cow Creek, vicinity of Redding, Shasta County, California.
Oenothera hispidula no. 307 (circa)

11 April—Sacramento River, Mill Creek, vicinity of Lassen's, Tehama County, California.
Gilia achilleifolia no number

12 April—Sacramento Valley, at Lassen's, near Vina, Tehama County, California.
Agoseris heterophylla no. 248

13 April—Near Lassen's, upper Sacramento, near Vina, Tehama County, California.
Mimulus guttatus no number (circa 315)

14 April—Sacramento River, at Lassen's, near Vina, Tehama County, California.
Lupinus albifrons no number
Quercus douglasii no. 341

16 April—Sacramento River, at Lassen's, near Vina, Tehama County, California.
Pogogyne zizyphoroides no. 285
Sanicula bipinnatifida no. 280 (circa)
Sedum pumilum no. 273 (circa)
Trifolium macraei no. 266

25 April—Antelope Creek, east of Red Bluff, Tehama County, California.
Bahia lanata var. *grandiflora* no. 333

25–26 April—Possibly Bear Creek, east of Redding, Shasta County, California.
Dudleya cymosa no. 338
Eriodictyon angustifolium no. 334
Quercus douglasii no. 341

27 April—Possibly Bear Creek, east of Redding, Shasta County, California.
Calochortus monophyllus no. 353
Ceanothus decumbens no. 357
Pedicularis densiflora no. 358

27–28 April—"Headwaters of Cow Creek," east of Redding, Shasta County, California.
Fritillaria recurva nos. 346, 348
Sanicula tuberosa no. 347

28 April—"Headwaters of Cow Creek," east of Redding, Shasta County, California.
Fremontia californica no. 384 (circa)
Garrya fremontii no. 369 (circa)
Prunus fremontii no. 370 (circa)
Ribes cf. *leptanthum* no. 372 (circa)
Viola nuttallii no. 373

29 April—Shasta County, California.
Salix lasiolepis no number

30 April—"Round Valley" vicinity of Lookout, Modoc County, California.
Hesperochiron californicus no. 379
Phlox hoodii no. 377 (circa)

1 May—Clear Lake, Modoc County, California.
Calycadenia tenella no. 380a
Leucocrinum montanum no. 380
Sisyrinchium douglasii no. 381 (circa)

4 May—McCrady (Lost River), Modoc County, California, or Klamath County, Oregon.
Smelowskia fremontii no. 384

5 May—Lost River, probably Klamath County, Oregon.
Lomatium dissectum no. 383

6 May—Klamath Lake vicinity, Klamath County, Oregon.
Betula glandulosa no. 393
Brodiaea elegans no. 486 (Denny's Creek)
Limnanthes douglasii no. 394 (circa)

20 May—At or near Lassen's, Tehama County, California.
Cercocarpus ledifolius no number
Delphinium nudicaule no. 414 (circa)
Fritillaria agrestis no. 397 (circa)
Fritillaria atropurpurea no. 411 (circa)
Lathyrus pauciflorus no. 416 (circa)
Lithophragma glabra no. 413 (circa)
Phlox speciosa no. 415 (circa)
Thlaspi montana no. 419 (circa)

22 May—At Lassen's, Deer Creek, Tehama County, California. (Note: Frémont cites specimens on this date from Zozah, Nozah, or Noza, possibly Noyah, river.)
Godetia amoena var. *albicaulis* no. 435
Perideridia oregana no. 487
Spraguea umbellata no. 466

22–23 May—At Lassen's, Deer Creek, Tehama County, California.
Ceanothus integerrimus nos. 410, 468 (Nozah River)
Cercocarpus ledifolius nos. 421, 459
Ribes cereum no. 447 (circa)
Trifolium macrocephalum no. 436 (circa)

23 May—Antelope Creek, east of Red Bluff, Tehama County, California.
Lilium canadense var. *puberulum* no. 490

25 May—At Lassen's, Deer Creek, Tehama County, California.
Monardella villosa no. 446
Trifolium variegatum no. 443 (circa)

26 May—At Lassen's, Deer Creek, Tehama County, California.
Calochortus luteus no. 433
Scutellaria siphocampyloides no. 434 (circa)
Sidalcea diploschpha var. *minor* no. 432 (circa)

27 May—At or near Lassen's, Deer Creek, Tehama County, California.
Cercis occidentalis no. 483
Fremontia californica no. 470 (circa)
Phacelia imbricata no. 472 (circa)

28 May—Probably Butte County, California (two days south of Lassen's).
Pogogyne douglasii no. 438

30 May—Camp at the Buttes, west of Yuba City, Sutter County, California.
Cryptantha intermedia no. 400
Plagiobothrys canescens no. 400 (circa)

4 June—Buttes, west of Yuba City, Sutter County, California.
Asclepias fremontii no. 477
Rhamnus californica no. 499 (circa)
Sida hederacea no. 476 (circa)

5 June—N bank of the American Fork, Sacramento County, California.
Antirrhinum vagans no. 495

14–15 June—Sutter's Landing, Sacramento, Sacramento County, California.
Quercus tinctoria var. *californica* no. 500
Philadelphus fremontii no. 511

3 or 13 September—Between Los Angeles and Sacramento, California.
Mimulus cardinalis no number

There are 197 dated or probably datable specimens from the third expedition, taken on at least 91 dates (out of approximately 360 possible). One should not infer from this that Frémont was more meticulous in recording data on this expedition than on the earlier ones. A large number of specimens (indicated by circa) have been estimated as to date and/or place of collection. The proportion of specimens with sufficient data to allow disposition in modern geographical terms is still abysmally small. By 14 June 1846, Frémont was embroiled in the California rebellion and beyond this time he collected very few plants; there is one specimen dated September 1846 and another dated 1847. Most of his California collections in 1846 came from north of the Feather River, along the valley of the Sacramento. The bulk of the collections apparently came from near Lassen's, Tehama County, California. He stayed at Lassen's for some days on three occasions, when the spring flowering was at its height and beyond. It is unfortunate that more of the 1846 specimens were not dated or provided with locality data. The rebellion in California put an end to Frémont's career as botanical explorer.

Fourth and Fifth Expeditions—1848–49, 1853–54

"I have good reasons for believing that I shall receive aid from the government in carrying on the work," Frémont wrote Torrey, "and am now making my arrangements in that expectation. Perhaps you will be able to give me the approximate amount which we shall require for our botany, as I should like to include it in the general estimate. Although Douglas, Nuttall, & Gambel have done a great deal yet I am persuaded that much remains to be done, and that such an expedition as I now propose to make would collect rich material for the work" (Frémont letter to Torrey, 12 March 1848, NY!, BRY!). He continued, "Perhaps we could safely base our estimate on eighty quarto or a hundred and fifty octavo plates." He had hired Richard Kern to accompany him as artist and hoped that beautiful drawings would result from the fourth expedition. A few such drawings were made by Edward Kern during the third expedition and have survived the years since; they are water color renditions of plants probably from near Lassen's in Tehama County, California.

Torrey (1853: 4) notes: "There was still another journey to California made by that zealous traveller [Frémont], the disastrous one commenced late in the year 1848. Even in this he gleaned a few plants, which, with all his other botanical collections he kindly placed at my disposal. I had hoped that arrangements would have been made by the Government for publication of such a general account of the Botany of California, but as there is no immediate prospect of such a work being undertaken, I have prepared this memoir on some of the most interesting new genera discovered by Colonel Frémont."

Although it is contended that the reason for the winter trip was to see if winter conditions would permit the building of a railroad, there is no reason to believe that Frémont had previously chosen to cross the Colorado Rockies in midwinter. He had clearly indicated that the expedition would be underway much earlier. The attempt to cross the mountains of Colorado in midwinter 1848–49 seems to have been due to other considerations. Why would one take a botanist if the trip was to be made in winter, when plants are not generally collectible? The expedition became, nevertheless, an opportunity for Frémont to regain the glow of his earlier successes, and ill-timed, ill-conceived, and ill-planned as it was, it did contribute something to the understanding of botany. The 50 or so plant specimens, none dated other than as to year, and that on labels modified from previous expeditions, were taken along the Gila River in Arizona (possibly also in Sonora) and in southern California.

It was on this trip that Frémont had arranged for a botanist to go along. That botanist, Frederick Creutzfeldt (spelled variously), accompanied the express party sent for help by John Charles, only to be rescued in turn by Frémont and his relief party on their way to the settlements for relief. Creutzfeldt had almost perished of exposure and starvation prior to being rescued, and there have been hints, often discounted, that some use had been made of fellow traveler Henry King's body for food following his death. Why Creutzfeldt was added to this expedition is open to speculation. Frémont must have had some reason to believe that a botanist's presence would add either prestige or much additional botanical information. Had the party succeeded in crossing the mountains they would have arrived in southern California during early springtime. Possibly Frémont had that in mind and remembered how pressed for time he had been on the third expedition. He could have employed a botanist to good effect on all of the expeditions. However, even following the rescue, when the party was traveling south into the springtime along the Gila track, and where plants were available for collection, Creutzfeldt was evidently not able to preserve plants taken for the purposes of John Charles's and John Torrey's proposed collaboration. In a letter to Torrey, 28 March 1850 (Spence 1984: 128), Frémont notes: "I shall be able to send a few plants to your daughter, which I have no doubt are of much interest, as being, some at least, entirely new. I had collected many fine plants along the Gila and in Sonora but the man [Creutzfeldt] to whom I entrusted their collection although professing to be a botanist, permitted them to get wet repeatedly and many are ruined & the rest he did not even label."

Probably Creutzfeldt (or Kreusfeldt) should receive some (or all of the) credit for the collection of plants taken on the fourth expedition; he was, after all, botanist of the expedition. His name, however, does not appear on any of the 1848–49 specimens. The only mention of him in the botanical appendix (Appendix I) is associated with a specimen of *Gentiana parryi* Engelm., collected by Creutzfeldt when on the Gunnison Expedition (Gray, 1862b: 256).

At least 10 new taxa were in the 1849 collection, from along the Gila, in Sonora, or along the lower Colorado, or in southern California: *Chorizanthe brevicornu* Torr., *Dichaeta fremontii* Torr. ex A. Gray; *Franseria albicaulis* Torr., *F. deltoidea* Torr., *Geraea canescens* Torr. & A. Gray in A. Gray; *Gilia demissa* A. Gray, *Hyptis emoryi* Torr. in Ives, *Lycium fremontii* A. Gray, *L. macrodon* A. Gray, and *Obione hymenelytra* Torr. The two *Franseria* species were published along with new taxa from the second and third expeditions in the Plantae Fremontianae, in volume six of Smithsonian Contributions to Knowledge (Torrey, 1853). The two species of *Lycium*, both authored by Asa Gray (1862a), appeared in Proceedings of the American Academy, volume 6, the *Gilia* in Proceedings of the American Academy, volume 8 (Gray, 1870a). The present writer has found 60 taxa taken with certainty on the fourth expedition (see family summary list, Appendix III) from among some 65 specimens. Possibly there are a few more specimens from this expedition at either NY or GH.

Frémont's illness delayed the start of the fifth expedition in 1853, which, like that of 1848–49, does not appear to have been intentionally set in winter. Since the traverse from the front range of Colorado to Parowan, Utah, required only slightly more than two months, the expedition commencing in early September could have crossed through the mountains before the end of the year 1853. In any event there would have been little opportunity to collect plant specimens. Starting late as it did on 1 November from the Saline Fork of the Kansas, it is little wonder that the botanical results of the fifth expedition are essentially nil. An excerpt reproduced by Spence (1984: 474) from the *Daily Alta California*, dated 21 April 1854, five days following Frémont's arrival, contains the following: "Col. Frémont has not had time to arrange his papers, and most of his calculations are still to be made, and we expect that when a detailed narrative of his journey shall be published, it will create a strong impression on the public mind in favor of the central route [for a railroad]. The season did not permit of extensive zoological, botanical or geological researches, yet a considerable portion of the journey having been made over country never before examined by civilized man, the report will no doubt add much to the present stock of knowledge about the country near the southern rim of the great basin." Unfortunately, the report was never written.

There are seven botanical collections and one additional species based on a literature citation known from the fifth expedition. The most important is that on which was based the genus *Syntrichopappus* A. Gray in Torr., and the species *S. fremontii* A. Gray in Torr., which was "gathered by Colonel Frémont (a single specimen) in his journey across the continent in 1853–4, probably in the spring of 1854, and somewhere between the Rocky Mountains and the Sierra Nevada" (Gray in Torrey, 1857). A note on the herbarium sheet at the Torrey Herbarium (microfiche BRY!) states: "Received from Col. Frémont Aug 12, 1854. Collected in spring of that year in his journey across the continent. The only specimen he brought home." The plant was undoubtedly collected somewhere in western Nevada or southeastern California. It is a low annual of warm to hot desert tracts, blooming early in the spring. The note by Torrey quoted above is misleading; there exists another specimen received on 12 Aug. 1854—*Cercocarpus ledifolius* (see Appendix I). A third specimen from this expedition is a fragment labeled *Sidalcea diplocypha* var. *minor*. The other known collections are *Pinus monophylla* at GH, *Stylomecon heterophylla* at NY, and *Coreopsis calliopsida* at NY. A seventh specimen, *Camissonia claviformis*, seems to have been taken on this expedition also (see discussion under *Oenothera claviformis* in Appendix I). Thus, even the final journey yielded some botanical information. *Syntrichopappus* was the nineteenth genus based on a collection by Frémont.

Frémont's apparently real lack of botanical training and understanding was compensated, in part at least, by his devotion as a plant collector. That he was a keen observer and continued to add to his collections plants not seen by him previously is unquestioned. The impressive list of plants taken by him includes great diversity in species, genera, families, and higher categories. The hardships associated with collection of plants on such expeditions were considerable. Wind, rain, cold and heat are experienced by all who collect plants, but in modern times a dry room is ordinarily nearby. For this the hide and cloth tents of the Frémont party were a poor alternative. Still Frémont persisted in taking plant specimens and in preserving them for posterity. Insect repellents, as we know them, were non-existent. Both men and animals were punished by insects and other vermin incessantly during much of each year. Preuss complained of mosquitoes more than once, but Frémont did not, rarely noting them at all. The taking and pressing of plants were only small duties among the myriad tasks of the expeditions. There were no containers useful for keeping specimens fresh for long periods of time prior to pressing. Drying facilities were poor, and maps were crude or were being produced only simultaneously with the collections. Record-keeping was, thus, simplified or lacking, but the specimens had to be kept in such condition that they would be usable by botanists. Few of the specimens taken were accompanied by locality information, at least by the time they reached the botanists who would interpret them. In spite of their quality, the plants allow one to glimpse times and places seen only by Frémont and his men.

The ultimate value of any plant collection depends on its accessibility to botanists, who interpret the specimens and determine their identity and relationships. Here Frémont made a valuable contribution; he made sure that the plants taken on his expeditions reached those most interested in them, those who could and would interpret them for future students of the flora of western North America. Torrey and Gray, and Watson later on, were the outstanding pioneers of botany of the American West. Preservation of the collections after the death of Torrey and Gray passed into the hands of institutions that have provided housing and care, and continue to make the specimens available to contemporary workers.

Torrey paid tribute to Frémont in the introduction to the Plantae Fremontianae. "The important services rendered to science by that distinguished traveller, Colonel Frémont, are known to all who have read the reports of his hazardous journeys. He has not only made valuable additions to the geographical knowledge of our remote possessions, but has greatly increased our acquaintance with the geology and natural history of the regions which he explored" (Torrey, 1853). That the expeditions were hazardous is unquestioned. The trails of the second, third, fourth, and fifth expeditions were each marked by graves of brave young men who threw in their lots with Frémont. Seldom, however, does Frémont emerge as the hero of any particular expedition, for others excelled him. His role in all of the expeditions appears to have one of delegation of responsibility; assignments were made to various members of the party. Those responsible for the various tasks then carried out their assignments, and when the responsible people functioned well so did the expedition. When the assignments were irresponsibly handled, the expeditions did not fare well.

Charles Preuss appears to this writer as having been the second most important person on the first and second expeditions, though he would surely decline the title of hero. He was a skilled and talented topographer, who was seldom content with events but did magnificent work. Preuss was with Frémont on the fourth expedition and went west with him into California in 1849. There he worked as a surveyor for a time. He suffered a sunstroke in 1850, and because of illness, returned to Washington City. He was invited to join the 1853–54 expedition but declined to accept another position, with the Williamson party on the Pacific Railroad Survey. Upon his return to Washington late in

1853 or early 1854 he became hopelessly ill and was unable to complete the survey work. "In a state of despondency he disappeared from his home on September 1, 1854. The following day his body was found hanging from a tree" (Gudde & Gudde, 1958: xxix). He is commemorated by *Astragalus preussii* A. Gray, the beautiful type of which was taken from the vicinity of the springs at Las Vegas, Nevada, on 3 May 1844.

The heroes of the expeditions were those that saddled the horses, packed and loaded the gear, and maintained the baggage of the party. Pack and riding animals have minds of their own. Becoming synchronized with their needs, personalities, and traits is a full-time job. Horses and mules go when and where they shouldn't, stop when they shouldn't, buck, kick, bite, and suffer. The animals get hungry and thirsty like the men who depend on them. They require rest and reasonably good treatment. Anyone who has worked with horses pays special tribute to the hardy men who depended on them for transport across the western frontier.

The botanical specimens collected by Frémont were taken at great cost in both human and animal lives. Whatever its quality, each should be regarded as a memento of the men and animals who suffered to make it possible.

ACKNOWLEDGEMENTS

This work grew out of a search for type specimens relevant to the botany of western North America. Many people have encouraged me in this seemingly endless and tedious task, whose moments of excitement have been, however, not unlike opening the wrapping on a new gift. Patricia Holmgren suggested the preparation of the work, following completion of my much smaller project on the contributions of John Charles Frémont to the flora of Utah. Others who gave encouragement and help include Arthur Cronquist and Rupert C. Barneby. Noel Holmgren allowed me to share his office at The New York Botanical Garden. Rupert C. Barneby aided me in finding critical specimens in the herbarium at New York and gave solace and refreshment at late afternoon breaks. He also read an initial copy of the manuscript. Arnold Tiehm selected the first of many Frémont plants from the herbarium at New York. His help is gratefully acknowledged. Jody Chandler and others at the library at Brigham Young University provided help with critical bibliographical materials. I acknowledge and thank Matthew Chatterley who provided the maps of the expeditions and enhanced the photograph of the original pencil illustration of *Arctomecon californicum*. Illustrations used in many of the figures were prepared by the graphics department of the Life Science Museum at Brigham Young University, where special thanks are given to Richard Weiss and Theodore Whitmoyer. The entire manuscript was edited professionally by Joan Abel, who greatly improved the quality of the presentation.

Walter Kittridge of the Gray Herbarium of Harvard University went beyond the call of duty in searching that huge collection for Frémont materials. His generosity is hereby gratefully acknowledged. Without his help the work would have been only half finished, since the Gray Herbarium is the other major repository for Frémont's plant specimens. James Solomon at the Missouri Botanical Garden guided workers there in the search for specimens taken by Frémont. He and his coworkers are hereby gratefully acknowledged. George F. Russell supervised the search for specimens at the U.S. National Herbarium. Thanks are extended to him and his colleagues who aided him.

I thank the numerous workers at The New York Botanical Garden who combed through the collection there following my August 1990 visit and found a great many specimens that round out this presentation. New York Botanical Garden staff members who have searched for Frémont specimens are: Lisa M. Campbell, Stephen P. Crisafulli, Laurence J. Dorr, James W. Grimes, Richard C. Harris, Noel H. Holmgren, Patricia K. Holmgren, Sarah Hunkins, Ann W. Hurst, Dhankumari Jaggernauth, Jacquelyn A. Kallunki, Maria Lucia Kawasaki, Linda D. Marschner, Veronica J. Masson, Michael Nee, Gysela Pacheco, John F. Pruski, Ivan Valdespino, and Eileen Whalen. Four of these staff members were supported by National Science Foundation grant BSR-8618970 to The New York Botanical Garden during the time they searched for Frémont specimens. These dedicated persons are herewith acknowledged and thanked for their help.

My former colleague at Brigham Young, Kaye H. Thorne, served as sounding board for this work, read portions of it critically, and helped always with the myriad tasks that accompany such a manuscript.

The librarians of The New York Botanical Garden and Center for Botanical Documentation, Carnegie Museum, are acknowledged and thanked for their help in securing photographs and letters, and for arranging for the rights to their publication in this work. The University of Oklahoma Press and University of Illinois Press gave permissions for use of quotes from various works listed in the Literature Cited section of this work. Both organizations are hereby acknowledged and thanked.

To my wife, Stella, I owe special gratitude and thanks for her long-suffering, while I recounted the Frémont sagas in seemingly endless discussions. Each time we crossed one of his routes through Utah the story of Frémont's trip through that segment of the state came to mind, and Stella would listen patiently to the recounting of the expedition or expeditions once again. I acknowledge my linguistically gifted sons for the translations of the abstract—Blaine Tree Welsh for the French and Martin Larson Welsh and Eric Richard Welsh for the Spanish. These, in addition to English, were the principal languages spoken on the Frémont expeditions. It is fitting that both be used in this work. The French translation was critically reviewed by Elizabeth Yim Cheung, of Faaa, Tahiti, and by Rupert C. Barneby.

The herbarium of Brigham Young University served as temporary home for Frémont specimens on loan from NY, GH, MO, and US. Photographs of many Frémont sheets were made at BRY by Theodore Whitmoyer, the negatives and photographs of which will be maintained permanently as a part of the collection. I wish to thank the personnel of the herbarium, the Life Science Museum, and Brigham Young University for their consideration and help in this work.

Acknowledgement is given also to the memory of John Charles and Jessie Benton Frémont, who lived the amazing experiences recounted in this book.

To the long-suffering and diligent Amy McPherson, who saw this manuscript through its labor pains, I am eternally grateful. Special thanks are given to Barbara Mack, who formatted the manuscript into its final pages, and entered corrections along the way. Marshall Crosby is acknowledged; he deserves credit for his time and effort in seeing this project finished.

Finally, I wish to express my gratitude to the kindness and aid of Peter H. Raven, without whom this work would never have been published.

Literature Cited

Abrams, L. 1923. Illustrated Flora of the Pacific States. Vol. I. Ophioglossaceae to Aristolochiaceae. Stanford: Stanford University Press.

______. 1944. Illustrated Flora of the Pacific States. Vol. II. Polygonaceae to Krameriaceae. Stanford: Stanford University Press.

______. 1951. Illustrated Flora of the Pacific States. Vol. III. Geraniaceae to Scrophulariaceae. Stanford: Stanford University Press.

______ & R. S. Ferris. 1960. Illustrated Flora of the Pacific States. Vol. IV. Bignoniaceae to Compositae. Stanford: Stanford University Press.

Bancroft, H. H. 1889. History of Utah — 1540–1887. San Francisco: The History Company.

Barkley, T. M. 1978. *Senecio* L. North Amer. Flora II. 10: 50–139.

Barneby, R. C. 1964. Atlas of North American *Astragalus*. Mem. New York Bot. Gard. 13: 1–1188.

Bassett, I. J. & C. W. Crompton. 1982. The genus *Chenopodium* in Canada. Canad. J. Bot. 60: 586–610.

Beaman, J. H. 1957. The systematics and evolution of *Townsendia* (Compositae). Contr. Gray Herb. 183: 1–151.

Beckwith, E. G. 1855. Reports of explorations and surveys, to ascertain the most practicable and economical route for a railroad from the Mississippi River to the Pacific Ocean. House Rep. Exec. Doc. Vol. 2, No. 91.

Bentham, G. 1839–57. Plantae Hartwegianae. London: W. Pamplin. [Facsimile edition. 1970. J. Cramer. Historia Naturalis Classica.]

______. 1846. *Penstemon*. Pp. 320–331 *in* A. P. de Candolle, Prodromus 10: 1–628.

______. 1846. *Mimulus*. Pp. 370–372 *in* A. P. de Candolle, Prodromus 10: 1–628.

______. 1856. *Eriogonum*. Pp. 6–21 *in* A. P. de Candolle, Prodromus 14: 1–706.

Bradford, N. 1984. Battles and Leaders of the Civil War. New York: Meridian.

Bigelow, J. 1856. Memoir of the Life and Public Services of John Charles Frémont. New York.

Brewer, W. H. 1880. List of persons who have made botanical collections in California. Pp. 553–559 *in* S. Watson, Botany. Vol. II. Geological Survey of California. Cambridge, Massachusetts: John Wilson & Son, University Press.

_____, S. Watson & A. Gray. 1876. Botany. Geological Survey of California. Vol. 1. Cambridge, Massachusetts: Welch, Bigelow, & Co., University Press.

Carter, H. L. 1968. Dear Old Kit: The Historical Christopher Carson. Norman: University of Oklahoma Press.

Carvalho, S. N. 1857. Incidents of travel and adventure from the Far West; with Col. Frémont's last expedition across the Rocky Mountains; including three months'

residence in Utah, and a perilous trip across the Great American Desert to the Pacific. New York: Derby & Jackson.
Cleaves, F. 1948. Rock of Chickamauga, the life of George H. Thomas. Norman: University of Oklahoma Press.
Coville, F. V. 1893. Botany of the Death Valley Expedition. Contr. U.S. Natl. Herb. 4: 1–318.
Cronquist, A. 1984. *Nama*. Pp. 194–197 *in* A. Cronquist, A. H. Holmgren, N. H. Holmgren, J. L. Reveal & P. K. Holmgren, Intermountain Flora. Vol. 4. New York Botanical Garden.
Decaisne, M. J. 1874. Mémoire sur la Famille des Pomacées. Nouv. Arch. Mus. Hist. Nat. 10: 115–192.
Delenbaugh, F. S. 1914. Frémont and '49. New York and London: G. P. Putnam's Sons.
Dorr, L. J. 1990. A revision of the North American genus *Callirhoë* (Malvaceae). Mem. New York Bot. Gard. 56: 1–74.
Durand, E. M. 1869. A sketch of the botany of the basin of the Great Salt Lake of Utah. Trans. Amer. Philos. Soc. 11: 155–180.
Eckenwalder, J. E. 1977. North American cottonwoods (*Populus*, Salicaceae) of sections *Abaso* and *Algeiros*. J. Arnold Arbor. 58: 193–208.
Egan, F. 1977. Frémont. Explorer for a Restless Nation. New York: Doubleday.
Eisenhower, J. S. 1989. So Far From God. The U.S. war with Mexico 1846–1848. New York: Doubleday.
Elmer, A. D. E. 1906. New and noteworthy western plants. III. Bot. Gaz. 41: 309–326.
Emory, W. H. 1848. Notes of a Military Reconnaissance from Fort Leavenworth, in Missouri, to San Diego, in California. Washington: Wendell and Van Benthuysen Printers.
Endlicher, S. 1847. Synopsis Coniferarum. Sangalli; Scheitlin & Zollikofer.
Epling, C. 1942. American species of *Scutellaria*. Univ. Calif. Publ. Bot. 20: 1–137.
Ertter, B. J. 1980. A revision of the genus *Oxytheca* (Polygonaceae). Brittonia 32: 70–102.
Estergreen, M. M. 1962. Kit Carson, A Portrait in Courage. Norman: University of Oklahoma Press.
Favour, A. H. 1962. Old Bill Williams. Norman: University of Oklahoma Press.
Foote, S. 1986. The Civil War, a Narrative. Fort Sumpter to Perryville. New York: Vintage Books.
Freeman, D., S. 1970. Lee's Lieutenants. Manassas to Malvern Hill. New York: Charles Scribner's Sons.
Frémont, J. B. 1878. A Year of American Travel. New York: Harper and Brothers Publishers.
Frémont, J. C. 1843. A report on an exploration of the country lying between the Missouri River and the Rocky Mountains, on the line of the Kansas and Great Platte Rivers. Washington, D. C., Senate Doc. 243, 27th Cong., 3rd sess.
______. 1845. Report of the exploring expedition to the Rocky Mountains in the year 1843, and to Oregon and North California in the years 1843–44. Washington, D.C.

Senate Doc. 461, 28th Cong., 2nd sess., pp. 1–327 (including: "Notice to the Reader." pp. 3–6; "A report on an exploration of the country lying between the Missouri River and the Rocky Mountains, on the line of the Kansas and Great Platte Rivers." pp. 9–101; and "A report of the exploring expedition to Oregon and North California, in the years 1843–'44." pp. 105–327).

______. 1848. Geographical Memoir upon Upper California, in Illustration of His Map of Oregon and California. Senate Misc. Doc. 148, 30th Cong., 1st sess., Washington, D.C., 1848, [Serial 511].

______. 1887. Memoirs of my life, by John Charles Frémont, Including the narrative of five journeys of Western Exploration, during the years 1842, 1843–4, 1845–6–7, 1853–4. Chicago and New York: Belford, Clark. [Note: the second volume covering the years 1848 to 1854 was never published.]

Gray, A. 1845. Characters of some new genera and species of plants of the natural order Compositae, from the Rocky Mountains and upper California. Boston J. Nat. Hist. 5: 105–111. (plate XIII).

______. 1848. *Geraea*, Torr. & Gray. Proc. Amer. Acad. Arts 1: 48–49.

______. 1849. Plantae Fendlerianae Novi-Mexicanae: An account of a collection of plants made chiefly in the vicinity of Santa Fe, New Mexico, by Augustus Fendler; with descriptions of the new species, &c. Mem. Amer. Acad. Arts II. 4: 1–116.

______. 1852. Plantae Wrightianae Texano-Neo-Mexicanae; an account of a collection of plants made by Charles Wright, A. M., in an expedition from Texas and New Mexico, in the summer and autumn of 1849, with critical notices and characters of other new and interesting plants from adjacent regions, and C. Smithsonian Contr. Knowl. 3, Art. 5, Part 1: 1–146.

______. 1859. In J. Torrey, Botany of the Boundary. Vol. 2, pp. 29–270 *in* W. H. Emory, United States and Mexican Boundary Survey. Washington: C. Wendel Printer.

______. 1862a. Characters of some new or obscure species of plants, of Monopetalous Orders, in the collection of the United States South Pacific Exploring Expedition under Captain Charles Wilkes, U.S.N. With various notes and remarks. Proc. Amer. Acad. Arts 6: 37–81.

______. 1862b. Enumeration of the plants of Dr. Parry's Collection in the Rocky Mountains. Amer. J. Sci. Arts II. 34: 249–397.

______. 1863. A revision and arrangement (mainly by the fruit) of the North American species of *Astragalus* and *Oxytropis*. Proc. Amer. Acad. Arts 6: 188–237.

______. 1865. Characters of some new plants of California and Nevada, chiefly from the collections of Professor William H. Brewer, Botanist of the State Geological Survey of California, and of Dr. Charles L. Anderson, with revisions of certain Genera or Groups. Proc. Amer. Acad. Arts 6: 519–556.

______. 1868. Characters of new plants of California and elsewhere, principally of those collected by H. N. Bolander in the State Geological survey. Proc. Amer. Acad. Arts 7: 327–401.

______. 1870a. Revision of the North American Polemoniaceae. Proc. Amer. Acad. Arts 8: 247–282.

______. 1870b. Miscellaneous botanical notes and characters. Proc. Amer. Acad. Arts 8: 282–296.
______. 1873. Characters of new genera and species of plants. Proc. Amer. Acad. Arts 8: 620–631.
______. 1874. Contributions to the botany of North America. II. Notes on Boraginaceae. Proc. Amer. Acad. Arts 10: 48–62.
______. 1878. Synoptical Flora of North America. 2(1): 1–402. New York.
Gudde, E. G. & E. K. Gudde. 1958. Charles Preuss Exploring with Frémont. Norman: University of Oklahoma Press.
Hafen, L. R. 1973. Broken Hand. Lincoln: University of Nebraska Press.
______ & A. W. Hafen. 1960. Frémont's Fourth Expedition. A Documentary Account of the Disaster of 1848–49, with Diaries, Letters, and Reports by Participants in the Tragedy. Glendale, California: The Arthur H. Clark Company.
Hall, H. M. 1928. The genus *Haplopappus*. Carnegie Inst. Washington. No. 389.
Hart, B. H. L. 1958. Sherman. New York: Frederick A. Praeger.
Hendrickson, R. 1990. Sumter. The First Day of the Civil War. New York: Laurel.
Herr, P. 1987. A Biography. Jessie Benton Frémont. New York: Franklin Watts.
Higgins, L. C. 1971. A revision of *Cryptantha* subgenus *Oreocarya*. Brigham Young University Sci. Bull., Biol. Ser. 13(4): 1–63.
Hine, R. V. 1982. In the Shadow of Frémont, Edward Kern and the Art of American Exploration, 1845–1860. Norman: University of Oklahoma Press.
Hitchcock, C. L. 1930. Revision of the North American species of *Godetia*. Bot. Gaz. 89: 331–361.
______. 1932. A monographic study of the genus *Lycium* of the Western Hemisphere. Ann. Missouri Bot. Gard. 19: 179–347.
Hooker, W. J. 1829–34. Flora Boreali-Americana. Vol. 1. London: Henry G. Bohn.
______. 1847. Catalogue of Mr. Geyer's collection of plants gathered in the upper Missouri, the Oregon Territory, and the intervening portion of the Rocky Mountains. London J. Bot. 6: 206–256.
Hyde, G. E. 1968. Life of George Bent Written from His Letters by George Hyde, Ed. Savoie Lottinville. Norman: University of Oklahoma Press.
Irving, W. 1986. The Adventures of Captain Bonneville, U.S.A. in the Rocky Mountains and the Far West. Norman: University of Oklahoma Press.
Jackson, D. 1973. The Expeditions of John Charles Frémont. Map portfolio (see Map Citations below). Urbana: University of Illinois Press.
______ & M. L. Spence. 1970. The Expeditions of John Charles Frémont. Vol. 1. Urbana: University of Illinois Press.
Jepson, W. L. 1907. A synopsis of the North American *Godetias*. Univ. Calif. Publ. Bot. 2: 319–354.
Kelman, W. M. 1991. A revision of *Fremontodendron* (Sterculiaceae). Syst. Bot. 16: 3–20.
Lewis, H. & M. E. Lewis. 1955. The genus *Clarkia*. Univ. Calif. Publ. Bot. 20(4): 241–392.

Locklear, J. H. 1990. A Post Rock Country specialty — Frémont's clematis. Unpublished mss. Hesston, Kansas: Dyck Arboretum of the Plains.
Long, E. B., ed. 1952. Personal Memoirs of U.S. Grant. Cleveland: World Publishing Company.
______. 1971. The Civil War Day by Day, an Almanac 1861–1865. New York: Da Capo Press.
McGregor, R. L., T. M. Barkley, R. E. Brooks, & E. K. Schofield. 1986. Flora of the Great Plains. Lawrence: University Press of Kansas.
McLaughlin, S. P. 1982. A revision of the southwestern species of *Amsonia* (Apocynaceae). Ann. Missouri Bot. Gard. 69: 336–350.
McKelvey, S. D. 1955. Botanical Exploration of the Trans-Mississippi West 1790–1850. Jamaica Plain, Massachusetts: Arnold Arboretum.
McPherson, J. M. 1988. Battle Cry of Freedom. New York: Ballentine Books.
Madsen, B. D. 1981. A Forty-niner in Utah. With the Stansbury Exploration to Great Salt Lake: Letters and Journal of John Hudson, 1848–50. Salt Lake City: University of Utah Library.
Miller, D. E. 1948. John C. Frémont in the Great Salt Lake Region. The Historian 11: 14–28.
Munz, P. A. 1928. Studies in Onagraceae I. A revision of the subgenus *Chylismia* of the genus *Oenothera*. Amer. J. Bot. 15: 223–240.
______. 1970. A California Flora. Berkeley: University of California Press.
Neff, A. L. 1928. John C. Frémont. Utah Educational Review 21: 432–33, 458–61.
Nevins, A., ed. 1956. Narratives of exploration and adventure by John Charles Frémont. New York: Longmans, Green.
Ottley, A. M. 1923. A revision of the Californian species of *Lotus*. Univ. Calif. Publ. Bot. 10: 189–305.
Ownbey, G. B. 1958. Monograph of the genus *Argemone* for North America and the West Indies. Mem. Torrey Bot. Club 21(1): 1–159.
Parish, S. B. 1923. *Cleomella obtusifolia* Torr. & Frém. Bull. S. Calif. Acad. Sci. 22: 12–14.
Payne, W. W. 1964. A re-evaluation of the genus *Ambrosia* (Compositae). J. Arnold Arbor. 45: 401–430.
Pennell, F. W. 1920. Scrophulariaceae of the Central Rocky Mountain States. Contr. U.S. Natl. Herb. 20(9): [i]–v, 313-381, vii–viii.
Peterson, K. M., & W. W. Payne. 1973. The genus *Hymenoclea* (Compositae; Ambrosieae). Brittonia 25: 243–259.
Porter, C. L. 1943. The genus *Amphipappus* Torr. and Gray. Amer. J. Bot. 30: 481–483.
Quaife, M. M. 1935. Kit Carson's Autobiography. Lincoln: University of Nebraska Press.
Raven, P. H. 1969. A revision of the genus *Camissonia* (Onagraceae). Contr. U.S. Natl. Herb. 37: 161–396.
Reveal, J. L. 1968. Some nomenclatural changes in *Eriogonum* (Polygonaceae). Taxon 17: 531–533.

______ & J. L. Reveal. 1985. The missing Frémont Cannon — An ecological solution. Madroño 32: 106–117.

Richardson, J. 1823. Botanical Appendix. *In* John Franklin. Narrative of a journey to the shores of the polar sea. London: John Murray.

Rodgers, A. D. 1942. John Torrey. A Story of North American Botany. Princeton: Princeton University Press.

Rolle, A. 1991. John Charles Frémont. Character as Destiny. Norman: University of Oklahoma Press.

Rudolph, E. D. 1969. Bryology and Lichenology. Pages 89–96 *in* J. Ewan, A Short History of Botany in the United States. New York: Hafner Publishing.

Rydberg, P. A. 1904. Studies on the Rocky Mountain flora — XII. Bull. Torrey Bot. Club 31: 555–575.

______. 1905a. Studies on the Rocky Mountain flora — XIV. Bull. Torrey Bot. Club 32: 123–140.

______. 1905b. *Philadelphus* L. North Amer. Flora 22: 162–175.

______. 1913. Studies on the Rocky Mountain flora — XXIX. Bull. Torrey Bot. Club 40: 461–485.

______. 1917. Flora of the Rocky Mountains and Adjacent Plains. New York: by the Author.

Shan, R. H. & L. Constance. 1951. The genus *Sanicula* (Umbelliferae) in the Old World and the New. Univ. Calif. Publ. Bot. 25: 1–78.

Spence, M. E. 1976. The Frémonts and Utah. Utah Hist. Quart. 44: 286–302.

______. 1984. The Expeditions of John Charles Frémont. Vol. 3. Travels from 1848 to 1854. Urbana: University of Illinois Press.

______ & D. Jackson. 1973a. The Expeditions of John Charles Frémont. Vol. 2. The Bear Flag Revolt and the Court-martial. Urbana: University of Illinois Press.

______ & ______. 1973b. The Expeditions of John Charles Frémont. Vol. 2, supplement. Proceedings of the Court-martial. Urbana: University of illinois Press.

Stansbury, H. (Capt.) 1852. Exploration and Survey of the Valley of the Great Salt Lake of Utah, Including a Reconnaissance of a New Route through the Rocky Mountains. Philadelphia: Lippincott, Grambo.

Thompson, D. W. 1988. Systematics of *Antirrhinum* (Scrophulariaceae) in the New World. Syst. Bot. Monogr. 22: 1–142.

Tiehm, A. 1987. Index to plants collected on Howard Stansbury's Expedition to the Great Salt Lake, 1849–1850. Brittonia 39: 86–95.

______ & F. A. Stafleu. 1990. Per Axel Rydberg: a biography, bibliography, and list of his taxa. Mem. New York Bot. Garden 58: 1–75.

Torrey, J. 1827. Some account of a collection of plants made during a journey to and from the Rocky Mountains in the summer of 1820, by Edwin P. James, M.D. Assistant Surgeon U.S. Army. Ann. Lyceum Nat. Hist. New York 2: 161–254.

______. 1843. Catalogue of plants collected by Lieut. Frémont, in his expedition to the Mountains. Pp. 79–94 *in* J. C. Frémont, A Report of an Exploration of the Country Lying Between the Missouri River and the Rocky Mountains, on the Line of the

Kansas and Great Platte Rivers. Senate Doc. 243, 27th Cong., 3rd sess. Washington, D.C. [Serial 416].

______. 1848. Appendix. Pp. 137–156 *in* W. H. Emory, Notes of a Military Reconnaissance, from Fort Leavenworth, in Missouri, to San Diego, in California. 30th Congress, 1st Session, Executive No. 7.

______. 1853. Plantae Frémontianeae; or, descriptions of plants collected by Col. J. C. Frémont in California. Smithsonian Contr. Knowl. 6(2): 1–24.

______. 1857. Description of the general botanical collections. Reports of Explorations and Surveys to ascertain the most practicable and economical route for a railroad from the Mississippi River to the Pacific Ocean 4: 63–181.

______. 1859. Botany of the Boundary. Vol. 2. Pp. 29–270 *in* W. H. Emory, United States and Mexican Boundary Survey. Washington: Cornelius Wendell, Printer.

______. 1861. IV. Botany. Pp. 1–30 *in* Colorado Exploring Expedition, Lieutenant J. C. Ives, Topographical Engineers. Washington: Government Printing Office.

______ & J. C. Frémont. 1845. Descriptions of some new genera and species of plants, collected in Captain J. C. Frémont's exploring expedition to Oregon and North California, in the years 1843–'44. Pp. 311–319 *in* J. C. Frémont, A Report of the Exploring Expedition to Oregon and North California, in the years 1843–'44. Senate Doc. 174, 28th Cong., 2nd sess., Washington, D.C.

______ & A. Gray. 1838. Flora of North America. Vol. 1. New York: Wiley and Putman.

______ & A. Gray. 1843. A Flora of North America 2(3): 393–504. New York: Wiley and Putnam.

______ & A. Gray. 1855. Report on the botany of the expedition. Explorations and Surveys for a Railroad route from the Mississippi River to the Pacific Ocean. War Department. Route near the Thirty-second Parallel of North Latitude, under command of Brevet Captain John Pope, Corps of Topographical Engineers. Pp. 157–185 *in* Rep. Explor. & Surv. Miss. to Pacific. 1853–54. Vol. II. Washington; A. O. P. Nicholson, Printer.

______ & A. Gray. 1870. A revision of the Eriogoneae. Proc. Amer. Acad. Arts 8: 145–200.

Tuckerman, E. 1855. Lichenes Americae Septentrionalis. Exsiccati. Fascic. III. et IV. Curante Edvardo Tuckerman, A. M. Boston, Nov. Ang. Typis Joh. Wilson et Fil.

______ 1858. Supplement to an enumeration of North American Lichenes; Part first, containing brief diagnoses of new species. Amer. J. Sci. Arts II. 25: 422–430.

Upham, C. W. 1856. Life, Explorations and Public Services of John Charles Frémont. Boston: Ticknor and Fields.

Wagner, W. L. 1983. New species and combinations in the genus *Oenothera* (Onagraceae). Ann. Missouri Bot. Gard. 70: 194–196.

______. 1984. Reconsideration of *Oenothera* subgenus *Gauropsis* (Onagraceae). Ann. Missouri Bot. Gard. 71: 1114–1127.

Watson, S. 1871. Botany. *In*: C. King, Report of the Geological Exploration of the Fortieth Parallel. Vol. 5. Washington: Government Printing Office.

______. 1873a. Revision of the extra-tropical North American species of the genus *Lupinus*. Proc. Amer. Acad. Arts 8: 517–548.

______. 1873b. Revision of the extra-tropical North American species of the genus *Potentilla* (excluding *Sibbaldia*, *Horkelia*, and *Ivesia*). Proc. Amer. Acad. Arts 8: 549–573.

______. 1873c. Revision of the extra-tropical North American species of the genus *Oenothera*. Proc. Amer. Acad. Arts 8: 573–618.

______. 1874. A revision of the North American Chenopodiaceae. Proc. Amer. Acad. Arts 9: 82–126.

______. 1875. Revision of the genus *Ceanothus* and descriptions of new plants. Proc. Amer. Acad. Arts 10: 333–350.

______. 1880. Botany. Geological Survey of California. Vol. 2 Cambridge, Massachusetts: John Wilson & Son.

Watson, T. J. 1977. The taxonomy of *Xylorhiza* (Asteraceae–Astereae). Brittonia 29: 199–216.

Welsh, S. L. 1982a. Utah plant types — historical perspective 1840 to 1981 — annotated list and bibliography. Great Basin Naturalist 42: 129–195.

______. 1982b. A species of *Cryptantha* (Boraginaceae) dedicated to the memory of F. Creutzfeldt. Great Basin Naturalist 42: 129–195.

______. 1987. History of botanical exploration in Utah: The Frémont era. Encyclia 63: 57–67.

______, N. D. Atwood, S. Goodrich, & L. C. Higgins. 1987. A Utah flora. Great Basin Naturalist Memoirs 9: 1–894.

Maps Cited

Frémont, J. C. [1843]. Map to illustrate an exploration of the country lying between the Mississippi River and the Rocky Mountains, on the line of the Nebraska or Platte River. By Lieut. J. C. Frémont, of the Corps of Topographical Engineers. E. Weber & Co., Lith.

Frémont, J. C. & C. Preuss. 1845. Map of the Exploring Expedition to the Rocky Mountains in the year 1842 and to Oregon & North California in the years 1843–44 by Brevet Capt. J. C. Frémont of the Corps of Topographical Engineers under the orders of Col. J. J. Abert. Chief of the Topographical Bureau. Lith. by E. Weber & Co., Baltimore Md.

Nicollet, J. N. & J. C. Frémont. 1843. Hydrographical basin of the upper Mississippi River from astronomical and barometrical observations, surveys, and information. by J. N. Nicollet in the years 1836, 37, 38, 39, and 40; assisted in 1838, 39, & 40 by Lieut. J. C. Frémont, of the Corps of Topographical Engineers under the superintendence of the Bureau of the Corps of Topographical Engineers and authorized by The War Department. Reduced and compiled under the direction of Col. J. J. Abert by Lieut W. H. Emory.

Preuss, C. 1846. Topographical map of the road from Missouri to Oregon, commencing at the mouth of the Kansas in the Missouri River and ending at the mouth of the Wallah-Wallah in the Columbia. In VII Sections. From the field notes and journal of Capt. J. C. Frémont, and from the sketches and notes made on the ground by his assistant Charles Preuss. Compiled by Charles Preuss, 1846, by order of the Senate of the United States. Lith. by E. Weber & Co., Baltimore.

Preuss, C. 1848. Map of Oregon and Upper California from the surveys of John Charles Frémont and other authorities drawn by Charles Preuss under the order of the Senate of the United States, Washington City 1848. Lith. by E. Weber & Co., Balto.

Appendix I

Botanical Collections

The list of plant names presented below is taken mainly from literature and from herbarium specimens. Plant specimens collected by Frémont were deposited historically in two main collections, the Torrey Herbarium of Columbia College now at The New York Botanical Garden (NY) and the Gray Herbarium of Harvard University (GH). Two other repositories, the U.S. National Herbarium (US), and the Missouri Botanical Garden (MO), received significant sets of Frémont's duplicates. The herbarium at NY was searched by the writer, albeit cursorily, in August 1990 and again in May of 1992. The NY collection was searched on a sheet by sheet basis by the herbarium staff at NY during 1990–92. The Gray Herbarium was investigated by the energetic and enthusiastic Walter Kittridge. Peter Raven and James Solomon directed the search of the Missouri Botanical Garden, and George Russell helped with the search at the U.S. National Herbarium.

Literature consulted includes papers by Torrey (1843, 1848, 1853, 1857, 1859, 1861), Torrey and Gray (1843, 1870), Torrey and Frémont (1845), Gray (1848, 1849, 1852, 1862a, 1862b, 1863, 1865, 1868, 1870a, 1870b, 1873, and 1874), Watson (1871, 1873a, 1873b, 1873c, 1874, 1875, 1880), and Bentham (1846, 1856). Rydberg (1904, 1905a, 1905b, 1913, and 1917) published new taxa based on Frémont materials. Two lichens collected by Frémont are included in a bound exsiccatae by Tuckerman (1855), and one of them, *Alectoria fremontii*, was later published by Tuckerman (1858). Tuckerman's contributions to North American lichenology are summarized by Rudolph (1969). The reports by Frémont (1843, 1845, 1848, and 1887) were studied for clues as to locality and plant species information. The best sources of unpublished data are, of course, the actual herbarium specimens taken by Frémont. A photographic record of most of the specimens examined for this work is on file in the herbarium of Brigham Young University (BRY).

Botanical results of only the 1842 first expedition were published in their entirety (359 taxa) or almost so (as additional 1842 specimens exist besides those published by Torrey); botanical summaries are lacking for the subsequent expeditions. The list presented below contains plant species taken by Frémont, taxa named in his honor, and a checklist of plant taxa identified from his collections. Twenty-two taxa were described in whole or in part from collections of the first expedition, 79 from the second (19 by Torrey and Frémont), 52 from the third, 10 from the fourth, 1 from the fifth, and 3 of unknown date, for a total of 167 taxa. The list also contains 19 new genera based in some part on Frémont material. Numerous Frémont specimens were discovered in the general collection at NY, where most of the types are segregated. Some type specimens in the following list bear numbers that have been regarded as collection numbers. The numbers were evidently attached to tagged fragments that corresponded to blanks in Frémont's notes. The identifications were added later by Torrey, and the same species, often the same sheet, will bear more than a single number, regardless of how many specimens are on the sheet or where the specimen was collected. Sometimes the same number was applied to several different species.

Type specimens from historical collections are often fragmentary. The dismal nature of many of Frémont's specimens was due to difficulties of collection, preservation, packaging, and transportation. Plant presses were, of necessity, few, and many specimens were evidently pressed several to a sheet. The specimens of *Swertia radiata* (Kellogg) Kuntze, taken on the first expedition, are of such a size as to fit within a press with dimensions 12 by 15 inches. Most are, however, much smaller. They served as the basis for botanical descriptions despite the flood on the Smoky Hill Fork of the Kansas, and the surviving specimens are about average for the period—they look like those taken by Nuttall, Geyer, Newberry, Douglas, and other contemporary collectors. Torrey, Gray, Watson, and Bentham, who described most of the taxa based on Frémont materials, were keen observers who were able to construct astute descriptions from meager and frequently damaged specimens. Specific or infraspecific taxa and new genera based on Frémont's collections include, respectively, 37 and 7 by Torrey, 34 and 2 by Gray, 19 and 5 by Torrey and Gray, 19 and 4 by Torrey and Frémont, and 13 species by Watson and 16 by Bentham. The small number described by others are 1 each by Decaisne, Liebman, and Jepson, and 6 by Rydberg. Some of the specimens were, and still are, in excellent condition, and those from the 1843–44 expedition, which suffered the flood on the Kansas, are not especially low in quality, although a few show indications of damage, possibly from wetting. It is probable that more than two-thirds of the collection was discarded by Torrey.

At present, the more serious problem is locating all of the specimens. This is due in part, at least, to changes in identification and to their subsequent refiling under new names. Some were exchanged by both Torrey and Gray, and others have been lost or merely discarded. The Frémont collections found at NY, GH, MO, and US are representative. It is difficult to believe, following the careful searches at the various herbaria, that many have been overlooked. Other specimens are at K and BM in England.

The botanical results of the expeditions depended on the partnership of collector Frémont and botanist patrons John Torrey and Asa Gray, but especially in that with John Torrey. Torrey was professor of chemistry at Columbia and Princeton and had pioneered in the establishment of a herbarium later deposited at Columbia, which included specimens taken by Thomas Drummond (1790–1835), David Douglas (1798–1834), John Richardson (1787–1865), Thomas Nuttall (1786–1859), Edwin James (1797–1861; see Torrey, 1827), Karl Andreas Geyer (Hooker, 1847), and others. John Richardson (1823) had accompanied Sir John Franklin on his exploration to the Polar Sea in 1817. Drummond had worked in the plains and mountains of Canada, and Douglas had collected in California, Oregon, Washington, and across the continent in 1825–26. The specimens taken by them formed much of the basis of the *Flora Boreali-Americana* of William Jackson Hooker (1829–34), who had sent representative specimens to Torrey. Nuttall's specimens, taken on a transcontinental trip with Nathaniel Wyeth in 1834, included materials critical to understanding the botany of western North America and had been treated in the *Flora of North America* by Torrey and his premier student, close friend, and collaborator, Asa Gray (Torrey & Gray, 1838).

Graduating with a medical degree in 1818, Torrey had joined others in founding the Lyceum of New York in 1817, and was interested in the herbarium of that society from its inception. He began at once, following establishment of the Lyceum, to publish on botany, and while he became a medical doctor his interests were not in the practice of medicine but divided between botany and chemistry. Three of his early publications in the *Annals of the Lyceum of New York* concerned the collection of Edwin James, taken on the Major Stephen H. Long Expedition to the Rocky Mountains in 1820. Those papers established his interest in the flora of the American West, an interest he would continue throughout his life (Rodgers, 1942: 52, 316). In 1827 Torrey accepted the chair of chemistry at the College of Physicians and Surgeons (a scion of Columbia College) in New York; botany had been added to the responsibility of the position.

The correspondence of Torrey with others concerned with botany and other sciences was already large and soon, in 1830, expanded to include a young medical student at Fairfield in upper New York state, Asa Gray. Gray had sent a collection of plants, many of them determined accurately, but some, as is usual, requiring correction. Torrey's response (Rodgers, 1942: 91) was cordial and encouraging. It began a lifelong association of the two most productive North American botanists of the 19th century. In the 1830s they began a project, never to be completed, on the flora of North America. Thomas Nuttall would be a major contributor of material and descriptions of hundreds of new taxa published in the flora. The Nuttall specimens would later be compared to Frémont's.

By the 1840s the work of Torrey was not only divided between botany and chemistry, but between Columbia and Princeton. At the beginning of his association with Princeton Torrey taught courses at Columbia during the winter and at Princeton during the summer. In 1824 he had married Eliza Richardson Shaw (Rodgers, 1942: 69), and they had four children. Moving back and forth with the family on very limited funds became difficult and financially oppressive. The family finally moved to Princeton, but not permanently.

Gray had come to New York and accepted an interim position at the herbarium of the Lyceum. He had stayed at Torrey's New York home on many occasions, sometimes for months. The two men had become close friends as well as collaborators. These two, along with George Engelmann at St. Louis, Missouri, received most of the collections from expeditions of exploration of the American West. The involvement begun by Torrey for the Long Expedition in the 1820s continued for five decades, well into the 1870s (see list of publications by both Torrey and Gray, in literature cited). Separately and collaboratively the team of Torrey and Gray would name and describe hundreds of species and dozens of genera.

Ultimately Gray accepted a position at Harvard University, following failure of the University of Michigan to provide funding for an anticipated position in botany. Torrey, at least, and probably Gray also, kept the specimens from the expeditions in his private herbarium and only later gave them to an institution. Early in the 1860s the job of moving the herbarium had become overwhelming, and Torrey had been thinking about its ultimate disposition. He made arrangements to transfer ownership to Columbia College, on condition that he receive five years of rent-free use of a house on campus, a house Torrey occupied for the final years of his life. The collection of Columbia College, some 600,000 sheets, was transferred to The New York Botanical Garden in 1895, four years following the founding of that institution. The proportion of the collection that was originally Torrey's is not known, but it must have been considerable (personal communication, Patricia Holmgren). The collections from the Frémont expeditions were a part of the Torrey Herbarium (with only occasional sheets from the Columbia and other herbaria), and they are currently at NY, with the exceptions of duplicates deposited at GH especially.

It was to Torrey and Gray that specimens trickled early on and then surged as more parties became involved in geographical and military reconnaissance of the American West. The specimens that came to Torrey, such as those from Frémont, were sorted into families, with certain of them (i.e., Compositae and other Gamopetalae) going to Asa Gray for determination and ultimate publication. Sometimes the two authors published the results jointly, but often as Torrey in or ex Gray or Gray in or ex Torrey. Specimens kept by Torrey were examined with great care, and were compared to those by Nuttall and Douglas, those communicated by Hooker (i.e., the Richardson collections), and others. Flowers of the most critical ones were carefully dissected by Torrey, and the parts drawn on small sheets of paper attached to the appropriate herbarium sheet. Often two or more collections by one, two, or more collectors were mounted on a single sheet. This practice, disconcerting to some later workers, allowed direct comparison.

The mounting sheets were generally of good-quality paper, but thin and approximately 11 by 15⅛ inches or slightly smaller. The herbarium paper has a look and a feel, a patina as it were, that is characteristic for the Frémont, Nicollet, Geyer, Xantus, Vasey, Nuttall, Douglas, and other contemporary collectors. A glance alerts the searcher to determine which of Frémont's contemporary collectors actually collected the specimen or whether it is one of Frémont's. Frémont specimens in the Torrey Herbarium, as distinguished (the sheets bear stamps indicating the source herbarium) from those of the Columbia Herbarium, were identified during searches of the general herbarium at NY by the printed, white labels; "Frémont's Expedition to the Rocky Mountains, 1842," "Frémont's Expedition to California, 1843–4" or "1845–7."

In some labeled specimens the designations 1843–4 or 1845–7, originally printed on the label, is marked out and the correct year is written in pen or pencil adjacent to the printed date. In others the printed designation is unchanged and the correct year, usually 1846, is written on the label. Occasional labels from 1843–4 are used for 1845–7 collections, and most of the 1849 labels have years from previous expeditions marked out and the number 49 written in ink. The few specimens from the 1853–54 expedition are labeled variously "Pac. R. R. Exp." (*Oenothera claviformis*), "Frémont's last (R. R.) Journey" (*Syntrichopappus fremontii*), "Frémont's last journey, 1853–54" (*Sidalcea diploscypha* var. *minor*), "Frémont's R. Road Expedn. 1853–54" (*Stylomecon heterophylla*), "Frémont's Rail Road Expedn. 1853–54" (*Coreopsis calliopsidea*), and "Frémont Coll., Rocky Mts., 1854" (*Pinus monophylla*).

Errors of labeling occur. Some specimens from the second expedition of 1843–44 are wrongly attributed to 1845–7 and vice versa. And in a few cases the hand-written data on the specimen are simply wrong. Specimens from California or from the Great Plains of Kansas bear labels indicating that they are from Colorado or Utah. Many specimens lack a printed label and are designated in various handwriting as "Frémont's 1st Expedn.," "Frémont's 2nd Expedn.," "Frémont's 3rd Expedn.," or merely "Frémont." Typically in the hand-written designations, the name Frémont followed by the expedition number is often, but not always, supplemented by a number and year marked in pencil. In four of the five expeditions the collections were scant, consisting of only sufficient material for one mounted sheet kept by Torrey. Wherever such were available, Gray retained a portion, currently on deposit at GH. However, some duplicates, especially from the third expedition, were sent elsewhere, for example to the Sartwell Herbarium. The Sartwell collection was donated to NY in 1982, and duplicates among them were given to BRY. Some specimens found their way from Torrey and Gray to Europe, where they were examined by George Bentham. Whether they were kept by him and are deposited in European herbaria is unknown to me. Certainly some are at Kew and others at The Natural History Museum.

Many of the specimens sent to Gray, some of which were obviously returned to Columbia, lack the usual printed label and bear Gray's handwriting, often with bibliographic citations or cryptic markings, e.g., KKKK, Sss, Tttt, etc. Evidently the designations by Gray allowed him to refer to specific specimens, not otherwise distinguishable by label data. Two printed labels bear the words "Geographical Memoir," indicating that the specimens are from the 1845–47 expedition. Occasional specimens from Gray, presumably, are marked "Ex herb. J. Torrey, Torr. & Gr. Flora N. Amer.," or "Syn. Fl. N. A.," indicating that the specimens were cited therein. A few specimens lack Frémont's name or a label designating the specimen as from one of his expeditions. There the handwriting and locality data, such as "Black Hills of the Platte, July 24," give an identity and provenance together that indicate a Frémont collection. Numerous specimens sought, but not found, at NY are in the collection at GH, evidently part of the arrangement between Torrey and Gray. There does not appear to be a logical place of deposition; Torrey's specialty groups are as likely to be at GH as at NY and the reverse is true for Gray's specialty groups. The Thurber Herbarium, now deposited at GH, and the Crooke and LeRoy (these came from Canby) Herbaria, now at NY, have occasional specimens not represented among the Frémont materials originally deposited at either GH or NY-Torrey.

Just as Torrey compared Frémont's collections with those of earlier workers, he also used them as a basis for comparison with later ones. In the first case, Frémont materials are mounted with those of Nuttall (see *Eriogonum ovalifolium*), and in the latter with those of Stansbury (see *Purshia tridentata*). Some sheets at both GH and NY have as many as five separate collections (or more) mounted together. Disconcerting as this practice of multiple mounts has been to some later botanists, the technique was a viable one for Torrey, Gray, and their associates. Many of the herbarium sheets with multiple mounts have been cut apart, leading those with an inquiring mind to wonder what was on the other part or parts.

Perhaps the most intriguing aspects of Torrey's sheets are the careful drawings, made following dissection of floral structures. Often the pistil, ovules, seeds, embryos, fruit, stamens (with detail of anthers), and corolla (laid out flat if sympetalous) are drawn. From these the descriptions could be derived readily. The technique of illustration and careful notation used by Torrey demonstrates his meticulous mind. Drawings of floral and other plant parts enabled him to construct descriptions and determine the taxonomic status of the particular specimen. The illustrations and minutely detailed descriptions often accompanying them are unmatched among the materials described by Gray. Torrey was the careful master botanist who typically cited the specimens on which the new species were based. On the other hand, Gray seldom illustrated the specimens as a part of the diagnosis of new taxa, and in some papers, at least, he failed to cite the materials examined. Torrey maintained a correspondence with other botanists, exchanged literature, and grasped for knowledge that seemed often to be beyond reach. More material was always needed, or better material, but even scraps were better than nothing. Occasional herbarium sheets at GH also have sketches of the plant parts, presumably drawn by Gray. The sketches are neat and well drawn, in contrast to the hurried scrawl of Gray's handwritten notes.

Both Torrey and Gray had counseled Frémont to take a botanist with him following the first expedition, when the plants were dumped in Torrey's lap. All things considered, the surviving specimens of the first expedition are not especially poor. Occasionally, when specimens were insufficient or immature, either Torrey or Gray would note, "Wait until there is more material!"

The type concept arose in the late 19th and early 20th centuries, and segregation of type specimens from the general herbarium at NY began during World War II, when bombardment from the sea was a possibility, and the removal of the most important specimens was deemed important, should evacuation be necessary. Many of the Frémont specimens thought to be types were hurriedly selected at that time, in an effort to locate as many historic type specimens as possible. Not all were found, and the search conducted during work leading to this book turned up a few types not previously segregated. Others were searched for diligently but not found, either at NY or at the other herbaria.

Lectotypification is a requirement for monographers, and some of the syntypes taken by Frémont have not been chosen as lectotypes. Taxa named by Gray should logically be lectotypified by material at the Gray Herbarium, and those by Torrey by material at The New York Botanical Garden. However, because of the uncertain deposition of materials such a method lacks the authority of practicality or reason. When Gray's taxa are best represented at NY the lectotype should be designated from there. Some taxa named by Torrey are represented by specimens only at GH, and these must be designated as holotypes. An attempt has been made by this writer to avoid designation of lectotypes. Rather, when only Frémont's material was noted in the protologue, and especially where it is accompanied by Torrey's drawings, the types have been cited as either holotype or isotypes. Specimens of species named early on, when Frémont's meager offerings were the only ones available, are mostly those designated herein as types. Later, as other collections were available, the Frémont specimens (syntypes) are only a portion of the material on which the taxon was based.

Lectotypes have sometimes been chosen by specialists from among later collections, and Frémont is sometimes cited first but included in a long list of other collectors. Selection of lectotypes for some names remains to be done. Where such have been chosen, and where this writer has been able to make those determinations, the author, place of publication, and place of deposition is noted. The first expedition list of names in the checklist presented below is from the Torrey appendix to Frémont's 1843 report (Frémont, 1843). They can be recognized by the lack of author's name (my choice) and are followed by the bibliographic citation "(Torrey, 1843)." Where it has been possible to determine the modern equivalents, such information is given following an equal sign (=), or equivalent sign (≡) for apparent nomenclatural synonyms, even when this results in a redundancy. Many of the names in the checklist are based on materials taken by Frémont on trips subsequent to the first. In any event, all specimens are cited, and all geographical information recorded on the label or on the sheet adjacent to the label (usually in pencil) is also given.

The search of the herbarium at NY by this writer was incomplete because the initial lists were developed from publications based on the existence, at least historically, of actual specimens. Intuitive guessing as to where specimens other than those cited in publications might be deposited led to discovery of some additional material, but a systematic search by me through all of the places of potential deposition was not possible. Nevertheless, the specimens found by me and others searching the herbarium at NY give evidence of the extent to which Frémont collected, even though the listing is undoubtedly incomplete. Walter Kittridge, Gray Herbarium, was successful in finding many Frémont collections, some in addition to those on the list developed from my previous literature and herbarium surveys. J. Pruski and others (see acknowledgements) continued the search at NY following my visit, and they were able to locate hundreds of additional specimens. As noted above, the list is built around the results of the 1842 expedition written by John Torrey. Specimens from the first expedition were expected to be almost entirely at NY, but many are deposited at GH. On his first expedition Frémont had no idea of the value of duplicate collections; consequently a disproportionate number of unicate specimens is deposited only at NY. The second expedition collections were probably short of duplicates also, some perhaps having been lost in the flood on the Kansas. Only on the third expedition were there sufficient duplicates to allow equable division between Torrey and Gray.

Collections of the first expedition were identified as representing 371 taxa; the second some 379 taxa, the third 458, the fourth 60, and the fifth 8. The total number of taxa from all collections, including 52 that are probably from the second or third expeditions, is 1064, although this is undoubtedly preliminary and incomplete. Some 58% of the species cited in the 1843 list are currently known from specimens found in the various herbaria. The disposition of the remainder is unknown.

There are occasional names in the checklist presented below that are not based on plant collections examined during the course of this investigation; they are those noted in the 1843 Torrey compilation especially, but there are also some mentioned in the text of the Frémont reports and elsewhere.

The locality information interpolated from dates of collection was derived from the maps of the routes of the expedition: 1842 (Frémont, 1843), 1843–44 (Frémont & Preuss, 1845; Preuss, 1846), and 1845–47 (Preuss, 1848). Latitude and longitude observations were correlated with modern maps where those of Frémont and Preuss are inadequate or in obvious error, as is occasionally the case.

The dates of the various expeditions are not always obvious in the species notations presented below. The first expedition was in 1842, the second during 1843–44, the third from 1845 to 1847, the fourth during 1848–49, and the fifth in 1853–54. Some specimens are assigned to one or the other of the expeditions by guesswork, but some cannot be assigned. Identification of taxa in the following list is based on original publications, on annotations of present and previous experts in various genera, and on contemporary taxonomic treatments of the floras of the Great Plains, Colorado, Utah, Wyoming, and California. Some few Frémont specimens have remained unidentified through the century and a half.

Some names on the labels of Frémont's collections were never published, and others are unknown in the literature in the combination noted on the labels. Such names and combinations are cited herein to record the status of botanical understanding during the mid- to late 19th century. The tentative names and combinations are not validated herein and are rejected by me as nomenclatural proposals. The names are useful insofar as they allow more ready recognition of a particular specimen, when label data of a distinctive nature are lacking. The manuscript names cited below were typically not italicized, but the author's names often were. The names are quoted verbatim in the checklist. The tentative names, and some of those included in the Frémont reports, show that Torrey was using best guesses for some of the plants, not unlike authors of much of the published botany of the present.

To the extent possible all specimens have been provided with modern names from the various floras, and if such determinations as I have made are found to be in error, I apologize now, with the hope of repenting later.

The endurance of names based on Frémont's collections reflects the botanical expertise of the authors, not that of John Charles Frémont. Some 123 taxa (75%) having basionyms typified by Frémont's collections are still recognized at taxonomic rank.

Specimens collected by Frémont are preserved in three major herbaria: the Gray Herbarium (GH), The New York Botanical Garden (NY), and the Missouri Botanical Garden (MO). A smaller number are at the U.S. National Museum (US), the Royal Botanical Gardens, Kew (K), and Brigham Young University (BRY, a gift from NY). The present repositories include specimens initially placed in other herbaria, i.e., Torrey, Thurber, Sartwell, Columbia, and occasionally others. These are cited following the herbarium designation to provide a historical perspective as to the flow of specimens through time to their present destinations. A following exclamation point (!) indicates that

I saw the specimen personally. Names in bold-face type are those named on the basis of Frémont's collections.

Annotated Checklist

Abies concolor (Gord. & Glend.) Lindley ex Hildebr. includes *Pinus alba* and white spruce

"FExCal, 1843–4. 426, July 20, 1843. Pinus (Abies) concolor. Rocky Mts. on [illegible] Peak [near head of Fountain Creek, El Paso County, Colorado]" (NY-Torrey!). "FExCal, 1843–4. Picea. Pinus (Abies) lasiocarpa Hook? [in pencil]" (NY-Torrey!). "Pinus n. sp.? Torr. Frémont's 2d Expedition.," "FExCal, No. 202. 1845. Abies," and "FExCal. 1846. Abies" (all three MO!). Frémont (1845: 233).

Abies douglasii = *Pseudotsuga menziesii* (Mirb.) Franco

Abies lasiocarpa (Hook.) Nutt. includes *Abies* near *balsamea*

"FExRM, 1842. Pinus (Abies) Balsamea? Wind River Mts. Aug. 13 [Sublette County, Wyoming]" (NY-Torrey!). "FExCal, 1845–7. 148. 1845. 'From the same bush as 147.' Abies Menziesii" (NY-Torrey!). "FExCal, 1845–7. 211. 1845" (NY-Torrey! and MO!). This sheet has a penciled note, "212 = Arkansas River," i.e., in Colorado. The numbering system is, so far, incomprehensible (see Appendix III).

Abronia fragrans Nutt. ex Hook. includes *Abronia mellifera*

"FExCal, 1845–47. Abronia fragrans Nutt. Ex Torrey" (GH-Thurber!); "FExCal, 1845–7. 447, 1845. Abronia fragrans" (GH! and MO!); and "FExCal, 1843–4" (GH!). "Abronia. Sandy Prairie. Frémont's 3d Exped. 227, 30th July 1845 [3 day's east of Bent's Fort]" (MO!).

Abronia mellifera = *A. fragrans* Nutt. ex Hook.

"North fork of the Platte, July 7–12 [1842]" (Torrey, 1843: 92). "FExRM, 1842. *Abronia mellifera* (mistake *A. fragrans*), July 12" [Note in Torrey's handwriting]; "Abronia fragrans. Upper Platte?, Frémont"; and "Frémont's 2nd Expedn. Probably from the Platte River" (all three NY-Torrey!). On 12 July 1842 the small group with Frémont camped near Greeley, Weld County, Colorado.

***Abronia* (*Tripterocalyx*) *micranthum* Torr.** in Frém., Rep. Explor. Exped. Rocky Mts. 92. 1843. (1st) = *Tripterocalyx micrantha* (Torr.) Hook.

Protologue locality: "Near the mouth of the Sweet Water river. Aug 1 [1842. Near Independence Rock, Natrona County, Wyoming]." Type: "FExRM, 1842. Bed of dry creek, August 1st" (holotype NY-Torrey!, Figure 16). This is undoubtedly the type sheet. It is accompanied by an excellent sketch of floral and fruit parts.

Abronia turbinata Torr. ex S. Wats., Rep. Explor. Exped. 40th Parallel, Bot. 5: 285. 1871.

"339, 1844. Frémont. April 23–24, 1844. Mohave River (Rio de los Animas) [San Bernardino County, California]" (NY-Torrey!). Sereno Watson annotated the Frémont material as "probably *A. turbinata*," and the material is mentioned provisionally by

Watson in the protologue, i.e., "Frémont's specimens from the Mohave River are probably the same" (Watson, 1871: 285).

Abronia umbellata Lam.
"FExCal, 1845–7. Qqqq, 1846. Abronia (Tripterocalyx) cycloptera, *with young fruit*" (NY-Torrey!). The sheet cited is annotated as *Abronia minor* Standley, presumably by Rydberg.

Abronia villosa S. Wats.
"FExCal, 1845–7. No. 1. 1847" (GH!). This is the same sheet as that cited under *Mirabilis multiflora* (see below). The sheet has plant fragments (some large) mounted on it. A corner has been removed and a paper glued to fill the gap. Adjacent to the cutout is a peduncle and inflorescence of *Abronia villosa*. The remaining plant fragments are *M. multiflora*. There is a second label in the lower left-hand corner of the paper, adjacent to two fragment envelopes, both containing fragments of *M. multiflora*.

Acacia = *Prosopis odorata* (Torr. in Frém.) Torr. & Frém. emend. Welsh, in part.
Frémont (1845: 260, 262, 266).

Acer glabrum Torr.
"Acer glabrum Torr. Frémont's 2nd Expedn." (NY-Torrey!).

Acer grandidentatum Nutt.
"FexCal, 1843–4. 305, 1845. Acer grandidentatum, Nutt.? 'Provost's Fork, where it enters Lake Mt.' [Mt. Timpanogas?]" (NY-Torrey!). The label bears the pencil notation "Wasatch." Frémont's large cavalcade was in Wasatch County, Utah, along the "Provost's Fork" on 2–3 October 1845.

Acer negundo L. includes *Negundo aceroides*, *N. californica*, and *N. fraxinifolia*
Frémont (1845: 21).

Acer negundo L. var. *californica* (Torr. & A. Gray) Sargent
"California, Frémont" and "FExCal, 1845–7. Ccc 1846" (both GH!; Ccc also at MO!). The first sheet is labeled simply as "Negundo," the second as "N. californica." "Frémont. 1846. On the border of the Cosumne River [Sacramento County, California] at Murphy's Farm, March 20, 1846" (NY-Torrey!).

Acerates angustifolius = *Asclepias stenophylla* A. Gray
"Big Blue river of the Kansas. June 20 [1842. Probably Marshall County, Kansas]" (Torrey, 1843: 91). "FExRM, 1842. June 29, 1842 [south of Cozad, Dawson County, Nebraska]" (NY-Torrey!). It is possible that "June 20" is an error for June 29.

Acerates auriculata Engelm. in Torr. U.S. and Mex. Bound. Bot. 160. 1859. = *Asclepias engelmanniana* Woodson
"It was also found Frémont on the upper Arkansas" (l.c.). "FExCal, 1845. Acerates Frémontii n.sp. Kansas River" (NY-Torrey!).

***Acerates latifolia* Torr. & Frém.** in Frém., Rep. Explor. Exped. Oregon & California 317. 1845. (2nd) = *Asclepias cryptoceras* S. Wats.

Protologue locality: "On Green river, a tributary of the Colorado of the West; June." Type: "Acerates latifolia, *Torr. & Frém.* Little Snake River, Upper mountains of California, 584. June. 1844" (holotype NY-Torrey!: microfiche BRY!). The Frémont party was at the Green River in Brown's Park, in Moffatt County, Colorado, on 8–9 June and on the Little Snake River on 10 June 1844. The sheet bears the notation: "= Asclepias—horn hidden in the hood. S.W." There is also an annotation label with the designation "Asclepias cryptoceras Watson. Syn. Fl. N. Amer."

Acerates longifolia = *Asclepias viridiflora* Raf.

"Big Blue river of the Kansas. June 20 [1842. Probably Marshall County, Kansas]" (Torrey, 1843: 91). "FExRM, 1842. June 22. A[cerates] longifolia" (NY-Torrey!). Frémont was along the Little Blue River of the Kansas, near Powell, Jefferson County, Nebraska, on 22 June 1842.

Achillea millefolium ≡ *Achillea millefolium* L.

"Upper Platte to the mountains [1842]" (Torrey, 1843: 87). The ubiquitous nature of this plant on the second expedition was noted by Frémont (1845: 119).

Achyrachaena mollis Schaeur

"FExCal, 1845–7. 269. 1846. Achyrachaena mollis, *Schauer*" (NY-Torrey!). The Frémont specimen is mounted on a sheet with three plants taken by Bigelow.

Actaea rubra (Ait.) Willd.

"Upper Platte [1842]" (Torrey, 1843: 83).

***Actinella depressa* Torr. & A. Gray** in A. Gray, Mem. Amer. Acad. II. 4: 100. 1849. (2nd) = *Hymenoxys torreyana* (Nutt.) Parker (*H. depressa* (Torr. & A. Gray) Welsh & Reveal) Protologue locality: "Rocky Mountains, apparently at a great elevation, the locality unknown, Col. Frémont; collected in the second expedition" Type: "FExCal, 1843–4. Mts. of California or Utah" (holotype GH!; isotype NY-Torrey!: microfiche BRY!). The specimen at NY has the 43–4 struck out and a 45–7 marked in pencil; the 1843–4 designation is undoubtedly correct. The GH material, labeled simply as "Frémont 2nd exped." was annotated as type of the taxon by K. F. Parker in 1946. The specimens were likely taken on 7 June 1844 in Uintah County, Utah, where the plants are known from modern collections. The type material at GH is annotated as "*Tetraneuris torreyana* (Nutt.) Greene" by K. F. Parker in 1946, and the NY isotype is so annotated by M. W. Bierner in 1991. Such being the case those plants passing under the designation of *H. depressa* elsewhere in Utah will require another name, a matter beyond the scope of this work. Indication of the Frémont type as belonging to *H. torreyana* helps clarify the problem of a type locality. All of the specimens passing under the name of *H. depressa* came from localities not visited by Frémont on any of his expeditions. He did pass through the area occupied by *H. torreyana*, when on Diamond Mountain, Uintah County, Utah and while still in a plant collecting mode (see itinerary in Chapter VII).

Actinella grandiflora Torr. & A. Gray in A. Gray, Boston J. Nat. Hist. 5: 109. 1845. (1st) = *Hymenoxys grandiflora* (Torr. & A. Gray) Parker

Protologue locality: "Mr. Frémont collected in his first journey on the Wind River Chain of the Rocky Mountains." "Wind River mountains" (Torrey, 1843: 87). Type: "Actinella grandiflora. n. sp. Wind River, Chain of the Rocky Mts., near snow line. Lieut. Frémont. Torr. & Gray, Flora, N. Amer." (holotype NY-Torrey!: microfiche BRY!). Materials came from present Sublette County, Wyoming, probably on 15 August 1842 (they were in the Wind River Mountains from 12–16 August 1842).

Actinella richardsonii Nutt. = *Hymenoxys richardsonii* (Hook.) Cockerell

"[This] exists in Frémont's third collection, apparently from the interior of the south part of Oregon" (Gray, 1849: 103).

Adenostoma fasciculatum Hook. & Arn.

"FExCal, 1845–7[1846]. Adenostoma fasciculata *Hook. & Arn.*" (NY-Torrey!). "FExCal, 1845–7. Nnn. 1846. Adenost." (GH! and MO!).

Aesculus californica (Spach) Nutt.

"FExCal, 465, 508, 1846. Aesculus Californica, *Nutt.*" (NY-Torrey!; BRY-Sartwell!; MO!); "Frémont's Exped. 1845–7[1846]" (GH-Thurber!); and "FExCal, 1845–7. 508. 1846" (GH!). Frémont (1848: 32) recorded this species on or about 28 April 1846, when he was in the vicinity of Redding, Shasta County, California.

Aesculus glabra Willd.

"FExCal, 10, 65, 1845" (NY-Torrey!). Someone has written "cultivated!" on the label. Certainly it could have been taken where indigenous in Kansas early in the third expedition during 1845. "Aesculus glabra Willd. Torr. North Amer. Cyper. Frémont's 3rd Expedn." (NY!). The latter sheet was annotated as *A. pavia* L. by J. W. Hardin in 1956, but seems to fit phases of *A. glabra* from eastern Kansas.

Agalinus aspera (Dougl.) Britt.

"Valley of the lower Platte, Sept. 1842. Frémont. Gerardia longifolia, *Nutt.*" (NY-Torrey!). This is mounted on the same sheet with *A. tenuifolia* (Vahl) Raf. (see citation under *Gerardia*).

Agalinus tenuifolia (Vahl) Raf. includes *Gerardia tenuifolia*

Agoseris aurantiaca (Hook.) Greene includes *Macrorhynchus troximonoides*

Agoseris glauca (Pursh) Dietr. includes *Troximon parviflorus*

"FExCal, 1843–4. 782, 1843. Macrorhynchus" (NY-Torrey!). "FExCal, 1845–7. 68. 1845. Troximon glaucum Nutt." (GH!).

Agoseris heterophylla (Nutt.) Greene var. *heterophylla*

"FExCal, 1845–7. 279. 1846. M. heterophyllus. Also M. Californicus; but no such ray achenes [note by Asa Gray]" and "FExCal, 1845–7. 248. 1846" (both GH!). The leaves of 248 have long linear-filiform lobes and narrow rachis, unlike other specimens of this species examined by me. "FExCal, 1843–4. 87. 1844. Macrorhynchus" (NY-Torrey!). Sheet number 87 at NY has a note "March 25th en route on the prairie." On 25 March 1844 Frémont moved from the Cosumne River in Sacramento County to the Mokelumne River and (?) Calavaras Creek, probably in San Joaquin County, California. "FExCal, 1845–7. 168 & 248, 1846. Macrorhynchus heterophyllus" and "FExCal, 1845–7. 183. 1846. Macrorhynchus heterophyllus" (both NY-Torrey!). Numbers 168, 248, and 183 are mounted on the same sheet but with only two labels. Adjacent to the label for the first two specimens is a note: "248. A new yellow flowering plant, open prairies Camp Lassen's farm. Sacto valley. latitude 40° April 12 [Tehama County, California]," and above the label for number 183 is another note: "183. Tow-al-um-ne River bottom, noticed but this specimen." The Toualumne River is in Stanislaus County, California, and was probably visited in March, 1846. "FExCal, 1845–7[1846]. Macrorhynchus heterophyllus" (US!).

Agrostis michauxiana = *A. perennans* (Walt.) Tuckerm.

"Little Blue river of the Kansas. June 22 [1842. Near present Powell, Jefferson County, Nebraska]" (Torrey, 1843: 94).

Agrostis perennans (Walt.) Tuckerm. includes *A. michauxiana*

***Alectoria fremontii* Tuckerm.**, Amer. J. Sci. Arts 25: 422, 1858. (3rd) = *Bryoria fremontii* (Tuckerm.) Brodo & D. Hawksworth (Opera Bot. 42: 136. 1977).

Protologue locality: "'Camp of Dec. 5, 6, 1854 [1845],' (Sierra Nevada), 'California, abundant on Pines,' *Col. Frémont*, (com. Torrey!)" Type: "FExCal, 1845–7. No. 491." 1845 (holotype NY-Columbia!). The label of the holotype contains several notations: "No. 491. 1845. Evernia sp. nov. E. T. E. fremontii. Tuckerm. Lich. Ex. no 52. 3rd Exped. Alectoria Fremonti. Supp. Supp. p. 422." The reference to the lichen exsiccatae is to a book of lichens from Tuckerman's private herbarium. The book "Lichenes Amerocae Septentrionalis Exsiccati. Fascic. III. et IV. curante Edvardo Tuckerman. 1855" is also extant at NY, and certainly contains an isotype of the taxon. The notation in the fascicle is as follows: "52. Evernia Fremontii, Tuckerm. mss. *Ad ramos Pini in montibus Californiae detexit*. C. Frémont; *comm. cl.* Torrey." This lichen is annotated "*Alectoria fremontii* Tuck." by I. M. Brodo (21 Dec. 1970).

Allenrolfea occidentalis (S. Wats.) Kuntze includes *Halostachys occidentalis* S. Wats. and *Spirostachys occidentalis* (S. Wats.) S. Wats.

"FExCal, 1843–4. 760. 1843. 'Eastern shore of ?Great Salt Lake.' 'Resembles Halocnemum—but the persistent scale-like processes of the rachis are not *true* scales—but portions of the rachis, not excavated—& separating as the axis elongates [Torrey note!]'" (NY-Torrey!). A "shrubby salicornia" is mentioned by Frémont on 5 (1845: 150) and 10 (1845: 157) September 1843, when the party was near present Brigham City, Box Elder County, and west of Ogden, Weber County, Utah, respectively. The species was described as *Halostachys occidentalis* by Watson (1871). Watson later (1874) transferred the species to *Spriostachys*, citing as collectors: "760 Frémont; Emory; 577, 1745 Wright; Stansbury; 100 Thurber; 139 Bigelow; Schott; Newberry; H. Engelmann; 467 Torrey; Palmer; 1191

Brewer; 994 Watson; Wheeler; Burgess," evidently in order of collection date. Indications are, thus, that Frémont was the first to collect the species.

Allium amplectens Torr.
"FExCal, Zzzz Gray. 1846" (NY-Torrey! and GH!). The sheet is annotated as *A. attenuifolium* Kell. by Sereno Watson. "FExCal, 396. 1845" annotated *A. occidentale* by Sereno Watson (NY-Torrey!). The type of this species was taken by Bigelow.

Allium peninsulare Lemmon ex Greene
"FExCal, 1845–7. 469. 1846" (GH!).

Allium reticulatum = *A. textile* Nels. & Macbr.
"Defiles in the Wind River mountains. Aug. 12–17 [1842. Sublette County, Wyoming]" (Torrey, 1843: 93).

***Allium serratum* S. Wats.**, Rep. Geol. Explor. U.S. 40th Parallel, Bot. 5: 487. 1871. (3rd) = *A. peninsulare* Lemmon ex Greene (fide D. W. McNeal, Jr. annotation label April 1983).
Protologue locality: "California; frequent. (Douglas, 1991 Hartweg, 469 Frémont, 345 Bridges, Bigelow, Wallace, Stillman, Rich, Bolander, Kellogg.)" Type: "FExCal, 469. 1846. Allium" (syntype NY-Torrey!).

Allium textile Nels. & Macbr. includes *Allium reticulatum*

Alnus incana Willd. includes *A. incana* var. *glauca* and *A. viridis*

Alnus incana Willd. var. *glauca* Ait. = *Alnus incana* Willd.
"It is 422 Frémont (1845)" (Watson, 1871: 324). "Frémont's 2nd Expedn. Alnus tenuifolia Nutt. Betula incana?" and "FExCal, 1845, 422, Alnus tenuifolia Nutt., Fruit not winged. White River [12–25 September 1845, Rio Blanco County, Colorado and Uintah County, Utah]" (both NY-Torrey!).

Alnus viridis = *A. incana* Willd.
Frémont (1845: 158).

Alternanthera? (*Endotheca*) *lanuginosa* Nutt. ≡ *Tidestromia lanuginosa* (Nutt.) Standley.
"FExCal, 455, 1845. Between Bent's Fort & Upper Pueblo [16–20 August 1845, Otero to Pueblo cos., Colorado]" (NY-Torrey!). "Aug. 15. Sandy Bottom of the Arkansas. Frémont's 3rd Exped." (GH!). On 15 August Frémont was still at Bent's Fort, Otero County, Colorado. "Colonel Frémont collected it on the upper Arkansas in his last [third] expedition" (Torrey in Emory, 1848: 150).

Amaranthus arenicola I. M. Johnst.
"FExCal, 1845. No. 138. July 4th [eastern Kansas, near the Santa Fe trail]. Acnida either tubericulata or tamarisana. Prairies" (NY-Torrey!). "Amaranthus. Frémont's 3rd Exped. 138. 1845" (MO!).

***Amarella ventorum* Rydb.**, Bull. Torrey Bot. Club 40: 463. 1913. (1st) = *Gentianella amarella* (L.) Boerner subsp. *acuta* (Michx.) J. M. Gillett

Protologue locality: "*Gentiana arctophila densiflora* Torr. Frémont's Rep. 94. 1845. Wyoming, Wind River Mts., 4 Aug. 1842 [southwest of Carmody Lakes, Frémont County, Wyoming], Frémont" Type: "Frémont's 1st Journey (Wind River Mts.) Augt. 4. 1842. Gentiana arctophila β densiflora" (holotype NY-Torrey!). The type sheet at NY bears the provisional epithet "Amarella Fremontii Rydb." in Rydberg's handwriting (Tiehm & Stafleu, 1990). "Ex spec. Frém. Hb. Torr. G. tenuis. Griseb" (probable isotype GH!). The sheet cited is from "Herb. A. Gray" and contains the notation "rare." The specimen is a fragment in an envelope.

***Amauria? dissecta* A. Gray**, Mem. Amer. Acad. II. 4: 104. 1849. (3rd) ≡ *Bahia dissecta* (A. Gray) Rydb.

Protologue locality: "A few miles east of Mora River; Aug. (537.) [Fendler] Also gathered in Frémont's third expedition, probably towards the head-waters of the Arkansas [1845]." Type: ? The party was at the headwaters of the Arkansas on 2 September 1845, in or near Lake County, Colorado. The Frémont material, if found, is a syntype.

Ambrosia deltoidea (Torr.) Payne includes *Franseria deltoidea*

Ambrosia dumosa (A. Gray) Payne includes *Franseria albicaulis*

Ambrosia tomentosa Nutt. includes *Franseria discolor* Nutt.

Amelanchier alnifolia Nutt. includes *A. diversifolia* var. *alnifolia*

The pomes of this species are referred to as service berries, which are juicy, sweet, bland, and mucilaginous, but nutritious. The berries of the related *A. utahensis* Koehne are often almost or quite dry at maturity and are not especially palatable. The pomes of *A. alnifolia* constituted a portion of the fruit diet of Indians, at least during years when production of fruit was abundant.

Amelanchier diversifolia var. *alnifolia* = *A. alnifolia* Nutt.

"Sweet Water of the Platte. Aug. 5 [1842. Southeast of Atlantic City, Frémont County, Wyoming]" (Torrey, 1843: 84).

Amelanchier utahensis Koehne

"FExCal, 1843–44, 542, 1844. A. alnifolia, Nutt.," "FExCal, 1845–7. 158. 1845"; "A. alnifolia, Nutt. Frémont's 2nd Expedn.," "Virgen River (probably Clark County, Nevada), 442, 1844. Frémont's 2nd Expedn.," and "FExCal, 1845–47, 464 & 412, 1846. Nnn. 1846. Dr. Gray. Amelanchier Canadensis var. alnifolia *T. & Gr.*" (all five NY-Torrey!).

Amole (or ammole)—*Chlorogalum pomeridianum* (DC.) Kunth

Frémont (1845: 249).

Amorpha canescens ≡ *A. canescens* Pursh

"Kansas and Lower Platte rivers. June 19–Sept. 20 [1842]" (Torrey, 1843: 84).

Amorpha fruticosa ≡ *A. fruticosa* L.
"From the Lower Platte to the mountains. Aug. 8–Sept. 19 [1842]" (Torrey, 1843: 84).

Amphicarpa bracteata (L.) Fern. includes *A. monoica*

Amphicarpaea monoica = *A. bracteata* (L.) Fern.
"North fork of the Platte. Sept. 4 [1842. West of Scotts Bluff, Scotts Bluff County, Nebraska]" (Torrey, 1843: 84).

***Amphipappus* Torr. & A. Gray** in A. Gray, Boston J. Nat. Hist. 5: 108. 1845. (2nd)
Type species: ***Amphipappus fremontii* Torr. & A. Gray** in A. Gray. Synonym: *Amphiachyris fremontii* (Torr. & A. Gray) A. Gray Proc. Amer. Acad. 8: 633. 1873.
Protologue locality: "Mr. Frémont collected this plant at several places along the Mohave River, &c., somewhere between California and the Rocky Mountains, in April." "Interior of California, in mountains between 35° and 36° N. latitude; particularly on the Mohave River and other tributaries of the Colorado; flowering in April" (Torrey, 1853: 17). Type: "FExCal, no. 336 & 413, 1844. Amphipappus Fremontii, Gray, in Bost. Jour. Nat. Hist. 5. p. 4" (lectotype GH!; isolectotype NY-Torrey!: microfiche BRY!). The GH specimen was chosen as lectotype in Porter (1943). The label data with the lectotype is simply "Frémont 2nd Exped." Probably the material on which this species was based came from San Bernardino County, California (Porter, 1943).

Amsinckia spectabilis Fisch. & Mey.
"Frémont's 2nd Expedn. 116 & 111, 1844" and "FExCal, 1845–7. 255. 1846. Amsinckia spectabilis *F. & Mey.* 'Fl. yellow.' Valley of the Sacramento" (both NY-Torrey!).

Amsinckia tessellata A. Gray
"Frémont's 2nd Expedn. 116, 111, 1844. Amsinckia. Frémont" and "FExCal, 1844. 285. Amsinckia lycopoides [marked out] *Lehm.* vermicosa" (both NY-Torrey!). Above the label of sheet 285 is a note: "Not at all *A. vermicosa*, but *tesselata*."

***Amsonia tomentosa* Torr. & Frém.** in Frém., Rep. Explor. Oregon & California 316. 1845. (2nd)
Protologue locality: "The specimens of this plant were without tickets; but they were probably collected west of the Rocky Mountains. They were without fruit." Type: "Amsonia tomentosa *Torr. & Frém.* Frémont's 2nd Expedn" (holotype NY-Torrey!). Type material likely came from Clark County, Nevada, in early May 1844. A drawing of a flower and floral parts based on the Frémont material is at NY! (Figure 18). The NY specimen is cited as holotype by McLaughlin (1982).

Anatherix viridis ≡ *Asclepias viridis* Walt.
"Big Blue river of the Kansas. June 20 [1842. Probably Marshall County, Kansas]" (Torrey, 1843: 91).

Andropogon nutans ≡ *Sorghastrum nutans* (L.) Nash in Small
"Laramie river, N. fork of the Platte. Sept. 3–4 [1842. Goshen County, Wyoming]" (Torrey, 1843: 94).

Andropogon scoparius ≡ *Schizachyrium scoparium* (Michx.) Nash in Small
"Lower Platte [1842]" (Torrey, 1843: 94).

Androsace filiformis Retz.
"Androsace filiformis Retz. Frémont's 1st Exp. Aug. 5. 1842" (NY-Torrey!). On 5 August 1842, Frémont and party were along the Sweet Water River, Frémont County, Wyoming. "Ex herb J. Torrey. Androsace occidentalis, *non Nutt.!* Torr. & Gr. Fl. N. Amer. Frémont's 1st Exp." (GH!). The specimen at GH is mounted with collections by Vasey, Nuttall, Hall and Harbour, Burke, and H. Engelmann.

Androsace occidentalis ≡ *A. occidentalis* Pursh
"Sweet Water river. Aug. 5 [1842. Southeast of Atlantic City, Frémont County, Wyoming]" (Torrey, 1843: 88). "FExRM, 1842. Androsace occidentalis, *Nutt.*" (NY-Torrey!).

Anemone patens L.
"Frémont's 2nd Expedn. 573. 1844. P. hirsutissima" (NY-Torrey!). "Herb. P. V. Le Roy, Peekskill, N. Y. Anemone Nuttalliana. Frémont" (NY-Columbia!).

Anemone tuberosa Rydb.
"FExCal, 1849. Anemone" (NY-Torrey!).

Anemopsis californica (Nutt.) Hook. & Arn.
"Frémont's 2nd Expedn. 585. 1844" (NY-Torrey!).

Anethum graveolens = *Perideridia gardneri* (Hook. & Arn.) Mathias

***Anisocoma* Torr. &. A. Gray** in A. Gray, Boston J. Nat. Hist. 5: 110. 1845. (2nd)
Type species: ***Anisocoma acaulis* Torr. & A. Gray** in A. Gray
Protologue locality: "The single specimen of this plant from which our figure is taken, was not accompanied by any ticket or number, by which its particular habitat may be ascertained" (Gray, 1845: 111). Type: "FExCal, 1843–4. March. Anisocoma acaulis, Gray, in Bost. Jour. Nat. Hist. 5. p. 7. tab. f. 7–11. Valley of the San Joachin—California" (holotype NY-Torrey!: microfiche BRY!; isotype fragment GH!). The label of the Frémont plant bears an annotation label "Anisocoma acaulis n. sp." That designation and the information on the label give supporting evidence of this particular specimen as the holotype. The specimen is mounted on a sheet with two other collections, one by Newberry and the other by Mr. Fitch. The GH material consists of fragments in an envelope. "Dry plains and hills, from Fort Tejon to the Colorado, and from the Sierra Valley of Western Nevada. First collected by Frémont" (Brewer et al., 1876: 431). The party was in the San Joaquin Valley from 24 March to 14 April 1844.

***Anogra cinerea* Rydb.**, Bull. Torrey Bot. Club 31: 570. 1904. (3rd) = *Oenothera latifolia* (Rydb.) Munz (fide Munz annotation).

Protologue locality: "Between Bent's Fort and Pueblo, Frémont 234, 1845." Type: "FExCal, 234, 1845. Same as 202, passing into Oe. pallida. Between Bent's Fort & Pueblo [i.e., 16–20 August 1845—Otero to Pueblo counties, Colorado]" (holotype NY-Torrey!).

Antennaria microphylla ≡ *A. microphylla* Rydb.

"July 10 2nd exped. [1843. St. Vrain's Fort, Weld County, Colorado]" (NY-Torrey!).

***Anticlea fremontii* Torr.**, Pacif. R. R. Rep. 4: 144. 1857. (3rd) ≡ *Zigadenus fremontii* (Torr.) S. Wats.

Protologue locality: "Mountains near Oakland, April 4, (in flower.) [Bigelow] . . . and by Colonel Frémont at Santa Cruz, (flowering in February,) and on the Uinta River, Utah; June, (in fruit.) [1844. Second expedition, at Fort Uintah, Uintah County, Utah]." Type: "FExCal, No. 157. 1846. In oak woods and in sandy places. Camp at Santa Cruz, Feb. 28 [i.e., Santa Cruz County, California]," and a second sheet identified as "Amanthium Fremontii [isotype]" (holotype NY-Torrey!: microfiche BRY!; isotype GH!) "Santa Cruz, California" (fide Abrams, 1923: 375). Both sheets at NY bear drawings and notes by John Torrey. Choice of a holotype from the Frémont materials is indicated by the presence of the drawings and by the epithet chosen for the species. The Utah specimens were not found, but they belong to some other species.

***Antirrhinum vagans* A. Gray**, Proc. Amer. Acad. 7: 375. 1868. (3rd) = *A. vexillo-calyculatum* Kellogg

Protologue locality: "Near San Francisco, valley of the Upper Sacramento, and other parts of California, collected by Frémont, Brewer, Bolander, Torrey, Heermann, &c." Type: "Frémont's 2d [3rd] Calif. Exped. 1845–47. Antirrhinum. Ex Torrey. No. 495. 1846" (syntype GH-Thurber!; MO!). "FExCal, 1845–7. 495. 1846. Antirrhinum cornutum, Benth. pl. Hartweg no. 1888? June 5th. N. bank of the American Fork [Sacramento County, California]" (syntype NY-Torrey!). The name is lectotypified by Thompson (1988) on the basis of Torrey 369(a) at GH. The specimen at NY is annotated by D. M. Thompson as *A. vexillo-calyculatum* subsp. *intermedium* D. Thompson. It bears a typical Torrey label with sketches of floral parts.

Antirrhinum vexillo-calyculatum Kellogg includes *A. vagans* A. Gray

Apios tuberosa = *A. americana* Medic.

"Forks of the Platte. Sept. 13 [1842. Lincoln County, Nebraska]" (Torrey, 1843: 84). "FExRM, 1842. Apios tuberosa. 'Junction camp. 13th September. Wild Potato; eaten by Indians & said to grow much larger. Forks of the Platte. 204'" (NY-Torrey!).

Aplectrum hyemale ≡ *A. hyemale* (Muhl.) Torr.

"On the Platte. June 29 [1842. South of Cozad, Dawson County, Nebraska]" (Torrey, 1843: 93). "FExRM, 1842. Aplectrum hyemale, *Nutt.*" (NY-Torrey!).

Aplopappus fremontii A. Gray, Proc. Acad. Sci. Phil. 1863: 65. 1864. Basionym: *Pyrrocoma foliosa* Torr. & A. Gray in A. Gray, Boston J. Nat. Hist. 5: 108. 1845.

Aplopappus spinulosus ≡ *Haplopappus spinulosus* (Pursh) DC.
"Fort Laramie, north fork of the Platte. Sept. 3 [1842. Goshen County, Wyoming]" (Torrey, 1843: 87). "River bottom. St. Vrain's Fort. July 10" [1842. Weld County, Colorado] (NY-Torrey!). "FExCal, 1845–7. Aplopappus spinulosus. Upper Arkansas [Colorado]"; "Frémont's 3rd Coll. 1845. 'July 19' [13 day's journey east of Bent's Fort, Kansas]"; and "FExCal, 1845–7. 417. 1845. A. spinulosus" (all three GH!). The latter two collections are on the same sheet.

***Aplopappus tortifolius* Torr. & A. Gray** in A. Gray, Boston J. Nat. Hist. 5: 109. 1845. (2nd) = *Xylorhiza tortifolia* (Torr. & A. Gray) Greene
Protologue locality: "It was gathered among the mountains of Upper California [by Frémont]." Type: "FExCal, 1843–4. Aplopappus tortifolius" (lectotype GH-Thurber!; isolectotype NY-Torrey!); and "Frémont's 2nd Exp." (isolectotype NY-Torrey!). The taxon was lectotypified by T. J. Watson (1977: 210) on the basis of the specimen at GH; a second sheet from GH! has two flowering Frémont specimens, from "Frémont's 2nd Exped." They are presumed to be isolectotypes. The lectotype is poorly chosen, based not on material from the Gray Herbarium per se. It is based, instead, on the material exchanged with Thurber. The other sheet at GH or one of those at NY would have been better selected. The species is locally common in the Mohave Desert vegetation of southern California, Nevada, and southwestern Utah.

Apocynum cannabinum ≡ *A. cannabinum* L.
"On the Platte [1842]" (Torrey, 1843: 90).

Aquilegia caerulea ≡ *A. caerulea* James in Long
"Wind River mountains [1842]" (Torrey, 1843: 83). "Aquilegia caerulea Torr. & Gray. Frémont's 1st Expedn. Aug 13–16 [1842. Wind River Mountains, Sublette County, Wyoming]" (NY-Torrey!). This aquilegia was noted also in Colorado by Frémont (1845: 285).

Arabis glabra (L.) Bernh.
"FExCal, 1845–7. Ss. 1845. Dr. Gray. Turritis glabra" and "FExCal, 125, 1845" (both NY-Torrey! and GH!).

Arbutus menziesii Pursh
Frémont (1887: 458).

***Arctomecon* Torr. & Frém.** in Frém., Rep. Explor. Exped. Oregon & California 312. 1845. (2nd)
Type species: ***Arctomecon californicum* Torr. & Frém.**
Protologue locality: "This remarkable plant was found in only a single station in the Californian mountains, on the banks of a creek; flowering early in May." Type: "FExCal, No. 429, May 3, 1844. It was the only one collected by Frémont at a place called Las

Vegas, near the Rio Virgin, then Utah—Lat 36°10′" (holotype NY-Torrey!: microfiche BRY!). "Discovered by *Frémont* on the banks of a creek in sterile soil near the southeastern border of the State [of California], but probably in Nevada. It has since been collected only by *Parry* in S. Utah [*A. humilis* Cov.]" (Brewer et al., 1876: 21). Evidently the specimen was lost; only a fragment and the original drawing remain (Frontispiece). The species is known only from Clark County, Nevada, from the vicinity of Las Vegas northeastward for only about sixty miles and as a disjunct in adjacent Arizona. Most of the eastern portion of its range lies to the south of the Frémont route. The type specimen was certainly collected on the banks of "two narrow streams of clear water, four of five feet deep [that] gush suddenly, with a quick current, from two large springs" at Las Vegas. The exact locality of the springs is unknown to the writer, but the species has been taken in modern times from saline-alkaline sites within the city limits of Las Vegas.

Arctostaphylos elegans Jepson?
"FExCal, 1845–7. 28, 1845. Arctostaphylos pungens var." (GH!).

Arctostaphylos glauca Lindley?
"California [1846?]. Frémont" (NY-Sartwell!).

Arctostaphylos manzanita Parry
"FExCal, 1845–7. 226 (no year on label)" (GH!). "FExCal, 1845–7. 226, 1845.

Arctostaphylos glauca? J. T[orrey] (US!).

Arctostaphylos mariposa Dudley
"FExCal, 1845–7. Zzzz. 1845" and "FExCal, 1845–7. 20. 1845" (both GH!). "FExCal, 1845–7. Arctostaphylos tomentosa. Zzz Gray. 1845. California" (**US!**).

Arctostaphylos patula Greene
"Frém. Calif. Exped. 1845–47[1846?]. Ex Torrey" (GH-Thurber!), and "Ex. Torr. (Frémont?) Arctostaphylos glauca (Lindl)" (GH!). "FExCal, 1845–7. 488, 1846" (MO!). "Frémont's 3rd Expedition, 368, 1846. Arctostaphylos glauca. California" (US!).

Arctostaphylos pungens H.B.K.
"FExCal, 1845–7[1846?]. Pinquam Creek, Utah Lake" (NY!). Pinquam Creek is probably American Fork river or creek, which drains from the Wasatch Mountains into the north side of Utah Lake, Utah County, Utah. The provenance is undoubtedy wrong; the species is known in Utah only from far to the south of Utah Lake, a region not visited by Frémont during his third expedition. Probably the specimen is from California, taken in 1846.

Arctostaphylos tomentosa (Pursh) Lindley
"Frémont's 2d Calif. Exped. 1845–47. 141. 1846. Ex Torrey" (GH-Thurber!). "FExCal, 1845–7. 142, 1846. A. tomentosa var. hispida" (GH!). "FExCal, 23 December 1845. Lake Fork of Tulare (word not clear) W. slope of Sierra Nevada" (NY-Torrey!). The sheet is annotated as "Arctostaphylos tomentosa v. serrulata Torr. & Gray, Fl. N. Amer." "FExCal, 1845–7. 145 1846. Arctostaphyulos tomentosa. In an oak grove at the camp

near Santa Cruz. A bush about 4 feet high. Feb. 26" (NY-Torrey!). The specimen from near Santa Cruz is mounted on a sheet with two other stems, one at least sent by Hooker.

Arctostaphylos uva-ursi ≡ *A. uva-ursi* (L.) Spreng.
"On a lake in the mountains. Aug. 12–17 [1842. Wind River Mountains, Sublette County, Wyoming]" (Torrey, 1843: 88). "Frémont's 1st Expedition" (NY-Torrey!). The Frémont specimen, a large leafy branch with roots, is mounted on the same sheet with a specimen from Franklin's Journey, Richardson, and one from the Rocky Mountains, by E. James.

***Arenaria brevifolia* Nutt. var. *californica* A. Gray**, Proc. Calif. Acad. 3: 101. 1864. (3rd).
Type locality: Type: "FExCal, 284. 1846" (NY-Torrey!).

Arenaria congesta ≡ *A. congesta* (Nutt.) Torr. & A. Gray
"Highest parts of the Wind River mountains. Aug. 13–16 [1842. Sublette County, Wyoming]" (Torrey, 1843: 83). "FExRM, 1842. Wind River Mountains. Aug. 13–16. Arenaria congesta *Nutt.*" (NY-Torrey!). "FExRM, 1842. Silene drummondii" (NY-Columbia!) and "Frémont. Arenaria congesta Nutt. ex. T. & G." (NY-LeRoy!). The Aug. 13–16 specimen is mounted on a sheet with one collected by Nuttall from "Columbia plains, also collected by Douglas Rocky Mountains," and one by Douglas from "Snake Country, Oregon."

Arenaria fendleri A. Gray
"Frémont's 2nd Expedn. Arenaria (Eremogone) Fendleri, Gray. Pl. Fend. p. 13?" (NY-Torrey!).

Arenaria hookeri Nutt. ex Torr. & A. Gray
"Frémont's 2nd Expedn. Arenaria Hookeri?" (NY-Torrey!).

***Argemone hispida* A. Gray**, Mem. Amer. Acad. 4: 5. 1849. (3rd?). includes *A. mexicana β albiflora*
Protologue locality: "Low, sandy places around Santa Fe; the stems 1 to 2 feet high, growing socially in great numbers; June, July [Fendler 16]. (Also on the Upper Arkansas, &c., Frémont, Wislizenus.)." Type: The Frémont specimen, if found, would be a syntype. Ownbey (1958: 69) cites such a specimen as being at GH: "FExCal, Frémont 8." The specimen has not been seen by me. The species is known from southeastern Wyoming, southward through central eastern Colorado to northwestern New Mexico.

Argemone mexicana β albiflora = *A. hispida* A. Gray
(Torrey, 1843: 83).

Aristida pallens = *A. purpurea* Nutt.
"On the Platte. June 29 [1842. South of Cozad, Dawson County, Nebraska]" (Torrey, 1843: 94).

Aristida purpurea Nutt. includes *A. pallens*
"FExCal, 1843–4. 167. 1843" (MO!).

Arnica angustifolia = *A. fulgens* Pursh
"Defiles of the Wind River mountains, from 7,000 feet and upwards. August 13–14 [1842. Sublette County, Wyoming]" (Torrey, 1843: 88).

Arnica fulgens Pursh includes *A. angustifolia*

Artemisia arbuscula Nutt.
"Artemisia arbuscula. R. Mts. Frémont" (NY-Columbia!).

Artemisia biennis Willd. includes *A. lewisii*
"On the Platte [1842]" (Torrey, 1843: 87). "FExRM, 1842. A. Lewisii? [J. Carey]. Platte. Frémont" and "Frémont's Exped. to the Rocky Mts. 1842. A. biennis. Torr. & Gray, Flora, N. Amer. Platte. Frémont" (both NY-Torrey!). The specimen was annotated as *Artemisia caudata* Michx. by Rydberg, but is obviously not perennial. The sheet labeled *A. lewisii* bears a note in pencil: "species considered fictitious by Dr. Gray in Syn. Flor. 369." John Carey was an associate of Torrey. "Torrey worked with Carey on the Frémont plants but as Carey had suffered financial losses and was despondent about them, Torrey, after sympathizing for a while and trying to help him, lost patience with him, and by March 9, 1843, finished the account himself for the plants of Frémont's first expedtion, and sent off a copy to Gray" (Rodgers, 1942: 155). There is little aside from the notation of Carey's name with this and another artemisia to indicate that he ever worked seriously with the Frémont collections.

Artemisia californica Less.
"FExCal, 1845–7. (0) Gray 1846. Artemisia Californica Less.! (& A. Fischerana Rep. Ledeb.). A. Gr." (NY!-Torrey).

Artemisia campestris L. subsp. *caudata* (Michx.) Hall & Clements includes *A. canadensis* (q.v.)

Artemisia cana Pursh
"On the Platte [1842]" (Torrey, 1843: 87). "FExRM, 1842. Upper Platte. A. cana." and "FExCal, 1845–7. 463, 1846. Artemisia cana. 'Not in my herb. From chars. probably A. Lindleyana, Bess.' A. Gr." (both NY-Torrey!). "FExCal, 1845–7[1845?]. Artemisia Lindleyana Bess. probably A.Gr[ay]" and "FExCal, 1845–7[1845?]. Artemisia tridentata" (both US!). "Plains of the Upper Missouri and Platte to the Rocky Mountains, *Lewis! Nuttall! Mr. Nicollet! Lieut. Frémont!*" (Torrey & Gray, 1843: 418).

Artemisia canadensis = *A. campestris* L. subsp. *caudata* (Michx.) Hall & Clements
"South fork of the Platte, and north fork, to Laramie river. July 4–Sept. 3 [1842]" (Torrey, 1843: 87). "Exped. to Wind River Mountains, 1842. A. Canadensis. Torr. & Gray, Flora, N. Amer. Platte. Frémont" and "Frémont's Exped. to the R. Mts. 1842. A. canadensis. Torr. & Gray, Flora, N. Amer. Platte. Frémont" (both NY-Torrey!). "FExCal, 296, 1845. A. canadensis *Gray*" (NY-Torrey!).

Artemisia filifolia Torr.

"South fork of the Platte, and north fork, to Laramie river. July 4–Sept. 3 [1842]" (Torrey, 1843: 87). "FExRM, 1842" (GH-Thurber!). "A. filifolia. Plains of the Platte, Frémont, 1842. A. filifolia *Torr*. Torr. & Gray, Flora, N. Amer." (NY-Torrey!). "Plains of the Platte, very abundant, *Dr. James! Nuttall! Lieut. Frémont!*" (Torrey & Gray, 1843: 418). "FExCal, 1845–7. 62, 1845" (GH!). "FExCal, 1845–47. No. 63. Aug. 22, 1845. Artemisia filifolia. *Torr*. 'Fontaine qui bouit' [Pueblo County, Colorado]" (NY-Torrey!). "FExCal, 1845–7[1845]. Artemisia filifolia *Torr.*" (US!).

Artemisia frigida Willd.

"Black Hills to the mountains [1842]" (Torrey, 1843: 87). "Frémont's Exped to the Rocky Mts. 1842. A. frigida. Wind R. Chain. 7000 feet. Frémont" (NY-Torrey!). "*A. frigida* var. *Gmelinana* Bess. Dry hills and rocks, Saskatchewan! and Missouri! to the Rocky Mountains, (Wind River Chain, at the altitude of 7000 feet, *Lieut Frémont!*)" (Torrey & Gray, 1843: 425). "FExCal, 1843–4. Artemisia frigida" (GH-Thurber!). "FExCal, 374, 1845. Artemisia frigida" (NY-Torrey!). "FExCal, 1845–7[1845]. Artemisia frigida" (US!).

Artemisia lewisii = *Artemisia biennis* Willd.

"On the Platte [1842]" (Torrey, 1843: 87). See specimen cited under *A. biennis*.

Artemisia longiloba (Osterh.) Beetle

"FExCal, 1843–4. 660. Artemisia arbuscula. Nutt. Muddy River, a tributary of Hams Fork [19 August 1843, Uinta County, Wyoming]" (NY-Torrey!).

Artemisia ludoviciana Nutt.

"Black Hills of the Platte. July 26 [1842. Deer Creek, near Glen Rock, Converse County, Wyoming]" (Torrey, 1843: 87). "Exped. to R. Mountains, 1842. A. Ludoviciana var. Torr. & Gray, Flora, N. Amer. Sweet Water River. Frémont" and "Exped. to Rocky Mts. 1842. A. ludoviciana. Plains of the Platte & c. Frémont" (both NY-Torrey). "Forms of A. ludoviciana. Upper Platte etc. Lieut. Frémont" (GH!). "Frémont's 3rd Exped. Artemisia ludoviciana. Upper Platte. Torr. & Gray, Fl. N. Amer." (US!). "FExCal, 266, 1843. Artemisia cana [J. Carey]" (NY-Torrey!).

Artemisia ludoviciana Nutt. var. *latifolia* Besser = *A. ludoviciana* Nutt.

"Wind River Chain of the Rocky Mountains, Lieut. Frémont [1842]" (Torrey & Gray, 1843: 420). "A. ludoviciana var. latifolia. Wind River Chain, high up. Frémont" (NY-Torrey!).

Artemisia nova A. Nels.

"FExCal, 1843–4. Artemisia trifida, Nutt." (NY-Torrey!).

Artemisia pedatifida Nutt.

"FExCal, 1843–4. Artemisia pedatifida" (NY-Torrey!).

Artemisia tridentata Nutt.

"On the Sweet Water, near the mountains [1842]" (Torrey, 1843: 87). "Frémont. Wind R. Chain, 1842. A. tridentata. Torr. & Gray, Flora, N. Amer." (NY-Torrey!). "Wind River Chain of the Rocky Mountains, *Lieut. Frémont!*" (Torrey & Gray, 1843: 418). "FExCal, 659, 1843–44, Artemisia tridentata. Muddy River, tributary of Ham's Fork [i.e., on 19 August 1843, in Uinta County, Wyoming]" (NY-Torrey!). "FExCal, 1843–4. A. tridentata" (GH-Thurber). This is the big sagebrush that covers vast areas of the West and was perceived as a monotonous plague by Frémont and his men.

Asarum canadense L.

Frémont (1887: 27, 28).

Asclepias cryptoceras S. Wats. includes *Acerates latifolia*

Asclepias engelmanniana Woodson includes *Acerates auriculata* Engelm.

***Asclepias fremontii* Torr. ex A. Gray**, Syn. Fl. N. Amer. 2(2): 93. 1878. (3rd) = *Asclepias eriocarpa* Torr. ex A. Gray

Protologue locality: "California, on the Upper Sacramento, Frémont, Newberry, &c." Type: "Frémont's Expedition to California 477, 1846. Upper Sacramento. June 4, Buttes Camp [i.e., west of Yuba City, Sutters County, California]" (holotype NY-Torrey!: microfiche BRY!; isotype fragments GH!]. "FExCal, 1845–7. 477, 1846. Asclepias speciosa Torr." (isotype GH!). This specimen was taken following the close of the official geographical exploration, prior to moving camp to the American Fork of the Sacramento River on 8 June 1846.

Asclepias incarnata L.

"Frémont's 2nd Expedition. Upper Platte" (NY-Torrey!).

Asclepias speciosa Torr.

"Forks of the Platte. July 2 [1842. Lincoln County, Nebraska]" (Torrey, 1843: 90). This species is cited in Torrey and Frémont (Frémont, 1845). Three sheets at NY-Torrey!: "Frémont 2 Exp. 513, 1843," "Platte Bottom, July 28. A. speciosa [1842. Near Evansville, Natrona County, Wyoming], Frémont," and "American Falls, Snake River, Sept. 24 [i.e., 1843. Power County, Idaho], 724 Frémont" Also, two mounts on one sheet: "Frémont's 3rd Exp. No 94, July 23 [1845, probably along Smoky Hill Fork, Kansas]" and "Smoky Hill Fork of the Kansas, No. 182, 1845" (also NY-Torrey! and MO!). "Near Bent's Fort [Otero County, Colorado]. Frémont. 3rd. Exp. (519. 1845)" (NY-Torrey!).

Asclepias stenophylla A. Gray includes *Polyotus angustifolius*

Asclepias tuberosa ≡ *A. tuberosa* L.

"Kansas river. June 19 [1842. Big Vermillion River, Pottawatomi County, Kansas]" (Torrey, 1843: 91).

Asclepias verticillata ≡ *A. verticillata* L.

"Forks of the Platte. July 2 [1842. Lincoln County, Nebraska]" (Torrey, 1843: 91).

Asclepias viridiflora Raf. includes *Acerates longifolia*

Asclepias viridis Walt. includes *Anatherix viridis*

"FExRM, 1842. June 20, 1842 Acerates paniculata, Nutt. Anantherix Nutt. [Big Blue River of the Kansas, Marshall County, Kansas]" (NY-Torrey!). "Rocky Mts. Frémont" (NY-Columbia!).

***Aster adscendens* var. *fremontii* Torr. & A. Gray**, Fl. N. Amer. 2: 503. 1843. (1st) ≡ *A. fremontii* (Torr. & A. Gray) A. Gray = *A. occidentalis* (Nutt.) Torr. & A. Gray

Protologue locality: "Wind River Chain of the Rocky Mountains, above 7000 feet, *Lieut. Frémont!*" Type: "A. adscendens. v. Fremontii. Torr. & Gray, Flora, N. Amer. Wind R. Chain, above 7000 feet [1842. Sublette County, Wyoming]. Frémont" (isotype NY-Torrey!, annotated by M. L. Dean, 1964: microfiche BRY!; holotype GH!, annotated by A. Cronquist 1940). A second sheet at GH!, labeled *Aster fremontii*, has the label data "Meadows and moist river banks, Wind River Mtn. July 21, 28." It is likely also an isotype of var. *fremontii*, but the dates are in error. Frémont was in the Wind River Mountains from 12–17 August 1842. "Wind River mountains, the highest summits to the limits of perpetual snow. Aug. 16" (Torrey, 1843: 86, as a nomen nudum). The material came from Sublette County, Wyoming. The sheet at NY has a second label adjacent to a solitary specimen with decumbent base, apparently belonging to the same species.

Aster andinus = *A. foliaceus* Lindley in DC. (annotated by K. L. Chambers in 1973).

"Near the snow line of the Wind River mountains. Aug. 16 [1842. Sublette County, Wyoming]" (Torrey, 1843: 87). "Wind Chain Mt., near snow line. Frémont's 1st Exped." (NY-Torrey!: microfiche BRY!).

Aster chilensis Nees

"FExCal, 1845–7. No. 167. Aster adscendens" (NY-Torrey!). The sheet is annotated as *Aster chilensis* by both Cronquist in 1943 and M. L. Dean in 1964. It was annotated as *Aster tweedyi* Rydb., evidently by Rydberg. "FExRM, 1842. 'Cannot name this' A.Gr. Wind River Mountains—high up" (NY-Torrey!).

Aster commutatus (Torr. & A. Gray) A. Gray

"FExCal, 1845–7. No. 64. 1844. Aster 'Nuttallii or new' 'Nuttall's specimen is poor' Dr. Gray" (NY-Torrey!). The specimen cited is mounted on a sheet with a slightly smaller plant with broader leaves, apparently not the same species. An anonymous notation *A. falcatus* occurs above the label, and the larger specimen bears an annotation label by Almut G. Jones (1973) as *Aster falcatus* Lindl. subsp. *commutatus* (Torr. & A. Gray).

Aster cordifolius = ?

"Lower Platte [1842]" (Torrey, 1843: 86).

Aster eatonii (A. Gray) T. Howell

"FExCal, 1845–7. Nos. 114 [crossed out] 375, 1845. Aster simplex? *AGr.* Upper Arkansas" (NY-Torrey!). The specimen is mounted on the same sheet as one of *A. occidentalis*.

Aster elegans = ?
"Wind River mountains [1842. Sublette County, Wyoming]" (Torrey, 1843: 87).

Aster ericoides L. includes *A. multiflorus β*

Aster falcatus = *A. chilensis* Nees
"Black Hills to the Sweet Water. July 30–Aug. [1842]" (Torrey, 1843: 86). "FExRM, 1842. August 3rd—'noon halt.' Aster falcatus I suppose. Compare in your *herb.* A.G." (NY-Torrey!). The specimen has been annotated by A. Cronquist as *A. chilensis* subsp. *adscendens* in 1943 and as *A. adscendens* by M. L. Dean in 1964.

Aster foliaceus Lindley includes *A. andinus*

Aster glacialis = *Erigeron simplex* Greene
"Near the snow line of the Wind River mountains. Aug. 16 [1842. Sublette County, Wyoming]" (Torrey, 1843: 87). "Aster glacialis, Nutt. Torr. & Gray, Flora, N. Amer. Small form. Wind Chain Mt. at snow line. Frémont" (NY-Columbia!). "Defiles of the Wind River Chain of the Rocky Mountains, and also just below the snow-line, *Lieut. Frémont!* With the above, Lieut. Frémont also collected a specimen of A. Andinus, *Nutt.*, A. integrifolius, *Nutt.*, &c." (Torrey & Gray, 1843: 503).

Aster glaucodes Blake includes *A. glaucus*

Aster glaucus = *A. glaucodes* Blake
"Wind River mountains [1842]" (Torrey, 1843: 87). "A. (Orthomeris) glaucus. Torr. & Gray, Flora, N. Amer. Wind R. Chain, 7000 Feet. Frémont" and "FExCal, 713, 313, 1844. Aster (Orthomeris) glaucus T., & Gr. Fl." (both NY-Torrey!). "A. (*Orthomeris*) glaucus.— Wind River Chain of the Rocky Mountains, at the elevations of 7000 feet or more, *Lieut. Frémont!*—A close congener of A. elegans (of which Lieut. Frémont gathered a single specimen near the same locality! (: rays several, small: achenia slightly hairy" (Torrey & Gray, 1843: 503).

Aster integrifolius = ?
"Basc of the Wind River mountains [1842]" (Torrey, 1843: 86). See the citation in the discussion of *A. glacialis*.

Aster laevis ≡ *A. laevis* L.
"North fork of the Platte [1842]" (Torrey, 1843: 86). "Frémont 371, 1845. Same as 394 1845. Aster, aff. adscendens [notation by Dr. Gray]" (NY-Torrey!: microfiche BRY!, identified as *A.* affinis *adscendens* Lindley); "FExCal, 1845–7. 394, 'Aster—new to all appearance. Gray. Upper Arkansas (Canon)" and "Utah Pass, Sheep River [Colorado, 28 August 1845]. Frémont notes" (both NY-Torrey!: microfiche BRY!), both annotated by M. L. Dean as *A. laevis* L. The coordinates for Sheep River, Utah Pass in the 1848 Frémont *Memoir* are 38°43′17″ latitude, 105°39′50″ longitude, probably in Chaffee County, Colorado.

Aster laxifolius = *A. chilensis* Nees

"On the Platte, from its mouth to the forks. Sept. 12–30 [1842]" (Torrey, 1843: 86).

Aster multiflorus β = *A. ericoides* L. sens. lat.

"Upper Platte, &c. [1842]" (Torrey, 1843: 86). Two sheets (NY-Torrey!): "FExRM, 1842, Aster multiflorus var. Upper Platte & Sweetwater" and "Frémont's [3rd] Expn. 72. 1845. A. multiflorus v. commutatus." "FExCal, 1845–7[1845]. Aster multiflorus. Turkey Creek" (US!). Frémont was at Turkey Creek, Kansas, on 11 July 1845.

Aster Novae-Angliae ≡ *A. novae-angliae* L.

"Lower Platte to the Wind River mountains. Aug 18–Sept. 24 [1842]" (Torrey, 1843: 87). "Valley of the Platte. Aug. 18. Frémont's 1st Coll." (GH!). On 18 August, Frémont was at the Little Sandy River, Sublette County, Wyoming. "FExCal, 1845–7. 31, 1845. A. novae-anglica" (GH!).

Aster novi-belgiae includes *A. laxifolius* = *A. chilensis* Nees (pro parte)

"Sweet Water of the Platte. Aug. 22 [1842. West of Devil's Gate, Frémont County, Wyoming]" (Torrey, 1843: 86). "FExRM, 1842. Valley of the North Fork of the Platte, between 'Red Buttes & Laramie's Fork.' 'A. nov.Belg.' A.Gr." (NY-Torrey!). This latter specimen has been annotated as *A. adscendens* by M. L. Dean in 1964. The annotation appears to be correct, and the specimen is herein assigned to *A. chilensis*. It seems that Gray was uncertain as to the identity of the asters included in the Frémont collections. They represented facets of the genus not within his previous experience. The genus consists of taxa whose edges are unclear because of morphological integradation, at least a part of which is due to hybridization. They are still difficult to determine with complete accuracy.

Aster oblongifolius ≡ *A. oblongifolius* Nutt.

"Lower Platte, &c. [1842]" (Torrey, 1843: 87). "Aster oblongifolius. Torr. & Gray, Flora, N. Amer. Frémont's 1st Expedn. 1842" and "Frémont, 498, 1845, Aster oblongifolius. Near Bent's Fort [i.e., 2–16 August, Otero County, Colorado]" (both NY-Torrey!).

Aster occidentalis (Nutt.) Torr. & A. Gray includes *A. adscendens* var. *fremontii* Torr. & A. Gray

"FExRM, 1842. Aster puniceus—dwarf.—? A. Gray. Lake in the Wind River Mountains" (NY-Torrey!). The specimens called *A. puniceus* by Gray are diminutive, but apparently belong here. "FExCal, No. 666 and 449, 1843. 449. Fontaine-qui-bouit [i.e., 12–18 July 1843, Fountain Creek, Pueblo County, Colorado]" and "666 Bear River, mouth of Smith's Fork, Aug 22 [1843. Lincoln County, Wyoming]" (both NY-Torrey!: microfiche BRY!). "FExCal, 1845–7. Nos. 114 [crossed out] 375, 1845. Aster simplex? *AGr*. Upper Arkansas" (NY-Torrey!). The specimen is mounted on the same sheet with one of *A. eatonii* (q.v.). "FExCal, 1845–7. No. 107. 1845. Aster" (NY-Torrey!).

Aster salsuginosus = *Erigeron peregrinus* (Pursh) Greene (q.v) pro parte
"Near the snow line of the Wind River mountains. Aug. 16 [1842. Sublette County, Wyoming]" (Torrey, 1843: 87). "Wind River Chain of the Rocky Mountains, above 7000 feet, *Lieut. Frémont!*" (Torrey & Gray, 1843: 503).

Astragalus agrestis Nutt. includes *A. hypoglottis*

Astragalus alpinus L. includes *Phaca astragalina*

***Astragalus arthu-schottii* A. Gray**, Proc. Amer. Acad. 6: 209. 1864. (2nd) = *A. lentiginosus* var. *variabilis* Barneby
Protologue locality: "Interior district between Utah and California; on the Mohave River, April 23, Frémont. Diluvial banks of the Colorado near its mouth, March 12, A. Schott. Boca Grande, Capt. E. K. Smith." Type: "Astragalus Schottii, n. sp. 338, 1844. April 23–24. Mohave River. Frémont's 2nd Expedn." (paratype NY-Torrey!). The Schott collection has been chosen as lectotype by Barneby (1964: 954). The Frémont material came from near Barstow, San Bernardino County, California.

Astragalus ceramicus Sheld. includes *Phaca longifolia*

Astragalus coulteri Benth.
"Probably collected in the arid region of the southeastern borders of the State, where it was found by *Frémont*" (Brewer et al., 1876: 147). *Astragalus arthu-schottii* A. Gray is annotated as *A. coulteri* Benth. by E.P.S[heldon].

Astragalus douglasii (Torr. & A. Gray) A. Gray
"California, near the coast, Douglas, Frémont, Brewer" (Gray, 1863: 216). "FExCal, 1845–7. 'Kkk. 1846. Dr. Gr.' Phaca Hookeriana?" (NY-Torrey!; GH!). The sheet at GH contains the label data: "Astragalus Douglasii. Phaca, Torr. & Gr."

Astragalus eucosmus Robins. includes *Phaca elegans*

***Astragalus fremontii* A. Gray ex Torr.**, Pacif. R. R. Rep. 4: 80. 1857. (2nd) ≡ *A. lentiginosus* var. *fremontii* (A. Gray) S. Wats.
Protologue locality: "Banks of the Rio Virgin, May 3, 1844, Frémont." Type: "No. 424, 1844. Frémont's 2nd Exp. Banks of the Rio Virgen, May 3rd. 'Flowers Purple.' Astragalus Fremontii" (holotype NY-Torrey!: microfiche BRY!; isotype GH!). Frémont was at Las Vegas, Clark County, Nevada, on 3 May 1844, not on the Virgin River! Substantial streams flowed from the springs at Las Vegas, and it is on the banks of these that the plant was presumably collected.

Astragalus gracilis ≡ *A. gracilis* Nutt.
"Forks of the Platte. July 2 [1842. Lincoln County, Nebraska]" (Torrey, 1843: 85).

Astragalus hypoglottis = *A. agrestis* Nutt.
"Sweet Water of the Platte. Aug. 5 [1842. Southeast of Atlantic City, Frémont County, Wyoming]" (Torrey, 1843: 85).

Astragalus kentrophyta (Nutt.) A. Gray includes *Kentrophyta montana*

Astragalus lentiginosus Dougl. var. *variabilis* Barneby
"Astragalus Schottii, n. sp. 338, 1844. April 23–24. Mohave River. Frémont's 2nd Expedn." (NY-Torrey!). "It was first collected in 1844, by Frémont, on the Mohave River" (Barneby, 1964: 949).

Astragalus mollissimus ≡ *A. mollissimus* Torr.
"Valley of the Platte. June 29 [1842. South of Cozad, Dawson County, Nebraska]" (Torrey, 1843: 85).

Astragalus parryi A. Gray
"I find in Dr. Torrey's herbarium a specimen collected by Frémont in his second expedition (station not recorded), with very ripe legumes" (Gray, 1863: 211). "Fr. Ex hb. Torr. Frémont's 2d. Expedition. Parryi" (GH!). The specimen at GH consists of a solitary mature fruit. No material has been found in the Torrey herbarium at NY.

***Astragalus preussii* A. Gray**, Proc. Amer. Acad. 6: 222. 1864. (2nd)
Protologue locality: "Banks of the Rio Virgen, a tributary of the Colorado in Nevada, near the eastern borders of California, in loose saline soil. Frémont, in second expedition, 1844. A well-marked species, named in memory of Frémont's able assistant in all his earlier explorations, Mr. Charles Preuss." Type: "Astragalus Preussii, n. sp. Banks of the Rio Virgen, California. Loose saline soil May 3rd, 1844. Frémont's 2nd Exped." (holotype NY-Torrey!: microfiche BRY!; isotype fragments (GH!)). Frémont was at the springs at Las Vegas, Clark County, Nevada, on 3 May 1844! The material at GH has the notation "leaflet, flower & legume from Hb. Torrey (Frémont's 2nd Expn.) A. Preussii, n. sp." Undoubtedly Gray was aware of the death of Preuss a decade prior to the actual naming of the species in his honor.

Astragalus spatulatus Sheldon
"Frémont's 2nd Expedition" (GH!). This is mounted on a sheet with presumed isotypes of *Homalobus brachylobus, H. caespitosus*, and *H. canescens* of Nuttall.

Astragalus tridactylicus A. Gray
"Frémont's 3rd Exped. No. 212, 1845. Arkansas River" (NY-Torrey!). Annotated by R. C. Barneby! Frémont was along the Arkansas in Colorado through most of August 1845.

Astragalus utahensis (Torr.) Torr. & A. Gray includes (?) *Phaca*
Frémont (1845: 156).

Atriplex argentea Nutt.
Three sheets NY-Torrey!: "FExRM, 1842. Atriplex argentea *Nutt.* Upper Platte, 'Cache Camp,' 28 July [1842. Near Evansville, Natrona County, Wyoming]"; and "FExCal, 97, 1845. Obione argentea? But the leaves are deltoid & toothed? Upper Missouri or Platte. Annual." The July 28 specimen is mounted with "Obione argentea *Moq.* 280 Geyer. Torr. & Gray, Flora, N. Amer. Upper Missouri. Nicollet, 1839."

***Atriplex breweri* S. Wats.**, Proc. Amer. Acad. 9: 119. 1874. (2nd) = *A. lentiformis* (Torr.) S. Wats.

Protologue locality: "Frémont; 459 Torrey; 75 Brewer." Type: "Frémont's 2nd Expedn. Atriplex Breweri S. Wats." (syntype NY-Torrey!).

Atriplex canescens (Pursh) Nutt.

"45, 94, 204, 211, 433 Frémont" (Watson, 1874: 120). Five sheets (NY Torrey!): "FExCal, 1845–47, Frémont 96, 209 (Sunday July 27th), 1845 [five days' journey east of Bent's Fort, Colorado]. Obione canescens *Moq.*"; "FExCal, 1845–47, 454, 33, 1845"; "Frémont 94, 211, 1845"; "FExCal, 1845–7, 433, 45, 1845, between Bent's Fort & Upper Pueblo [i.e., Otero, Crawley, or Pueblo cos, Colorado, 16–20 August 1845]"; and "Frémont 1845." The final specimen is mounted with three stems of *A. tridentata* Kuntze taken on 15 September 1850 by Howard Stansbury. Two sheets GH!: "Frémont's 2nd Exped. [a single stem with leaves and staminate flowers]" and "FExCal, 1845–7. 45, 1845 [mounted on a sheet with two stems by Hall and Harbour taken in 1862]." "FExCal, 1845–7. No. 24 [?], 1845" (MO!).

Atriplex confertifolia (Torr. & Frém.) S. Wats.

"24, 761, 767 Frémont" (Watson, 1874: 119). "FExCal, 1845–47[1845]"; and "Frémont's 2nd Expedn." (both NY-Torrey!). Both specimens are cited again under *Obione confertifolia*, q.v. "Frémont" (NY-LeRoy!). The specimen at NY LeRoy consists of a sprig of an early flowering staminate plant. It is mounted on the same sheet with a pistillate specimen of *A. polycarpa*. "FExCal, 1845–7. 24. 1845. Obione" (US!). "FEx Cal, 1845–7. 24. 1845. A. confertifolia. Shores of Utah Lake" (GH!).

Atriplex endolepis S. Wats.

"Frémont" (Watson, 1874: 120).

Atriplex gardneri (Moq.) Dietr. includes *A. nuttallii* S. Wats.

The name *A. nuttallii* is an illegitimate substitute for *A. gardneri*, which Watson found objectionable, it being an orthographic variant. He included specimens from several different species, as the genus is currently understood, within the concept of *A. nuttallii.*

Atriplex hymenelytra (Torr.) S. Wats. includes *Obione hymenelytra* Torr., q.v.

"Frémont" (Watson, 1874: 120). Two sheets NY-Torrey!: "Frémont's 2nd Expedn. [probably from the Mohave of California or Nevada]" and "Frémont's [4th] Expedn. California, Gila [1849]." The sheets are cited again and discussed under *Obione hymenelytra.*

Atriplex nuttallii S. Wats. = *A. gardneri* (Moq.) Dietr.

"Frémont" (Watson, 1874: 116).

Atriplex polycarpa (Torr.) S. Wats. includes *Obione polycarpa* Torr.

"Frémont" (NY-LeRoy!). There is a second sheet at NY-LeRoy! that has a branch of a staminate specimen of *A. confertifolia* (q.v.).

Atriplex powellii S. Wats.

"Frémont 621, 1843. On the Sweet Water. Aug. 'Can this be a state of Obione argentea?'" (NY-Torrey!). The specimen "621 Frémont" was included initially, at least under *A. argentea* (Watson, 1874: 115).

Baeria chrysostoma Fisch. & Mey.

"FExCal, 1845–7. 169, 1846. Burrielia gracilis. DC." (GH!; a second sheet GH-Lowell!). "California, Frémont. 1849. Style app. truncato-capitata absque setula" (GH!).

Baeria fremontii (Torr.) A. Gray includes *Dichaeta fremontii* Torr. ex A. Gray

"Frémont" (Watson, 1880 1: 377).

Baeria minor (DC.) Ferris includes *Lasthenia minor* (DC.) Ornduff

Bahia dissecta (A. Gray) Rydb. includes *Amauria dissecta* A. Gray

***Bahia lanata* var. *grandiflora* A. Gray**, Bot. Calif. 1: 381. 1876. (3rd) ≡ *Eriophyllum lanatum* var. *grandiflorum* (A. Gray) Jepson

Protologue locality: no type information was given by Gray, i.e., it is the Frémont material by inference. Type: "FExCal, 333, 1846. 'April 25. Frequent along road.' Probably on Antelope Creek, a tributary of the Sacramento River, Calif'" (isotype NY-Torrey!: microfiche BRY!). The Frémont party was probably at Bear Creek, east of Redding, Shasta County, California, on 25 April 1846.

Baileya multiradiata Harv. & A. Gray

"Interior of California near Hernandez' [Resting] Spring, Frémont [Inyo County, California, 29 April 1844]" (Gray, 1849: 106). "FExCal, 1849. Baileya multiradiata Harv. & Gray" (NY-Torrey!). The notation "multiradiata Harv. & Gray" appears to be in Rydberg's handwriting; the specimen bears the stamp "Examined for North American Flora," typical of specimens examined by Rydberg.

***Baileya multiradiata* Harv. & A. Gray var. *nudicaulis* A. Gray**, Syn. Fl. N. Amer. 1(2): 318. 1884. (2nd) ≡ *B. multiradiata* Harv. & A. Gray

Protologue locality: "*Baileya multiradiata*, Harv. & Gray, l.c., mainly.—Same range or more southern. (adj. Mex.)." Type: "Frémont's 2nd Exped., 1844. Baileya (DC.) nudicaulis" (isotype NY-Torrey!: microfiche BRY!). The writing on the label appears to be that of Asa Gray.

Balsam pine = *Abies* sp.

Frémont (1845: 180).

***Balsamorhiza bolanderi* A. Gray**, Proc. Amer. Acad. 7: 356. 1868. (3rd) ≡ *Wyethia bolanderi* (A. Gray) W. Weber

Protologue locality: "Shady hillsides, at Auburn, April, 1865, Bolander. [This, as now appears, was collected in 1844 by Frémont on the Upper Sacramento, and later by Major Rich.]." Type: "FExCal, 1843–4. No. 7. 1844. March 12th. Balsamorhiza ovata—a new species" (syntype NY-Torrey!). The Frémont specimen was taken while the party was recuperating and refitting at their camp at the mouth of the American Fork River, Sacramento River, Sacramento County, California. The brackets in the above quote are as they appeared in the protologue, not editorial comments.

Balsamorhiza deltoidea Nutt. var. *glabrescens* (Benth.) Torr.
"This was also collected by Frémont in his second journey, and is mentioned in the account of some new Compositae of that collection (in Bost. Jour. Nat. Hist.) as a new Balsamorhiza, if not a form of B. deltoidea" (Torrey, 1857: 103).

Balsamorhiza hookeri Nutt. var. *neglecta* (W. Sharp) Cronq.
"FExCal, 1843–4. 553, 1844. Balsamorhiza incana" (NY-Torrey!). The tentative identification of the specimen was verified by W. M. Sharp, who annotated the sheet in 1934. The Frémont number 553 fits within a sequence of numbers that appear to have come from the Uinta Basin of Utah. The var. *neglecta* simulates *B. incana* in having densely woolly-villous involucres. The variety is locally common in both Duchesne and Uintah counties, through which Frémont and party passed on 1–5 June 1844.

Balsamorhiza macrophylla Nutt.
"FExCal, 1845–7. 282. 1846. Balsamorhiza macrocephala *Nutt.*" (NY-Torrey!). Above the label is a penciled note: "Named by Dr. Gray.—but—I find not the name in any of Nuttall's papers. J. T." Where this specimen came from, and whether it was taken on the third expedition, is open to question. The specimen is in spring flowering condition, and might have come from northern Utah—on the second, not the third, expedition.

Balsamorhiza sagittata ≡ *B. sagittata* (Pursh) Nutt.
"Wind River mountains [1842. Sublette County, Wyoming]" (Torrey, 1843: 87). "Balsamorhiza sagittata. *Nutt.* Torr. & A. Gray, Flora, N. Amer. Rky Mts. Frémont" (NY-Torrey!). "FExCal, 1843–4. 580. 1844. Balsamorhiza—'helianthoides or sagittata' *A.Gr.*" (NY-Torrey!).

Baptisia leucantha ≡ *B. leucantha* Torr. & A. Gray
"Kansas river [1842]" (Torrey, 1843: 85).

Barbarea orthoceras Ledeb.
"FExCal, 224, 1845. Barbarea vulgaris [crossed out] praecox" (NY-Torrey! and GH!). The sheet at GH has a second collection: "FExCal, 1845–7. Rr. 1846" (GH!).

Batschia Gmelini = *Lithospermum carolinense* (Walt.) MacMillan
"Little Blue river of the Kansas [1842. On 21 or 22 June]" (Torrey, 1843: 85). "FExRM, 1842, June 20 [probably Marshall County, Kansas], on the Platte" (NY-Torrey!). On 22 June 1842 Frémont was on the Big Blue River of the Kansas, probably in Jefferson County, Nebraska.

Beckmannia eruciformis = *B. syzigachne* (Steud.) Fern.
"North fork of the Platte. July 22 [1842. Mouth of La Bonte Creek, near Orin, Converse County, Wyoming]" (Torrey, 1843: 94). "FExRM, 1842" (GH-Thurber!).

Beckmannia syzigachne (Steud.) Fern. includes *Beckmannia eruciformis*

Beloperone californica Benth.

As *Sericographis californica* (Torrey, 1859: 125) in "Southern part of California; Frémont." "Along the southeastern borders of the State [California] (*Frémont*,)" (Brewer et al., 1876: 589). "FExCal, 1849. Sericographis Californica. Returning from California—probably collected in N. Mex. or Sonora" (NY-Torrey!). The note on the sheet at NY is in error, the specimen having been taken on the route to California. It is mounted on a sheet with specimens taken by Thurber and Newberry. "Spec. Frémont. 1849. ex Hb. Torr." (GH!). The Frémont fragments are in an envelope mounted on a sheet with collections by E. L. Greene, Kellogg, and George Thurber.

Berberis aquifolium = *Mahonia repens* (Lindley) G. Don

(Torrey, 1843: 83). "Berberis Aquifolium, *Ph.* Frémont's 2nd Expedn.," "FExCal, 1845–7. 345. 1846. Berberis aquifolium," and "Berberis Aquifolium. Frémont 530, 1844. Utah Lake [Utah County, Utah], May 20 (Rocky places)" (all three NY-Torrey!). Either the date 20 May or the locality Utah Lake is in error. Frémont was at Utah Lake on 24, 25, 26 May 1844; on 20 May he was south of Fillmore, Millard County, Utah.

***Berberis fremontii* Torr.**, Rep. U.S. Mex. Bound., Bot. 30. 1859. (2nd) = *Mahonia fremontii* (Torr.) Fedde

Protologue locality: "This species was first discovered by Frémont, in 1844, on the tributaries of the Rio Virgen, in southern Utah." Type: "Berberis trifoliata [crossed out] *Moric.*? pinnata, *Lag.* [crossed out]. Fremontii n. sp. Tributaries of the Virgin River. May. 5 feet high. Frémont's 2nd Exped. 432, 1844" (holotype NY-Torrey!). This plant, strikingly adorned with clusters of yellow flowers in springtime, was probably collected on or near the Muddy River, Clark County, Nevada.

Berberis trifoliata Moricand. = *Mahonia fremontii* (Torr.) Fedde

"Colonel Frémont found it on the tributaries of the Virgin River" (Torrey, 1856: 64).

Berula erecta (Huds.) Cov. var. *incisum* (Torr.) Cronq. includes *Sium* (?) *incisum*

Betula glandulosa ≡ *B. glandulosa* Michx.

"On a lake in the Wind River mountains. Aug. 12–17 [1842. Sublette County, Wyoming]" (Torrey, 1843: 93). "FExRM, 1842. Betula glandulosa (nana)" (NY-Torrey!). "FExCal, 1845–7. 393. 1845. Betula glandulosa Michx." (GH! and NY-Torrey!); the NY specimen bears the additional information "Valley of the Klamath. Common"; the correct year is, therefore, probably 1846.

Betula occidentalis ≡ *B. occidentalis* Hook.

"On a lake in the Wind River mountains. Aug. 12–17 [1842. Sublette County, Wyoming]" (Torrey, 1843: 93). "FExRM, 1842. Wind River Mountains. Betula occidentalis, *Hook.* [crossed out], fontinalis Sargent" and "Frémont's 2nd Expedn. 483. 1844" (both NY-Torrey!). "Frémont's 2d Expedition. (Torrey). 'B. alba. var. papyracea humilis' Regel!" (GH!).

Bidens connata ≡ *B. connata* Muhl.
"Upper Platte [1842]" (Torrey, 1843: 87).

***Blitum californicum* S. Wats.**, Proc. Amer. Acad. 9: 101. 1874. (2nd) ≡ *Chenopodium californicum* (S. Wats.) S. Wats.
Protologue locality: "California, from the Sacramento to Fort Tejon and San Diego." Type: "Frémont's 2nd Exped. Pericarp adhering to the seed. Seed vertical [other notes illegible]. Blitum. seems different from rubrum" (syntype NY-Torrey!). "Coulter; Frémont; Bigelow; Parry; Torrey; 104 Xantus; 244, 1065 Brewer; 448 Cooper; 855 Kellogg & Harford" (Watson, 1874: 101).

Box elder = *Acer negundo* L.
Frémont (1845: 21).

Braya (Torrey, 1843: 83) = *Smelowskia calycina* C. A. Meyer in Ledeb.

Brickellia grandiflora ≡ *B. grandiflora* (Hook.) Nutt.
"North fork of the Platte. Sept. 4 [1842. West of Scotts Bluff, Scotts Bluff County, Wyoming]" (Torrey, 1843: 86). "Brickellia grandiflora, Torr. & Gray, Flora, N. Amer. N. Fork of Platte, Frémont [1842, probably as cited above]" (NY-Torrey!).

Brodiaea californica Lindley
"FExCal, 1845–7[1846]. Brodiaea grandiflora—var. elatior, floribus majoribus, *Benth.*" (GH!). "Brodiaea. Frémont. 1846. California" (NY-Torrey!). The latter sheet has attached a typical drawing of anthers and pistils by Torrey.

Brodiaea elegans Hoover
"Denny's Creek [Klamath Lake, Klamath County, Oregon, 6 May 1846], 486, 1846. Frémont. Triteleia laxa [both crossed out] Brodiaea. 'The root is cooked by the Indians'" (NY-Torrey!). The specimen is accompanied by an excellent diagnostic drawing of floral parts by Torrey.

Brodiaea hyacinthina (Lindley) Baker
"FExCal, 319. 1846. Hesperoscordium lacteum *Lindl.* Allium. San Joachin & Sacramento Vallies" (NY-Torrey!). An original tag is attached: "Flowers white. Prairies between Sacramento and San Joaquin." Additionally there is an attached sheet of Torrey's sketches of flowers and floral parts.

Brodiaea lutea (Lindley) Mort.
"FExCal, 1843–4. 395 & 429, 1846" (NY-Torrey!).

***Brodiaea multiflora* Benth.**, Pl. Hartw. 339. 1857. (2nd) = *Triteleia grandiflora* Lindley
Protologue locality: "In valle Sacrament. Huc referenda specimina Jefroyana, n. 1125, Frémontiana, n. 225." Type: "Frémont's 3rd Exped., 225, 1844 [1846?] (=222), Provost's Fork, Utah Lake. Brodiaea multiflora, *Benth. pl. Hartw.* B. parviflora Torr." (syntype NY-Torrey!; GH!). The specimen at GH has the notation "225, 1845," but it lacks the detail on the Torrey specimen at NY. Under his discussion of *B. grandiflora*, Torrey (1857:

149) notes: "The same plant was collected also by Colonel Frémont on Utah Lake." Despite the dates 1844 and 1845 on the labels, the collection was undoubtedly taken in 1846 in northern California. The specimens are in full flower, consistent with the spring flowering time of Frémont's visit to northern California in 1846. Frémont's numbered specimens sometimes give a clue as to collection locality, even though they are far from absolute in making determinations. Number 225 fits within the 1846 number sequence along with several geographically misplaced specimens, i.e., 218 *Camissonia graciliflora* (labeled from Bent's Fort) and 222 *Lomatium dasycarpum* (with label information from Utah Lake, Utah and Piney Creek, Colorado). All were collected in northern California in the modern sense.

Brodiaea peduncularis S. Wats.
"Collected by Douglas, Frémont, and in Lake County by Dr. Torrey" (Watson, 1880, 2: 155).

Bromus ciliatus ≡ *B. ciliatus* L.
"On the Platte. June–Aug. [1842]" (Torrey, 1843: 94).

Bryoria fremontii (Tuckerman) Brodo & D. Hawksworth includes *Alectoria fremontii* Tuckerman

Buchloe dactyloides (Nutt.) Engelm. includes *Sesleria dactyloides*

Bur-clover = *Medicago*?
Frémont (1848: 17).

Burrielia fremontii (Torr.) Benth. includes *Dichaeta fremontii* Torr. ex A. Gray

Cacalia tuberosa = *C. plantaginea* (Raf.) Shinners
"Upper Platte [1842]" (Torrey, 1843: 88). "Cacalia tuberosa. Platte, 22 June 1842 [near Powell, Jefferson County, Nebraska]. Frémont." (NY-Torrey!).

Calandrina ciliata (R. & P.) DC. var. *menziesii* (Hook.) Macbr.
"FExCal, 160, 1846. March 2nd. Calandrina Menziesii" (NY-Torrey!).

***Calliachyris* Torr. & A. Gray** in A. Gray, Boston J. Nat. Hist. 5: 110. 1845. (2nd)
Type species: ***Calliachyris fremontii* Torr. & A. Gray** in A. Gray ≡ *Layia fremontii* (Torr. & A. Gray) A. Gray
Type locality: "Mr. Frémont gathered the plant in the mountains of California in March." Type: "FExCal, 88. 1844. Layia fremontii, Gray, in Fendl. pl. p. (note). *Calliachris Frémontii Gray* in Bost. jour. nat. hist." (holotype NY-Torrey!: microfiche BRY!). A notation "Calliachris Fremontii" is written on a small piece of paper glued above the printed label at NY. The holotype is mounted on a sheet with a collection by Mr. Rich and 318 of Frémont (see citation under *Layia*). There is a sheet at GH, probably by Frémont, that bears the following information: "Her. A. Gray. Calliachyris Fremontii. Layia (55. Calliachyris)." Below the label is the name "Calliachyris Fremontii Torr. & Gr." All notations are in Gray's writing.

Callirhoe alcaeoides (Michx.) A. Gray

"Frémont's 3rd Exp. C. macrorhiza—ined. M. pedata var? umbellulata—[and other notes partially illegible]. Torr. & Gray, Fl. N. Amer. No. 54. Open prairie, July 8th, near Santa Fe road [Kansas, 1845]" (NY-Torrey!). The information starting with the "No. 54" is recorded on a narrow strip of paper, evidently Frémont's method of transmitting locality data to Torrey. The huge entourage moved west along the Santa Fe Road to the vicinity of the Smoky Hill Fork of the Kansas, which they ascended to Colorado. No map of the early part of the journey was published, and it is not known where they were on particular dates. The treatment by Dorr (1990) is instructive as regards the species of *Callirhoë*.

Callirhoe involucrata (Torr. & A. Gray) A. Gray includes *Malva involucrata*.

"I have for several years had this handsome species in cultivation in the Cambridge Botanic Garden, from seeds taken from specimens gathered by Col. Frémont. It forms a very large root, which stands the winter well in the open air. The showy flowers are cherry-red with a tinge of purple, deeper colored and one third smaller than in C. Papaver, and are produced from spring until late in Autumn. On prolonged flowering stems the upper leaves are abortive, and a membranaceous bract, formed of the two united stipules, subtends the peduncle" (Gray, 1849: 17). "Malva involucrata. Bot. Garden Cambridge, 1845. Dr. Gray. Seeds from Frémont" (NY-Torrey!). "Malva involucrata. Frémont. Bot. Gard. 1846" (GH- Thurber!).

Callirhoe involucrata (Torr. & A. Gray) A. Gray var. *lineariloba* (Torr. & A. Gray) A. Gray

"Frémont's 3rd Exped. Var. of Malva involucrata" (GH!).

Callirhoe pedata (Nutt.) A. Gray includes *C. digitata* sensu A. Gray non Nutt.

Calocedrus decurrens (Torr.) Florin includes *Libocedrus decurrens* Torr.

This is probably the "tall cedar" noted by Frémont (1845: 233).

Calochortus kennedyi Porter

"Frémont's 2nd Exp. No. 402, 1844. Rocky bed of a creek on the upper part of Mohave River. May 1, 1844" (NY-Torrey!). Either the date or the provenance is in error. On 1 May the Frémont party was in the Charleston Mountains, Clark County, Nevada.

Calochortus luteus Dougl. ex Lindley

"Calochortus luteus? Frémont's 3rd Exped. No. 433, 1846. Near Peter Lassen's. Northern California [i.e., Tehama County, California]," "FExCal, 209, 213 } 27 March 1846. Oak plains & open uplands of the Feather River [Yuba County, California] = 1981 *Hartweg*" and "FExCal, 321. 1846. Calochortus. Upper Sacramento. 'Pet. yellow, with a blood red spot on the inside'" (all three collections NY-Torrey!). A badly stained watercolor, bearing the label "433, 1846, Frémont. Calochortus luteus? Near Peter Lassen's, May 26, 1846," marked "Stanley" is also at NY. "FExCal, 1845–7. 360. 1846" (GH!). The sheet at GH is annotated as *C. luteus* × *superbus* by Marion Ownbey in June 1939.

Calochortus monophyllus (Lindley) Lem.
"FExCal, 353. 1846. April 27. Calochortus nitidus [both crossed out]. Along the road, on a small stream, at head of Lower Valley of Sacramento [probably Bear Creek, near Redding, Shasta County, California]. 'Inside of petals entirely covered with moss-like hairs; yellow'" (NY-Torrey!). "FExCal, 1845–7. 353. 1846" (GH!). The sheet bearing the number 353 at GH is annotated as *C. luteus* Douglas ex Lindley by Marion Ownbey in June 1939. Undoubtedly the annotation is correct. "FExCal, 1845–7. Hhhh [crossed out] 1845 [1846]. 321" (GH!). This sheet is unquestionably *C. monophyllus.*

Calochortus nuttallii Torr.
"Frémont's 2nd Expedn. 541. 1844" (NY-Torrey!).

Calochortus superbus Purdy ex Howell
"FExCal, 332, 419, 1846. Calochortus venustus, *Dougl.*" (NY-Torrey!).

Calochortus venustus Dougl. ex Benth.
"FExCal, 1849" (NY!).

Caltha leptosepala DC.
"Frémont's 2nd Expedn." (NY-Torrey!).

***Calycadenia fremontii* A. Gray** in Torr. Rep. U.S. Mex. Bound., Bot. 100. 1859. (3rd)
Protologue locality: "California, (the particular station not recorded;) Col. Frémont." Type: "Frémont's Expedition to California 1845–7. Calycadenia Frémontii sp. nov." [holotype NY-Torrey! (annotated type by D. D. Keck in 1935); microfiche BRY!, 2 sheets NY and 1 NY Crooke; isotype GH! (annotated as isotype by D. D. Keck in 1935), two sheets; isotype US!]. The one sheet at GH is labeled "L. 1846." A second sheet at GH (Thurber!) lacks any detailed locality information, but bears several notations: "Some fl. leaves with glands at tip; others not. Connects with Osmadenia Nutt. Hemizonia (Calycadenia) Frémontii. Calycadenia Frémontii. n. sp. = H. multiglandulosa var. sparsa" (all in the writing of Asa Gray). "Known only from the vicinity of Chico, Butte County, California" (Abrams & Ferris, 1960: 190). "Frémont" as *Hemizonia fremontii* A. Gray (Watson, 1880, 1: 365). Frémont was at Lassen's on Deer Creek, Tehama (adjacent to Butte) County, California, and vicinity from late March to 5 April, 11–20 April, and 22–25 May 1846.

Calycadenia multiglandulosa DC.
"FExCal, 505, 1846. Calycadenia cephalotes DC. Hemizonia multiglandulosa Gray var. cephalotes" (NY!; microfiche BRY!; GH!; GH-Lowell!). "FExCal, 1845–7 [1846]. Calycadenia cephalotes, DC? 'A stumpy form' AGray" (NY-Torrey!). The latter specimen is mounted on a sheet with one by John L. Le Conte from "Southern Upper California."

***Calycadenia pauciflora* A. Gray** in Torr. Rep. U.S. Mex. Bound., Bot. 100. 1859. (3rd)
Protologue locality: "California; Col. Frémont." Type: "FExCal, 1845–7 [1846]. Calycadenia uniradiata n. sp." (holotype GH!; isotypes NY-Torrey!, microfiche BRY!, 3 sheets; NY-Crooke!; GH-Lowell!; US!). The holotype specimen at GH is labeled "W.

1846," and bears the notations "Ray only one. Disk fl. 3. Hemizonia (Calyc.) pauciflora. Calycadenia pauciflora n.sp." in Gray's writing. "California. Collected by Frémont" (Abrams, 1951: 190).

Calycadenia tenella (Nutt.) Torr. & A. Gray
"FExCal, 1845–7. May 1, 1846 [Clear Lake, Modoc County, California]. 380(a). Headwaters of the Sacramento. Calycadenia tenella? larger than usual. J. T." (NY-Torrey!). A pencil notation, probably by Gray, is also on the label, "380(a) 1846. Gray."

Calycanthus occidentalis Hook. & Arn.
"FExCal, 1845–7. 494, 1846. Calycanthus occidentalis" (NY-Torrey!; GH!; MO!).

Calylophus serrulatus (Nutt.) Raven includes *O. serrulata* Nutt.

Calyptridium monandrum Nutt. in Torr. & Gray
"FExCal, 1843–4. Calyptridium monandrum, *Nutt.*" (NY-Torrey!). This is a rather common plant of the Mohave Desert tracts traversed by Frémont in April and early May of 1844. The sheet is mounted with collections by Nuttall and Newberry.

Calyptridium umbellatum (Torr.) Greene includes *Spraguea umbellata* Torr.

Calystegia sepium ≡ *C. sepium* (L.) R. Br.
"Forks of the Platte. July 2 [1842. Lincoln County, Nebraska]" (Torrey, 1843: 90). "*Frémont's Exp. to the Wind River Mts.* Calystegia sepium. July 2, 1842" (NY-Torrey!). "Calystegia. Turkey Creek. Frémont's 3d Expedn. 108. 11 July 1845" (MO!).

Campanula rotundifolia ≡ *Campanula rotundifolia* L.
"Lower Platte [1842]" (Torrey, 1843: 88).

Camissonia bistorta (Nutt.) Raven includes *Oenothera gauraeflora*
"FExCal, 1849. Oenothera gauraeflora" (NY-Torrey!). "Frémont 172, 1845, in part" (GH!). The species is endemic to southern California and northern Baja California.

Camissonia boothii (Dougl.) Raven subsp. *alyssoides* (Hook. & Arn.) Raven includes *Oenothera alyssoides* Hook. & Arn.
"Oenothera. Ex herb. Torrey—Frémont" (GH!). The specimen was annotated by P. H. Raven in 1966–67.

Camissonia boothii (Dougl.) Raven subsp. *desertorum* (Munz) Raven
"Frémont's 2nd Exped. Oe. alyssoides, *H. & A.* Sandy uplands of the Mohave River. April 24 [San Bernardino County, California], 337, 1844" (NY-Torrey!). There are two specimens on the sheet annotated by Sereno Watson as (A) *O. gauraeflora* and (B) *O. alyssoides*. The former has denticulate leaves and the latter has entire ones. Both are within the range of subspecies *desertorum*, and both were annotated as such by P. H. Raven in 1964. The subspecies is a southern California endemic.

Camissonia breviflora (Torr. & A. Gray) Raven includes *Oenothera nuttallii* Torr. & Gray

Camissonia campestris (Greene) Raven
"166, 1844 [Frémont's 2nd Expedition]. n. sp. Gr. Probably Oe. Dentata" (NY-Torrey!). "FExCal, 172. 1846. cf Oe. dentata" (GH!). The species is a California endemic, from the Bay region southward.

Camissonia claviformis (Torr. & Frém.) Raven includes *Oenothera claviformis* Torr. & Frém.

Camissonia claviformis (Torr. & Frém.) Raven subsp. *aurantiaca* (S. Wats.) Raven includes *Oenothera scapoidea* var. *aurantaica* S. Wats.
"FExCal, 1849. Oenothera (Chylismia) clavaeformis" (NY-Torrey!). The subspecies is restricted to western Arizona, southern California, and southern Nevada. Likely the specimen cited was taken in southern California.

Camissonia contorta (Dougl.) Kearney
"FExCal, 1843–4 [struck out] 5. 219" (GH!). The specimens (mounted with those of Lyall, Macoun, Spalding, and Suckley) are annotated by Peter H. Raven.

Camissonia dentata (Cav.) Reiche includes *Oenothera dentata* Cav.

Camissonia graciliflora (Hook. & Arn.) Raven
"FExCal, 1845. 218. R. graciliflora var." (GH!; NY!). The specimen at NY-Torrey has the following data: "Oenothera graciliflora *Hook. & Arn.* 'Shorter tube to calyx' Gray. Arkansas River, above Pueblo, mouth of Canyon." The party was at Fountain Creek on 20 August and two days west of there on 22 August, when probably in the vicinity of Canon, Pueblo County, Colorado. The NY-Torrey specimen is mounted on a sheet with the Nuttall type.

Camissonia micrantha (Hornem.) Raven includes *Oenothera micrantha* Hornem. ex Spreng.

Camissonia ovata (Nutt.) Raven includes *Oenothera ovata* Nutt. ex Torr. & A. Gray

Cardamine angulata Hook.
"FExCal, 1845–7. 151 & 154, 1846. Feb. 23, Cardamine angulata? Summit of Coast mountains [Wildcat Ridge, Santa Cruz County, California], in rich soil" (NY-Torrey!).

Cardamine cordifolia A. Gray
"FExCal, 429, 1845. Cardamine cordifolia. Gray, Pl. Fendl. [Mem. Amer. Acad. 4: 9. 1849] 4 or 5th camp beyond Bent's Fort [19 or 20 August 1845, probably Pueblo County, Colorado]" (NY-Torrey!).

Carduus leucographis = ?
Observed on 25 June 1842, a day's travel south of the Platte, probably in Adams County, Nebraska.

Carex atrata ≡ *C. atrata* L.
"Alpine region of the Wind River mountains, near perpetual snow. Aug. 15 [1842. Sublette County, Wyoming]" (Torrey, 1843: 94).

Carex aurea ≡ *C. aurea* Nutt.
"Little Blue river of the Kansas. June 22 [1842. Near Powell, Jefferson County, Nebraska]" (Torrey, 1843: 94). "Carex aurea *Nutt.* Frémont's 1st Exp." (NY!).

Carex barbarae Dewey includes *C. sitchensis*

Carex festucacea ≡ *C. festucacea* Schkuhr.
"On the Kansas. June [1842]" (Torrey, 1843: 94).

Carex panicea = ?
"Alpine region of the Wind River mountains, near perpetual snow. Aug. 15 [1842. Sublette County, Wyoming]" (Torrey, 1843: 94).

Carex sitchensis = *C. barbarae* Dewey
Frémont (1845: 258; 1887: 367).

***Carpenteria* Torr.**, Smiths. Contr. 6(2): 12. 1853. (3rd)
Type species: ***Carpenteria californica* Torr.**
Protologue locality: "Sierra Nevada of California, probably on the head waters of the San Joachin [Joaquin]." Type: "FExCal, 1845–47. Carpenteria Californica Torr." (holotype NY-Torrey!; isotype GH!). While Torrey states that the material came from the headwaters of the "San Joachin," the collection locality is actually at Grapevine Spring, Fresno County, California (fide Spence, 1984). A sheet containing drawing and analysis accompanies the type specimen (Figures 17 and 19). Frémont was on King's River, Fresno County, California, in late December 1845 and early January 1846. I have been unable to determine when he was along that river later in 1846. The plant blooms in June and July. However, the specimens forming the basis of the genus and species are in fruit. "The only specimens of this plant brought home by Colonel Frémont, were in fruit; but I found attached to them a few withered and imperfect flowers. These materials, however, were sufficient to show the essential characters of nearly all the organs" (Torrey, 1853: 13). The label of the specimen at GH contains the notes: "Only 3 specms. of this—all poor. Flower in a loose term. panicle," in Gray's writing, and "Pubescence of 2 kinds; one of longer straight, somewhat barbed hairs—the other of short crisped hairs. Cal. valvate. Cor. imbricate (pet. 5) Stam. 5 or more. Leaves opposite, entire, no stipules. Caps. 4–8-celled, septicidal; exocarp separating from the endocarp. Cells 2-seeded; seeds collat. anatrop?," in Torrey's writing.

Carum gairdneri ≡ *Perideridia gairdneri* (Hook. & Arn.) Mathias

***Carum kelloggii* A. Gray**, Proc. Amer. Acad. 7: 43. 1868. (3rd) = *Perideridia oregana* (S. Wats.) Mathias
Protologue locality: "California near the coast: San Jose, Brewer (8320; Oakland, Bolander; Bolinas, Dr. Kellogg. [Also collected, I find, by Frémont, in 1846, only in

flower, but with thick farinaceous roots, as in *C. Gairdneri*]." Type: "FExCal, 1845–7. 487, 1846" (syntype GH!). The sheet is annotated as "Carum Kellogii Gray." A modern annotation label affixed by Chuang and Constance identifies the material as *Perideridia oregana* (S. Wats.) Mathias. "FExCal, 1845–7. 487. 184[6]5. Edosmia Gardneri. Upper Sacramento, May 22. The Indians use the roots as food & collect them in considerable quantities" (syntype NY-Torrey!, mounted on sheet with a Nuttall specimen).

Carya tomentosa Nutt.?
"No. 24. Near the Creek. July 3d, 1845 [near Santa Fe Road, Kansas]. Frémont's 3rd Expedn. 1845–7" (NY-Torrey!).

Cassia chamaecrista ≡ *C. chamaechrista* L.
"Mouth of the Platte. Sept. 30 [1842. Sarpy or Cass cos., Nebraska" (Torrey, 1843: 85).

Castilleja affinis Hook. & Arn.
"FExCal, 1845–7. 114. 1845" and "FExCal, 1845–7. 327. 1846. C. affinis" (both GH!; No. 327 also MO!).

Castilleja chromosa A. Nels.
"FExCal, 1845–7. 474. 1846" (GH!). The specimen is annotated as *C. chromosa* A. Nels. by N. H. Holmgren, 1967.

Castilleja flava S. Wats.
"5 Aug. River bottom, upper Sweetwater. Frémont's 1st Exp." (NY-Torrey!). The sheet is annotated as Castilleja flava S. Wats by F. W. P[ennell] 1921. Presumably Pennell also wrote the note in pencil on the sheet: "[on August 5, 1842, Frémont was along the North Platte River in Carbon Co., Wyoming, see Report p. 322.]." The map of the expedition, however, shows the party at a locality in Frémont County, Wyoming, on that date.

Castilleja latifolia Hook. & Arn.
"FExCal, 1845–7. Cccc 1846. Castilleja latifolia *H. & Arn.* Gr[ay]" (NY-Torrey!). The label also contains a cryptic penciled note: "Uncertain whether this belongs to the Frémont specimens or to another plant."

***Castilleja linariifolia* Benth.** in DC., Prodr. 10: 532. 1846. (1st)
Protologue locality: "in montibus Scopulosis (Frémont!). (v.s. herb. Torrey)." Type: "FexRM 1842. Aug. 25–31. Castilleja linariaefolia Benth. Named by Bentham" (holotype NY!, and two paratypes, one dated as for the holotype, the other is dated "13–14 Aug."; microfiche BRY!; isotype GH!). F. W. Pennell placed a note on one of the sheets at NY stating: "Collected along the north slope of the Black Hills (= Laramie Mountains) in present Converse or Platte counties, Wyoming." On 25 August Frémont was near present Alcova, Natrona County, Wyoming, and on 31 August they reached Fort Laramie, Goshen County, having traversed through Converse and Platte counties. The paratype taken on 13–14 August came from the Wind River Mountains, present Sublette County, Wyoming.

Castilleja miniata = *C. rhexifolia* Rydb.

"Wind River mountains. Aug. 13–16 [1842. Sublette County, Wyoming]. There are two or three other species of this genus in the collection, which I have not been able to determine" (Torrey, 1843: 88). "FExCal, 1842. Castilleja miniata" (NY-Torrey!). The sheet is annotated by N. H. Holmgren in 1966 as *C. rhexifolia* Rydb.

Castilleja pallida = *C. sulphurea* Rydb.

"Sweet Water river. Aug. 8 [1842. Frémont County to Little Sandy Creek, Sublette County, Wyoming]" (Torrey, 1843: 88). "FexRM 1842. Aug. 13–16 [Sublette County, Wyoming]. Castilleja pallida. The specific name by Bentham" (NY-Torrey!).

Castilleja rhexifolia Rydb. includes *C. miniata*

Castilleja stenantha A. Gray, Syn. Fl. N. Amer. 2(1). 1878.

"FExCal, 1845–7. Bbbb. 1846" (GH!; MO!). This specimen is mounted on a sheet with Bigelow specimens taken in 1854 and with a stem of Hartweg 1897, the latter the presumed holotype of the species (GH!). The Hartweg material is the only specimen cited with certainty in the original description (Gray, 1878: 295).

Castilleja sulphurea Rydb. includes *C. pallida*

"FExCal, 1845–7. 361. 1845. Castilleia" (NY-Torrey!).

Ceanothus americanus var. *sanguineus* = *C. americanus* L.

"Frémont's 1st Expedn. Kansas River. Ceanothus Americanus" (NY-Torrey!). "On the Platte [1842]" (Torrey, 1843: 84).

Ceanothus cuneatus (Hook.) Nutt.

"FExCal, 1845–7. Ceanothus cuneifolius (crossed out) cuneatus. San Joaquin Valley. Abundant in thickets along the woods. March 11, 1846. Frémont [San Benito County, California]" (NY-Torrey!; BRY-Sartwell!). "263, 1844. Frémont's 2nd Exp." and "450, 1844. Frémont's 2nd Exp." (both NY-Torrey!). "FExCal, 1845–7. 211, 1846. (Ceanothus cuneatus)" (MO!).

***Ceanothus decumbens* S. Wats.**, Proc. Amer. Acad. 10: 335. 1875. (3rd) = *C. diversifolius* Kellogg

Protologue locality: "Frequent in the mountains of Central California, from the Mariposa Grove northward; collected by Frémont (n. 357), Bigelow (*C. sorediatus* of Whipple's Report, Stillman, Brewer (n. 1624), Bolander (n. 6331), and Torrey n. 69)." Type: "FExCal, 1845–7. 357. 1846" (syntypes NY-Torrey!, GH!). The specimen at NY bears the additional information "Ceanothus sorediatus Hook. Shrub 2–5 ft. Fl. blue. Upper Sacramento" and the date "April 27"; it is mounted with another collection by Frémont ("FExCal, 1845–7. Aaa. 1846. Dr. Gray") and one of some other species by C. C. Parry from the Emory Mexican Boundary Survey. On 27 April 1846 the Frémont party was at or near Bear Creek, east of present Redding, Shasta County, California.

Ceanothus diversifolius Kellogg

"FExCal, 1843–4. Ceanothus sorediatus, *Hook.*" (NY-Crooke!).

Ceanothus herbaceus Raf. includes *C. mollissimus*

Ceanothus integerrimus Hook. & Arn.
"FExCal, 1849. Ceanothus. near integerrimus" (NY-Torrey!). The "near integerrimus" is written on the label in pencil in Torrey's hand. Below the label is the notation, also by Torrey, "or var. of C. divaricatus (var. integrifolius)." The material consists of two stem fragments in flower, but with only one complete leaf. They are mounted on a sheet with a branch of *C. velutinus* Dougl. by C. C. Parry. "FExCal, 1845–7. 468, 1846" (NY!). A second sheet at NY-Torrey! has a single flowering stem. It is labeled: "FExCal, 410, 468, 1846. Ceanothus integerrimus *Hook. & Arn.* Nozah River." The plant was likely taken during the period 20–23 May 1846 near Lassen's, Tehama County, California.

Ceanothus mollissimus = *C. herbaceus* Raf.
"Near the Kansas river. June 19 [1842. Big Vermillion River, near Pottawatomi County, Kansas]" (Torrey, 1843: 84). "Frémont's 1st Expedn., June 19, 1842. Ceanothus mollissimus T. & Gr. n. sp. See Hartweg. 'Afternoon march'" (NY-Torrey!).

Ceanothus prostratus Benth.
"Colonel Frémont collected the same on the Upper Sacramento in 1846" (Torrey, 1857: 75). Four sheets (NY-Torrey!): "FExCal, 1845–7. 359. 1846. 'Ceanothus rigidus [crossed out] prostratus, with large leaves. Seems to be the same as 359, 1846, but not rooting'"; "FExCal, 1845–47. 359. 1846. Ceanothus prostratus, Benth. Upper Sacramento. 'Ceanothus prostratus Benth. β. ilicifolius, or a nearly allied species'"; and "FExCal, 461, 1846. Ceanothus prostratus, *Benth.*" "FExCal, 1845–47 [1846]. Ceanothus prostratus Benth. Pl. Hartweg. var.? ex Torrey. (359–1846) (GH-Thurber!)" and "FExCal, 1845–7. 493, 1846" (GH!).

Ceanothus cf. *thyrsiflorus* Esch.
"California. Frémont. Ex herb. J. Torrey. Ceanothus integrifolius, Torr. & Gr. Fl. N. Amer." (NY-Sartwell!); "FExCal, Bbb, 1846. Ceanothus" (NY-Torrey!).

Ceanothus velutinus ≡ *C. velutinus* Dougl.
"Summit of the Wind River mountains [1842. Sublette County, Wyoming, 13–15 August]" (Torrey, 1843: 84). "Ceanothus velutinus *Dougl.* Frémont's 1st Expedn. 1842" (NY-Torrey!).

Cedar = name assigned variously to *Juniperus, Thuja, Calocedrus*, and others.

Celtis crassifolia = *C. occidentalis* L.
"Lower Platte [1842]" (Torrey, 1843: 93; Frémont, 1845: 17).

Celtis occidentalis L. includes *C. crassifolia*

Celtis reticulata Torr.
This is the species of hackberry referred to by Frémont (1845: 150) at Pole Patch, Weber County, Utah.

Centaurium venustum (Gray) Robins.
"FExCal, 1845–7. Pppp. 1846" (GH!).

Ceratoides lanata (Pursh) J. T. Howell includes *Eurotia lanata* Pursh
"Frémont's 1st Expedition, Aug. 18–25. 1842 [Frémont and Natrona cos., Wyoming]"; "Frémont's expedition to California, 1845–7. 42, 1845" (NY-Torrey!; NY- Sartwell!; GH!; MO!). A pencil sketch illustrating details of flowers, fruit, and embryo accompanies the sheet bearing the first two specimens cited above (Figure 20).

Ceratoides lanata (Pursh) J. T. Howell var. *subspinosa* (Rydb.) J. T. Howell.
"Frémont's 2nd Expedn. Frémont 440, 1844. Eurotia lanata" (NY-Torrey!). "Frémont's 2nd Exped." (GH!).

Cerasus virginiana ≡ *Prunus virginiana* L.
"Upper North fork of the Platte. July 30 [1842. Near Alcova, Natrona County, Wyoming]" (Torrey, 1843: 85). "FexRM 1842. C. Virgin" (GH!).

Cercidium floridum Benth. ex A. Gray
"FExCal, 1849. Cercidium floridum, Torrey, not *Benth.* 'Palo verde'" (NY-Torrey!).

Cercis occidentalis Torr. ex A. Gray
"FExCal, 1845–7. No. 181. 1846. Cercis occidentalis, *Torr.* with flowers only. California," "FExCal, 1845–7. April 8th, 1846. Cercis occidentalis, *Torrey.* Between Cow Creek & the Sacramento, young leaves, flowers & young fruit [near Redding, Shasta County, California]. Young leaves, flowers & young fruit," and "FExCal, 483, 1846. Mar. [or May?] 27. Cercis occidentalis, Torr. 'Bois rouge—Frequent along streams on the upper part of the Sacramento. Saw it near Virgin River'" (all three NY-Torrey!). Specimen 483 at NY has the following notation: "*Cercis occidentalis* Torr. ex Gray (Bost. J. Nat. Hist. 6: 177. 1850) is based on C. siliquastrum. var. Benth. Pl. Hartw. no 1706, p. 307. NY has Hartweg isotype. Frémont material is mentioned in Gray's discussion but not explicitly cited or identified. Presumably this and adjoining Frémont gatherings are those Gray examined. I do not regard them as syntypes. Duane Isely, 1972." I agree with Isely. "FExCal, 1845–7. Cercis occidentalis Torr. & Gr. California" (MO!).

Cercocarpus ledifolius Nutt.
"FExCal, 1845–7. Peraphyllum ramosissimum *Nutt.* Upper Sacramento, May 20, 1846" (NY-Torrey!). On 20 May 1846 the Frémont party was at or near Lassen's, Tehama County, California. "FExCal, 1845–7. 459. 1846" (MO!). "FExCal, 1845–7. 421 & 459. 1846. Cercocarpus ledifolius Nutt. 'Mountain Privet' 'Rhubarb Tree' On the Sacramento, 22–3 May [at Lassen's, Tehama County, California], very abundant" (NY-Torrey!). "'Mountain Mahogany' of the Mormons. Recd. from Col. Frémont (in New York) August 12, 1854" (NY-Torrey!). The latter two are mounted on the same sheet at NY Torrey.

Cercocarpus montanus Raf. includes *C. parvifolius*

Cercocarpus parvifolius = *C. montanus* Raf.

"Bitter creek, North fork of the Platte. 22 July [1842. Platte County, Wyoming]" (Torrey, 1843: 85). "Cercocarpus parvifolius, *Nutt.* Frémont's 1st Expedn. 1842" and "Frémont's 2nd Exp. Kansas" (both NY-Torrey!). "Cercocarpus fothergilloides. Frémont's 2d Expedition" (MO!).

Chaenactis douglasii (Hook.) Hook. & Arn.

"FExCal, 1843–4. 789. 1843. Chaenactis achilleaefolia. Valley of Snake River, Oct. 6. 1843 [Snake River, probably Elmore County, Idaho] = Stansbury's Salt Lake plant, but not A. lutea Pl. Fend." (NY-Torrey!). The materials consist of two, vegetative basal rosettes, in keeping with the lateness of the season. They are from that portion of the trip wherein the specimens were all supposedly later lost when a mule carrying the pack of plants plunged over a precipice into a raging torrent and was killed, the pack not recovered.

***Chaenactis fremontii* A. Gray**, Proc. Amer. Acad. 19: 30. 1883. (2nd)

Protologue locality: "California. Frémont." Type: "FExCal, 357, 1844" (holotype GH!; isotype NY-Torrey!: microfiche BRY!). The label of the NY specimen has the notation in pencil below the collection number "or 359" and the name "Chaenactis Frémonti, A. Gray." The GH specimen is labeled merely "Frémont's 2nd Exped.," but bears descriptive notations by Gray.

***Chaenactis heterocarpha* Torr. & A. Gray** in A. Gray, Mem. Amer. Acad. II. 4: 98. 1849. (3rd)

Protologue locality: California, Frémont (third expedition), Hartweg (no. 1792). Type: "FExCal, 1845–7. 299, 1846. Chaenactis heterocarpha T. & Gr." (holotype NY- Torrey!: microfiche BRY!; isotype GH!). The sheet at GH has three specimens mounted on it; Frémont's, Hartweg 1792 (a paratype), and a collection by A. Gray from Chico, taken in 1885. There is a second Frémont sheet at NY-Torrey! with two plants and two numbers: "180, 1846" and "291, 1846," accompanied with a label, "Frémont's 3rd Exped. I suspect Chaenactis glabriuscula *DC.*" A note of unknown authorship states, "Probably *Isosyntype Chaenactis heterocarpha* Gray. Pl. Fendl. 98, 1849."

Chaenactis heterocarpha Torr. & A. Gray in A. Gray var. *tanacetifolia* (A. Gray) A. Gray

"On the Sacramento and its tributaries, Ukiah, &c., *Frémont*" (Brewer et al., 1876: 389).

Chamaebatia Benth., Plantae Hartw. 308. 1849.

Type locality: "1712. (392). *Chamaebatia foliolosa*, gen. nov. Rosacearum. In montibus Sacramento." Type: "California. Hartweg" (GH! probable holotype). "The plant on which this genus was founded was first discovered by Colonel Frémont, in his second expedition, while traversing the Sierra Nevada and other parts of California, early in the year 1844, as well as in his third expedition. His specimens were too imperfect for description. It was afterwards found in good condition, but without mature fruit, by the well known and zealous botanical collector, Mr. [Carl Theodor] Hartweg [1812–1871].

Mr. Bentham kindly offered me the privilege of describing this fine new genus, but I thought the right fairly belonged to him, as he first determined its character and affinities. I have but little to add to the accurate description which he has given to it in his Plantae Hartwegianae" (Torrey, 1853: 11).

Chamaebatia foliolosa Benth.

"Higher parts of the Sierra Nevada, as well as on the sides of the foothills, in great abundance: Colonel Frémont" (Torrey, 1853: 11). "FExCal, 37 and 52, 1844. Feb 24–25 [Sierra Nevadas, probably Eldorado County, California]" & "March 25, 'N. gen. Rosaceae,' Mokelemnes [San Joaquin County, California], Sierra Nevada & Roi de Mar, Calif. Chamaebatia" (all three NY-Torrey!). This latter sheet has a fragment envelope: "Fl. of Chamaebatia. Dec 6, 1845. Frémont [two days' journey west of Donner Pass, probably Placer County, California]." The name "Mokelumne" has several spelling variants on the labels; it is not corrected here. "FExCal, 1845–7. Dec. 6., 1845" (GH!). On 6 December 1846 Frémont and party were two days west of Donner Pass, probably in Placer County, California.

Chenopodium album L. = *C. album* L. var. *berlandieri* (Moq.) Mack. & Bush.

"North fork of the Platte. July 12 [1842. Near Greeley, Weld County, Colorado]" (Torrey, 1843: 91). "Frémont" (Watson, 1874: 96). Two sheets NY-Torrey!: "Chenopodium album? Frémont's 1st Expedn. July 10, 1842, seed lentic, thin edge, 'valley of S. Platte' [St. Vrain's Fort, present Weld County, Colorado]," mounted with "Frémonts Expedition to California, 239, 1845, July 29th Grand River, Utah. [The Frémont party was four days' march east of Bent's Fort, which is in Otero County, Colorado, on 29 July 1845, not on the Grand River, which was crossed in Colorado, not Utah, much later in the trip.]

Chenopodium californicum (S. Wats.) S. Wats. ≡ *Blitum californicum* S. Wats.

Chenopodium dessicatum A. Nels. includes *C. pratericola* Rydb.

***Chenopodium fremontii* S. Wats.**, Rep. Geol. Explor. U.S. 40th Parallel, Bot. 5: 287. 1871. (1st)

Protologue locality: "Collected by Frémont on the north Platte upon his first expedition. Truckee and Monitor Valleys and on the foot-hills and ridges of the East Humboldt Mountains, Nevada; 4–800 feet altitude; July, August. [Watson] (973)." Type: "Chenopodium Frémontii Wats. Frémont's 1st Expedn. July 1842" (syntype NY-Torrey!: microfiche BRY!). The name is lectotypified illogically by Bassett and Crompton (1982: 598) on the basis of Watson 973, East Humboldt Mts., July 1867. The Frémont collection cited above would have been an obvious good choice. It bears a small sheet of drawings of a flower with enclosed seed.

Chenopodium hybridum L.

"FExCal, 1845–7. 189. 1845. Chenopodium. 'Seems to be the same as No. 142 Frém. but leaves broader & none toothed. The seeds are larger than in C. hybridum'" and

"FExCal, 1845–7. No. 142, 1845. Chenopodium subspicatum. Nutt. gen. i. p. 199?" (both NY-Torrey!).

Chenopodium leptophyllum Nutt. ex Moq. includes *C. zosterifolium*
"Frémont" (Watson, 1874: 95).

***Chenopodium olidum* S. Wats.**, Proc. Amer. Acad. 9: 95. 1874. (3rd) = *C. album* L.
Protologue locality: "382 Frémont; 718, 721, 725 Fendler; Hall & Harbour; 970 Watson; Hall, cult. from Powell's seeds; 258 Wolf." Type: "FExCal, 382, 1845. 'Forks of the White River. Frémont's notes. Colo.' [labeled *Endolepis suckleyi* S.W.]" [Frémont's party was along the White River in Colorado (Rio Blanco County,) and Utah (Uintah County) 12–25 Sept. 1845] (two isotypes NY-Torrey!); and "FExCal, 1845–7. 382. 1845" (holotype GH!).

Chenopodium pratericola Rydb. = *C. dessicatum* A. Nels.
"Chenopodium. Seed lentic (biconvex) the edge acute, shining. Platte Bottom, 29 June 1842 [south of Cozad, Dawson County, Nebraska]. Frémont" (NY-Torrey!).

Chenopodium subglabrum (S. Wats.) A. Nels.
"Horse Creek, 14 July [1842. North of Cheyenne, Laramie County, Wyoming] Frémont" (NY-Torrey!).

Chenopodium zosterifolium = *Chenopodium leptophyllum* Nutt. ex Moq.
"Platte? [1842]" (Torrey, 1843: 91). "Frémont's 1st Exped. Aug 12–17. [1842, Wind River Mountains, Sublette County, Wyoming]. Chenopodium zosterifolium Hook. Fl. B. Am. or a n. sp. Seeds glabrous. Seed horizontal" (NY-Torrey!).

Chlorogalum pomeridianum (DC.) Kunth = ammole or soap plant
Three specimens and labels on one sheet, (NY-Torrey!): "Frémont's 2nd Exped. N 14. 1844. Chlorogalum pomeridianum"; "FExCal, valley of the upper Sacramento—439. 1846"; "1844 (14) Sutters Fort, 81. Mokelumne River. Chlorogalum pomeridianum, *Lindl.* Ammole—Soap plant. used for making mats."; "FExCal, 1844 (14, Sutter's Fort [Sacramento County, California])", and "81. Mokelemne River [probably San Joaquin County, California}. 25–26 March." Two sheets (three collections) are at GH! (No. 349 also at MO!): Frémont's 2nd Expedn. 56 and 81. 1844. "Ammole" and "FExCal, 1845–7. 349, 1846. Chlorogalum pomeridianum, *Kth.*" The sheet taken at Sutter's Fort was amidst hurried preparation for the homeward journey.

***Chorizanthe brevicornu* Torr.**, Rep. U.S. Mex. Bound., Bot. 177. 1859. (4th)
Protologue locality: "On the Gila River, March, Parry,; also collected by Col. Frémont on the same River." Type: "Probably from the Gila. Col. Frémont [1849, fourth expedition] (Figure 21; syntype NY-Torrey!)." There are two tiny plants mounted on a sheet at NY-Torrey! with the note quoted above. "S. E. California to the Gila and Nevada, Frémont" (Torrey & Gray, 1870: 196). J. L. Reveal (personal communication) considers the Parry specimen at NY to be the holotype.

Chrysopsis villosa (Pursh) Nutt. includes *C. hispida* and *C. mollis* = *Heterotheca* (q.v.)

Chrysopsis hispida = *Heterotheca villosa* (Pursh) Shinners
"On the Platte [1842]" (Torrey, 1843: 87).

Chrysopsis mollis = *Heterotheca villosa* (Pursh) Shinners
"On the Platte [1842]" (Torrey, 1843: 87).

Chrysothamnus nauseosus (Pallas) Britt. includes *Linosyris graveolens*

Chrysothamnus viscidiflorus (Hook.) Nutt. includes *Linosyris viscidiflora*

Cicuta maculata ≡ *C. maculata* L.
"Lower Platte [1842]" (Torrey, 1843: 86).

Cirsium altissimum ≡ *C. altissimum* (L.) Spreng.
"Lower Platte [1842]" (Torrey, 1843: 88). "C. altissimum. End of Sept. Lower Platte, Lieut. Frémont, 1842" (NY!). The label has the printed notation "Torr. & Gray Flora, N. Amer."

Cirsium canescens Nutt.
"FExCal, 1843–4. Cirsium" (NY-Torrey!).

Cirsium undulatum (Nutt.) Spreng.
"FExCal, 1845–7. No. 86. 1845. Cirsium undulatum. Douglasii, DC). Turkey Creek [Kansas, 11 July 1845]" (NY-Torrey!).

Cirsium Virginianum = *C. altissimum* (L.) Spreng.

Citrullus lanatus (Thunb.) Mats. & Nakai
"Aug. 14. No. 37. Arkansas bottom (sandy). Frémont's 3rd Exp." (NY-Torrey!). This, the cultivated water melon, was either taken from cultivation or escaped from cultivation at Bent's Fort, Otero County, Colorado.

Clarkia arcuata (Kellogg) Nels. & Macbr. includes *Godetia hispidula* (S. Wats.) S. Wats.
"FExCal, 1846. Ppp. Oenothera (Godetia) tenella Cav.? Sacramento Valley, April 9th 1846 [Cow Creek, vicinity of Redding, Shasta County, California" and "Frémont's 3rd Exped. 307. 1846" (two on same sheet NY-Torrey!).

Clarkia concinna (Fisch. & Meyer) Greene
"FExCal, 1845–7. 430. 1846. Eucharidium concinnum, *Fisch. & Mey.*" (GH! and NY-Torrey!).

Clarkia gracilis (Piper) Nels. & Macbr. subsp. *albicaulis* (Jepson) Lewis & Lewis includes *Godetia amoena* var. *albicaulis* Jepson

Clarkia purpurea (Curtis) Nels. & Macbr.
"FExCal, 1845–7. 441. 1846. Oe. viminea" (GH!; NY-Torrey!; MO!); "FExCal, 1845–7. 484. 1846. Oenothera (Godetia)" (NY-Torrey!); and "FExCal, 1845–7. Rrr 1846. Oenothera (Godetia)" (GH!). The Rrr 1846 sheet, labeled "Oe. purpurea," is duplicated at NY-Torrey!

Clarkia unguiculata Lindley
"FExCal, 1845–7. 482. 1846. Clarkia elegans" (GH!, MO!, and NY-Torrey!).

***Clematis fremontii* S. Wats.**, Proc. Amer. Acad. 10: 339. 1875. (2nd)
Protologue locality: "This well-marked species, the western representative of *C. ochroleuca*, was first collected by Frémont (no. 194) on his second expedition, but without note of the locality. It was rediscovered during the past season by Louis Watson, M.D., in the neighborhood of Ellis, Kansas." Type: "FExCal, 1843–44. 194. Clematis Frémontii, Wats. n. sp." (holotype NY-Torrey!; isotype GH!). "Frémont's clematis occurs in a 15 county area in north-central Kansas. It is most abundant in the counties of Cloud, Jewell, Lincoln, Mitchell, Osborne, Ottawa, Russell and Smith. Rocky prairie hilltops and roadcuts through the limestone hills of this region are where it is most often found. Aside from a handful of locations in extreme southern Nebraska, the only other place where it occurs outside of Kansas is in the eastern Ozarks of Missouri" (Locklear, 1990).

Clematis hirsutissima Pursh var. *hirsutissima*
"Frémont's 2nd Expedn." and "567, 1844. Frémont's 2nd Exp." (both NY-Torrey!).

Clematis hirsutissima Pursh var. *scottii* (Porter) Erickson
"FExCal, 1843–4" (NY-Torrey!).

Clematis lasiantha Nutt. in Torr. & A. Gray
"But it [the female] has since been found by Colonel Frémont" (Torrey, 1859: 61); "FExCal, 335 and 504, 1846. Clematis lasiantha, *Nutt.*" (NY-Torrey!; 335 also MO!) and "California, Frémont. Ex herb. J. Torrey. Clematis lasiantha, *Nutt.* Torr. & Gr. Fl. N. Amer." (NY-Sartwell!). "Frémont's California Expedition 1845–47 [1846]. C. lasiantha Nutt." and "FExCal, 1845–7. 235. 1846. C. lasiantha, *Nutt.*" (both GH!).

Clematis ligusticifolia Nutt. in Torr. & A. Gray
"Frémont? 2nd exp" (NY-Torrey!) and "Clematis ligusticifolia. California, Frémont" (NY-Sartwell!). "FExCal, 1845–7. 269. 1845" (GH!).

Clematis Virginiana
"Valley of the Platte. June, July [1842]" (Torrey, 1843: 83).

Cleome integrifolia = *C. serrulata* Pursh
"From the Lower Platte nearly to the mountains. June 29 [south of Cozad, Dawson County, Nebraska], July 2 [Forks of the Platte, Lincoln County, Nebraska], Aug. 21 [1842, Sweetwater River near Jeffery City, Frémont County, Wyoming]" (Torrey, 1843: 83).

Cleome serrulata Pursh includes *C. integrifolia*
"FExCal, 33, 39, & 150. 1845" (NY-Torrey!; 39 also MO!).

***Cleomella obtusifolia* Torr. & Frém.** in Frém., Rep. Exped. Rocky Mts. 311. 1845. (2nd)
Protologue locality: "On the American fork of the Sacramento river; March." Type: "On the American Fork of the Sacramento, 1844" (holotype NY-Torrey!: microfiche

BRY!). Parish (1923) contends logically that the type locality is east of the Sierra Nevada in the Mohave Desert, not along the American Fork of the Sacramento.

***Coleogyne* Torr.**, Smiths. Contr. 6(2): 8. 1853. (2nd)
Type species: ***Coleogyne ramosissima* Torr.** (l.c.). Protologue locality: "Sources of the Mohave and Virgin rivers, tributaries of the Colorado of the West, in the mountains of Southern California. Flowering in April and May." Type: "FExCal, 1843–4. 409. N. gen. of Chrysobalaneae. 'A yellow-flowering shrub,' Camp of Apr. 30–May 1, 1844" (holotype NY- Torrey!: microfiche BRY!; isotype GH!). Frémont camped that night at Stump Spring, Pahrump Valley, Clark County, Nevada. The GH specimen bears only the notation "Int. California. Frémont." "Coleogyne ramosissima Torr. 409, 1844 & 443, 1844. Frémont" (isotype and paratype NY-Torrey!). A third sheet at NY-Torrey! [paratype] has three mounted stems and three illustrations, one of them "Sprague's." but there is no label information except that the Torrey sketch contains the notation "443, 1844."

***Collinsia bartsiifolia* Benth.** in A. DC., Prodr. 10: 318. 1846. (2nd)
Protologue locality: "in montibus Scopulosis (Frémont!)." Type: "Frémont 86. 1844. Herb. A. Gray. C. bartsiaefolia Benth.!" (holotype GH!). The note following the comparison by Bentham of this species with the related *C. bicolor*, "(v.s. comm. a cl. A. Gray)" lends credence to the identification of this material as typical. A second sheet at GH bears specimens by both Hartweg (No. 1885) and by Frémont ("FExCal, 1845–7. 175, 1846" GH!). Possibly the Frémont specimen is an isotype, but Bentham did not cite a particular number with the protologue.

Collinsia heterophylla Buist ex Grah.
"FExCal, 232–242, 246, 1846. Collinsia grandiflora" (NY-Torrey!). "FexRM 1842. Collinsia" (NY-Sartwell!). The species occurs in California, not along the track of Frémont in 1842; it was very likely taken in 1846 in California and is probably a duplicate of part of the 232–242, 246 material. "Collinsia bicolor. California, Frémont" (NY-Sartwell!). This is also a duplicate of part of the 232–242, 246 material. "Collinsia. California, Frémont" (GH- Thurber!). "FExCal, 246 and 242, 1846" (GH!).

Collinsia sparsiflora Fisch. & Mey.
"FExCal, 1845–7. 234, 1845[1846]" (GH!).

Collomia linearis Nutt.
"Collomia linearis Nutt. California. Frémont's 2nd Expedn. named by Bentham)" (NY-Torrey!). "Herb. A. Gray. Collomia linearis, *Nutt.* Torr. & Gray, Fl. N. Amer. Frémont's 2nd Exped." (GH!).

Comandra umbellata (L.) Nutt.
"Comandra. Frémont's 2nd Exped. 76. 1843. on the Kansas, and 596, 1844" (two on same sheet NY-Torrey!).

Convallaria stellata L. ≡ *Smilacina stellata* (L.) Desf.
Frémont (1845: 273).

Conyza canadensis (L.) Cronq. ≡ *Erigeron canadensis*

***Cordylanthus laxiflorus* A. Gray**, Rep. U.S. Mex. Bound., Bot. 120. 1859. (2nd) = *C. maritimus* Nutt. var. *canescens* (A. Gray) Jepson
Protologue locality: Rocky hills, Sonora, Mexico; Thurber. Also Great Salt Lake; Col. Frémont, 1843. Type: "Frémont, 759, shore of the Great Salt Lake, Sept. 11, 1843 [west of Ogden, Weber County, Utah]" (holotype NY-Torrey!). "Near Great Salt Lake, (Frémont)" (Watson, 1874: 233). The herbarium sheet bears an attached sheet with illustrations of floral parts by Torrey and the following notation: "Cordylanthus maritimus Nutt.? Shore of Salt Lake. Frémont. Sept 11, 1843." At the bottom of the sheet written in pencil is the notation "Cordylanthus, n. sp.?"

Cordylanthus rigidus (Benth.) Jepson var. *filifolius* (Nutt.) Macbr.
"Frémont's 3rd Expedition. California. Santa Cruz Valley? 1846" (NY-Torrey!; MO!).

Coreopsis californica (Nutt.) H. K. Sharsmith
"FExCal, 1849. & 286. 1844. Leptomyne" (NY-Torrey!). The meaning of the note "& 286. 1844" is recondite. The solitary specimen by Frémont is multiply mounted with two by Bigelow and one by Coulter. The specimen by John Charles is here assigned to the 1849, fourth expedition.

Coreopsis calliopsidea (DC.) A. Gray
"Frémont's Rail Road Exped. 1853–54. Coreopsis (Agarita) calliopsidea, Gray" (NY-Torrey!). The specimen, a solitary head, is attached to a small sheet of critical diagnostic drawings by Torrey.

Coreopsis tinctoria ≡ *C. tinctoria* Nutt.
"On the Platte [1842]" (Torrey, 1843: 87). "Platte, Frémont Coreopsis tinctoria. Torr. & Gray, Flora, N. Amer." (NY-Torrey!). "FExCal, 1845–7 [1846]. Coreopsis tinctoria" (US!).

Cornus circinata = ?
"On the Platte [1842]" (Torrey, 1843: 86).

Cornus nuttallii Aud.
"FExCal, 1845–7. 374, 1846. Cornus Nuttallii" (NY-Torrey!).

Cornus stolonifera = *C. sericea* L.
"On a lake in the Wind River mountains. August 12–17 [1842. Sublette County, Wyoming]" (Torrey, 1843: 86). "Frémont's 2nd Exped." (NY!).

Corydalis aurea Willd.
"Frémont's 2nd Exp. 563, 1844" and "FExCal, 1849" (both NY-Torrey!). "FExCal, 1845–7. 175. 1845. C. aurea" (GH!).

Coryphantha vivipara (Nutt.) Britt. & Rose
"= Mammillaria vivipara. Frémont's 2nd Expedition. 1843–4" (NY-Torrey!).

Cosmidium gracile = *Thelesperma megapotamicum* (Spreng.) Kuntze
"Upper Platte [1842]" (Torrey, 1843: 87). "Cosmidium gracile! Torr. & Gray, Flora, N. Amer. Prairies, Upper Platte, Frémont! 22 Juillet, haute, Prairies" (NY-Torrey!). On 22 July 1842 Frémont and party was at Horseshoe Creek, near present Glendo, Platte County, Wyoming.

Cotyledon farinosa (Lindley) Benth. & Hook.
"It probably also includes a more northern form with longer pedicels, collected on upper tributaries of the Sacramento (*Frémont*)" (Brewer et al., 1876: 212). "FExCal, 1845–7. 489. 1846" (MO!). A note above the label indicates: "upper tributaries of the Sacramento fide label in Gray herbarium."

Cowania mexicana DC.
"'Mountains of California along the Virgen River' (*Frémont*, probably in Southern Nevada)" (Brewer et al., 1876: 175).

Cowania plicata D. Don
This species tentatively is cited in the Torrey and Frémont botanical report (Frémont, 1845: 314): "Specimens of this plant, without a ticket, were in the collection; doubtless obtained in California. It may prove to be a distinct species from the Mexican plant, for the leaves are more divided than they are described by Don, and the flowers are smaller."

***Cowania stansburyana* Torr.**, Exped. Great Salt Lake 378. 1852. (2nd)
Protologue locality: "Stansbury's Island, Salt Lake." Type: Stansbury's collection from the Great Salt Lake (NY?). Frémont's material cited here under *Purshia mexicana* var. *stansburyana* is at least a syntype. Both *C. plicata* and *C. mexicana* (see above) refer to the collection by Frémont. That material is further cited with the protologue of *C. mexicana* var. *stansburyana*: "C. foliis pinnatifido 5–7-lobatis, lobis oblongis; floribus flavis. *C. plicata?* Torr. in Frém. 2d Report, p. 314; not of Don. Colonel Frémont collected this plant in the mountains of California, along the Virgin River, a tributary of the Colorado."

Crataegus douglasii Lindley
"Near Utah Lake. Crataegus. 511, 1844. Frémont's 2nd Expedn." (NY-Torrey!). The hawthorns along the Bear River (Frémont, 1845: 132) and the thorn thickets near the Great Salt Lake belong to this species (Frémont, 1845: 151). The specimen cited belongs to variety *rivularis* (Nutt.) Sargent. Frémont was camped near Utah Lake, Utah County, Utah, on 24–26 May 1844.

Crepis glauca = *C. runcinata* (James) Torr. & A. Gray
"Upper Platte [1842]" (Torrey, 1843: 88). "Sweet Water River—Upper Platte, Frémont, July 31, 1842 [Natrona County, Wyoming]. Torr. & Gray, Flora, N. Amer." (NY-

Torrey!). "Plains of the Upper Platte, *Nuttall! Lieut. Frémont!*" (Torrey & Gray, 1843: 488).

Crepis modocensis Greene
"Frémont's Expedition, 1843–4. California" (NY-Columbia!). The specimen, determined by F. V. Coville, May 18, 1894, as *C. scopulorum* Coville, bears a note by Coville. "From Frémont's itinerary it appears likely that this specimen was collected in the Wind River mountains of Wyoming." If that is so, the year of collection is wrong. The data on the label is followed here, and the plant is assigned to the second expedition.

Crepis occidentalis Nutt.
"FExCal, 1843–4. Crepis occidentalis, *Nutt.*" (NY-Torrey!).

Croton capitatus Michx. ≡ *Pilinophytum capitatum*

Croton procumbens Esch.
Sandy places in various parts of California; Parry, Rich, Le Conte, Frémont (Torrey, 1859: 195).

Croton texensis (Klotzsch) Muell.-Arg. in DC. includes *Hendecandra multiflora* Torr. in Frém.
"FExCal, 1845–7. Wwww 1846. Gray" (GH!).

Cruciferae = *Oxystylis lutea* Torr. & Frém.
Frémont (1845: 262).

Cryptantha celosioides (Eastw.) Payson includes *Myosotis glomerata*

Cryptantha flava (A. Nels.) Payson
"Frémont's 2nd Expedn. 557. 1844. Eritrichium leucophaea. Seems intermediate between flavocinereum and glomeratus. Style ½ as long as the corolla. On the Uinta River. June 1st [?] [the party reached the Uinta River, Uintah County, Utah on 3 June 1844]" (NY- Torrey!). The species was ultimately named *Oreocarya flava* A. Nelson.

Cryptantha fulvocanescens (A. Gray) Payson includes *Eritrichium glomeratum* var. *fulvocanescens*

Cryptantha humilis (A. Gray) Payson
"Wasatch Mts., 1844, Frémont" (Higgins, 1971: 46). "Frémont's 2nd Expedn. Flowers very white. W. side of Wahsatch Mts. 550, 1844 & 464, 1844. Frémont. Eritrichium" and "Frémont's 2nd Expedn. Western side of Wahsatch Mts. May 21, 522, 1844. Eritrichium" (NY-Torrey!). The Preuss map of the 1843–44 route indicates that the camp of 21 May was at or near present-day Fillmore, Millard County, Utah.

Cryptantha intermedia (A. Gray) Greene
"FExCal, 1845–7. 400. 1846. Eritrichium muriculatum? Sacramento Valley, camp at the 'Buttes.' May 30" (NY-Torrey!). The "Buttes" is in Sutter County, California. A

second label with a drawing of a mature achenes and note is attached; "Nutlets 4, homomorphous, ovate, acute, erect-granular-tuberculate."

Cryptantha aff. *leiocarpa* (Fisch. & Meyer) Greene
"FExCal, 1849. Krynitzkya. E. leiocarpum?" (NY-Torrey!). The specimen is in early bud and lacks critical diagnostic characters. It was examined by Larry C. Higgins, who placed it with the group of species centering on *C. leiocarpa*, with which it had been placed tentatively by Torrey more than a century ago.

Cryptantha micrantha (Torr.) Johnston
"FExCal, 376. 1844. Eritrichium (Piptocalyx micrantha). Sandy uplands of the Mohave" (NY-Torrey!).

Cryptantha thyrsiflora (Greene) Payson
"Frémont's 2nd Expedn. Label lost. California?" and "FExCal, 1844. 300. 1844. Eritrichium glutinosum" (both on same sheet NY-Torrey!). The former is accompanied by a careful drawing of flowers and fruit, and includes notes; the latter has illegible pencil notes. "FExCal, 1845–7. Krynitzkia glomerata, Gray, 437. 1845" (GH!). The Frémont material at GH is mounted with a specimen by H. Engelmann taken in 1854.

Cryptantha sp.
"Frémont's 2nd Expedn. Eritrichium. Looks like plebium [?]—but leaves too narrow" (NY-Torrey!). Larry C. Higgins has indicated (personal communication) that this specimen likely is an immature specimen of *C. intermedia.*

Cucurbita foetidissima H.B.K.
"Frémont 185, and No. 198. Pond Sandy, July 25th, and No. 202. Pond Sandy. July 25th" (NY-Torrey!; 202 also MO!). This material, though not marked as such, came from the third expedition on 25 July 1845, when the party was on the Smoky Hill Fork of the Kansas, still in Kansas.

Cuscuta indecora Choisy
"FExCal, 1843–4. 485, 1843. Sent to Engelmann. Cuscuta decora B *Engelm.* Indian Country west of Arkansas" (NY-Torrey!; MO!). The dodder is apparently parasitic on *Heterotheca villosa* (Pursh) Shinners.

Cycloloma atriplicifolium (Spreng.) Coult. includes *C. platyphyllum*

Cycloloma platyphyllum Moq. = *C. atriplicifolium* (Spreng.) Coult.
"North fork of the Platte. Sept. 4 [1842. West of Scotts Bluff, Scotts Bluff County, Nebraska]" (Torrey, 1843: 91). Two sheets at NY-Torrey!: "Cycloloma platyphyllum (occ) Moq. Chen. 18. Kochia dentata Willd. Sept. 4. a la traverse de la Platte. Frémont 1842"; and "Cycloloma platyphylla. Frémont's 1st Expedn., 1842." "Ex Herb. J. Carey. Cycloloma platyphyllum. Moq. Chen. North Fork of the Platte, Frémont's 1st Journey (ex Torrey!)" (GH!). This latter sheet is mounted with collections of Wright and Henry Engelmann. "Frémont" (Watson, 1874: 92).

Cymopterus bulbosus A. Nels.

"Frémont's 2nd Expedn. 594, 1844" (NY-Torrey). This is mounted on the same sheet with *C. longipes* (q.v.) and was likely taken with it in the Uinta Basin during late May or early June 1844. That there were two entities mounted on the same sheet is indicated by notations in Gray's handwriting; "Cymopterus montanus" is written in pencil below the specimen of *C. bulbosus*, and "C. glaucus, or probably campestris" is written beside one portion of *C. longipes*. That specimen is likewise annotated by Sereno Watson as "= C. campestris—apparently."

Cymopterus longipes S. Wats.

"Frémont's 2nd Expedn. 594, 1844" (NY-Torrey!).

Cymopterus montanus Nutt. = *C. bulbosus* A. Nels (sensu Frémont specimen)

In his discussion of this species, Gray (1849: 57), notes the collection of "a specimen gathered by Frémont in his second expedition (in herb Torr.), with perfectly mature fruit." And further "In Frémont's specimen the carpophore is seen to be free and 2-parted."

Cynoglossum grande Dougl. ex Lehm.

"FExCal, 1845–7. 216. 1846. Cynoglossum grande. *Dougl.* Banks of the Sacramento" (NY-Torrey! and GH-Thurber!). The sheet at GH lacks the number 216.

Cyperus acuminatus Torr. & Hook.

"Frémont's 3rd Exped. No. 161. 1845" (NY-Torrey!). "FExCal, 56. 1845" (NY-Torrey!).

***Dalea arborescens* Torr. ex A. Gray**, Mem. Amer. Acad. II. 5: 316. 1854. (2nd) ≡ *Psorothamnus arborescens* (Torr.) Barneby

Protologue locality: "Mountains of San Fernando, a southern branch of the Sierra Nevada, California; April, Frémont." Type: "Frémont's 2nd Exped. April 15, 1844. 'Mts of San Fernando, a southern continuation of the Sierra Nevada. A small tree.' Dalea arborescens, *Torr. n.sp.*" (holotype NY-Torrey!: microfiche BRY!; isotype GH!; fragment US!). The NY holotype bears the notation "Dalea arborescens, Torr. in Gray. Pl. Thurber." On 15 April 1844 the Frémont party was on the east side of Oak Creek Pass south of Tehachapi Pass, Kern County, California. "Collected only by Frémont at eastern base of the San Fernando Mountains" (Brewer et al., 1876: 142).

***Dalea fremontii* Torr. ex A. Gray**, Mem. Amer. Acad. II. 5: 316. 1854. (2nd) ≡ *Psorothamnus fremontii* (Torr.) Barneby

Protologue locality: "Mountains of the Pah-Utah country, S. W. California, on rocks; May, Frémont." Type: "FExCal, 1843–4. May 5. 417, 1844. Dalea Frémontii. May 5, 1844. Pah Utah Country." (holotype NY-Torrey!: microfiche BRY; isotype [May 5] GH!; MO!). The holotype has the usual diagnostic sketch sheet provided by Torrey. "Frémont's 2nd Expedn. Top of a large rock, at Muddy Creek. 417, 1844 (May 5th). Mts of S.W. California [crossed out]. Pah-Utah Country" (isotype NY-Crooke!). The isotype has both flowers and leaves and is in much better condition than the holotype. Why it was exchanged to the Crooke herbarium is not known. The type was collected on 5 May 1844, when Frémont's party was encamped on the Muddy River in Clark County, Nevada. His party was being threatened by Indians at the time. This is the plant called *Psoralea* by Frémont (1845: 262) on 25 April 1844.

***Dalea nana* Torr.** in A. Gray, Mem. Amer. Acad. N. Ser. 4: 31. 1849. (3rd)
Protologue locality: "Sandy soil, Willow Bar, on the Cimarron; August. Collected in the same region by Frémont in 1845; also by Lindheimer and Mr. Wright in Western Texas in 1847." Type: "Frémont 3rd Exped. 1845(?)" (syntype GH!). "Dalea. Frémont's 3d Expedit. 221. 1845" (syntype MO!). "FExCal, 1845–7. Dalea nana sp. nov. Torr. Gray pl. Fendl. no. 130. Sandy prairies. July 30th 1845" [three days journey east of Bent's Fort, Colorado] (syntype NY-Torrey!). The sheet bears the notation "Frémont was at Bent's Fort on the Arkansas – La Junta, Otero Co., Colo., on Aug 2, 1845. RCB[arneby]."

Dalea oligophylla (Torr.) Shinners includes *Petalostemon candidum*

Dalea purpurea Vent. includes *Petalostemon purpureum* and *P. violaceum*

Darlingtonia brachypoda = *Desmanthus leptolobus* Torr. & A. Gray
"On the Platte. Sept. 17 [1842. One days' journey west of Grand Island, Nebraska]" (Torrey, 1843: 85).

Datura wrightii Regel
"FExCal, 1845–7. Nnnn, 1846. Gray. Datura meteloides" (NY-Torrey!).

Daucus pusillus Michx.
"FExCal, 1845–7. 425. 1846. Daucus pusillus" (NY-Torrey! and GH!).

Delphinium hesperium A. Gray
"FExCal, 1846. Delphinium simplex B. *Hook.*" (NY-Torrey!). "FExCal, 1845–7. 485. 1846" and "FExCal, 1845–7. 423. 1846" (both GH!).

Delphinium nudicaule Torr. & A. Gray
"FExCal, 1845–7. 414 & 449, 1846. Delphinium nudicaule var.——" (NY-Torrey!; MO!). "FExCal, 1845–7. 449, 1846" (GH!).

Delphinium nuttallianum Pritz. ex Walp.?
"FExCal, 1845–7. 249. 1846. Delphinium menziesii" (NY-Torrey!). "California, Frémont. Ex herb. J. Torrey. Delphinium patens. Torr. & Gr. Fl. N. Amer." (NY-Sartwell!). This second sheet has a large flowering stem that appears to be *D. nuttallianum*, but a second smaller stem does not. "107, 1844. Frémont. D. scopulinum" (NY-Torrey!).

Delphinium parryi A. Gray? = (? *D. hesperium* see above)
"FExCal, 1845–7. 423, 1846. Delphinium simplex *Hook.*—var.)" (NY-Torrey!). The sheet bears an annotation label, presumably by Gray "D. distichum var. Frémontii. Syn. Fl. N. Amer." A search of the *Delphinium* treatment in that publication has not revealed any such name.

Delphinium variegatum Torr. & A. Gray

"FExCal, 1845–7. 199. 1846. Delphinium variegatum T. & Gr. = D. decorum Fisch. & Mey—fide Gray, in Pl. Wright II. p. 8" (NY-Torrey! and GH!). "Frémont's Expedition to California, 1845–7. 505. 1846" (GH!).

Dendromecon rigida Benth.

"FExCal, 1845–7. 1846. Dendromecon rigidum, *Benth.*" (NY-Torrey!; NY-Sartwell!; GH!). The GH label includes the notation "Mn. 1846." "FExCal, 1849. Dendromecon rigidum, *Benth. Col. Frémont.*" (NY-Crooke!).

Deschampsia caespitosa ≡ *D. caespitosa* (L.) Beauv.

"Alpine region of the Wind River mountains. Aug. 13–14 [1842. Sublette County, Wyoming]" (Torrey, 1843: 94).

Desmanthus leptolobus Torr. & A. Gray includes *Darlingtonia brachypoda*

Desmodium acuminatum = *D. glutinosum* (Muhl.) Wood

"Little Blue River of the Kansas, June 22 [1842. Near Powell, Jefferson County, Kansas]" (Torrey, 1843: 88).

Dicentra chrysantha (Hook. & Arn.) Walp.

"FExCal, 1849. Dielytra. 'Summit of Rushy [?] (Grisly?) Mountains, bordering Bend River (Pajaro) June'" (NY-Torrey!). The hand-written locality data help little in understanding when the fourth expedition actually ended or where the specimen likely came from. The label information is, however, the most complete of any of the 1848–49 expedition specimens. The species is evidently endemic to southern California and Baja California.

Dicentra formosa (Andr.) Walp.

"FExCal, 339 & 352, 1846. Dielytra formosa. Noza River, a tributary of the upper Sacramento" (NY-Torrey!; 352 also MO!). "FExCal, 1845–7. 339, 1846. D. formosa, DC." (GH!).

***Dichaeta fremontii* Torr. ex A. Gray**, Mem. Amer. Acad. II. 4: 102. 1849. (3rd) ≡ *Baeria fremontii* (Torr) A. Gray

Protologue locality: "California, Frémont (1846)." Type: "FExCal, 1845–7, 289, 1846. Burrielia (Dichaeta Frémontii. Torr.) Baeria (Dichaeta) Frémontii" (holotype GH!) and "FExCal, 1845–7. 260 1/2. Dichaeta Frémontii n. sp. T. & Gr. Pl. Fend. 102 (illegible word)" (isotype GH-Lowell!) "FExCal, 1849. Buriellia" (NY-Torrey!).

Dichelostemma californicum (Torr.) Wood ≡ *Strophiolirion californicum* Torr.

Dichelostemma pulchellum (Salisb.) Heller

"Frémont. 131, 1844" (NY-Torrey!). "Frémont 131, 1844. Caliveras Creek, March 24 [San Joaquin County, California]. Dichelostemma capitatum" and "173, 1846. Frémont. Brodiaea congesta—(capitata). Banks of Ausumne [Cosumne?] River, Valley of San Joachin, March 14, 1846 [Sacramento County, California]" (both NY-Torrey!). Both herbarium sheets bear attached sketches of floral parts by Dr. Torrey. Number 173, dated 14 March, was likely taken on 24 March or later. On 14 March the party was still in camp near Sutter's, Sacramento County.

Dietaria = *Machaeranthera*
Frémont (1845: 147).

Dietaria coronopifolia = *Machaeranthera tanacetifolia* (H.B.K.) Nees
"On the Platte [1842]" (Torrey, 1843: 87). "Dietaria coronopifolia. Torr. & Gray, Flora, N. Amer. Platte, Frémont. Sept 3, 1842 [Fort Laramie, Goshen County, Wyoming]" (NY-Torrey!).

Dietaria pulverulenta = *Machaeranthera canescens* (Pursh) A. Gray
"On the Platte [1842]" (Torrey, 1843: 87).

Dietaria viscosa = *Machaeranthera bigelovii* (A. Gray) Greene (q.v.), pro parte.
"On the Platte [1842]" (Torrey, 1843: 87).

Distichlis spicata (L.) Greene ≡ *Uniola spicata*
"FExCal, 1843–4" (GH!). There is a note written on the sheet: "Delta of Bear River, in Great Salt Lake, Sept 3, 1843. See Frémont's Report, p. 149." The author of the note is unknown; the citation on that date is to *Uniola spicata*. "FExCal, 1843–4" (2 sheets: GH! and GH-Thurber!). "Uniola stricta Torr. Salt marshes near the Great Salt Lake in North eastern California. Frémont's 2d Expedt. No. 672. Sept 1843" (MO!). "FExCal, 1843–4. 1843" (US!). This is the salt grass or herbe salée of Frémont's reports.

Ditaxis lanceolata (Benth.) Pax & K. Hoffm.
"FExCal, 1849. Aphora lanceolata, *Engelm.* Probably from the Gila (Sonora)" (NY-Torrey!). The plant probably came from southern California, not from the Gila. The species distribution includes western Arizona but is not reported from as far east as the Gila.

Dodecatheon clevelandii Greene
"California, Frémont. Ex herb. J. Torrey. D. meadia var. Californica. Torr. & Gr. Fl. N. Amer." (NY-Sartwell!). "Ex Herb. H. P. Sartwell, M.D. Dodacheon Meadii. California. Frémont" (GH-Sartwell!).

Dodecatheon conjugens Greene includes *D. meadia*
"Frémont's 2nd Expedn. 34. 1844" (NY-Torrey!). "No. 105. Febry 23, 1846 [Wild Cat Ridge, Santa Cruz County, California]. D. meadia. Frm. Exped to Calif—1845–47. Dodecatheon Meadia. ex Torrey" (GH-Thurber!); "FExCal, 1845–7. 137. 1845" (GH!; MO!).

Dodecatheon dentatum = *D. jefferyi* van Houtte
"Defiles of the Wind River mountains. Aug. 13–16 [1842. Sublette County, Wyoming]" (Torrey, 1843: 88). The name *D. dentatum* was applied by Frémont to several species of the genus. It is mentioned at various points in his first and second reports.

Dodecatheon hendersonii A. Gray
"Frémont's 2nd Exped." (GH!).

Dodecatheon jefferyi van Houtte includes *D. dentatum* pro parte
"Dodecatheon dentatum *Hook.* Frémont's 1st Exp. Aug. 3–16. 1842. 'Defiles of the Wind river mountains'" (NY-Torrey!).

Dodecatheon meadia = *D. conjugens* Greene pro parte

Dodecatheon pulchellum (Raf.) Merr. includes *D. dentatum* pro parte
"Frémont's 2nd Exp. 482. 1844" (NY-Torrey!).

Dudleya cymosa (Lem.) Britt. & Rose
"FExCal, 1845–7. 338, 1846. Escheveria lanceolata? Upper tributaries of the Sacramento, Camp 25–26 April [Bear Creek, east of Redding, Shasta County, California]. Same as have in the vicinity of 'Antelope Creek'" (NY-Torrey!). "FExCal, 1845–7. 489. 1846. Escheveria lanceolata? 'Upper tributaries of Sacramento'" (GH!; MO!). The material at MO has been labeled tentatively as both *lanceolata* and *farinosa.*

Echinocereus triglochidiatus Engelm.
"Frémont's 2nd Expedition. = Cer. phoeniceus (Engelm.!)" (NY-Torrey!).

***Echinospermum (Lappula) fremontii* Torr.** in A. Gray, Expl. Surv. R. R. Miss. Pac. 1853–55. 12(2): 46. 1860. (2nd) = *L. squarrosa* (Retz.) Dumort
Protologue locality: "Colonel Frémont collected this plant in his second journey (1844) on Pass creek, near the southern extremity of the Sierra Nevada." Type: "Frémont's 2nd Expedn. April 13th, 1844. 'Creek of the Pass' in the Sierra Nevada. Echinospermum Frémontii sp. nov. Prickles in a double marginal series & smaller ones on the keels. Perhaps distinct from E. Lappula" (holotype NY-Torrey!). Frémont moved from the Kern River to Oak Creek Pass on 13 April 1844, Kern County, California. The species is adventive from Eurasia, having been introduced very early during exploration of the New World.

Edosmia gairdneri ≡ *Perideridia gairdneri* (Hook. & Arn.) Mathias
"Frémont's 1st Exp., Edosmia gairdneri. August 7th, noon halt [1842. Stillwater River, adjacent to South Pass, Frémont County, Wyoming]" (NY-Torrey!). "San it, delicious root resembling sweet potatoe, Menny bushels dug every year, low land. June 26" "Frémont?" (packet with root fragments GH!). The note quoted here appears to be in the same handwriting as that of the label accompanying *Ipomoea leptophylla* at NY (q.v.), and it is the same as that of the August 5th specimen. The spelling is certainly not that of Frémont. On 26 June, however, Frémont was at or in Kearney County, Nebraska, far to the east of the known distribution of *Perideridia.* "Without fruit" (Torrey, 1843: 86).

Elaeagnus argentea Pursh
"On a lake in the Wind River mountains. August 12–17 [1842. Sublette County, Wyoming]" (Torrey, 1843: 92). "Wyoming Territory, (Frémont.)" (Watson, 1871: 319).

Elymus canadensis ≡ *E. canadensis* L.
"Little Blue river of the Kansas. June 22 [1842. Near Powell, Jefferson County, Nebraska]" (Torrey, 1843: 94).

Elymus virginicus = *E. canadensis* L.
"Big Blue river of the Kansas. June 20 [1842. Probably Marshall County, Kansas]" (Torrey, 1843: 94). "FExRM, 1842" (MO!).

***Emplectocladus* Torr.**, Smiths. Contr. 6(2): 10. 1853. (2nd)
Type species: ***Emplectocladus fasciculatus* Torr.** ≡ *Prunus fasciculata* (Torr.) A. Gray
Protologue locality: "Sierra Nevada of California; probably in the southern part of the range. The only specimens of this plant brought by Colonel Frémont had unfortunately lost their labels, so that we have no certain information as to its precise station, and of the size which it attains. Neither, for want of fruit, can we determine its nearest affinities. It is probable, however, that the genus belongs to the Tribe Dryadeae. In many respects it resembles Adenostoma of that tribe, but it differs in the even calyx without glands in the throat; in being almost destitute of a style, as well as in the mode of inflorescence, the form of the ovary, &c. There may also be considerable difference in the fruit, as the appearance of the ovary seems to indicate." Type: "California. Labels not found. Frémont's 2nd Exp." (holotype NY-Torrey!). The sheet at GH bears a note "at them and I enclose a small piece of Emplectocladus from Frémont's specimen. No other locality on label" (isotype fragment GH!). The specimen at GH is certainly a portion of the type; it is in a fragment envelope mounted on a sheet with four extraneous collections. It bears the label, "Herb. Torr. Herbarium Columbia College, fourth and Madison Avenue." The holotype sheet bears two small sheets of drawings, the smaller of which has several diagnostic notes. One of the notations reads "N. genus, allied to Adenostoma & Purshia." There is another notation on the sheet proper: "N. G.? near Adenostoma." These and the detailed sketches are indicative, along with the Torrey discussion with the original description, of the nature of the specimen as holotype.

Encelia eriocephala A. Gray, Proc. Amer. Acad. 8: 657. 1873. = *Geraea canescens* Torr. & A. Gray in A. Gray
"Fort Mohave, Fort Yuma and elsewhere along the Colorado and vicinity, *Coulter*, *Frémont*" (Brewer et al., 1876: 352).

Encelia frutescens A. Gray
"Gravelly ravines, &c. southeastern borders of California and adjacent parts of Arizona, Nevada, and Utah, *Frémont*" (Brewer et al., 1876: 352).

Ephedra nevadensis S. Wats. includes *E. occidentalis* pro parte

Ephedra occidentalis = *E. nevadensis* S. Wats. pro parte
Frémont (1845: 217).

Epilobium angustifolium L. includes *E. spicatum*

Epilobium ciliatum Raf. includes *E. coloratum*

Epilobium coloratum = *E. ciliatum* Raf.
"Black Hills of the Platte to the Sweet Water river. Aug. 4–31 [1842]" (Torrey, 1843: 85).

Epilobium spicatum = *E. angustifolium* L.
"From the Red Buttes to the Wind River mountains. Aug. 13–31 [1842]" (Torrey, 1843: 85).

Epinettes des prairies = *Grindelia squarrosa* (Pursh) Dun. in DC.
Frémont (1845:140).

Equisetum arvense ≡ *E. arvense* L.
"On a lake in the Wind River mountains. Aug. 12–17 [1842. Sublette County, Wyoming]" (Torrey, 1843: 94).

Equisetum hyemale ≡ *E. hyemale* L.
"FExCal, 1845–7 [probably 1846]. 304" (NY-Torrey!). The specimen is annotated as "Equisetum × ferrissii Clute" by R. L. Hauke. This name became a catchall for "rushes" in the Frémont journals, including probably species of *Juncus, Scirpus*, and grasses. The name "prele" is applied at least in part to *Equisetum.*

Equisetum laevigatum A. Br.
"FExCal, 1845–7 [both the 5 and the 7 marked out]. 430 [possibly 1846]" (NY-Torrey!).

Equisetum telmateia Ehrh.
"FExCal, 1845–7 [1846]" (NY-Torrey!).

Eriastrum diffusum (A. Gray) H. L. Mason
"423, 1844. Frémont. Gilia (bollomioides) diffusa n. sp. Torr. & Gray, Fl. N. Amer." (NY-Torrey!). Evidently this is the material that was later named *Gilia filifolia* var. *diffusa* A. Gray, but without citation of collections or collectors (Gray 1873). Adjacent to the plant is a note in Gray's writing: "This, the original G. diffusa, is not the one later so called."

Erigeron bellidiastrum ≡ *E. bellidiastrum* Nutt.
"On the Platte [1842]" (Torrey, 1843: 87).

Erigeron canadensis ≡ *Conyza canadensis* (L.) Cronq.
"On the Platte, from near its mouth to the Red Buttes. Latter part of September to July 30 [1842]" (Torrey, 1843: 87).

Erigeron engelmannii A. Nels.
"Frémont 2nd Exp." (NY-Torrey!).

Erigeron foliosus Nutt.
"FExCal, 1845–7. 498. 1846. Erigeron Douglasii" and "FExCal, 1845–7 [1846]. Erigeron Douglasii" (both NY-Torrey!).

Erigeron glabellum [*glabellus*] ≡ *E. glabellus* Nutt.
"On the Platte [1842]" (Torrey, 1843: 87). "E. glabellum. Torr. & Gray, Flora, N. Amer. Wind R. Mountains. Frémont. 7 August [South Pass, Frémont County, Wyoming]" and "FExCal, 1843–4. Erigeron glabellum B. asperum" (both NY-Torrey!).

Erigeron glaucus Ker.
"FExCal, 1845–7. Ii. 1846. Dr. Gray" (NY-Torrey!; GH!).

Erigeron macranthum [*macranthus*] ≡ *E. speciosus* (Lindley) DC. var. *macranthus* (Nutt.) Cronq.
"On the Platte [1842]" (Torrey, 1843: 87). "A. salsuginosus B. Torr. & Gray, Flora, N. Amer. Wind R. Chain. Frémont" and "Erigeron macranthum, *Nutt.* Torr. & Gray, Flora, N. Amer. Platte. Frémont" (both NY-Torrey!).

Erigeron peregrinus (Banks) Greene
"A. salsuginosus, *Richards*. Torr. & Gray, Flora, N. Amer. Wind R. Chain, near 7000 feet. Frémont" (NY-Torrey!). The two specimens of *E. peregrinus* are mounted on the same sheet with a single plant tentatively identified as *E. subtrinervis* (q.v.).

Erigeron pumilus Nutt. subsp. *concinnoides* Cronq.
"FExCal, 1843–4. 448, 1844. Erigeron concinhum (A.Gr)" (NY-Torrey!).

Erigeron simplex Greene includes *Aster glacialis*

Erigeron speciosus (Lindley) DC. var. *macranthus* (Nutt.) Cronq. includes *E. macranthus*

Erigeron strigosum [*strigosus*] ≡ *E. strigosus* Muhl. ex Willd.
"On the Platte [1842]" (Torrey, 1843: 87). "FExCal, 1845–7. 99. 1845. Erigeron tenue" (NY-Torrey!; GH!). "FExCal, 1845–7. Erigeron Philadelphicum" (US!).

Erigeron subtrinervis Rydb. ex Port. & Britt.?
"FExCal, 1845–7. 95 & 97, 1845. Erigeron between glabellum & speciosum J. T." (NY-Torrey!). See also *E. peregrinus* above.

Eriodictyon angustifolium Nutt.
"Eriodyction?? Frémont's 2nd Exp. 306. 1844" and "FExCal, 1845–47. 334, 1846. April 25–26 [East of Redding, Shasta County, California]. E. californicum." (both NY-Torrey!).

Eriogonum alatum Torr. in Sitgr.
"In montibus Scopulosis in regione superiore fl. Platte meridionalis et Bahia Salada [South Park] (Frémont!)" (Bentham, 1856: 6). "FExCal, 1843. 425. Eriogonum (Pterygonum) alatum, *Torr.* Upland prairies, sandy soil. Sources of the Platte" (NY-Torrey!). "FExCal, 1845. 288. Bahia Salada [South Park, Colorado, 2 Sept. 1845]" (NY-Torrey!). The 288 sheet has attached a small sheet of detailed drawings by Torrey.

Eriogonum annuum ≡ *E. annuum* Nutt.

"North fork of the Platte. September 4 [1842. West of Scotts Bluff, Scotts Bluff County, Nebraska]" (Torrey, 1843: 92). "No. 239. Dry Fork, July 29th Sand [probably 3rd expedition, 1845, when ca 3 days east of Bent's Fort, Colorado]"; the tag also bears a second notation "Piney Creek of Grand River [Eagle County, Colorado, but well out of the range of the species]" (Figure 22); "Frémont's 3rd Exp. (105) 1845" (NY-Torrey!) and "Between Bent's Fort and upper Puebla [Otero to Pueblo cos., Colorado], 454, Eriogonum annuum *Nutt.* [16–20 August] 1845" (NY-Sartwell!; GH!, but without the locality information). "FExCal, 1845. 230. Betweeen Bent's Fort & Pueblo [16–20 August 1945]" (NY-Torrey!, mounted on the type sheet of *Eriogonum annuum* Torr. with the Nuttall isotype from Arkansas]. "In Arkansas usque ad mont. Scopulosis Frémont!" (Bentham, 1856: 19).

Eriogonum brevicaule Nutt.

"FExRM, 1842, 13 & 14 August [Sublette County, Wyoming]. Eriogonum brevicaule *Nutt. Benth. in DC. Prodr.* 'Seems to be exactly E. brevicaule Nutt. spec. of Geyer (Oregon 139) in Herb Gray named by Bentham. It was afterwards sent to Mr. Bentham & is the plant quoted by him as Frémont's (excl. syn. E. fremontii)'" (Torrey, 1843: 92). This is the basis for the name *Eriogonum fremontii* Torr. ex Benth. in DC. (q.v.), which was published as a synonym. "fl Platte superioris (Gordon! Geyer! n 139 Frémont!) *E. fremontii* Torr. in Frém. report)" (Bentham, 1856: 18). "FExRM, 1842. 'Eriogonum fremontii *Torr.* Aug. 26–31 [From near Alcova, Natrona Co., through Converse and Platte, into Goshen Co., Wyoming]'" (three sheets, two with detailed Torrey drawings NY-Torrey!). "Frémont's 2d Exped. E. Frémontii, *Torr.* in pl Frém. Exped. = brevicaule, Nutt." (GH!).

Eriogonum caespitosum Nutt.

"Horse-shoe creek, upper north fork of the Platte. July 22 [1842. Platte County, Wyoming]" (Torrey, 1843: 92). "Rocky Mountains, Nuttall, Frémont, &c." (Torrey & Gray 1870: 157). "FExCal, 1844, 470, Eriogonum caespitosum *Nutt.* May 16, Wasatch Mountains [near Little Salt Lake, Iron County, Utah]" (NY-Torrey!).

Eriogonum cernuum Nutt.

"Scopulosis in regione fl. Platte super. Frémont!" (Bentham in DC., 1856: 21). "FExCal, 1845. 289. Eriogonum cernuum Nutt. [crossed out]. deflexum sp. nov. 'Bahia Salada' [Bayou Salada is South Park, Chaffee or Lake counties, Colorado, 2 September 1845]" (NY-Torrey!). The sheet has attached to it a small paper with detailed drawings by Torrey. "FExCal, 1845–7. 289. 1845. Eriogonum cernuum, Nutt." (GH!).

***Eriogonum cordalum* Torr. & Frém.** in Frém., Rep. Explor. Exped. Oregon & California 317. 1845. (2nd)

Protologue locality: "With the preceding [*E. subreniforme*], from which it is easily distinguished by the form of its leaves and color of the pubescence." The Frémont party was along the lower elevation portions of the Sacramento, i.e., the American River, during the period 6–22 March 1844, but the material more likely came from east of the Sierra

Nevada, in the Mohave Desert. The name is evidently a misspelling of "*cordatum*" (see Torrey & Gray, 1870). No authentic material was found at NY. It is cited by Bentham (1856: 21) as "In California." Torrey and Gray (1870) report the sheet lost. Reveal (1969) cites this name as a nomen in synonymy with *Eriogonum trichopes* Torr. in Emory. The description is sufficiently vague as to potentially represent other taxa as well. If adequately typified, the name would most certainly replace one in current use.

***Eriogonum corymbosum* Benth.** in DC., Prodr. 14: 17. 1856. (3rd)

Protologue locality: "In itinere Californico propre Grand-River (Frémont!)." Type: "FExCal, 1845, 248, on road, day we reached Grand River. Woody bush in a Draw [illegible word]" (holotype NY-Torrey!; isotype GH!). The GH label lacks the notation of the NY specimen. "Utah (Frémont and Gunnison) and New Mexico" (Watson, 1871: 303). "Utah and W. New Mexico, Frémont, Beckwith, Newberry (San Juan River, in Macomb's Expedition), Whipple" (Torrey & Gray, 1870: 171). Frémont was never on the Grand (i.e., Colorado) River in Utah; he intersected it in Colorado during 4–11 September 1845. It is probable, as J. L. Reveal (personal communication) contends, that it was taken on 4 September 1845 in or near Eagle County, Colorado, near Yarmony, northeast of Piney Creek.

Eriogonum dichotomum Dougl. = *E. niveum* Dougl. ex Benth.

"Forma paniculis magis virgatis, *E. strictum*, var. *lachnostegia*, Benth. in DC. [q.v.]. Interior of Oregon, and Utah, Douglas, Nuttall, Frémont" (Torrey & Gray, 1870: 175).

Eriogonum effusum Nutt.

"Platte superioris (Nutt.! Frémont!)" (Bentham, 1856: 18). "Eriogonum. Torr. & Gray, Flora, N. Amer. Frémont's 1st Exped. 1842" (NY-Sartwell!). "FExRM, 1842. July 24th Apres midi, Buttes de Sables [Converse County, Wyoming]" (GH-Thurber!). The handwriting, ink, etc. appear to be the same as on the specimen of *Ipomoea leptophylla* at NY!, which lacks a Frémont label. "FExCal, 1843–4. E. effusum. E. microthecum, var. effusum," "Frémont's 2nd Expedn. E. effusum," and "FExCal, 1843. 591. 'Heights above N. Fork of the Platte. E. effusum'" (all NY-Torrey!). "FExCal, 1845. 486. E. brevicaule Nutt. E. Frémontii, Torr." and "FExCal, 1845–7. 486. 1845. E. effusum var. rosmarinoides, Benth.?" (GH!). The latter sheet is placed here because it has the same number as the former, but might be mislabeled, perhaps being a duplicate (hence an isotype) of var. *rosmarinoides* Benth., q.v. It is probable that number 486 was taken at or near Bent's Fort, Otero County, Colorado.

***Eriogonum effusum* Nutt. *β? rosmarinoides* Benth.** in DC., Prodr. 14: 18. 1856. (3rd) ≡ *E. effusum* var. *rosmariniodes* Benth. in DC.

Protologue locality: "In California (Frémont!). (v. s. m h. Torr. et Hook.)." Type: "Frémont's Expedition to California, 1845, 181, July 24, clay cliffs (Probably in the [illegible word])" (holotype NY-Torrey!; GH!; seen by J. L. Reveal at K, MIN, and MO). During the fourth week in July 1845 the Frémont expedition was along the Smoky Hill Fork, Kansas. The variety is known from only six counties in Kansas (fide J. L. Reveal, personal communication), four along the Smoky Hill Fork: Ellis, Trego, Gove, and Logan. The specimens undoubtedly came from one of these.

Eriogonum elongatum Benth.
"In California (Frémont!)" (Bentham, 1856: 14). "Part of SSSS. Frémont. E. elongatum" (GH!).

Eriogonum fasciculatum Benth. var. *foliosum* (Nutt.) S. Stokes
"FExCal, 1845–7. Eriogonum fasciculatum. Rrrr, 1846. Gray. J. T. Eriogonum Fasciculatum, *Benth.* also. ? E. rosmarinifolium, Nutt. pl. Gambel." (NY-Torrey!; NY-Sartwell!; GH!; MO!).

Eriogonum fasciculatum Benth. var. *polifolium* (Benth.) Torr. & A. Gray includes *E. polifolium* Benth.

Eriogonum fremontii Torr. ex Benth. in DC., Prodr. 14: 18. 1856 (pro syn.). = *E. brevicaule* Nutt.
"Sweet Water river, Aug. 7 [1842. Adjacent to South Pass, Frémont County, Wyoming]" (Torrey, 1843: 92), a nomen nudum. (pro syn. *E. brevicaule* Nutt.).

Eriogonum gracile Benth.
"In California (Frémont!)" (Bentham, 1856: 17). "FExCal, 1845–7. Tttt. 1846. Gray. Eriogonum vimineum (crossed out) gracile. Part of Frémont cited in DC.!" (GH!; NY!). There are two small sheets of Torrey's drawings attached, the upper one notes: "1210 Expl = Frémont, 1846 ssss."

***Eriogonum inflatum* Torr. & Frém.** in Frém., Rep. Explor. Exped. Oregon & California 317. 1845. (2nd)
Protologue locality: "The plant was found on barren hills in the lower part of North California." Type: "392, 1844. Frémont. April 25, 1844. Barren hills, Calif." (holotype NY-Torrey!: microfiche BRY!; isotype K, fide J. L. Reveal, personal communication). This remarkable species with inflated stems was first mentioned by Frémont (1845: 260) on 24 April, while the party was along the Mohave River, in San Bernardino County, California. The Frémont party was at Agua de Tomaso or Bitter Spring, west of present Baker, San Bernardino County, California, on 25 April 1844. "In montibus Scopulosis Frémont!" (Bentham, 1856: 20). "Eriogonum inflatum Torr. in Frém. 2nd Report. Frémont!" (isotype GH!). "FExCal, 1849. Eriogonum inflatum" (NY-Torrey!).

Eriogonum maculatum A. Heller
"FExCal, 1844. near Agua de Tomaso, a trib. of the Colorado, about lat. 35° N" (NY-Torrey!). The specimen was likely taken on 25 or 26 April 1844; the spring is near present Baker, San Bernardino County, California. The specimen is mounted on a sheet with a Douglas isotype of *Eriogonum angulosum* Benth.

Eriogonum niveum Dougl. ex Benth. includes *E. strictum* var. *lachnostegium* Benth. in DC.

***Eriogonum nudum* Dougl. ex Benth. var. *pubiflorum* Benth.** in DC., Prodr. 14: 13. 1856. (3rd)

Protologue locality: "In California (Frémont!)." Type: "Frémont's Expedition to California, 1846. 502. Eriogonum (truncatum) n. sp.—nudum Dougl.? probably. E. nudum var. pubiflorum, Benth." (holotype NY-Torrey!; isotypes GH!, US!, and at MIN and K, fide J. L. Reveal, personal communication). "California, Frémont, Rich, Heermann, Horn, & C." (Torrey & Gray, 1870: 167).

***Eriogonum obtusum* Benth.** in DC., Prodr. 14: 15. 1856. (3rd) = *E. racemosum* Nutt.

Protologue locality: "In montibus Scopulosis ad Decharge du lac (Frémont!)" (l.c.). Type: "FExCal, 1845–7. 5? 301. 'Discharge du Lac' (near Rocky Mts?) [Colorado or Utah?]. E. n. sp. obtusum. near E. ramosum *Nutt.* but leaves broader and more obtuse" (holotype NY-Torrey!). The sheet has attached a small plate of Torrey's sketches of floral parts, labeled "301. 1845. Fremont."

Eriogonum ovalifolium ≡ *E. ovalifolium* Nutt.

"Horse-shoe creek, upper north fork of the Platte. July 22 [1842. Platte County, Wyoming]" (Torrey, 1843: 92). Two sheets (three collections) NY-Torrey!: "Eucycla purpurea, *Nutt.*! in Jour Acad. Phil. n. ser. FExCal, 1843–44, June 5th, 536, 1844, Uinta Plains, Frémont [Uintah County, Utah, east of present Whiterocks]." Two additional Frémont collections are mounted on the type (NY-Torrey!) sheet of *E. ovalifolium* Nutt.: "FExRM, 1842, July 22, Horseshoe Creek, upper N. Fork of the Platte [near Glendo, Platte County, Wyoming]," and "Frémont's 1st Exped. 22 July 1842." The sheet is annotated "Eucycla purpurea Nutt."; "E. purpureum"; and "ovalifolium β purpureum."

Eriogonum parvifolium = ?

Noted by Torrey (1843 catalogue preface).

***Eriogonum polifolium* Benth.** in DC., Prodr. 14: 12. 1856. (2nd) ≡ *E. fasciculatum* var. *polifolium* (Benth.) Torr. & A. Gray

Protologue locality: "In Sierra Nevada Californiae (Frémont!)." Type: "Frémont's Expedition to California, 1844. Sierra Nevada. Apr. 13 [Owens River, near Bakersfield, Kern County, California]" (syntype NY-Torrey!). "FExCal. E. polifolium. Las Vegas. May 3, 1844, 427, 1844 [Clark County, Nevada]" (NY-Torrey!). There is an attached sheet of Torrey's drawings.

***Eriogonum polyanthum* Benth.** in DC., Prodr. 14: 12. 1856. (3rd)

Protologue locality: "In California (Frémont!)." Type: "Frémont's Expedition to California, 1846, 495. Eriogonum sphaerocephalum *Dougl.*" (holotype NY-Torrey!; istoypes GH!, GH-Thurber!, GH-Lowell!). The Thurber specimen at GH lacks a number and is similar to the following; "Eriogonum sphaerocephalum. From Frémont. Torrey" (isotype NY-Sartwell!). J. L. Reveal indicates (personal communication) that there are isotypes at K, MO, and US. He considers the species to be valid, related to, and probably with, other serpentine species, but known only from the Frémont collection.

Eriogonum purpureum (Nutt.) Benth. = *E. ovalifolium* Nutt.
"In montibus Scopulosis (Nuttall! Burke! Frémont!)" (Bentham, 1856: 10).

Eriogonum racemosum Nutt. includes *E. obtusum* Benth. in DC.
"N. New Mexico and Utah, Fendler, Frémont" (Torrey & Gray, 1870: 175).

***Eriogonum reniforme* Torr. & Frém.** in Frém., Rep. Explor. Exped. Oregon & California 317. 1845. (2nd)

Protologue locality: "On the Sacramento River; March." The party was in the vicinity of the lower reaches of the Sacramento River, i.e., the American River, from 6–24 March 1844. The locality is cited by Torrey and Gray (1870: 184) as "S. E. California, probably on the Mohave, Frémont" [i.e., San Bernardino County, California]. Type: "Eriogonum reniforme, Torr. in Frém. 2nd Report. Frémont, 1844" (NY-Torrey!: microfiche BRY!). The sheet at NY has attached a plate of Torrey's sketches of floral parts. "In itinere Californico (Frémont!)" (Bentham, 1856: 21). The species is known in California today only from the Mojave Desert, where it extends as far north as eastern Kern County, along Frémont's route. More likely it was collected in April in Kern County, given the age of the specimen.

Eriogonum roseum Dur. & Hilg. includes *E. virgatum* Benth. in DC.

Eriogonum sphaerocephalum Dougl. ex Benth. = *E. polyanthum* Benth. in DC.

***Eriogonum strictum* Benth. var. *lachnostegium* Benth.** in DC., Prodr., 14: 16. 1856. (2nd) = *E. niveum* Dougl. ex Benth.

Protologue locality: "In collibus ad Snake River (Frémont!) (vs. in h. Torr)." Type: "Frémont's Expedition to California, 1843. no 786. Eriogonum strictum var. lachnostegium, Benth.! in herb *Torr.* Hills, Snake River, Oct 6[(?) 1843. Hills by the Snake River [possibly Elmore County, Idaho]" (holotype NY-Torrey!; isotype GH!).

Eriogonum thomasii Torr.
"Fort Mohave (Frémont, locality not given)" (Torrey & Gray, 1870: 184).

Eriogonum umbellatum ≡ *E. umbellatum* Torr.

"Sweet Water river, Aug. 7 [1842. Adjacent to South Pass, Frémont County, Wyoming] 153" (Torrey, 1843: 92). "FExRM, 1842. Eriogonum umbellatum, Torr. in Ann. Lyc. 2. p. 241" (NY-Torrey!). There is a drawing (Figure 23) of *E. umbellatum* at NY!, labeled: "Drawing made from Frémont specimen of 1842." "FExCal, 1843. 608. Eriogonum umbellatum Torr. in Ann. Lyc. not of Benth." (GH!). The GH sheet has a duplicate of the drawing mounted on it. "FExCal, 1843. 400" (two collections NY-Torrey!). The label bears the notations in faded pencil "Upper Platte. July 23[?]." Frémont and party were at St. Vrain's Fort, present Weld County, Colorado on 23 July 1843. The specimen number 400 is mounted on the same sheet as: "FExCal, 1845–7. 153, 1845." According to J. L. Reveal (personal communication) there is an 1842 specimen with the number 153 in the herbarium at Michigan State University (MSC).

***Eriogonum umbellatum* Torr. var. *majus* Benth.** in DC., Prodr. 14: 11. 1856. (3rd)
Protologue locality: "In montibus Scopulosis region sup. fl. Platte, Sweetwater, etc. (Gordon! Frémont! Burke! Geyer! n 241 et 403)" (l.c.). Two sheets (syntypes): "Frémont's Expedition to California, 1845, 237. near head of Arkansas River [probably early September, in or near Lake County, Colorado]"; and "Frémont's Expedition to California, 1845, 94 & 99" (NY-Torrey!). Reveal (1969: 532) designated Geyer 403 (K) as lectotype.

Eriogonum vimineum Dougl. ex Benth.
"Frémont's 2nd Expedn. 1844. California. Remarkably proliferous" (NY-Torrey!). "In California (Frémont!)" (Bentham, 1856: 17).

***Eriogonum virgatum* Benth.** in DC., Prodr. 14: 16. 1856. (3rd) = *E. roseum* Dur. & Hilg.
Protologue locality: "In California (Frémont!)." Type: "Frémont's Expedition to California, 1846. Eriogonum gracile Bth. n. sp. near E. vimineum. DC. prod. XIV p. 17" (holotype NY-Torrey!; two isotypes GH!, GH-Lowell!; MO!). "California, on the plains, usually more northern than the preceding [*E. elongatum*], Frémont, &c." (Torrey & Gray, 1870: 177). The GH and MO labels bear the notation "Ssss. 1846." The name has been long associated with the annual, *E. roseum* Dur. & Hilg., with which *E. virgatum* is placed as a synonym. However, one of the sheets at GH has a root, and the plant is definitely the perennial, *E. elongatum.*

Eriophyllum lanatum (Pursh) Forbes var. *achillioides* (DC.) Jepson
"FExCal, 1845–7. Bb. 1846. Dr. Gray. Bahia lanata B tenuifolia" (NY-Torrey!).

Eriophyllum lanatum var. *grandiflorum* (A. Gray) Jepson includes *Bahia lanata* var. *grandiflora* A. Gray

Eritrichium canescens (Benth.) A. Gray ≡ *Plagiobothrys canescens* Benth.
"California—Frémont" (Gray, 1874).

***Eritrichium crassicepalum* Torr. & A. Gray**, Pacific R.R. Rep. 2: 171. 1855. ≡ *Cryptantha crassisepala* (Torr. & A. Gray) Greene
Protologue locality: "On the Pecos, Llano Estacado, &c.; by Frémont on the Upper Platte. It is the same as No. 640 of Fendler's New Mexican collection." Type: "Frémont's Expedition to the Rocky Mountains, 1842. July 2nd, 1842. Eritrichium crassisepalum *Torr.* Forks of the Platte" (syntype NY-Torrey!).

***Eritrichium glomeratum* DC. var. (?) *fulvocanescens* A. Gray ex S. Wats.**, Rep. Geog. Explor. 40th Parallel, Bot. 5: 2483. 1871. (2nd) ≡ *Cryptantha fulvocanescens* (A. Gray) Payson
Protologue locality: "It is 632 Fendler, from New Mexico, (E. fulvocanescens, A. Gray, Ms. in Herb.,) and 467, 522 and 577 Frémont, (1844,) probably collected in Utah." The taxon is lectotypified on "632 Fendler" (see Higgins, 1971: 42). Number 522 has been identified as a specimen of *Cryptantha humilis* (q.v.). The Frémont materials are syntypes.

Erodium cicutarium (L.) L'Her.
"Frémont's 2d Exped." (GH!); "Frémont's 2nd Expedn. 66, 1844" (NY-Torrey!); "FExCal, 1845–7. 165. 1846. Erod." (GH!). This species is cited many times in the expedition of 1843–44 especially; it is also cited variously as alfalferia or geranium.

Erodium macrophyllum Hook. & Arn.
"FExCal, 1843–4. 85. 1844. Geranium [crossed out]. Between Kosumne [Cosumne] & Mokelemne Rivers—Valley of Joaquin" (NY-Torrey!). During the third expedition the name "*geranium*" appears in the journal account, possibly based in large part on this species.

Erysimum asperum ≡ *E. asperum* (Nutt.) DC.
"South fork of the Platte. July 4 [1842. Ca. 40 miles west of Platte forks, Keith County, Nebraska]" (Torrey, 1843: 83). "Erysimum asperum. July 4, 1842. Frémont's 1st Expedn," "Toualumne sink [Stanislaus County, California], March 1846. Frém. 3rd Exp.," and "Arkansas River, above Pueblo. Frémont's 3rd Exped" (all three NY-Torrey!).

Erysimum cheiranthoides ≡ *E. cheiranthoides* L.
"Black Hills. July 23 [1842. Near Orin, Converse County, Wyoming]" (Torrey, 1843: 83).

Eschscholzia caespitosa Benth.
"FExCal, 305. 1846" (NY-Torrey!).

Eschscholzia californica Cham.
"Frémont's 2nd Expedn., 5, 1844," "Frémont. 401. 1846. E. leptandra, and from east of Sierra Nevada," and "FExCal, 203, 1846" (all three NY-Torrey!). "California. Frémont. Ex herb. J. Torrey. Torr. & Gr. Fl. N. Amer." (GH-Thurber!); "FExCal, 1845. 233. 1846. E. Californica" (GH!; MO!); and "FExCal, 1845–7. 401. 1846. E. Californica" (GH!). Frémont (1848: 19). This, the state flower of California, is cited on numerous occasions in both the 1843–44 and 1845–47 expeditions, always in glowing terms, and sometimes being compared by Frémont with the "gold" of California.

Eschscholzia crocea = *E. californica* Cham.
Frémont (1845: 244).

Eschscholzia glyptosperma Greene?
"FExCal, 1849" (NY-Torrey!).

Esparcette = *Hedysarum*? or *Oxytropis*?
Frémont (1845: 115).

Eucrypta micrantha (Torr.) Heller
"FExCal, 1849" (NY-Torrey!).

***Eunanus fremontii* Benth.** in A. DC., Prodr. 10: 374. 1846. (2nd) ≡ *Mimulus fremontii* (Benth.) A. Gray
Protologue locality: "in montibus Scopulosis (Frémont!)." Type: "Frémont's 2nd Expedition" (NY-Torrey!: microfiche BRY!). "Southern California (erroneously stated as Rocky Mountains)" (Abrams, 1951: 752).

Eupatorium maculatum L. includes *E. purpureum*

Eupatorium purpureum = *E. maculatum* L.
Frémont (1845: 150).

Euphorbia albomarginata Torr. & A. Gray
"Frémont's 2nd Expedn. Euphorbia albomarginata, *Torr. & Gray*" and "FExCal, 1849. Euphorbia albomarginata *Torr. & Gray*" (both NY-Torrey!). The 1849 Frémont specimen, likely collected by Fredrick Creutzfeldt, is mounted on a sheet with collections by Schott and Major Thomas (from Fort Yuma). Major George H. Thomas was promoted to General during the Civil War and is known as "The Rock of Chicamauga." "FExCal, 1845–7. Wwww. 1846" (MO!).

Euphorbia corollata ≡ *E. corollata* L.
"On the Kanzas [1842]" (Torrey, 1843: 92).

Euphorbia fendleri Torr. & Gray
"428, 1844. Frémont's 2nd Expedn." (NY-Torrey!).

Euphorbia marginata ≡ *E. marginata* Pursh
"Forks of the Platte. September 11 [1842. Lincoln County, Nebraska]" (Torrey, 1843: 92). "FExRM, 1845–6. 23, 1845. = 112, 241. Euphorbia marginata, *Pursh.* Sandy places, July 30." (NY-Torrey!). The sheet at NY has two plants, one in flower, the other past flower.

Euphorbia missurica Raf.
"FExCal, 1845. No 102 & 234—July 30. Dry Fork [three days journey east of Bent's Fort, Colorado]" (NY-Torrey!).

***Euphorbia montana* Torr. *β robusta* Torr.,** U.S. and Mex. Bound. Bot. 192. 1859. (1st) = *Euphorbia brachycera* Engelm. in Emory?
Protologue locality: "Var. *β*., on the upper Platte; James, Nuttall, Frémont; is a much shorter plant." (Torrey, 1859). Type: "FExRM, 1842. Euphorbia montana *β*. Engelmann" (syntype NY-Torrey!).

Euphorbia obtusata = ?
"Little Blue river of the Kanzas [1842. 22 or 23 June]" (Torrey, 1843: 92).

Euphorbia polygonifolia = ?
"South Fork of the Platte. July 4 [1842. Ca. 40 miles west of Platte forks, Keith County, Nebraska]" (Torrey, 1843: 92).

Eurotia lanata (Pursh) Moq. ≡ *Ceratoides lanata* (Pursh) J. T. Howell
See specimen citations under *Ceratoides lanata* (Pursh) J. T. Howell. "Red Buttes to the mountains. Aug. 18–25" (Torrey, 1843: 91). "42, 440 Frémont" (Watson, 1874: 121).

Eustoma russellianum = *E. grandiflorum* (Raf.) Shinners

Eustoma grandiflorum (Raf.) Shinners
"Ex herb. J. Torrey. Eustoma Russelianum. Torr. & Gr. Fl. N. Amer. Frémont's 1st Expedn." (mounted with a collection by H. Engelmann, GH!). "Lisianthus Russelianus *Hook.* Eustoma Russelianum. Frémont's Expedn. to the Rocky Mts. 1842. North Fork of the Platte" and "Frémont's 2nd Exp. 1844? July 9" (two on same sheet NY-Torrey!). The question on the year of collection places doubt as to provenance; whether 9 July 1843 or 9 July 1844, the specimen came either from in or near El Paso County, Colorado, or from western Kansas.

Eutoca sericea ≡ *Phacelia sericea* (Graham) A. Gray
"Wind River mountains [1842. 12–17 Aug. Sublette County, Wyoming]!" (Torrey, 1843: 89). "FExRM, 1842" (NY-Torrey!).

Evernia vulpina Ach. = *Letharia columbiana* (Nutt.) Thoms. (fide Clayton Newberry, BRY, 8 April 1991)
"53. Evernia vulpina, Ach. *Tuckerm. Syn. p.* 11. *In montibus Californiae legit cl.* Frémont; *comm. cl.* Torrey" (NY Lichenes Sept. Curanes E. Tuckerman. Fascic. III. IV. 1855!).

Evolvulus nuttallianus Roem. & Schult.
"239, 1843. [and] 235 & 237, 1843. Frémont's 2nd Exped." (NY-Torrey!). The sheet has three separate collections, two mere branches, 239, and entire plants, 235 and 237.

Ferula dissoluta S. Wats. (a new name for *Leptotaenia dissecta* Nutt., i.e., *Lomatium dissectum* (Nutt.) Math. & Const., q.v.)
"Klamath Lake (*Frémont*)" (Brewer et al., 1876: 271).

Festuca = *Elymus* sp.
Frémont (1845: 176, 270). The bunch grasses common through much of Frémont's journeys are mainly species of *Elymus* sens. lat. (including *Agropyron*).

Festuca nutans = *F. obtusa* Biehler
"On the Kansas [1842. In June]" (Torrey, 1843: 94).

Festuca obtusa Biehler includes *F. nutans*

Festuca ovina ≡ *F. ovina* L.
"Alpine region of the Wind River mountains. Aug. 13–14 [1842. Sublette County, Wyoming]" (Torrey, 1843: 94).

Flax = *Linum perenne* L. (q.v.)

Fouquieria splendens Engelm.
"FExCal, 1849. Fouquieria" (NY-Torrey!). The Frémont fragments are mounted on a sheet with others by Emory and Wright.

***Frankenia jamesii* Torr. ex A. Gray**, Proc. Amer. Acad. 8: 622. 1873. (2nd)
Protologue locality: "Eastern base of the Rocky Mountains, on rocks and bluffs, Colorado Territory, James in Long's Expedition, Frémont; near Pueblo, Brandegee, J. H. Redfield, E. L. Greene. Western borders of Texas, C. Wright, no. 626.—Wright's specimen is out of flower. It is named as above by Dr. Torrey in my herbarium, on comparison with a fragment collected half a century ago by Dr. James, which he had recently determined, but had not published. It is now characterized from excellent specimens in full bloom, collected on bluffs of the Arkansas, near Pueblo, by my excellent correspondent, Rev. E. L. Greene." Type: "Frémont's Expedition to California, May 1st (408) 1844. Shrub one foot high; flowers white. Tributaries of the Colorado, near the 116° W. longitude" (syntypes NY-Torrey!, NY!), also "408, 1844. Frémont" (GH!). On 1 May 1844 Frémont was at Mountain Spring, Clark County, Nevada, far west of the known distribution of the species. Likely it came from near Pueblo, Pueblo County, Colorado, near Fountain Creek, along which Frémont traveled from 12–19 July 1843. Wright 626 at GH was designated lectotype by M. A. Whalen (annotation label); the Wright material at NY would be an isolectotype. The choice of lectotype is unfortunate; it is poor material as noted by Asa Gray above. A better choice would have been the Greene specimen cited by Gray.

Frankenia salina (Mol.) I. M. Johnst.
"Frémont's 3rd Exp. Prep. 1. Ex herb. J. Torrey. Torr. & Gr. Fl. N. Amer." and "Frémont's Expedition 1845–47 [1846]" (both GH!). "FExCal, 1845–7. DC vi. Benth. Frankenia grandiflora" (NY-Torrey!). "FExCal, 1845–7. Xx. 1846" (MO!).

***Franseria albicaulis* Torr.**, Smiths. Contr. 6(2): 16. 1853. (4th) = *Ambrosia dumosa* (A. Gray) Payne
Protologue locality: "Southern California [Arizona], probably on the Gila: Colonel Frémont. It was also found, without flower or fruit, by Major Emory, on the sandhills of the Gila; and is the plant referred to in my botanical appendix to his Report, as an apparently new species of Ambrosia." Type: "Frémont's Expedition to California, 1849. Franseria albicaulis Torr. sp. nov." (holotype NY-Torrey!: microfiche BRY!; isotype GH!). The material at NY was cited as type by Payne (1964: 423). The material at GH is mounted on a sheet with several other collections and bears the information "Frémont 1849."

***Franseria deltoidea* Torr.**, Smiths. Contr. 6(2): 15. 1853. (4th) ≡ *Ambrosia deltoidea* (Torr.) Payne
Protologue locality: "On the Gila River, S. California [Arizona]; collected by Colonel Frémont, in returning [to California] from his fourth journey. Found also by Dr. C. C. Parry, on the same river." Type: "Frémont's Expedition to California, 1849, Franseria deltoidea sp. nov." (holotype NY-Torrey!; isotype GH!). This specimen (Figure 24), the

best choice for the type (Payne, 1964: 421), was found by the writer in the general collection. The Frémont flowering branch is mounted on a sheet with two other collections: "Schott 111.59. Sonora Gila valley Las Lomas. v. 855" and "C. C. Parry 549, near Tucson, Sonora, April 1852." The label of the Frémont specimen bears typical Torrey anatomical sketches of flowers and parts. Frémont was in Arizona, along the Gila, on his fourth expedition in 1849, but specimens of this species in the NY type collection are by Emory 1846 and Parry 1852 (NY-Torrey!: microfiche BRY!). Presumed duplicates of the Parry and Frémont specimens are at GH!, mounted on a sheet with a large specimen by Palmer.

Franseria discolor = *Ambrosia tomentosa* Nutt.

"Near the Wind River mountains [1842]" (Torrey, 1843: 87). "Also gathered by Frémont on the Platte in the Wind River chain of the Rocky Mountains" (Gray, 1849: 80). "Franseria discolor Nutt. N. Platte near Rky. Mts. Frémont. Torr. & Gray, Flora, N. Amer." (GH!). The Frémont specimens (flowering branch and leaf) are mounted on a sheet with three other collections, one of them from the Rocky Mts. by Nuttall, a possible type fragment of *Franseria discolor* Nutt.

***Franseria dumosa* A. Gray** in Frém., Rep. Explor. Exped. Oregon & California 316. 1845. (2nd) ≡ *Ambrosia dumosa* (A. Gray) Payne

Type locality: "On the sandy uplands of the Mohahve [Mohave] river, and very common in all that region of North California. Flowering in April." Type: "Frémont's Expedition to California, 374, 1844. Franseria dumosa Gray, in Frémont's 2nd Report. Sandy uplands of the Mohave River—very common in all that region of North California" (isotype NY-Torrey!: microfiche BRY!). The Mohave River is completely within San Bernardino County, California. Frémont was along the Mohave River from at least 20–24 April 1844.

Frasera speciosa = *Swertia radiata* (Kellogg) Kuntze

"Defiles of the Wind River mountains. Aug. 13–14 [1842. Sublette County, Wyoming]" (Torrey, 1843: 90). "Frasera speciosa, Hook. Wind River Mountains, Aug. 13–14, 1842. Lt. Frémont" (two sheets at NY-Torrey!). "Frémont's 1st Exped." (GH!). "Frasera speciosa Hook. Frémont's 2d Expedition" (MO!).

Fraxinus americana L.

Frémont (1845: 109).

Fraxinus latifolia Benth.

"FExCal, 1846. 497. Fraxinus oregana, *Nutt.* Near Keysers, Bear River [probably Yuba County, California]. June" (NY-Torrey!; GH!). "FExCal, 1845–7. 479. 1846" (GH!). The sheet 479 at GH bears an annotation on the label in pencil: "[497 in Torrey's own set.]." The sheet is likely a duplicate of both of the above, and the number difference due to a transposition.

Fraxinus platycarpa = *F. americana* L.

"Lower Platte [1842]" (Torrey, 1843: 91).

***Fremontia* Torr.** in Frém., Rep. Expl. Exped. Rocky Mts. 91. 1843. (1st) = *Sarcobatus* Nees in Max.

Type species: *Batis vermiculatus* Hook.

Type locality: "FExRM, 1842. *Fremontia vermicularis*, Torr. July 30 [1842. Near Alcova, Natrona County, Wyoming]—Excursion to the *Pass*. n. gen. not in Moq. Tand. Chenop." (generitype NY!). There is a second sheet at NY! The generic name was certainly typified by Torrey on the basis of Frémont's material taken on the "excursion." It is academic, and perhaps impossible, that a genus be typified apart from its included species. The sheet is accompanied by a series of detailed sketches of the flowers and parts (Figure 28).

Fremontia vermicularis Torr. in Frém., Rep. Explor. Exped. Rocky Mts. 91. 1843. = *Sarcobatus vermiculatus* (Hook.) Torr. in Emory

Protologue type: "Upper north fork of the Platte, near the mouth of the Sweet Water. 30 July." "Excursion to the Pass [1842. Near Alcova, Natrona County, Wyoming] Frémont" (NY-Torrey!). This epithet is clearly a new combination for *Batis* ? *vermiculatus* Hook., as *F. vermicularis* (Hook.) Torr. (i.e., *vermiculatus*, either Torrey transposed the "t" in *vermiculatus* as an "r," or it is a typographic error. In any event, the spelling *vermicularis* is merely an orthographic variant). The species was reported as being widespread in the West in Torrey and Frémont (Frémont, 1845).

***Fremontia* Torr.**, Proc. Amer. Assoc. Advancem. Sci. 4: 191. 1851, not *Fremontia* Torrey in Frémont, 1843. (3rd) ≡ *Fremontodendron* Coville (1893: 74). Contr. U.S. Natl. Herb. 4: 74. 1893. Basionym for Fremontiaceae J. G. Agardh., Theoria Syst. Pl. 264. Apr.–Sep. 1858. ("Fremontieae"), nom. illeg. (Art. 18.3).

Type species: ***Fremontia californica* Torr.** ≡ *Fremontodendron californicum* (Torr.) Coville.

Protologue locality: "Sources of the Sacramento, in the northern part of the Sierra Nevada of California. Also hill-sides, Mariposa County, especially near the gold works of the Merced Company; flowering in May.—Rev. Mr. A. Fitch." Type: "Frémont's Expedition to California, 1845–7. Frémontia Californica Torr. 470. 1846. 'Mr. Sprague's drawing was taken from this specimen J. T.'" [lectotype NY-Torrey! (Kelman, 1991): microfiche BRY!; isolectotype MO!]. There are two other sheets in the type collection at NY, numbers 384 and 470. Specimen 384 is presumed to be a syntype (i.e., paratype); the other sheet, 470, is an isolectotype. "Southern Nevada, (Frémont)" (Watson, 1871: 267). "On a small head water of Cow Creek," Shasta County, California (Coville, 1893). "FExCal, 1845–7. Frémontia Californica. Specimen without label—evidently gathered late in the season" (NY-Torrey!).

Fremontodendron Coville, Contr. U.S. Natl. Herb. 4: 74. 1893.

Synonym: *Fremontia* Torr. (Torrey, 1853).

Fritillaria agrestis Greene

"FExCal, 1843–4. 397, 1846. Near Lassen's, upper Sacramento. Fruit of Fritillaria Kamtschatica" (NY-Torrey!). The label is from the second expedition, but the collection is from the third.

Fritillaria atropurpurea Nutt.

"FExCal, 411, 1846. Fritillaria 'lanceolata, var. minoribus *Benth. Pl. Hartw.*,' 2005 Hartweg, Calif. is the same but with broader leaves. Fork of the upper Sacramento, among the pines" (NY-Torrey!). The nomenclatural notes made by Torrey give an indication of the progression of ideas as new specimens became available for comparison.

Fritillaria liliacea Lindley?

"FExCal, March 1846. Toualumne River [Stanislaus County, California]. Fritillaria" (NY-Torrey!; GH!).

***Fritillaria pluriflora* Torr.** in Benth., Pl. Hartw. 338. 1857. (3rd)

Protologue locality: "In locis per tempus pluviorum inundatis, in valle Sacramento." Type: "FExCal, 1845–7. 213. 1846. Fritillaria pluriflora, Torr. in *Benth. Hart.* Feather River, Calif." (holotype GH!). "On the upper Sacramento (Hartweg), and on the Feather River, Frémont" (Watson, 1880 2: 169). The sheet at GH has both the collection by Frémont (213, 1846) and by Hartweg (no. 1981) mounted together (and with a superfluous Burgess collection). It seems clear that Bentham, in ascribing the species to Torrey, gives an implied typification to the material available to Torrey (i.e., the Frémont specimens) and that the Hartweg material was secondary. The entire citation by Bentham (1839–1857) follows: "1981 (258). Fritillaria (Amblirion) pluriflora, Torr. Pl. Frém.—Flores rosei.—In locus per tempus pluviorum inundatis, in valle Sacramento." The Frémont material at GH should be regarded as the holotype, until such a time as that at NY is located. The Hartweg materials should be treated as syntypes or paratypes. "FExCal, 1843–4. Fritillaria" (NY-Torrey!). This specimen is clearly not a portion of the type material; Frémont was not in the Sacramento Valley in 1844, except at the junction of the Sacramento with the Amercan River.

Fritillaria pudica (Pursh) Spreng.

"FExCal, 1843–4. Xxxx. Fritillaria pudica, *Hook. fl. Bor.-Am.*" (NY-Torrey!; GH!; MO!). The three Frémont specimens on the NY sheet, two with bulbs as well as flowers, are mounted on a sheet with a Nuttall specimen from "Herb. Wyeth" and a plant with two flowers from Promontory Range (Box Elder County, Utah), April 12/50 by Capt. Howard Stansbury.

***Fritillaria recurva* Benth.**, Pl. Hartw. 340. 1857. (3rd).

Protologue locality: "In montibus Sacramento. Occurrit etiam inter Fremontianas sub num. 348." Type: "Frémont's Expedition to California, 348. 1846. 'The rice-root plant.' 'Scarlet bell-flower.' Fritillaria recurva *Benth.* On a small headwater of Cow Creek [Shasta County, California], Sierra of the Sacramento. 28–29. April" (NY-Torrey!, mounted on same sheet with Frémont 346!).

Gaillardia aristata Pursh
Frémont (1845: 119).

Gaillardia pinnatifida Torr.
"Frémont's Expedition to California, 1845–47. Gaillardia pinnatifida" (GH!).

Gaillardia pulchella Foug.
"Frémont's 2nd Expedition. 1843–4. No. 464. Gaillardia pulchella" (two sheets NY-Torrey!).

Galium aparine L.
"FExCal, 1845–7. 317. 1846. Galium" (NY-Torrey!).

Galium boreale ≡ *G. boreale* L.
"Upper part of the north fork of the Platte. Aug. 12–31 [1842]" (Torrey, 1843: 86). "Galium boreale. Frémont's 1st Exp. Aug. 26–31" (NY-Torrey!).

Galium circaezans Michx.
"Galium circaezans. Frémont's 3rd. Expedition. June 20, 1845" (NY-Torrey!).

Galium concinnum Torr. & A. Gray
"FExCal, 1845–7. 530. 1845. Galium concinnum, T. & G." (NY-Torrey!).

Galium nuttallii A. Gray
"FExCal, 1845–7. Xxx, 1846. Galium. Gray. California" (NY-Torrey!).

Garrya elliptica = *G. fremontii* Torr. pro parte
The plant indicated by Frémont (1845: 268) under the name of *G. elliptica*, along the Virgin River on 6 May 1844, is certainly not this species and probably not even a *Garrya*. The species is also noted by Frémont (1845: 253).

***Garrya fremontii* Torr.**, Pacif. R. R. Rep. 4: 136. 1857. (3rd)
Protologue locality: "Colonel Frémont found on the Upper Sacramento, 'above the Great Canon,' in 1846, a Garrya nearly allied to this species [*Garrya wrightii* Torr.]." Type: "Frémont's Expedition to California, 1845–7. 369, 1846. Garrya Frémontii n. sp. 'Upper Sacramento above the Great Canon. Shrub 4 feet high'" (holotype NY-Torrey!: microfiche BRY!; isotypes GH!; MO!). "On the head of Cow Creek, Shasta County, California" (Abrams, 1951: 287). Frémont defined the lower (i.e., Great Canyon) Sacramento from the upper as being marked by the position of Mt. Shasta.

Gaura coccinea Pursh
This species was cited by Torrey and Frémont (Frémont, 1845). Four sheets NY-Torrey!: "Frémont's 1st Exped., July 4, 1842. Gaura coccinea [ca. 40 miles west of Platte Forks, Keith County, Nebraska]"; "Frémont's 2nd Expedn., 301, 1843"; "Frémont's 2nd Expedn., 430, 1843. Gaura sp."; and "Frémont's 2nd Expedn."

Gayophytum diffusum Torr. & Gray
This species was cited by Torrey and Frémont (Frémont, 1845). "On Snake River, Oregon, Oct. 7th. [Elmore County, Idaho] 782. 1843. Frémont. Gayophytum diffusum" (NY-Torrey!). "Fragments. 782. Frémont" (GH!).

Gentiana affinis ≡ *G. affinis* Griseb. in Hook.
"North fork of the Platte. Sept. 9 [1842. Near Keystone, Keith County, Nebraska]" (Torrey, 1843: 90). Three sheets NY-Torrey!: "Gentiana affinis. Upper Platte. Frémont"; "Frémont's 1st Exp. Gentiana affinis"; and "Frémont's Expedition to California, 1845–7. Headwaters of the upper Arkansas, No. 128. 1845 [2 September in or near Lake County, Colorado]. Gentiana. (also GH!)." One sheet NY-Columbia!: "FExCal, 360, 1843"; and one sheet each (NY-Sartwell!, NY-Torrey!, MO!): "FExRM, 1842. Gentiana affinis, *Griseb.*" The specimen at MO has a typical Frémont tag attached, "8 August, Camp. Little Sandy [Sublette County, Wyoming]." Possibly the others are from there also.

Gentiana arctophila β densiflora = *Gentianella amarella* (L.) Borner subsp. *acuta* (Michx.) J. M. Gillette?
"Sweet Water of the Platte. Aug. 4 [1842. Southwest of Carmody Lake, Frémont County, Wyoming]" (Torrey, 1843: 90). The type of Rydberg's *Amarella ventorum* (q.v.), was based on this collection.

Gentiana calycosa Griseb. in Hook. includes *G. pneumonanthe*

***Gentiana fremontii* Torr.** in Frém., Rep. Explor. Exped. Rocky Mts. 90. 1843. (1st) = *G. prostrata* Haenke in Jacq.
Protologue locality: "Wind River Mountains [1842. Sublette County, Wyoming, 12–17 August]." Type: "Gentiana Frémontii, Torr. in Rep. Frémont's 1st Exped." (holotype NY-Torrey!: microfiche BRY!).

Gentiana parryi Engelm.
"FExCal, 360. 1843" (NY-Columbia! and GH!). Gray (1862b: 256) cites this collection: "The plant of Kreusfeldt [Fredrick Creutzfeldt], in Gunnison's Expedition, referred to *G. affinis* in the second volume of the Pacific Railroad Report, is of this species, but with narrower leaves, and Frémont's No. 360 (1845) is a small-leaved form of it, which also occurs in Mr. Howard's collection (Herb Acad. Philad.), in one instance with a six-lobed corolla."

Gentiana pneumonanthe = *G. calycosa* Griseb. in Hook.
"Laramie river to Little Sandy creek in the mountains. July 12–Aug. 8 [1842]" (Torrey, 1843: 90).

Gentiana prostrata Haenke in Jacq. includes *G. fremontii*

Gentianella amarella (L.) Borner includes *Gentiana arctophila β densifolia*

***Geraea* Torr. & A. Gray ex A. Gray**, Proc. Amer. Acad. 1: 48. 1848. (2nd)
Type species: ***Geraea canescens* Torr. & A. Gray** in A. Gray
Protologue locality: "California, *Frémont, Coulter*." Type: "Frémont 2d Coll. 293, 1844, April 13. (Creek of the Pass, Sierra Nevada) [Kern River to the pass, Kern County, California]" (holotype NY-Torrey!: microfiche BRY!, the sheet contains a second collection "FExCal 1849," doubtlessly from the troublesome fourth expedition of 1848–49.

Geranium caespitosum James includes *G. fremontii* Torr. ex A. Gray
"G. fremontii. Frémont No. 42. (1845?)," "Specimen sent to Sprague to figure. Geranium Frémontii T. & Gr. Frémont's Expedn.," and "FExCal, 61. 1845" (all three NY-Torrey!). The latter specimen was annotated "*Geranium parryi* (Engelm.) Heller" for the *North American Flora*. For a review of the nomenclature of this taxon see Welsh (1987).

Geranium cicutarium ≡ *Erodium cicutarium* (L.) L'Her in Ait.
Frémont (1848: 20).

Geranium fremontii Torr. ex A. Gray, Pl. Fendl. 26. 1849. = *G. caespitosum* James
"Black Hills. Aug. 26–31 [1842]" (Torrey, 1843: 84). The name was merely mentioned by Torrey; there is no description, i.e., it was published as a nomen nudum. Gray (1849) evidently indicated the Fendler material from "bottom lands of the Mora River [New Mexico], among shrubs" as the basis of the species. The Frémont material is cited only parenthetically and provisionally: "(Also in the Raton Mountains, Lieut. Abert, and probably farther north and west by Col. Frémont.)" "Frémont's Expedn. 'Specimen sent to Sprague to figure'" (NY-Torrey!). The sheet is certainly what Torrey had in mind to be named after Frémont. It bears the notation "Geranium Frémontii T&Gr."

Gerardia tenuifolia ≡ *Agalinus tenuifolia* (Vahl) Raf.
"Lower Platte. July 22 [1842. Horseshoe Creek, near Glendo, Platte County, Wyoming]" (Torrey, 1843: 89). "Gerardia longifolia *Nutt.* Valley of the lower Platte, Sept. 1842. Frémont" (NY-Torrey!).

Geum canadense Jacq. includes *G. virginianum*

Geum triflorum Pursh
"390, 1846 (3rd Exp.)" and "Frémont's 2nd Expedn." (same sheet NY-Torrey!).

Geum virginianum = *G. canadense* Jacq.
"Kansas river. June 20 [1842. Big Blue River, probably Marshall County, Kansas]" (Torrey, 1843: 85).

Gilia achilleifolia Benth.
"FExCal, 241, 1846, Gilia capitata. April 5th, Gilia achilleaefolia. Sacramento River [at Lassen's, near Vina, Tehama County, California]" (NY-Torrey!; GH!; MO!) and "FExCal, 1845–7. Mill Creek of the Sacramento, April 11, 1846 [vicinity of Lassen's, Tehama County, California]. Gilia achilleaefolia Benth." (GH!; NY-Torrey!; MO!). "Herb.

A. Gray. Gilia achilleaefolia Torr. & Gray, Fl. N. Amer. Hort. Cantab. Anno 1849. e sem. Frém. 3d Exp." (GH!). The last cited collection was grown from seed at Cambridge, taken from a Frémont collection, presumably one of the others noted above.

Gilia aggregata (Pursh) Spreng. includes *G. pulchella* Dougl.

"Gilia. California, Frémont" and "Gilia pulchella California. Frémont" (both NY-Sartwell!); "FExCal, 1845–7 [1846?]. Gilia tenuiflora?" (GH!, probable duplicate of the NY collection); "Ex herb. J. Torrey. Torr. & Gr. Fl. N. Amer. Frémont's 1st Expedn. Gilia pulchella, Dougl." (GH!); and "Frémont's 1st Expedn. Upper Sweet Water River (Rocky Pass), Aug. 20, 1842 [East of South Pass, Frémont County, Wyoming]" (NY-Torrey!; GH!). "Frém. 2d Exped. Gilia pulchella Dougl." and "Frémont's 2nd Expedn. Gilia pulchella" (both NY-Torrey!).

***Gilia aurea* Nutt. var. *decora* A. Gray**, Proc. Amer. Acad. 8: 264. 1870. (2nd) ≡ *Linanthus aureus* (Nutt.) Greene subsp. *decorus* (A. Gray) H. L. Mason

Protologue locality: "California, Frémont." Type: "G. decora, A. G. olim. Frémont 2nd Exped." (holotype GH!; isotype NY-Torrey!). The sheet at GH contains three collections, one by Smart and two by Frémont. The upper "G. decora A. G. olim Frémont 2nd Exped." and "Frémont n' Exped." The uppermost is proposed as holotype. The sheet at NY contains more complete information: there are three numbered specimens "344, 1844, 345, 1844, and 324, 1844" all from California. The sheet is labeled "Linanthus (Dactyl.) decorus, n. sp. (in Gray's writing) Torr. & Gray, Fl. N. Amer." In the lower right corner is the designation "Gilia aurea var. decora," below a cryptic note "named by Bentham." It is very difficult to determine which of the specimens at NY are exact duplicates of the GH materials. "'California.' Collected by Frémont" (Abrams, 1951: 419). "The variety on Monte Diablo (*Brewer*), and in the southern part of the State [California], *Frémont*, &c." (Brewer et al., 1876: 490).

Gilia congesta Hook.

"Frémont's 2nd Expedn." (NY-Torrey!). The sheet bears two labels: "Gilia sp. n. near G. congesta. [named by Bentham] Frémont's 2nd Expedn." and "G. (Thyrsogilia) Frémontii. Torr. & Gray, Fl. N. Amer." The second label is followed by a note: "It is only a form of Gilia congesta." The brackets in the above quote belong there: the information is not editorial.

***Gilia demissa* A. Gray**, Proc. Amer. Acad. 8: 263. 1870. (4th) ≡ *Linanthus demissus* (A. Gray) Greene

Protologue locality: "S. E. California and adjacent part of Arizona, Frémont; mouth of Diamond River, Newberry (*G. dactylophyllum*, n. sp. in Ives Exped: 22); near Fort Mohave, Cooper." Type: "FExCal 1849. Gilia demissa, n. sp. Navarretia?" (NY-Torrey!: microfiche BRY!). Abrams (1951: 424) cites *G. dactylophyllum* Torr., Ives Rep. 22. 1860, as a "nomen confusum."

Gilia inconspicua ≡ *G. inconspicua* (J. E. Sm.) Sweet
"Goat Island, upper N. fork of the Platte. July 30 [1842. Near Alcova, Natrona County, Wyoming]" (Torrey, 1843: 89).

Gilia latiflora (A. Gray) A. Gray
"San Diego and Los Angeles Counties, Frémont, Wallace, Palmer 1876, n. 466" (Watson, 1880 2: 466). Basionym: *G. tenuiflora* Benth. var. *latiflora* A. Gray, Proc. Amer. Acad. 8: 278. 1870. "The variety, Los Angeles, &c., *Frémont, Wallace*" (Brewer et al., 1876: 498).

Gilia (*Cantua*) *longiflora* = *G. longiflora* (Torr.) G. Don.
"Sand Hills of the Platte. July 8 [1842. South Platte, near Brush, Morgan County, Colorado]" (Torrey, 1843: 89). "Sand hills of the Platte, 20 miles below the Forks. Sept. 16, 1842 [Lincoln County, Nebraska]. Frémont" (NY-Torrey!).

Gilia minutiflora Benth.
"And Wyoming, on the Upper Platte, Nuttall, Frémont" (Gray, 1840: 277). "Frémont. ex Hb. Torr." (GH!).

***Gilia nuttallii* A. Gray**, Proc. Amer. Acad. 8: 267. 1870. (?) ≡ *Linanthastrum nuttallii* (A. Gray) Ewan
Protologue locality: "Rocky Mountains of Colorado and Utah to the Sierra Nevada in California, Nuttall, Frémont, Anderson, Brewer, Watson." Type: "Nuttall, Bear River Hills" (holotype GH); the Frémont material, if found, would be a paratype.

Gilia pulchella = *G. aggregata* (Pursh) Spreng. (q.v.)
"Upper part of the Sweet Water near the mountains. Aug. 7–20 [1842]" (Torrey, 1843: 89).

Gilia setosissima (Torr. & A. Gray) A. Gray, Proc. Amer. Acad. 8: 271. 1870. ≡ *Langloisia setosissima* (Torr. & A. Gray) Greene
"Arizona and S. E. California on the Mohave, &c., Coulter, Frémont" (Gray, 1870a).

Gilia sinuata Dougl.
"California—Frémont's 2nd Exp. Gilia pygmaea [crossed out] n.sp. Torr. & Gray, Fl. N. Amer." (NY!).

Gilia spicata Nutt.
"Rocky Mountains, Colorado, Nuttall, Frémont" (Gray, 1870: 275). "574. (1844) 2d Exped. Herb. A. Gray. Gilia congesta, Hook. Gilia (thyrsogilia) Frémont" (GH!). The material at GH is multiply mounted with collections of *Gilia congesta* taken by various workers, i.e., S. Watson (2 sheets), E. L. Greene, and H. L. Bolander. The specimen by Frémont was annotated by Constance and Rollins in 1936 as *Gilia spicata*. Possibly the sheet bearing the number 574 placed herein with *G. congesta* is indeed *G. spicata* also.

***Gilia stenothyrsa* A. Gray**, Proc. Amer. Acad. 8: 276. 1870. (2nd)

Protologue locality: "Utah, in a 'cedar forest,' Uintah Mountains, Frémont." Type: "Frémont's 2nd Exped. 556, 1844. Among the cedars between Duchesne and Lake Fork, June and H. N. Bolander." The Frémont label has been pasted over, but the words "Gilia (Thyrsogilia) 1st [Duchesne County, Utah]. Frémont" can be seen through the paper (holotype NY-Torrey!: microfiche BRY!).

***Gilia tenuiflora* Benth. var. *latiflora* A. Gray**, Proc. Amer. Acad. 8: 278. 1870. (2nd) ≡ *G. latiflora* (A. Gray) A. Gray

Protologue locality: "Los Angeles County? Frémont, Wallace." Type: "California. Frémont's 2nd Exped. Gilia patens, n. sp. mss = G. tenuiflora var. latiflora" (isotype NY-Torrey!: microfiche BRY; holotype GH!). The Frémont holotype is mounted on the same sheet with the Wallace specimens, both of which lack leaves. The leaves mounted separately and presumed to be part of the Wallace material do not, unfortunately, belong to this taxon. Also associated with the Frémont holotype are two fragment envelopes, the upper labeled: "Ex spec. Hb. Torr. Frémont's 2nd Exped. Herb. A. Gray. Gilia patens. n. sp. Torr. & Gray, Fl. N. Amer."; the lower labeled, "Perhaps G. patens; but the tube of the corolla shorter. Calyx less cupulate," and the holotype proper labeled, "Frémont's 2nd Exped. Formally named. 'G. pygmaea n.sp.,' G. sinuata, large corolla, i.e., G. inconspicua var." The name "Gilia tenuiflora var. latiflora" is written above the Frémont specimens and is annotated with that name by Sereno Watson. The fragment envelopes apparently do not contain the type material. "Los Angeles County" (Abrams, 1951: 467). Frémont was in Los Angeles County in April 1844.

Gilia tricolor Benth.

"G. tricolor. California. Frémont" and "No. 26. California, March 8, 1844" and "Frémont. 75, 1844" (all three NY-Torrey!). Frémont 26 and 75 are only tentatively assigned to this species. On 8 March 1844 the Frémont party was still east of Sutter's along the reaches of the American River. "FExCal, 1845–7. 310. 1846. Gilia tricolor" (GH!; MO!).

Githopsis pulchella Vatke

"FExCal, 1846" (NY-Torrey!; BRY-Sartwell!); "FExCal, 1845–7. Yyy 1846" (GH!); and "Frémont's 2d [3rd?] Calif. Exped—1845–47 [1846?]. Githopsis specularioides, Nutt. Prismatocarpus. ex Torrey" (GH!). The NY 1846 sheet has two collections, one by J. M. Bigelow, annotated by N. Morin as *G. pulchella* Vatke, and the other (seven specimens in all) as *G. specularioides* Nutt. The latter designation agrees with that on a sketch sheet by Torrey that overlaps two of the tiny specimens.

Glaux maritima ≡ *G. maritima* L.

"Upper North fork of the Platte. July 31 [1842. Near Independence Rock, Natrona County, Wyoming]" (Torrey, 1843: 88).

Glyceria striata (Lam.) A. S. Hitchc. includes *Poa nervata*

Glycyrrhiza lepidota = *G. lepidota* Pursh
"From near the Kansas river to the Black Hills of the Platte. June 21–July 25 [1842]" (Torrey, 1843: 84). Frémont (1845: 150).

Gnaphalium palustre ≡ *G. palustre* Nutt.
"Sweet Water river [1842]" (Torrey, 1843: 88).

***Gnaphalium strictum* A. Gray** in Torr., Pacif. R. R. Rep. 4: 110. 1857. (1st)
Protologue locality: "Banks of the Rio Grande, near Albuquerque; October" [Bigelow], but also "To this apparently well-marked species belongs a specimen gathered by Frémont, in his first expedition, on the Sweet-water of the Platte [1842]. Its strict and virgate stems and inflorescence, and the very narrow leaves, distinguish it at once from G. uliginosum and any allied species." It seems probable that the specimen cited as *G. uliginosum* (see below) is the same as that included by Torrey with *G. strictum* in 1857. Type: "Collected by Dr. J. M. Bigelow" (holotype GH!); "Gnaphalium strictum n. s. Sweet Water. N. Platte, Lieut. Frémont" (syntype GH!).

Gnaphalium uliginosum ≡ *G. uliginosum* L.
"Sweet Water river [1842]" (Torrey, 1843: 88).

***Godetia amoena* (Lehm.) G. Don var. *albicaulis* Jepson**, Univ. Calif. Publ. Bot. 2: 329. 1907. (3rd) ≡ *Clarkia gracilis* (Piper) Nels. & Macbr. subsp. *albicaulis* (Jepson) Lewis & Lewis
Protologue locality: "Mrs. Bidwell, May, 1878, no. 122; *Frémont*, no. 435, 1846, both Kew Herbarium." Syntype: "FExCal, 1845–7. 435. 1846. Oenothera (Godetia) Lindleyi. Denny's Creek. May 22" (GH!; NY-Torrey!; MO!). The materials at GH and NY are beautiful flowering specimens, and, unless the Bidwell material at Kew is equally representative of the taxon, the Frémont specimens could well serve as lectotype, a proposal not made here. Denny's Creek is in Klamath County, Oregon, but Frémont was at Lassen's, Tehama County, California, on 22 May 1846.

Godetia hispidula (S. Wats.) S. Wats., Proc. Amer Acad. 8: 599. 1873. = *Clarkia arcuata* (Kellogg) Nels. & Macbr.
"Sacramento and Tulare Valleys, *Frémont*" (Brewer et al., 1876: 231).

Grains de boeuf = *Shepherdia argentea* (Pursh) Nutt.
Frémont (1845: 47).

Grayia polygaloides Hook. & Arn. = *G. spinosa* (Hook.) Moq.
"Frémont" (Watson, 1874: 122). Two sheets NY-Torrey!: "Grayia polygaloides, Hook. & Arn. Westerly slope of the Sierra Nevada, southern extremity, Frémont's 2nd Expedition"; and "Grayia spinosa. Frémont's 2nd Expedn."

Grindelia squarrosa ≡ *G. squarrosa* (Pursh) Dunal in DC.

Grindelia squarrosa var. *serrulata* (Rydb.) Steyerm.
"Upper north fork of the Platte, and on the Sweet Water. July 22–Aug 21 [1842]" (Torrey, 1843: 87). "Grindelia squarrosa. Torr. & Gray, Flora, N. Amer. Platte, Frémont [1842]" (GH!; NY-Torrey!).

Grindelia squarrosa (Pursh) Dunal in DC. var. *squarrosa*
"Frémont's 3rd Expedition [1845]" (NY-Torrey!).

Gutierrezia euthamiae = *G. sarothrae* (Pursh) Britt. & Rusby
"Laramie river, upper north fork of the Platte. Sept. 3 [1842. Goshen County, Wyoming]" (Torrey, 1843: 87). "Gutierrezia Euthamiae. Torr. & Gray, Flora, N. Amer. Platte, Frémont. 1st Exp. [probably the specimen referred to by Torrey]," "FExCal, 1845–7. No. 54, 1845, Gutierrezia divaricata," "FExCal, 1843–4. 398, 1844. Linosyris viscidiflora ? *AGr.* [followed by penciled notes]" "Surely not. J. T. Aplopap. laricifol?" (all three NY-Torrey!). Collection 398 is mounted on a sheet with a branch, past flower, of *Haplopappus linearifolius* DC. (q.v.). "FExCal, 1845–7. No. 54, 1845. G. euthamiae var. divaricaties. capit. paucis." (GH!). "FExCal, 1845–7. Gutierrezia divaricata Nutt. Arkansas River [Colorado, 1845]" (GH-Lowell!). There is a sheet at NY-Torrey! with the designation "Frémont. (uncertain locality)" and without a year or expedition of collection. *Gutierrezia sarothrae* (Pursh) Britt. & Rusby includes *G. euthamiae*.

Habenaria dilatata (Pursh) Hook. includes *Platanthera leucophaea*

Habenaria hyperborea (L.) R. Br. in Ait. includes *Platanthera hyperborea*

Hackberry = *Celtis*
Frémont (1845: 16).

Hackelia floribunda (Lehm.) I. M. Johnst.
"Frémonts 2d Calif. Exped. 1845–47 [likely 1844]. Ex. Torrey. No. 437?" (GH!). "California? Frémont's 2nd Exp. Echinospermum floribundum *Hook.*" (NY-Torrey!). The label of the second expedition material at NY-Torrey has a drawing of the lateral margin of the nutlet, showing the prickles in a single row.

Hackelia patens (Nutt.) I. M. Johnst.
"Frémont's 2nd Expedn., 497, 1844. Frémont. Echinospermum floribundum" (NY-Torrey!). The number and year is followed by a notation (3?), and the word mistake is penciled in lightly adjacent to the year. "Frémont's 2nd Expedn. Echinospermum floribundum" (NY-Torrey!).

Halostachys occidentalis S. Wats., Rep. Explor. 40th Parallel, Bot. 5: 293. 1871. ≡ *Allenrolfea occidentalis* (S. Wats.) Kuntze

Haplopappus annuus (Rydb.) Cory
"FExCal, 1845–7. 35. 1845. Arkansas [illegible]. Aplopappus rubiginosus. Syn Fl. N. Amer." (GH!).

Haplopappus ciliatus (Nutt.) DC.
"FExCal, 1845–7. 185. 1845. Aplopappus ciliatus, *DC.* Prionopsis ciliata, *Nutt.*" (NY-Torrey!; MO!).

Haplopappus fremontii A. Gray includes *Aplopappus fremontii* A. Gray, based on: *Pyrrocoma foliosa* Torr. & A. Gray in A. Gray.

Haplopappus linearifolius DC.
"FExCal, 1843–4. 398, 1844" (NY-Torrey!). See *Gutierrezia sarothrae* specimen 398, for more complete label information; the two are mounted on the same sheet.

Haplopappus spinulosus (Pursh) DC. includes *Aplopappus spinulosus*

Haplopappus venetus (H.B.K.) Blake
"FExCal, 1845–7. 1846. Aplopappus Menziesii [California]" (NY-Torrey!). The specimen is annotated anonymously as subsp. *vernonioides* (Nutt.) Hall.

Hawthorn = *Crataegus douglasii* Lindley (q.v.)

Hedyotis nigricans (Lam.) Fosberg
"Kansas. Frémont" (NY-Torrey!).

Hedysarum boreale Nutt.
This is the most likely candidate for the plant called esparcette or *Onobrychis sativa* in the Frémont report (1845: 115).

Helianthella uniflora = *Wyethia scabra* Hook.
"Wind River mountains [1842. Sublette County, Wyoming]" (Torrey, 1843: 87). "Wind R. Chain, Frémont. Helianthella uniflora, Torr. & Gray, Flora, N. Amer." and "Unknown Helianthella or Wyethia. Torr. & Gray, Flora, N. Amer. Wind R. Chain, Frémont. R. Mts. 31 July 1842 [one day east of Independence Rock, Natrona County, Wyoming]" (both NY-Torrey!). Obviously Gray was not familiar with either *Helianthella* or *Wyethia*.

Helianthus maximiliani ≡ *H. maximiliani* Schrad.
"Black Hills of the Platte. July 26 [1842. Near Glen Rock, Converse County, Wyoming]" (Torrey, 1843: 87). "Platte, Frémont. H. Maximiliani. Torr. & Gray, Flora, N. Amer." (NY-Torrey!).

Helianthus nuttallii Torr. & A. Gray
"Upper Platte, Frémont [1st exped, 1842]. Helianthus Nutt.? Torr. & Gray, Flora, N. Amer." and "FExCal, 1843–4. 148. 1843. Helianthus Maximiliani" (both NY-Torrey!).

Helianthus petiolaris ≡ *H. petiolaris* Nutt.
"Black Hills of the Platte. July 26 [1842. Near Glen Rock, Converse County, Wyoming]" (Torrey, 1843: 87). "Platte, Frémont [1842]. Helianthus petiolaris. Torr. & Gray, Flora, N. Amer.," "He. petiolaris Frémont. Platte, 29 June [1842, Dawson County, Nebraska]," and "FExCal, 1843–4. Helianthus. 'Singular sp. with lanceolate & appendiculate chaff.' A.Gr." (all three NY-Torrey!). "Frémont-s Expedition to California,

1845–7. No. 34, 1845" (GH!; NY-Torrey!). The specimen at NY-Torrey has the date "August 18, 1845" and the notation "Arkansas Bottoms." The Frémont party was between Bent's Fort, Otero County, and Upper Pueblo, Pueblo County, Colorado, on that date. Frémont (1887: 431) noted a helianthus on Antelope Island in the Great Salt Lake.

Heliotropium convolvulaceum (Nutt.) A. Gray
"FExCal, 1845–7. No. 100. Frémont 1845. Euploca convolvulacea *Nutt.*," (NY-Torrey!; NY-Sartwell!; MO!); "Frémont's Exped." (NY!); "Frémont's 2nd Exped" (NY-Torrey!). Frémont 100 is mounted on the same sheet as the holotype of *Euploca grandiflora* Torr. The Second Expedition sheet has a small specimen of the species taken on Abert's Expedition, July 28, 1846.

Heliotropium curassavicum L.
"Frémont's 2nd Expedn. 436, 1844 and 299, 1844" and "FExCal, 1845–7. LlIl. 1846. Heliotropium Curassavicum. California" (both NY-Torrey! and the second also GH! and MO!).

Hemizonia congesta DC. subsp. *luzulifolia* (DC.) Babc. & Hall includes *H. luzulifolia* DC.
"FExCal, 1845–7. (v) Dr. Gray. 1846. Hemizonia viscosissima n. sp. T. & Gr." (NY-Torrey!). "FExCal, 1845–7. Hemizonia luzulaefolia. v. 1846" (GH!).

Hemizonia fremontii (A. Gray) A. Gray ≡ *Calycadenia fremontii* A. Gray
"Frémont" (Watson, 1880 1: 365). "California, *Frémont*. The station unknown" (Brewer et al., 1876: 365).

Hemizonia pauciflora (A. Gray) A. Gray ≡ *Calycadenia pauciflora* A. Gray
"California, *Frémont*: the station unknown. Both species [this and *H. fremontii*] were collected in 1845, and have not since been met with" (Brewer et al., 1876: 365).

Hemizonia pungens (Hook. & Arn.) Torr. & A. Gray subsp. *laevis* Keck
"FExCal, 1845–7[1846]. Hemizonia n.sp." (GH-Lowell!).

Hemizonia pungens (Hook. & Arn.) Torr. & A. Gray subsp. *septentrionalis* Keck
"FExCal, 1845–7. 478, 1846. Foothills of the upper Sacramento. Hemizonia sp. nov. aff. pung." (NY-Torrey!).

Hemizonia ramosissima Benth.
"FExCal, 1845–47. (S.) Dr. Gray 1846. Hemizonia fasciculata Nutt. Pl. Gamb. 'In Bot. Mex. Bound. Dr. Gray refers this to H. ramosissima'" (NY-Torrey!).

***Hemizonia virgata* A. Gray** in Torr., Rep. U.S. Mex. Bound. Bot. 100. 1859. (3rd) ≡ *Holocarpha virgata* (A. Gray) Keck
Protologue locality: "California, probably on the Sacramento; Col. Frémont." Type: "FExCal, 1845–7" (holotype GH!; isotypes NY-Torrey!; US!). The specimen at GH includes the designation "2. 1846. Hemizonia virgata n. sp." It was annotated as "holotype" by Vernon Bates in 1985. There is another specimen, possibly by Frémont, at NY-Torrey!: "Calycadenia. California. Frémont, or Dr. Stillman. Seems different any

of the others. J. G. May 1872." It is annotated as *Holocarpha virgata* by both D. D. Keck (in 1952) and by R. E. Palmer (in 1982).

Hemlock spruce = *Tsuga* (most likely *T. heterophylla*, but also *T. mertensiana*).

***Hendecandra* (?) *multiflora* Torr. in Frém.**, Rep. Exped. Rocky Mts. 92. 1843. (1st) = *Croton texensis* (Klotzsch) Muell.-Arg. in DC.

Protologue locality: "Laramie river, north fork of the Platte. Sept. 3–11" [i.e., Goshen County, Wyoming, east into Nebraska]. Type: "FExRM, 1842. July 2nd [forks of the Platte, Lincoln County, Nebraska]. North Fork of the Platte [1842]" (holotype NY-Torrey!: microfiche BRY!, 3 sheets). "FExRM, 1842" (isotype GH-Thurber!). "Hendecandra. Frémont's 3d Expedit. 146. 1845" (MO!).

Heracleum lanatum ≡ *H. lanatum* Michx.

"Alpine regions of the Wind River mountains. August 12–17 [1842. Sublette County, Wyoming]" (Torrey, 1843: 86). "FExRM, 1842. Aug. 13. Heracleum lanatum" (NY-Torrey!). The specimen at NY consists of a single leaf attached to a portion of the root crown.

Herbe salée = salt grass

Frémont (1845: 21).

Hesperocallis undulata A. Gray, Proc. Amer. Acad. 7: 391. 1867.

"FExCal, 1843–4. No 363, 1844. Sandy and gravelly uplands of the Mohave River, April 24–25 [San Bernardino County, California]" (NY-Torrey!: microfiche BRY!). This specimen is in the type collection at NY but is apparently not a type. The type location is given by Gray as: "Desert plains at Jessup Rapids, Arizona or New Mexico; 'the bulb eaten by Indians,' Prof. Newberry. Gravelly plains at Fort Mohave, Dr. J. G. Cooper."

Hesperochiron californicus (Benth.) S. Wats.

"California. Frémont's 2nd Exped." and "FExCal, 1845–7. 379. 1846. Upper Sacramento, above the great Canon [vicinity of Lookout, Modoc County, California]. April 30/46. open pine woods & prairies" (both on same sheet NY-Torrey!; also number 379 at MO!). The sheet bears a small sheet of detailed illustrations of floral parts by Torrey.

Heteromeles arbutifolia (Ait.) Roem. includes *H. fremontiana* Decaisne

***Heteromeles fremontiana* Decaisne**, Nouv. Arch. Mus. Hist. Nat. 10: 144. 1874. (3rd) = *H. arbutifolia* (Ait.) Roem.

Protologue locality: "*Loc. nat.* California (Frémont!)." Type: "FExCal, 1845–7. 501. 1846. Photinia arbutifolia *Lindl.*" (? isotype NY-Torrey!; MO!). The complete citation by Decaisne is: "Heteromeles Frémontiana. C. ramulis floriferis floribusque puberulis.—Differt a praecedente floribus minoribus." The preceding is "Heteromeles arbutifolia, Roem., *Syn.*, III. p. 405."

Heterotheca villosa (Pursh) Shinners

"Platte, Frémont, 1842, July 14 [Horse Creek, Laramie County, Wyoming] & 22 [Horseshoe Creek, Platte County, Wyoming]. Chrysopsis mollis Nutt. too near C. foliosa. Torr. & Gray, Flora, N. Amer." (two collections same sheet), "Platte, Frémont, Aug. 4 [1842. Sweetwater River, Frémont County, Wyoming], Chrysopsis hispida. Torr. & Gray, Flora, N. Amer.," "FExCal, 1843–4. 482. 1843. C. foliosa *Nutt.*," "FExCal, 1843–4. Chrysopsis foliosa. Near Fort Laramie [not in vicinity of Fort Laramie on the second expedition]," "FExCal, 1845–7[1846?]. Chrysopsis canescens—(connecting with *C. foliosa Nutt.*)," "FExCal, 1845–7. 62. 1845. Chrysopsis hispida—'same as of Coll. II (1843–4),'" and "Upper Missouri, Lt. *Frémont*. Chrysopsis canescens, passing into C. foliosa, Nutt." "FExCal, 1845–7. Chrysopsis canescens. 'very hispid variety' *Dr. Gray*, Upper Platte, no. 77, 1845 & 528 1845" (all nine NY-Torrey!; 62 also MO!). The specimens represent a portion of the huge range of variation within *H. villosa*, and no attempt is made herein to indicate infraspecific taxa involved. Also, this plant was collected secondarily, as the host plant of *Cuscuta indecora* Choisy (q.v.).

Hoita macrostachya (DC.) Rydb.

"FExCal, 1846. Mmm = young. Psoralea macrostachya, *DC.* Torr. & Gray. Fl. 1. p. 689," "Frémont-s Expedition to California, 1845–7. Lll. 1846. Dr. Gray. Psoralea macrostachya," and "FExCal, 1843–4. Mmm. = Lll? 1846" (all three NY-Torrey!; Lll also MO!).

Hoita orbicularis (Lindley) Rydb.

"FExCal, 496. 1846 & ? Nnn. Psoralea Near the American Fork, in a grassy hollow" (NY-Torrey!; MO!).

Holocarpha virgata (A. Gray) Keck includes *Hemizonia virgata* A. Gray in Torr.

Hordeum jubatum ≡ *H. jubatum* L.

"Forks of the Platte. July 2 [1842. Lincoln County, Nebraska]" (Torrey, 1843: 94).

Horse-chestnut = *Aesculus californica* (Spach) Nutt.

Frémont (1848: 32).

***Hosackia argophylla* A. Gray var. (?) *fremontii* A. Gray**, Proc. Acad. Nat. Sci. Philadelphia 1863: 347. 1864. (3rd) ≡ *Lotus argophyllus* var. *fremontii* (A. Gray) Ottley (1923), includes *Hosackia fremontii* (A. Gray) Abrams

Protologue locality: "Eastern side of Sierra Nevada" (l.c.). "Sierra Nevada, California" (fide Abrams, 1944: 550). "Found east of the Sierras by Frémont, probably in Nevada" (Watson, 1871: 62). Type: "California. Frémont's 3rd Exped. Iii (a) 1846. Hosackia tomentosa, *Benth.*" (holotype NY-Torrey!; isotype GH!). "FExCal, 1843–4. Hosackia argophylla, *Gray* 'On rocks, western side of the Sierra Nevada'" (NY-Torrey!). Only cryptic hints allow designation of a holotype. The sheet designated here as holotype has both leaflets and flowers, both mentioned in the protologue, even though it lacks definitive geographical data. The sheet has an attached sheet with detailed drawings of a calyx and legume by Torrey, and contains the notation "Hosackia." The 1843–4 sheet has no leaflets and equivocal geographical data.

Humulus lupulus L. var. *neomexicanus* Nelson & Cockerell
"FExCal, 1845–7. 67. 1845" (GH!).

Hydrophyllum capitatum Dougl.
"Oregon and Washington Territory, (371 Frémont, 326 Geyer &c." (Watson, 1871: 249). "FExCal, 371, 1846. Hydrophyllum capitatum, *Dougl.* Upper Sacramento, above the Great Canyon (i.e., north of Mt. Shasta)" (NY-Torrey!; GH!).

***Hymenoclea* Torr. & A. Gray** in A. Gray, Mem. Amer. Acad., n.s. 4: 79. 1849. (2nd)
Type species: ***Hymenoclea salsola* Torr. & A. Gray** in A. Gray
Protologue locality: "Sandy saline uplands near the Mohave River, in the interior desert of California, Frémont" (l.c.). "Sandy saline uplands, near the Mohave River, Southern California; flowering in August." and "The only specimens of this plant which I have ever seen, were collected by Colonel Frémont, in the place above mentioned. Afterwards another species of the same genus was discovered by Major Emory on the Gila River, and is briefly noticed in the Botanical Appendix of his Report, under the name of H. monogyra, *Torr. & Gray*. The same plant has since been found in California by Colonel Frémont; at Ojito, in New Mexico, by the late Dr. Gregg; and in Texas by Mr. Charles Wright" (Torrey, 1853: 14–15). Type: "Frémont's Expedition to California 298, 400, 1844" (lectotype NY-Torrey!: microfiche BRY!, 2 plants on one sheet). The number 400 has been designated as lectotype by Peterson and Payne (1973). "San Bernardino County, California" (fide Abrams & Ferris, 1960: 145). Frémont was along the Mohave River from 19 to 25 April 1844. There is a sheet at GH with three collections of this species and excellent illustrations of flowers and associated parts, one by Cooper, one by Newberry (in an envelope), and the third by an unidentified collector, but probably by Frémont, and if so an isolectotype. "FExCal, 1849. Hymenoclea. Seems to be a young state of H. monogyra—in which the scales of the fertile invol. are ovate & acute" (NY-Torrey!). This last cited specimen bears an annotation "Hymenoclea salsola T. & G. ex Gray v. pentalepis (Rydb.) L. Benson. Specimen immature—but probably this variety—fruits with relatively few wings"—Kathleen M. Peterson Apr. 11, 1973. "FExCal, 1845. 401. 1845. Hymenoclea Salsola Torr. & Gr. Pl. Frem. p. 14. t.8. On the Mohave River. Aug. 1845" (probable syntype MO!). The sheet at MO was undoubtedly taken in 1844; Frémont was not on the Mohave River at any time in 1845.

Hymenopappus corymbosus ≡ *H. scabiosaeus* L'Her. var. *corymbosus* (Torr. & A. Gray) B. L. Turner

Hymenopappus filifolius Hook. var. *cinereus* (Rydb.) Johnston
"FExCal, 1843–4. Hymenopappus luteus *Nutt.* Scarcely! Colo." (NY-Torrey!). The specimen bears an annotation label by B. L. Turner dated 1953, with the notation "Terrible Specimen!!!" The plant, an entire clump with thick taproot and numerous

caudices with basal leaves and short stems, appears to have been one of those soaked during the flood of the Kansas; it was not well collected, however.

Hymenopappus scabiosaeus L'Her. var. *corymbosus* (Torr. & A. Gray) B. L. Turner includes *H. corymbosus*
"Upper Platte [1842]" (Torrey, 1843: 87). "Hymenopappus corymbosus. Platte. Frémont" (GH!). "Platte, Frémont. 23 June 1842 [Little Blue River of the Kansas, near Adams County, Nebraska]. Hymenopappus corymbosus. Torr. & Gray, Flora, N. Amer." (NY-Torrey!).

Hymenopappus tenuifolius Pursh
"FExCal, 1843–4. Hymenopappus filifolius, with a pretty strong pappus" (NY-Torrey!). The identification on the label is in Gray's hand. The specimen was likely taken in western Kansas during the return portion of the journey during 1844.

Hymenoxys acaulis (Pursh) Parker
"FExCal, 107. 1845. Actinella argentea, Gray" (NY-Torrey!).

Hymenoxys grandiflora (Torr. & A. Gray) Parker includes *Actinella grandiflora*

Hymenoxys richardsonii (Hook.) Cockerell includes *Actinella richardsonii*
"FExCal, 1843–4. Actinella Richardsonii. var." (NY-Torrey!). "FExCal, 1845–7. 369. 1845. Actinella Richardsonii var." (GH-Lowell!) and "FExCal, 1845–7. 369 & 404, 1845. Actinella Richardsonii var. floribunda" (GH!).

Hymenoxys torreyana (Nutt.) Parker includes *Actinella depressa*

Hypericum concinnum Benth.
"FExCal, 1846. Hypericum concinnum *Benth. pl Hartw.*" (NY-Torrey!; BRY-Sartwell!). "FExCal, 1845–47[1846]. Hypericum concinnum Benth. Pl. Hartweg. Ex Torrey" (GH-Thurber!). "Frémont's 3rd Expedition [1846]. Hypericum concinnum, *Benth.* California" (US!).

Hypericum sphaerocarpum Michx.
"No. 34. Near a Branch. July 6th, 1845. Gravelly Swale. Frémont" and three with one label on one sheet "FExCal, 1845. = 33 & 49, 523, 504" (all NY-Torrey!). The label for No. 34 is the original tag by Frémont. A folded tag still wrapped around the stem of the largest plant on the second sheet bears the information "No. 51. Near a Branch. July 5." On 5 and 6 July 1845 the Frémont party was along the Santa Fe Trail, Kansas.

Hypopeltis obtusa ≡ *Woodsia obtusa* (Spreng.) Torr.
"On the Platte [1842]" (Torrey, 1843: 94).

***Hyptis emoryi* Torr.** in Ives, Rep. Colorado R. 4: 20. 1861. (4th)
Protologue locality: "This plant was first detected on the Lower Gila, by Major Emory, while accompanying the military expedition of General Kearney to California in 1846. It was afterwards found in the same region by Col. Frémont." Type: "Calif. Frémont. 1849" (syntype GH!) and "FExCal, 1849" (probably duplicate of the former; syntype

NY-Torrey!). The NY specimen bears several descriptive notations in Torrey's handwriting and is designated as "H. Emoryi Torr.," also in Torrey's hand. "Gravelly ravines of the Mohave (*Frémont*)" (Brewer et al., 1876: 591).

Impatiens capensis Meerb. includes (?) jewel-weed
Frémont (1887: 27–28).

***Ipomoea leptophylla* Torr.** in Frém., Rep. Exped. Rocky Mts. 90. 1843. (1st)
Protologue locality: "Forks of the Platte to Laramie river, July 4–Sept. 3 [1842]." Type: "'22 Juillet. Matin. Coulees de Sable.' Ipomoea leptophylla Torr. Frémont's Expedn." (holotype NY-Torrey!). The sheet has attached to it a note in Torrey's writing [see Figure 25], with an analysis of the features of the plant. It is undoubtedly the type sheet, although the other sheets presumably studied by Torrey are in better flowering condition. Camp for the night of 22 July was at Horseshoe Creek, near present Glendo, Platte County, Wyoming. There is a presumed Frémont collection "July 24, N. F. of Platte" at NY-Torrey! that lacks a Frémont designation or label. It is a beautiful plant in full flower. The handwriting on the specimen dated July 24th is a near match for that on the sheet of *Eriogonum effusum* at GH! and to that of the holotype, both of which bear a Frémont designation. "Upper Platte. Frémont. July 1842" (NY!). "Frémont's 3rd Exped. [1845]" and "Herb. A. Gray. Hort. Cantab. 1853. e sem. Frémont" (both GH!). The first cited GH specimen is accompanied by a print of the species from the Emory report; the second, though grown from seed, is a close match to the NY July 24 material. "Ipomoea leptophylla Torr. in Frem. 1st Report. Fremont's 2d Expedition. Plains near the Rocky Mountains" (MO!). There is a watercolor print of this species in the herbarium at NY-Torrey! partially colored and bearing misleading information, i.e., "July 19–1842 [1845?], No. 63K, Frémont's Expedn (3rd)." By whom it was drawn, colored, and labeled is not known, but if from 1845, as probable, by Edward Kern.

Iris missouriensis ≡ *I. missouriensis* Nutt.
"Sweet Water river. Aug. 3 [1842. West of Jeffery City, Frémont County, Wyoming]" (Torrey, 1843: 93). "FExRM, 1842. Aug. 3d. Avant midi en route" (GH!). "Frémont's Expedn. 1842. Iris Missouriensis *Nutt.*?" and "Frémont's 2nd Expedn. 488. 1844. 'Ashley's Fork [Uintah County, Utah] of Green River, & every river since the Du Chene [Duchesne]. June 6'" (both NY-Torrey!). Iris was also recorded by Frémont (1845: 285) in Colorado.

Isomeris arborea Nutt.
"Frémont's 2nd Expedn." (NY-Torrey!). The sheet at NY-Torrey is mounted on a sheet with a Nuttall type. "FExCal, 1845–7. Oo. 1846" (GH!; MO!; NY-Torrey!).

Iva axillaris ≡ *I. axillaris* Pursh
"Sweet Water river. Aug. 3 [1842. West of Jeffery city, Frémont County, Wyoming]" (Torrey, 1843: 87). "Iva axillaris, Torr. & Gray, Flora, N. Amer. Platte. Frémont" (NY-Torrey!). "Frémont's 2nd Exped." (GH!). The Frémont specimen at GH, a flowering branch, is mounted on a sheet with collections by Geyer, Burke, Suckley, Torrey, Coulter,

and Lyall. The NY sheet bears an annotation by I. J. Bassett dated 1960 as "*Iva axillaris* Pursh var. *robustior* Hook."

Jewel weed = *Impatiens capensis* Meerb.
Frémont (1887: 27, 28).

Joshua tree = *Yucca brevifolia* Engelm. (q.v.)

Juncus echinatus = ?
"North fork of the Platte. Sept. 4 [1842. West of Scotts Bluff, Scotts Bluff County, Nebraska]" (Torrey, 1843: 94).

Juncus effusus = ?
Frémont (1845: 252).

Juniperus communis L.
"FExRM, 1842. Juniperus communis, *L.*" and "Frémont 2nd Exp. No. 87. 1843" (same sheet NY-Torrey!).

Juniperus occidentalis Carr.
"FExCal, 1845–7. 387, [18]46. Juniperus" (NY!; MO!). The sheet at MO was annotated by George Engelmann, March 1874, as "Junip. occidentalis var. pleiosperma."

Juniperus scopulorum Sargent
"Frémont's 2nd Exped. 526. 1843. Juniperus virg. var. ? Rocky hill sides, among Red Buttes of disintegrated granite, 30 July" (NY!). Frémont was near the headwaters of the Laramie River, Larimer County, Colorado, on 30 July 1843.

Juniperus virginiana ≡ *J. virginiana* L.
"Lower Platte [1842]" (Torrey, 1843: 93). "Frémont's 1st Expedn. Ex herb. J. Torrey. Juniperus Virginiana. Torr. & Gr. Fl. N. Amer." (NY!).

Kallstroemia californica (S. Wats.) Vail
"Kalstroemia [word illegible]. Frémont's Exped to Calif." (NY-Sartwell!).

Keckiella breviflora (Lindley) Straw.
Three sheets NY-Torrey!: "FExCal, 1845–7, kkkk 1846. Penstemon breviflorus Gray"; "FExCal, 1845–7. Penstemon breviflorus, Lindl. bot. reg. t. 1946. Benth, in DC. prodr. 10. p. 329"; and "Frémonts 3rd Exped. Penstemon breviflorus *Benth.*" One sheet GH!: "FExCal, 1845–7. Near Monterey [Monterey County, California], Jan 31. 1846. Diplacus glutinosus." The Frémont specimen is mounted with a Bigelow specimen, and with Hartweg 1889.

Kentrophyta montana = *Astragalus kentrophyta* (Nutt.) A. Gray
"Laramie river to the Sweet Water. July 14–Aug. 5 [1842]" (Torrey, 1843: 85). "FExRM, 1842. Kentrophyta montana *Nutt.*" (GH!). "Frémont's 2nd Exp." (NY-Torrey!). The specimen at NY has attached a small sheet of paper with detailed drawings of flower parts and the notation "Kenorus viridis Nutt."

Koeleria cristata = *K. macrantha* (Ledeb.) Schult. in Schult. & Schult.
"Big Blue river of the Kansas, and on the Platte as high as Laramie river. June 20–July 22 [1842]" (Torrey, 1843: 94).

Kooyah = tobacco root = *Valeriana edulis* Nutt. ex Torr. & A. Gray
This was noted by Frémont (1845: 135) as the principal edible root of Indians of the western mountain regions. It was said to be nutritious, but had an odor not unlike a wet bed. Preuss found it objectionable, to say the least.

Krameria parvifolia Benth.
A shrubby member of the genus *Krameria* was taken by Frémont on the Virgin River during the period 6–10 May 1844 (see account in botanical report by Torrey and Frémont, in Frémont, 1845). The species could well have been collected during the stop east of present Littlefield, Mohave County, Arizona, on the day Jean Baptiste Tabeau was killed by Indians. On that day Frémont had been "arranging plants." Also "Southern Nevada, (Frémont.)" (Watson, 1871: 417). "Between Calif. & Rky Mts.? Frémont 1849" (GH!). The 1849 gathering likely came from Arizona.

Lactuca tatarica (L.) C. A. Meyer includes *Mulgedium pulchellum*

Langloisia setosissima (Torr. & A. Gray) includes *Navarretia setosissima*

Lappula occidentale (Wats.) Greene
"FExCal, 1849. Echinospermum patulum" (NY-Torrey!).

Lappula squarrosa (Retz.) Dumort includes *Echinospermum* (*Lappula*) *fremontii* Torr. in A. Gray

Larch = *Larix occidentalis* Nutt.
Frémont (1845: 187, 202).

Larix occidentalis Nutt. includes *Pinus larix*

Larrea mexicana Moric. = *L. tridentata* (DC.) Cov.
"Southern Nevada" (Watson, 1871: 418).

Larrea tridentata (DC.) Cov. includes *Zygophyllum californicum* and *L. mexicana*
"Larrea. Frémont's 2d Expedn." (GH!). "341. Zygophyllum n. sp.? Fremont. 1844" (MO!).

Lasthenia fremontii (Torr. & A. Gray) Greene includes *Baeria fremontii* (Torr.) A. Gray

Lasthenia minor (DC.) Ornduff ≡ *Baeria minor* (DC.) Ferris
"Frémont's 3rd Expedition, 109, 1846. Burriellia chrysostoma" (NY-Torrey!).

Lathyrus linearis = *Vicia americana* Muhl. ex Willd. var. *minor* Hook. (q.v.)
"On the Platte, from its confluence with the Missouri, to Fort Laramie. Sept. 2–30 [1842]" (Torrey, 1843: 84).

Lathyrus pauciflorus Fern. subsp. *brownii* (Eastw.) Piper
"FExCal, 416. 1846. Lathyrus parvifolius S. Wats. 'At the meadow coral in fork of the upper Sacramento'" (NY-Torrey!).

Lathyrus polymorphus Nutt.
"FExCal, 1843–4. 36, 1843. Lathyrus ornatus, Nutt." (NY-Torrey!).

Lathyrus watsonii White
"FExCal, 256. 1846. Lathyrus watsoni White" (NY-Torrey!).

Layia fremontii (Torr. & A. Gray) A. Gray, Mem. Amer. Acad. n.s. 4: 103. 1849. Basionym: *Calliachyris fremontii* Torr. & A. Gray
"California, Frémont (in his second, and also in the third expedition)" Gray, 1849. "FExCal, 1843–4, 88. 1844" (also cited under *Calliachyris fremontii*; mounted on same sheet with collection from "Prairies of the Sacramento Valley, Mr. Rich." "FExCal, 1845–7. 318, 1845[6]") and "FExCal, 1845–7[1846]" (both NY-Torrey!).

Layia glandulosa (Hook.) Hook. & Arn.
"FExCal, 1843–4. Layia glandulosa—but the achenia not very hairy. Pappus shorter than the flowers" (NY-Torrey!). The note on the label is in Gray's hand. The three specimens are mounted on the same sheet with a fragment envelope and sketches of floral parts, with notes by Torrey. Both fragment envelope and the small sheet of sketches bear notations. "From a ornate specimen rcd in a letter from Frémont, May 4, 1848 & returned to him. Calif.? Below the envelope is written" "L. platyg." "FExCal, 1845–7. 177, 1846. Layia elegans T. & G.," and "Frémont's 2nd Exped. Layia elegans. Nutt. ex char. pappi" (both GH!). "FExCal, 1845–7. 177, 1846" (GH-Lowell!).

Layia platyglossa (Fisch. & Mey.) A. Gray
"FExCal, 176, 1846. Layia platyglossa" (NY-Torrey!). "FExCal, 1845–7. m. 1846. Layia (Calliachris) platyglossa" (GH!).

Lepachys columnaris = *Ratibida columnifera* (Nutt.) Woot. & Standl.
"Little Blue river of the Kansas. June 26 [1842. Frémont was on the Little Blue on 22–23 June and on the Platte River, Kearney County, Nebraska, on 26 June]" (Torrey, 1843: 87). "Platte. Frémont 1st Journey" (NY-Torrey!; GH!). The NY specimen label includes: "Lepachys columnaris. Torr. & Gray, Flora, N. Amer. on Platte. Frémont."

Lepechinia calycina (Benth.) Epling in Munz
"FExCal, 1849. Sphacele sp. nov. near S. calycina" (NY-Torrey!).

***Lepidium alyssoides* A. Gray**, Mem. Amer. Acad., n.s. 4: 10. 1849. (3rd)
Protologue locality: "Mountain valleys, from Santa Fe eastward to Rabbit's Ear Creek; Aug. [Fendler 46]. Also recently collected (in the Rocky Mountains?) by Col. Frémont." Syntype: "FExCal, 1845–7. 480, 1845" (GH!; NY Torrey!). The specimen label of the NY sheet is annotated "Lepidium alyssoides, Gray in pl Fendl." Adjacent to the sheet is the notation "near Bent's Fort." Frémont was at Bent's Fort, Otero County, Colorado, from 2–16 July 1845.

***Lepidium flavum* Torr.**, Pacif. Railr. Rep. 4: 67. 1857. (2nd)

Protologue locality: "Sandy places near the Mohave Creek; March 13 [taken by John Bigelow]. These are early specimens of a minute depressed plant, in flower only. But a single specimen was gathered by Frémont, in the same region, in his second expedition, from which the fruit is here characterized." Type: "Frémont's 2nd Exped." (holotype GH!). Both the Bigelow and Frémont materials were taken in present San Bernardino County, California, which Frémont traveled within from 18 to 24 April 1844. Specimens by Bigelow and Frémont are mounted on the same sheet at GH, with others by Hayden, Watson, and Parry. The three tiny Bigelow specimens are in very early flower and are accompanied by a label characterized by Torrey's drawings. The label shows illustrations of two fruits, one cutaway to show the arrangement of two ovules, which could only have come from the Frémont specimen. The label data includes the following: "Fl. yellow. Branching from the root. Mohave Creek, Calif. Bigelow. Stam. 6, tetradynamous, one ovule in each cell." "Collected by Frémont near Mohave Creek Western Arizona" (Watson, 1871: 30).

***Lepidium fremontii* S. Wats.**, Botany [Fortieth Parallel] 5: 30. 1871. (2nd)

Protologue locality: "Gathered by Frémont on the Mohave River in 1844." Type: "Frémont's 2nd Exp. 316, 1844. Sandy bottom of creek, pass in the mts., in bunches 2 feet high. April 17–18 camp" (holotype NY-Torrey!: microfiche BRY!). The party was near present Victorville, San Bernardino County, California, when they camped on 17 April. "Frémont's 2nd Exp. April 25–27 (Camp), 390, 1844, Mohave River" (paratypes GH!; NY-Torrey!). The party was at Bitter Spring, near present Baker, San Bernardino County, California, on 25–27 April, awaiting the return of Carson and Godey, who were in pursuit of Indians with stolen horses.

Lepidium ruderale = *L. virginicum* L.

"On the Platte. June 29 [1842. South of Cozad, Dawson County, Nebraska]" (Torrey, 1843: 83).

Lepidium virginicum L. includes *L. ruderale*

"393, 1843. Frémont's 2nd Expedn." (NY-Torrey!).

Leptodactylon pungens (Torr.) Nutt.

"On the hills, Duchesne Fork, Utah 484, May 31, 1844 [Duchesne County, Utah]. Frémont. Gilia (L.) pungens" (microfiche BRY!; specimen GH!).

Leptotaenia multifida (see Frémont, 1845: 156). = *Lomatium dissectum* (Nutt.) Math. & Const.

"Frémont's 2nd Expedn., Island in Great Salt Lake, 764, 1843 [9 September. Disappointment, now Frémont, Island, Weber County, Utah]" (NY-Torrey!). The sheet bears the handwritten notations: "Leptotaenia multifida. Probably P. dasycarpum smoothed with age. Probably Leptotaenia (platycarpa) of Torr. A. Gr."

Lespedeza capitata ≡ *L. capitata* Michx.
"Mouth of the Platte. Sept. 30 [1842. Sarpy or Cass cos., Nebraska]" (Torrey, 1843: 84).

Lesquerella fremontii Rollins & Shaw, Gen. Lesquerella N. Amer. 228. 1973.
Protologue locality: Wyoming, Frémont Co., Wind River Mts., 5 miles east of Atlantic City, calcareous gravel ridge, 8,200 ft. Ripley & Barneby 8931 (holotype CAS); isotypes (NY, US). The species was named "for John Charles Frémont, early explorer and topographer of the area where it grows."

Lesquerella ludoviciana (Nutt.) S. Wats.
"V. ludoviciana, *DC.* Upper S. Fork of Platte, 273. 1843. Frémont's 2nd Expedn." (NY-Torrey!; GH!). The plant likely came from Colorado. The specimen at GH is in a fragment envelope labeled, "V. Ludoviciana, Upper S. Fork of Platte, 273, 1843. Frémont's 2nd Exped. *Hb. Torr.*"

Letharia columbiana (Nutt.) Thoms. includes *Evernia vulpina* Ach.

Leucocrinum montanum Nutt. ex A. Gray
"FExCal, 1846. May 1st. 380. Leucocrinum montanum Nutt. Near Klamath Lake, Northern California, open rocky ground" (NY-Torrey!). On 1 May 1846 Frémont and party were at Clear Lake, present Modoc County, California. "FExCal, 1845–7. 380. 1846. Leucocr." (GH!).

Lewisia rediviva Pursh
"FExCal, 1849. Lewisia rediviva" (NY-Torrey!).

Liatris aspera Michx. includes *L. scariosa*

Liatris glabrata = *L. squarrosa* (L.) Michx.

Liatris punctata ≡ *L. punctata* Hook.
"Black Hills of the Platte. Aug. 29 [1842. One day's journey west of La Bonte Creek, Converse County, Wyoming]" (Torrey, 1843: 86). "L. punctata, *Hook.* Torr. & Gray, Flora, N. Amer. N. Fork of the Platte. Frémont" and "FExCal, 1843–4. Liatris punctata" (both NY-Torrey!). "L. punctata Hook. Torr. & Gray, Flora, N. Amer. N. Fork of the Platte. Frémont. 1st Exped." and "FExCal, 1845–7. 48. 1845" (on same sheet GH!). "FExCal, 1845–7. Liatris punctata. Platte" (Bost. Soc. Nat. Hist. GH!). Frémont was not on the Platte during the third expedition of 1845–47.

Liatris scariosa = *L. aspera* Michx.
"Lower part of the platte. Sept. 27 [1842. Three day's journey west of Platte mouth, eastern Nebraska]" (Torrey, 1843: 86).

Liatris spicata = (?) *L. lancifolia* (Greene) Kittell
"North fork of the Platte. Sept. 4 [1842. West of Scotts Bluff, Scotts Bluff County, Nebraska]" (Torrey, 1843: 86). "Liatris spicata (Platte) Frémont. Torr. & Gray, Flora, N. Amer." (NY-Torrey!).

Liatris squarrosa var. *intermedia* = *L. squarrosa* (L.) Michx.

"On the Platte [1842]" (Torrey, 1843: 86). "*L. squarrosa* v. Torr. & Gray, Flora, N. Amer. Platte, *Lieut. Frémont.*" (NY-Torrey!).

***Libocedrus decurrens* Torr.**, Smithsonian Contr. Knowl. 6(2): 7. 1853. (2nd) ≡ *Calocedrus decurrens* (Torr.) Florin

Protologue locality: "Upper waters of the Sacramento, particularly in Lat. 38°41′ to about 41° N. Lat., where it was found (without fruit) by the botanists of the United States Exploring, and by Dr. G. W. Hulse." Type: "Frémont's 2nd Exp. *Thuya gigantea* Nutt. No. 33, 1844. Feb. 25. Probably distinct from the Oregon plant. The leaves are narrower and with a longer base, & serrulate on the margins. This is the large cedar of the upper part of the mts., a new variety? Measured one of 120 ft. They were frequently greater size, & 120–130 ft in the gen! ht. Tolerably numer[ous] on the highest parts of the Sierra, nearly to the summits—going as high as any other timber. Thuja (Calli[illegible]) decurrens sp. nov. Frémont" (holotype NY-Torrey!: microfiche BRY!, one of three specimens on sheet). The Frémont party was in present Eldorado County, California, on 25 February. The journal entry of 25 February mentions measuring a large tree. The note and annotation by Torrey indicate that this was indeed a part of his concept of the new species.

***Lilium canadense* L. var. *puberulum* Torr.**, Pacif. Railr. Rep. 4: 146. 1857. (3rd) = *L. humboldtii* Roezl. & Leichtl.

Protologue locality: "Colonel Frémont found it on Antelope Creek, one of the tributaries of the Upper Sacramento [east of Red Bluff, Tehama County, California], and it is No. 2004 of Hartweg's California collection." Type: "FExCal, 1843–4. May 23 (490), 1846. Border of meadows. Antelope Creek [east of Red Bluff, Tehama County, California], a tributary of the Upper Sacramento (lat. 40°). Lilium. = 2004 Hartw. Calif. (in herb Gray)" (holotype NY-Torrey!).

Lilium philadelphicum L.

"Upper Platte. No. 451, 1843. Frémont's 2nd Exped.. Lilium philadelphicum?" (NY-Torrey!).

Limnanthes alba Benth.

"FExCal, 1846. E. Limnanthes alba Benth. Pl. Hartw. [mounted on same sheet with Hartweg No. 1677]" (NY-Torrey!).

Limnanthes douglasii R. Br. var. *rosea* (Hartw.) Mason

"Limnanthes douglasii. 121, 1844. 'Calabra Creek' Frémont's 2nd Expedn." and "FExCal, 1843–4. *286, 1846*. Limnanthes rosea Benth. *pl. Hartw.*" (both NY-Torrey!). The second sheet cited has only one plant, but two labels. The other label is by Bigelow. Who collected the specimen, pretty though it is, is moot. "FExCal, 1846. N. 394. Limnanthes. 'Tlamath Lake'" (NY-Columbia!). This latter specimen consists of tangled stems still with the Frémont note "394—1846" attached. "FExCal, 1845–7. 229. 1845" (MO!).

Limonium californicum (Boiss.) Heller
"FExCal, 1845–7. Aaaa. Statice Californica, Boiss. 1846. Gray" (NY-Torrey! and GH!).

Linanthastrum nuttallii (A. Gray) Ewan includes *Gilia nuttallii* A. Gray

Linanthus androsaceus (Benth.) Greene
"Frémont's 3rd Exped. 245, 1846. Gilia grandiflora v. androsacea" (NY-Torrey!; MO!; GH!). The specimen at GH is labeled "Gilia (Leptosiphon) androsaceus."

Linanthus aureus (Nutt.) Greene subsp. *decora* (A. Gray) H. L. Mason includes *Gilia aurea* var. *decora* A. Gray

Linanthus bicolor (Nutt.) Greene
"Herb. P. V. Le Roy, Peerskill, N. Y. Gilia tenella. Frémont" (NY-Columbia!).

Linanthus demissus (A. Gray) Greene includes *Gilia demissa*

Linanthus dianthiflorus (Benth.) Greene
"FExCal, 1849. Fenzlia" (NY Torrey!). The two tiny Frémont specimens are mounted on the same sheet with those by Parry (Emory), Coulter, [from] Hooker, and Maj. Rich.

Linanthus dichotomus Benth.
"73, 1844. Frémont. Linanthus dichotomus. Torr. & Gray, Fl. N. Amer.," "Frémont's 2nd Exp. Calif. Linanthus simplex *n. sp.* Torr. & Gray, Fl. N. Amer.," "179 & 309 California, Frémont. Gilia (Linanthus) dichotoma" and "FExCal, 1849. Gilia (Linanthus) dichotoma" (all four NY-Torrey!). "FExCal, 1845–7. 309. 1846. Gilia dichotoma Benth." (GH!; MO!).

Linanthus harknessii (Curran) Greene
"FExCal, 1845–7. Mmmm 1846. Gray. Gilia pharnaceoides *Benth.*" (NY-Torrey!). "Linanthus. Gilia pharnaceoides. Frémont's Exped." (NY-Princeton!).

Linosyris graveolens = *Chrysothamnus nauseosus* (Pallas) Britt. var. *glabratus* (A. Gray) Cronq.
"Sweet Water river. Aug. 20 [1842. Southwest of Carmody Lakes, Frémont County, Wyoming]" (Torrey, 1843: 87). "Linosyris dracunculoides! Torr. & Gray, Flora, N. Amer. Sweet Water of Platte. Frémont [1842, probably as above]'" (NY-Torrey!). "FExCal, 1845–7[1845]. Linosyris graveolens. Upper Arkansas [Colorado]" (GH-Lowell!). "FExCal, 1845. 17, 1845. Arkansas bottom. L. graveolens. Bigelovia graveolens. [Colorado]" and "FExCal, 1845–7. 160. 1845" (on same sheet GH!). "FExCal, 1845–7. Linosyris graveolens" (US!).

Linosyris viscidiflora ≡ *Chrysothamnus viscidiflorus* (Hook.) Nutt.
"Upper Platte [1842]" (Torrey, 1843: 87). "L. viscidiflora. Wind R. Chain Rky. Mts. Frémont" (NY-Torrey!; GH!).

Linum californicum Benth.
"Linum Californicum. California, Frémont. 475, 1846. 'Small white flowers'" (NY-Torrey!).

Linum perenne ≡ *L. perenne* L. includes flax or blue flax
"Black Hills to the Sweet Water of the Platte. Aug. 2–31 [1842]" (Torrey, 1843: 84). "FExRM, 1842. Linum perenne" and "FExCal, 1845–7. 80, 86, 1845. L. perenne" (both GH!). Blue flax was mentioned several times in the report of the second expedition.

Linum rigidum ≡ *L. rigidum* Pursh
"North fork of the Platte. July 8 [1842. South Platte, near Brush, Morgan County, Colorado]" (Torrey, 1843: 84).

Linum rigidum Pursh var. *berlandieri* (Hook.) Torr. & A. Gray
"FExCal, 1845–7. Eee, 1846. Linum rigidum" (GH!). "Linum rigidum var.? 207. 1845. Frémont. Prairies—sandy. July 27. Probably from the sources of the Arkansas" (NY-Torrey!). On 27 July 1845, Frémont was five days' journey east of Bent's Fort, probably in eastern Colorado.

Lippia cuneifolia ≡ *L. cuneifolia* (Torr.) Steud.
"N. fork of the Platte. July 12 [1842. Near Greeley, Weld County, Colorado]" (Torrey, 1843: 89).

Lithophragma glabra Nutt.
"Pine forests on small tributaries of the Upper Sacramento, California, Frémont [1846. 3rd expedition]" (Gray, 1865: 533). "FExCal, 1845–7. 413. 1846. Lithophragma heterophylla (marked out) glabra? Pine forests, on small tributaries of the Upper Sacramento. End of May" (NY-Torrey!). "FExCal, 1845–7. 413. 1846. Lithophragma tenella, *Nutt.* var. (L. glabra, Nutt.!). In mountains of upper Sacramento" (GH!; MO!).

Lithospermum carolinense (Walt.) MacMillan includes *Batschia gmelinii* q.v.
"FExRM, 1842. June 20. on the Platte [Big Blue River of the Kansas, probably Marshall County, Kansas]." Lithospermum hirtum, *Lehm.* = L. gmelini (Michx.) (NY-Torrey!).

Lithospermum incisum Lehm.
"FExCal, 1843–4. 287. 1843. Lithospermum breviflorum Engelm. & Gray. Sandy soil, upper South Fork of the Platte River [Colorado]" (NY Torrey!).

***Lithospermum multiflorum* Torr. ex A. Gray**, Proc. Amer. Acad. Arts 10: 51. 1875. (2nd)
Protologue: "L. multiflorum Torr. in herb.; S. Wats. Bot. King (adnot), p. 238." Type: "Frémont's 2nd Expedn. 442, 1843. July 20, 1843 [near head of Fountain Creek, north of Colorado Springs, El Paso County, Colorado]. Lithospermum multiflorum Torr. = Fendl. N. Mex. 627" (syntype NY-Torrey!) The reference by Gray to Watson (1871) clearly indicates the syntypes of this entity. That citation (Watson, 1871: 238) is as follows: "295 Parry and 441 Hall & Harbour, (referred to this species,) are the same as

627 Fendler, (L. multiflorum, Torr., Ms. in Herb.,) 1562 Wright, at least in part, and 442 Frémont, 1843, . . ."

Lobelia cardinalis L.
"FExCal, 1845–7. 1845. Lobelia cardinalis? Texensis?" (NY-Torrey!).

Lobelia siphilitica L.
"North fork of the Platte. Sept. 4 [1842. West of Scotts Bluff, Scotts Bluff County, Nebraska]" (Torrey, 1843: 88).

Lobelia spicata ≡ *L. spicata* Lam.
"On the Lower Platte. June 28 [1842. South of Lexington, Dawson County, Nebraska]" (Torrey, 1843: 88).

Lomatium sp.
There are two sheets at NY-Columbia! noted variously as *Lomatium* or *Cymopterus*. They are: "FExCal, 1845–7. 139. Feb. 1846. Valley of San Jose [annotated by M. Mathias, 1936, as 'Cymopterus?']" and "FExCal, 1849. Cymopterus ? Lomatium."

Lomatium dasycarpum (Torr. & A. Gray) Coult. & Rose subsp. *tomentosum* (Benth.) Coult. Theobald
"FExCal, 1845–7. 222. 1845[1846]. Peucedanum tomentosum. Utah Lake. 'First Camp on Piney Fork'" (NY-Torrey!). The label data are wrong; the species and subspecies are confined to California, and the number 222 fits within the sequence of specimens taken in northern California in 1846.

Lomatium dissectum (Nutt.) Math. & Const.
"FExCal, 1845–47. *Leptotaenia dissecta* of S. Watson. Hillside of Tlamath Lake, May 5th, frequent for some time back. Root large" (NY-Torrey!); and "FExCal, 1845–7. 383, 1846. Hillside of Klamath Lake. May 5. Root Large. Frequent for some time back" (GH!). The specimens at GH and NY are practically identical. In his Memoirs, Frémont (1878) states that he arrived at Klamath Lake on 6 May 1846; on 5 May he was probably still along Lost River, Klamath County, Oregon. The specimen 383 at NY bears a notation on the label: "Leptotaenia dissecta Nutt. f. S. Watson." That at GH is annotated as "Ferrula (Leptotaenia, Nutt.)" by S. W. (Sereno Watson).

Lomatium grayii Coult. & Rose
"Frémont's 2nd Expedn. 595. 1843. Upper Platte. Neb." (NY-Torrey!). Frémont was in portions of the upper Platte in Colorado (South Platte and tributaries) and in Wyoming (Sweet Water), but not in Nebraska, during 1843.

Lomatium triternatum (Pursh) Coult. & Rose
"FExCal, 1845–7. 376. 1846. Peucedanum triternatum" (NY-Torrey!).

Lomatium utriculatum (Nutt.) Coult. & Rose
"Frémont's 2nd Expedn. 47, 1844 [annotated by M. Mathias]," "Frémont's 2nd Expedn. 62, 1844," "FExCal, 1845–7. 237. 1846. Peucedanum utriculatum. Upper

Sacramento. 'Bears are fond of it,'" and "FExCal, 1843–4. 197. 1846. Peucedanum marginatum, Benth. Gravelly soil on the Mokelumne River [San Joaquin County, California], March 19" (all four NY-Torrey!). "FExCal, 1845–7. 237. 1846. Peucedanum utriculatum" (GH!).

Lomatogonium rotatum (L.) Fries
"Frémont's 3rd Expedition, Headwaters of the Arkansas [Colorado]. Pleurogyne rotata, *Griseb.*" (NY-Torrey!). "Ex Herb. George Thurber. Pleurogyne. Frémont's Second [Third] California Expedition. 1846–7[1845]. No. 252" (GH!).

Lonicera interrupta Benth.
"FExCal, 1845–7[1846]. WWW Gray. Lonicera subspicata. California" (NY-Torrey!).

Lotus argophyllus var. *fremontii* (A. Gray) Ottley includes *Hosackia fremontii* var. *fremontii* (A. Gray) Abrams

Lotus purshianus (Benth) Clements & Clements
"FExCal, 1846. Hhh. Hosackia floribunda" (NY-Torrey!).

Lotus rigidus (Benth.) Greene
"FExCal, 1849. H. puberula" (NY-Torrey!). The label is covered completely by notes in Torrey's writing.

Lotus scoparius (Nutt.) Ottley
"Frémont's 2nd Expedn." and "FExCal, 431, 1846. Symatium junceum" (both NY-Torrey!).

Lupinus albifrons Benth.
"112, 129, 262 Frémont" (Watson, 1873: 540). Five sheets NY-Torrey!: FExCal, 1843–4. Iii 1845. L. Douglasii"; "Frémont's 2nd Expedn. Upland prairie of the Mokelumne. In large bunches. Abundant. 112 and 129. 1844. versicolor? [probably San Joaquin County, California, 25–26 March]"; "112, 1844, 129, 1844. Frémont. Shrub. Banks of the Mokelumne. some branches 4 ft high. Possibly 18–20 feet circumference, Frémont's 2nd Expedn. 1844"; "Frémont's Expedition to California. L. versicolor?? Lassen's farm, April 14, 1846. White flowers"; and "FExCal, 1846. Lupinus. Fl. blue. Upper Sacramento Valley. April 8 [Cow Creek, Shasta County, California]." Lassen's farm was along Deer Creek, near present Vina, Tehama County, California. This species was noted several times by Frémont (1845: 248–49).

Lupinus albifrons Benth. var. *douglasii* (Agardh.) C. P. Smith includes *L. douglasii*

Lupinus argenteus Pursh?
"April 23–24. 333. 1844. Mohave River [San Bernardino County, California]. Frémont's 2nd Exp." (NY-Torrey!). The specimen appears to be one of the early-flowering phases of lupine, similar to large-flowered materials of sandy tracts east of the Mohave.

Lupinus argenteus Pursh var. *argenteus*
"Near L. parviflorus? Frémont's 2nd Expedn. July 31st. On the upper Platte. 535, 1843" (NY-Torrey!). Frémont was at a tributary of the Laramie River, in present southwestern Albany County, Wyoming, on 31 July 1843.

Lupinus argenteus Pursh var. *argophyllus* (A. Gray) S. Wats. ≡ *L. caudatus* Kellogg var. *argophyllus* (A. Gray) Welsh
"Frémont" (Watson, 1873: 541), includes *L. ornatus* of Torrey and Frémont: 89 in part, fide Watson (l.c.). "FExRM, 1842. 'Lupinus decumbens ? [L.] ornatus ? Gray' Sweetwater River. Aug. 1st" (NY-Torrey!). The Frémont party camped near Independence Rock, Natrona County, Wyoming, on 1 August 1842.

Lupinus argenteus Pursh var. *decumbens* (Torr.) S. Wats.
"Frémont" (Watson, 1843: 541).

Lupinus bicolor Lindley
"L. micrantha Dougl or ? bicolor. Frémont's 2nd Exp. Uplands on the Mokelumne [probably San Joaquin County, California] among oaks in hard clayey soil. 25 March. Also when first entered Sacramento Valley. 78. 1844" and "FExCal, 242, 1846. Lupinus gracilis or micranthus. Fl. blue. April 5 [Lassen's, near Vina, Tehama County, California]. Prairies, abundant. upper Sacramento" (both NY-Torrey!). The latter sheet is annotated as "*L. micranthus* Var. *bicolor*" by Sereno Watson. The second expedition dates are difficult to follow for the first several days after the party left Sutter's. Specimens were taken, reputedly at both Mokelumne River and (?) Calavaras Creek at the camp of 25–26 March.

Lupinus caespitosus Nutt. in Torr. & A. Gray = *L. lepidus* Dougl. var. *utahensis* (S. Wats.) C. L. Hitchc.
"No. 253 Frémont" (Watson, 1873: 541).

Lupinus caudatus Kellogg var. *argophyllus* (A. Gray) Welsh includes *L. argenteus* var. *argophyllus* (A. Gray) S. Wats.

Lupinus caudatus Kellogg var. *caudatus*
"FExCal, 406, 1845. Lupinus. 'Lake Fork, Grand River (near the Rocky Mts.)'" (NY-Torrey!), Frémont was along tributaries of the Grand River, Colorado, from 4 to 11 Sept. 1845.

Lupinus chamissonis Esch.
"FExCal, 1845–7. Lupinus albifrons ? Near Monterey [Monterey County], Cal. Jany. 21. 1846" (NY-Torrey!).

Lupinus concinnus Agardh. var. *arizonicus* S. Wats.
"Frémont" (Watson, 1873: 541).

Lupinus densiflorus Benth.
"147, 453, 473 Frémont" (Watson, 1873: 542). "Frémont's 2nd Expedn. Mar. 29, 147, 1844. Stanislaus River [Stanislaus County, California], in oak woods"; and "FExCal, 453 and 473 [same sheet], 1846. Lupinus Menziesii or densiflorus. Plains of Sacramento. Frequent. large" (all three NY-Torrey!).

Lupinus douglasii Agardh.
"Frémont" (Watson, 1873: 542).

Lupinus laxiflorus Dougl. = *L. argenteus* Pursh var. *argenteus*
"Frémont" (Watson, 1873: 543). "FExRM, 1842. Wind River Mountains, 1842. [Sublette County, Wyoming]. 'Lupinus laxiflorus ? A. Gray'"; and "FExRM, 1842. Wind River Chain of the Rocky Mountains, 7000 ft. Lupinus laxiflorus. Scarcely L. laxif. upper lip of calyx not saccate" (both NY-Torrey!).

Lupinus lepidus Dougl. var. *utahensis* (S. Wats.) C. L. Hitchc. includes *L. caespitosus* Nutt. in Torr. & Gray

Lupinus leucophyllus ≡ *L. leucophyllus* Dougl. ex Lindley
"Wind River mountains, and Sweet Water of the Platte. Aug. 4–21 [1842]" (Torrey, 1843: 85). "No. 737 Frémont" (Watson, 1873: 543). "FExRM, 1842. Lupinus leucophyllus? Wind River Mountains" and "L. leucophyllus. Frémont's 2nd Exped. Rolling ridges, Bannack River, upper Snake, Sept 17, (734) 1843 [Bannock River, Power County, Idaho]" (both NY-Torrey!).

Lupinus leucopsis
This name is included in the Torrey list of 1843, presumably as a synonym, of *L. ornatus* (see below).

Lupinus micranthus Dougl.
"No. 78 Frémont" (Watson, 1873: 544).

Lupinus ornatus = *L. caudatus* var. *argophyllus* (A. Gray) Welsh
"Wind River mountains, and Sweet Water of the Platte. August 4–21 [1842]" (Torrey, 1843: 85). Gray (1849: 37–38), under discussion of *L. decumbens* var. *argophyllus*, notes: "A characteristic of the species is the saccate, almost spurred, base of the calyx, which is quite as conspicuous as in L. laxiflorus, next to which it should be placed. The same plant was gathered near the sources of the Platte [Wyoming] in the first expedition of Col. Frémont, and forms part of what was called L. ornatus in the Botanical catalogue of that expedition." The specimen was not found at NY.

***Lupinus ornatus* Dougl. var. *glabratus* S. Wats.**, Proc. Amer. Acad. Arts 8: 528. 1873. (2nd) = *L. plattensis* S. Wats.
Protologue locality: "Common in the Rocky Mountains of Colorado." "No. 578 Frémont; 95 Hall & Harb.; 104 Vasey; Gordon; Greene" (Watson, 1873: 545). Type: "On hills between the branches of St. Vrain's Fork [probably Muddy Creek, Carbon County, Wyoming] of the Green River waters, 578. 1844. Frémont's 2nd Expedn." (holotype

NY-Torrey!). The specimen is annotated "L. ornatus, var. glabratus" by Sereno Watson. The specimen was likely taken in Carbon County, Wyoming, on or about 12 June 1844.

Lupinus parviflorus Nutt. = *L. argenteus* Pursh
"Collected in the Rocky Mountains, near the sources of the Snake River, by Nuttall, Frémont, (No. 413, 1845,) and Tolmie" (Watson, 1871: 54).

Lupinus plattensis S. Wats. includes *L. ornatus* var. *glabratus* S. Wats.

Lupinus pusillus Pursh
"103, 296 Frémont" (Watson, 1873: 547). One sheet with two labels and specimens at NY-Torrey!: "Frémont's 2nd Expedn., 296, 1843"; and "Frémont 1843, 3rd Exp. (103) 1845."

Lupinus sparsiflorus Benth.
"FExCal, 1849. Lupinus hirsutissimus ? Same as Fitch from the Gila" (NY-Torrey!).

***Lycium fremontii* A. Gray**, Proc. Amer. Acad. Arts 6: 46. 1862. (4th)
Protologue locality: "Interior of California or country east of it, Frémont, Coll. Exped. 1849." Type: "FExCal, 1849. Lycium Frémontii, n.sp." (holotype NY-Torrey!: microfiche BRY!). The type sheet bears careful analytical drawings by Torrey. The name on the label appears to be in Gray's hand. This taxon occurs from San Diego County, California, east into southern Arizona, and southward into Baja California and Sonora (Abrams, 1951: 667).

***Lycium macrodon* A. Gray**, Proc. Amer. Acad. Arts 6: 45. 1862. (4th)
Protologue locality: "California, in the interior? Coll. Frémont in Expedition to California, 1849, Herb Torr." (l.c.). Type: "FExCal, 1849. Lycium macrodon, n. sp. Gray [in Gray's writing]" (holotype NY-Torrey!: microfiche BRY!). Hitchcock (1932: 310) states: "The type was very probably collected in southern Arizona."

Lycium pallidum Miers
"New Mexico and adjacent parts of Arizona, Fendler (670, 668b), Bigelow, Thurber, Frémont, Newberry" and "Forma β: filamentis tuboque corollae intus pilosulis (sp. Thurber) vel hirsutis (spec. Frémont e Rio Virgen)" (Gray, 1862a: 45). Hitchcock (1932: 301) includes the following citation: "bottom land of the Santa Clara River, western New Mexico or southern Utah?, May 11, 1843–44, Frémont 474 (NY)." "Frémont's Expedition to california, 474, 1844. Lycium? Western New Mexico. On bottom land of the Santa Clara River, sandy soil, very abundant. May 11" (NY-Torrey!). The NY mount of the Frémont specimen bears a label with the following information: "Lycium pallidum Miers, same as Fendler 679, From Rio Sa Clara, California, Frémont 474." "Ex spec. coll. Frémont" (GH!, a flower in an envelope). The GH fragment is mounted on a sheet with collections by Fendler (No. 670), Newberry, and Palmer. The Fendler and Newberry collections are cited on annotation labels affixed as "Cotypes" of the *Lycium pallidum* Miers. Frémont camped on the Santa Clara River, present Washington County, Utah, on

11 May 1844. This is the first known plant taken from the flora of Washington County, Utah.

***Lycium torreyi* A. Gray**, Proc. Amer. Acad. Arts 6: 47. 1862. (2nd)
Protologue locality: "Texas, on the Rio Grande, to Fort Yuma, interior of California, along the Mexican boundary, collected by Frémont, Major Thomas, Thurber, Bigelow, Schott, and Wright." Type: "FExCal, 1843–44. Lycium Torreyi, A.G." (syntype NY-Torrey!: microfiche BRY!). Abrams (1951) cites the type locality as "Fort Yuma, California." Hitchcock (1932: 282) selects as type of the species a collection by George H. Thomas ["Fort Yuma, Cal. Mar 3rd, 1855" NY-Torrey!], Rock of Chickamauga of Civil War fame (Cleaves, 1948) from Fort Yuma, California.

Lycopus americanus Muhl. in Bart. includes *L. sinuatus*

Lycopus sinuatus = *L. americanus* Muhl. in Bart.
"On the Platte [1842]" (Torrey, 1843: 89).

Lygodesmia juncea ≡ *L. juncea* (Pursh) D. Don
"Upper Platte [1842]" (Torrey, 1843: 88). "Plains of the Missouri and Platte to the Rocky Mountains, *Lewis? Nuttall! Dr. James! Lieut. Frémont!*" (Torrey & Gray, 1843: 484). "Herb. A. Gray. Lygodesmia juncea. Frémont 3rd Exped. 1845" (GH!). "Lygodesmia juncea. galls. Frémont's 3d Expedit. 90. 1845" (MO!).

Lysimachia ciliata ≡ *L. ciliata* L.
"Forks of the Platte. July 2 [1842. Lincoln County, Nebraska]" (Torrey, 1843: 88).

Machaeranthera bigelovii (A. Gray) Greene
"Dietaria viscosa Nutt. ex char. [illegible words] Frémont" (NY-Torrey!).

Machaeranthera canescens (Pursh) A. Gray includes *Dietaria viscosa, D. pulverulenta*, and probably others pro parte.
Three specimens and labels on one sheet and the final two on another, all GH!: "FExCal, 1845–7. 36, 367, 481 [Dietaria] viscosa Nutt., 1845." Each label bears one of the numbers, i.e., 36 or 367, or 481. "FExCal, 1845–7. 365, 1845" and "FExCal, 1845–7. 105, 1845. D. pulverulenta *Nutt.*" "FExCal, 1843–44. No. 10. 1843. Machaeranthera sessiliflora *Dietaria sessiliflora*, Nutt. 'June 2. Noon halt. Bottom land of the Creek. Open ground (no timber) very rich soil'" (NY-Torrey!). The date of "June 2" makes no sense. The party did not leave Westport until 10 June 1843.

***Machaeranthera fremontii* Rydb.**, Bull. Torrey Bot. Club 32: 123. 1905. (2nd) = *M. canescens* var. *glabra* A. Gray (annotation B. L. Turner)
Protologue locality: "Platte Waters, 20 July 1844 [1843], Frémont 421." Type: "FExCal, 421, 1844[1843]. July 20 [El Paso County, Colorado]. Black soil of river bottom (Platte Waters) among tall plants" (NY-Torrey!). The 1844 date is not tenable; the number sequence is wrong, a not unusual situation, but it fits with that of 1843, not 1844.

Machaeranthera tanacetifolia (H.B.K.) Nees includes *Dietaria coronopifolia*
"FExCal, 1845–7. No. 6. 1845. Dietaria coronopif." and "Platte. Frémont. Dietaria coronopifolia" (both GH!).

Macrorhynchus (*Stylopappus*) *troximonoides* = *Agoseris aurantiaca* (Hook.) Greene
"Defiles of the Wind River mountains [1842]" (Torrey, 1843: 88). "On the Wind River Chain at the elevation of 7000 feet and more, *Lieut. Frémont!*. We have described the fruit from the single specimen collected by Lieut Frémont; which alone exhibits it fully developed" (Torrey & Gray, 1843: 491).

Madrona = *Arbutus menziesii* Pursh
Frémont (1848: 37).

Mahonia repens (Lindley) G. Don includes *Berberis aquifolium*

Mahonia fremontii (Torr.) Fedde includes *Berberis fremontii* and *B. trifoliata*

Malacothamnus fremontii (Torr.) Greene includes *Malvastrum fremontii*

Malva involucrata ≡ *Callirhoe involucrata* (Torr. & A. Gray) A. Gray
"Little Blue river of the Kansas. June 23 [1842. Near Adams County, Nebraska]" (Torrey, 1843: 84). "Frémont. [illegible note and date]" (GH-Thurber!); "Frémont's 3rd Exped. [1845]" (GH!). The Thurber sheet at GH is annotated as var. *involucrata*, and the 3rd Exped. sheet as var. *lineariloba* (Torr. & A. Gray) A. Gray. Both annotations are by L. J. Dorr.

Malva pedata ≡ *Callirhoe pedata* (Nutt.) A. Gray
"Big Blue river of the Kansas. June 21 [1842. Near Marshall County, Kansas]" (Torrey, 1843: 84).

Malva rotundifolia = *Sidalcea candida* A. Gray pro parte

Malvastrum coccineum var. ***elatum* E. G. Baker**, J. Bot. 29: 171. 1891. (3rd)
Protologue locality: "United States. *Wright*, No. 41. *Frémont*, No. 411." Type: "Frémont's Expedition to California 411, 1845. Sphaeralcea new. (S. pedata call it). Moving Fork, *1st* Camp. Utah" (syntypes NY-Torrey!: microfiche BRY!; GH!; US!). Frémont 411 is also the type of *Sphaeralcea pedata* A. Gray, q.v.

***Malvastrum fremontii* Torr. ex A. Gray**, Mem. Amer. Acad. Arts, n.s. 4: 21. 1849. (3rd)
≡ *Malacothamnus fremontii* (Torr.) Greene
Protologue locality: "Interior of California, Frémont." Type: "FExCal, 428, 1846. Malvastrum fremontii Torr. in Gray Pl. Fendl." (lectotype NY-Torrey!, see Torrey ex A. Gray, Syn. Fl. N. Amer. 1(1): 31. 1897; isotype GH!). The two GH sheets "Ex herb. J. Torrey. Malvastrum Frémontii, *Torr. in Pl. Fendler.* Frémont's 3rd Expedn. 428, 1846" and "FExCal, 1845–7. Malvastrum Frémontii Torr. in Gr. pl. Fendl. p. 21 [GH-Thurber!]" are annotated as *Malacothamnus fasciculatus* (Nutt) Greene subsp. *exfibulosus* (Jepson) Bates.

Malvella leprosa (Ortega) Krap. includes *Sida hederacea* Torr.

Manzanita or mansanita = *Arbutus menziesii* Pursh
Frémont (1887: 475–77).

Marah fabaceus (Naud.) Greene includes *Melothria* of Frémont?
Four sheets NY-Torrey!: "Frémont's 2nd Expn. March 15, 114, 1844. Mouth of the American Fork, Sacramento [Sacramento County, California]," mounted with "152, 1844, March 28, Camp on Stanislaus River [Stanislaus County, California]"; "Frémont's 2nd Expedn. Camp 25th –26 March, 80, 1844 [Mokelumne River?, San Joaquin (?) County, California]"; "FExCal, 1845–7. Ttt. 1846. Dr. Gray. These specimens were in a small thin folio book. not numb? Echinocystis occidentalis?"; and "FExCal, 1845–7. 1846. Sss Dr. Gray. Santa Cruz, sea coast. Lat 57°. Differs from No 80, 1844. 1. Young fruit echinate with long soft spines. 2. ovary 4-celled, with a single ovule in each cell." The sheet with number 80 designation has three small sheets of Torrey's drawings of floral parts and features of the ovary. Two sheets GH!: "FExCal, 1845–7. Sss 1846"; and "FExCal, 1845–7. Ttt. 1846." Frémont was at Santa Cruz, Santa Cruz County, California, on 28 February 1846. The Sss sheet at GH was annotated by K. M. Stocking in 1949 as "*Marah oreganus* (T. & G.) Howell."

Mariposas = *Calochortus*
Frémont (1887: 479).

***Meconella californica* Torr. & Frém.** in Frém., Rep. Exped. Rocky Mts. 312. 1845. (2nd)
Protologue locality: "On American fork of the Sacramento river. Frémont." Type: "American Fork of the Sacramento. No. 39 & 44. Frémont [1844]. Meconella Californica Torr. & Frém. in 2nd Report" (holotype NY-Torrey!).

Megarrhiza muricata (Kellogg) S. Wats.
"Specimens collected by *Frémont*, (from the Mokelumne River to the Upper Sacramento), may belong here" (Brewer et al., 1876: 242). This may be synonymous with *Marah fabaceus* cited above.

Melampodium cinereum DC.
"A still more slender-leaved form was gathered at Paso del Norte by Dr. Wislizenus, and intermediate states by him on the Cimarron and by Frémont on the upper Arkansas" (Gray, 1849: 78). Frémont was on the upper Arkansas in August and early September 1845.

Menispermum canadense ≡ *M. canadense* L.
"On the Platte [1842]" (Torrey, 1843: 83).

Mentha arvensis L. includes *M. canadensis*
"FEXRM, 1842, July 10th [St. Vrain's Fort, Weld County, Colorado]" (NY-Torrey!).

Mentha canadensis = *M. arvensis* L.
"North fork of the Platte. July 14 [1842. North of Cheyenne, Laramie County, Wyoming]" (Torrey, 1843: 89).

Mentzelia albicaulis (Dougl.) Torr. & A. Gray
"Frémont's 2nd Exp. M. albicaulis v. gracile, *Nutt.*" (NY-Torrey!).

Mentzelia nuda (Pursh) Torr. & A. Gray
"North fork of the Platte. July 14 [1842. North of Cheyenne, Laramie County, Wyoming]" (Torrey, 1843: 86). Five specimens on four sheets (NY-Torrey!): "Mentzelia nuda—but flowers bracteolate in one spec. Frémont's 1st Expedn., 14 July 1842 [Horse Creek, north of Cheyenne, Laramie County, Wyoming]"; "10 petals, nearly equal. Frémont's 3rd Expedition, Ex herb. J. Torrey. Mentzelia nuda. Torr. & Gr. Fl. N. Amer. August 22, 1845, Platte River [on 22 August 1845 Frémont was along the upper Arkansas, west of present Pueblo, Pueblo County, Colorado]"; "Frémonts 3rd Exped., July 19, 1845, no 149. Mentzelia (Bartonia) nuda *T. & Gr.* [on 19 July Frémont was 13 days east of Bent's Fort, probably in western Kansas]"; "Frémonts 3rd Expedn., Upper Arkansas, 31 July 1845 [on this date Frémont was three day's east of Bent's Fort, Colorado]"; "FExCal, Aug. 22, 1845. Mentzelia." The 31 July 1845 specimen is also at MO!, but there it bears the number 243.

Mentzelia oligosperma Nutt.
"Mentzelia oligosperma. Frémont's 3d Expedit. 123. 15 July 1845 [Smoky Hill Fork, Kansas]" (MO!; NY!).

Mentzelia pumila Nutt.
"FExCal, 1845–7. 416. 1845. M. pumila, *Nutt.*" (GH!). The specimen is in rather poor condition and its determination is questionable. It is mounted with a specimen from "Colorado of the Oregon" by Nuttall.

Mentzelia tricuspis A. Gray
"FExCal, 1849. Mentzelia" (NY-Torrey!).

Mertensia ciliata (James) G. Don includes *Pulmonaria ciliata*

Mesembryanthemum crystallinum L.
"Collected also by *Frémont*" (Brewer et al., 1876: 251). "FExCal, 1845–7. Vv. 1846 (sent before as Prep. 2)" [mounted on same sheet as "Prep 2. Ex herb J. Torrey. Torr. & Gr. Fl. N. Amer. Frémont's 3rd Exp."] (GH!). "FExCal, 1846. Rep 2 Vv. Apr. Mesembryanthemum" (NY Torrey!; MO!). "Frémont's 3rd Expedition [1846]. Mesymbryanthemum. California" (US!).

Microsteris gracilis (Hook.) Greene
"Collomia gracilis, *Dougl.* 4, 1844. Frémont's 2nd Expedn. California," "Frémont's 2nd Exped. California," and "FExCal, 313 and 230. 1846" (all three NY-Torrey!). "Frémont's Expedition 1845–47[1846]. Collomia gracilis Dougl. ex Torrey" (GH!).

Mimosa nuttallii (DC.) Barneby includes *Schrankia angustifolia* and *S. nuttallii*

Mimulus alsinoides = *Mimulus glabratus* H.B.K. (see *M. jamesii β fremontii* below)
"Defiles of the Wind River mountains. Aug. 13–16" [1842. Sublette County, Wyoming] (Torrey, 1843).

Mimulus aurantiacus Curtis
"FExCal, 1845–7. 509, 1846. Diplacus glutinosus. 'Some mistake about the number'"; and "Frémont's 3rd exped. 510, 1846. Diplacus glutinosus. Near rocks. Flowers yellow. American Fork. June [Sacramento County, California]" (both NY-Torrey!; and also at MO!). "FExCal, 1845–7. 510. 1846. Mimulus glutinosus" (GH!).

Mimulus cardinalis Dougl. ex Benth.
"Frémont's 3rd Expedition. Sept. 3, 1846" (NY-Torrey!). The date is difficult to read, either Sept. 3, 1846 or Sept. 13, 1846. In neither event is it clear where Frémont was during those times. He was in southern California on both dates.

Mimulus fremontii (Benth.) A. Gray includes *Eunanus fremontii* Benth. in DC.
"Southern part of the State [California], *Coulter, Frémont* (his specimens probably from the San Joaquin Valley or farther south," (Brewer et al., 1876: 565).

Mimulus glabratus H.B.K. subsp. *fremontii* (Benth.) Pennell includes *Mimulus jamesii β fremontii* Benth. in DC.

Mimulus guttatus DC.
"FExCal, 315, 1846. Mimulus luteus. Sacramento Valley" and "Frémont's 3rd Expedition. Near Lassen's [Tehama County, California], Upper Sacramento. April 13, 1846. Mimulus luteus" (both NY-Torrey!; the latter also at MO!).

***Mimulus jamesii β fremontii* Benth.** in DC., Prodr. 10: 371. 1846. (1st) = *M. glabratus* subsp. *fremontii* (Benth.) Pennell
Protologue locality: "β. fremontii, pedicellis gracilibus folio longioribus, floribus minoribus. In montium Windriver praeruptis (Frémont!). M. alsinoides Torr.! in Frém. rep. p. 88. non Dougl. (v. in Herb Torrey)." Type: "FEXRM, 1842. July 14 [in pencil]" (holotype NY-Torrey!). It is clear from the citation by Bentham, quoted above, that the name was based on materials in the Torrey herbarium. On 14 July 1842 the Frémont party reached Horse Creek, present Laramie County, Wyoming.

Mimulus lewisii ≡ *M. lewisii* Pursh
"Defiles of the Wind River mountains. Aug. 13–16 [1842. Sublette County, Wyoming]." "FEXRM, 1842. Mimulus Lewisii. Wind River Mountains, Augt. 13–16" (NY-Torrey!).

Mimulus rubellus A. Gray in Torr.
"FExCal, 1849. Mimulus rubellus?" (NY-Torrey!).

Mirabilis jalapa L. probably = *M. multiflora* (Torr.) A. Gray in Torr.
This name might apply to more than one species of *Mirabilis* in the Frémont reports.

Mirabilis multiflora (Torr.) A. Gray in Torr.
"FExCal, 1845. No. 1. Augt. 20th [Fountain Creek, Pueblo County, Colorado]. Arkansas bottom. Quamoclidion multiflorum"; "Frémont's 2nd Expedn. Mirabilis multiflorus Torr." (both NY-Torrey! and the latter also as fragments GH!). "Frémont's 2nd Expedn. 'Arkansas bottom,'" mounted on the same sheet with "FExCal, 1845–7. No. 1. 1847" (both GH!). If the 1847 date is correct, Frémont continued to collect following his involvement in the California rebellion. It seems more likely that the year is wrong, and it should be 1845, a duplicate of the first cited specimen.

Mirabilis nyctaginea (Michx.) MacMillan includes *Oxybaphus nyctaginea*
"FExCal, 1845–7. 51, 1845" (GH!).

Mohavea viscida A. Gray in Torr.
Gray (in Torrey, 1857: 122) mentions only the Bigelow collection from "Mohave Creek, California; March 2" with the original description. However, the following quote indicates that his was not the earliest collection: "Gravelly banks from Fort Mohave to Fort Yuma on the Colorado, and adjacent parts of Arizona, first found by Coulter and Frémont" (Brewer et al., 1876: 552).

Monarda fistulosa ≡ *M. fistulosa* L.
"On the Platte [1842]" (Torrey, 1843: 88).

Monarda pectinata Nutt.
"FEXRM, Monarda aristata, *Nutt.* 1842. July 2nd [forks of the Platte, Lincoln County, Nebraska]" (NY Torrey!). "Ex herb. J. Torrey. Monarda. Torr. & Gr. Fl. N. Amer. Fremont's 2nd Expedn." (US!).

Monardella candicans Benth.
"Frémont's Expedition 1845–47[1846]. Monardella candicans Benth. Pl. Hartweg. ex Torrey" (GH-Thurber!); "[Frémont] 506. 1846. ex herb. J. Torrey. Torr. & Gr. Fl. N. Amer." (GH!), mounted on sheet with Bigelow's specimen from Knights Ferry, Stanislaus, and with Pl. Hartweg no. 1911, Mns. Sacramento, an isotype of the species (!). Bentham (1839–57: 330) notes the type locality as: "in locis aridis montium Sacramento." "FExCal, 1845–7. 506, 1846. Monardella candicans *Benth. Hartw.*" (US!). The sheet at US was annotated as *Monardella lanceolata* by L. R. Abrams in 1912.

Monardella lanceolata A. Gray
"Frémont's Expedition 1845–47[1846]. ex Torrey" (GH-Thurber!). This sheet also has mounted on it a specimen of *M. candicans* Benth.

Monardella villosa Benth.
"Frémont's Expedition 1845–47[1846]. Monardella fremontii. Ex Torrey" (GH-Thurber!), and "Frémont's 3rd Exp. 446. 1845[6]. Ex herb. J. Torrey. Torr. & Gr. Fl. N. Amer." (GH!). Both sheets are annotated by Carl Epling as subsp. *subserrata* (Greene) Epling, and the latter bears a notation by Epling: "Mountains of the upper Sacramento." "FExCal, 1845–7. 446, 1846. (once named M. Frémontii Torr.), Lassen's

(upper Sacramento) May 25 [Tehama County, California]. = Calif. Rose in herb Gray" (NY-Torrey!; GH!; MO!; US!). "M. Frémontii Torr." was evidently a provisional name, never published.

Monolepis chenopodioides Moq. = *M. nuttalliana* (Schultes) Greene
"Blitum Nuttallianum Roem. & Schult. Frémont's 2nd Expedn" (NY-Torrey!). "477 Frémont" (Watson, 1874: 102). "FExCal, 1845–7. 477. 1845. Monolepis" (GH!; NY-Torrey!). The NY specimen is labeled "Blitum Nuttallianum, *Roem. & Schult. Moq. Chenop.* Near Bent's Fort." Frémont was at Bent's Fort [Otero County, Colorado] from 2 to 16 August 1845.

Monolepis nuttalliana (Schultes) Greene includes *M. chenopodioides* Moq.(?)

***Monoptilon* Torr. & A. Gray** in A. Gray, Boston J. Nat. Hist 5: 106. 1845. (2nd)
Type species: ***Monoptilon bellidiforme* Torr. & A. Gray** in A. Gray
Protologue locality: "It was probably gathered in the southern ranges of the Rocky Mountains." Type: "FExCal, 1843–4" (holotype NY-Torrey!; isotype fragments GH!). The materials at GH consist of two flower heads in an envelope, subtended by a note and two illustrations of the species. The note in Gray's hand reads: "All the rest is in Herb. Torrey!." This species is, however, a Mohave desert plant, likely taken by Frémont either in San Bernardino County, California, or Clark County, Nevada.

Montia perfoliata (Donn) Howell
"10, 1844. (March 12). Fremont's 2nd Exp." and "67, 1844. Fremont's 2nd Expedn." (both NY-Torrey!).

Mosses = ? lichens, in some part.
Mosses were noted by Frémont (1848: 18) on 21 December 1845.

Mulgedium pulchellum = *Lactuca tatarica* (L.) C. A. Meyer
"Black Hills of the Platte. July 25–31 [1842]" (Torrey, 1843: 88). "Alluvial soil, & c., from the Upper Missouri and Platte, *Nuttall! Mr. Nicollet! Lieut. Frémont!*" (Torrey & Gray, 1843: 498).

Musenium tenuifolium ≡ *Musineon tenuifolium* Nutt. ex Torr. & A. Gray
"Alpine region of the Wind River mountains [1842. 12–16 August. Sublette County, Wyoming]" (Torrey, 1843: 86). "Wind River Mountains. Musineum tenuifolium" (NY-Torrey!).

Myosotis glomeratus = *Cryptantha celosioides* (Eastw.) Payson (q.v.)
"Forks of the Platte. July 2 [1842. Lincoln County, Nebraska]" (Torrey, 1843: 89).

***Myrica hartwegii* S. Wats.**, Proc. Amer. Acad. Arts 10: 350. 1875. (3rd)
Protologue locality: "Collected by Hartweg (n. 1958) on the Sacramento, by Frémont, and on the south fork of the Merced near Clark's Station by Mr. Muir, who describes it as a small bush six feet high." Syntype: "No. 24, 1845. Fremont's 3rd Expedition" (US!;

NY!). The specimen at NY is dated 21 December 1845, "Borders of the San Joaquin River, near the foot hills. Dec."

Myriophyllum heterophyllum Michx.?

"FExCal, 1845–7. No. 29. 1845. Myriophyllum" (NY-Torrey!). The specimen is only tentatively identified; previous annotations by S. G. Aiken in 1981 and E. N. Nelson and R. W. Couch in 1984, tentative also, place the specimen with *M. hippuroides* Nutt. ex Torr. & A. Gray, a California species. The specimen most likely was taken in Kansas, however.

***Nama demissa* A. Gray**, Proc. Amer. Acad. Arts 8: 283. 1870. (2nd)

Protologue locality: "Dry or desert regions of Nevada, Frémont, Anderson, Torrey, Watson in King's expedition; forms with ample corolla sometimes twice the length of the calyx." "Western Nevada, (Frémont, Anderson, Torrey.)" (Watson, 1871: 259). "(*Frémont*, Nev., is the first specimen cited.)" (Cronquist in Cronquist et al., 1984: 196). The specimen likely came from Clark County, Nevada. No Frémont material was found in the collections of the various herbaria searched during this research.

Nasturtium palustre = *Rorippa islandica* (Oed.) Borbas

"Black Hills of the Platte. July 26–August [1842]" (Torrey, 1843: 83). "FEXRM, 1842. Camp, mouth of Deer Creek, 26 July [near Glen Rock, Converse County, Wyoming]" (NY Torrey!).

Navarretia pubescens (Benth.) Hook. & Arn.

"Frémont's Expedition to California 1845–7. Sr56 [or 456]. 1846" and "Frémont 325, Sacramento Valley—1846. Navarretia pubescens, *Hook. & Arn.*" (NY-Torrey!; BRY-Sartwell!). "Frémont. Calif. No. 456. 1846. Navarretia" and "FExCal, 1845–7. 456. 1846. Navarretia pubescens, *Hook. & Arn.*" (both NY-Torrey!); and "Frémont's 2[3]d Calif. Exped. 1846–47, Navarretia pubescens. ex Torrey" (GH!).

***Navarretia setosissima* Torr. & A. Gray ex Torr.** in Ives, Rep. Colorado R. 4: 22. 1861. (2nd) ≡ *Langloisia setosissima* (Torr.) Greene.

Protologue locality: "This well-marked species (which is nearly allied to N. Schottii) was first collected in 1844, near the Rio Virgen, toward the great Californian desert, and again in 1848." Type: "Frémont's Expedition to California 414, 1844, April 30. Most westerly part of N. Mex. near the Virgin river. Sandy and stony ground" (lectotype NY-Torrey!: microfiche BRY!; isolectotype GH!). "(Frémont 414, 'most westerly part of N.M., near the Virgin R.,' actually referring to the Virgin River of Utah; lectotype at NY)" (Cronquist in Cronquist et al., 1984: 186). The camp on 30 April was at present Stump Spring, Clark County, Nevada. The isolectotype at GH is mounted adjacent to a fragment (!) labeled "Frémont, 1849."

Navarretia viscidula Benth.

"FExCal, 1845–8. 507. 1846. Navarretia viscidula, *Benth.*" (NY-Torrey!; GH!).

Negundo aceroides = *Acer negundo* L.

"August 28th. Forche a la Prele, among the Black Hills (Platte Valley). [1842. West of Douglas, Converse County, Wyoming]" (NY-Torrey!). "On the lower part of the Platte [1842]" (Torrey, 1843: 84). The specimen is labeled "Negundo fraxinifolium." The species was variously called *N. aceroides* or *N. fraxinifolium* in the Frémont reports.

Negundo californicum Torr. & A. Gray ≡ *Acer negundo* var. *californica* (Torr. & A. Gray) Sargent

Negundo fraxinifolium = *Acer negundo* L.

***Nemophila fremontii* Elmer**, Bot. Gaz. 41: 319. 1906. ≡ *Nemophila pulchella* var. *fremontii* (Elmer) Constance

Protologue locality: "no. 4901, collected in May 1903, on Frémont's Peak of the Gabilan mountains, San Benito County, California." "Frémont's Peak, San Benito County, California" (Abrams, 1951). This is one of two species named in Frémont's honor but not based in some part on his collections (see also *Lesquerella fremontii*).

Nemophila heterophylla Fisch. & Mey.

"FExCal, 1845–7. 250. 1846. Nemophila parviflora, *Benth.*" (GH!). The Frémont gathering at GH is mounted with specimens by Hartweg, Thurber, and Kellogg. Annotated as such by Lincoln Constance in 1938. "Nemophila—hardly parviflora. Leaves pinnatifid & sep. deeply 3–5 toothed. Frémont's 2nd Expedn. 42. 1844. May [or Mar.] 4. American Fork of the Sacramento" (NY-Torrey!). The date is difficult to read; either alternative is impossible for the 1844 expedition, if the provenance is correct!

Nemophila insignis = *N. menziesii* Hook. & Arn.

Frémont (1848: 19).

Nemophila maculata Benth. ex Lindley

"FExCal, 1845–7. 231. 1846. Nemophila maculata—Valley of the San Joaquin, Calif. April" (GH!; NY-Torrey!). "FExCal, 1849. Nemophila maculata. 'Summit of Coast Range of Mts.—between the vallies of the San Joaquin & Monterey Rivers'" (NY-Torrey!). All annotated by Lincoln Constance in 1938.

Nemophila menziesii Hook. & Arn.

"FExCal, 1845–7. 162. 1846. Nemophila Menziesii, H. & A." (GH-Thurber!; NY-Torrey!) and "FExCal, 1845–7. 312. 1846. Nemophila insignis" (GH!; NY-Torrey!). "Frémont, Calif. 217. 1845[6]. Nemophila insignis" (NY-Torrey!). All annotated by Lincoln Constance in 1938. Specimen 312 is mounted on a sheet with collections by Hartweg and Douglas. The Douglas specimens are isotypes of *Nemophila insignis* Benth. The species was noted by Frémont (1848: 19) on 12 February 1846.

***Nicolletia* A. Gray** in Frém., Rep. Exped. Rocky Mts. 315. 1845. (2nd)

Type species: ***Nicolletia occidentalis* A. Gray**

Protologue locality: "On the banks of the Mohahve river, growing in naked sands; flowering in April." Type: "FExCal, 1843–4. Nicolletia occidentalis Gray in Frémont's

2nd Exped." (holotype NY-Torrey!: microfiche BRY!). The holotype consists of three stem fragments, with some florets in a fragment envelope. "Nicolletia occidentalis. Torr. & Gray. Frémont's 2d Expedition" (isotype GH!). The isotype at GH is in very poor condition, as if it had been wet following collection. It is one of the survivors of the flood of the Kansas. "FExCal, 1843–4. 220, 1844. Nicolletia occidentalis Gray" (isotype NY!). The species was evidently taken in San Bernardino County, California, where it is known as "hole-in-the-sand plant."

Nicotiana bigelovii (Torr.) S. Wats.

"FExCal, 1846. Nicotiana quadrivalvis. Lassen's [Tehama County, California]—Upper Sacramento. 'Brought to les jeunes gens to smoke, by the indians'" (NY-Torrey!).

Nycterium luteum = *Solanum rostratum* Dun.

"South fork of the Platte. July 4 [1842. Ca. 40 miles west of Platte Forks, Keith County, Nebraska]" (Torrey, 1843: 90). "Solanum loatum *Dunal*. Nycterium luteum *Doner* [crossed out]. Frémont's 1st Exp." (NY-Torrey!).

***Obione confertifolia* Torr. & Frém.** in Frém., Rep. Exped. Rocky Mts. 318. 1845. (2nd) ≡ *Atriplex confertifolia* (Torr. & Frém.) S. Wats. includes *Obione rigida* Torr. & Frém.

Protologue locality: "On the borders of the Great Salt Lake." Type: "Obione confertifolia, *Torr. & Frém.* in Frém. 2nd Reprt. (1845). Borders of the Great Salt Lake [near mouth of Weber River, Weber County], Utah. 761. 1843" (holotype NY-Torrey!). This species is noted in the discussion of the journey on 10 September 1843, when the Frémont party was returning from the boat trip to Disappointment [Frémont] Island. It was probably taken on the trip from the water's edge to the camp on the lower Weber River, in Weber County, Utah. The holotype consists of a single branch in young fruit. The sheet bears the notation in Torrey's handwriting, "Obione rigida var. confertifolia n.sp. (crossed out) T. & F." Below the notation is a drawing of a fruiting bract, with one side folded back, and an ovary. This is clearly the specimen on which the species was based. There is a second sheet at NY-Torrey!: "Frémont's 2nd Expedn." with the notation "Grayia or near it." The specimen has male inflorescence fragments and clearly is not a portion of the type collection.

Obione coriacea Moq. = *Atriplex canescens* (Pursh) Nutt.

This species is compared by Torrey and Frémont (Frémont, 1845) with *Obione confertifolia* (see above). It does not occur in the West.

***Obione hymenelytra* Torr.**, Pacif. Railr. Rep. 4: 129. 1857. (4th) ≡ *Atriplex hymenelytra* (Torr.) S. Wats.

Protologue locality: "This species was found by Dr. Parry and by Colonel Frémont on the Gila." Type: "FExCal, 1849. Obione hymenelytra, n. sp." (holotype NY-Torrey!). "FExCal, Gila [1849]" (NY-Crooke!; GH!) A third sheet, "Frémont's 2nd Expedition," is at NY-Torrey! Except for the sheet designated as holotype, the Frémont materials from 1849 are scanty, consisting mainly of fruiting bracts (isotypes NY!; GH!) and a branchlet of equivocal source (GH!). The holotype at NY bears all of the accoutrements of a Torrey type specimen, except for illustrations. It bears a descriptive label in Torrey's handwriting and the name *Obione hymenelytra* n. sp. on the label. The specimen was annotated as type by G. D. Brown in 1951.

Obione rigida Torr. & Frém. in Frém., Rep. Exped. Rocky Mts. 318. 1845, nom. nud. = *Atriplex confertifolia* (Torr. & Frém.) S. Wats.

Intended type: "Obione rigida T. & F. On an island [Frémont Island] in Great Salt Lake [Weber Co., Utah], Frémont 767, 1843" (NY-Torrey!). The name was published without a description and is a nomen nudum. The specimen was taken on 9 September 1843, when Frémont and his boating party were on Disappointment (Frémont) Island in the Great Salt Lake. It seems clear from the notation that Torrey intended, at least initially, to name the species *O. rigida*, with the specimen taken later on "borders of the Great Salt Lake" as var. *confertifolia* of that species. Reasons for change of mind are not apparent, but Torrey abandoned the epithet *rigida* in favor of *confertifolia*. The application of the same number, in this case 767, to two sheets of the same taxon is in keeping with the practice of Frémont, at least occasionally, of using the number to indicate a species and not a collection. The sheet bears drawings of bracts, fruit, seed, and embryo, roughly sketched by Dr. Torrey.

Oenothera albescens (Lindley) S. Wats.

"Frémont" (Watson, 1873c: 601).

Oenothera albicaulis Pursh

"North Forks of the Platte. July 14 [1842. North of Cheyenne, Laramie County, Wyoming]" (Torrey, 1843: 85). This species was cited by Torrey and Frémont (Frémont, 1845). "FExCal, 46, 1845, Arkansas River [August 1845]. Oenothera pinnatifida, *Nutt.*" (NY-Torrey!).

Oenothera albicaulis Pursh var. *nuttallii* Engelm.

"202, 234, 751, 753 Frémont" (Watson, 1873c: 601).

Oenothera alyssoides Hook. & Arn. = *Camissonia boothii* (Dougl.) Raven subsp. *desertorum* (Munz) Raven pro parte

This species was cited by Torrey and Frémont (Frémont, 1845). "No. 337 Frémont, in part" (Watson, 1873c: 602).

Oenothera amoena Lehm.

"Nos. 408, 435 Frémont" (Watson, 1873c: 602).

Oenothera biennis = *O. villosa* Thunb. (q.v.)

"Black Hills to the Sweet Water River. July 23–August 4 [1842]" (Torrey, 1843: 85).

Oenothera biloba Durand

"Frémont" (Watson, 1873c: 604).

Oenothera breviflora Torr. & A. Gray = *Camissonia breviflora* (Torr. & A. Gray) Raven
"Frémont" (Watson, 1873c: 605). Includes *O. nuttallii* Torrey in Frémont's report, fide Watson. "Upper Sweetwater River. Frémont's 1st Exped. 1842" (NY-Torrey!).

Oenothera caespitosa Nutt. var. *navajoensis* (Wagner, Stockhouse & Klein) Cronq. includes *O. montana*

***Oenothera canescens* Torr. & Frém.** in Frém., Rep. Exped. Rocky Mts. 314. 1845. (2nd)
Protologue locality: "This species was collected (we believe) on the upper waters of the Platte [1–4 July 1843; Wagner 1984]." Type: "Frémont's 2nd Exped. Oe. (Euoenothera, near subsect. Gauropsis) canescens, *Torr. & Gr.* ined." (holotype NY-Torrey!: microfiche BRY!); and "FExCal, 1843–4" (isotype GH!). "Oenothera. Frémont's Exped. 192. 25 July 1845 [Smoky Hill Fork?, Kansas]" (MO!).

***Oenothera claviformis* Torr. & Frém.** in Frém., Rep. Exped. Rocky Mts. 314. 1845. (2nd) ≡ *Camissonia claviformis* (Torr. & Frém.) Raven
Protologue locality: "Grows with the preceding, [i.e., with *Cowania plicata*] 'Specimens of this plant, without a ticket, were in the collection; doubtless obtained in California'" Type: "Oenothera (Chylismia) n. sp.! clavaeformis Torr. & Frém. *not numbered*. Frémont's 2nd Exped." (holotype NY-Torrey!, annotated as type by P. Raven in 1959: microfiche BRY!). According to Raven (1969), the type variety grows in western Inyo County, eastern Kern County, northern Los Angeles County, western San Bernardino County, and northern Riverside County, California, almost entirely on the Mohave Desert. The species was lectotypified by Munz (1928: 236) on the basis of a specimen cited by him as "Frémont's Pac. R. R. Exp., 1843–44," probably collected in California. Raven (1969: 217) cites a collection at NY Torrey, not seen by me, labeled "Frémont's Pacific R. Road Expedition, 1853–54 (Probably collected in California)." The specimen is likely the same as that cited wrongly by Munz as being dated 1843–44. More than one of the few specimens taken on the 1853–54 expedition are referred to as taken on the Pacific Railroad Expedition. The publication of the taxon in 1845 precludes the possibility of specimens from 1853–54 being included as portions of the type. This 1854 specimen adds another species to the lamentably small list taken by Frémont on his fifth and last expedition.

***Oenothera deltoides* Torr. & Frém.** in Frém., Rep. Exped. Rocky Mts. 315. 1845. (2nd)
Protologue locality: Not given. Type: "Oe. (Euoenothera, Onagra) n. sp. (put next to Oe. jamesii). Oenothera deltoides, Torr. & Frém. in Frém. 2nd Report, p. 315" (holotype NY-Torrey!: microfiche BRY!). No type specimen information accompanied the publication of the species, but the plant is common in sandy stretches between Las Vegas, Nevada, and Littlefield, Mohave County, Arizona. The plant could have come from that general area.

Oenothera dentata Cav. = *Camissonia campestris* (Greene) Raven pro parte
"Nos. 166, 172 Frémont" (Watson, 1873c: 606). The number 166 is definitely *C. campestris*.

Oenothera drummondii = *Oe. missouriensis* Sims
"Black Hills. July 26 [1842. Deer Creek, near Glen Rock, Converse County, Wyoming]" (Torrey, 1843: 85).

***Oenothera fremontii* S. Wats.**, Proc. Amer. Acad. Arts 8: 587. 1873. (2nd)
Protologue locality: "Collected by Frémont on his second expedition (locality not given)." This plant is cited in McGregor et al. (1986) as *Oenothera macrocarpa* Nutt. subsp. *fremontii* (S. Wats.) W. L. Wagner, Frémont's evening primrose. It is endemic to Nebraska (Antelope, Cedar, Franklin, Webster counties) and west central Kansas. The taxon is questionably lectotypified by Parry 79 (GH) from "White rock on Smoky Hill River, Elsworth, Russell, Ellis, Trego, Cove, or Logan county, Kansas, 7–23 June 1867" (Wagner, 1983). "Frémont's 3d Exped. 1845. Oe. Missouriensis v. incana" (GH!). "Frémont's 2nd Exp. Oe. missouriensis var. or n. sp.???" and "Oe. missouriensis, 81, 1843. Frémont's 2nd Expedn." (both NY-Torrey!). One of the two Frémont specimens from the second expedition would have been better selected as lectotype.

Oenothera gauraeflora Torr. & A. Gray = *Camissonia bistorta* (Nutt.) Raven
"No. 337 Frémont, in part" (Watson, 1873c: 608).

Oenothera graciliflora Hook. & Arn. ≡ *Camissonia graciliflora* (Hook. & Arn.) Raven
"FExCal, 218, 1845, Arkansas River above Pueblo, mouth of Canon! Oe. graciliflora var." (NY-Torrey!; GH!). Note on specimen by Peter Raven: "Locality must be in error." "218 Frémont" (Watson, 1873c: 608).

***Oenothera hispidula* S. Wats.**, Proc. Amer. Acad. Arts 8: 599. 1873. (3rd) ≡ *Godetia hispidula* (S. Wats.) S. Wats.
Protologue locality: "Sacramento and Tulare Valleys, collected by Frémont, Pratten, and Rattan." Type: "FExCal, 1845–7. Ppp. 1846. Oe. hispidula" (holotype GH!). "No. 307, and Ppp., Frémont;" (Watson, 1873c: 609). "Sacramento Valley" (Abrams, 1951: 188). "Without locality: *Frémont p.p.p.* in 1846, cited as typical material *G. hispidula*" (Hitchcock, 1930: 351). No Frémont material was found at NY. H. and M. E. Lewis (1955) regard this as a synonym of *Clarkia arcuata* (Kellogg) Nels. & Macbr.

Oenothera latifolia (Rydb.) Munz includes *Anogra cinerea* Rydb. and *O. pinnatifida* Nutt.
"Oenothera albicaulis pubescens. Frémont's 3d Exped. 178. 1845" (MO!).

Oenothera micrantha Hornem. ex Spreng. ≡ *Camissonia micrantha* (Hornem.) Raven
"Frémont" (Watson, 1873c: 610).

Oenothera missouriensis Sims includes *O. macrocarpa* Nutt. subsp. *macrocarpa*
"Blue river of the Kansas. June 19–20 [1842. Near Marshall County, Kansas]" (Torrey, 1843: 85). This species was cited by Torrey and Frémont (Frémont, 1845). "Oenothera. Frémont's 3d Exped. 108. 1845" (MO!). "Nos. 81, 108 Frémont"; (Watson, 1873c: 610).

Oenothera montana Nutt. = *O. caespitosa* Nutt.
This species was cited by Torrey and Frémont (Frémont, 1845). "Frém. 2d. Exped. Torr. Oe. montana, *Nutt.*" (GH!).

Oenothera nuttallii = *Camissonia breviflora* (Torr. & A. Gray) Raven
"Upper part of the Sweet Water [1842]" (Torrey, 1843: 85). "Oenothera Nuttallii, *T. & Gr.* Upper Sweetwater River, Frémont's 1st Exped. 1842" (NY-Torrey!).

Oenothera ovata Nutt. ex Torr. & A. Gray ≡ *Camissonia ovata* (Nutt.) Raven
"FExCal, 1843–4 [struck out]. 125. 1846. Oe. (Primulopsis) ovata Nutt." (GH!). "FExCal, 1845–7. No. 125. Feb. 25, 1845. Oenothera (Primulopsis) ovata *Nutt.*" (NY-Torrey!). The date as to year at least is wrong. "No. 125 Frémont" (Watson, 1873c: 611).

Oenothera pallida Lindl.
"Oenothera trichocalyx *Nutt.* 30 July 1842. Frémont's 1st Exp. North fork of Platte, Wyoming, near junction of Platte & Sweetwater [note above label]" (NY-Torrey!, mounted on sheet with a Nuttall isotype of *Oenothera trichocalyx* Nutt.). "Oenothera albicaulis glabra. Frémont's 3d Exped. 222. 1845" (MO!).

Oenothera pinnatifida Nutt. = *O. latifolia* (Rydb.) Munz
"Nos. 45, 267 Frémont" (Watson, 1873c: 611). "FExCal, 1843–4. Oenothera pinnatifida, *Nutt.* Republican Fork of the Kansas River, June 27/43 [Republican Fork of Kansas, Kansas]" and "Oe. albicaulis, Nutt. Frémont's 3rd Ex. 20 July [1845, Smoky Hill Fork (?), Kansas]" (both NY-Torrey!).

Oenothera rhombipetala ≡ *O. rhombipetala* Nutt. ex Torr. & A. Gray
"On the Platte. September 18–20 [1842. Grand Island to east of Grand Island, Nebraska]" (Torrey, 1843: 85). "Platte. Frémont. Oe. rhombipetala" (GH!). "River Kansas, Frémont. 1844 [eastern Kansas, returning from second expedition]. Oe. rhombipetala" (NY-Torrey!).

***Oenothera scapoidea* Nutt. var. *aurantaica* S. Wats.**, Proc. Amer. Acad. Arts 8: 595. 1873. (?) ≡ *Camissonia claviformis* subsp. *aurantiaca* (S. Wats.) Raven
Protologue locality: "Southern California and Arizona" [p. 595] and "No. 180 Coulter, in part; 374 Parry; Frémont; Bigelow; Newberry; Cooper; Thomas; Almendinger [p. 613]." Type: "Fort Mohave, Mohave County, Arizona, 1861, J. G. Cooper (lectotype GH; Munz, 1928: 237)." The Frémont specimen (see *Camissonia claviformis* subsp. *aurantiaca*) is a syntype.

Oenothera serrulata ≡ *Calylophus serrulatus* (Nutt.) Raven
"On the Kanzas and Platte. June–July 14 [1842]" (Torrey, 1843: 85). "17, 201, 455 Frémont" (Watson, 1873c: 613). Three specimens (NY-Torrey!): "Serrulata. Frémont 455, 1843"; "FExCal, 17, 1843. Oenothera serrulata, *Nutt.*"; and "Frémont's 3rd Expedition, 201, 1845. Branch of Smoky Hill Fork [? western Kansas during late July 1845]. Oenothera serrulata, *Nutt.*"

Oenothera serrulata Nutt. var. *spinulosa* Torr. & A. Gray
"Frémont" (Watson, 1873: 613).

Oenothera speciosa ≡ *O. speciosa* Nutt.

"Big Blue river of the Kanzas. June 19–20 [1842. Near Marshall County, Kansas]" (Torrey, 1843: 85). Three specimens on two sheets NY-Torrey!: "Frémonts Expedition to California, 537, 1845. Oenothera"; "FExCal, 532, 1845. Oenothera"; and "FExCal, July 1843. Oenothera speciosa." "Frémont I." (GH!). The Frémont specimen at GH is mounted on a sheet with two specimens labeled "Hort. Bot. 1842, Oenothera Speciosa, *Nutt*. Torr. & Gray, Flora, N. Amer." The Frémont plant is likely a duplicate of that cited by Torrey as having been collected on June 19–20.

Oenothera trichocalyx = *O. pallida* Lindley

"North fork of the Platte. July 30 [1842. Near Alcova, Natrona County, Wyoming]" (Torrcy, 1843: 85).

Oenothera villosa Thunb.

"Oenothera biennis, var. canescens (fide Gray). Frémont's 1st Exped. July 1842" (NY-Torrey!). The sheet bears the annotation "*Oenothera villosa* Thunb. var. *villosa*" by W. Dietrich in 1981.

Olione [Obione] *canescens* ≡ *Atriplex canescens* (Pursh) Nutt.

"Upper north fork of the Platte. July 26 [1842. Deer Creek, near Glen Rock, Converse County, Wyoming]" (Torrey, 1843: 91).

Onobrychis arenaria = ? *Hedysarum boreale* or *Oxytropis* species

Onobrychis sativa = ? *Hedysarum boreale* or *Oxytropis* species

Onosmodium molle ≡ *O. molle* Michx.

"On the Platte. June 29 [1842. South of Cozad, Dawson County, Nebraska]" (Torrey, 1843: 89). "FEXRM, 1842. June 26. Platte Ridge [Kearney County, Nebraska]. Onosmodium molle, *Mx.*" (NY-Torrey!).

Onosmodium occidentale Mack. = *O. molle* Michx.

Opuntia missouriensis = *O. polyacantha* Haw.

"Forks of the Platte. July 2 [1842. Lincoln County, Nebraska]" (Torrey, 1843: 86). "Frémont's 2nd Expedition, 275, 1843–44 Opuntia Missouriensis. named by Engelmann" (NY-Torrey!). The sheet bears a broken cladode, a mature one with etiolated sprouts, a juvenile cladode, a flower, and a fruit. The fruit lacks glochids and belongs to another species, possibly to *O. macrorhiza* Engelm.

Opuntia polyacantha Haw. includes *O. missouriensis*

Oreophila myrtifolia = *Pachystima myrsinites* (Pursh) Raf.

"Summit of the Wind River mountains. Aug. 13–14 [1842. Sublette County, Wyoming]" (Torrey, 1843: 84). "FExCal, 1843–4. Pachystima myrsinites, *Raf.*," "Oreophila myrtifolia, Nutt. *Torr. & Gr. fl. N. Am. 1. p. 258.* Frémont's 2nd Expedn. & 3rd Expedn. 375. 1846" and "FExCal, 1846. Oreophila myrtifolia, *Nutt.*" (all four NY-Torrey!). The first cited specimen is mounted on a sheet with a specimen by T.

Nuttall from the Rocky Mountains. "FExCal, 1845–7. 156. 1845" (GH!). The Frémont specimen at GH is mounted with collections by Thomas Nuttall and Karl Geyer.

Orobanche fasciculata ≡ *O. fasciculata* Nutt.
"South fork of the Platte. July 4 [1842. Ca. 40 miles west of Platte forks, Keith County, Nebraska]" (Torrey, 1843: 89).

Orobanche ludoviciana Nutt.?
"Pinquam Creek, Utah Lake. Frémont's 3rd Exped. July 29, 1845" (NY-Torrey!). Pinquam Creek is American Fork river or creek, which enters the north side of Utah Lake, Utah County, Utah. However, on 29 July 1845 Frémont and his huge party were still four days east of Bent's Fort, Colorado, i.e., the provenance or the date is wrong.

Orobanche californica Cham. & Schlecht. subsp. *jepsonii* (Munz) Heckard
"FExCal, 1845–7. Eeee 1846. Dr. Gray. Phelipaea California, *Don. Syst. Orobanche Californica* Cham. & Schlech." (NY-Torrey!).

Oryngium aquaticum of Frémont, ? possibly ≡ *Orontium aquaticum* L.

Orthocarpus lithospermoides Benth.
"FExCal, 1845–7[1846]. Orthocarpus lithospermoides" (NY-Sartwell!). "FExCal, 1845–7. 479, 1846. O. lithospermoides"; "FExCal, 1845–7. 421. 1846" (both GH!); and "Frémonts 2d Cal. Exped. 1846. 437. Orthocarpus lithospermoides" (GH-Thurber!; MO!).

Orthocarpus luteus ≡ *O. luteus* Nutt.
"Sweet Water river. Aug. 5 [1842. Southeast of Atlantic City, Frémont County, Wyoming]" (Torrey, 1843: 88). "FEXRM, 1842. Orthocarpus luteus, Nutt. 'River bottom,' Aug. 5" (NY-Torrey!, this and the following). The three specimens from the 1842 expedition are mounted on the same sheet with two other plants subtended by a label: "FExCal, 1845–7. 75. 1845 Orthocarpus" (also GH!).

Orthocarpus purpurascens Benth.
Three Frémont labels on one sheet: "FExCal, 1845–7. 174, 303, 422. 1846. Orthocarpus purpurascens" (all GH!). "FExCal, 1845–7. 422, 1846. Orthocarpus. 'Throughout the San Joaquin & Sacramento vallies.' 'Flowers rose color'" and "FExCal, 1843–4. 232, 1844. April 10 [northeast of Bakersfield, Kern County, California]. Orthocarpus" (both NY-Torrey!). The label has another one attached with the notation "Orthocarpus purpurascens?" Below the note is another notation: "Named by Bentham. See DC. Prodr." "FExCal, 1845–7. 272, 303, & 311. 1846. Orthocarpus" and "Frémont 2d. 122. 1844" (both NY-Torrey!).

Oxalis stricta ≡ *O. stricta* L.
"On the Kansas. June [1842]" (Torrey, 1843: 84).

Oxybaphus nyctaginea ≡ *Mirabilis nyctaginea* (Michx.) MacMillan
"Kansas river, June 20 [1842. Big Blue River, near Marshall County, Kansas]" (Torrey, 1843: 91). "FEXRM, 1842. Oxybaphus Nyctaginea" (GH-Thurber!).

Oxyria reniformis = *O. digyna* (L.) Hill

"Alpine region of the Wind River mountains. August 13–16 [1842. Sublette County, Wyoming]" (Torrey, 1843: 92). "FEXRM, 1842. Wind River Mountains" (NY-Torrey!). The label of the specimen at NY-Torrey bears faintly the name "Oxyria reniformis Hook." "FEXRM, 1842. O. digyna, Hill" (GH-Thurber!).

Oxystylis **Torr. & Frém.** in Frém., Rep. Exped. Rocky Mts. 312. 1845. (2nd) Type species: ***Oxystylis lutea*** **Torr. & Frém.**

Protologue locality: "On the Margoza [Amargosa] river, at the foot of a sandy hill; only seen in one place, but abundant there. The specimens were collected on the 28th of April, and were in both flower and fruit." Type: "Frémont's 2nd Expedn. No. 386. 1844. Bottom of Margoza at the foot of a sandy hill—only seen in one place but abundant there. April 28th" (holotype NY-Torrey!). On 28 April the Frémont party had reached the Amargosa, "a large creek of salt and bitter water, running in a westerly direction." The locality is in San Bernardino County, California. This is probably the plant indicated by Frémont (1845: 262) as "a remarkable new genus of *cruciferae*." The holotype sheet has affixed a small sheet of Torrey's drawings and notes, again demonstrating the care with which he dissected and illustrated plants prior to preparing the description of new taxa.

Oxytheca perfoliata **Torr. & A. Gray**, Proc. Amer. Acad. Arts 8: 191. 1873. (2nd)

Protologue locality: "Nevada, Frémont, second Expedition." "Unionville, Humboldt, and Tucker Valleys, on the border of the desert, May to July 1860, S. Watson, in King's expedition?" Type: "Oxytheca perfoliata n. sp. Fremont's 2nd Expedn." (syntype NY-Torrey!). This species has been lectotypified (Ertter, 1980: 83–84) on a collection by "Sereno Watson (no. 1043 June 1868)" (NY-Torrey!: microfiche BRY!).

Oxytropis lambertii ≡ *O. lambertii* Pursh

"Big Blue river of the Kansas to the forks of the Platte. June 20–July 2 [1842]" (Torrey, 1843: 85). Two sheets NY-Torrey!: "Oxytropis Lambertii. Torr. & Gray, Flora, N. Amer. Upper Platte. Frémont's 1st Expedn, 1842. June 27 [Kearney County, Nebraska]"; and "Oxytropis Lambertii. Torr. & Gray, Flora, N. Amer. Frémonts 1st Expedn." "FExCal, 1845–7. 140. 1845. O. Lambertii" (GH!). Both *O. lambertii* and *O. sericea* are likewise candidates for the esparcette or *Onobrychis sativa* of Frémont's 1845 report (see also *Hedysarum boreale*).

Oxytropis plattensis = *O. lambertii* Pursh?

"Goat island of the upper Platte. July 31 [1842. East of Independence Rock, Natrona County, Wyoming]" (Torrey, 1843: 85). This locality, if right, is at the edge of the range of *O. lambertii*, but is within that of *O. nana* Nutt.

Oxytropis sericea Pursh

"FExCal, 1845–7, 368. 1845. Oxytropis Lambertii, var. sericea (= O. sericea Nutt.!)" (GH!). There are two labels and two plants on the sheet. One label bears the notation: "For Dr. Gray."

Pachypodium integrifolium ≡ *Thelypodium integrifolium* (Nutt.) Endl. in Walp.
"North fork of the Platte. September 4 [1842. West of Scotts Bluff, Scotts Bluff County, Nebraska]" (Torrey, 1843: 83). ["Pachypodium integrifolium Nutt. (Thelypodium) T. & Gr. On the Platte, Sept. 4, Nebraska], 1842. Frémont's 1st Exped" (NY-Torrey!).

Pachystima myrsinites (Pursh) Raf. includes *Oreophila myrtifolia*

Paeonia brownii Dougl. ex Hook.
"FExCal, 1846" (NY-Torrey!). The Frémont specimen is on a sheet with one by Douglas. "FExCal, 1845–7. 367, 1846" (GH!). The specimen at GH is mounted with a collection by Hartweg (no. 1636).

Palo Colorado = *Sequoia sempervirens* (D. Don) Endl.
Frémont (1843: 36–37).

Parnassia fimbriata ≡ *P. fimbriata* Koenig & Sims
"Little Sandy creek, defiles of the Wind River mountains. Aug. 8 [1842. Sublette County, Wyoming]" (Torrey, 1843: 83). "Fimbriata. Frémont's 1st Journey" (NY-Torrey!). The Frémont gathering is mounted on a sheet with two specimens from Franklin's Journey, from Hooker.

Paronychia jamesii Torr. & A. Gray
"FExCal, 1843–4. 493/43. July 28 [northern Larimer County, Colorado]. Paronychia jamesii T. & G." (NY-Torrey!).

Parvisedum pumilum (Benth.) Clausen includes *Sedum pumilum* Benth.

Pectis angustifolia Torr.
"FExCal, 1843–4. No. 511" (NY-Torrey!). "Fine specimens of this rare plant were gathered on the Upper Arkansas by Frémont, in his second expedition, and by Lieut. Abert" (Gray, 1849: 61). "Frémont's 2d Exped. [1843–4]" and "Frémont's 3rd Exped. 1845" (same sheet GH!). The two Frémont collections at GH are mounted on a sheet with others by Thurber, Fendler, Wright, Edwards, and Hayden. "Dysodia. Fremont's 3rd Exped. 235. 1845" (MO!).

Pectocarya chilensis DC. var. *californica* Torr.
Under discussion of this *Pectocarya* Torrey notes: "P. pencillata was found in California by Frémont in his second expedition" (Torrey, 1857: 124).

Pedicularis densiflora Benth.
"FExCal, 1845–7. Upper Sacramento, April 27 [Bear Creek, Shasta County, California]. G[ray]. alpha 358. 1846. Pedicularis densiflora, *Benth.*" (NY-Torrey!; BRY-Sartwell!; MO!). The sheet at NY has a drawing of floral parts attached.

Pedicularis groenlandica Retz. includes *P. surrecta*

***Pedicularis procera* A. Gray**, Amer. J. Sci. Arts 84: 251. 1862. (3rd)

Protologue locality: Parry 252 "Shaded hill-sides, not uncommon in scattered localities. Also collected by Frémont in 1845, and in the Sandia Mountains further south, by Dr. J. M. Bigelow; but only in fruit." Type: "Parry 252, Shaded hill-sides, headwaters of Clear Creek, E. of Middle Park, Colo., in 1861" (syntype NY!). "FExCal, 1845–7. 119. 1845. Pedicularis procera n. sp." (syntype GH!). "FExCal, 1845–7. 478. 1845. Pedicularis Frémonti n. sp. Near Bent's Fort" (probable syntype NY-Torrey!). The label bears the manuscript name "*Pedicularis fremontii* n. sp." The name was never published. "Frémont's 2nd Exped. 'Pedicularis too poor probably *P. densiflora*'" (NY-Torrey!). The sheet from the second expedition was not cited by Gray.

Pedicularis surrecta = *P. groenlandica* Retz.

"Defiles of the Wind River mountains. Aug. 13–16 [1842. Sublette County, Wyoming]" (Torrey, 1843: 89). "FExRM 1842. Pedicularis surrecta, *Benth.*" (two sheets NY-Torrey!).

Pediomelum cuspidatum (Pursh) Rydb.

"FExCal, 1843–4. 171. 1843. Psoralea cuspidata" (NY-Torrey!).

Pediomelum esculentum (Pursh) Rydb. includes *Psoralea esculenta* Pursh

Pellaea mucronata (D. C. Eaton) D. C. Eaton

"Frémont. 60. 1844. 'Feb 30th. American Fork in the mountains'" (NY!). There being no such date as 30 February, the specimen was either taken on 29 February or 1 March 1844. In any event Frémont was moving ahead with the advance party, hurrying to Sutter's for relief of the expedition. Probably they were still in Eldorado County, California.

Peltiphyllum peltatum (Torr.) Engelm.

"Saxifraga peltata, Torr. Noza River, upper Sacramento, Frémont. 1846" and "FExCal, 1845–7. Noza River. A handsome water-plant, growing in the river where the water was six inches deep & the current swift. Saxifraga peltata *Torr. in Benth. pl. Hartw.*" (both NY Torrey!). This is likely a portion of the material on which the concept of *Saxifraga peltata* Torr. was based, to be published later but not cited, in Bentham's Plantae Hartwegiana.

Penstemon albidum ≡ *P. albidus* Nutt.

"Forks of the Platte. July 2 [1842. Lincoln County, Nebraska]" (Torrey, 1843: 88). "July 1842, Frémont. Frémont 1st Exped. P. albidum" (NY-Torrey!).

Penstemon alpinus Torr.

"Versus montes Scopulosos (iter Longii! Frémont!)" (Bentham, 1846).

***Penstemon ambiguus β foliosus* Benth.** in DC., Prodr. 10: 321. 1846. (2nd) = *P. ambiguus* Torr.

Protologue locality: "Frémont's 2nd Expedn. No. 623, 1844." Type: "Frémont's notes 623, 'On the highest level prairie, July 7, 1844.'" "Probably Cheyenne County, Colo. P.

ambiguus β foliosus Benth.!" (holotype NY-Torrey!; isotype GH!). On 7 July 1844, Frémont was nearing the end of his second expedition. "Penstemon. Frémont's 3rd Exped. 229. 1845" (MO!). The sheet is annotated by F. W. Pennell in 1934.

Penstemon angustifolius Nutt. includes *P. caeruleum*

Penstemon azureus Benth.
"FExCal, 1845–7[1846]. P. azureus, Benth. var. angustissimus Gray" (NY-Torrey!). "FExCal, 1845–7. 407. 1846. P. azureus, *Benth.*" (GH!).

Penstemon breviflorus Lindley
"FExCal, 1845–7. Kkkk. 1846" (GH!).

Penstemon buckleyi Pennell
"Frémont's 3rd Exp. 118. 1845. July 12" (NY-Torrey!). On 12 July 1845 the Frémont party was one day west of Turkey Creek, Kansas. The Buckley penstemon is restricted to sandy soil, particularly dunes in north-central Kansas, where encountered by Frémont, and elsewhere in the plains south to central Texas.

Pentstemon caeruleum ≡ *P. caeruleus* Nutt. = *P. angustifolius* Nutt.
"South fork of the Platte. July 4" (Torrey, 1843: 88). "Frémont's 1st Exped. July 4, 1842. Wind River Mts. P. caeruleus, *Nutt.*" (NY-Torrey!; GH!). On 4 July 1842 Frémont was 40 miles west of the Platte forks, South Platte, Keith County, Nebraska. The sheet at GH! contains the following note by Asa Gray: "Not quite Torrey's Frémont. July 4. Wind River Mts, which has pubescent stem, ciliate leaves, &c., & C. = Bradbury's & Nuttalls from Platte. Hb. Acad."

Penstemon caeruleus Nutt. = *P. angustifolius* Nutt. pro parte
"It [pubescence of stem] is evident in that of Frémont from the Wind River Mountains, in Dr. Torrey's herbarium" (Gray, 1862a: 61). "ad flum. Platte (Frémont!)" (Bentham, 1846). This is the same as that cited above.

Penstemon caespitosus Nutt.
In discussing *P. pumilus* Nutt., Gray (1862a: 67) notes: "Frémont's specimen, referred here in the Prodromus, must belong to the preceding species (i.e., to *P. caespitosus*)." "Frémont 2nd Expedn. *P. caespitosus, Nutt.* see Parry for good specims. Named by Bentham Penstemon pumilus" (NY-Torrey!).

Penstemon centranthifolius Benth.
"In montibus Scopulosis (Frémont!)" (Bentham, 1846).

Penstemon cobaea Nutt.
"Platte (Frémont!)" (Bentham, 1846). "Penstemon Cobaea Nutt. Frémont's 1st Exped. July 20, 1842 [Fort Laramie, Goshen County, Wyoming]" (NY-Torrey!). "Frémont 2d. Coll. P. cobaea, *Nutt.*" (GH!).

***Penstemon fremontii* Torr. & A. Gray**, Proc. Amer. Acad. Arts 6: 60. 1862. (2nd)
Protologue locality: "'On the Uinta plains, very abundant and in large patches. June 5, 1844.' Frémont." Type: "On the Uinta plain, very abundant and in large fields, June 5th 1844, Frémont no. 540. 1844. P. Frémontii, n. sp." (holotype NY-Torrey!: microfiche BRY; isotype GH!). On 5 June 1844 the Frémont party traveled from the vicinity of Whiterocks to Vernal, placing the type locality within Uintah County, Utah. The specimen at NY was annotated as type by F. W. Pennell in 1916.

Penstemon heterophyllus Lindley
"FExCal, 1845–7. 407 and Ffff. 1846. P. heterophyllus, Lindl." (both on same sheet GH!; Ffff also NY-Torrey!). The specimens were annotated as subsp. *purdyi* (McMinn) Keck by D. D. Keck in 1931. "Penstemon heterophyllus, *Lindl.* var. fide *Gray*. California—Frémont" (NY-Torrey!). There are two stems mounted on the NY sheet; one has a knotted strip of paper bearing the notation "407—1846." The sheet is at least partly coordinate with the materials at GH. There is a second sheet at NY-Torrey! with another Frémont "California, 407—1846" mounted with specimens by both C. C. Parry (Emory's Mexican Boundary Survey) and Shelton.

Penstemon laricifolius Hook. & Arn.
"In montibus Scopulosis (Frémont!)" (Bentham, 1846). "Frémont no 553 (No. of year uncertain, probably 1844)" (two sheets NY-Torrey!). This is mounted on the sheet with an isotype of *P. laricifolius*, and it is annotated by F. W. Pennell as *P. exilifolius* A. Nels. "Herb. A. Gray. Torr. & Gray, Fl. N. Amer. Frémont. No 533. 1843. P. laricifolius" (GH!). The Frémont material at GH is mounted on a sheet with a probable isotype of the species by Tolmie from the "Snake Country." One of the NY sheets has a note by F. W. Pennell: "No. 533 coll. Jul. 31, 1843. Collected near upper Laramie R. in Albany Co. Wyoming."

Pentstemon micranthum = ?
"Sources of the Sweet Water, near the mountains. Aug 7" (Torrey, 1843: 89).

***Penstemon nitidus β major* Benth.** in DC., Prodr. 10: 323. 1846 (2nd)
Protologue locality: "In montibus Scopulosis (Frémont!) v. in herb Torrey)." Type: "Hill sides of Duchesne Fork [Duchesne County, Utah], May 31, 1844. 485, 1844. Frémont. *P. pachyphyllus* A. Gray n. sp." (holotype NY-Torrey!). The taxon was treated at specific rank later and bears the name *P. pachyphyllus* A. Gray ex Rydb.

***Penstemon pachyphyllus* A. Gray ex Rydb.**, Fl. Rocky Mts. 770, 1066. 1917. (2nd) See *P. nitidus β major* Benth. in DC.

Penstemon rydbergii A. Nels.
"FExCal, 1845–7. No. 101. 1844. Penstemon confertus (procerus) v. violacea. The numbers in Frémont's rep. do not commence so low as 101. This plant is probably from the Arkansas [in Colorado]" (NY-Torrey!).

***Penstemon secundiflorus* Benth.** in DC., Prodr. 10: 325. 1846. (2nd)
Protologue locality: "In montibus Scopulosis (Frémont!)" (l.c.). Type: "Named by Bentham. Frémont 2nd Exped. Penstemon secundiflorus!" (holotype NY-Torrey!: microfiche BRY!). A notation is written on the sheet as follows: "This is only *P. acuminatus* Dougl. small. A. G[ray]. 1852."

***Penstemon strictus* Benth.** in DC., Prodr. 10: 324. 1846. (1st)
Protologue locality: "In montibus Scopulosis ad fontes Fl. Sweetwater (Frémont!)." Type: "Frémont's 1st Expedn. (Rocky Mountains) Wind River Range, 1842. August 7, 1842 [adjacent to South Pass, Frémont County, Wyoming]" (holotype NY-Torrey!).

***Penstemon watsonii* A. Gray**, Syn. Fl. N. Amer. 2(1): 267. 1878. (3rd)
Protologue locality: "Mountains of W. Colorado, Utah, and Nevada (*Frémont, Parry, Watson, Wheeler, Vasey, Ward,* &c.), to borders of Arizona, *Palmer*" (l.c.). Syntype: "FExCal, 1845–7. 210, 1845 and 409, 1845" (two sheets, GH!). Both sheets bear the name "Penstemon watsonii" written on a label bearing the printed designation "Syn. Fl. N. Amer." The species has been lectotypified on Watson 773, Austin, Lander Co., Nevada, July 1865 (NY) by Pennell, 1920: 365. There is a third sheet at GH-Thurber! that appears to be a duplicate of the 409 material.

Perideridia gairdneri (Hook. & Arn.) Mathias includes *Edosmia gairdneri*

Perideridia oregana (S. Wats.) Mathias includes *Carum kelloggii* A. Gray

Petalostemon candidum = Dalea oligophylla (Torr.) Shinners
"Red Buttes. July 29 [1842. Near Casper, Natrona County, Wyoming]" (Torrey, 1843: 84).

Petalostemon purpureum ≡ Dalea purpurea Vent.

Petalostemon violaceum = Dalea purpurea Vent.
"Big Blue river of the Kansas, &c. June 21 [1842. Near Marshall County, Kansas]" (Torrey, 1843: 84).

Peteria thompsonae S. Wats.
Frémont's 2nd Expedition. Probably from the mountains of Utah or of California (NY-Torrey!). That this specimen was an enigma to Torrey is indicated by a cryptic note, "spiny Spiny Stipules! J. T." A second note on the sheet, probably written by Gray, notes, "Something very doubtful." The two stems lack flowers, the racemes are reduced to rachis and bracts. The spiny stipules are apparent. This seems to be the earliest collection of the species.

Petrophytum caespitosum (Nutt.) Rydb.
"Spiraea caespitosa *Nutt.* 585. 1844. Frémont's 2nd Exp." (NY-Torrey!).

Phaca = Astragalus utahensis (Torr.) Torr. & A. Gray
Frémont (1845: 156).

Phaca astragalina = *Astragalus alpinus* L.
"Highest summits of the Wind River mountain. Aug. 15 [1842, the day Frémont reached the summit, Sublette County, Wyoming]" (Torrey, 1843: 85).

Phaca (Orophaca) digitata = *Astragalus* sp.
"Little Sandy river. Aug. 8 [1842. Half day's ride west of South Pass, Sublette County, Wyoming]" (Torrey, 1843: 85).

Phaca elegans = *Astragalus eucosmus* Robins.
"Goat island of the Upper Platte. July 31 [1842. East of Independence Rock, Natrona County, Wyoming]" (Torrey, 1843: 85).

Phaca longifolia = *Astragalus ceramicus* Sheld.
"Phaca longifolia, *Nutt.* Wind River mountains Aug. 12–17 [1842. Sublette County, Wyoming]" (Torrey, 1843: 85). "Frémont's 2nd Expedn. 290. 1843" (NY-Torrey!).

Phacelia cicutaria Greene
"FExCal, 1845–7. 402. 1846. Phacelia tanacetifolia, *Benth.*" (GH!; NY-Torrey!), also, "Herb A. Gray. from 402, 1846. Phacelia tanacetifolia. Hort. Cantab. Anno 849. e sem Frémont 3d ex" (NY-Torrey!), and "FExCal, 1845–7. 186. 1846" (NY-Torrey!).

Phacelia distans Benth.?
"Frémont's 2nd Expedn. Sacramento Valley. 72, 1844" (NY-Torrey!).

Phacelia douglasii (Benth.) Torr.
"FExCal, 1845–7. 171. 1846. Phacelia Douglasii (*Eutoca* Benth.)" (GH!; NY-Torrey!). "Frémont's 2nd Exp. 155. 1844. San Joaquin, Calif. Eutoca Douglasii, *Benth.*" (NY-Torrey!).

***Phacelia fremontii* Torr.** in Ives, Rep. Colorado R. 4: 21. 1861. (2nd)
Protologue locality: "This was collected by Colonel Frémont in his journey to California in 1843,44, probably in the interior of that state, or in western New Mexico." Type: "California. Frémont 2nd Exp.?" (NY-Torrey!: microfiche BRY!). "Southern California, (Frémont)" (Watson, 1871: 254).

Phacelia hastata Dougl. ex Lehm. includes *P. leucophylla* Torr. in Frém.

Phacelia imbricata Greene
"FExCal, 1845–7. 472. 1846. Phacelia circinata, *Jacq.*" (NY-Torrey!).

***Phacelia leucophylla* Torr.** in Frém., Rep. Exped. Rocky Mts. 89. 1843. (1st) = *P. hastata* Dougl. ex Lehm.
Protologue locality: "Goat Island, upper North fork of the Platte. July 30 [1842, near Alcova, Natrona County, Wyoming]." Type: "FExRM 1842. Frémont's 1st Exped. 30 July, on road to Goat Island, in sandy soil" (holotype NY-Torrey!: microfiche BRY). This locality is within Natrona County, Wyoming. The type sheet has two small sheets of detailed drawings by Torrey.

Phacelia linearis (Pursh) Holz.
"FExCal, 1843–4. 505. 1844. Eutoca Menziesii, *R. Br.* 'Spanish Fork, near Utah Lake [Utah County, Utah].' May 27, 1844" (NY-Torrey!).

Phacelia menziesii Torr. = *P. linearis* (Pursh) Holz.
"And Utah, (505 Frémont, Stansbury.)" (Watson, 1871: 254).

Phacelia nemoralis Greene?
"FExCal, 1845–7. 186. 1846. Phacelia" (NY-Princeton!).

Phacelia sericea (Graham) A. Gray includes *Eutoca sericea*
"FExRM 1842. Eutoca sericea, Lehm.?" (NY-Torrey!). "Frémont's 2nd Journey. Phacelia sericea" (NY-Torrey!).

Phacelia tanacetifolia Benth.
"Herb. A. Gray Hort. Cantb. Anno 1849. e sem. Frém. 3rd Ex." (GH!); "Herb. A. Gray. Hort. Cantab. Anno 1849. e Hort. Humb." and "FExCal, 1845–7. 254. 1846. P. tanacetifolia" (same sheet GH!; the latter also at MO!).

Philadelphus californicus Benth.
"Frémont collected fine specimens of this plant on the rocky banks of the American River; June 14, 1846 [Sutter's Landing, Sacramento, Sacramento County, California]" (Torrey, 1857: 90). This is probably the same as below.

***Philadelphus fremontii* Rydb.**, N. Amer. Fl. 22: 165. 1905. (3rd) = *P. lewisii* subsp. *californicus* (Benth.) Munz
Protologue locality: "On the north fork of the American River, California, in 1846, Frémont 511." Type: "FExCal, 511, 1846. Philadelphus Lewisii. cfr. P. Californicus Benth. pl. Hartw. no. 1723. Dr. Gray says this is = Bentham's plant. North branch of the American River, on rocky banks. June 14–15 [1846, Sutter's Landing, Sacramento, Sacramento County, California]. A shrub 8–12 feet high" (holotype NY-Torrey!: microfiche BRY!; isotype MO!). The specimens were taken while Frémont awaited Lieutenant Gillespie, who was bringing supplies requisitioned from the Navy, following return of the party from Oregon. He was not so distracted by the political events as to refrain from collecting plants entirely.

Phleum alpinum ≡ *P. alpinum* L.
"Alpine region of the Wind River mountains. Aug. 13–14 [1842. Sublette County, Wyoming]" (Torrey, 1843: 94). "FExRM, 1842" (MO!).

Phlox aculeata A. Nels.
"Frémont's 2nd Exped. *P. linearifolia* n. sp. Plains of the Boise River. Style long—cells of ovary 1-ovul. J. T. [named by Bentham] Phlox sp. n. Frémont 784, 1843" (NY-Torrey!; GH!). The brackets are as quoted; the sheet at NY also contains a bracketed "[Thurber]."

Phlox andicola E. Nels.

"FExCal, 1843–4" and "FExRM 1842. July 8. Phlox Hoodii *Torr in Frém. Rep. non Rich.* humilis. Upper N. Fork of the Platte [actually South Platte, near Brush, Morgan County, Colorado]" (both NY-Torrey! and the 1842 specimen also at GH!). A second collection by Frémont is mounted on the same sheet at GH. It is: "Frémont, 2d Expedition. Phlox 'very near *P. humilis*, but appears different' Benth in herb Torr." (GH!). The specimen is annotated as "P. multiflora A. Nelson var. depressa E. Nelson" by R. H. W. in 1922.

Phlox austromontana Coville var. *austromontana*

"FExCal, 1843–4. May 10th. 447. 1844. Phlox Douglasii, Hook. forma pubescens. Pass in the Virgin River" (NY-Torrey!). The pass spoken of is almost certainly that at the head of Castle Cliff Wash, Washington County, Utah, which Frémont and party traversed on 10 May 1844. The sheet also contains an annotation label "Phlox Douglasii Hook., below which is the note: Named by Bentham. J. T." "Frémont. 468. 1844. May 15th. Phlox Frémontii—Thurb. n. sp. = P. Douglasii Hook? 'On low hills, among the Artemisias & c. A frequent plant; almost characteristic.' Santa Clara" (NY-Torrey!). On 15 May 1844, Frémont and party camped at the north end of Cedar Valley, Iron County, Utah, at a spring. The "Santa Clara" designation on the label appears to be superfluous. The plant labeled as "Phlox Frémontii" also bears a tiny annotation label with the information "Phlox sp. n? [Benth].," which, of course, was correct. Coville named it many years later, on the basis of other materials.

There is a second specimen tentatively assigned here also, bearing the label information, "Frémont's 2nd Expedn. with No 468, 1844} May 15—Santa Clara River, Thurb. n.sp. P. acerosa sp. n." (NY-Torrey!). The plant has a small annotation sheet bearing drawings and notes typical of materials examined critically by Torrey. The annotation, partly in ink ("Style long; ovary with the cells 1-ovule[d]" and "May 15—on the Santa Clara"), and partly in pencil ("The specimen with pungent, narrowly subulate leaves is probably different from the others—but there are other younger leaves which are broader & less rigid. The pungent leaves may be vestiges from previous season"). Above the small, bluish label is the note, "The leaves are in a *weathered* condition." And, there are two annotations, *P. douglasii* Hook., and *Leptodactylon caespitosum* Nutt. E. O. W[herry].

Phlox hoodii ≡ *P. hoodii* Richards.

"North fork of the Platte. July 8 [1842. South Platte, near Brush, Morgan County, Colorado]" (Torrey, 1843: 89). "Phlox Hoodii Dougl. = Phlox canescens, Torr. & Gr. Frémont's 2nd Exped." (NY-Torrey!; GH-Thurber!; MO!); "FExCal, 1845–7. 377. 1846. Phlox canescens, T. & Gr. in Beckwith's Rep. Head waters of the Sacramento." (GH!). The last cited specimen might have come from Modoc County, California. It bears a subnote "same as (crossed out) likely P. Douglasii minus n. Gr[ay] var.," in Gray's writing.

Phlox longifolia Nutt.
"FExCal, 1843–4. Near camp of 1–2 May, 431, 1844. Sandy soil. Sources of the Rio Virgen [Mountain Spring, Charleston Mountains, Clark County, Nevada]. Phlox pumila, Thurb. n.sp. 'sp. n.' *Benth.* See Thurber's figure in his notes on Phlox. style long. Phlox sp. n. [named by Bentham]" (NY-Torrey!). I have been unable to find places of publication of any species based on collections by Frémont by either Thurber or Bentham.

Phlox muscoides = *P. pulvinata* (Wherry) Cronq.
"Immediately below the region of perpetual snow, on the Wind River mountains. Aug. 15 [1842. Sublette County, Wyoming]" (Torrey, 1843: 89).

Phlox pilosa ≡ *P. pilosa* L.
"Big Blue river of the Kansas. June 20 [1842. Near Marshall County, Kansas]" (Torrey, 1843: 89). "FExRM 1842. Phlox pilosa *Linn.* style short. June 20th" (NY-Torrey!). "Frémont's 3rd Exped. No. 15. Phlox pilosa, *Linn.*? Prairies. June 30, 1845 [four days' journey west of Westport, Kansas, along the Santa Fe trail]" (NY-Torrey!).

Phlox pulvinata (Wherry) Cronq. includes *P. muscoides*
"FExRM 1842. Phlox muscoides, *Nutt.* rather Hoodii? = P. caespitosa, Nutt. Wind River Mountains: limits of perpetual snow. Aug. 15 [Sublette County, Wyoming]" (NY-Torrey!). The changes of names on the label indicate the frustration of identification of caespitose phloxes.

Phlox speciosa Pursh
"Phlox. California. Frémont" (NY-Sartwell!); "Frémont's 2nd [3rd?] Calif. Exped. 1846–47. Phlox elegans Thurb. ex Torrey" (GH!); "FExCal, 1845–7. 415, 1846. = 448, 1846. Canyon of the Upper Sacramento" (NY-Torrey!; MO!, GH!, mounted on the same sheet with the following); "FExRM 1846. 448 = 415. 1846. Phlox elegans, *H.* (2 ovules in a cell) ? J. T. I was mistaken, there is but one. J. T. Highlands of the Upper Sacramento. Abundant & very handsome. Frémont" (NY-Torrey!). The sheet again shows the frustration of working with caespitose phlox species. It has attached a small sheet of Torrey's analytical drawings, with notations, and a blue annotation label: "*P. elegans*, n. sp. cannot make out '2 ovules in a cell'—The spc. from Bigelow seems to be a broad-leaved form of the same." There is another note on the sheet: "material worked over by Torrey."

Phoradendron flavescens (Pursh) Nutt. var. *macrophyllum* Engelm. in Rothr.
"Frémont 106, 1844" (NY-Torrey!).

Phyllodoce breweri (A. Gray) Heller
"FExCal, 1845–7. Dec. 29, 1845. No. 40. Bryanthus Breweri, *Gray.* Abundant at the sources of Lake Fork of the San Joachin [King's River, Fresno County, California]" (NY-Torrey!).

Phyllodoce empetriformis ≡ *P. empetriformis* (J. E. Smith) D. Don
"Defiles of the Wind River mountains. Aug. 13–16 [1842. Sublette County, Wyoming]" (Torrey, 1843: 88).

Physalis hederifolia A. Gray
"FExRM 1842. Physalis pubescens? July 2nd" (NY-Torrey!). The sheet bears annotations as *P. hederifolia* by both P. A. Rydberg and U. T. Waterfall, the latter as var. *comata* (Rydb.) Waterfall.

Physalis lobata Torr.
"FExCal, 299, 1843. Physalis lobata Torr." (NY-Torrey!).

Physalis pubescens = *P. hederifolia* A. Gray (q.v.)
"Upper North fork of the Platte. July 23 [1842. La Bonte Creek, near Orin, Converse County, Wyoming]" (Torrey, 1843: 90).

Physalis pumila = *P. virginiana* Miller
"Upper North fork of the Platte. July 23 [1842. La Bonte Creek, near Orin, Converse County, Wyoming]" (Torrey, 1843: 90). "FExRM 1842. Physalis pumila, *Nutt.* High prairies. June 23" (NY-Torrey!). The specimen at NY is likely the exact one cited by Torrey (1843), but the date is wrong. On 23 June 1842 the Frémont party was along the Little Blue River of the Kansas, near Adams County, Nebraska.

Physaria acutifolia Rydb. includes *Vesicaria didymocarpa* (q.v.)
"Vegas, Pah Utah Country, 420, 1844, Frémont's 2nd Expedn.," "Base of Wahsatch Mts. 519, 1844. Frémont's 2nd Expedn.," and "FExCal, 463. 1845" (all three NY-Torrey!).

Physaria sp.
"FExCal, 1849" (NY-Torrey!).

Physostegia parviflora Nutt. ex A. Gray
"Frémont's 2nd Exped. 35. 1843. 'On the Snake River &c.' Physostegia parviflora Nutt." (NY-Torrey!).

Picea engelmannii Parry ex Engelm.
"FExCal, 1845–7. 117, 235, 1845[6], Feb. 22. Abies" (NY-Torrey!); "FExCal, 1845–7. 174. 1845. Abies Menziesii, *Dougl.* Camp at western foot of the Coast Mountains (Cuesta de los gatos) [Santa Cruz County, California]. In rich soil, among small oaks & redwoods (Taxode) only 6–7 feet high" (NY-Torrey!). Frémont was almost certainly not at the Cuesta de los Gatos any time in 1845. He was there during 22–25 February of 1846.

Pilinophytum capitatum ≡ *Croton capitatus* Michx.
"Forks of the Platte [1842]" (Torrey, 1843: 92).

Pinus (*Abies*) *alba* = *Abies concolor* (Gord. & Glend.) Lindley ex Hildebr.
"Defiles of the Wind River mountains. Aug. 13–14 [1842. Sublette County, Wyoming]" (Torrey, 1843: 93).

Pinus near *balsamea* = *Abies lasiocarpa* (Hook.) Nutt.
"Defiles of the Wind River mountains. Aug. 13–14 [1842. Sublette County, Wyoming]" (Torrey, 1843: 93).

Pinus colorado = *Pinus ponderosa* Dougl. ex P. & C. Lawson

Pinus edulis Engelm.
Great forests of this two-needle pinyon pine were traversed by Frémont both in 1844 and 1845, but they were not cited in his reports.

Pinus flexilis James in Long includes *Pinus* undetermined.

Pinus fremontiana Endl., Synopsis Conif. 183. 1847. = *P. monophylla* Torr. & Frém.
"Habitat in Californiae borealis montibus inter 111–120° Long. Occ." (Endlicher, 1847). This is merely a new name for *P. monophylla.*

Pinus lambertiana Dougl. = sugar pine
Frémont (1845: 203; 1887: 479).

Pinus larix = *Larix occidentalis* Nutt.
Frémont (1845: 178).

Pinus monophylla Torr. & Frém. in Frém. includes *Pinus monophyllus*

***Pinus monophyllus* Torr. & Frém.** in Frém., Rep. Exped. Rocky Mts. 319. 1845. (2nd) ≡ *Pinus monophylla* Torr. & Frém. in Frém.

Protologue locality: "This tree, which is remarkable among the true pines for its solitary leaves is extensively diffused over the mountains of Northern California, from long. 111° to 120°." Type: "Frémont's Expedition to California 367, 1844" (holotype NY-Torrey!: microfiche BRY!). "Frémont's 2d Exped." (isotype GH!). The sheet at GH has two obviously different collections, one marked "California, *Frémont.* ex herb. J. Torrey," and the other designated simply as "Frémont 2d Exped." A portion of the second specimen is in a large fragment envelope. "Frémont 367, Masonic Mts., Mineral County, Nev." (fide Cronquist et al., 1972: 232). "Col. Frémont found extensive forests of the tree in his first expedition [to California], as well as in his journey of 1853–54" (Torrey, 1859: 208). "Frémont Coll, Pinus monophylla *Torr.* Ex herb. Torr. Rocky Mountains, 1854" (GH-Thurber!).

Frémont (1845: 221) first noted this species on 24 January 1844, when an aged Indian brought a few pounds of its seeds to the camp. At that time his party was in camp in present Lyon County, Nevada. He does not mention that the plant was collected there, and a date of collection does not accompany the specimen. The route of the expedition on 24 January 1844 was generally along the East Fork of the Walker River in present Lyon County, which is adjacent to Mineral County, Nevada. The place of collection of the type material is, thus, subject to conjecture. However, the species was mentioned again on 19 April 1844 (Frémont, 1845: 258), and the number 367 fits within the sequence of numbered specimens taken between 17 and 27 April, when the second expedition was within San Bernardino County, California, as was suggested by McKelvey (1955: 872).

While the numbers are not always conclusive evidence of provenance, it seems almost certain that San Bernardino County includes the type locality of *Pinus monophylla*.

Pinus ponderosa Dougl. ex P. & C. Lawson includes *P. colorado* and *P. rigida*
"FExRM 1842. Pinus rigida? Lower Platte. no cones. Is it not rather P. ponderosa?" (NY-Torrey!). Frémont (1845: 82) referred to this species as red pine.

Pinus quadrifolia Parry
"Pinus Llaveana Schiede & Depp. Cal. Frémont" (NY-LeRoy!).

Pinus rigida = *P. ponderosa* Dougl. ex P. & C. Lawson
"Lower Platte [1842]" (Torrey, 1843: 93).

Pinus (?) *sabiniana* Dougl.
"A remarkable species of pine" Frémont (1887: 475).

Pinus undetermined = *Pinus flexilis* James in Long
"Defiles of the Wind River mountains. Aug. 13–14 [1842. Sublette County, Wyoming]. Between P. Strobus and P. Lambertiana. Leaves in 5's, 1½–2 inches long, rigid, No cones" (Torrey, 1843: 93).

Pisang = *Yucca brevifolia* Englem.
This is the name applied to the species by Preuss (Gudde & Gudde, 1958: 123).

Plagiobothrys canescens Benth. includes *Eritrichium canescens*
"FExCal, 1845–7. 400. 1846. Plagiobothrys canescens *Bth.* Eritrichium canescens Gray" (GH!). This specimen is mounted on the same sheet as specimens by Brewer and those that are at least portions of the type of the species, i.e., Hartweg 1871 (GH!). "FExCal, 1845–7. Eritrichium canescens.? 'S of the calyces (all?) in fruit enlarged & opened out. Nutlets strongly corrugated transversely & carinate on the base" (NY-Torrey!).

Plagiobothrys nothofulvus A. Gray
"Frémont's 2nd Expedn. 16. 1844" (NY-Torrey!).

Plagiobothrys tenellus (Nutt.) A. Gray
"FExCal, 1843–4. 166. 1846. Eritrichium canescens" (NY-Torrey!).

Plagiobothrys tener (Greene) I. M. Johnst.
"FExCal, 1845–7. 287. 1846. Eritrichium scouleri, A. DC." (GH!). The specimen is so annotated by L. C. Higgins.

Plagiobothrys sp.
"Frémont's 2nd Expedn. 3, 1844. Eritrichium" (NY-Torrey!).

Plantago eriopoda ≡ *P. eriopoda* Torr.
"Mouth of the Sweet Water. July 31 [1842. Near Alcova, Natrona County, Wyoming]" (Torrey, 1843: 91). "Frémont's 1st Expedn. Plantago eriopoda" (NY-Torrey!). "Herb. A. Gray. Plantago eriopoda, *Torr.* Frémont, 2d Exped." (GH!)

Plantago gnaphaloides = *P. patagonica* Jacq.
"Little Blue river of the Kansas [1842, 22–23 June]" (Torrey, 1843: 91). "FExCal, 283. 1844. Plantago gnaphaloides, *Nutt.*" and "FExCal, 1843–4" (both NY-Torrey!).

Plantago insularis Eastw.
"California, *Frémont, 1844*" and "California, Frémont, 1848 [1849?]" (both same sheet NY-Columbia!). The sheet bears the annotation "Plantago ovata Forsk. Det. K. Rahn, 1975."

Plantago patagonica Jacq. includes *P. gnaphaloides*
"Frémont, 3d Coll." (GH!).

Platanthera hyperborea ≡ *Habenaria hyperborea* (L.) R. Br. in Ait.
"Laramie river to the Red Buttes. Aug. 26–31 [1842]" (Torrey, 1843: 93).

Platanthera leucophaea = *Habenaria dilatata* (Pursh) Hook.
"Black Hills. July 27 [1842. East of Evansville, probably in Natrona County, Wyoming]" (Torrey, 1843: 93).

Platanus occidentalis = *P. racemosa* Nutt.
Frémont (1845: 255; 1848: 23).

Platanus racemosa Nutt. includes *P. occidentalis*
Frémont (1845: 255). Three sheets NY-Torrey!: "Frémont's Expedition to California 1843–4 Platanus californica"; "FExCal, 1846, No. 110. P. racemosa. Lake Fork, near camp where Pablo's mule was killed by the Indians [A mule was killed by Indians on 31 December 1845—see Frémont, 1887: 450]"; and "FExCal, 1849" [mounted on the sheet with that of 1846]. Frémont (1887: 448) mentions Lake Fork (Tulare Lake River, now Kings River), on 22 December 1845, as being called by the Mexicans Río de los Reyes; it is in Fresno County, California. "FExCal, 1845–7. 210, 1846" and "Frémont's 2d Exped." (both GH!). "No. 99. 1844. Herb. Frémont. Platanus racemosa. Frémont's 2d Expedition. J. Torrey" (MO!).

Platystemon californicus Benth.
"FExCal, 1846. 304. Platystemon Californicum Benth. Torr. & Gr. Fl. I. 65." (MO!). "FExCal, 1849" (NY-Torrey!).

Plectritis macrocera Torr. & A. Gray var. *grayii* (Suksd.) Dyal
"FExCal, 1845–7. 316, 1846 and 314, 1846 (the small specm.). Plectritis" (both same sheet NY-Torrey!). "Frémont's 2nd Expedn. (Banks of Utah Lake) [Utah County, Utah, 24–26 May 1844]" (NY-Torrey!).

Poa crocata = *P. palustris* L.
"On the Kansas [1842]" (Torrey, 1843: 94).

Poa fendleriana (Steud.) Vasey
"Frémont's 2nd Exp. 529, [18]44" (GH!).

Poa laxa = *P. lettermannii* Vasey

Poa lettermannii Vasey includes *P. laxa*
"FExRMt, 1842. Poa laxa. Dwarf form. Wind River Mts—near the snow" (NY-Columbia!).

Poa nervata = *Glyceria striata* (Lam.) A. S. Hitchc.
"On the Kansas [1842]" (Torrey, 1843: 94).

Poa palustris L. includes *P. crocata*

Pogogyne douglasii Benth.
"FExCal, 1845–7. 438, 1846. Pogogyne Douglasi, *Benth.* Upper Sacramento, May 28 [probably Butte County, California]" (NY-Torrey!; US!).

Pogogyne zizyphoroides Benth.
"FExCal, 1845–7. 285, 1846. Pogogyne. Upper Sacramento. Lassens. April 16, 1846 [Tehama County, California]" (NY-Torrey!; MO!). The two tiny Frémont specimens at NY are mounted on the same sheet with an isotype of *P. zizyphoroides*.

Polanisia dodecandra (L.) DC. includes *P. trachysperma*

Polanisia trachysperma, *β* = *P. dodecandra* (L.) DC.
"Black Hills of the Platte. July 23 [1842. Near Orin, Converse County, Wyoming]" (Torrey, 1843: 83).

Polemonium caeruleum = *P. caeruleum* L. var. *occidentale* (Greene) Davidson
"Red Buttes on the Upper N. fork of the Platte [1842. 29 July, adjacent to Casper, Natrona County, Wyoming]" (Torrey, 1843: 89). "Polemonium caeruleum. Frémont's 1st Expedition, Wind River Mountains [1842. 12–17 August, Sublette County Wyoming]" (NY-Torrey!).

Polemonium caeruleum β humile = ?
"Highest parts of the mountains, near perpetual snow. Aug. 13–15 [1842. Sublette County, Wyoming]" (Torrey, 1843: 89).

Polyctenium fremontii (S. Wats.) Greene includes *Smelowskia fremontii*

Polygala alba ≡ *P. alba* Nutt.
"Forks of the Platte. July 2 [1842. Lincoln County, Nebraska]" (Torrey, 1843: 83). "P. alba, Nutt. 153, 1843. Frémont's 2nd Expedn." (NY-Torrey!).

Polygala cornuta Kellogg
"FExCal, 1845–7. Yy. 1846 Dr. Gray. Polygala cucullata *Benth. pl. Hartw.*" (NY-Torrey!).

Polygonum amphibium ≡ *P. amphibium* L.
"Sweet Water river. August 4 [1842. Southwest of Carmody Lake, Frémont County, Wyoming]" (Torrey, 1843: 92). "FExRM 1842. August. Polygonum amphibium" (NY-Torrey!).

Polygonum aviculare ≡ *P. aviculare* L.
"North fork of the Platte. Sept. 4 [1842. West of Scotts Bluff, Scotts Bluff County, Nebraska]" (Torrey, 1843: 92). "FExRM 1842. Aug. 4 [Sweetwater River, Frémont County, Wyoming]. Polygonum aviculare." (NY-Torrey!). There is a discrepancy in the dates. The citation in Torrey (1843: 92) indicates "with the preceding," i.e., with *Polygonum persicaria*, which was taken on Sept. 4, 1842. The date on the label is assumed to be correct. The plant is in vegetative condition and is annotated by J. F. Brenckle as *Polygonum buxiforme* Small. Certainly it is within the concept of *P. aviculare* sens. lat.

Polygonum bistortoides Pursh
"FExRM 1842. Valley of the Lower Platte. Polygonum" (NY-Torrey!).

Polygonum californicum Meissn.
"FExCal, 1843. Polygonum coarctatum" (NY-Torrey!).

Polygonum persicaria ≡ *P. persicaria* L.
"North fork of the Platte. Sept. 4 [1842. West of Scotts Bluff, Scotts Bluff County, Nebraska]" (Torrey, 1843: 92). "FExRM 1842. Polygonum Persicaria? Aug. 18–25" (NY-Torrey!).

Polygonum viviparum ≡ *P. viviparum* L.
"Black Hills. July 26 [1842. Deer Creek, near Glen Rock, Converse County, Wyoming]" (Torrey, 1843: 92).

Polyotus angustifolius = *Asclepias stenophylla* A. Gray

Polyotus longifolia = *Asclepias* (?) *longifolia*

Polytaenia nuttallii ≡ *P. nuttallii* DC.
"On the Kanzas. June 20 [1842. Big Blue River, probably Marshall County, Kansas]" (Torrey, 1843: 86).

Populus = *Populus fremontii* S. Wats.
This is the "Populus, differing from any in Michaux's Sylva" (Frémont, 1845: 253).

Populus angustifolia ≡ *P. angustifolia* James ex Torr.
"Sweet Water river. Aug. 21 [1842. Near Jeffery City, Frémont County, Wyoming]" (Torrey, 1843: 93). "Populus angustifolia *Torr.* Aug. 21. 1842. Frémont's 1st Expedn." (NY-Columbia!). "Frémont's 2nd Expedn." (NY-Torrey!). "FExCal, 1845–47[1845]. Populus angustifolia. Ex Torrey" (GH-Thurber!). The NY-Columbia sheet bears a notation in pencil "Bear River Valley." The notation is incorrect. This is the species noted by Frémont (1845: 287) on 24 June 1844, south of South Park, Colorado.

Populus canadensis = *P. deltoides* Marsh and *P. fremontii* S. Wats.

Populus deltoides Marsh includes *P. canadensis* and *P. monilifera*
"Frémont's 2nd Expedn. 412, 1843. Frequent" (NY-Torrey!). The sheet bears the J. E. Eckenwalder 1975 annotation *Populus deltoides* Marsh subsp. *monilifera* (Ait.) Eckenw.

***Populus fremontii* S. Wats.**, Proc. Amer. Acad. Arts 10: 350. 1875. (3rd)
Protologue locality: "Collected by Frémont (n.243, 244 of 1846) on Deer Creek at 'Lassens' in the upper Sacramento Valley." Type: "Frémont's Expedition to California 243, 244, 1846, on the upper Sacramento" [isolectotype NY-Torrey!: microfiche BRY!; lectotype (243) (Eckenwalder, 1977: 200) GH!]. "Deer Creek, Tehama County, California" (fide Abrams, 1923: 487). Frémont was at Lassen's, near present Vina, Tehama County, California, in late March and early April, 11–20 April, and 22–25 May, 1846. However, the numbers 243 and 244 fit within a sequence of specimens probably collected on 5 April. Frémont referred to this cottonwood as "sweet" as opposed to the "liard amer" of the East. The lectotype has the notation "Populus Frémontii, n. sp." The isolectotype at NY bears the annotation "P. Frémontii, Watson. S.W." "Herbarium of Columbia College, New York. Frémonts [leaves only]" (NY-Columbia) and "P. moniliforme. Frémont's 2nd Expedn. 186, 1843 [with additional illegible pencil notation]" (NY-Torrey!). The last cited sheet evidently has two separate collections, both from the second expedition. The notation for the fruiting twig is lost amidst the blackish oxidant of the paper.

Populus monilifera = *P. deltoides* Marsh
"Lower Platte [1842]" (Torrey, 1843: 93; Frémont, 1845: 17). "Populus monilifera ? Frémont's 1st Expedn. Grand Island, Lower Platte, Sept. 19, 1842 [Kearney County, Nebraska]" (NY-Torrey!).

Populus tremuloides ≡ *P. tremuloides* Michx.
"Lake in the Wind River mountains" (Torrey, 1843: 93). "Frémont's Expedition to the Rock Mountains, 1842. Populus tremuloides. August 12–17 [1842. Sublette County, Wyoming]" (NY-Torrey!).

Potentilla anserina ≡ *P. anserina* L.
"Black Hills of the Platte to the mountains. Aug. 4–15 [1842. Frémont or Sublette County, Wyoming]" (Torrey, 1843: 85). "FExRM 1842. Potentilla Anserina" (GH!). "Herbarium of Geo. V. Nash. Potentilla Anserina, L. Rocky Mts. Frémont, 1842" (NY-Thurber!) and "Frémont's 2nd Expedn. Potentilla anserina?" (NY-Torrey!).

Potentilla arguta ≡ *P. arguta* Pursh
"Little Blue river of the Kansas, and Black Hills of the Platte. June 23–Aug. 28 [1842]" (Torrey, 1843: 85).

Potentilla diversifolia = *P. gracilis* Dougl. ex Hook. (q.v.)
"Sweet Water of the Platte to the mountains. Aug. 4–15 [1842]" (Torrey, 1843: 85).

Potentilla effusa Dougl.
"FExCal, 1845–7. 389, 1845. Potentilla effusa" (NY-Torrey!).

***Potentilla etomentosa* Rydb.**, Bull. Torrey Bot. Club 24: 8. 1897. (3rd) = *P. gracilis* var. *glabrata* Lehm.
Protologue locality: "California. Frémont no. 162. 1846 (Type); J. S. Newberry (Williamson Expedition); Munson & Hopkins, 1889; Coville & Funston, no. 1399, 1891." (See also the citation under *Potentilla gracilis* Dougl. var. *rigida* (Nutt.) S. Wats. below.) Type: "FExCa, 1845–7. 162, 1846" (holotype NY-Torrey!).

Potentilla fissa Nutt.
"Potentilla fissa Nutt.? Frémont's 2nd Exp." (NY-Torrey!). The sheet is annotated by P. A. Rydberg as *Potentilla fissa* Nutt.

Potentilla fruticosa ≡ *P. fruticosa* L.
"Sweet Water of the Platte to the mountains. Aug. 4–15 [1842]" (Torrey, 1843: 85).

Potentilla glandulosa Lindley
"Frémont" (Watson, 1873b: 567).

Potentilla gracilis ≡ *P. gracilis* L.
"Wind River mountains, near perpetual snow. Aug. 13–14 [1842. Sublette County, Wyoming]" (Torrey, 1843: 85). "Wyoming Territory (Frémont)" (Watson, 1871: 88). "Potentilla gracilis Dougl. Frémont's 1st Expedn. Aug. 13, 1842" and "FExRM 1842, August 7 [adjacent to South Pass, Frémont County, Wyoming] '*Potentilla gracilis* var. *diversifolia*'" (both NY-Torrey!). The first cited specimen is assigned to var. *pulcherrima* (Lehm.) Fern.

Potentilla gracilis Dougl. var. *elmeri* (Rydb.) Jepson includes *P. pectinisecta* Rydb.
"Frémont's 2nd Expedn." (NY-Torrey!). The specimen is annotated "Potentilla pectinisecta n. sp." by P. A. Rydberg.

Potentilla gracilis Dougl. var. *glabrata* Lehm. includes *P. etomentosa* Rydb. and *P. gracilis* var. *rigida* (Nutt.) S. Wats.

Potentilla gracilis Dougl. var. *rigida* (Nutt.) S. Wats. = *P. gracilis* var. *glabrata* Lehm.
"No. 162 Frémont" (Watson, 1873b: 568).

Potentilla gracilis Doug. var. *pulcherrima* (Lehm.) Fern.
"FExCal, 1845–7. 104. 1845. Potentilla" (NY-Torrey!). The sheet bears the annotation "Potentilla pulcherrima Lehm." by P. A. Rydberg.

***Potentilla pectinisecta* Rydb.**, Bull. Torrey Bot. Club 24: 7. 1897. (2nd) = *P. gracilis* var. *elmeri* (Rydb.) Jepson

Protologue locality: "*Arizona*: E. Palmer, no. 145, 1877. *Wyoming*: C. E. Sheldon, no. 72, 1844; Frémont, 2d exp. [and others]." Syntype: "Frémont's 2nd Expedn." (NY-Torrey!). Rydberg had access to all of the Frémont specimens during his more than three decades at the New York Botanical Garden. The use of binomials exclusively by him is a trademark. Unfortunately Rydberg did not designate a type for this taxon as he did for *P. etomentosa*, published on the same page of the *Bulletin*.

Potentilla pensylvanica L. var. *glabrata* (Lehm.) S. Wats. includes *P. sericea β glabrata* Lehm.

"No. 326 Watson; Frémont" (Watson, 1873b.: 571). "P. sericea β glabrata. Frémont's 1st Expedn. Aug. 4, 1842 [Sweetwater River, Frémont County, Wyoming]" (NY-Torrey!).

Potentilla plattensis Nutt.

"No. 564 Frémont" (Watson, 1873b: 571). "Frémont's 2nd Expedn. Park Mountains, sources of the North Fork of the Platte, Camp 16–17 June, 564. 1844 [North Park, Jackson County, Colorado]" (NY-Torrey!).

***Potentilla pseudosericea* Rydb.**, Mem. Dept. Bot. Columbia Univ. 2: 98. 1898. (3rd) = *P.* cf. *pensylvanica* L.

Protologue locality: "*Nevada:* Shockley, No. 502, 1888. *Rocky Mountains:* Nuttall; Fremont, No. 218, 1845–7." Syntype: "FExCal, 1845–7. 218. 1845. Arkansas River above Pueblo, mouth of canyon [circa 21 August 1845, Pueblo County, Colorado]" (NY-Torrey!).

Potentilla sericea β glabrata ≡ *P. pensylvanica* var. *glabrata* (Lehm.) S. Wats.

"Sweet Water of the Platte to the mountains. Aug. 4–15 [1842]" (Torrey, 1843: 85).

Prele = *Equisetum*

Frémont (1845: 15).

Prosopis glandulosa Torr. includes *P. odorata* Torr. & Frém. pro parte (discordant type)

"Fremont's 2nd Expedition" (MO!). This is an inflorescence of *P. glandulosa.*

***Prosopis odorata* Torr. & Frém.** in Frém., Rep. Exped. Rocky Mts. 313. 1845. (2nd)

Protologue locality: "A characteristic tree in the mountainous part of Northern California, particularly along the Mohahve and Virgen rivers, flowering the latter part of April. 419, 1844." Type: "Frémont's 2nd Exped." (holotype NY-Torrey!: microfiche BRY!; GH!, two sheets). Other writing on the sheet is illegible. Frémont (1845: 260) first noted this species, which he called acacia, on 24 April along the Mohave River in San Bernardino County, California, where it is adequately characterized and named as *Spirolobium odoratum* Torr. (q.v.). He mixed the collection of the honey mesquite, *Prosopis glandulosa* Torr., with that of the screwbean mesquite, later named *P. pubescens* Benth.; hence, the name *P. odorata* as described on page 313 was based on discordant type material and has been rejected. The plate accompanying the report (see Figure 26) illustrates a flowering branch of *P. glandulosa* and the fruit of *P. pubescens*. Because of the discordant type material the name *P. odorata* has been relegated to synonymy of both *Prosopis pubescens* Benth. and *P. glandulosa* Torr. Torrey (1857: 82) notes: "Prosopis odorata, *Torr. in Frém. Rep., p. 313, t. 1,* is a var. of P. glandulosa, (in flower only,) with the pods of Strombocarpa pubescens. The error arose from the mixing of specimens in Frémont's collections." However, the epithet was published twice in the Frémont (1845) report, the first time on page 260, where it is adequately characterized as applicable only to the screwbean. The correct name for the species, as herein interpreted, is *Prosopis odorata* (Torr. in Frém.) Torr. & Frém. in Frém. emend. Welsh (see citation under *Spriolobium odoratum*).

Prosopis pubescens Benth. = *P. odorata* (Torr. in Frém.) Torr. & Frém. in Frém. emend. Welsh.
"Southern Nevada, (Frémont;)" (Watson, 1871: 420). "Coll. Frémont [1844]" (GH!).

Prunus fasciculata (Torr.) A. Gray includes *Emplectocladus fasciculata* Torr. q.v.
"In Southern Sierra Nevada (*Frémont*)" (Brewer et al., 1876: 168).

***Prunus fremontii* S. Wats.**, Bot. Calif. 2: 442. 1880. (3rd)
Protologue locality: "Coast Ranges of Southern California; Oriflamme Canyon, San Diego County, California (D. Cleveland); Also collected by Frémont in 1846, locality uncertain." Type: "FExCal, 1845–7. 370. 1846" (isotype NY-Torrey!; holotype GH!). The GH sheet bears the notation "P. fremontii, Watson n. sp.," evidently in Watson's hand. The label on the NY isotype bears the identification "Prunus subcordata Benth. pl. Hartw. 1710." A second, unnumbered, sheet at NY-Crooke! is "FExCal, 1845–7. Prunus subcordata, Benth. pl. *Hartw.*"

Prunus ilicifolia (Nutt.) Walp.
"368, 1844. Frémont's 2nd Exp. Cerasus ilicifolius" (NY-Torrey!).

Prunus virginiana L. includes *Cerasus virginiana*

Psathyrotes ramosissima (Torr.) A. Gray
"And in Arizona on the Gila, Emory, Frémont, Thurber, Parry" (Brewer et al., 1876: 409). "Frémont. 1849" (GH!; NY-Torrey!). *Psathyrotes ramosissima* is based on *Tetradymia (Polydymia) ramosissima* Torr. in Emory (Torrey, 1848: 145). The type was taken by Emory along the Gila River in Arizona. The Frémont specimen at GH is multiply mounted with numerous other collections—Cooper, Parry, Palmer, Thurber. The Frémont designation is written in pencil on a fragment envelope, bearing the notation "Polydymia. Torr.!" The envelope contains a small specimen and a label with the notation "Polydymia. Emoryi report. Valley of the Gila." The specimen at NY Torrey is likewise multiply mounted, with specimens by Thurber (674, River Gila) dated June 1852 and two stems by Schott ("Compos. No. 28").

Pseudotsuga menziesii (Mirb.) Franco includes *Abies* pro parte
"Frémont's 2d. Exped. Abies douglasii" (GH!). Two sheets!

Psoralea argophylla ≡ *Psoralidium argophyllum* (Pursh) Rydb.
"Little Blue river. June 23 [1842. Near Adams County, Nebraska]" (Torrey, 1843: 84). "Psoralea incana, *Nutt. argophylla*, Pursh. Frémont's 3rd Exped. June 30, 1845" (NY-Torrey!). The date is the earliest known for specimens taken on the third expedition; it was collected four days west of his camp at Westport, on the Santa Fe trail, in eastern Kansas. "Psoralea argophylla. Frémont's 3d Exped. 15. 1845" (MO!). It is likely that this is a duplicate of the 30 June 1845 specimen at NY-Torrey.

Psoralea campestris = *Psoralidium tenuiflorum* (Pursh) Rydb.
"Forks of the Platte. July 2 [1842. Lincoln County, Nebraska]" (Torrey, 1843: 84). "FExRM 1842. Psoralea campestris—smooth variety?" (two sheets GH-Thurber!).

Psoralea = *Psorothamnus fremontii* (Torr.) Barneby
Frémont (1845: 262).

Psoralea esculenta Pursh ≡ *Pediomelum esculentum* (Pursh) Rydb.
Frémont (1845: 262).

Psoralea floribunda = *Psoralidium tenuiflorum* (Pursh) Rydb.
"Forks of the Platte. July 2 [1842. Lincoln County, Nebraska]" (Torrey, 1843: 84). "Frémont's expedition to California, 1844. No. 6, 184. Psoralea floribunda" (NY-Torrey!).

Psoralea lanceolata ≡ *Psoralidium lanceolatum* (Pursh) Rydb.
"Black Hills of the Platte. July 24 [1842. Between Labonte and La Prele creeks, Converse County, Wyoming]" (Torrey, 1843: 84).

Psoralea tenuiflora ≡ *Psoralidium tenuiflorum* (Pursh) Rydb.
"Forks of the Platte. Sept. 12 [1842. Lincoln County, Nebraska]" (Torrey, 1843: 84). "FExCal, 101, 1845. Psoralea tenuiflora, Pursh. Turkey Creek" (NY-Torrey!). "FExRM 1842" (GH!) and "Frémont's 1st Exped. Ex herb. J. Torrey. Torr. & Gr. Fl. N. Amer." (GH-Thurber!).

Psoralidium argophyllum (Pursh) Rydb. includes *Psoralea argophylla Pursh*

Psoralidium lanceolatum (Pursh) Rydb. includes *Psoralea lanceolata* Pursh

Psoralidium tenuiflorum (Pursh) Rydb. includes *Psoralea tenuiflora* Pursh

Psorothamnus emoryi (A. Gray) Rydb.
"FExCal, 1849" (NY-Torrey!).

Psorothamnus fremontii (Torr.) Barneby includes *Dalea fremontii* Torr.

Psorothamnus schottii (Torr.) Barneby
"FExCal, 1849" (NY-Torrey!).

Psorothamnus spinosus (A. Gray) Barneby
"FExCal, 1849. Dalea spinosa, Gray. Fl. blue, glandular sepals—so says Dr. Parry" (NY-Torrey!).

Ptelea trifoliata L.

"Frémont's Expedition to California 1845, no. 55. Ptelea trifoliata var. 'doubtless collected east of the R. Mts.'" (NY-Torrey!). This sheet is annotated by Torrey: "The early portion of Frémont's list of localities was not sent to me."

***Pterochiton* Torr. & Frém.** in Frém., Rep. Exped. Rocky Mts. 318. 1845. (2nd)

Type species: ***Pterochiton occidentale* Torr. & Frém.** in Frém. (l.c.) ≡ *Atriplex canescens* (Pursh) Nutt. var. *occidentale* (Torr. & Frém.) Welsh & Stutz

Protologue locality: "The precise locality of this plant we cannot indicate, as the label was illegible; but it was probably from the borders of the Great Salt lake." Type: "Pterochiton occidentale Torr. & Frém." [locality data is missing from the type specimen] (holotype NY-Torrey!: microfiche BRY!). The herbarium sheet bears a folded sheet of paper with the usual careful and detailed drawings of bracts, embryo, and seed, and the designation "Pterochiton." In the lower right corner of the sheet is written "Frémont, N. Gen. Pterocalyx," and at the bottom center the words "Pterochiton occidentale, Torr. & Frém." The sheet contains three branches, with the bracts mainly fallen away.

Pulmonaria ciliata ≡ *Mertensia ciliata* (James) G. Don

"Defiles in the Wind River mountains. Aug. 13–15 [1842. Sublette County, Wyoming]" (Torrey, 1843: 89).

Purshia mexicana (D. Don) Welsh var. *stansburyana* (Torr.) Welsh

"No. 444, 1844. Frémont's 2nd Expedition" (NY-Torrey!). The sheet bears the name "Cowania Stansburyana" in Torrey's hand. There is also an attached sketch of floral and fruit characteristics. See discussion under *Cowania stansburyana*.

Purshia tridentata (Pursh) DC.

"Sweet Water river, &c. Aug. 12–Sept. [1842]" (Torrey, 1843: 85). The sheet at NY-Torrey! has two labels, one for the 1842 Wyoming collection and a second from the 1843–44 expedition. The label for the latter plant includes: "Purshia tridentata, DC. Eastern slope of the Sierra Nevada, lat. 34°27′ long. 117°13′, April 17–18, 1844. Torr. & Gray, Fl. N. Amer." The Sierra Nevada site is near Victorville, San Bernardino County, California. "Purshia tridentata, DC. Collected on Captn. Frémont's 2d Expn. to Oregon & Nor. California, 1843–4" (NY-Sartwell!). The Sartwell sheet is likely a duplicate of the 1843–44 specimen cited previously. "*Purshia tridentata* formed a conspicuous object in several parts of the route, not only east of the mountains, but in Oregon and California" (Torrey & Frémont, in Frémont, 1845). This species was noted repeatedly during the second expedition.

***Pycnanthemum californicum* Torr.** in Durand, J. Acad. Philad. II. 3: 99. 1855. (3rd)

Protologue locality: "Gathered by Colonel Frémont, (1846)" (Torrey, 1857: 122). Type: "FExCal, 1845–7[1846]" (NY-Torrey!: microfiche BRY!). The Frémont specimen is mounted on a sheet with two other collections, one by Mr. Shelton and the other by Rev. A. Fitch, both cited merely as from "California." Two small sketch sheets are attached to the herbarium sheet, showing drawings typical of those on Torrey types: "near Nevada City [Nevada County, California]" (fide Abrams, 1951: 658).

***Pyrrocoma foliosa* Torr. & A. Gray** in A. Gray, Boston J. Nat. Hist. 5: 108. 1845. (2nd) = *Haplopappus fremontii* A. Gray (i.e., *Haplopappus*)

Protologue locality: "It was gathered among the mountains of Upper California" (but implied by Gray in letter to Torrey as along the Arkansas River, in Colorado). Type: "FExCal, 414. 1843. Pyrrocoma foliosa Gray, in Bost. Jour. nat. hist. 5. p.—" (isotype NY-Torrey!: microfiche BRY!; holotype GH!). The specimen at GH is designated simply "Frémont's 2nd Exped." It is annotated as holotype by D. E. Boufford 1982. See Hall (1928) for distribution of the species.

Quercus agrifolia Nee

"FExCal, 1845–7. 247. 1846. Quercus agrifolia? Mountains of California" and "FExCal, 1845–7. 300, 1846. Quercus agrifolia, Nee. Between Cow Creeks of the Sacramento" (same sheet NY-Torrey!). The sheet from "between Cow Creeks" was likely taken on 8 or 9 April 1846, near Redding, Shasta County, California. "FExCal, 1845–7. 227. 1845. Quercus agrifolia. Q. Wislizeni. fol. latioribus. 'An evergreen oak, 2 feet in diameter. 7th April, 1846. No. 227'" (GH!). It is possible that "227" is in fact a mistake for "247."

Quercus alba = *Q. gambelii* Nutt.

(Frémont, 1845: 118, 148; 1887: 183).

***Quercus chrysolepis* Liebm.**, Overs. Kongel. Danske Vidensk. Selsk. Forh. Medlemmers Arbeider, 1854: 173. 1854. (3rd)

Protologue locality: "Coll. Hartw. n. 1962 in hb. Hook.! Coll. Frémont n. 29, n. 48, n. 51, n. 214 a. in hb. Hook. Coll. W. Lobb. n. 109 hb. Hook.! California." Syntypes: "FExCal, 1845–7. 48, Dec. 1845. Quercus chrysolepis, Liebm." and (mounted on same sheet) "FExCal, 1845–7. No. 29. Dec. 1845. Quercus chrysolepis Lieb." (both GH!). The sheet has a second label above the left side label: "High granite (white) ridge, 9400 ft. above the sea. A live oak, 7–8 feet high. No. 29. Dec. 26. 1845." This is the same information that appears on a label of a syntype at NY-Torrey!: "FExCal, 1845–7. No. 29. Dec. 26, 1845. High granite ridge of the Sierra Nevada, 9400 feet above the sea. A shrub 7–8 feet high." There are two specimens on loan from NY. Both are labeled as "Q. emoryi." The first has the notation, "This is probably referred by Liebmann to Q. chrysolepis for it was sent to Hooker and it is the only Californian oak described by Liebmann with such small leaves. "6'''-2½" x 4'''-10"." The second sheet, "Ex herb. J. Torrey. Quercus emoryi. Torr. & Gr. Fl. N. Amer. Frémont's 2nd Expedition," lacks any notation. There are five additional specimens of this species, mounted on four sheets, at NY-Torrey!: "On a stream in the Sierra Nevada, February 25, 1844 (No. 22). Frémont 2nd Exped. Quercus chrysolepis, Liebm." and "FExCal, 1845–7, 364. 1846. 'Leaves more acute than in No. 35, some finer toothed'" (both same sheet), "FExCal, 1845–7. No. 22. Dec. 24–25, 1845 [King's River, Fresno County, California]. Quercus densiflora, *Hook. & Arn.*," and "FExCal, 1845–7. No. 35. Dec. 26, 1845. Quercus densiflora *Hook. & Arn.*

'Sierra Nevada, on a high granite ridge (9400 ft) [also Fresno County]," and "FExCal, 1845–7. Dec. 5, 1845. Sierra Nevada. Quercus." On 5 December 1845 the party was one day's march west of Donner's Pass, probably in Placer County, California. "Quercus wislizenius. foliis persist. parvis integris. Fremont 214. 1846. Q. chrysolepis Liebm. (spec. valid & det.) [and a descriptive note]" (MO!). "FExCal, 1845–7 [Dec.?, 1845]. Singular galls grow on this species. Mountains of California" (GH!). "FExCal, 1845–7 [Dec.?, 1845]" (GH-Thurber!). The holotype material should be among the materials deposited in the herbarium of Hooker (presumably now at Kew).

Quercus douglasii Hook. & Arn.

"FExCal, 1845–7[1846?]. Mountains of California" (GH-Thurber!); "FExCal, 1845–7. 341, 1846. Quercus douglasii Hook. (fide Torrey & G[eorge] E[ngelmann])" (GH!; NY-Torrey!). The NY specimen bears the notation "Camp of April 25–26." Camp for that night was two days' ride north of Lassen's, probably in southernmost Shasta County, California. "FExCal, 1845–7. 28, 1845" (GH!; NY-Torrey!). The latter specimen bears the name of *Q. douglasii* on the label, and the notation "Valley of the Upper Sacramento," but the plant was taken early in springtime (it is still in flower) and might belong to some other species. "Frémont's 2nd Exp. 314, 1844. April 14th, Sierra Nevada" (NY-Torrey!). On 14 April 1844 Frémont was at Oak Creek Pass, Kern County, California. "FExCal, 1845–7 [1846?]. Quercus Douglasii" (NY-Columbia!). "Frémont's 2nd Expedn. [3rd, 1846?]" (NY-Torrey!).

Quercus dumosa Nutt.?

"FExCal, 1845–7. 228, 1845. Quercus Garryana (crossed out) Douglasii" (GH!).

Quercus gambelii Nutt. includes *Q. alba* sensu Frémont.

There are two sheets, with three labels, at NY-Torrey!: "FExCal, 464, 1843, Fontaine que Bouit [Fountain Creek, 12–18 July 1843, Pueblo County, Colorado]"; "FExCal, 52, 1845. Arkansas [Colorado, 1–22 August 1845]. Quercus"; and "Frémont's 2nd Expedn. May 28, 506, 1844, Spanish Fork in the Uintas(?) [Utah County, Utah]" (Figure 27). "Frémont's 2nd Exp. Arkansas [faded pencil]. Q. Fendleri Liebm. = No. 808 Fendl- (in herb Gray) & seems to be intermediate between Q. Fendleri & Q. Gambelii" (NY-Torrey!). The two specimens on the sheet seem to represent one of the numerous hybrids between *Q. gambelii* and one or more of other oaks.

Quercus kelloggii Newb. = California black oak, includes *Q. tinctoria* var. *californica*

"FExCal, 1845–7. Quercus nigra (crossed out) tinctoria. 'near Bent's Fort.' 529, 1845" (NY-Torrey!). The notation "near Bent's Fort" is written on the label in pencil and might represent an error in labeling; the specimen looks like *Q. kelloggii* and was filed in that species folder at NY.

Quercus lobata Nee = Valley oak, includes *Q. longiglanda* of Frémont (see below)

There are five sheets at GH!: "FExCal, 1845. No. 7. Quercus. Stanislaus River [Stanislaus County, California]—in groves—A large oak"; "FExCal, 1845–7. 253. 1846. Quercus hindsii"; "FExCal, 1845. Dec. 23, near the 'Lake Fork' [King's River, Fresno

County, California] of the Joachin. 3 feet in diameter"; "FExCal, 1845. No. 14. Cosumne River [Sacramento County, California]. 'Bottoms'" (also NY-Torrey!); and "FExCal, 1845–7[1846]." "Quercus. Frémont's Expedition to California. River Merced. 17 xii. 1845. No. 4" and "Quercus. Frémont's Expedition to California. Bottom of Lake fork [King's River, Fresno County, California]. 22 xii. 1845. no. 8" (both GH-Thurber!; no. 8 also NY-Torrey! mounted with No. 14). The specimens taken in December 1845 were during the search by Frémont for the remainder of his party under direction of Kern, Talbot, and Walker, in present Fresno County, California. "Lake Fork" of Frémont was later named King's River. "March 29. Stanislaus River [Stanislaus County, California]. 149, 1844. Fremont's 2nd Expedn."; "Fremont's 2nd Expedn. [illegible] of California"; "April 13 & 14 [Kern County, California]. 284. 1844. Fremont's 2nd Expedn." (all three NY-Torrey!). Specimen 149 consists of two branches in early leaf.

***Quercus longiglanda* Torr. & Frém.** in Frém., Geogr. Mem. Calif. 15, 17. 1848. (3rd) = *Q. lobata* Nee

Protologue locality: "The eastern (which is the fertile) side of the valley is intersected with numerous, streams, forming large and very beautiful bottoms of fertile land, wooded principally with white oaks (*quercus longiglanda*, Torr. & Frém.) in open groves of handsome trees, often five or six feet in diameter, and sixty to eighty feet high" (Frémont, 1848: 15), and "We encamped in one of these bottoms, in a grove of large white oaks previously mentioned, as *quercus longiglanda (Torr. & Frém.)*. This oak is a new species, belonging to the division of white oaks, distinguished by the length of its acorn, which is commonly an inch and a half, and sometimes two inches. This long acorn characterizes the tree, which has accordingly been specified by Dr. Torrey as *quercus longiglanda*—(long-acorn oak.)" (Frémont, 1848: 17). A footnote accompanies the page 17 quote: "The names of plants mentioned in this memoir rest on the authority of Dr. Torrey, by whom the specimens have been examined." Type: "Quercus macradenia—(longiglanda) Torr. in Frém. geogr. mem. of Calif. Sacramento to Capt. Sutter's" (holotype NY-Torrey!); and "Quercus [tuberculosa] Hindsii (lobata). Sacramento to Capt. Sutter's" [the acorn thicker than in the first] (isotype NY-Crooke!). Under *Q. hindsii* Benth., Torrey (1857: 138) notes: "Q. longiglanda, *Torr. in Frémont's Geogr. Mem. of Calif.* Plains near Marysville, Feather River California." The 1848 reports are repeated by Frémont (1887: 440, 442) in his memoir. The name has essentially been ignored, probably considered as unpublished. The form of the publication in the 1848 memoir leaves little doubt that the plant was formally proposed as a new species, and the description, meager as it is, cannot apply to any other California oak. Additionally the epithet is supported by type specimens that verify both the name "longiglanda" and the placement of the name in synonymy of *Q. lobata*. Further justification is given by the Torrey bibliographical citation noted above, and by the existence of a watercolor drawing of the species at NY-Torrey!, with the data: "Quercus longiglanda *Torr. & Frém.* Frémont's Exp. 1845–7. Drawn by *Kerne*."

Quercus macrocarpa Michx.

"FExCal, 1845–7. 39 and 41. 1845. July 5th [near Santa Fe road, Kansas]. Quercus macrocarpa (g[George] e[Engelmann]" (two sheets NY-Torrey!).

***Quercus tinctoria* Bartram** var. ***californica* Torr.**, Pacif. Railr. Rep. 4: 138. 1857. (3rd). = *Q. kelloggii* Newb.

Protologue locality: Hillsides Napa Valley [Bigelow]. Type: "FExCal, 1845–7. April 8, 1846. = Quercus tinctoria var. Californica. 'Sacramento Bottom, above Cow Creek' [Shasta County, California, April 1846]. Tree to 50 feet high"; "FExCal, 1845–7. June 14 [1846]. Quercus tinctoria, var. Californica, Torr. Near N. Branch of the American Fork [near Sutter's, Sacramento County, California]"; and "FExCal, 1845–7. 500. 1846. sp. nov. Torrey 1850" (three probable syntypes NY-Torrey!). "FExCal, 1845–7. 500. 1846. Quercus tinctoria var. Californica, Torr. in Whipp. rep.,—rubra Liebm.,—Kelloggii Newberry" (syntypes GH!; GH-Thurber!).

Quercus turbinella Greene

This is probably the oak referred to by Frémont (1845: 265) at Mountain Spring, Nevada.

Quercus wislizenii A. DC. = Interior live oak

Four sheets (five collections) NY-Torrey!: "FExCal, Dec. 25, 1845, an abundant evergreen oak [Sierra Nevada, King's River, Fresno County, California]" (also GH!); "FExCal, 1845–7. Dec. 25. 1845. Sierra Nevada, Sources of Lake Fork of Joachin" (also GH-Thurber!); "FExCal, Mokulemnes River (a), 1846. Hooker. Quercus agrifolia, *Nee*"; [sheet 3 left side] "FExCal, 1845–7, Dec 17, 1845, No. 15. Quercus agrifolia, Nee. 'Species of holly or live oak. Very frequent along the Valley (Joachin)' [Stanislaus County, California, also GH!]"; and [sheet 3 right side] "FExCal, 1845–7. Quercus agrifolia, Nee. Mokulemnes River, Dec 15, 1845 [San Joaquin County, California]"; and "FExCal, 1845–7. Quercus agrifolia, Nee," "FExCal, 1845–7. No. 16. Dec. 24–5, 1845. From a tree 25 ft. high. Foothills of the Sierra Nevada. elev. 2200 ft. [King's River, Fresno County, California]" (GH-Thurber!). "Quercus. FExCal, 1846. No. 365" (GH!). "Quercus. Frémont's Expedition to California. Mokelemni river. 18.iii.1846 [San Joaquin County, California]" (GH-Thurber!). Frémont's fascination with the oaks of California is manifested in the large number of specimens collected. It is noted, however, that they could be collected without dismounting from a horse.

Rafinesquia californica Nutt.

"Found also by Frémont on the Mohave river and other parts of California" (Gray, 1859: 106). "FExCal, 1844. 332 & 335. Mohave River. April 23, 1844. Rafinesquia Californica, *Nutt.*" and "FExCal, 1845–7[1846, unless a duplicate of the above]. Rafinesquia" (two labels on same sheet NY-Torrey!).

Ranunculus alismifolius Geyer

"Frémont's Expedition to California, 1845–7. Ll. 1846. Dr. Gray. Ranunculus alismaefolius. Benth. pl. Hartw. no. 1607" (NY-Torrey!; GH!).

Ranunculus californicus Benth.
"Frémont gathered the latter in 1846, near San Jose [Santa Clara County, California]" (Torrey, 1857: 62). "FExCal, 1845–7, 140, 1846. Specm. sent to Dr. Gray = 138. R. californicus. Benth." (NY-Torrey!; GH!). "Santa Cruz Mountains [Santa Cruz County], Calif. 1846. Frémont" (NY-Torrey!).

Ranunculus cymbalaria ≡ *R. cymbalaria* Pursh
"Upper Platte. July 31, August [1842. East of Independence Rock, Natrona County, Wyoming]" (Torrey, 1843: 83).

Ranunculus rhomboideus Goldie
"Frémont's 2nd Expedn. Ranunculus rhomboideus, *Goldie*" (NY-Torrey!). This is a Great Plains species.

Ranunculus scleratus ≡ *R. scleratus* L.
"Valley of the Sweet Water river. August 18–29 [1842]" (Torrey, 1843: 83).

Ratibida columnifera (Nutt.) Woot. & Standl. includes *Lepachys columnaris*

Rhamnus californica Esch.
"FExCal, 1843–4 [crossed out]. 499(a) 1846. Buttes—upper Sacramento. June [Sutter County, California, 30 May to 4 June 1846]. Rhamnus. Shrub 18 feet high" and "FExCal, 1845–7[1846]. 499. Rhamnus oleifolius. Buttes of upper Sacramento. June. Shrub with many branches—18 ft." (both NY-Torrey!; 499 also MO!).

Rhamnus crocea Nutt. ex Torr. & Gray
"FExCal, 1849. Rhamnus near croceus. Pet. 0" (NY-Torrey!). The specimen likely came from Arizona. It is mounted with two other stems from Monterey, by Major Rich.

Rhododendron occidentale (Torr. & A. Gray) A. Gray
"FExCal, 1845–7. 409. 1846. Azalea Californica" (GH!).

Rhus aromatica Ait. var. *trilobata* (Nutt.) A. Gray includes *R. trilobata* Nutt.
"Frémont's 2nd Exp. 453, 1844" (NY!); "Frémont 49, 1845" (NY-Torrey!; NY-Sartwell!; GH!; BRY!); "Frémont 1845. Neil's Fork of the Sacramento, in banks of the river" (NY-Torrey!; BRY!); and "FExCal, 1845–7. Aug. 22. 1845. (no number). Fontaine qui bouit. R. canadensis var. mollis. Syn. Fl. N. Amer." (GH!). Fountain Creek joins the Arkansas River in Pueblo County, Colorado. "FExCal, 49, 1845. Rhus trilobata" (MO!).

Rhus glabra L.
Observed by Frémont in Utah, on Pole Patch, north of Ogden, Weber County, Utah (Frémont, 1845: 150).

Rhus trilobata = *R. aromatica* Ait.
"Red Buttes. July 29 [1842. Adjacent to Casper, Natrona County, Wyoming]" (Torrey, 1843: 84).

Ribes aureum Pursh
"Frémont's 1st Expedn. Aug. 5, 1842 [southeast of Atlantic City, Frémont County, Wyoming]" (NY-Torrey!). This species was referred to as Lewis and Clark's currant by Frémont (1845: 164). "502, 1844. Frémont's 2nd Expedn." (NY-Torrey!). The sheet contains the notation "Spanish Fork of Uintah River, Utah." The second expedition was in Spanish Fork, Utah County, Utah, on 27 and 28 May 1844. "FExCal, 1845–7. 490. Near Bent's Fort [Otero County, Colorado, 2–16 Aug. 1845]" (NY-Torrey!).

Ribes cereum ≡ *R. cereum* Dougl.
"Sweet Water of the Platte. August 2–4 [1842. Between Devil's Gate, Natrona County and Southwest of Carmody Lake, Frémont County, Wyoming]" (Torrey, 1843: 86). "FExCal, 1846. 447. Ribes cereum" (NY-Torrey!; GH!; MO!).

Ribes echinatum Dougl.
Torrey (1843: 86) includes this species under the discussion of *R. lacustre*, indicating that it is "perhaps a distinct species."

Ribes inerme Rydb.
"Frémont's 2nd Expedn. 569. 1844" (NY-Torrey!).

Ribes irriguum = *R. oxycanthoides* L. var. *setosum* (Lindley) Dorn
"Sweet Water of the Platte. August 2–4 [1842. Between Devil's Gate, Natrona County and Southwest of Carmody Lake, Frémont County, Wyoming]" (Torrey, 1843: 86). "Ribes irriguum, *Dougl.* Aug. 5th 1842" (NY-Torrey!).

Ribes lacustre ≡ *R. lacustre* (Pers.) Poir. ex Lam.
"Sweet Water of the Platte. August 2–4 [1842. Between Devil's Gate, Natrona County and Southwest of Carmody Lake, Frémont County, Wyoming]" (Torrey, 1843: 86). "Ribes lacuste B. (R. echinatum, *Dougl.*). 'perhaps good species.' Aug. 13–14, 1842. Fremont's 2nd Exp." (NY-Torrey!). Either the date 1842 is in error or the expedition number is wrong.

Ribes cf. *leptanthum* A. Gray
"FExCal, 1845–7. 372. 1846. Ribes" (NY-Torrey!). The specimen lacks flowers and fruit, and the identification is tentative. The names *Grossularia roezlii* (Regel) Coulter & Britton (probably by Rydberg), *Ribes amietum* Greene, and *R. californicum* A. Gray, as well as a faint notation "probably leptanthum Gray," appear on the sheet. "Frémont's 2nd Expedn. 257, 1844. Frémont" (NY-Torrey!).

Ribes sanguineum Pursh var. *glutinosum* (Benth.) Loud.
"FExCal, 1845–7. 159. 1846. Ribes glutinosum *Benth.* Near Santa Cruz, California [Santa Cruz County, probably on 28 February 1846]" (NY-Torrey!).

Romneya coulteri Harvey
"Romneya Coulteri Harvey in Hook. Lond. jour. bot. 4. p. 74. t. 3. California. Frémont. 1846" (NY-Torrey!). "FExCal, 1845–7. Nn. Dr. Gray. Romneya Coulteri" (GH!; GH-Thurber!).

Rorippa islandica (Oed.) Borbas includes *Nasturtium palustre*

Rosa blanda = *R. acicularis* Lindl. and *R. arkansana* Porter
"Lower Platte [1842]" (Torrey, 1843: 85). "FExRM, 1842. Rosa blanda [= *R. acicularis]*" and "FExRM, 1842. blanda. June 24 [= *R. arkansana*]" (both NY-Torrey!).

Rosa foliolosa ≡ *R. foliolosa* Nutt.
"Lower Platte [1842]" (Torrey, 1843: 85).

Rosa woodsii Lindley
"Torr. & Gray, Flora, N. Amer. Frémont's 1st Exped. Lake in Wind River Chain of R. Mts." and "R. foliolosa var. leiocarpa T. & Gr. On the Platte. Frémont's 1st Exped." (both NY-Torrey!).

Rubus deliciosus Torr.
"Kansas. 1844. Frémont's 2nd Expedn." (NY-Torrey!).

Rubus idaeus L. includes *R. strigosus*
"FExCal, 1845–7. 159, 1845" and "FExCal, 1845–7. 267, 1845" (both NY-Torrey!). Written on the sheet is the note "Piney Fork, 2d or 3d Camp. Frémont's field notes." Piney Creek is in Eagle County, Colorado. Frémont was there sometime during the period 4–11 September 1845. The specimen belongs to the North American phase of the species known as subsp. *melanolasius* (Dieck.) Focke.

Rubus strigosus = *Rubus idaeus* L.
"Defiles of the Wind River mountains. Aug 12–17 [1842. Sublette County, Wyoming]" (Torrey, 1843: 85). "Rubus strigosus. A.Gr. Hardly. J.T. Frémont's 1st Expedn. Aug. 12–17. 1842" (NY-Torrey!). The notations on the label show the evolution of thought regarding names for plants from the American West. Gray provided the name, and Torrey thought otherwise but did not provide another designation.

Rubus ursinus Cham. & Schlecht.
"FExCal, 1845–7. 239. 1846. Rubus ursinus. Coral Creek, near Hyde's Ford of the Sacramento" (NY-Torrey!).

Ruellia humilis Nutt.
"Frémont's 3rd Exp. July 11th 1845. Turkey Creek [Kansas]" (NY-Torrey!).

Rumex hymenosepalus Torr.
This is undoubtedly the "*rumex venosus*" employed by Frémont and his men to allay thirst while crossing portions of the Mohave Desert on 4 May 1844 (Frémont, 1845: 266).

Rumex maritimus L. var. *fuegineus* (Phil.) Dusen
"FExCal, 1845. N. 426. Rumex maritimus. '4th or 5th camp above Bent's Fort'" (NY-Torrey!; GH!). This would have been taken on the 19th or 20th of August, probably in Pueblo County, Colorado.

Rumex occidentalis S. Wats.
"FExCal, 1845. 384. Rumex domesticus? Forks of the White River [probably Rio Blanco County, Colorado]. R. longifolius, Meisn. in DC. Prodr.?" (NY-Torrey!).

Rumex salicifolius ≡ *R. salicifolius* Weinm.
"Black Hills. July 26 [1842. Near Glen Rock, Converse County, Wyoming]" (Torrey, 1843: 92). "FExRM, 1842. Rumex salicifolius, *Weinm.* Mouth of Deer Creek. July 26 [near Glen Rock, Converse County, Wyoming]" (NY-Torrey!).

Rumex venosus Pursh
"FExCal, 586, 1844. Rumex venosus." (NY-Torrey!; GH!). The GH material consists of two fruiting bracts in a packet. The Frémont gatherings at NY are mounted with a collection by James of Long's Expedition.

Sagittaria sagitifolia = *Sagittaria cuneata* Sheldon
"On the Kansas [1842]" (Torrey, 1843: 93). "Platte Bottom, 29 June. Fremont's Expedition to the Rocky Mountains, 1842. S. variabilis?" (GH!).

***Salazaria mexicana* Torr.**, Rep. U.S. Mex. Bound., Bot. 133. 1859. (2nd)
Protologue locality: "Ravines, Chihuahua, below Piendro del Norte, near the Rio Grande; Parry. This remarkable plant was first discovered by Col. Frémont, in 1844, on the Rio de los Angelos, a branch of the Rio Virgen, western New Mexico; but the specimens were too much injured for description." Type: "FExCal, 1843–4. 433, 1844. May 4th. Salazaria Mexicana, *Torr.* Near Vegas, Utah [actually Las Vegas, Clark County, Nevada]. 'Shrub 3 ft. high, very branching; flower reddish black. Rare'" (syntype NY-Torrey!). "Southern Nevada, (Frémont)" (Watson, 1871: 237).

Salicornia herbacea L.
"677 Frémont" (Watson, 1874: 124). "Frémont's 2nd Expedn, 677, 1843" (NY-Torrey!). Frémont (1845) notes this species in his journal entry for 4 September 1843, when the party was on the Bear River, Box Elder County, Utah. The three Frémont plants are mounted with a single branch by Abert.

Salix amygdaloides Anderss.
"FExRM, 1842. Horse Creek, July 14 [north of Cheyenne, Laramie County, Wyoming]"; "FExRM, 1842. Salix amygdaloides, And.! M.S.B. 1887. Camp on the Platte"; "FExCal, 1845. 402 (a). Salix nigra Marsh v. Wrightii, And. forma. 'On road day we left Canon Arkansas River, Aug. 28th' 'Frémont's notes'" (three sheets NY-Torrey!). The locality information indicates a provenance in Frémont County, Colorado, and gives an indication that Torrey had some additional information from Frémont as to locality data, probably on scraps of paper attached to the plant.

Salix exigua Nutt.
"FExCal, 1845–7. 402 (b) 1845. Salix. S. sessilifolia, Nutt. var. Hindsiana, Anderss." (NY-Torrey!).

Salix glauca L.
"FExRM, 1842. Salix. Wind River Mountains. Aug. 13–16 [Sublette County, Wyoming]" and "FExCal, 170. 1845. Salix desertorum, Rich." (both NY-Torrey!).

Salix interior = *S. exigua* Nutt.

Salix lasiandra Benth.
"Frémont's 3rd Expedition. At foot of Coast Mts. opposite Monterey, California" (NY-Torrey!). The sheet bears the notation "Salix." It is annotated *S. lasiandra* Benth. by M.S.B[ebb] 1887. The specimens are staminate.

Salix lasiolepis Benth.
"Frémont's 3rd Exped. Upper Sacramento, California, April 2, 1846 [Deer Creek, Tehama County, California]" (NY-Torrey!). The specimen is excellent; it has numerous pistillate catkins. The sheet bears the annotation "S. lasiolepis Benth. var. Bigelovii Bebb" by MSB[ebb] 1887.

Salix longifolia = *S. exigua* Nutt. pro parte
"On the Platte [1842]" (Torrey, 1843: 92). "FExRM, 1842. Salix longifolia *Muhl.* On the Platte" and "FExCal, 1845. 187. Salix" (both NY-Torrey!). "Salix longif. Frémont's 3d Expedit. 187. 1845" (MO!).

Salix lutea Nutt.
"FExRM, 1842. Salix Muhlenbergii? Grand Island, Sept. 19 [probably Hall County, Nebraska]" (NY-Torrey!). The name on the plant label is "Salix muhlenbergii?." The specimen bears the annotation "S. cordata Muhl. M.S.B[ebb] 1887."

Salix melanopsis Nutt.
Observed by Frémont in California?

Salix monticola Bebb. ex. Coult.?
"FExCal, 1845. 402. Salix" (NY-Torrey!). The number 402, as 402, 402 (a), and 402 (b) all refer to different species.

Salix muhlenbergii = *S. lutea* Nutt.
"On the Platte [1842]" (Torrey, 1843: 92). See *S. lutea* above for the disposition of this citation.

Salix myricoides = *S. scouleriana* Barratt in Hook.
Frémont (1845: 252).

Salix nigra Marsh.
"Collected by Frémont in Utah" (Watson, 1880: 83).

Salix scouleriana Barratt in Hook. includes *S. myricoides*

Salvia azurea ≡ *S. azurea* Lam.
"Kansas river and forks of the Platte. June 19–29 [1842], July 2 [1842. Lincoln County, Nebraska]" (Torrey, 1843: 89).

Salvia carduaca Benth.
"FExCal, 1845–7. 178. 1846. Salvia gossypina, *Benth. pl. Hartw.* Carduacae var. ?" (NY-Torrey!; MO!).

Salvia dorrii (Kellogg) Abrams subsp. *pilosa* (A. Gray) Epling
"FExCal, 1843–4. No. 349. (Apr. 17, 1844) and 407 or 409. 1844. May 1 [Clark County, Nevada]. Audibertia 'Flowers blue'" (NY-Torrey!).

Salvia mellifera Greene
"Near Monterey [Monterey County], Calif. Jany 31, 1846. Frémont" (NY-Torrey!).

Salvia reflexa Hornem.
"FExCal, 1845. Salvia lanceolata, *Willd.*. No. 200 and 201, July 25, 1845 [Smoky Hill Fork (?), Kansas]" (both on same sheet NY-Torrey!; 200 also MO!).

Sanicula arctopoides Hook. & Arn.
"California. Frémont's 3rd Exp. Ex herb. J. Torrey. Torr. & Gr. Fl. N. Amer." (NY-Torrey!). "FExCal, 1845–7. 156. 1846. S. arctopoides" (GH!).

Sanicula bipinnatifida Dougl.
"Frémont's 2nd Exp. 51, 1844. Sanicula bipinnatifida Hook. & Arn.," "FExCal, 1845–7. 280, 1846. Sanicula bipinnatifida," and "FExCal, 1845–7. Sanicula bipinnatifida" (all three NY!). "FExCal, 1845–7. 259. 1846. S. bipinnatifida" (GH!).

Sanicula graveolens Poeppig
"FExCal, 1845–7. Uuu 1846. Sanicula nevadensis Wats." (NY-Torrey!).

Sanicula tuberosa **Torr.**, Pacif. Railr. Rep. 4: 91. 1857. (2nd)
Protologue locality: "Hillsides, Duffield's Ranch, Sierra Nevada; April–May [Dr. Bigelow]." "This remarkable species was first collected by Colonel Frémont in 1844 on the American river, and afterwards on the upper waters of the Sacramento, but without fruit." Syntype: "Sanicula tuberosa Torr. Hills of the American Fork of the Sacramento, early in March. Fremont's 2nd Expedn. 44. 1844" (NY-Torrey!). "FExCal, 1845–7, 347. 1846" (syntype GH!). The Frémont material is mounted on a sheet with two others by Bigelow (one the lectotype, see Shan & Constance, 1951: 73; the other probably not a type) and one by Bolander. "FExCal, 1845–7. 347, 1846. Sanicula tuberosa Torr. 'Headwaters of Cow Creek [east of Redding, Shasta County, California], Sierra of the Sacramento. April 27–28'" (syntype NY-Torrey!). It is clear from the notation quoted above that Torrey considered both the 1844 and 1846 collections by John Charles.

Sarcobatus vermiculatis (Hook.) Torr.
"Frémont 41" (Watson, 1874: 86). This plant was designated by Torrey as *Frémontia vermicularis*, but the generic name could not stand because of the earlier named *Sarcobatus*. Frémont was evidently proud of having his name commemorated, and he mentioned the genus on numerous occasions. Greasewood is a common component of saline bottomlands in the west, and it was through and in these bottomlands that Frémont and his men traveled and camped. "California. Frémont" (NY-Sartwell!); "FExCal,

1845–7[1845]. Frémont" (NY!); "Frémont's 2nd [1st] Exped. 30 July—on excursion to the Pass [1842. Near Alcova, Natrona County, Wyoming, see citations under *Frémontia*]" (NY-Torrey!). "FExCal, 1845–7. 401, 1845" (GH!).

***Sarcodes* Torr.**, Smithsonian Contr. Knowl. 6(2): 17. 1853. (3rd)
Type species: ***Sarcodes sanguinea* Torr.** (l.c.)
Protologue locality: "Valley of the Sacramento; the precise locality not recorded, but probably on the Yuba River [probably Yuba County]." Type: "FExCal, 1845–7[1846]. N. gen. Sarcodes sanguinea, *Torr.* To be drawn by Sprague" (holotype NY-Torrey!: microfiche BRY!; isotype GH!).

Satureja douglasii (Benth.) Briq.
"FExCal, 1846. Micromeria" (NY-Torrey!); "FExCal, 1845–7. Gggg 1846" (GH!; MO!); and "Frémont's 2d [3rd?] Cal. Expedition 1846–47. Micromeria. Dr. Gray?" (GH-Thurber!).

Saxifraga californica Greene
"Frémont's 2nd Expedn." (NY-Torrey!).

Saxifraga peltata Torr. ≡ *Peltiphyllum peltatum* (Torr.) Engler in Engler & Prantl
"Along and in the beds of quick-flowing streamlets, through the Sierra Nevada from Mariposa County northward to the head-waters of the Sacramento (Pickering & Brackenridge, Frémont, Hartweg, &c.)" (Brewer et al., 1876: 193).

Schrankia angustata = *Mimosa nuttallii* (DC.) Barneby
"Kansas and Platte rivers. June 19–Sept. [1842]" (Torrey, 1843: 85). Frémont (1845: 108) cites this name in journal entry of 16 June 1843.

Schrankia nuttallii (DC.) Standl. ≡ *Mimosa nuttallii* (DC.) Barneby
"Schrankia. Frémont's 3rd Expedition, 1845" (NY-Torrey!). "FExRM, 1842. Schrankia" (GH!; GH-Thurber!).

Scirpus acutus Muhl. ex Bigel. includes tules?

Scirpus californicus (C. A. Meyer) Steud. includes *S. lacustris*

Scirpus lacustris = *S. californicus* (C. A. Meyer) Steud.
Frémont (1845: 252).

Scrophularia californica Cham. & Schlecht.?
"FExRM, 1842. Scrophularia. no label—but doubtless from California" (NY-Torrey!). The specimen, though accompanied by an 1842 label, is likely, as the label information indicates, from California, probably in 1846.

Scutellaria antirrhinoides Benth.
"We have the same variety, collected in California by Frémont (1846) and by Rev. A. Fitch" (Torrey, 1857: 123). "Scutellaria antirrhinoides. California. Frémont" (NY-Sartwell!).

***Scutellaria antirrhinoides* var. *californica* A. Gray**, Proc. Amer. Acad. Arts 8: 396. 1872. (3rd) ≡ *S. californica* (A. Gray) A. Gray

Protologue locality: "This has been collected by Frémont, Bigelow, Bolander, Rattan, Bridges, and Torrey; and Hartweg's no. 1918, referred by Bentham to *S. angustifolia*, is a narrow-leaved form of it." Type: This taxon has been lectotypified by Epling (1942: 31): "I consider Bolander's specimen from Anderson Valley [California] to be the standard." "FExCal, 1845–7, Iiii. 1846" (syntype GH!, GH-Thurber!; MO!; US!). This might well be the same as that cited under the species name above.

Scutellaria galericulata ≡ *S. galericulata* L.

"North fork of the Platte. July 10 [1842. St. Vrain's Fort, Weld County, Colorado]" (Torrey, 1843: 89). "FExRM, 1842. Scutellaria galericulata. July 10" (NY-Torrey!).

Scutellaria parvula Michx. var. *leonardii* (Epling) Fern.

"No. 200, 1843. Frémont's 2nd Exped." (NY-Torrey!). The variety is known from the Plains States.

Scutellaria siphocampyloides Vatke

"Frémont's Expedition 1845–47" (GH-Thurber!). "FExCal, 1845–7. 434, 1846. Scutellaria angustifolia *Ph.*?" (NY-Torrey!; MO!; US!).

Sedum integrifolium (Raf.) A. Nels. ex Coult. & Nels. includes *S. rhodiola*

Sedum lanceolatum Torr.

"Frémont's 2nd Expedn." (NY-Torrey!).

Sedum obtusatum A. Gray

"FExCal, 1845–7. Dec. 4th. 1846[1845]. Echeveria—n. sp.? Pass [Donner Pass, Placer County, California] at the head of the Salmon Trout River & Ebo River" (NY-Torrey!).

Sedum pumilum Benth. ≡ *Parvisedum pumilum* (Benth.) Clausen

"It was also collected by *Frémont*" (Brewer et al., 1876: 210). "FExCal, 1845–7. 273. 1846. Sedum pumilum sp. n. Benth." (GH!). "FExCal, 1845–7. 273. 1846. Sedum sparsiflorum? 'Fleshy plant with yellow flowers.' Upper Sacramento. Sedum pumilum Benth. Pl. Hartw. p. 310 (1849)" (NY-Torrey!, mounted on sheet with specimens by Fitch and Bigelow).

Sedum rhodiola ≡ *S. integrifolium* (Raf.) A. Nels. ex Coult. & A. Nels.

"On a lake in Wind River mountains. August 12–17 [1842. Sublette County, Wyoming]" (Torrey, 1843: 86). "FExRM, 1842. Sedum Rhodiola. Wind River Mountains, Aug. 13–16 [1842. Sublette County, Wyoming]" (NY-Torrey!). "FExRM, 1842. Sedum Rhodiola" (GH!). This is likely a duplicate of that at NY-Torrey.

Selaginella bigelovii Underwood

"FExCal, 1843–4. Lycopodium (Selaginella) rupestris?" (NY-Columbia!).

Selaginella hansenii Hieronymus

"FExCal, 1845–7" (NY-Torrey!).

Senecio californicus DC.
"FExCal, 1845–7. (N.) Gray. 1846. Senecio Californicus" (NY-Torrey!).

Senecio cymbalaroides Buek
"Senecio subnudus, *DC.* Torr. & Gray, Flora, N. Amer. Wind River Chain, 7000 Ft &c. Frémont 1842" (NY-Torrey!).

Senecio douglasii DC. var. *douglasii*
"Frémont's Expedition to California, 1845–7, No. 9. Dec. 1845. Senecio filifolius? '*En route*, among foot hills of the sierra between the auxumne and forks of the upper San Joaquin'" (NY-Torrey!).

Senecio eremophilus Richards. includes *S. ambrosioides* Rydb.
"FExCal, 1845–7. 380. 1845. Senecio eremophilus, Richards." (NY-Torrey!). The sheet has the notation "Bahia Salada." "Also met with by Frémont, in his second expedition" (Gray, 1849: 108).

***Senecio eurycephalus* Torr. & A. Gray** in A. Gray, Mem. Amer. Acad., n.s. 4: 109. 1849. (3rd)
Protologue locality: "California, Frémont; also Hartweg." Type: "Frémont's Expedition to California 326, 1846. n. sp. Senecio eurycephalus" (isotype NY-Torrey!: microfiche BRY!; holotype GH!). Prior to the description of the species, Gray (1849) states: "Another unpublished Californian species, which was gathered by Frémont in his third expedition, is." The NY isotype is labeled: "Senecio eurycephalus T. & Gr. ined. Gr. pl. Fendl." The "Gr. pl. Fend." was obviously added later.

***Senecio filifolius* β *fremontii* Torr. & A. Gray**, Fl. N. Amer. 2: 444. 1843. (1st) = *S. riddellii* Torr. & A. Gray (Barkley, 1978).
Protologue locality: "β. On the Lower Platte, near the 'Chimney,' *Lieut. Frémont!* [1842. 5 September, camp was just west of Chimney Rock, still in Scotts Bluff County, Nebraska]." Type: "Senecio filifolius β. Torr. & Gray, Flora, N. Amer. Lower Platte, Frémont 1842" (holotype NY-Torrey!: microfiche BRY!). "Lower Platte [1842]" (Torrey, 1843: 88).

***Senecio fremontii* Torr. & A. Gray**, Fl. N. Amer. 2: 445. 1843. (1st)
Protologue locality: "On the Wind River Chain of the Rock Mountains, just below the limits of perpetual snow, *Lieut. Frémont!*." Type: "Senecio Frémontii. Torr. & Gray, Flora, N. Amer. Wind River Chain, Rky Mts. Near perpetual snow. Lieut. Frémont" (isotype NY-Torrey!: microfiche BRY!; holotype GH!). "Highest parts of the mountains, to the region of perpetual snow. Aug. 15 [1842. Sublette County, Wyoming]" (Torrey, 1843: 88). Sublette County, Wyoming, includes the type locality.

Senecio hydrophilus Nutt. β
"On a lake in the Wind River mountains. Aug. 12–17 [1842. Sublette County, Wyoming]" (Torrey, 1843: 88). "β. Borders of a lake in the Wind River Chain of the Rocky Mountains, *Lieut. Frémont!*" (Torrey & Gray, 1843). "Senecio hydrophilus Nutt.

β. Torr. & Gray, Flora, N. Amer. Lake in Wind R. Chain, Rky. Mts. Frémont" (NY-Torrey!; GH!). The expedition was in the Wind River Mountains on 12–17 August 1842. "(1845) Hort. Cantab. e sem. Frémont. S. hydrophyllus Nutt." (NY!; GH!). The specimen at NY contains the notation "Senecio hydrophilus. Bot. gard Cambridge. Seed from Frémont. 1845." "No. 357. 1843. Senecio hydrophilus *Nutt.* Frémont's 2nd Expedn." (NY-Torrey!).

***Senecio lanceolatus* Torr. & A. Gray**, Fl. N. Amer. 2: 440. 1843. (1st) = *S. serra* Hook.
Protologue locality: "Along the North Fork of the Platte, *Lieut. Frémont!*." "North fork of the Platte and Sweet Water" (Torrey, 1843: 88). Type: "N. Fork of the Platte. Frémont [1842]" (isotype NY-Torrey!: microfiche BRY!; holotype GH!).

***Senecio multilobatus* Torr. & A. Gray** in A. Gray, Mem. Amer. Acad. n.s. 4: 109. 1849. (2nd)
Protologue locality: "Abundant on the Uintah River, in the interior of California, Frémont (second expedition)." Type: "Frémont's Expedition to California 549, 1844. Senecio multilobatus T. & Gr. in Gray. pl. Fendl. p. 109. June 3rd. On an island in the main Uinta river, near the Fort. An abundant plant" (isotype NY-Torrey!: microfiche BRY!; holotype GH!). The fort, Fort Roubideau, was near present White Rocks, Uintah County, Utah.

Senecio rapifolius Nutt.
"Sweet Water river and North Fork of the Platte, Lieut. Frémont?" (Torrey & Gray, 1843: 441). "North fork of the Platte and Sweet Water" (Torrey, 1843: 88). "S. rapifolius, Nutt.! Torr. & Gray, Flora, N. Amer. Aug. 4, 1842. Frémont" (NY-Torrey!).

Senecio riddellii Torr. includes *Senecio filifolius β. fremontii* Torr. & A. Gray
"Senecio. Frémont's Exped. 170. 18 July 1845 [branch of Smoky Hill Fork, Kansas]" (MO!).

Senecio serra Hook. includes *S. lanceolatus* Torr. & A. Gray
"FExCal, 1845–7. 1846? No. 96. 'Senecio Serra Hook.? but with none of the leaves cordate at the base' A.Gr." (NY-Torrey!).

***Senecio spartioides* Torr. & A. Gray**, Fl. N. Amer. 2: 438. 1843. (1st)
Protologue locality: "Upper Platte; on a steep sand-bank of the Sweet-water River, *Lieut. Frémont!* Aug.–Sept." Type: "Sand Bank, Cache Broad Camp, Sweet Water R. Aug. 21 [1842. Vicinity of Jeffery City, Frémont County, Wyoming]. Frémont" (holotype NY-Torrey!: microfiche BRY!). "FExRM, 1842. Senecio spartioides T. & G. Sweetwater River, Aug." (isotype GH!) "Sweet Water river. Aug. 21" (Torrey, 1843: 88).

Senecio subnudus DC. = *S. cymbalarioides* Buek (q.v.)
"Defiles of the Wind River mountains, from 7,000 feet upwards. August 13–14 [1842. Sublette County, Wyoming]" (Torrey, 1843: 87).

Senecio triangularis Hook. *β* Torr. & A. Gray, Fl. N. Amer. 2: 441. 1843.
"*β*. Wind River Chain of the Rocky Mountains, about lat. 42°, at the altitude of 7000 feet, *Lieut. Frémont!*." "Defiles of the Wind River mountains, from 7,000 feet upwards. August 13–14 [1842. Sublette County, Wyoming]" (Torrey, 1843: 87).

Sequoia sempervirens (Lamb.) Endl. includes *Taxodium*, cypress, palo colorado
"FExCal, 1845–7[1846]. 'Red-Wood—Higher parts of the Coast Mountains between San Jose & Santa Cruz'" (NY-Torrey!). "Ex herb. J. Torrey. Taxodium sempervirens. Frémont's 3rd Expedn." (GH!). Frémont (1887: 457).

Service berry = *Amelanchier alnifolia* Nutt. mainly (q.v.)

Sesleria dactyloides ≡ *Buchloe dactyloides* (Nutt.) Engelm.
"Sesleria dactyloides. Frémont 2nd" (GH!). The Frémont staminate material is multiply mounted with collections by Berlandier and Drummond, and with a printed plate from Emory's Report. "Sesleria dactyloides. No. 166 & 195. Fremont's 2d. expedition. 1843" (MO!).

Sesuvium verrucosum Raf.
"626, 1844, Frém. 2nd Exped. Sesuvium" (NY-Torrey!).

Shepherdia argentea "Grains de boeuf." ≡ *S. argentea* (Pursh) Nutt.
"Upper north fork of the Platte, from the Red Buttes to the mouth of the Sweet Water. Aug. 24–28 [1842]" (Torrey, 1843: 92). "Ex herb. J. Torrey. Shepherdia argentea. Frémont's 2nd Exp."; and "Shepherdia argentea *Nutt.* Frémont's 1st Exped. July 24–28, 1842" (both NY-Torrey!). On 24 July the party was at La Bonte River, Converse County, Wyoming, and on 28 July half-a-days's ride east of Red Buttes, Natrona County, Wyoming. Red Buttes was not reached until 29 July and the mouth of the Sweetwater until 31 July, 1842. "28 July—Platte bottoms, Grains de Boeuf, Jaune" (GH-Thurber!). The writing on a small paper tag appears to be the same as that on the specimens of both *Perideridia gairdneri* and *Ipomoea leptophylla*. The date corresponds to data on the second Frémont sheet at NY, cited above. The information relating this to Frémont is on the label, "Ex Herb. George Thurber. Shepherdia argentea, Nutt. Frémont's Expedition."

Shepherdia canadensis ≡ *S. canadensis* (L.) Nutt.
"On a lake in the Wind River mountains. August [1842. 12–17 August, Sublette County, Wyoming]" (Torrey, 1843: 92).

Sibbaldia procumbens ≡ *S. procumbens* L.
"Wind River mountains, near perpetual snow. Aug. 13–14 [1842. Sublette County, Wyoming]" (Torrey, 1843: 85). "Sibbaldia procumbens. Frémont's 1st Expedn. Aug 13, 1842. Wind River Mountains" (NY-Torrey!).

Sida coccinea ≡ *Sphaeralcea coccinea* (Nutt.) Rydb.
"Little Blue river to the South fork of the Platte. June 22–July 4 [1842]" (Torrey, 1843: 84). "Ex herb. J. Torrey. Frémont's 1st Expedition. Torr. & Gr. Fl. N. Amer. Sida coccinea" (NY-Columbia!) and "On the Platte. Frémont's 1st Exp. June 29. 1842 [south

of present Cozad, Dawson County, Nebraska]" (and both NY-Torrey!). "FExCal, 1845–47[1845]. Malvastrum coccineum Gray" (GH-Thurber!).

Sida hederacea Torr. = *Malvella leprosa* (Ortega) Krap.

Gray (1849: 23) cites: "California, Haenke, Coulter, Frémont." "FExCal, 476, 1846. Sida obliqua. Sida (Pseudo-malvastrum) hederacea, Torr. in Gr. pl. Fendl. p. 23. Malva plicata var obliqua Nutt." (NY-Torrey!; GH!).

***Sidalcea candida* A. Gray**, Mem. Amer. Acad. Arts, n.s. 4: 24. 1849. (3rd) includes *Malva rotundifolia* pro parte?

Protologue locality: "Along Santa Fe Creek; June, July [Fendler]." "A remarkable variety of this fine species, having larger cauline leaves with a very open sinus, and subsessile flowers, was gathered by Col. Frémont in his third expedition, probably in the Rocky Mountains" (Gray, 1849: 24). Syntypes: "Sidalcea candida Gray, Pl. Fendl. Rocky Mt. Frémont" (NY-Columbia!; BRY!); "FExCal, 407, 109, 45, 110, 410, 177, 92, 130, 1845. Sidalcea candida Gray var. Pl. Fend. no. 80" (NY-Torrey!). "FExCal, 1845–7. 410, 1845. Sidalcea candida var.? Pl. Fendl." (GH!); and "FExCal, 1845–47[1845?]. Sidalcea candida Gray Pl. Fendl. var." (GH-Thurber!). The two sheets at GH are annotated by C. L. Hitchcock as *S. candida* var. *glabrata* C. L. Hitchc.

***Sidalcea diploscypha* Torr. & A. Gray *β minor* A. Gray**, Mem. Amer. Acad. Arts, n.s. 4: 19. 1849. (3rd) = *S. diploscypha* Torr. & A. Gray

Protologue locality: "β. California, Frémont, Hartweg." Type: "FExCal, 1845–7. 432, 1846. Sidalcea diploscypha Gray β minor. 1848. Syn. Fl. N. Amer." (holotype GH!; isotype NY-Torrey!; isotype US!). There is a fragment of a specimen at NY-Torrey! with a tiny note clipped to its base: "Frémont's last journey—the only specimen. Carpels uniovulate. Malvastrum. 1853–54." The label, written by Asa Gray, contains the following: "Apparently a Malvastrum., but one I do not recognize. Keep it till it turns up in better condition and more of it. A[sa]. G[ray]. Sidalcea diplocypha var. minor."

Sidalcea humilis Hook. & Arn.

"Var. β humilior, foliis omnibus indivisis seu vix lobatis rotundato-reniformibus basi pl. m. truncatis. —California, Douglas, Frémont, Hartweg" (Gray, 1849: 20). "FExCal, Ww. 1846. Sidalcea humilis ? A. Gr." (NY-Torrey!; GH!). The Frémont material is annotated by C. L. Hitchcock as *S. malviflora* subsp. *laciniata* C. L. Hitchc. "FExCal, 81, 82, 1845. S. malvaeflora (humilis, olim)" (NY-Torrey!).

Sidalcea malviflora (DC.) A. Gray includes *S. humilis* Hook. & Arn.

Silene acaulis ≡ *S. acaulis* L.

"Wind River mountains, at the limits of perpetual snow [1842. 15 August. Sublette County, Wyoming]" (Torrey, 1843: 83).

Silene drummondii = *Lychnis drummondii* (Hook.) S. Wats. and *Arenaria congesta* Nutt. ex. Torr. & Gray

"Highest parts of the Wind River mountains. Aug. 13–16 [1842. Sublette County, Wyoming]" (Torrey, 1843: 83). "Frémont's 1st Expedn. Aug. 13–16 [1842. Sublette County, Wyoming]. 1842. Silene Drummondii *Hook.*" (NY-Torrey!).

Simmondsia chinensis (Link) C. K. Schneid.

"FExCal, 1849. Simmondsia californica Nutt. in Lond. jour. bot. 3. p." (NY-Torrey!).

Simsia (*Geraea*) *canescens* Torr. & A. Gray ≡ *Geraea canescens* Torr. & A. Gray

"Interior of California, Frémont, Coulter" (Gray, 1849: 85).

Sisymbrium auriculatum A. Gray

"FExCal, 1849. Thelypodium auriculatum. fide S. Watson" (NY-Torrey!). The specimen is fragmentary, in early flower, and has pinnatifid leaves. Its identification is uncertain, but undoubtedly wrong; the species is known from west Texas and Mexico.

Sisyrinchium anceps = ?

"North fork of the Platte. July 12 [1842. Actually near Greeley, Weld County, Colorado]" (Torrey, 1843: 93).

Sisyrinchium douglasii A. Dietr.

"FExCal, 1843–4. 381. 1846. Sisyrinchium grandiflorum, Dougl." (NY-Torrey!).

***Sium* (?) *incisum* Torr.** in Frém., Rep. Exped. Rocky Mts. 86. 1843. (1st) = *Berula erecta* var. *incisum* (Torr.) Cronq.

Protologue locality: "North fork of the Platte. July 12 [1842. Near Greeley, Weld County, Colorado]." Type: "Sium ? incisum, Torr. in Frém. 1st *Report*, p. 90. Frémont's 1st Expedition. July 1842" (NY-Torrey!: microfiche BRY!).

***Smelowskia fremontii* S. Wats.**, Proc. Amer. Acad. Arts 11: 123. 1876. (3rd) ≡ *Polyctenium fremontii* (S. Wats.) Greene

Protologue locality: "Collected by Frémont on hills near Klamath Lake." Type: "FExCal, 384, 1846. Hills around Lake Klamath. May 4 [Mcrady (Lost) River, Modoc County, California, or Klamath County, Oregon; Frémont did not reach Klamath Lake until 6 May 1846]" (holotype NY Torrey!: microfiche BRY!; isotypes GH!, GH-Thurber!, US!).

Smelowskia calycina C. A. Meyer includes *Braya* sp.

Smilacina stellata ≡ *S. stellata* (L.) Desf. includes *Convallaria stellata* L.

"From the Laramie river to the Red Buttes. Aug. 26–31 [1842]" (Torrey, 1843: 93).

Solanum douglasii Dunal in DC.

"Frémont's 3rd Exped. Solanum—n.sp. (physaloides). Probably from the sources of the Platte, near the mountains" and "FExCal, 1845–7. Pppp. 1846. Gray. P-3a. Solanum? Better a Physalis—but peduncle many-flowered" (both NY-Torrey!). Despite the notation on the label of the first cited sheet, the specimen seems clearly to have come from California.

Solanum parishii Heller

There are two labels, but only one plant: "FExCal, 1845–7. 294. 1846. Solanum umbelliferum Esch." and "294, 1846. Frémont. Solanum Californicum (umbelliferum). 'Fl. purple with yellow [illegible word]. On naked and very loose sandy on borders of waterbed—in descending the Lake Fork & afterwards in Santa Cruz Mts, more Frequently" (NY-Torrey!).

Solanum rostratum Dunal includes *Nycterium luteum*

"Kansas, Frémont. Frémont's 2nd Expedn." (NY-Torrey!).

Solanum umbelliferum Eschs.

"FExCal, 1845–7. No. 120. Feb. 26, 1846. Solanum umbelliferum. Santa Cruz [Santa Cruz County], California—'A shrub. Flowers blue or purple, with yellow anthers'" (NY-Torrey!). The information noted on the label is written over another set of information: "Frémont's 3rd Exped. No. 76. 1846. Sandy Shore." There are three stems mounted on the sheet; another one of which is also accompanied by data: "*Frémont's 3rd Exped.* California.—Santa Clara?" Possibly the overwritten information goes with one of the others, all of which appear to be separate collections of the same species.

Solanum xantii ≡ *S. xantii* A. Gray

This is the *Solanum* cited by Frémont on 16 April 1844.

Solidago canadensis L.

This is cited by Frémont (1845: 158) along Willard Creek, Box Elder County, Utah.

Solidago gigantea var. *β* = *S. gigantea* Ait.

"From the Platte to the mountains [1842]" (Torrey, 1843: 87).

Solidago incana Torr. & A. Gray

"Sweet Water river [1842]" (Torrey, 1843: 87). "A well-marked dwarf state of S. incana, only a span high, with roundish leaves, but less hoary than the plant of Nicollet, was collected on the Upper Arkansas in Frémont's third expedition" (Gray, 1849: 75).

Solidago missouriensis ≡ *S. missouriensis* Nutt.

"Fort Laramie, north fork of the Platte. Sept. 3 [1842. Goshen County, Wyoming]" (Torrey, 1843: 87). "S. Missouriensis, Nutt. dwarf form. Torr. & Gray, Flora, N. Amer. N. Platte, Frémont [probably the specimen cited above]" and (on same sheet) "S. Missouriensis var. Torr. & Gray, Flora, N. Amer. Wind River Chain, high up. Frémont" (NY-Torrey!).

Solidago mollis Bartl.

"FExCal, 1845–7. Ff. 1845. Dr. Gray. Solidago multiradiata *Nutt.* thirsoidea E. Mey. T. & Gr." and (two on same sheet) "Herb A. Gray. S. incana var. or new. Frémont 1845.

Sent by Dr. McDowell. Torr. & Gray, Fl. N. Amer." and "FExCal, 1845–7. 190. 189 is the same J. T. Solidago incana July 25, 1845." (all three NY-Torrey!).

Solidago multiradiata Ait.
"S. virga-aurea v. multiradiata. Torr. & Gray, Flora, N. Amer. Wind R. Chain, near snow line. Frémont" and "S. virga-aurea. v. Torr. & Gray, Flora, N. Amer. Wind R. Chain, near perpet. snow. Frémont" (both on same sheet NY-Torrey!).

Solidago rigida ≡ *S. rigida* L.
"North forth [fork] of the Platte [1842]" (Torrey, 1843: 87). "Solidago rigida. Torr. & Gray Flora, N. Amer. North Platte. Frémont" (NY-Torrey!). The specimen bears an annotation as subsp. *humilis* (Porter) Heard & Semple, by S. Heard and J. C. Semple in 1986.

Solidago speciosa ≡ *S. speciosa* Nutt.
"Upper Platte [1842]" (Torrey, 1843: 87).

Solidago virga-aurea var. *multiradiata* ≡ *S. multiradiata* Ait.
"Wind River mountain, from the height of 7,000 feet, to perpetual snow [1842. 13–15 August. Sublette County, Wyoming]" (Torrey, 1843: 87). "S. virga-aurea v. multiradiata. Torr. & Gray, Fl. N. Amer. Wind River Mts., near snow line. Frémont" (two on one sheet GH!).

Sophora nuttalliana Turner
"Sophora. Frémont's 2nd Expedn. (a) 297, 1843. 'Omitted in the list! 296 was Platte bottom'" and "(b) 206, 1843, June 25, Upper Platte [actually a tributary of the Republican River, in or near Rawlins County, Kansas]" (two collections same sheet NY-Torrey!).

Sorghastrum nutans (L.) Nash includes *Andropogon nutans*

Spartina cynosuroides = (?) *S. pectinata* Link.
"Little Blue river of the Kansas. June 22 [1842. Near Powell, Jefferson County, Nebraska]" (Torrey, 1843: 94).

Specularia amplexicaulis = *Triodanus perfoliata* (L.) Nieuw.
"Little Blue river of the Kansas [1842 on 22 or 23 June]" (Torrey, 1843: 88).

Sphaeralcea ambigua A. Gray
"FExCal, 1849. Malvastrum Munroanum ?" (NY-Torrey!).

Sphaeralcea coccinea (Nutt.) Rydb. includes *Sida coccinea* and *Malvastrum coccineum*

Sphaeralcea emoryi Torr. in A. Gray
"FExCal, 1849. Malvastrum Munroanum" (NY-Torrey!). This specimen is mounted on the same sheet with *S. ambigua* noted above.

Sphaeralcea grossulariifolia subsp. *pedata* (Torr.) Kearney includes *S. pedata* Torr. in A. Gray

Sphaeralcea lindheimeri A. Gray
"Central California (*Frémont*)" (Brewer et al., 1876: 86).

Sphaeralcea pedata **Torr.** in A. Gray, Mem. Amer. Acad. Arts, n.s. 4: 23. 1849. (3rd) = *S. grossulariifolia* subsp. *pedata* (Torr.) Kearney
Protologue locality: "California. Frémont." Type: "Frémont's Expedition to California 411, 1845. Sphaeralcea new. (S. pedata call it). Moving Fork, *1st* Camp. Utah" (holotype NY-Torrey!: microfiche BRY!; isotype GH!; isotype US!). The NY holotype has the label information "Sphaeralcea pedata Torr. in Gray pl. Fendl. No. 98 (adnot). p. 23." It also bears a sheet of drawings by A. Mariolle about 1905. The sheet at GH has two specimens with slightly differing labels; one is marked "Herbarium Benthianum, 1854," and both lack the note Moving Fork, etc. Under discussion of *Sphaeralcea miniata*, A. Gray (1849: 23) notes: "S. pedata, Torr. ined., gathered in Frémont's third expedition, has 3–5-sected leaves; the divisions all cuneiform, 3-lobed and incised." "Moving Fork" has not been identified, but probably is a tributary of the White River in western Colorado where Frémont and party traveled from 4 to 11 September 1845. Frémont number 411 is also a syntype of *Malvastrum coccineum* var. *elatum* E. G. Baker (q.v.).

Spiraea ariaefolia var. *discolor* Pursh
This plant is cited in Torrey and Frémont (Frémont, 1845) from "upper waters of the Platte." It is regarded today within the genus *Holodiscus*.

Spiranthes cernua ≡ *S. cernua* (L.) Rich.
"Sweet Water river. Aug. 7 [1842. Adjacent to South Pass, Frémont County, Wyoming]" (Torrey, 1843: 93).

Spiranthes romanzoffiana Cham.
"Frémont's 2nd Expedn. 610, 1843. Frémont" (NY-Torrey!).

Spirolobium odoratum **Torr.** in Frém., Rep. Exped. Rocky Mts. 260. 1845. (2nd) ≡ *Prosopis odorata* (Torr. in Frém.) Torr. & Frém. in Frém. emend. Welsh, *P. pubescens* Benth.
Protologue locality: "The caravans sometimes continue below, to the end of the river, from which there is a very long *journada* of perhaps sixty miles, without water. Here a singular and new species of acacia, with spiral pods or seed vessels, made its first appearance; becoming henceforward, for a considerable distance a characteristic tree. It was here comparatively large, being about 20 feet in height, with a full and spreading top, the lower branches declining towards the ground. It afterwards occurred of smaller size, frequent in groves, and very fragrant. It has been called by Dr. Torrey *spirolobium odoratum*." Type: "Frémont's 2nd Exped." (holotype NY-Torrey!: microfiche BRY!; GH!, two sheets; MO!). Other writing on the sheet is illegible. Only that portion of the type collection in fruit, i.e., the spiral pods, serve as type of this entity (Frémont, 1845: 260, 264).
Frémont mixed two species of *Prosopis* in his collection of "acacia": *P. glandulosa* Torr., the honey mesquite, which has long compressed pods; and another, the screwbean,

which has tight spirally twisted pods. The mixed material formed the basis of *Prosopis odorata* Torr. & Frém., but not of *Spirolobium odoratum*, whose identity is adequately characterized in the Frémont narrative on page 260. The name *P. odoratum* has been relegated to synonymy, because the flowering material belonged to the honey mesquite and the fruiting portion to the screwbean. Torrey belatedly recognized the mixed nature of the collection (see citation of *Prosopis odorata*). It is certain, however, from the description of the plant and of the pods, that Frémont clearly had the screwbean mesquite in mind. The honey mesquite seldom grows to the proportions described by Frémont. It is evident, however, that both Frémont and Torrey had in mind the screwbean mesquite when they used the name "*spirolobium odoratum*." A case can be made for recognition of the place of publication of the epithet being page 260 of the 1845 report instead of page 313. The plant is adequately described and characterized, and the application of the name is unequivocal. In spite of discordant type materials ultimately being used by Torrey to base the combination *Prosopis odorata*, the *Code* allows selection of a portion of the discordant materials as type in some instances at least. Certainly, *Spirolobium odoratum* Torr. in Frém., has priority over *Prosopis pubescens* Benth. *Prosopis odorata* Torr. & Frém. in Frém. can be looked upon as an inadvertant new combination of *Spirolobium odoratum* Torr. in Frém., although simultaneously published. The correct designation for the species is *Prosopis odorata* (Torr. in Frém.) Torr. & Frém. in Frém. emend. Welsh.

Spirostachys occidentalis (S. Wats.) S. Wats. Syn: *Halostachys occidentalis* S. Wats. ≡ *Allenrolfea occidentalis* (S. Wats.) Kuntze q.v.

"760 Frémont" (Watson, 1874: 126). "FExCal, 1843–44. Eastern shore of Great Salt Lake, Frémont 760, 1843 [Weber or Box Elder Cos., Utah]" (NY-Torrey!).

***Spraguea* Torr.**, Smiths. Contr. Gen. 6(2): 4. 1853. (3rd)

Type species: ***Spraguea umbellata* Torr.** ≡ *Calyptridium umbellatum* (Torr.) Greene

Protologue locality: "Forks of the Zozah [Noyah?] river, in the foothills of the Sierra Nevada of Northern California, in flower and fruit, May 22 [1846. at Lassen's, near Vina, Tehama County, California]. Other specimens not ticketed were in the collection, perhaps taken on the same ground a little earlier in the season." Type: "Frémont's Expedition to California 466, 1846. n. gen. Forks of the Nozah River, in Foothills of Sierras" (holotype NY-Torrey!: microfiche BRY!; isotype GH!). There is a sheet of drawings for this species at NY also. The drawings are labeled "Herb. Torr. N. Gen. Portulacaceae." "FExCal, 1845–7. 1846. Portulac. New genus. Spraguea umbellata, *Torr.*" (isotype NY-Torrey!). "Spraguea umbellata Torr. Pl. Frémont. California. Frémont" (isotype NY-Sartwell!). "FExCal, 1845–47. Spraguea umbellata Torr. Ex. Torr. original stock. ex herb. George Thurber" (GH-Thurber!); this is apparently also an isotype of the species.

Stachys albens A. Gray

"FExCal, 1845–7. 1846. Stachys albens Gray" (NY-Torrey!).

Stachys aspera = *S. palustris* L.

"Forks of the platte. July 2 [1842. Lincoln County, Nebraska]" (Torrey, 1843: 89). "Stachys aspera. Frémont's 1st Journey" (NY-Torrey!).

Stachys palustris L. includes *S. aspera*

Stanleya integrifolia = *S. pinnata* (Pursh) Britt. pro parte

Stanleya integrifolia James
"Frémont 423, 1845. Bent's Fort [Otero County], Colorado. Large root perennial throwing up several stems. Stanleya" (NY-Torrey!; GH!). The party stayed at Bent's Fort from 2 to 16 August 1845. "Frémont's Expedition, 1845–7[1845]" (GH!). "Frémont's 2nd Expedn." (NY-Torrey!). The material called *S. integrifolia* by Frémont (1845: 265) in the Mohave Desert is likely *S. pinnata.*

Stanleya pinnata (Pursh) Britt. includes *S. integrifolia* pro parte
"FExCal, 15, 1845, Frémont. Root perennial" (NY-Torrey!).

Stellaria longipes Goldie
"Frémont's 2nd Expedn. S. longipes, Goldie" (NY-Torrey!).

Stenosiphon linifolius (Nutt.) Heynh. includes *S. virgatum*

Stenosiphon virgatum = *S. linifolius* (Nutt.) Heynh.
This species was cited by Torrey and Frémont (Frémont, 1845).

Stephanomeria paniculata Nutt.
"FExCal, 1845–7. x. 1846.. S. paniculata. Nutt. var. (S. virgata. Benth.)" (GH!).

Stephanomeria runcinata ≡ *S. runcinata* Nutt.
"Upper Platte [1842]" (Torrey, 1843: 87). "Plains of the Platte at the base of the Rocky Mountains, *Dr. James! Lieut. Frémont!*" (Torrey & Gray, 1843: 472). "Stephanomeria runcinata *Nutt.* Torr. & Gray, Flora, N. Amer. Upper Platte, near Rky Mts. *Frémont*" (NY!). The sheet now bears a cutout from another herbarium sheet, with three mounted fragments.

Stipa hymenoides Trin. = Indian ricegrass
This is probably the source of the grass seed noted by Carvalho (1857: 168).

Streptanthus carinatus Wright?
"FExCal, 1849. Streptanthus" (NY-Torrey!). If the identification is correct (as so annotated by T. J. Crovello in 1975), the plant should have been taken in New Mexico. It is mounted on a sheet with a sprig of *Thelypodiopsis sagittata* (Nutt.) Schulz, taken by Capt. Stansbury at Salt Lake (in 1850).

Streptanthus cordatus Nutt. in Torr. & A. Gray
"We have specimens of this plant collected in California by Colonel Frémont" (Torrey, 1857: 65).

Streptopus amplexifolius (L.) DC.
"FExCal, No. 91. 1845" (NY-Torrey!).

Strombocarpa ≡ *Prosopis pubescens* Benth.

***Strophiolirion californicum* Torr.**, Pacif. Railr. Rep. 4: 149. 1857. (3rd) ≡ *Dichelostemma californicum* (Torr.) Wood

Protologue locality: "In rocky places, Knight's Ferry, Stanislaus River, May, (in flower and fruit) [Dr. J. M. Bigelow]; also at Sonora, Mokelumne Hill; Valley of the Sacramento, Colonel Frémont, Mr. Rich, and Dr. Stillman." Type: "California. [1845] Frémont? Stropholirion Californicum, Torr." (syntype NY-Torrey!). The sheet has sketches of floral parts in an attached envelope; at least part of the drawings are attributed to the Stillman collection.

Stylomecon heterophylla (Benth.) G. Taylor

"Frémont's R. Road Expedn. 1853–54. Meconopsis" (NY-Torrey!).

***Styrax californica* Torr.**, Smithsonian Contr. Knowl., 6(2): 4. 1853. (3rd) ≡ *S. officinalis* L. var. *californica* (Torr.) Rehder

Type locality: "Foot-hills, from Calaveras County, to the Upper Sacramento, first collected by Frémont" (Torrey, 1853; Brewer et al., 1876: 470). Type: "FExCal, 1845–7[1846]. Styrax californicum, *Torr.* From small volume of collection of Frémont's 3rd Expedition in California. Upper Sacramento" (holotype NY-Torrey!: microfiche BRY!); "Ex herb. J. Torrey. Coll. Frémont. Styrax californicum Torr. & Gr. Fl. N. Amer." (isotype GH!). The holotype sheet has remnants of a relaxed flower and a fragment envelope with floral parts. "Upper Sacramento River, collected by Frémont" (Abrams, 1951: 346).

Suaeda calceoliformis (Hook.) Moq. includes *S. depressa* var. *erecta*

***Suaeda depressa* S. Wats.** var. ***erecta* S. Wats.**, Proc. Amer. Acad. Arts 9: 90. 1874. (1st) = *S. calceoliformis* (Hook.) Moq.

Protologue locality: "From the Saskatchewan to Central Colorado and Northern Nevada; Kern County, Southern California (Blake)." Type: "Frémont's 1st Expedition, July 1842. Suaeda maritima" (syntype NY-Torrey!). "FExRM, 1842. Suaeda maritima" (syntype ? GH!).

Suaeda fruticosa Forsk.

"This is 522 Frémont from the Sweetwater in central Wyoming," (Watson, 1871: 285).

Sueda [Suaeda] maritima = *S. calceoliformis* (Hook.) Moq. pro parte

"North fork of the Platte. Sept. 4 [1842. West of Scotts Bluff, Scotts Bluff County, Nebraska]" (Torrey, 1843: 91). "Sueda maritima. Frémont's 1st Exp." (MO!).

***Suaeda torreyana* S. Wats.**, Proc. Amer. Acad. Arts 9: 88. 1874. (1st)

Protologue locality: "In alkaline soils from the North Fork of the Platte (Fremont) to Northern Nevada, and south to Northern Mexico and Southern California." Syntypes: "Suaeda fruticosa Moquin, Torr.? Perhaps only an annual! Frémont's 1st Expedition, July 1842" and "Suaeda linearis Torr.? Chenopodina linearis. Seed horizontal & vertical. Stam. 5. Styles 4. N. Fork of the Platte near the Sweetwater. Fremont's 2nd Expedn. Aug. 8,

1843 [Carbon County, Wyoming]. 622" (NY-Torrey!). "622 Fremont" (Watson, 1874: 88).

Swertia perennis β obtusa = *S. perennis* L.
"From Laramie River to the Big Buttes [1842]" (Torrey, 1843: 90). "Swertia perennis Hook. Fl. Bor.-Am. Frémont's 1st Exp. Aug. 20–31, 1842" (NY-Torrey!).

Swertia radiata (Kellogg) Kuntze includes *Frasera speciosa*
"FExCal, 1843–4. 583. 1844. Frasera. 'St. Vrain's Fork [Battle Creek, Carbon County, Wyoming].—& on all the mountain streams till we entered the Park [North Park, Colorado], were [where] it disappeared. June. The Snake Indians use the root in wounds. Frém." (two sheets NY-Torrey!). Frémont was on St. Vrain's Fork on 12 June 1844.

Symphoricarpos occidentalis ≡ *S. occidentalis* Hook.
"North fork of the Platte. July 10–Aug. 31 [1842]" (Torrey, 1843: 86). "Ex herb. J. Torrey. Symphoric. occidentalis. Torr. & Gr. Fl. N. Amer. Frémont's 1st Exp." (GH!). "Frémont's 2nd Expedn., 402, 1843" (NY-Torrey!). "Symphoricarpus occidentalis. Frémont's 3d Expedit. No. [illegible]. 1845" (MO!).

Symphoricarpos oreophilus A. Gray includes *S. vulgaris*
"Frémont's 2nd Expedn. 603, 1843 & 212, 1844" (NY-Torrey!).

Symphoricarpos vulgaris = *Symphoricarpos oreophilus* A. Gray
"Defiles of the Wind River mountains. August 13–14 [1842. Sublette County, Wyoming]" (Torrey, 1843: 86).

***Syntrichopappus fremontii* A. Gray** in Torr., Pacif. Railr. Rep. 4: 106. 1857. (5th)
Type species: *Syntrichopappus fremontii* A. Gray in Torr.
Protologue locality: "Gathered by Colonel Frémont (a single specimen) in his journey across the continent in 1853–4, probably in the spring of 1854, and somewhere between the Rocky Mountains and the Sierra Nevada." Type: "Received from Col. Frémont Aug. 12, 1854. Collected in spring of that year in his journey across the continent. The only specimen he brought home" (isotype NY-Torrey!: microfiche BRY!). Evidently he also picked up several other species on that expedition (see Chapter VIII). "In the desert region of the Southeastern borders of the State [California] and in S. Nevada and Utah (*Frémont*)" (Brewer et al., 1876: 395). The fragments sent by Torrey to Asa Gray (GH!) serve as holotype. The fragments are accompanied by diagnostic sketches of flowers and floral parts, which appear to have been drawn by Torrey, on a small sheet of paper. The paper includes the designation 1854 and "Frémont's last (R. R.) Journey." The fragment envelope and drawing of the Frémont material is mounted on a sheet with others taken by Palmer, Bishop, Smith, Newberry, Parry, and Cooper.

Talinum parviflorum ≡ *T. parviflorum* Nutt. in Torr. & A. Gray
"Little Blue river of the Kansas. June 26 [1842]" (Torrey, 1843: 84). The provenance cited by Torrey requires explanation. The specimen (see next) is from the Platte Ridge, taken on the traverse from the head of the Little Blue to the Platte, Kearney County,

Nebraska. "Talinum parviflorum, *Nutt.* Frémont's 1st Ex., Platte Ridge, June 26" (NY-Torrey!).

Taxodium = *Sequoia sempervirens* (D. Don) Endl.
Frémont (1848: 36). John Charles was awed by the size of these trees, about which he writes eloquently, especially on the third expedition.

Taxus brevifolia Nutt.
"Taxus brevifolia. Frémont's 2nd Exped. 1843–44" (NY-Torrey!).

Tetradymia canescens DC. includes *T. inermis* Nutt.
"Sweet Water river, from its mouth to the highest parts of the Wind River mountains [1842]" (Torrey, 1843: 88). "Wind River Chain, alt. 7000 feet. Frémont" and "Tetradymia inermis. Nutt. Hills, upper Platte near Deer Creek, Aug. 27 [1842]. Lieut. Frémont" (same sheet GH!). Deer Creek enters the North Platte near Glenrock, Converse County, Wyoming. "Also east of the Rocky Mountains on hills of the upper part of the North Fork of the Platte, near Deer Creek; and on the Wind River Chain at the height of 7000 feet, *Lieut. Frémont!*" (Torrey & Gray, 1843: 447).

Teucrium canadense ≡ *T. canadense* L.
"On the Platte [1842]" (Torrey, 1843: 89).

Thalictrum cornuti = *T. dasycarpum* Fisch. & Ave.-Lall.
"Platte [1842]" (Torrey, 1843: 83). "22d June. Sur la petite Riv. ou l'on dine. Frémont's 1st Exp. 1842" (NY-Torrey!).

***Thalictrum megacarpum* Torr. ex Rydb.**, Fl. Rocky Mts. 290. 1917. (1st) = *T. occidentale* A. Gray
Protologue locality: "Upper Platte. August 26–31 [1842]" (Torrey, 1843: 83). Type: "Thalictrum megacarpum T&Gr. n. sp. Frémont's 1st Exp. Aug. 26–31. 1842 [Natrona, Converse, Platte, and Goshen counties, Wyoming]" (holotype NY-Torrey!: microfiche BRY!).

Thalictrum occidentale A. Gray includes *T. megacarpum* Torr. ex Rydb.
"North Fork of the Platte, 571, 1844. Frémont's 2nd Expedn." (NY-Torrey!).

***Thamnosma* Torr. & Frém.** in Frém., Rep. Exped. Rocky Mts. 313. 1845. (2nd)
Type species: ***Thamnosma montana* Torr. & Frém.** in Frém.
Protologue locality: "It grows in the passes of the mountains, and on the Virgen river in Northern California. The greater part of it was already in fruit in the month of May." Type: "Frémont's 2nd Expedn. 405, 1844. May 2, 1844"; also "Mohave River" (holotype NY-Torrey!: microfiche BRY!). "Southern Nevada, (Frémont;)" (Watson, 1871: 418). There are two stems mounted on the type sheet. One of them is marked "Mohave River." The camp of 2 May 1844 was at a spring near present Blue Diamond, Clark County, Nevada.

Thelesperma filifolium (Hook.) A. Gray
"FExCal, 1843–4. Thelesperma filifolium" (NY-Torrey!). The specimen evidently belongs to var. *intermedium* (Rydb.) Shinners.

Thelesperma megapotamicum (Spreng.) Kuntze includes *Cosmidium gracile*

Thelypodiopsis elegans (Jones) Rydberg
"Frémont's 2nd Expedn." (NY-Torrey!). This likely came from the Uinta Basin, Utah, during the first week of June 1844.

Thelypodium integrifolium (Nutt.) Endl. includes *Pachypodium integrifolium*

Thermopsis macrophylla Hook. & Arn.
"Thermopsis fabacea. FExCal, 1845–7. 153. 1846" (GH!).

Thermopsis montana ≡ *T. montana* Nutt. in Torr. & A. Gray
"Sweet Water river. Aug. 5 [1842. Southeast of Atlantic City, Frémont County, Wyoming]" (Torrey, 1843: 85). "Thermopsis montana, Nutt. Frémont's 1st Expedn. 1842, Aug. 5. river bottoms Camp 5–6" (NY-Torrey!). "Frémont's 2nd Expedn." (NY-Torrey!). "Thermopsis. Frémont's 2nd Expedn. Waters of the Spanish Fork [Utah County, Utah], Uinta, May 27–31. 504, 1844" (NY-Torrey!). Frémont moved through the counties of Utah, Wasatch, and Duchesne, Utah, during the period outlined. The species was also reported by Frémont (1845: 285) from the mountains of Colorado.

Thlaspi montanum L.
"561. 1844. Headwaters of the Platte. New [North] Park [Jackson County, Colorado, 16–17 June 1844]. Frémont's 2nd Expedn." (NY-Torrey!) and "FExCal, 1845–7. 417. 1846. Tributaries of the Upper Sacramento, in pine forests" (NY-Torrey!; GH!; GH-Thurber!; MO!).

Thuya gigantea = *Thuja plicata* or *Calocedrus decurrens*
Frémont (1848: 31; 1887: 440).

Thysanocarpus curvipes Hook.
"43, 1844. March 5 [Placer (?) County, California], first appearance; vallies among undulating hills on the river (American Fork of Sacramento River). Frémont's 2nd Exp." (NY-Torrey!). This is mounted on a sheet with "69, 1843. 'Camp on Buck creek (of the Kansas) Creek bottom—very rich.'" The solitary plant associated with that provenance appears to be a *Thysanocarpus*, a genus not known from Kansas. The provenance is likely in error. "FExCal, 1846. 306. Thysanocarpus" (NY-Torrey!; GH!) and "FExCal, 1846. Thysanocarpus—mixed with T. radicans. J. T." (NY-Torrey!). "Frémont's 2d Exped." (GH!).

Thysanocarpus radians Benth.
"FExCal, 1845–7. Qq. 1846. Dr. Gray. Thysanocarpus radians Benth. pl. Hartw. 1651" (NY-Torrey!). "FExCal, 1845–7. Qq. 1846. Thysanocarpus" (GH!; MO!). The Frémont

plant is mounted on a sheet with a collection by Brewer and one by Hartweg (no. 1651), which is an isotype of the species.

Tidestromia lanuginosa (Nutt.) Standley includes *Alternanthera lanuginosa*

Tobacco root = *Valeriana edulis* Nutt. ex Torr. & A. Gray

***Townsendia fremontii* Torr. & A. Gray ex A. Gray**, Boston J. Nat. Hist. 5: 106. 1845. = *T. incana* Nutt.

Protologue locality: "Among the plants of the Asteroid tribe, I notice a new species of a very marked and characteristic genus of the Rocky Mountain Region, viz. Townsendia;—a genus founded by Hooker upon a single species, but to which Nuttall has since added four more, and still others will doubtless reward the exertions of future explorers. The present addition (Townsendia Frémontii, *Torr. & Gray, ined.*) resembles T. incana, *Nutt.* but has longer and narrower leaves, and larger heads even than T. sericea, *Hook.* The bristles of the pappus are also somewhat scariously fringed toward the base, so as to become almost squamellate." Type: "FExCal, 1843–4. No. 548. 1844 [ca. 3 June, Uintah County, Utah]. Townsendia Frémontii, Gray, in Bost. Jour. Nat. hist. 5. p. 2." (holotype NY-Torrey!). Beaman (1957: 123), monographer of *Townsendia*, notes: "Original material: apparently collected in Wyoming by Frémont on his first expedition in 1842 (GH)," but does not indicate that he has seen the material. The entire citation by Gray is reproduced above; the description, though meager, is sufficient to characterize the plant, which is, as Gray suspected, a phase of the widespread *T. incana* Nutt.

Townsendia grandiflora Nutt.

"FExCal, 1843–4. Townsendia grandiflora" (NY-Torrey!). The Frémont specimen is mounted on a sheet with one by Dr. G. W. Hulse and an isotype of the species by Thomas Nuttall.

Toxicodendron diversilobum (Torr. & A. Gray) Greene

"FExCal, 1845–7. 298. 1846. Rhus diversiloba" (NY-Torrey!; GH!). The specimen at GH is mounted with collections by T. J. Howell, Dr. Coulter, and L. J. Xantus de Vesey. The Frémont material is a tiny fragment.

Toxicodendron rydbergii (Small) Greene

"178, 1843. Frémont's 2nd Expedn." (NY-Torrey!).

Tradescantia occidentalis (Britt.) Smythe includes *T. virginica*

"FExRM, 1843 [1842]" (NY-Torrey!). The correct date for this sheet is likely 1842, not 1843. The locality information is hand written, but is in the form of the 1842 label information, not that of 1843. The mounting sheet has been cut apart; its other half is cited below and has the correct year of collection.

Tradescantia virginica = *T. occidentalis* (Britt.) Smyth

"Kansas and Platte [1842]" (Torrey, 1843: 94). "FExRM, 1842. Tradescantia Virginica var. angustifolia" (NY-Torrey!).

Trichoptilium incisum (A. Gray) A. Gray
"Gravelly hills, of the Colorado desert region near Fort Yuma, Mohave, &c., *Frémont*" (Brewer et al., 1876: 395). "Int. California. Frémont. 1849" (GH!). The Frémont collection is in the upper left corner of the sheet, which bears also collections by Palmer, Schott, Cooper, Parry, and Thurber. The last is the holotype of *Psathyrotes incisa* A. Gray.

Trichostema lanatum Benth.
"FExCal, 1846. Trichostema lanatum, *Benth.* Coast Range of mountains" (NY-Torrey!).

Trichostema lanceolatum Benth.
"FExCal, 1845–7. Hhhh. 1846. Trichostema lanceolatum, *Benth.*" (GH!; NY-Torrey!).

Trifolium depauperatum Desv.
"FExCal, 1843–4 [crossed out], 235. Morin's fork of the Uinta, 1845. Trifolium" (NY-Torrey!, MO!). The label data is contradictory. The species is known only from California and South America, and the locality information is thus superfluous, even though Frémont and party were along the Uinta River late in 1845. The specimen is in full flower and was taken in spring or summer.

Trifolium longipes Nutt. var. *longipes*
"Trifolium longipes, *Nutt.* Frémont's 2nd Expedn. 587, 1844" (NY-Torrey!).

Trifolium macraei Hook. & Arn.
"Frémont. 3rd Exped. High prairies, Lassen's [Tehama County, California], April 16, 266. 1846" (NY-Torrey!).

Trifolium macrocephalum (Pursh) Poir.
"FExCal, 1845–7. Fff, 1846. Dr. Gray. Trifolium megacephalum" (NY-Torrey!; GH!; MO!) and "FExRM, 1846 [label modified from 1842 expedition]. Trifolium megacephalum" (NY-Crooke!). The NY Crooke specimen is probably a duplicate of the Fff, 1846 sheet.

Trifolium microcephalum Pursh
"FExCal, 1843–4. 426. 1846. Trifolium microcephalum" (NY-Torrey!; MO!).

Trifolium tridentatum Lindley
"Frémont's 2nd Expedn." and "FExCal, 1843–4. Ddd 1846. Trifolium fimbriatum. 88" (both NY-Torrey!; Ddd also MO!). A plant with a confusing label is on this sheet also. It is mounted on a partial sheet cut from a larger one. The information follows: "FExCal, 1843–4 [marked out]. 236 [probably 1846], Head of Ark. River in the R. Mts." (NY-Torrey!). Above the label is a penciled note by E. L. G. [Edward L. Greene?] as follows: "True tridentatum of Calif. and it cannot come from 'head of Ark. River.'"

Trifolium variegatum Nutt.
"FExCal, 443, 1846. Trifolium variegatum" (NY-Torrey!; MO!).

Trillium chloropetalum (Torr.) Howell
"Frémont's Expedition to California. Gggg. 1846. Trillium" and "FExCal, 1845–7. Yyyy 1846. Gray. Trillium" (both NY-Torrey!; Yyyy also **GH!**).

Tripterocalyx micrantha Torr. in Frém. includes *Abronia (Tripterocalyx) micrantha*
"FExCal, 1843–4. Abronia cycloptera. Near Pike's Peak. July 12 [Fountain Creek, Pueblo County, Colorado]" (NY-Torrey!).

Triteleia grandiflora Lindley includes *Brodiaea multiflora* Benth. (q.v.)
"Frémont's 2nd Expedn. Calavaras Creek [probably San Joaquin County, California], March 25–26, 79 & 41, 1844" (NY-Torrey!).

Triteliea laxa Benth.
"FExCal, 1843–4, Seubertia laxa Kth. {184, 260, 1846. Seubertia laxa, *Kth.* Prairies between Stanislaus & Mokelumnes, March 16–17, & Valley of the American Fork" (NY-Torrey!; 184 also MO!). The materials taken on 16–17 March 1846 probably came from San Joaquin County, the other from Sacramento County. "Triteliea laxa. Frémont's 2nd Expedn. Good soil, river bottom, Cosumne R. [Sacramento County, California], 24–25 March, 98, 1844. Frémont" (NY-Torrey!).

Tropidocarpum gracile Hook.
"FExCal, 203, 1846. Tropidocarpum—n. sp.? Sept. perfect?" (NY-Torrey!; GH!).

Troximon parviflorum Nutt. = *Agoseris glauca* (Pursh) Raf.
"Sweet Water river, near the mountains [1842]" (Torrey, 1843: 88). "Frémont's 1st Expedn. 1842. Troximon parviflorum, *Nutt.* Torr. & Gray, Flora, N. Amer. July 31 [one day's journey east of Independence Rock, Natrona County, Wyoming], near Rocky Mts. Frémont" (NY-Torrey!). "Plains of the Platte to the Rocky Mountains, *Nuttall! Lieut. Frémont!*" (Torrey & Gray, 1843: 490).

Tsuga heterophylla (Raf.) Sargent = hemlock spruce

Tsuga mertensiana (Bong.) Carr. = hemlock spruce

Ulmus fulva = *U. rubra* Muhl.
"Lower Platte [1842]" (Torrey, 1843: 93).

Ulmus rubra Muhl. includes *U. fulva*

Umbellularia californica (Hook. & Arn.) Nutt.
"FExCal, 1845–7. Oreodaphne. Torrey 1850" (NY-Torrey!). "FExCal, 1845–7. Uuuu, 1846" (GH!).

Uniola spicata ≡ *Distichlis spicata* (L.) Greene
Frémont (1845: 149) did not discern that this was the plant referred to by him as "herbe salee" or salt grass, possibly because the plants bore pistillate inflorescences. Certainly he recognized salt grass as it grew in saline, moist sites over much of his route from Nebraska westward on the second expedition in 1843–44.

Vaccinium myrtilloides = *V. scoparium* Leiberg
"Wind River mountains, in the vicinity of perpetual snow. Aug. 15 [1842. Sublette County, Wyoming]" (Torrey, 1843: 88). "Vaccinium Myrtillus L. β microphyllum Hook. Wind R. Mts. Frémont. Near the snow line. Aug. 15. Torr. & Gray, Fl. N. Amer." (GH!).

Vaccinium myrtillus L. = *V. scoparium* Leiberg

Vaccinium scoparium Leiberg includes *V. myrtillus* and (?) *V. uliginosum*

Vaccinium uliginosum = *V. scoparium* Leiberg
"Wind River mountains, in the vicinity of perpetual snow. Aug. 15 [1842. Sublette County, Wyoming]" (Torrey, 1843: 88).

Valeriana edulis Nutt. in Torr. & A. Gray
"Valeriana edulis, *Nutt., Torr. & Gr. fl. 2. p. 48.* 'Tobacco Root or Black Root.' Frémont's Catalogue. Frémont's 2nd Expedn. (Banks of Utah Lake, most of the Rocky Mountains)" (NY-Torrey!). Frémont was at Utah Lake, Utah County, Utah, on 24–26 May 1844. Mounted with the *Valeriana* specimens is a single stem of *Plectritis macrocera* (q.v.). Frémont (1845) notes this species of *Valeriana* on several occasions.

Verbena bipinnatifida Nutt. var. *latilobata* Perry
"FExCal, 1845–7. Verbena Aubletia, Jacq." (NY-Torrey!). "Verbena. Prairie. Frémont's 3d Exped. 147. 19 July 1845" (MO!).

Verbena bracteata ≡ *V. bracteata* Lag. & Rodr.
"N. fork of the Platte. July 12 [1842. Near Greeley, Weld County, Colorado]" (Torrey, 1843: 89). "Frémont 1842, 12 July. Evening camp. Verbena bracteata" (NY-Torrey!).

Verbena canadensis (L.) Britt.
"FExCal, 1849. Verbena Drummondii" (NY-Columbia!).

Verbena hastata ≡ *V. hastata* L.
"N. fork of the Platte. July 12 [1842. Near Greeley, Weld County, Colorado]" (Torrey, 1843: 89).

Verbena stricta ≡ *V. stricta* Vent.
"N. fork of the Platte. July 12 [1842. Near Greeley, Weld County, Colorado]" (Torrey, 1843: 89). "Verbena stricta. North Fork of the Platte" (NY-Torrey!).

Vernonia fasciculata ≡ *V. fasciculata* Michx.
"On the Platte [1842]" (Torrey, 1843: 86). "Platte. Frémont. 1842. Vernonia fasciculata, *Michx.* (fol. latioribus)" (NY-Torrey!). The sheet was annotated as belonging to subsp. *corymbosa* (Schwein.) Jones by S. B. Jones in 1971.

Veronica alpina β = *V. wormskjoldii* R. & S.
"Alpine region of the Wind River mountains [1842. 13–15 August. Sublette County, Wyoming]" (Torrey, 1843: 88). "Frémont's 1st Exped. On Aug 14 & 15, 1842. Veronica alpina ? 'Frémont was on the Wind River mts, Wyoming, on Aug. 15, ascending Frémont

Peak'"' [note's author unknown]. (NY-Torrey!). "V. Wormskjoldii R. & S." is written to the right of the label.

Veronica wormskjoldii R. & S. includes *V. alpina β*

Vesicaria didymocarpa = *Physaria acutifolia* Rydb.
"North fork of the Platte, above the Red Buttes [1842]" (Torrey, 1843: 83). "Frémont's 1st Expedn. 30 June 1842" (NY-Torrey!).

Vicia americana Muhl. ex Willd.
"FExCal, 238, 257, 1846. Vicia" and "FExCal, 238, 1846[5?], near Grand River [Colorado]. Vicia" (both NY-Columbia!). Frémont crossed the drainage of the Grand [Colorado] River in early September 1845.

Vicia americana Muhl. ex Willd. var. *minor* Hook. includes *Lathyrus linearis*
"FExRM, 1842. Lathyrus linearis. Upper Platte" (NY-Torrey!).

Viola adunca J. E. Sm. ex Rees
"Viola longipes Nutt. Frémont's 2nd Expedn." and "FExCal, Uu 1846" (both NY-Torrey!).

Viola chrysantha = *V. douglasii* Steud.
Frémont (1845: 19).

Viola douglasii Steud. includes *V. chrysantha*

Viola nuttallii Pursh
"FExCal, April 28, 373, 1846. Sources of the Sacramento, Sierra Nevada" (NY-Torrey!; MO!). On 28 April 1846 Frémont and party were at the headwaters of Cow Creek, east of Redding, Shasta County, California. The specimen bears two annotations, one on a Syn. Fl. N. Amer. label "Probably V. praemorsa," in Gray's hand, and the other "Viola probably nearest to Bakeri Greene or some western form of V. Nuttallii" by J. Clausen in 1936.

Viola purpurea Kellogg
"V. nuttallii? Platte River. 1845. No. 132. Frémont's 3rd Exped." (NY-Torrey!). The sheet was annotated by E. Brainerd as *V. purpurea* in 1917. A notation written adjacent to the specimen notes "probably Wyoming; but Frémont's 3rd expedition did not follow the Platte River." The author of the note is unknown, but the assertion is correct. Either the Platte locality is wrong or the year and number of the expedition are incorrect.

Vitis riparia ≡ *V. riparia* Michx.
"Grand island of the Platte. Sept. 19 [1842. Probably Hall County, Nebraska]" (Torrey, 1843: 84). "168, 1845. Frémont's 3rd Exped. Branch of Smoky Hill Fork, July 18" (NY-Torrey!).

White cedar = ? *Thuja* sp.

Woodsia obtusa (Spreng.) Torr. includes *Hypopeltis obtusa*

Wyethia bolanderi (A. Gray) W. A. Weber includes *Balsamorhiza bolanderi* A. Gray

Wyethia helenioides DC.
"And with the fruitful head three inches in diameter, occurs in the Californian collections made by Frémont in 1846" (Gray, 1849: 82). "FExCal, 1845–7. 3. 1846. Wyethia (Alarconia) helenioides" (GH!; NY-Torrey!).

Wyethia scabra Hook. includes *Helianthella uniflora*

Yampah = *Perideridia*
This is the "*anethum graveolens*" of Frémont's (1845: 124) report.

Yerba buena = *Satureja douglasii* (Benth.) Briq.
Frémont (1845: 249).

Yucca angustifolia = *Y. glauca* Nutt.
"Laramie river. July 14 [1842. North of Cheyenne, Laramie County, Wyoming]" (Torrey, 1843: 93). "FExCal, 438, 1845. Divide between Smoky Hill Fork and Arkansas River [Colorado]. Yucca angustifolia. Young plant" (NY-Torrey!). The specimen consists of a rosette and caudex.

Yucca brevifolia Engelm. in S. Wats. includes *Y. draconis* var. *arborescens* Torr. = Joshua tree
"FExCal, no. 271. 1844. Yucca. 'Forming a forest, on a sandy plain on the eastern side of the Pass. April 15 [Kern County, California]'" (NY-Torrey!). The epithet *brevifolia*, adequately characterizing the species, is a new name for Torrey's var. *arborescens*. Certainly Torrey had the Frémont material from the Mohave long prior to publication of *Yucca draconis* var. *arborescens* in the *Pacific Railroad Report* of 1857. That he did not include it as part of the basis of the variety is indicated by the brief description wherein the leaves are described as being "about 3½ inches long," as in the extant Bigelow collection at NY-Torrey, which is much shorter than the two leaves taken by Frémont. Preuss (Gudde & Gudde 1958: 123) referred to this plant, the Joshua tree, as "Pisang."

Yucca draconis var. *arborescens* Torr. = *Y. brevifolia* Engelm. in S. Wats.

Yucca glauca Nutt. includes *Y. angustifolia*

Zigadenus fremontii (Torr.) S. Wats. includes *Anticlea fremontii* pro parte = (?) *Z. paniculata* (Nutt.) Wats.
"Collected by Frémont on the Uinta River, Utah [June 1844], and found from California to Washington Territory" (Watson, 1871: 343).

Zigadenus glaucus = ?
"Sweet Water river. Aug. [1842]" (Torrey, 1843: 93). This is likely *Z. paniculatus* (Nutt.) Wats.

Zygophyllum californicum = *Larrea divaricata* (DC.) Cov.
Frémont (1845: 257, 264).

Doubtful and Excluded Taxa and Unidentified Specimens

Besseya bullii (Eaton) Rydb.

"FExCal, 1843–4. Synthris" (NY!). The sheet is accompanied by an elaborate Latin description and citation of geographical distribution. The folded sheet bears diagnostic illustrations and notations. Mentioned in the geographical notes are both Illinois and Iowa. Frémont was not in either of those places or elsewhere within the known range of the species in 1843–44. Likely the specimen is by Geyer, or by some other collector, and is mislabeled.

Unidentified

"FExCal, 1843–4. 200, 1844. Artemisia 'pycnocephala' J. Carey" The label has the notation "no. J. T." above it. It is not an *Artemisia*. The specimen is vegetative, with several stems arising from a superficial caudex and taproot. The stems and juvenile leaves are covered with hairs.

APPENDIX II

FRÉMONT'S EPONYMY

Alectoria fremontii Tuckerman
Amphipappus fremontii Torr. & A. Gray in A. Gray
Anticlea fremontii Torr.
Aplopappus fremontii A. Gray
Asclepias fremontii Torr. ex A. Gray
Aster adscendens var. *fremontii* Torr. & A. Gray
Astragalus fremontii A. Gray ex Torr.
Berberis fremontii Torr.
Calliachris fremontii Torr. & A. Gray
Calycadenia fremontii A. Gray
Chaenactis fremontii A. Gray
Chenopodium fremontii S. Wats.
Clematis fremontii S. Wats.
Dichaeta fremontii Torr. ex A. Gray
Echinosperumum fremontii Torr. in A. Gray
Eriogonum fremontii Torr. ex Benth.
Eunanus fremontii Benth. in A. DC.
Fremontia Torr. in Frém.
Fremontia Torr.
Fremontiaceae J. G. Agardh, nom. illeg.
Fremontodendron Coville
Garrya fremontii Torr.
Geranium fremontii Torr.
Gentiana fremontii Torr. in Frém.
Hosackia argophylla var. *fremontii* A. Gray
Lepidium fremontii S. Wats.
Lesquerella fremontii Rollins & Shaw
Lycium fremontii S. Wats.
Machaeranthera fremontii Rydb.
Malvastrum fremontii Torr. ex A. Gray
Oenothera fremontii S. Wats.
Penstemon fremontii Torr. & A. Gray
Phacelia fremontii Torr. in Ives
Philadelphus fremontii Rydb.
Populus fremontii S. Wats.
Prunus fremontii S. Wats.
Senecio filifolius var. *fremontii* Torr. & A. Gray
Senecio fremontii Torr. & A. Gray
Smelowskia fremontii S. Wats.
Syntrichopappus fremontii A. Gray in Torr.
Townsendia fremontii A. Gray

APPENDIX III

TAXON SUMMARY BY FAMILY, GENUS, SPECIES, AND DEPOSITION

In the following list, families, genera, and species are arranged alphabetially under the seven divisions of vascular plants, with Frémont's two lichens listed at the end. Each expedition has its own column for information about plants collected on that expedition, with the final "unknown" column for plants of unknown expedition. The number in parentheses after the names of families indicates the number of species in the list. Abbreviations used in the list are as follows: numeral prior = expedition number; 0 = expedition unknown; N = NY; G = GH; M = MO; U = US; B = BRY; L = Literature; numeral following = number of specimens; no numeral following = 1; * prior, new genus; * following, new taxon with basionym resting on Frémont material; (*) included synonym, based on Frémont material.

EQUISETOPHYTA			
Equisetaceae (4)			
Equisetum arvense	1-L		
Equisetum hyemale			3-N
Equisetum laevigatum			3-N
Equisetum telmateia			3-N
LYCOPODIOPHYTA			
Selaginellaceae (2)			
Selaginella bigelovii		2-N	
Selaginella hansenii			3-N
POLYPODIOPHYTA			
Polypodiaceae (2)			
Pellaea mucronata		2-N	
Woodsia obtusa	1-L		
GNETOPHYTA			
Ephedraceae (1)			
Ephedra nevadensis		2-L	
PINOPHYTA			
Cupressaceae (6)			
Calocedrus decurrens *		2-N,L	
Juniperus communis	1-N	2-N	
Juniperus occidentalis			3-N,M
Juniperus scopulorum		2-N	

Juniperus virginiana	1-N					
Thuja gigantea			3-L			
Pinaceae (13)						
Abies concolor	1-L	2-N2,M	3-M2			
Abies lasiocarpa	1-N		3-N2,M			
Larix occidentalis		2-L				
Picea engelmannii			3-N2			
Pinus flexilis	1-L					
Pinus lambertii		2-L				
Pinus monophylla *		2-N,G3			5-G	
Pinus ponderosa	1-N	2-L				
Pinus quadrifolia						0-N
Pinus sabiniana(?)			3-L			
Pseudotsuga menziesii		2-G2				
Tsuga heterophylla		2-L				
Tsuga mertensiana		2-L				
Taxaceae (1)						
Taxus brevifolia		2-N				
Taxodiaceae (1)						
Sequoia sempervirens			3-N,G			
MAGNOLIOPHYTA						
Magnoliatae.-						
Acanthaceae (2)						
Beloperone californica				4-G		
Ruellia humilis			3-N			
Aceraceae (4)						
Acer glabrum		2-N				
Acer grandidentatum			3-N			
Acer negundo	1-N					
Acer negundo var. californica			3-N,G2,M			0-G
Aizoaceae (2)						
Mesembryanthemum crystallinum			3-N,G2,M,U			
Sesuvium verrucosum		2-N				
Amaranthaceae (2)						
Amaranthus arenicola			3-N,M			
Tidestromia lanuginosa			3-N,G			
Anacardiaceae (4)						
Rhus aromatica var. *trilobata*	1-L	2-N	3-N2,G2,B,M			
Rhus glabra		2-L				
Toxicodendron diversilobum			3-N,G			
Toxicodendron rydbergii		2-N				
Apiaceae (20)						
Berula erecta var. *incisum* *	1-N					

Cicuta maculata	1-L			
Cymopterus bulbosus		2-N		
Cymopterus longipes		2-N		
Daucus pusilla			3-N,G	
Heracleum lanatum	1-N			
Lomatium sp.			3-N	4-N
Lomatium dasycarpum ssp. *tomentosum*			3-N	
Lomatium dissectum		2-N	3-N,G	
Lomatium grayii		2-N		
Lomatium triternatum		2-N		
Lomatium utriculatum		2-N2	3-N2G	
Musineon tenuifolium	1-N			
Perideridia gairdneri	1-N,G		3-N	
Perideridia oregana (*)			3-N,G	
Polytaenia nuttallii	1-L			
Sanicula arctopoides			3-N,G	
Sanicula bipinnatifida		2-N	3-N2G	
Sanicula graveolens			3-N	
Sanicula tuberosa *		2-N	3-N,G	
Apocynaceae (2)				
Amsonia tomentosa *		2-N		
Apocynum cannabinum	1-L			
Aristolochiaceae (1)				
Asarum canadense			3-L	
Asclepiadaceae (9)				
Asclepias cryptoceras *		2-N		
Asclepias engelmanniana			3-N	
Asclepias eriocarpa (*)			3-N,G	
Asclepias speciosa	1-N	2-N2	3-N2,M	
Asclepias stenophylla	1-N			
Asclepias tuberosa	1-L	2-N		
Asclepias verticillata	1-L			
Asclepias viridiflora	1-N			
Asclepias viridis	1-N2			
Asteraceae (175)				
Achillea millefolium	1-L			
Achyrachaena mollis			3-N	
Agoseris aurantiaca	1-L			
Agoseris glauca	1-N	2-N	3-N,G	
Agoseris heterophylla		2-N	3-N3,G2,U	
Ambrosia deltoidea *				4-N,G

Ambrosia dumosa *		2-N		4-N,G	
Ambrosia tomentosa	1-G				
* *Amphipappus fremontii* *		2-N,G			
* *Anisocoma acaulis* *		2-N,G			
Antennaria microphylla		2-N			
Arnica fulgens	1-L				
Artemisia arbuscula					0-N
Artemisia biennis	1-N2				
Artemisia californica			3-N		
Artemisia campestris ssp. *caudata*	1-N2		3-N		
Artemisia cana	1-N		3-N,U2		
Artemisia filifolia	1-N,G		3-N,G,U		
Artemisia frigida	1-N	2-G	3-N,U		
Artemisia longiloba		2-N			
Artemisia ludoviciana	1-N3,G	2-N	3-U		
Artemisia nova		2-N			
Artemisia pedatifida		2-N			
Artemisia tridentata	1-N	2-N,G			
Aster chilensis	1-N3		3-N		
Aster commutatus		2-N			
Aster cordifolius	1-L				
Aster eatonii			3-N		
Aster elegans	1-L				
Aster ericoides	1-N		3-N,U		
Aster foliaceus	1-N				
Aster glaucodes	1-N	2-N			
Aster integrifolius	1-L				
Aster laevis	1-L		3-N3		
Aster novae-angliae	1-G		3-G		
Aster oblongifolius	1-N		3-N		
Aster occidentalis (*)	1-N3,G2	2-N2	3-N2		
Baeria chrysostoma			3-G2	4-G	
Baeria fremontii *			3-G2	4-N	
Baeria minor			3-N		
Bahia dissecta *			3-?		
Baileya multiradiata		2-L		4-N	
Baileya multiradiata var. *nudicaulis* *		2-N			
Balsamorhiza deltoidea var. *glabrescens*		2-L			
Balsamorhiza deltoidea		2-L			
Balsamorhiza hookeri		2-N			

Balsamorhiza macrophylla			3?-N			
Balsamorhiza sagittata	1-N	2-N				
Bidens connata	1-L					
Brickellia grandiflora	1-N					
Cacalia plantaginea	1-N					
* *Calliachris fremontii* *		2-N2,G?				
Calycadenia fremontii *			3-N3,G3,U			
Calycadenia multiglandulosa			3-N2,G2			
Calycadenia pauciflora *			3-N4,G2,U			
Calycadenia tenella			3-N			
Carduus leucographis	1-L					
Chaenactis douglasii		2-N				
Chaenactis fremontii *		2-N,G				
Chaenactis heterocarpha *			3-N3,G			
var. *tanacetifolia*						0-L
Chrysopsis villosa	1-N3	2-N3	3-N3,M			
Chrysothamnus nauseosus						
var. *glabratus*	1-N		3-G3,U			
Chrysothamnus viscidiflorus	1-N,G					
Cirsium altissimum	1-L					
Cirsium canescens		2-N				
Cirsium undulatum			3-N			
Conyza canadensis	1-L					
Coreopsis californica				4-N		
Coreopsis calliopsidea					5-N	
Coreopsis tinctoria	1-N		3-U			
Crepis modocensis		2-N				
Crepis occidentalis		2-N				
Crepis runcinata	1-N					
Encelia frutescens						0-L
Erigeron bellidiastrum	1-L					
Erigeron engelmannii		2-N				
Erigeron foliosus			3-N2			
Erigeron glabellus	1-N	2-N				
Erigeron glaucus			3-N2			
Erigeron peregrinus	1-N					
Erigeron pumilus						
ssp. *concinnoides*		2-N				
Erigeron simplex	1-N					
Erigeron speciosus						
var. *macranthus*	1-N2					
Erigeron strigosus	1-N		3-N,G,U			
Erigeron subtrinervis	1-N2		3-N			

Eriophyllum lanatum					
var. *achillaeoides*			3-N		
var. *grandiflorum* *			3-N		
Eupatorium maculatum	1-L				
Gaillardia aristata					0-L
Gaillardia pulchella		2-N2			
* *Geraea canescens* *		2-N		4-N	
Gnaphalium palustre	1-G2				
Gnaphalium uliginosum (*)	1-L				
Grindelia squarrosa					
var. *serrulata*	1-N,G				
var. *squarrosa*			3-N		
Gutierrezia sarothrae	1-N	2-N	3-N,G2		0-N
Haplopappus ciliatus			3-N,M		
Haplopappus fremontii *		2-N,G			
Haplopappus linearifolius		2-N			
Haplopappus spinulosus	1-N		3-G3		
Haplopappus venetus			3-N		
Helianthella uniflora	1-N2				
Helianthus maximiliani	1-N				
Helianthus nuttallii	1-N	2-N			
Helianthus petiolaris	1-N2	2-N	3-N,G		
Hemizonia luzulifolia			3-N,G		
Hemizonia pungens					
ssp. *laevis*			3-G		
ssp. *septentrionalis*			3-N		
Hemizonia ramosissima			3-N		
Holocarpha virgata			3-N,G,U		
* *Hymenoclea salsola* *		2-N2,M		4-N	
Hymenopappus filifolius					
var. *cinereus*		2-N			
Hymenopappus scabiosaeus					
var. *corymbosus*	1-N,G				
Hymenopappus tenuifolius		2-N			
Hymenoxys acaulis			3-N		
Hymenoxys grandiflora *	1-N				
Hymenoxys richardsonii		2-N	3-G2		
Hymenoxys torreyana (*)		2-N,G			
Iva axillaris	1-N	2-N			
Lactuca tatarica	1-L				
Layia fremontii *		2-N	3-N2		
Layia glandulosa		2-N,G	3-G2		
Layia platyglossa			3-N,G		

Liatris aspera	1-L				
Liatris lancifolia	1-N				
Liatris punctata	1-N,G	2-N	3-G2		
Liatris squarrosa	1-N				
Lygodesmia juncea	1-L		3-G,M		
Machaeranthera bigelovii	1?-N				
Machaeranthera canescens	1-L	2-N	3-G5		
var. *glabra* (*)		2-N			
Machaeranthera tanacetifolia	1-N		3-G2		
Machaeranthera sp.	1-L				
Melampodium cinereum			3-L		
* *Monoptilon bellidiforme* *		2-N,G			
* *Nicolletia occidentalis* *		2-N2,G			
Pectis angustifolia		2-N,G	3-G,M		
Psathyrotes ramosissima				4-N,G	
Rafinesquia californica		2-N	3-N		
Ratibida columinfera	1-N,G				
Senecio californicus			3-N		
Senecio cymbalarioides	1-N				
Senecio douglasii			3-N		
Senecio eremophilus		2-L	3-N		
Senecio eurycephalus *			3-N,G		
Senecio fremontii *	1-N,G				
Senecio hydrophilus	1-N2,G2	2-N			
Senecio multilobatus *		2-N,G			
Senecio rapifolius	1-N				
Senecio riddellii (*)	1-N		3-M		
Senecio serra (*)	1-N,G		3-N		
Senecio spartioides *	1-N,G				
Senecio triangularis	1-L				
Solidago canadensis		2-L			
Solidago gigantea	1-L				
Solidago incana	1-L		3-L		
Solidago missouriensis	1-N2				
Solidago mollis			3-N3		
Solidago multiradiata	1-N2,G2				
Solidago rigida	1-N				
Solidago speciosa	1-L				
Stephanomeria paniculata			3-N		
Stephanomeria runcinata	1-N				
* *Syntrichopappus fremontii* *					5-N,G
Tetradymia canescens	1-G2				
Thelesperma filifolium		2-N			

Thelesperma megapotamicum	1-N			
Townsendia incana (*)	1-N,G	2-N		
Townsendia grandiflora		2-N		
Trichoptilium incisum				4-N
Vernonia fasciculata	1-N			
Wyethia bolanderi *		2-N		
Wyethia helenioides			3-G,N	
Wyethia scabra	1-N2			
Xylorhiza tortifolia *		2-N2,G3		
Balsaminaceae (1)				
Impatiens capensis			3-L	
Berberidaceae (2)				
Mahonia fremontii *		2-N		
Mahonia repens	1-L	2-N2	3-N	
Betulaceae (3)				
Alnus incana		2-N	3-N	
Betula glandulosa	1-N		3-N,G	
Betula occidentalis	1-N	2-N,G		
Boraginaceae (31)				
Amsinckia spectabilis		2-N2	3-N	
Amsinckia tessellata		2-N2		
Cryptantha crassisepala *	1-N			
Cryptantha celosioides	1-L			
Cryptantha fendleri				4-N
Cryptantha flava		2-N		
Cryptantha fulvocanescens *		2-L2		
Cryptantha humilis		2-N2		
Cryptantha intermedia			3-N	
Cryptantha leiocarpa		2-N		
Cryptantha micrantha		2-N		
Cryptantha thyrsiflora		2-N2	3-G	
Cryptantha sp.		2-N		
Cynoglossum grande			3-N,G	
Hackelia floribunda		2-N,G		
Hackelia patens		2-N2		
Heliotropium convolvulaceum		2-N2	3-N2,M	
Heliotropium curassavicum		2-N	3-N,G,M	
Lappula occidentale				4-N
Lappula squarrosa (*)		2-N2		
Lithospermum carolinense	1-N			
Lithospermum incisum		2-N		
Lithospermum multiflorum *		2-N		
Mertensia ciliata	1-L			

Onosmodium molle	1-N				
Pectocarya chilensis		2-L			
Plagiobothrys sp.		2-N			
Plagiobothrys canescens			3-N,G		
Plagiobothrys nothofulvus		2-N			
Plagiobothrys tenellus			3-N		
Plagiobothrys tener			3-G		
Brassicaceae (27)					
Arabis glabra			3-N2,G2		
Barbarea orthoceras			3-N,G		
Cardamine angulata			3-N		
Cardamine cordifolia			3-N		
Erysimum asperum	1-N		3-N2		
Erysimum chieranthoides	1-L				
Lepidium alyssoides *			3-N,G		
Lepidium flavum *		2-G			
Lepidium fremontii *		2-N2,G			
Lepidium virginicum	1-L	2-N			
Lesquerella ludoviciana		2-N,G			
Physaria sp.				4-N	
Physaria acutifolia	1-N	2-N2	3-N		
Polyctenium fremontii (*)			3-N,G2,U		
Rorippa islandica	1-N				
Sisymbrium auriculatum				4-N	
Smelowskia calycina	1-L				
Stanleya integrifolia		2-N	3-N2,G		
Stanleya pinnata			3-N		
Strephanthus carinatus				4-N	
Streptanthus cordatus					0-L
Thelypodiopsis elegans		2-N			
Thelypodium integrifolium	1-N				
Thlaspi montana		2-N	3-N,G2,M		
Thysanocarpus curvipes		2-N2G	3-N2G		
Thysanocarpus radians			3-N,G,M		
Tropidocarpum gracile			3-N,G		
Buxaceae (1)					
Simmondsia chinensis				4-N	
Cactaceae (3)					
Coryphantha vivipara		2-N			
Echinocereus triglochidiatus		2-N			
Opuntia polyacantha	1-N				
Calycanthaceae (1)					
Calycanthus occidentalis			3-N,G,M		

Campanulaceae (6)					
Campanula rotundifolia	1-L				
Githopsis pulchella			3-N,B,G		
Lobelia cardinalis			3-N		
Lobelia siphilitica	1-L				
Lobelia spicata	1-L				
Triodanus perfoliata	1-L				
Canabinaceae (1)					
Humulus lupulus					
var. *neomexicanus*			3-G		
Capparidaceae (5)					
Cleome serrulata			3-N,M		
Cleomella obtusifolia *		2-N			
Isomeris arborea		2-N2,G,M			
* *Oxystylis lutea* *		2-N			
Polanisia dodecandra	1-L				
Caprifoliaceae (3)					
Lonicera interrupta			3-N		
Symphoricarpos occidentalis	1-G	2-N	3-M		
Symphoricarpos oreophilus	1-L	2-N2			
Caryophyllaceae (8)					
Arenaria brevifolia					
var. *californica* *			3-N		
Arenaria congesta	1-N3				
Arenaria fendleri		2-N			
Arenaria hookeri		2-N			
Lychnis drummondii	1-N				
Paronychia jamesii		2-N			
Silene acaulis	1-L				
Stellaria longipes		2-N			
Celastraceae (1)					
Pachystima myrsinites	1-L	2-N2	3-N2,G		
Chenopodiaceae (26)					
Allenrolfea occidentalis		2-N			
Atriplex argentea	1-N		3-N		
Atriplex canescens					
var. *occidentalis* *	1-L	2-N,G	3-N5,G,M		
Atriplex confertifolia *		2-N4	3-N,U		0-N
Atriplex endolepis					0-L
Atriplex hymenelytra *		2-N3,G2		4-N,G	
Atriplex gardneri					0-L
Atriplex lentiformis (*)		2-N			
Atriplex polycarpa					0-N2

Atriplex powellii		2-N	
Ceratoides lanata			3-N2,G,M
ssp. *subspinosa*		2-N,G	
Chenopodium album			
ssp. *berlandieri* (*)	1-N		3-N3,G
Chenopodium californicum *		2-N	
Chenopodium dessicatum	1-N		
Chenopodium fremontii *	1-N		
Chenopodium hybridum			3-N2
Chenopodium leptophyllum	1-N		
Chenopodium subglabrum	1-N		
Cycloloma atriplicifolium	1-N2,G		
Grayia spinosa		2-N2	
Monolepis nuttalliana		2-N	3-N,G
Salicornia herbacea		2-N	
Sarcobatus vermiculatus (*)	1-N		3-N2,G
Suaeda calceoliformis *	1-N,G,M		
Suaeda torreyana *	1-N2		
Convolvulaceae (3)			
Calystegia sepium	1-N		3-M
Evolvulus nuttallianus		2-N3	
Ipomoea leptophylla *	1-N3	2-M	3-G2
Cornaceae (3)			
Cornus circinata	1-L		
Cornus nuttallii			3-N
Cornus sericea	1-L	2-N	
Crassulaceae (6)			
Cotyledon farinosa			3-M
Dudleya cymosa			3-N,G,M
Sedum integrifolium	1-N,G		
Sedum lanceolatum		2-N	
Sedum obtusatum			3-N
Sedum pumilum			3-N,G
Cucurbitaceae (3)			
Citrullus lanatus			3-N
Cucurbita foetidissima			3-N,M
Marah fabaceus		2-N3	3-N2,G2
Cuscutaceae (1)			
Cuscuta indecora		2-N,M	
Elaeagnaceae (3)			
Elaeagnus argentea	1-L		
Shepherdia argentea	1-N	2-G	
Shepherdia canadensis	1-N		

Ericaceae (13)					
Arbutus menziesii			3-L		
Arctostaphylos elegans			3-G		
Arctostaphylos glauca			3?-N		
Arctostaphylos manzanita			3-G,U		
Arctostaphylos mariposa			3-G2,U		
Arctostaphylos patula			3-G2,M,U		
Arctostaphylos pungens			3-N	4-N	
Arctostaphylos tomentosa			3-G2,N2		
Arctostaphylos uva-ursi	1-N				
Phyllodoce breweri			3-N		
Phyllodoce empetriformis	1-N				
Vaccinium scoparium	1-G				
Vaccinium uliginosum	1-L				
Euphorbiaceae (12)					
Croton capitatus	1-L				
Croton procumbens					0-L
Croton texensis (*)	1-N3,G		3-G,M		
Ditaxis lanceolata				4-N	
Euphorbia albomarginata		2-N	3-M	4-N	
Euphorbia brachycera (*)	1-N				
Euphorbia corollata	1-L				
Euphorbia fendleri		2-N			
Euphorbia marginata	1-L		3-N		
Euphorbia missurica			3-N		
Euphorbia obtusata	1-L				
Euphorbia polygonifolia	1-L				
Fabaceae (88)					
Amorpha canescens	1-L				
Amorpha fruticosa	1-L				
Amphicarpaea bracteata	1-L				
Apios americana	1-N				
Astragalus sp.	1-L				
Astragalus agrestis	1-L				
Astragalus alpinus	1-L				
Astragalus ceramicus	1-L	2-N			
Astragalus douglasii			3-N,G		
Astragalus eucosmus	1-L				
Astragalus gracilis	1-L				
Astragalus kentrophyta	1-G	2-N			
Astragalus lentiginosus					
var. *fremontii* *		2-N,G			
var. *variabilis* (*)		2-N			

Astragalus mollissimus	1-L				
Astragalus parryi		2-G			
Astragalus preussii *		2-N,G			
Astragalus tridactylicus			3-N		
Astragalus utahensis		2-L			
Baptisia leucantha	1-L				
Cassia chamaechrista	1-L				
Cercidium floridum				4-N	
Cercis occidentalis			3-N3,M		
Dalea nana *			3-N,G,M		
Dalea oligophylla	1-L				
Dalea purpurea	1-L				
Desmanthus leptolobus	1-L				
Desmodium glutinosum	1-L				
Glycyrrhiza lepidota	1-L				
Hedysarum boreale?		2-L			
Hoita macrostachya			3-N3,M		
Hoita orbicularis			3-N,M		
Lathyrus pauciflorus					
ssp. *brownii*			3-N		
Lathyrus polymorphus		2-N			
Lathyrus watsonii			3-N		
Lespedeza capitata	1-L				
Lotus argophyllus					
var. *fremontii* *		2-N	3-N,G		
Lotus purshianus			3-N		
Lotus rigidus				4-N	
Lotus scoparius		2-N	3-N		
Lupinus albifrons		2-N2	3-N3		
Lupinus albifrons					
var. *douglasii*		2-L			
Lupinus argenteus	1-N	2-N2			
var. *argenteus*	1-N2				
var. *decumbens*					0-L
Lupinus bicolor		2-N	3-N		
Lupinus caudatus					
var. *argophyllus*	1-N				
var. *caudatus*			3-N		
Lupinus chamissonis			3-N		
Lupinus concinnus					
var. *arizonicus*					0-L
Lupinus densiflorus		2-N	3-N2		
Lupinus lepidus					

var. *utahensis*					0-L
Lupinus leucophyllus	1-N	2-N			
Lupinus micranthus					0-L
Lupinus plattensis (*)		2-N			
Lupinus polyphyllus		2-N			
Lupinus pusillus		2-N	3-N		
Lupinus sparsiflorus				4-N	
Mimosa nuttallii	1-G2		3-N		
Onobrychis arenaria		2-L			
Onobrychis sativa		2-L			
Oxytropis lambertii	1-N2		3-G		
Oxytropis plattensis	1-L				
Oxytropis sericea			3-G2		
Pediomelum cuspidatum		2-N			
Pediomelum esculentum		2-L			
Prosopis glandulosa		2-N,G,M			
Prosopis odorata (*)		2-N,G2			
Psoralidium argophyllum	1-L		3-N,M		
Psoralidium lanceolatum	1-L				
Psoralidium tenuiflorum	1-N,G2	2-N			
Psorothamnus arborescens *		2-N,G,U			
Psorothamnus emoryi				4-N	
Psorothamnus fremontii *		2-N2,G,M			
Psorothamnus schottii				4-N	
Psorothamnus spinosus				4-N	
Sophora nuttalliana		2-N2			
Strombocarpa odorata *		2-L			
Thermopsis macrophylla			3-G		
Thermopsis montana	1-N	2-N2			
Trifolium depauperatum			3-N,M		
Trifolium longipes		2-N			
Trifolium macraei			3-N		
Trifolium macrocephalum			3-N2,G,M		
Trifolium microcephalum			3-N,M		
Trifolium tridentatum		2-N	3-N3,M		
Trifolium variegatum			3-N,M		
Vicia americana			3-N2		
var. *minor*	1-N				
Fagaceae (10)					
Quercus agrifolia			3-N2,G		
Quercus chrysolepis *		2-N	3-N7,G3,M		
Quercus douglasii		2-N2	3-N2,G3		
Quercus dumosa			3-G		

Quercus gambelii		2-N2	3-N2	
Quercus kelloggii (*)			3-N4,G2	
Quercus lobata (*)			3-N7,G7	
Quercus macrocarpa			3-N2	
Quercus turbinella		2-L		
Quercus wislizenii			3-N5,G6	
Fouquieriaceae (1)				
Fouquieria splendens				4-N
Frankeniaceae (2)				
Frankenia jamesii *		2-N,G		
Frankenia salina			3-N,G2,M	
Fumariaceae (3)				
Corydalis aurea		2-N	3-G	4-N
Dicentra chrysantha				4-N
Dicentra formosa			3-N,G,M	
Garryaceae (1)				
Garrya fremontii *			3-N,G,M	
Gentianaceae (10)				
Centaurium venustum			3-G	
Eustoma grandiflorum	1-N,G	2-N		
Gentiana affinis	1-N2,M	2-N3	3-N,G	
Gentiana calycosa	1-L			
Gentiana parryi		2-N,G		
Gentiana prostrata (*)	1-N			
Gentianella amarella ssp. *acuta* (*)	1-N,G			
Lomatogonium rotatum			3-N,G	
Swertia perennis	1-N			
Swertia radiata	1-N2,G	2-N,M		
Geraniaceae (3)				
Erodium cicutarium		2-N,G	3-G	
Erodium macrophyllum		2-N		
Geranium caespitosum			3-N3	
Hippocastanaceae (2)				
Aesculus californica			3-N,G2,B,M	
Aesculus glabra			3-N2	
Hydrophyllaceae (19)				
Eriodictyon angustifolium		2-N	3-N	
Eucrypta micrantha				4-N
Hesperochiron californicus		2-N	3-N,M	
Hydrophyllum capitatum			3-N,G	
Nama demissa *		2-L		
Nemophila heterophila		2-N	3-G	

Nemophila maculata		2-N,G		4-N
Nemophila menziesii			3-N3,G2	
Phacelia cicutaria			3-N3,G	
Phacelia distans		2-N		
Phacelia douglasii		2-N	3-N,G	
Phacelia fremontii *		2-N		
Phacelia hastata (*)	1-N			
Phacelia imbricata			3-N	
Phacelia linearis		2-N		
Phacelia menziesii			3-M	
Phacelia nemoralis			3-N	
Phacelia sericea	1-N	2-N		
Phacelia tanacetifolia			3-G3,M	
Hypericaceae (2)				
Hypericum concinnum			3-N,B,G,U	
Hypericum sphaerocarpum			3-N4	
Juglandaceae (1)				
Carya tomentosa			3-N	
Krameriaceae (1)				
Krameria parviflora		2-L		4-N
Lamiaceae (31)				
Hyptis emoryi *				4-N,G
Lepechinia calycina				4-N
Lycopus americanus	1-L			
Mentha arvensis	1-N			
Monarda fistulosa	1-L			
Monarda pectinata	1-N	2-U		
Monardella candicans			3-G2,U	
Monardella lanceolata			3-G	
Monardella villosa			3-N,G3,M,U	
Physostegia parviflora		2-N		
Pogogyne douglasii			3-N,U	
Pogogyne zizyphoroides			3-N,M	
Pycnanthemum californicum *			3-N2	
Salazaria mexicana *		2-N		
Salvia azurea	1-L			
Salvia carduacea			3-N,M	
Salvia dorrii		2-N		
Salvia mellifera			3-N	
Salvia reflexa			3-N2,M	
Satureja douglasii			3-N,G2,M	
Scutellaria antirrhinoides			3-N	
Scutellaria californica *			3-G2,M,U	

Scutellaria galericulata	1-N					
Scutellaria parvula var. *leonardii*		2-N				
Scutellaria siphocampyloides			3-N,G,M,U			
Stachys albens			3-N			
Stachys palustris	1-N					
Teucrium canadense	1-L					
Trichostema lanatum			3-N			
Trichostema lanceolatum			3-N,G			
Trichostema lanatum			3-N			
Lauraceae (1)						
Umbellularia californica			3-N,G			
Limnanthaceae (2)						
Limnanthes alba			3-N			
Limnanthes douglasii var. *rosea*		2-N2	3-N,M			
Linaceae (4)						
Linum californicum			3-N			
Linum perenne	1-G		3-G2			
Linum rigidum	1-L					
var. *berlandieri*			3-N,G			
Loasaceae (5)						
Mentzelia albicaulis		2-N				
Mentzelia nuda	1-N		3-N4,M			
Mentzelia oligosperma			3-M			
Mentzelia pumila			3-G			
Mentzelia tricuspis				4-N		
Malvaceae (14)						
Callirhoe alcaeoides			3-N			
Callirhoe involucrata	1-L		3-N,G2			
Callirhoe pedata	1-L					
Malacothamnus fremontii *			3-N,G2			
Malvella leprosa			3-N,G			
Malvastrum fremontii *			3-N			
Sidalcea candida *			3-N2,G2,B			
Sidalcea diploscypha (*)			3-N,G,U		5-N	
Sidalcea malviflora			3-N2,G			
Sphaeralcea ambigua				4-N		
Sphaeralcea coccinea *	1-N3		3-G			
Sphaeralcea emoryi				4-N		
Sphaeralcea grossulariifolia ssp. *pedata* *			3-N,G2,U			
Sphaeralcea lindheimeri						0-L
Menispermaceae (1)						

Menispermum canadense	1-L					
Myricaceae (1)						
Myrica hartwegii *			3-U			
Nyctaginaceae (8)						
Abronia fragrans	1-N2	2-N,G	3-G2,M2			
Abronia turbinata		2-N				
Abronia umbellata			3-N			
Abronia villosa			3-G			
Mirabilis jalapa		2-L				
Mirabilis multiflora		2-N,G2	3-N,G			
Mirabilis nyctaginea	1-G		3-G			
Tripterocalyx micrantha *	1-N					
Oleaceae (2)						
Fraxinus americana	1-L					
Fraxinus latifolia			3-N,G2			
Onagraceae (44)						
Calylophus serrulatus		2-N2	3-N			
Camissonia bistorta			3-G	4-N		
Camissonia boothii						
ssp. *alyssoides*						0-G
ssp. *desertorum*		2-N				
Camissonia breviflora	1-N					
Camissonia campestris		2-N	3-G			
Camissonia claviformis *		2-N			5-L	
ssp. *aurantiaca* *				4-N		
Camissonia contorta		2-G				
Camissonia dentata						0-L
Camissonia graciliflora			3-N2,G			
Camissonia micrantha						0-L
Camissonia ovata			3-N,G			
Clarkia arcuata			3-N2			
Clarkia concinna			3-N,G			
Clarkia gracilis						
ssp. *albicaulis* *			3-N,G,M			
Clarkia purpurea			3-N3,G2,M			
Clarkia unguiculata			3-N,G,M			
Epilobium angustifolium	1-L					
Epilobium ciliatum	1-L					
Gaura coccinea	1-N	2-N3				
Gayophytum diffusum		2-N,G				
Godetia hispidula *			3-G			
Oenothera albescens						0-L
Oenothera albicaulis	1-L		3-N			

var. *nuttallii*						0-L
Oenothera amoena						0-L
Oenothera biennis	1-L					
Oenothera biloba						0-L
Oenothera brachycarpa						
ssp. *fremontii* *		2-N2	3-G			
Oenothera caespitosa						
var. *navajoensis*		2-G				
Oenothera canescens *		2-N,G,M				
Oenothera deltoidea *		2-N				
Oenothera gauriflora						0-L
Oenothera latifolia (*)		2-N	3-N2,M			
Oenothera macrocarpa						
ssp. *fremontii* *		2-G,M				
Oenothera missouriensis	1-L		3-M			
Oenothera nuttallii	1-L					
Oenothera pallida	1-N		3-M			
Oenothera pinnatifida						0-L
Oenothera rhombipetala	1-G	2-N				
Oenothera speciosa	1-G	2-N	3-N2			
Oenothera villosa	1-N					
Stenosiphon linifolius		2-L				
Orobanchaceae (3)						
Orobanche californica						
ssp. *jepsonii*			3-N			
Orobanche fasciculata	1-L					
Orobanche ludoviciana			3-N			
Oxalidaceae (1)						
Oxalis stricta	1-L					
Paeoniaceae (1)						
Paeonia brownii			3-N,G			
Papaveraceae (10)						
* *Arctomecon californicum* *		2-N				
Argemone hispida *			3-L			
Dendromecon rigida			3-N3,G			
Eschscholzia caespitosa			3-N			
Eschscholzia californica		2-N	3-N2,G3,M			
Eschscholzia glyptosperma				4-N		
Meconella californica *		2-N				
Platystemon californicus			3-M	4-N		
Romneya coulteri			3-N,G2			
Stylomecon heterophylla					5-N	
Plantaginaceae (3)						

Plantago eriopoda	1-N	2-G			
Plantago insularis		2-N		4-N	
Plantago patagonica	1-L	2-N2	3-G		
Platanaceae (1)					
Platanus racemosa		2-N,G,M	3-N,G	4-N	
Plumbaginaceae (1)					
Limonium californicum			3-N,G		
Polemoniaceae (36)					
Collomia linearis		2-N,G			
Eriastrum diffusum		2-N			
Gilia achilleifolia			3-N2,G3,M2		
Gilia aggregata	1-N,G2	2-N2	3-N,G		
Gilia congesta		2-N			
Gilia inconspicua	1-L				
Gilia latiflora *		2-N,G			0-L
Gilia longiflora	1-L				
Gilia minutiflora					0-G
Gilia sinuata		2-N			
Gilia spicata		2-G	3-G		0-L
Gilia stenothyrsa *		2-N			
Gilia tricolor		2-N3	3-G,M		
Langloisia setosissima *		2-N,G		4-G	
Leptodactylon pungens		2-G			
Linanthastrum nuttallii *					0-L
Linanthus androsaceus			3-N,G,M		
Linanthus aureus ssp. *decorus* *		2-N,G			
Linanthus bicolor					0-N
Linanthus demissus *				4-N	
Linanthus dianthiflorus				4-N	
Linanthus dichotomus		2-N2	3-N,G,M	4-N	0-N
Linanthus harknessii			3-N2		
Microsteris gracilis		2-N2	3-N,G		
Navarretia pubescens			3-N4,B,G		
Navarretia viscidula			3-N,G		
Phlox aculeata		2-N,G			
Phlox andicola	1-N,G	2-N,G			
Phlox austromontana		2-N2			
Phlox hoodii	1-L	2-N,G,M	3-G		
Phlox longifolia		2-N			
Phlox pilosa	1-N		3-N		
Phlox pulvinata	1-N				
Phlox speciosa			3-N3,G3,M		

Polemonium caeruleum	1-N				
var. *humile*	1-L				
Polygalaceae (2)					
Polygala alba	1-L	2-N			
Polygala cornuta			3-N		
Polygonaceae (43)					
Chorizanthe brevicornu *				4-N	
Eriogonum alatum		2-N	3-N		
Eriogonum annuum	1-L		3-N5,G		
Eriogonum brevicaule	1-N3	2-G			
Eriogonum caespitosum	1-L	2-N			
Eriogonum cernuum			3-N,G		
Eriogonum cordalum *		2-L			
Eriogonum corymbosum *			3-N,G		
Eriogonum dichotomum					0-L
Eriogonum effusum	1-N,G	2-N3	3-G		
var. *rosmarinoides* *			3-N,G		
Eriogonum elongatum					0-G
Eriogonum fasciculatum					
var. *foliosum*			3-N,G,M		
var. *polifolium* *		2-N2			
Eriogonum gracile			3-N,G		
Eriogonum inflatum *		2-N,G		4-N	
Eriogonum maculatum (*)		2-N2			
Eriogonum niveum (*)		2-N,G			
Eriogonum nudum					
var. *pubiflorum* *			3-N,G,U		
Eriogonum ovalifolium	1-N2	2-N3			
Eriogonum parvifolium	1-L				
Eriogonum racemosum (*)			3-N		0-L
Eriogonum reniforme *		2-N			
Eriogonum roseum (*)			3-N,G2,M		
Eriogonum sphaerocephalum					0-L
Eriogonum thomasii					0-L
Eriogonum umbellatum		2-N3,G			
var. *majus* *			3-N2		
var. *polyanthum* *			3-N2,G3		
Eriogonum vimineum		2-N			
Oxyria digyna	1-N,G				
Oxytheca perfoliata		2-N			
Polygonum amphibium	1-N				
Polygonum aviculare	1-N				
Polygonum bistortoides	1-N				

Polygonum californicum		2-N			
Polygonum persicaria	1-N				
Polygonum viviparum	1-L				
Rumex hymenosepalus		2-L			
Rumex maritimus					
var. *fuegineus*			3-N,G		
Rumex occidentalis			3-N		
Rumex salicifolius	1-N				
Rumex venosus		2-N,G			
Portulaceae (6)					
Calandrina ciliata					
var. *menziesii*			3-N		
Calyptridium monandrum		2-N			
Calyptridium umbellatum *		2-N2,G2			
Lewisia rediviva				4-N	
Montia perfoliata		2-N2			
Talinum parviflorum	1-N				
Primulaceae (9)					
Androsace filiformis	1-N,G				
Androsace occidentalis	1-N				
Dodecatheon clevelandii			3-N,G		0-N
Dodecatheon conjugens		2-N	3-G2,M		
Dodecatheon hendersonii		2-G			
Dodecatheon jefferyi	1-N				
Dodecatheon pulchellum		2-N			
Glaux maritima	1-L				
Lysimachia ciliata	1-L				
Pyrolaceae (1)					
* *Sarcodes sanguinea* *			3-N,G		
Ranunculaceae (23)					
Actaea rubra	1-L				
Anemone patens		2-N			
Anemone tuberosa				4-N	
Aquilegia caerulea	1-N				
Caltha leptosepala		2-N			
Clematis fremontii *		2-N,G			
Clematis hirsutissima					
var. *hirsutissima*		2-N2			
var. *scottii*		2-N			
Clematis lasiantha			3-N2G2,M		
Clematis ligusticifolia		2-N2	3-G		
Clematis virginiana	1-L				
Delphinium hesperium			3-N,G2		

Delphinium nudicaule			3-N,G,M			
Delphinium nuttallianum		2-N	3-N2			
Delphinium parryi?			3-N			
Delphinium variegatum			3-N,G2			
Ranunculus alismaefolius			3-N,G			
Ranunculus californicus			3-N2,G			
Ranunculus cymbalaria	1-L					
Ranunculus rhomboideus		2-N				
Ranunculus sceleratus	1-L					
Thalictrum dasycarpum	1-N					
Thalictrum occidentale (*)	1-N	2-N				
Rhamnaceae (10)						
Ceanothus americanus	1-N					
Ceanothus cuneatus		2-N2	3-N,B,M			
Ceanothus diversifolius (*)		2-N	3-N2,G			
Ceanothus herbaceus	1-N					
Ceanothus integerrimus			3-N,M	4-N		
Ceanothus prostratus			3-N4,G2			
Ceanothus thyrsiflorus			3-N2			0-N
Ceanothus velutinus	1-N					
Rhamnus californica			3-N2,M			
Rhamnus crocea				4-N		
Rosaceae (40)						
Adenostoma fasciculatum			3-N,G,M			
Amelanchier alnifolia	1-L	2-L				
Amelanchier utahensis		2-N3	3-N2			
Cercocarpus ledifolius			3-N2,M		5-N	
Cercocarpus montanus	1-N	2-N,M				
Chamaebatia foliolosa		2-N3	3-N,G			
* *Coleogyne ramosissima* *		2-N3,G				
Crataegus douglasii		2-N				
Geum canadense	1-L					
Geum triflorum		2-N	3-N			
Heteromeles arbutifolia (*)			3-N,M			
Holodiscus sp.		2-L				
Petrophytum caespitosum		2-N				
Potentilla anserina	1-N,G	2-N				
Potentilla arguta	1-L					
Potentilla effusa			3-N			
Potentilla fissa		2-N				
Potentilla fruticosa	1-L					
Potentilla glandulosa						0-L
Potentilla gracilis	1-L	2-N				

var. *elmeri* (*)		2-N		
var. *glabrata* (*)		2-N	3-N	
var. *pulcherrima*	1-N		3-N	
Potentilla pensylvanica			3-N	
var. *glabrata*	1-N		3-N	
Potentilla plattensis		2-N2		
Prunus fasciculata *		2-N,G		
Prunus fremontii *			3-N2,G	
Prunus ilicifolia		2-N		
Prunus virginiana	1-G			
Purshia mexicana				
var. *stansburyana* (*)		2-N		
Purshia tridentata	1-N	2-N2		
Rosa acicularis	1-N			
Rosa arkansana	1-N			
Rosa foliolosa	1-L			
Rosa woodsii	1-N2			
Rubus deliciosus		2-N		
Rubus idaeus	1-N		3-N2	
Rubus ursinus			3-N	
Sibbaldia procumbens	1-N			
Rubiaceae (6)				
Galium aparine			3-N	
Galium boreale	1-N			
Galium circaezans			3-N	
Galium concinnum			3-N	
Galium nuttallii			3-N	
Hedyotis nigricans				0-N
Rutaceae (2)				
Ptelea trifoliata			3-N	
* *Thamnosma montana* *		2-N		
Salicaceae (14)				
Populus angustifolia	1-N	2-N	3-G	
Populus deltoides	1-N	2-N		
Populus fremontii *		2-N	3-N,G	
Populus tremuloides	1-N			
Salix amygdaloides	1-N2		3-N	
Salix exigua	1-N		3-N2,M	
Salix glauca			3-N2	
Salix lasiandra			3-N	
Salix lasiolepis			3-N	
Salix lutea	1-N			
Salix melanopsis			3-L	

Salix monticola			3-N	
Salix nigra				0-L
Salix scouleriana			3-L	
Santalaceae (1)				
Comandra umbellata		2-N2		
Saururaceae (1)				
Anemopsis californica		2-N		
Saxifragaceae (13)				
* *Carpenteria californica* *			3-N,G	
Lithophragma glabra			3-N,G,M	
Parnassia fimbriata	1-N			
Peltiphyllum peltatum			3-N2	
Philadelphus lewisii ssp. *californicus* (*)			3-N,M	
Ribes aureum	1-N	2-N	3-N	
Ribes cereum	1-L		3-N,G,M	
Ribes echinatum	1-L			
Ribes inerme		2-N		
Ribes lacustre	1-N			
Ribes leptanthum		2-N	3-N	
Ribes oxycanthoides var. *setosum*	1-N			
Ribes sanguineum var. *glutinosum*			3-N	
Saxifraga californica		2-N		
Scrophulariaceae (52)				
Agalinus aspera	1-N			
Agalinus tenuifolia	1-N			
Antirrhinum vexillo-calyculatum (*)			3-N,G,M	
Castilleja affinis			3-G2,M	
Castilleja chromosa			3-G	
Castilleja flava	1-N			
Castilleja latifolia			3-N	
Castilleja linariifolia *	1-N3,G			
Castilleja rhexifolia	1-N			
Castilleja stenantha			3-G,M	
Castilleja sulphurea			3-N	
Collinsia bartsiifolia *		2-G	3-G	
Collinsia heterophylla			3-N3,G2	
Collinsia sparsiflora			3-G	
Cordylanthus maritimus (*)		2-N		
Cordylanthus rigidus ssp. *filifolius*			3-N	

Keckiella breviflora			3-N3,G		
Mimulus aurantiacus			3-N2,G,M2		
Mimulus cardinalis			3-N		
Mimulus fremontii *		2-N			
Mimulus glabratus					
ssp. *fremontii* *	1-N				
Mimulus guttatus			3-N2,M		
Mimulus lewisii	1-N				
Mimulus rubellus				4-N	
Mohavea viscida		2-L			
Orthocarpus lithospermoides			3-N,G3,M		
Orthocarpus luteus	1-N3,G		3-N,G		
Orthocarpus purpurascens		2-N2	3-N2,G3		
Pedicularis densiflora			3-N,B,M		
Pedicularis groenlandica	1-N2				
Pedicularis procera *		2-N	3-N,G		
Penstemon albidus	1-N				
Penstemon alpinus		2?-L			
Penstemon ambiguus					
var. *foliosus* (*)		2-N,G	3-M		
Penstemon angustifolius	1-N,G				
Penstemon azureus			3-N,G		
Penstemon breviflorus			3-G		
Penstemon buckleyi			3-N		
Penstemon caespitosus		2-N			
Penstemon centranthifolius					0-L
Penstemon cobaea	1-N	2-G			
Penstemon fremontii *		2-N,G			
Penstemon heterophyllus			3-N3,G2		
Penstemon laricifolius		2-N2,G			
Penstemon micranthus	1-L				
Penstemon pachyphyllus * (*)		2-N			
Penstemon rydbergii		2-N			
Penstemon secundiflorus *		2-N			
Penstemon strictus *	1-N				
Penstemon watsonii *			3-G3		
Scrophularia californica?			3?-N		
Veronica wormskjoldii	1-N				
Solanaceae (13)					
Datura wrightii			3-N		
Lycium fremontii *				4-N	
Lycium macrodon *				4-N	
Lycium pallidum		2-N,G			

Lycium torreyi *		2-N			
Nicotiana bigelovii			3-N		
Physalis hederifolia var. *comata*	1-N				
Physalis lobata		2-N			
Physalis virginiana	1-N				
Solanum douglasii			3-N2		
Solanum rostratum	1-N	2-N			
Solanum umbelliferum			3-N3		
Solanum xantii		2-L			
Sterculiaceae (1)					
* *Fremontodendron californicum* *			3-N3,M		
Styracaceae (1)					
Styrax californica *			3-N,G		
Ulmaceae (3)					
Celtis occidentalis	1-L				
Celtis reticulata		2-L			
Ulmus rubra	1-L				
Valerianaceae (2)					
Plectritis macrocera var. *grayii*		2-N	3-N2		
Valeriana edulis		2-N			
Verbenaceae (6)					
Lippia cuneifolia	1-L				
Verbena bipinnatifida			3-N,M		
Verbena bracteata	1-N				
Verbena canadensis				4-N	
Verbena hastata	1-L				
Verbena stricta	1-N				
Violaceae (4)					
Viola adunca		2-N	3-N		
Viola douglasii		2-L			
Viola nuttallii			3-N,M		
Viola purpurea			3-N		
Viscaceae (1)					
Phoradendron flavescens var. *macrophyllum*		2-N			
Vitaceae (1)					
Vitis riparia	1-L		3-N		
Zygophyllaceae (2)					
Kallstroemia californica					0-N
Larrea tridentata		2-G,M			
LILIATAE					
Alismaceae (1)					

Sagittaria sagitifolia	1-L				
Commelinaceae (1)					
Tradescantia occidentalis	1-N2				
Cyperaceae (7)					
Carex atrata	1-L				
Carex aurea	1-N				
Carex barbarae		2-L			
Carex festucacea	1-L				
Carex panicea	1-L				
Scirpus acutus		2-L			
Scirpus californicus		2-L			
Haloragaceae (1)					
Myriophyllum heterophyllum?			3-N		
Iridaceae (3)					
Iris missouriensis	1-N,G	2-N			
Sisyrinchium anceps	1-L				
Sisyrinchium douglasii			3-N		
Juncaceae (2)					
Juncus echinatus	1-L				
Juncus effusus			3-L		
Liliaceae (35)					
Allium amplectens			3-N2G		
Allium peninsulare (*)			3-N,G		
Allium textile	1-L				
Brodiaea californica			3-N,G		
Brodiaea elegans			3-N		
Brodiaea hyacinthina			3-N		
Brodiaea lutea			3-N		
Brodiaea peduncularis					0-L
Calochortus kennedyi		2-N			
Calochortus luteus			3-N3,G		
Calochortus monophyllus			3-N,G2		
Calochortus nuttallii		2-N			
Calochortus superbus			3-N		
Calochortus venustus				4-N	
Chlorogalum pomeridianum		2-N3,G2	3-N,G,M		
Dichelostemma californicum *		2-N			
Dichelostemma pulchellum		2-N2			
Fritillaria agrestis			3-N		
Fritillaria atropurpurea			3-N		
Fritillaria liliacea			3-N,G		
Fritillaria pluriflora *		2-N	3-G		
Fritillaria pudica		2-N,G,M			

Fritillaria recurva *			3-N2		
Hesperocallis undulata		2-N			
Leucocrinum montanum			3-N,G		
Lilium humboldtii (*)			3-N		
Lilium philadelphicum		2-N			
Smilacina stellata	1-L				
Streptopus amplexifolius			3-N		
Trillium chloropetalum			3-N2,G		
Triteleia grandiflora (*)		2-N,G			
Triteleia laxa		2-N	3-N,M		
Yucca brevifolia		2-N			
Yucca glauca	1-L		3-N		
Zigadenus fremontii *			3-N,G		
Zigadenus glaucus	1-L				
Orchidaceae (5)					
Aplectrum hyemale	1-N				
Habenaria hyperborea	1-L				
Habenaria dilatata	1-L				
Spiranthes cernua	1-L				
Spiranthes romanzoffiana		2-N			
Poaceae (20)					
Agrostis perennans	1-L				
Aristida purpurea	1-L	2-M			
Beckmannia syzigachne	1-G				
Bromus ciliatus	1-L				
Buchloe dactyloides		2-G,M			
Deschampsia caespitosa	1-L				
Distichlis spicata		2-G3,M,U			
Elymus canadensis	1-M				
Festuca obtusa	1-L				
Festuca ovina	1-L				
Glyceria striata	1-L				
Hordeum jubatum	1-L				
Koeleria macrantha	1-L				
Phleum alpinum	1-M				
Poa fendleriana		2-G			
Poa palustris	1-L				
Schizachyrium scoparium	1-L				
Sorghastrum nutans	1-L				
Spartina pectinata	1-L				
Stipa hymenoides?					5-L
LICHENS					
Bryoria fremontii * (a lichen)			3-N		

Letharia columbiana (a lichen) 0-N
Unknown (2) 1-N 3-M

	1st	2nd	3rd	4th	5th	unk	total
Total taxa	371	379	458	60	8	47	-----
Total specimens	460	552	990	65	9	48	2,129

Taxon summary	Families	Genera	Taxa
Lichens	2	2	2
Ferns & allies	3	4	8
Conifers	4	13	22
Liliatae	9	44	77
Magnoliatae	90	383	955
Totals	108	448	1,064

APPENDIX IV

COLLECTIONS FOR THE SECOND AND THIRD EXPEDITIONS BY YEAR, NUMBER, DATE, AND LOCALITY

1843—76 numbered specimens:

10 Machaeranthera canescens; 2 Jun
17 Calylophus serrulatus
35 Physostegia parviflora; on the Snake, Idaho
36 Lathyrus polymorphus
76 Comandra umbellata
81 Oenothera canescens
87 Juniperus communis
148 Helianthus nuttallii
153 Polygala alba
171 Pediomelum cuspidatum
178 Toxicodendron rydbergii
194 Clematis fremontii
200 Scutellaria powellii
206 Sophora nuttalliana; 25 Jun; Rawlins Co., KS
235 Evolvulus nuttallianus
237 Evolvulus nuttallianus
239 Evolvulus nuttallianus
266 Artemisia ludoviciana
273 Lesquerella ludoviciana; S Fork of the Platte
275 Opuntia polyacantha
287 Lithospermum incisum
290 Astragalus ceramicus
296 Lupinus pusillus
Sophora nuttalliana
297 Sophora nuttalliana
299 Physalis lobata
300 Cryptantha thrysiflora
301 Gaura coccinea
357 Senecio hydrophilus
360 Gentiana parryi
360 Gentiana affinis
393 Lepidium virginicum
400 Eriogonum umbellatum; 23 Jul; Weld Co., CO
403 Symphoricarpos occidentalis
412 Populus deltoides
414 Haplopappus fremontii
425 Eriogonum alatum
426 Abies concolor; 20 Jul; El Paso Co., CO
430 Gaura coccinea
442 Lithospermum multiflorum; 20 Jul; El Paso Co., CO
449 Aster occidentalis; 12–18 Jul; Pueblo Co., CO
451 Lilium philadelphicum
455 Calylophus serrulatus; 12–18 Jul; Pueblo Co., CO
464 Quercus gambelii
469 Gaillardia pulchella
482 Heterotheca villosa
485 Cuscuta indecora
487 Juniperus communis
493 Paronychia jamesii; 28 Jul; Larimer Co., CO
513 Asclepias speciosa
526 Juniperus scopulorum; 30 Jul; Larimer Co., CO
553 Penstemon laricifolius; 31 Jul; Albany (?) Co., WY
591 Eriogonum effusum
595 Lomatium grayi
603 Symphoricarpus oreophilus
608 Eriogonum umbellatum
610 Spiranthes romanzoffianum

621 Atriplex powellii; 12 Aug; Fremont Co., WY
622 Suaeda torreyana; 8 Aug; Carbon Co., WY
659 Artemisia tridentata; 19 Aug; Uinta Co., WY
660 Artemisia longiloba; 19 Aug; Uinta Co., WY
666 Aster occidentalis; 22 Aug; Lincoln Co., WY
672 Distichlis spicata; 3 Sep?; Box Elder (?) Co., UT
677 Salicornia herbacea; 4 Sep?; Box Elder (?) Co., UT
724 Asclepias speciosa; 24 Sep; Power Co., ID
734 Lupinus leucophyllus; 17 Sep; Bannock Co., ID
759 Cordylanthus maritimus; 11 Sep; Weber Co., UT
760 Allenrolfea occidentalis; 5 Sep?; Box Elder Co., UT
761 Atriplex confertifolia; 10 Sep; Weber Co., UT
764 Lomatium dissectum; 9 Sep; Weber Co., UT
767 Atriplex confertifolia; 9 Sep; Weber Co., UT
782 Gayophytum diffusum; 7 Oct; Elmore Co., ID
Agoseris glauca
784 Phlox aculeata; Plains of the Boise R., ID
786 Eriogonum niveum; 6 Oct; Elmore Co., ID
789 Chaenactis douglasii; 6 Oct; Elmore Co., ID

Probably 1843—52 unnumbered specimens:
Abies concolor
Abronia fragrans
Antennaria microphylla; 10 Jul; St. Vrain's Fort, Weld Co., CO
Artemisia frigida
Artemisia pedatifida
Artemisia tridentata
Acer glabrum
Alnus incana
Astragalus spatulatus
Atriplex canescens
Atriplex confertifolia
Cirsium canescens
Clematis ligusticifolia
Croton texensis
Cryptantha thrysiflora
Distichlis spicata; 3 Sep; Box Elder Co., UT
Eriogonum effusum
Eustoma grandiflorum; 9 Jul
Gaura coccinea
Helianthus petiolaris
Heliotropium convolvulaceum
Heterotheca villosa
Hymenopappus tenuifolius
Iva axillaris
Liatris punctata
Lupinus argenteus
Mirabilis multiflora
Monarda pectinata
Obione confertiflora
Oenothera canescens
Oenothera fremontii
Oenothera latifolia
Pachystima myrsinites
Pedicularis procera
Penstemon secundiflorus
Phlox andicola

Populus angustifolia
Potentilla anserina
Potentilla fissa
Potentilla gracilis
Potentilla pectinisecta
Pyrrocoma foliosa
Quercus gambelii
Ranunculus rhomboideus
Rubus deliciosus
Senecio hydrophyllus
Sesleria dactyloides
Shepherdia argentea
Stanleya integrifolia
Thelesperma filifolium
Townsendia grandiflora
Tripterocalyx micrantha; 12 Jul; Pueblo Co., CO

1844—175 numbered specimens:

3 Plagiobothrys sp.
4 Microsteris gracilis
5 Eschscholzia californica
7 Balsamorhiza bolanderi; 12 Mar; Sacramento Co., CA
10 Montia perfoliata; 12 Mar; Sacramento Co., CA
14 Chlorogalum pomeridianum; Sacramento Co., CA
16 Plagiobothrys nothofulvus
22 Quercus chrysolepis; 25 Feb; Sierra Nevada, CA
26 Gilia tricolor; 8 Mar; American River, CA
33 Libocedrus decurrens; 25 Feb; Eldorado Co., CA
34 Dodecatheon conjugens
37 Chamaebatia foliosa
39 Meconella californica; ca. 4–8 Mar; Eldorado Co., CA
41 Triteleia grandiflora; 25–26 Mar; San Joaquin Co., CA
42 Nemophila heterosepala; 4 Mar; American Fork, CA
43 Thysanocarpus curvipes; American Fork, CA
44 Sanicula tuberosa
Meconella californica; ca. 4–8 Mar; Eldorado Co., CA
47 Lomatium utriculatum
51 Sanicula bipinnatifida
52 Chamaebatia foliosa
56 Chlorogalum pomeridianum
60 Pellaea mucronata; 30 (29) Feb; Eldorado Co., CA
62 Lomatium utriculatum
66 Erodium cicutarium
67 Montia perfoliata
69 Thysanocarpus curvipes (probably 1844)
72 Phacelia distans; Sacramento Valley, CA
73 Linanthus dichotomous
75 Gilia tricolor
78 Lupinus bicolor
79 Triteleia grandiflora; 25–26 Mar; San Joaquin Co., CA
80 Marah fabaceus; 25–26 Mar; San Joaquin Co., CA
81 Chlorogalum pomeridianum; 25–26 Mar; San Joaquin Co., CA
85 Erodium macrophyllum
86 Collinsia bartsiifolia
87 Agoseris heterophylla; 25 Mar; San Joaquin Co., CA
88 Calliachris fremontii
98 Triteleia laxa; 24–25 Mar; Sacramento Co., CA
99 Platanus racemosa
101 Penstemon rydbergii; Colorado?
106 Phoradendron flavescens
107 Delphinium nuttallianus
111 Amsinckia spectabilis
112 Lupinus albifrons

114 Marah fabaceus; 15 Mar; Sacramento Co., CA
116 Amsinckia spectabilis
121 Limnanthes douglasii; Calabra Cr.
122 Orthocarpus purpurascens
129 Lupinus albifrons; 25–26 Mar; San Joaquin Co., CA
131 Dichelostemma californicum; 24 Mar; San Joaquin Co., CA
147 Lupinus densiflorus; 29 Mar; Stanislaus Co., CA
149 Quercus lobata; 29 Mar; Stanislaus Co., CA
152 Marah fabaceus; 28 Mar; Stanislaus Co., CA
155 Polygala alba
166 Camissonia campestris
173 Dichelostemma pulchellum; 14(?) Mar; Sacramento Co., CA
200 Indet
212 Symphoricarpus oreophilus
220 Nicolletia occidentalis; Kern Co., CA
232 Orthocarpus purpurascens; 10 Apr; Kern Co., CA
235 Trifolium depauperatum
Eriogonum maculatum; 25–26 Apr; San Bernardino Co., CA
257 Ribes cf. leptanthum
263 Ceanothus cuneatus
271 Yucca brevifolia; 15 Apr; Kern Co., CA
280 Quercus lobata
283 Plantago patagonica
286 Coreopsis californica
293 Geraea canescens; 13 Apr; Kern Co., CA
298 Hymenoclea salsola; 13 Apr; Kern Co., CA
299 Heliotropium curassavicum
304 Equisetum hyemale
306 Eriodictyon angustifolium
314 Quercus douglasii; 14 Apr; Kern Co., CA
316 Lepidium fremontii; 17–18 Apr; San Bernardino Co., CA
324 Gilia aurea var. decora
332 Rafinesquia californica; 23 Apr; San Bernardino Co., CA
333 Lupinus argenteus; San Bernardino Co., CA
334 Eriodictyon angustifolium; 25–26 Apr; San Barnardino Co., CA
335 Rafinesquia californica; 23 Apr; San Bernardino Co., CA
337 Camissonia boothii; 24 Apr; San Bernardino Co., CA
338 Astragalus arthu-schottii; 23 Apr; San Bernardino Co., CA
341 Larrea tridentata
344 Gilia aurea var. decora
345 Gilia aurea var. decora
349 Salvia dorii; 17 Apr; San Bernardino Co., CA
357 Chaenactis fremontii
363 Hesperocallis undulata; 24–25 Apr; San Bernardino Co., CA
367 Pinus monophylla; 17–18 Apr; San Bernardion Co., CA
368 Prunus ilicifolia
374 Ambrosia dumosa; 23–24 Apr; San Barnardino Co., CA
375 Cryptantha micrantha
386 Oxystylis luteus; 28 Apr; San Bernardino Co., CA
390 Lepidium fremontii; 25–27 Apr; San Bernardino Co., CA
392 Eriogonum inflatum; 25 Apr; San Bernardino Co., CA
397 Haplopappus linearifolius
398 Gutierrezia sarothrae
400 Hymenoclea salsola

401 Hymenoclea salsola
402 Calochortus kennedyi; 1 May?
405 Thamnosma montana; 2 May; Clark Co., NV
407 Salvia dorrii; 1 May; Clark Co., NV
408 Frankenia jamesii; provenence wrong
409 Coleogyne ramosissima; 1 May; Clark Co., NV
414 Langloisia setosissima; 30 Apr; Clark Co., NV
417 Dalea fremontii; 5 May; Clark Co., NV
419 Prosopis odorata
419 Physaria acutifolia; Pah, UT
420 Physaria acutifolia; base of Wasatch
423 Eriastrum diffusum
424 Astragalus fremontii; 3 May; Clark Co., NV
427 Eriogonum fasciculatum var. polifolium; 3 May; Clark Co., NV
428 Euphorbia fendleri
429 Arctomecon californicum; 3 May; Clark Co., NV
430 Equisetum laevigatum
431 Phlox longifolia; 1–2 May; Clark Co., NV
432 Berberis fremontii
433 Salazaria mexicana; 4 May; Clark Co., NV
436 Heliotropium curassavicum
437 Hackelia floribunda; ?
440 Ceratoides lanata
442 Amelanchier utahensis; Virgin R.
443 Coleogyne ramosissima
444 Purshia mexicana
447 Phlox austromontana; 10 May; Washington Co., UT
448 Erigeron pumilus
450 Ceanothus cuneatus
453 Rhus aromatica
464 Potentilla plattensis; 16–17 Jun; Jackson Co., CO
467 Cryptantha fulvocanescens
468 Phlox austromontana; 15 May; Iron Co., UT
470 Eriogonum caespitosum; 16 May; Iron Co., UT
474 Lycium pallidum; 11 May; Washington Co., UT
482 Dodccathcon pulchcllum
483 Betula occidentalis
484 Leptodactylon pungens; 31 May; Duchesne Co., UT
486 Eriogonum effusum?
485 Penstemon pachyphyllus; 31 May; Duchesne Co., UT
488 Iris missouriensis; 6 Jun; Uintah Co., UT
497 Hackelia patens
502 Ribes aureum; 27–28 May; Utah Co., UT
504 Thermopsis montana; 27–31 May; Utah Co., UT
505 Phacelia linearis; 27 May; Utah Co., UT
506 Quercus gambelii; 28 May; Utah Co., UT
511 Crataegus douglasii
522 Cryptantha humilis; 21 May; Millard Co., UT
529 Poa fendleriana
530 Mahonia repens; 24 May; Utah Co., UT
536 Eriogonum ovalifolium; 5 Jun; Uintah Co., UT
540 Penstemon fremontii; 5 Jun; Uintah Co., UT
541 Calochortus nuttallii
542 Amelanchier utahensis
548 Townsendia incana

549 Senecio multilobatus; 3 Jun; Uintah Co., UT
553 Balsamorhiza incana; provenance?
556 Gilia stenothrysa; 1 Jun; Duchesne Co., UT
557 Cryptantha flava
Ribes leptanthum
560 Cryptantha humilis
561 Thlaspi montana; 17 Jun; Jackson Co., CO
563 Corydalis aurea
564 Potentilla plattensis; 16–17 Jun; Jackson Co., CO
567 Clematis hirsutissima
569 Ribes inerme
571 Thalictrum occidentale
573 Anemone patens
574 Gilia spicata
577 Cryptantha fulvocanescens
578 Lupinus plattensis; ca. 12 Jun; Carbon Co., WY
580 Balsamorhiza sagittata
583 Swertia radiata; 12 Jun; Carbon Co., WY
584 Acerates latifolia; 10 Jun; Moffatt Co., CO
585 Petrophytum caespitosum
Anemopsis californica
586 Rumex venosus
587 Trifolium longipes
594 Cymopterus bulbosus
596 Comandra umbellata
623 Penstemon ambiguus; 7 Jul; Cheyenne Co., CO
626 Sesuvium verrucosum

Probably 1844—85 unnumbered specimens:

Anisocoma acaulis; San Joaquin Valley, CA
Aplopappus tortifolius; Mohave Desert?
Artemisia nova; Uinta Basin?
Amphipappus fremontii; Mohave Desert?
Amsonia tomentosa; Mohave Desert?
Anticlea sp.; Fort Uinta, Uintah Co., UT
Arenaria fendleri
Arenaria hookeri
Astragalus preussii; 3 May; Las Vegas, Clark Co., NV
Atriplex breweri
Atriplex hymenelytra; Mohave Desert?
Blitum californicum
Caltha leptosepala
Calyptridium monandrum; Mohave Desert?
Ceanothus diversifolius
Ceratoides lanata
Clematis hirsutissima
Cleomella obtusifolia; Mohave Desert?
Collinsia linearis
Cornus sericea
Coryphantha vivipara
Crepis modocensis
Crepis occidentalis
Cryptantha humilis
Cryptantha sp.
Dalea arborescens; 15 Apr; Kern Co., CA
Dodecatheon hendersonii
Echinocereus triglochidiatus; Mohave Desert?
Echinospermum fremontii; 13 Apr; Kern Co., CA
Emplectocladus fasciculatus; Mohave Desert
Erigeron glabellus
Eriogonum cordalum; (CA)
Eriogonum polifolium; 13 Apr; Kern Co., CA

Eriogonum reniforme
Eriogonum vimineum
Eunanus fremontii; Mohave Desert?
Euphorbia albomarginata; Mohave Desert
Fritillaria pluriflora
Fritillaria pudica
Geum triflorum
Gilia aggregata
Gilia aurea var. decora; Mohave Desert
Gilia congesta
Gilia sinuata; Mohave Desert?
Gilia tenuiflora var. latiflora; Mohave Desert?
Grayia spinosa
Hackelia floribunda
Hackelia patens
Hesperochiron californicum
Hoita macrostachya
Hosackia argophylla var. fremontii
Hymenopappus filifolius
Hymenoxys richardsonii
Isomeris arborea
Layia glandulosa
Lepidium flavum
Lotus scoparius
Mentzelia albicaulis
Microsteris gracilis
Monoptilon bellidiforme; Mohave Desert
Nicolletia occidentalis; Mohave Desert
Oenothera claviformis; Mohave Desert?
Oenothera deltoides; Mohave Desert?
Oxytheca perfoliata; Mohave Desert
Penstemon caespitosus
Phacelia fremontii; Mohave Desert
Phacelia sericea
Phlox hoodii
Plantago insularis
Plantago patagonica; Mohave Desert?
Platanus racemosa; CA
Plectritis procera
Prosopis odorata
Purshia tridentata; 17–18 Apr; San Bernardino Co., CA
Quercus chrysolepis
Saxifraga californica
Sedum lanceolatum
Selaginella bigelovii
Spirolobium odoratum; Mohave Desert
Stellaria longipes
Taxus brevifolia
Thelypodiopsis elegans; Uinta Basin, UT
Thermopsis montana
Valeriana edulis
Viola adunca

1845: Third Expedition—Kansas, Colorado.

List #1. Westport, Kansas to Pueblo, Colorado—106 numbered species:

15 Psoralidium argophyllum; 30 Jun; E KS
Phlox pilosa; 30 Jun; E KS
23 Euphorbia marginata
24 Carya tomentosa; 3 Jul; E KS
31 Aster novae-angliae
33 Hypericum sphaerocarpum
34 Hypericum sphaerocarpum
35 Haplopappus annuus
36 Machaeranthera canescens
39 Quercus macrocarpa; 5 Jul; E KS

41 Quercus macrocarpa; 5 Jul; E KS
48 Liatrus punctata
49 Hypericum sphaerocarpum
51 Hypericum shpaerocarpum; 5 Jul; E KS
54 Callirhoe alcaeoides; 8 Jul; KS
56
65 Aesculus glabra
67 Humulus lupulus
68 Agoseris glauca
72 Aster ericoides
75 Orthocarpus luteus
76 Solanum umbelliferum
80 Linum perenne
81 Oenothera missouriensis
86 Cirsium undulatum; Turkey Creek, KS
90 Lygodesmia juncea
93 Asclepias speciosa; 23 Jul; Smoky Hill Fork, KS
94 Asclepias speciosa; 23 Jul; Smoky Hill Fork, KS
95 Erigeron subtrinervis
96 Atriplex canescens
97 Atriplex argentea
100 Heliotropium convolvulaceum
102 Euphorbia missurica
103 Lupinus pusillus
104 Potentilla gracilis
105 Eriogonum annuum
107 Hymenoxys acaulis
108 Oenothera missouriensis
Calystegia sepium; 11 Jul; Turkey Creek, KS
112 Euphorbia marginata
118 Penstemon buckleyi; 12 Jul; W Turkey Creek, KS
123 Mentzelia oligosperma; 15 Jul; Pawnee Rock, KS
138 Amaranthus arenicola; 4 Jul; E KS
140 Oxytropis lambertii
142 Chenopodium hybridum
146 Croton texensis
147 Verbena bipinnatifida; 19 Jul; Smoky Hill Fork?, KS
149 Mentzelia nuda; 19 Jul; Smoky Hill Fork?, KS
150 Cleome serrulata
161 Cyperus acuminatus; 15 Jul; KS (Pawnee Rock?)
168 Vitis riparia; 18 Jul; Smoky Hill Fork, KS
170 Senecio riddellii; 18 Jul; Smoky Hill Fork, KS
178 Oenothera latifolia
181 Eriogonum effusum; 24 Jul; Smoky Hill Fork, KS
182 Asclepias speciosa
185 Haplopappus ciliatus
189 Solidago mollis; 25 Jul; Smoky Hill Fork?, KS
190 Solidago mollis; 25 Jul; Smoky Hill Fork?, KS
192 Oenothera canescens; 25 Jul; Smoky Hill Fork?, KS
198 Cucurbita foetidissima; 25 Jul; Smoky Hill Fork?, KS
201 Salvia reflexa; 25 Jul; Smoky Hill Fork?, KS
Calylophus serrulata
202 Salvia reflexa; 25 Jul; Smoky Hill Fork?, KS
Cucurbita foetidissima; 25 Jul; Smoky Hill Fork?, KS
207 Linum rigidum; 27 Jul; E CO
209 Atriplex canescens; 27 Jul; E CO
211 Atriplex canescens
212 Astragalus tridactylicus
218 Potentilla pensylvanica; 21 Aug; Pueblo Co., CO
221 Dalea nana; 30 Jul; E Bent's Fort, CO
222 Oenothera pallida

224 Barbarea orthoceras
227 Abronia fragrans; 30 Jul; E Bent's Fort, CO
229 Penstemon ambiguus
230 Eriogonum annuum; 16-20 Aug; Bent's Fort to Pueblo, CO
234 Oenothera latifolia
Euphorbia missurica; 30 Jul; E Bent's Fort, CO
235 Anogra cinerea; 16-20 Aug; Bent's Fort to Pueblo, CO
Pectis angustifolia
239 Chenopodium album; 29 Jul; E Bent's Fort, CO
Eriogonum annuum; 29 Jul; E Bent's Fort, CO
241 Euphorbia marginata; 30 Jul; E Bent's Fort, CO
243 Mentzelia nuda; 31 Jul; E Bent's Fort, CO
423 Stanleya integrifolia; Bent's Fort, CO
426 Rumex maritimus; 19-20 Aug; Pueblo Co., CO
429 Cardamine cordifolia; 19-20 Aug; Pueblo Co., CO
430 Equisetum laevigatum
437 Cryptantha thrysiflora
438 Yucca angustifolia; E CO
447 Abronia fragrans
454 Atriplex canescens
455 Tidestromia lanuginosa; 16-20 Aug; Bent's Fort to Pueblo, CO
463 Physaria acutifolia
477 Monolepis nuttalliana; Bent's Fort, CO
478 Pedicularis procera
480 Lepidium alyssoides; Bent's Fort, CO
481 Machaeranthera canescens
486 Eriogonum effusum
490 Ribes aureum; Bent's Fort, CO
498 Aster oblongifolia; 2-16 Aug; Bent's Fort, CO
504 Hypericum sphaerocarpum
519 Asclepias speciosa
523 Hypericum sphaerocarpum
528 Chrysopsis villosa
530 Galium concinnum
532 Oenothera speciosa
537 Oenothera speciosa

1845, Westport to Pueblo—16 unnumbered specimens:

Aesculus glabra
Asclepias engelmanniana
Callirhoe involucrata
Gaillardia pinnatifida
Galium circaezans; 20 Jun; Westport, KS?
Gutierrezia sarothrae
Haplopappus spinulosus; 19 Jul; Smoky Hill Fork, KS
Ipomoea leptophylla
Lobelia cardinalis
Lygodesmia juncea
Mentzelia nuda; 31 Jul; E Bent's Fort, CO
Mentzelia oligosperma (dup # 123?); 15 Jul; KS
Oenothera latifolia; 20 Jul; Smoky Hill Fork, KS
Psoralidium argophyllum; 30 Jun; E KS
Ruellia humilis; 11 Jul; Turkey Creek, KS
Tidestromia lanuginosa; 15 Aug; Bent's Fort, Otero Co., CO

List # 2. Pueblo, Colorado, to Wasatch County, Utah—103 numbered specimens:

1 Mirabilis multiflora; 20 Aug; Pueblo Co., CO
15 Stanleya pinnata
17 Chrysothamnus nauseosus
24 Atriplex confertifolia; October; Shores, Utah Lake, UT
33 Atriplex canescens
33 Cleome serrulata
34 Helianthus petiolaris; 18 Aug; Bents Fort to Pueblo, CO
39 Cleome serrulata
42 Geranium caespitosum
Ceratoides lanata
45 Sidalcea candida
46 Oenothera albicaulis
49 Rhus aromatica
51 Mirabilis nyctaginea
52 Quercus gambelii; Arkansas R.
54 Gutierrezia sarothrae
55 Ptelea trifoliata; Colorado?
61 Geranium caespitosum
62 Heterotheca villosa
Artemisia filifolia
63 Artemisia filifolia; 22 Aug; Pueblo Co., CO
77 Chrysopsis villosa
86 Linum perenne
91 Streptopus amplexifolius
92 Sidalcea candida
94 Eriogonum umbellatum
94 Atriplex canescens
99 Eriogonum umbellatum
Erigeron strigosus
105 Machaeranthera canescens
107 Aster occidentalis
109 Sidalcea candida
110 Sidalcea candida
117 Picea engelmannii
109 Sidalcea candida
110 Sidalcea candida
119 Pedicularis procera
125 Arabis glabra
128 Gentiana affinis; ca. 2 Sep; Lake Co., CO
130 Sidalcea candida
132 Viola purpurea
137 Dodecatheon conjugens
147 Abies lasiocarpa
148 Abies lasiocarpa
153 Eriogonum umbellatum
156 Pachystima myrsinites
158 Amelanchier utahensis
159 Rubus idaeus
160 Chrysothamnus nauseosus
161 Potentilla gracilis
167 Aster chilensis
170 Salix glauca
172 Camissonia bistorta
174 Picea engelmannii
175 Corydalis aurea
177 Sidalcea candida
186 Populus fremontii
187 Salix glauca
202 Abies concolor
210 Penstemon watsonii
211 Abies lasiocarpa
237 Eriogonum unbellatum var. majus; near head of Arkansas River, in or near Lake Co., CO
248 Eriogonum corymbosum; 4-11 Sep; Grand R., CO
257 Vicia americana; Grand R. vic., CO
267 Rubus idaeus
269 Clematis ligusticifolia
288 Eriogonum alatum; South Park, CO
289 Eriogonum cernuum; South Park, CO
296 Artemisia campestris
301 Eriogonum racemosum
304 Equisetum hyemale

305 Acer grandidentatum; 2-3 Oct; Wasatch Co., UT
334 Collinsia sparsiflora
345 Clematis lasiantha
361 Castilleja sulphurea
365 Machaeranthera canescens
367 Machaeranthera canescens
368 Oxytropis sericea
369 Hymenoxys richardsonii
371 Aster laevis
374 Artemisia frigida
375 Aster eatonii
Aster occidentalis
380 Senecio eremophilus; South Park, CO
382 Chenopodium album
384 Rumex occidentalis; White R., Rio Blanco (?) Co., CO
389 Potentilla effusa
393 Betula glandulosa
Aster laevis; 28 Aug; Utah Pass, CO
396 Allium amplectens
402 Salix amygdaloides; 28 Aug; Fremont Co., CO
Salix monticola
Salix exigua
404 Hymenoxys richardsonii
406 Lupinus caudatus; 12-25 Sep; White R., CO-UT
407 Salix candida
409 Penstemon watsonii
410 Sidalcea candida
411 Sphaeralcea grossulariifolia
413 Lupinus argentea
416 Mentzelia pumila
417 Haplopappus spinulosus
422 Alnus incana; 12-25 Sep; White R., CO-UT
401 Sarcobatus vermiculatus
464 Amelanchier utahensis (wrong year)

1845, Pueblo, Colorado, to Utah—15 unnumbered specimens:
Arabis glabra; Ss
Artemisia ludoviciana
Callirhoe involucrata
Chrysothamnus nauseosus
Eriogonum annuum; Grand R, Eagle Co., CO
Erysimum asperum; Arkansas R, above Pueblo, CO
Grindelia squarrosa
Heterotheca villosa
Linum rigidum
Lomatogonum rotatum; Head of Arkansas, CO
Mentzelia nuda; 22 Aug; Pueblo, CO (Arkansas not Platte)
Populus angustifolia
Rhus aromatica; 22 Aug; Pueblo, CO
Sarcobatus vermiculatus
Sphaeralcea coccinea

1845–1846 (California)

1845—30 numbered specimens:
491 Alectoria fremontii; 5-6 Dec; Placer Co., CA
2 Hemizonia virgata
3 Wyethia helianthoides
4 Quercus lobata; 17 Dec; River Merced, CA
6 Machaeranthera tanacetifolia
7 Quercus lobata; Stanislaus Co., CA
8 Quercus lobata; 22 Dec; Fresno Co., CA
9 Senecio douglasii; 9 Dec; Sacramento Co., CA
10 Aesculus glabra
14 Quercus lobata; Sacramento Co., CA

15 Quercus wislizenii; 17 Dec; Stanislaus Co., CA
16 Quercus wislizenii; 24-25 Dec; Fresno Co., CA
20 Arctostaphylos tomentosa; 23 Dec; Fresno Co., CA
22 Quercus chrysolepis; 24-25 Dec; Fresno Co., CA
24 Myrica hartwegii; 21 Dec; Fresno Co., CA
28 Quercus douglasii
Arctostaphylos elegans
29 Quercus chrysolepis; 26 Dec; Fresno Co., CA
35 Quercus chrysolepis; 26 Dec; Fresno Co., CA
40 Phyllodoce breweri; 29 Dec; Fresno Co., CA
Trifolium tridentatum
45 Quercus chrysolepis; Dec
48 Quercus chrysolepis; Dec
51 Quercus chrysolepis
52 Alectoria fremontii
76 Solanum umbelliferum
81 Sidalcea humilis
82 Sidalcea humilis
88 Trifolium tridentatum
96 Senecio serra

1845, California—7 unnumbered specimens:
Arctostaphylos mariposa
Carpenteria californica
Chamaebatia foliolosa; 6 Dec; Placer Co., CA
Quercus chrysolepis; 5 Dec; Sierra Nevada, Placer Co., CA
Quercus wislizenii; 25 Dec; King's R, Fresno Co., CA
Quercus wislizenii; 15 Dec; Mokelumnes R, CA
Sedum obtusum; 4 Dec; Placer Co., CA

1846—248 numbered specimens:
100 Chaenactis heterocarpa
105 Dodecatheon conjugens; 23 Feb; Santa Cruz Co, CA
109 Lasthenia minor
110 Platanus racemosa; 31 Dec; Fresno Co., CA
114 Castilleja affinis
120 Solanum umbelliferum; 26 Feb; Santa Cruz Co., CA
125 Oenothera ovata; 25 Feb; Santa Cruz Co., CA
138 Ranunculus californica; Santa Cruz Co., CA
139 Lomatium sp.; Feb
140 Ranunculus californica; Santa Cruz Co., CA
141 Arctostaphylos tomentosa
Arctostaphylos tomentosa
145 Arctostaphylos tomentosa; 26 Feb; Santa Cruz Co., CA
151 Cardamine angulata; 23 Feb; Santa Cruz Co., CA
153 Thermopsis macrophylla
154 Cardamine angulata; 23 Feb; Santa Cruz Co., CA
155 Amsinckia spectabilis
156 Sanicula arctopoides
157 Anticlea fremontii; 28 Feb; Santa Cruz Co., CA
159 Ribes sanguineum; Santa Cruz Co., CA
160 Calandrina ciliata var. menziesii; 2 Mar; Santa Cruz Co., CA
162 Nemophila menziesii
Potentilla etomentosa
165 Erodium cicutarium
166 Plagiobothrys tenellus

168 Agoseris heterotricha
169 Baeria chrysostoma
171 Phacelia douglasii
172 Camissonia campestris
173 Dichelostemma pulchellum; 14 Mar; Sacramento Co., CA
174 Orthocarpus purpurascens
175 Collinsia bartsiifolia
Salvia carduaca
176 Layia platyglossa
177 Layia glandulosa
178 Salvia carduaca
179 Linanthus dichotomus
181 Cercis occidentalis; 8 Apr; Shasta Co., CA
183 Agoseris heterotricha
184 Triteleia laxa; 16-17 Mar; San Joaquin Co., CA
186 Phacelia cicutaria
197 Lomatium utriculatum; 19 Mar; San Joaquin Co., CA
199 Delphinium variegatum
203 Eschscholzia californica
Tropidocarpum gracile
209 Calochortus luteus; 27 Mar; Yuba Co., CA
210 Ceanothus cuneatus
Platanus racemosus
213 Fritillaria pluriflora
Calochortus luteus; Tehama Co., CA
216 Cynoglossum grande
217 Nemophila menziesii
218 Camissonia graciliflora; misplaced, not from Bent's Fort
222 Lomatium dasycarpum
225 Triteleia multiflora; Utah Lake (provenance?, likely California)
226 Arctostaphylos manzanita
227 Quercus agrifolia; 7 Apr; Shasta Co., CA
228 Quercus douglasii
229 Limnanthes douglasii
230 Microsteris gracilis
231 Nemophila maculata; Apr; San Joaquin Valley?
232 Collinsia heterophylla
233 Eschscholzia californica
234 Collinsia sparsiflora
235 Clematis lasiantha
Trifolium depauperatum
236 Trifolium tridentatum
237 Lomatium utriculatum
238 Vicia americana
239 Rubus ursinus; Sacramento R., CA
241 Gilia achilleifolia; 5 Apr; Tehama Co., CA
242 Collinsia heterophylla
Lupinus bicolor; 5 Apr; Tehama Co., CA
243 Populus fremontii; 5 Apr; Tehama Co., CA
244 Populus fremontii; 5 Apr; Tehama Co., CA
245 Limnanthes androsaceus
246 Collinsia heterophylla
247 Quercus agrifolia; 7 Apr; Shasta Co., CA
248 Agoseris heterophylla
249 Delphinium nuttallianum
250 Nemophila heterophylla
252 Lomatogonium rotatum
253 Quercus lobata
254 Phacelia tanacetifolia
256 Lathyrus watsonii
257 Vicia americana
259 Sanicula bipinnatifida
260 Triteleia laxa; 16-17 Mar; Sacramento Co., CA
260½ Dichaeta fremontii
266 Trifolium macraei; 16 Apr; Tehama Co., CA
269 Achyrachaena mollis

272 Orthocarpus purpurascens
273 Sedum pumilum; ?16 Apr; Upper Sacramento, CA
279 Agoseris heterophylla
280 Sanicula bipinnatifida;16 Apr; Tehama Co., CA
282 Balsamorhiza macrophylla
284 Arenaria brevifolia var. californica
285 Pogogyne zizyphoroides; 16 Apr; Tehama Co., CA
286 Limnanthes douglasii
287 Plagiobothrys tener
289 Dichaeta fremontii
291 Chaenactis heterocarpha
294 Solanum parishii
298 Toxidendron diversilobum; ?8 Apr; Shasta Co., CA
299 Chaenactis heterocarpha
300 Quercus agrifolia; 8-9 Apr; Shasta Co., CA
301 Eriogonum racemosum; Klamath Co., OR
303 Orthocarpus purpurascens
304 Platystemon californicus
305 Eschscholzia caespitosa
306 Thysanocarpus curvipes
307 Oenothera hispidula; ?9 Apr; Sacramento Valley, CA
309 Linanthus dichotomous
310 Gilia tricolor
311 Orthocarpus purpurascens
312 Nemophila menziesii
313 Microsteris gracilis
314 Plectritis macrocera
315 Mimulus guttatus; Sacramento R., CA
316 Plectritis macrocera
317 Galium aparine
318 Calliachyris fremontii; Sacramento Valley, CA
319 Brodiaea hyacintha
321 Calochortus luteus
326 Senecio eurycephalus
327 Castilleja affinis
332 Calochortus suberbus
333 Eriophyllum lanatum; 25 Apr; Shasta Co., CA
334 Eriodictyon angustifolia; 25 Apr; Shasta Co., CA
338 Dudleya cymosa
339 Dicentra formosa; Noza R., Tehama Co., CA
341 Quercus douglasii
345 Mahonia repens
346 Fritillaria recurva; 27–28 Apr; Shasta Co., CA
347 Sanicula tuberosa; 27–28 Apr; Shasta Co., CA
348 Fritillaria recurva; 27–28 Apr; Shasta Co., CA
346 Chlorogalum pomeridianum
352 Dicentra formosa; Noza R., Tehama Co., CA
353 Calochortus monophyllus; 27 Apr; Shasta Co., CA
357 Ceanothus decumbens; 27 Apr; Shasta Co., CA
358 Pedicularis densiflora; 27 Apr; Shasta Co., CA
359 Ceanothus prostratus
360 Calochortus luteus
364 Quercus chrysolepis
365 Quercus wislizenii
366 Paeonia brownii
368 Arctostaphylos patula
369 Garrya fremontii
370 Prunus fremontii
371 Hydrophyllum capitatum
372 Ribes cf leptanthum
373 Viola nuttallii; 28 Apr; Shasta Co., CA
374 Cornus nuttallii
375 Pachystima myrsinites
376 Lomatium triternatum

377 Phlox hoodii; Head of Sacramento, CA
379 Hesperochiron californicus; 30 Apr; Modoc Co., CA
380 Leucocrinum montanum; 1 May; Modoc Co., CA
Calycadenia tenella; 1 May; Modoc Co., CA
380a Calycadenia tenella; 1 May; Modoc Co., CA
381 Sisyrinchium douglasii
383 Lomatium dissectum; 5 May; Klamath Co., OR
384 Fremontia californica
Smelowskia fremontii; 4 May; Modoc Co., CA
385 Pogogyne zizyphoroides; 16 Apr; Tehama Co., CA
387 Juniperus occidentalis
390 Geum triflorum
393 Betula glandulosa; 6 May; Klamath Co., OR
394 Limnanthes douglasii; 6 May; Klamath Lake, Klamath Co., OR
395 Brodiaea lutea
396 Allium amplectus
397 Fritillaria agrestis; Near Lassen's, Tehama Co., CA
400 Cryptantha intermedia; 30 May; Sutter Co., CA
Plagiobothrys canescens
401 Exchscholzia californica
402 Phacelia cicutaria
407 Penstemon heterophyllus
Penstemon azureus
409 Rhododendron occidentale
410 Ceanothus integerrimus; 20–23 May; Nozah R., near Lassen's, Tehama Co., CA
411 Fritillaria atropurpurea
412 Amelanchier utahensis
413 Lithophragma glabra; ?20 May; Near Lassen's, Tehama Co., CA
414 Delphinium nudicaule
415 Phlox speciosa; ?20 May; Near Lassen's, Tehama Co., CA
416 Lathyrus pauciflorus; ?20 May; Near Lassen's, Tehama Co., CA
417 Thlaspi montana; ?20 May; Near Lassen's, Tehama Co., CA
419 Calochortus superbus
421 Orthocarpus lithospermoides
Ceanothus decumbens
Cercocarpus ledifolius; 22–23 May; Lassen's, Tehama Co., CA
422 Orthocarpus purpurascens
423 Delphinium hesperium
425 Daucus pusillus
426 Trifolium macrocephalum
428 Malvastrum fremontii
429 Brodiaea lutea
430 Clarkia concinna
431 Lotus scoparius
432 Sidalcea diploscypha
433 Calochortus luteus; 26 May; Lassen's, Tehama Co., CA
434 Scutellaria siphocampyloides
435 Godetia amoena var. albicaulis; 22 May; Shasta Co., CA
437 Orthocarpus lithospermoides
438 Pogogyne douglasii; 28 May; Butte Co., CA
439 Chlorogalum pomeridianum
441 Clarkia purpurea
443 Trifolium variegatum; ?28 May; Butte Co., CA
446 Monardella villosa; 25 May; Tehama Co., CA
447 Ribes cereum

448 Phlox speciosa
449 Delphinium nudicaule
453 Lupinus densiflorus
456 Navarretia pubescens
459 Cercocarpus ledifolius
Ceanothus decumbens
463 Artemisia cana
466 Spraguea umbellata; 22 May; Tehama Co., CA
468 Ceanothus integerrimus
469 Allium peninsulare
470 Fremontia californica
472 Phacelia imbricata
473 Lupinus densiflorus
474 Castilleja chromosa
475 Linum californicum
476 Malvella leprosa
477 Asclepias fremontii; 4 Jun; Sutter Co., CA (Buttes Camp)
478 Hemizonia pungens; CA
479 Orthocarpus lithospermoides
Fraxinus latifolia
(perhaps a transposition of 497, q.v.)
482 Clarkia unguiculata
483 Cercis occidentalis; 27 May; Tehama Co., CA
484 Clarkia purpurea
485 Delphinium hesperium
486 Brodiaea elegans; 6 May; Klamath Co., OR
487 Perideridia kelloggii; 22 May; Shasta Co., CA
488 Arctostaphylos patula
489 Dudleya cymosa
490 Lilium canadense; 23 May; Tehama Co., CA
493 Ceanothus decumbens
494 Calycanthus occidentalis
495 Eriogonum umbellatum
Antirrhinum vagans; 5 Jun; Sacramento Co., CA
496 Hoita orbicularis
497 Fraxinus latifolia (see also 479)
498 Erigeron foliosus
499 Rhamnus californica; Jun; Buttes, Sutter Co., CA
500 Quercus tinctoria
var. californica; 14 Jun; Sutter's, Sacramento Co., CA
501 Heteromeles fremontiana
502 Eriogonum nudum
504 Clematis lasiantha
505 Calycadenia multiglandulosa
Delphinium variegatum
506 Monardella candicans
507 Navarretia viscidula
508 Aesculus californica
509 Mimulus aurantaicus
510 Mimulus aurantaicus
511 Philadelphus fremontii; 14–15 June; Sutter's, Sacramento Co., CA

1846—95 unnumbered specimens:
Artemisia californica
Calycadenia fremontii; L
Calycadenia multiglandulosa
Calycadenia pauciflora
Castilleja latifolia; Cccc
Castilleja stenantha; Bbbb
Ceanothus decumbens; Aaa
Ceanothus prostratus
Centaurium venustum; Pppp
Cercocarpus ledifolius; 20 May; Near Lassen's, Tehama Co., CA
Clarkia arcuata; Ppp
Clarkia purpurea; Rrr
Clematis lasiantha
Cordylanthus rigidus; Santa Cruz V., Santa Cruz Co., CA
Coreopsis tinctoria
Croton texensis; Wwww
Datura wrightii; Nnnn

Delphinium hesperius
Dendromecon rigidum; Nn
Dichaeta fremontii
Equisetum telematia
Erigeron douglasii
Erigeron glaucus; Ii
Erigeron strigosus??
Eriogonum fasciculatum var. foliosum; Rrrr
Eriogonum gracile; Ssss & Tttt
Eriogonum virgatum; Ssss
Eriophyllum lanatum; Bb
Erysimum asperum; Mar; Toualumne sink, Stanislaus Co., CA
Euphorbia albomarginata; Wwww
Frankenia salina; Xx
Fritillaria liliacea; Toualumne R, Stanislaus Co., CA
Galium nuttallii; Xxx
Gilia achilleifolia; 11 Apr; Lassen's, Tehama Co., CA
Githopsis pulchella; Yyy
Godetia hispidula; Ppp
Haplopappus venetus
Heliotropium curassavicum; Llll
Hemizonia congesta
Hemizonia pungens
Hemizonia ramosissima; S
Hoita macrostachya; Lll
Hypericum concinnum
Isomeris arborea
Keckiella breviflora; Kkkk
Keckiella breviflora; 31 Jan; Monterey Co., CA
Layia fremontii
Limonium californicum; Aaaa
Linanthus harknessii; Mmmm
Lomatium dissectum; 5 May; Klamath hillside, Klamath Co., OR
Lonicera interrupta
Lupinus albifrons; 8 Apr; Shasta Co., CA
Lupinus albifrons; 14 Apr; Tehama Co., CA
Lupinus chamissonis; 21 Jan; Monterey Co., CA
Marah fabacea; Sss
Marah fabacea; Ttt
Mesembryanthemum crystallinum; Vv
Mimulus cardinalis; 3 or 13 Sep
Mimulus guttatus; 13 Apr; Tehama Co., CA
Monardella candicans
Monardella lanceolata
Monardella villosa
Nicotiana bigelovii; Tehama Co, CA
Orobanche californica; Eeee
Pedicularis densiflora; 27 Apr; Shasta Co., CA
Peltiphyllum peltatum; Tehama Co., CA
Penstemon azureus
Penstemon breiflorus; Kkkk
Polygala cornuta; Yy
Pycnanthemum californicum
Quercus tinctoria var. californica; 8 Apr; Cow Cr., Shasta Co., CA
Quercus tinctoria var. californica; 14 Jun; Near Sutter's, Sacramento Co., CA
Ranunculus alismifolius; Ll
Romneya coulteri; Nn
Salix lasiandra; Coast ranges, opposite Monterey, CA
Salix lasiolepis; 29 Apr; Deer Creek, Tehama Co., CA
Salvia mellifera; 31 Jan; Monterey Co., CA

Sanicula graveolens; Uuu
Sarcodes sanguinea
Satureja douglasii; Gggg
Scutellaria antirrhinoides; Iiii
Senecio californica; N
Sequoia sempervirens; Coast mts., San Jose-Santa Cruz, CA
Solanum douglasii
Spraguea umbellata; Nozah R., Tehama Co., CA
Stachys albens
Stephanomeria paniculata; x
Styrax californica; Upper Sacramento
Thysanocarpus radians; Qq
Trichostemma lanceolatum; Hhhh
Trichostemma lanatum
Trifolium macraei; Deer Creek, Tehama Co., CA
Trifolium macrocephalum; Fff
Trillium chloropetalum; Yyyy
Umbellularia californica; Uuuu

Index of the Narrative

This index is to the people, places, things, and events recounted in the narrative of the expeditions, and of the people and new taxa only in the account of the Botany of the Expeditions. Plant names contained in the Botany of the Expeditions are in alphabetical order in the various appendices, which often contain more detailed information on localities and dates. New genera based on Frémont's collections are in bold italics.